COMPUTATIONAL CELL PHYSIOLOGY

WITH EXAMPLES IN PYTHON

STEPHEN M. BAYLOR, M.D.
PROFESSOR EMERITUS OF PHYSIOLOGY
UNIVERSITY OF PENNSYLVANIA

COMPUTATIONAL CELL PHYSIOLOGY

COMPUTATIONAL CELL PHYSIOLOGY
WITH EXAMPLES IN PYTHON

Copyright © 2020 Stephen M. Baylor

First Edition (Revised and Expanded) 2020

All rights reserved. No part of this book may be reproduced or transmitted in any form or by any means, electronic or mechanical, including photocopying, recording or by any information storage and retrieval system, without written permission from the author.

Design and layout | Emily de Rham

Printed and bound via Kindle Direct Publishing.

ISBN: 978-1661705145

ACKNOWLEDGMENTS

The author acknowledges two eminent physiologists who were important mentors to him in the study of physiology: Clay M. Armstrong, M.D., Professor Emeritus in the Department of Physiology at the University of Pennsylvania, and W. Knox Chandler, M.D. (1933 to 2017), a long-time Professor in the Department of Cell and Molecular Physiology at Yale University. Both scientists made seminal contributions to the study of nerve and muscle physiology, including electrical signaling on cell membranes and chemical signaling within the cell volume. Both coupled a remarkable conceptual understanding of their subjects with carefully-executed experiments as they carried out their laboratory work to reveal the mechanisms of the cell processes under study. Both took meticulous efforts in the write up of their work so that their published articles were clear and complete.

The author acknowledges two excellent books: "Nerve, Muscle, and Synapse" by Bernard Katz, 1970 winner of the Nobel Prize in Physiology or Medicine, which led the author to consider the idea of a research career in cell physiology, and "Computational Physics" by Mark Newman, Distinguished University Professor of Physics at the University of Michigan, which planted the seed that led to the development of this book.

The author thanks Dr. Clay Armstrong and Dr. Paul De Weer for permission to use their source materials related to the topics in Chapter 2 (Dr. De Weer) and Chapters 5 and 14 (Dr. Armstrong). The author also thanks those who made helpful comments on the manuscript, including, Dr. Paul De Weer, Dr. Stephen Hollingworth, Dr. Toshinori Hoshi, Dr. Philip Nelson, and Dr. Brian Salzberg. The author particularly thanks Dr. Denis Baylor for comments and encouragement. The author acknowledges the important contribution of Emily de Rham in assisting in the design and layout of the book.

TABLE OF CONTENTS

Preface xv

CHAPTERS

Chapter 1. Introduction to Physiology 1

    1.1 What is Physiology? 1
    1.2 Extracellular Fluid (ECF) and Intracellular Fluid (ICF) 3
    1.3 Homeostasis 5
    1.4 More about the Cell Membrane 8
    1.5 Cell Membrane Potential (V_m) 12
    1.6 The Concentration of Free Ca^{2+} Ions 13
    1.7 Introduction to Signaling Mechanisms 14
    1.8 Cell Signaling via Voltage and Calcium 15
    1.9 What Happens When a Healthy Cell Membrane is Damaged? 16
    1.10 Exercises 19

Chapter 2. Diffusion, Osmosis, and Membrane Permeability 21

    2.1 Simple Diffusion 21
    2.2 Membrane Permeability 26
    2.3 Relation between Lipid Solubility and Membrane Permeability 29
    2.4 Exceptions to the Lipid-solubility Rule 31
    2.5 Osmosis (The Diffusion of Water) 35
    2.6 Application of Osmotic-pressure Laws to Living Cells 38
    2.7 Exercises 41

Chapter 3. Introduction to *Python* 43

    3.1 A Program that Plots a One-dimensional Diffusion Profile 43
    3.2 A Program that Plots a Two-dimensional Diffusion Profile 51
    3.3 A Program that Permits Input and Output of Text and Numbers 55
    3.4 Further Examples with a One-dimensional Diffusion Profile 58
    3.5 Comparison of a One-dimensional Diffusion Profile with an
          Experimental Data Set 60
    3.6 Exercises 65

Chapter 4. Elements of *Python* 67
4.1 Data Types 67
4.1.1 Constants and Variables 68
4.1.2 Strings 68
4.1.3 Lists 69
4.1.4 Tuples 70
4.1.5 Numbers 71
4.1.5.1 Integers 71
4.1.5.2 Floating-point Numbers 71
4.1.5.3 Complex Numbers 72
4.1.6 Arrays of Numbers 73
4.2 Expressions and Statements 74
4.3 The Assignment Statement 75
4.4 Control Statements 76
4.4.1 The While Statement 77
4.4.2 The If Statement -- and the Elif and Else Statements 77
4.4.3 The For Statement 78
4.5 User-defined Functions 80
4.6 More on Arrays 81
4.6.1 Creating One-dimensional Arrays 81
4.6.2 Creating Multi-dimensional Arrays 82
4.6.3 Reshaping Arrays 83
4.6.4 Stacking Arrays 84
4.6.5 Flattening Arrays 84
4.6.6 Slicing Arrays 84
4.7 Order of Operations 85
4.8 *Python* Shortcuts 85
4.9 Programming Style 86
4.10 Simulated Diffusion Using a Random-number Generator 87
4.11 Exercises 96

Chapter 5. Introduction to Electrophysiology 99
5.1 Membrane Voltage (V_m) 99
5.2 The Origin of Membrane Voltages 101
5.3 Charge and Current 102
5.4 Capacitors and Capacitive Current 105

5.5 The Nernst Equation 108
5.6 Conductance 109
5.7 Resistance 110
5.8 Driving Force 110
5.9 The Time to Charge a Capacitor 112
5.10 Exercises 115

Chapter 6. Osmotic Balance in Cells **117**
6.1 A Model of Osmotic Balance in Cells 117
6.2 A Digression on Systems of Ordinary Differential Equations 120
6.3 A *Python* Model of Osmotic Balance in Cells 126
6.4 Program Notes 131
6.5 Physical Interpretation of the Model 137
6.6 Other Time-dependent Responses in the Model 140
6.7 Response of the Model in the Absence of Na/K Pumping 140
6.8 Exercises 142

Chapter 7. Passive Electrical Properties of Cells **145**
7.1 A Simple Circuit Model of a Cell at Rest 145
7.2 Kirchhoff's Laws for Electrical Circuits 148
7.3 Techniques Used to Study the Electrical Properties of Cells 148
7.4 Theoretical Response of a Cell Membrane to a Step of Current 151
7.5 Theoretical Response of a Cell Membrane to a Step in Voltage 156
7.6 A More Realistic Membrane Equivalent Circuit for a Resting Cell 163
7.7 Membrane Conductance vs. Membrane Permeability 165
7.8 One-dimensional Cable Theory 167
7.9 Exercises 173

Chapter 8. The Action Potential in Nerve Axons **177**
8.1 A Brief Survey of Action Potentials 177
8.2 The Action Potential in the Squid Giant Axon 179
8.3 The Voltage-clamp Technique Applied to the Squid Giant Axon 180
8.4 The Membrane Action Potential 183
8.5 The Hodgkin-Huxley Model 184
8.6 Simulation of Action Potentials with the HH Model 190
8.7 Simulation of Voltage-clamp Experiments with the HH Model 198

8.8 Voltage Dependence of G_{Na} and G_K 205
8.9 First Measurements of Channel Gating Currents in Squid Axons 206
8.10 Exercises 209

Chapter 9. Reaction Schemes and Kinetic Equations **215**
9.1 The Law of Mass Action 215
9.2 An Example with Ca^{2+} as a Reactant 216
9.3 The Kinetics of Ca^{2+} Binding in Response to a Change in $[Ca^{2+}]$ 221
9.4 Competitive Binding: Steady-state 222
9.5 A Steady-state Equivalence between Ca^{2+} and Mg^{2+} Effects on Binding 226
9.6 Competitive Binding: Kinetics 227
9.7 Cooperative Binding and the Hill Equation 229
9.8 A Kinetic Scheme for the Ca^{2+} Pump of the Sarcoplasmic Reticulum 234
9.9 Structure of EF-hand Ca^{2+} Binding Sites within Proteins 242
9.10 Exercises 246

Chapter 10. More on Ion Channels **251**
10.1 Ion-channel Families 251
10.2 Structural Motifs of Ion Channels 256
10.3 Single-channel Recording from Artificial Bilayers 261
10.4 Single-channel Recording with the Patch-clamp Technique 263
10.5 A Digression on the Poisson Probability Distribution 266
10.6 First Simulation of the Results in Figure 10.4*c* 268
10.7 A More-complete Simulation of the Results in Figure 10.4*c* 271
10.8 A Digression on a Poisson Process 272
10.9 Models of Channel-gating Activity 274
10.10 Other Examples of Single-channel Recording 277
10.11 Exercises 286

Chapter 11. Synaptic Transmission at the Neuromuscular Junction **291**
11.1 Chemical vs. Electrical Synapses 291
11.2 Components of a Chemical Synapse 292
11.3 Anatomy of the Neuromuscular Junction 294
11.4 Functional Details of the Neuromuscular Junction 298
11.5 Miniature Endplate Potentials 300
11.6 Statistics of Mepps and Epps 302

11.7 Ca^{2+}-dependence of Neurotransmitter Release 307
11.8 Why Are Not All Synapses Electrical? 310
11.9 Exocytosis 312
11.10 Exercises 316

Chapter 12. Excitation-Contraction Coupling in Skeletal Muscle **323**
12.1 Introduction to Skeletal Muscle 323
12.2 Introduction to Excitation-contraction Coupling 325
12.3 A Quick Tour of the Steps in EC Coupling 327
12.4 Overview of the Structure of Skeletal Muscle Fibers 328
12.5 Electrophysiology of Skeletal Muscle 332
12.6 T-tubular Depolarization to SR Ca^{2+} Release 336
12.7 The Rise in Myoplasmic Free $[Ca^{2+}]$ 340
12.8 Recovery Processes after a Twitch 345
12.9 Voltage-clamp Studies of EC Coupling 346
12.10 Calcium Sparks 350
12.11 Exercises 357

Chapter 13. Calcium Dynamics in Skeletal Muscle Cells **361**
13.1 Model Preview 361
13.2 A *Python* Program that Models Ca^{2+} Dynamics during EC Coupling 366
13.3 Model Estimates in Response to a Train of Action Potentials 385
13.4 Exercises 387

Chapter 14. The Muscle Reflex Arc: A Peak into the Nervous System **393**
14.1 A Quick Tour of the Muscle Reflex Arc 393
14.2 Details of the Stretch Reflex 396
14.3 More about Myelination 403
14.4 Reciprocal Innervation 406
14.5 The Golgi Tendon Organ 407
14.6 Pathology Affecting the Muscle Reflex Arc 408
14.7 Exercises 410

APPENDICES

A. Installation of *Python* 3 411

B. Derivation of Fick's First and Second Laws of Diffusion 417

C. Derivation of the Nernst Equation 421

D. Fitting of Model Parameters in *Python* 425

E. Kinetic Response of V_m in a One-dimensional Linear Cable 431

F. Calculation of a Propagated AP with the HH Model 441

G. Physical Constants and Common Units 453

REFERENCES 455

INDEX 471

PREFACE

The goals of this book are twofold: (i) to introduce students to important concepts and mechanisms in cell physiology and (ii) to pursue a selection of topics to the quantitative level, with equations, computer simulations, and exercises. The subjects considered are basic ones and illustrate the power of quantification in elucidating the underlying physical mechanisms. The subjects also supply an essential background for understanding the function of organs and systems. The material is suitable for self-study or for a one- or two-semester course for advanced undergraduates or early graduate students. My hope is that this book will convince students that a quantitative approach to the study of physiology is worthwhile, powerful, and enjoyable -- and that it will help them to develop habits of thinking quantitatively.

The mathematical background assumed is largely presented in standard college-level mathematics courses -- and, increasingly, in high-school math courses -- and includes calculus and some differential equations. While many quantitative ideas in physiology can be addressed with pencil and paper or with a hand calculator, a fuller exploration often requires calculations by computer. This becomes particularly convenient if done with a powerful and easy to use computer language that incorporates graphical display. An example of such a language is *Python*, the language that has been chosen for the examples in this book.

Python has several advantages for students of the physical and biological sciences: it is free; it is available for Windows, Mac, and Unix platforms; it is easy to install; it has a simple syntax that makes it easy to learn; it has many powerful 'libraries' and 'packages' that can be called into action when greater functionality is needed; in most installations, it is an interpreted language. The last feature, which contrasts with compiled languages such as Fortran, C, and C++, renders *Python* user-friendly at the outset, thus providing a tool with which to begin useful scientific calculations with a minimum number of side issues. Furthermore, a plethora of on-line resources about *Python* is readily available. With these resources, an answer to a specific question about programming syntax or a programming error can often be found within a minute or less.

Many good books are available for learning *Python*. If that is the reader's aim, he/she should seek one of those books. This book focuses on principles of cell physiology, particularly as encountered in experimental studies of nerve, muscle and endocrine cells, i.e., the family of so-called 'excitable' cells, which use action potentials to control their activity and whose resting state, as in all cells, is controlled by ion channels and ion pumps. Enough *Python* is introduced here to enable the student to become comfortable with the basics of the language and permit this book to have a self-contained flavor in the writing of *Python* programs. As the student builds confidence in *Python*, mastery of more complicated features of the language should become straightforward.

A number of topics in this book involve "bio-electricity", which is the subject of how charged ions and molecules participate in the functioning of the organelles, cells, and tissues of the body. Chapter 5 provides a review of important electrical concepts that are essential for understanding the laws of electricity as applied to biology. These concepts provide essential background for much of the material presented in the later chapters. Because bio-electricity is based on the laws of physics, the computational abilities of a programming language like *Python* are well-suited for addressing quantitative topics related to bio-electricity.

This book also includes some important appendices:

Appendix A describes how to install a working *Python* environment on the student's computer. The one we recommend is supplied in conjunction with a program called *Anaconda Navigator*, which includes an "integrated development environment" (IDE) called *Spyder*. Within this environment, programs can be edited, saved, run, and debugged.

Appendix B gives a derivation of Fick's first and second laws of diffusion, which are used and discussed in various chapters of the book.

Appendix C gives a derivation of the Nernst equation, one of the pillars for the understanding of bio-electricity in cells.

Appendix D give examples of how *Python* can be used to carry out a least-squares fit of the parameters of a quantitative model to an experimental data set.

Appendix E examines the solution to the kinetic problem in one-dimensional linear cable theory of how membrane potential changes at different times and distances from the site at which a maintained current step is injected into the cable.

Appendix F illustrates the use of the Hodgkin-Huxley model of membrane excitability to calculate a propagated action potential in a squid giant axon. The *Python* program presented here extends the material in Chapter 8, in which the Hodgkin-Huxley model is used to calculate a membrane action potential in a squid axon.

Appendix G tabulates physical constants, experimental quantities, and commonly-used units related to the material in this book.

[Note: Since the original edition of this book was published in January, 2020, Appendices D - G have been added, as have a number of exercises and several *Python* programs. A number of small changes and corrections have also been made to the text,]

Stephen M. Baylor
Philadelphia, Pennsylvania
October 30, 2020

RECOMMENDED READING

A. Related to Cell Physiology

Nerve, Muscle, and Synapse
   by Bernard Katz

Ion Channels of Excitable Membranes
   by Bertil Hille

B. Related to the use of *Python* in quantitative scientific applications

A Student's Guide to Python for Physical Modeling
   by Jesse M. Kinder and Philip Nelson

Computational Physics
   by Mark Newman

CHAPTER 1

INTRODUCTION TO PHYSIOLOGY

This chapter introduces important ideas in the study of physiology, particularly cell physiology. This material provides general background for many topics and computational examples considered in later chapters.

1.1 WHAT IS PHYSIOLOGY?

Physiology is the study of how the body functions. It has both important factual and conceptual bases. A major benefit of studying physiology for students of biology, bio-engineering, medicine, nursing, and the medical sciences is that physiology fosters a mechanistic, rather than empirical, approach to thinking about how the body functions under normal conditions and what may happen when cells, tissues, and organs malfunction.

Because physiology is a broad and complex subject, this book must focus on a few major themes and try to divide them into digestible units, each with their own computational examples. One way to sub-divide physiology relates to the ease of visualization of the underlying biological entities. If we rely simply on the naked eye and gross dissection, we can see the major organ systems of the body, including the skeletal muscles, brain, nerves, heart, lungs, kidneys, gastro-intestinal tract, and reproductive system. Hence we have the subject of organ and tissue physiology.

If we use a light microscope, we can see the individual cells that make up the tissues -- hence the subject of cell physiology. The latter might be further divided into (1) 'general' cell physiology, concerned with the functioning of most/all cell types -- for example, how does a cell retain essential constituents and maintain a stable resting state, how does it use the electric potential across its surface membrane to help take in nutrients and discharge wastes, how does the cell respond to changes in energy needs, and how does the cell react if its surface membrane is damaged; and (2) 'specialized' cell physiology, concerned with the specializations that allow, say, nerve cells, muscle cells, lung cells, gastrointestinal cells, and kidney cells to accomplish their unique functions -- including electrical signaling, muscle contraction, gas exchange, digestion, and secretion.

With the electron microscope, one can visualize many important sub-cellular components, including the surface membrane (also called the 'cell membrane', 'plasma membrane', and 'plasmalemma'), the mitochondria, the endoplasmic reticulum, the Golgi apparatus, the nucleus, and the cytoskeleton (Fig. 1.1). A study of the particular functions of these and related entities might be called 'organellar' physiology. Underlying all of these levels, we know that cell and tissue functions are heavily influenced by the properties and behavior of individual molecules, particularly proteins, including enzymes, ion channels, ion pumps, receptor proteins, vesicle fusion proteins, motor proteins, cyto-skeletal proteins, and myriad regulatory proteins -- hence the subject of 'molecular' physiology.

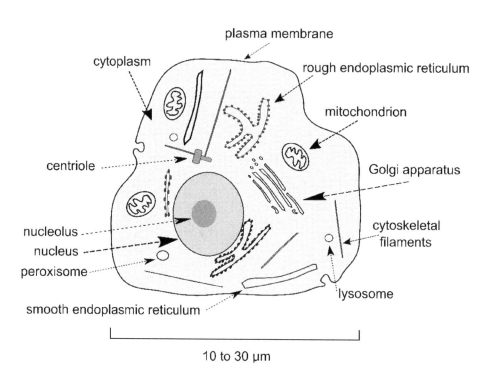

Figure 1.1 Schematic thin section revealing important components of a generic animal cell. [After Alberts et al. (1994).]

Intimately related to all levels of function are many other molecular species, including small inorganic ions such as sodium (Na^+), potassium (K^+), chloride (Cl^-), bicarbonate (HCO_3^-), calcium (Ca^{2+}), magnesium (Mg^{2+}), and protons (H^+); small organic molecules such as the twenty naturally-occurring amino acids; adenosine triphosphate (ATP) and other high-energy phosphates; glucose and other sugars; cyclic nucleotides; phospholipids; neurotransmitters such as acetylcholine, norepinephrine, and glutamate; large molecules such as RNA and DNA; and arrays of molecules such as microfilaments, microtubules, and desmosomes.

In this book, we will use single cell physiology as our anchor point. Single cells are relatively accessible experimentally and provide the environment for a "downward" look into the activities of smaller units of organization, including organelles and individual molecules. A knowledge of how individual cells function is also essential for an "upward" view of the functioning of the tissues and organs from which the cells are derived. A major challenge to all who study physiology is to try to integrate one's understanding across many levels of organization, from the molecular to the organismal.

The topics considered in this book include some that apply to all cells, such as maintenance of a stable resting state and avoidance of the tendency to swell and die. A larger focus is on the remarkable mechanisms found in the specialized cells known as 'electrically-excitable' cells, i.e., nerve, muscle, and endocrine cells. These cells use high-speed electrical and chemical signals to control activities such as nerve-nerve communication, perception and thought, voluntary movement, motor reflexes, the beating of the heart, and the secretion of hormones. Without these mechanisms, life as we know it, with thoughts and actions, would not be possible. Another reason to study excitable cells is that they include some of the largest cells in the body, so they are some of the best-understood cell types of all. Interleaved among these subjects will be a variety of computational examples and exercises in *Python*.

1.2 EXTRACELLULAR FLUID (ECF) AND INTRACELLULAR FLUID (ICF)

Multi-cellular organisms evolved from uni-cellular organisms that were exposed to ions at the concentrations found in seawater or brackish water. It is not surprising, therefore, that cells exist surrounded by a "mini-sea" of ions resembling that in seawater, although not as concentrated. They also contain within their interiors their own unique "mini-sea" of ions.

It is useful to know the approximate ionic composition and the amounts of water found within the extracellular and intracellular fluid compartments of typical mammalian cells. Body water makes up 50-60% of body weight. It can be divided into that in the extracellular fluid, which is approximately 40% of total body water, and that in the intracellular fluid, which is approximately 60% of the total.

Fig. 1.2 gives an overview of the concentrations of the major substances in the ECF and the ICF of humans. Most of these substances carry an electric charge; inevitably, this makes the subject of electrophysiology an important one. In Fig. 1.2, the ECF is divided into plasma (A, the non-cellular component of blood) and the interstitial fluid (B, the fluid that directly bathes the cells other than blood cells). As shown in Fig. 1.2, the ionic composition of these two components is similar but very different from that of the ICF (C). The interstitial fluid accounts for approximately 75% of the water in the ECF and the plasma approximately 20%. The other ~5% is in spaces surrounded by epithelia -- the so-called transcellular fluid, which includes synovial fluid and cerebrospinal fluid.

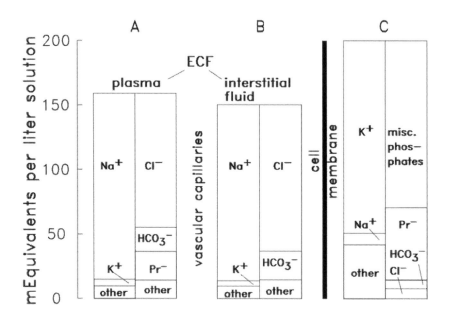

Figure 1.2 A summary of the major constituents found in the ECF (A and B) and ICF (C). In each of the double columns in A, B, and C, cations are shown on the left and anions on the right. For a univalent substance, an equivalent is equal to a mole. [After Barrett et al. (2004).]

The dominant cation (positively-charged substance) in the ECF is Na^+, with a concentration of about 140 mM, whereas the concentration of K^+ is low, 4-5 mM. The reverse is found in the ICF, where $[K^+]$ is high, about 140 mM, and $[Na^+]$ is low, 5-10 mM. The concentrations of the various anions (negatively-charged substances) in the two fluids are also very different. Cl^- is the dominant anion in the ECF, whereas $[Cl^-]$ is low in the ICF. In the ICF, the majority of anionic charges are found on (i) proteins (denoted by Pr^- in Fig. 1.2), the majority of which carry a net negative charge at neutral pH; (ii) phosphate compounds, including ATP, phosphocreatine (PCr), and inorganic phosphate (Pi); and (iii) other small metabolites. So, the ions in the ECF are largely the small inorganic ions Na^+ and Cl^-, whereas those in the ICF are largely K^+ and larger anions, including proteins and phosphates.

1.3 HOMEOSTASIS

For a complicated organism like a vertebrate animal to survive, many specialized cells, tissues, and organs are required to work together to provide food and oxygen for all cells, to eliminate wastes, and to respond to the unexpected. To achieve these ends, the cells and organs must provide a stable internal environment within the body, i.e., maintain "homeostasis" (literally, "same/similar condition"). If a stable internal environment cannot be maintained within both the ECF and ICF, it is likely that organ systems will fail and the animal will die. An important principle used by the body to achieve internal homeostasis is the principle of *negative feedback*. A negative feedback system is a collection of elements that work together to keep a quantity or variable of interest approximately constant. Because there are many variables in the body that need to be kept within reasonable bounds (e.g., body temperature; blood pressure; blood and tissues levels of glucose, oxygen, pH, sodium, potassium, calcium, etc.), the body has many different negative feedback systems that are all working simultaneously and largely independently.

The elements of a negative feedback system include (Fig. 1.3):
- a set point (or desired value) of the variable being controlled;
- a sensor that monitors the current value of the variable and sends this information to a decision center (or "integrating" center);
- the integrating center, which compares the current value of the variable with the set point and decides whether to send an "outgoing" signal to an "effector" to take an action to restore the value of the variable towards its set point;
- the effector, whose actions adjust the value of the controlled variable.

An example is the negative feedback system that controls blood pressure. (For very important variables like blood pressure, there may be feedback redundancy, i.e., more than one system -- or components in more than one anatomic location -- to control the variable.) Under normal resting conditions, the blood pressure in the arteries varies during each heart beat between maximum and minimum values -- the systolic and diastolic pressures -- of approximately 100-130 mm Hg (millimeters of mercury) systolic and 70-80 mm Hg diastolic.

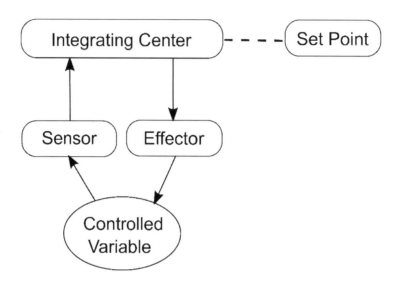

Figure 1.3 Components of a negative-feedback system.

The carotid sinus, located within the walls of the internal carotid artery, contains important sensors ('baroreceptors') that keep track of the arterial blood pressure (Fig. 1.4). Similar baroreceptors are also found in the walls of the nearby arch of the aorta, which receives the blood ejected by the left ventricle.

These sensors are in fact nerve endings of specialized cells in the afferent limb of the autonomic nervous system. The higher the pressure, the more these nerves will "fire", i.e., generate conducted electrical signals called 'actions potentials' (APs), which go to the central nervous system (CNS) to report information about the current values of the blood pressure.

The CNS will use this information, in concert with other information, to decide whether blood pressure should be lowered. If so, the CNS will send outgoing electrical and chemical signals that will cause slowing of the heart rate and/or dilation of appropriate blood vessels, which will lower blood pressure. Reciprocal events, with opposite effects on the heart and vasculature, will occur if blood pressure falls below the set point.

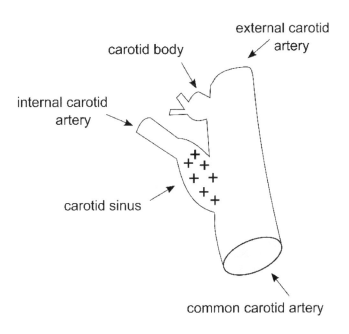

Figure 1.4 The carotid sinus at the base of the internal carotid artery contains sensors (+) that help regulate blood pressure. The nearby carotid body contains sensors that respond to the levels of oxygen, carbon dioxide, and pH in the blood. [After Barrett et al. (2004).]

The proper functioning of the negative feedback systems that maintain the internal homeostasis of the organism depends, in turn, on the stability of the cells that make up these systems, i.e., on cellular homeostasis. Thus, cell properties, including the concentrations of the intracellular constituents, must be kept within narrow bounds. For most cells, maintaining internal stability requires a substantial expenditure of energy, with many background activities being carried out in parallel. These include transporting constituents between the ICF and ECF, metabolizing substrates, maintaining the cell's supply of ATP, synthesizing a steady stream of proteins, and moving these proteins to the appropriate location in the cell. Cell homeostasis involves a steady-state, not an equilibrium. An equilibrium implies that the status quo can be maintained without the expenditure of energy. An equilibrium for all components of a cell is equivalent to cell death.

A basic requirement of cell homeostasis is the prevention of diffusive mixing of the extracellular and intracellular constituents, i.e., cells must retain what is needed and keep out what is not. This task, in the first instance, falls to the cell's surface membrane, which strongly limits the diffusive and other movements of most constituents between the inside and outside of the cell. Necessarily, some counterproductive movements do take place. Cells then use chemical energy, largely in the form of ATP -- often directly, by means of enzymes that use ATP; sometimes secondarily, by other pathways -- to reverse these counterproductive movements. If ATP levels should fall, the cell's contents will begin to move away from their normal steady state, an early sign of which is the uptake of salt and water, which causes cell swelling. If this process continues unchecked, the endpoint will be cell death.

1.4 MORE ABOUT THE CELL MEMBRANE

The cell's surface membrane consists of lipid and protein molecules, the proportions of which vary somewhat from one cell type to another. On average, the cell membranes of vertebrates are roughly 50% lipid and 50% protein.

The lipid molecules in membranes are mostly phospholipids (Fig. 1.5, left). These have a phosphate group near one end (the "head" of the molecule) and two long chain fatty acids at the other (the "tail" of the molecule), with a glycerol backbone in between. The head of the molecule is 'hydrophilic', i.e., prefers to be in a polar or water environment whereas the fatty acid tail is 'hydrophobic', i.e., prefers to be in a non-polar/non-water environment.

The phospholipid molecules are organized into a double leaflet (Fig. 1.5, right), with their hydrophobic tails facing each other in the interior and the hydrophilic head groups facing the water solutions on the two sides of the double leaflet. This creates a very effective barrier to the movement of many substances across the lipid portion of the membrane, including:
(i) large molecules like nucleic acids and proteins;
(ii) most charged molecules and atoms, including charged amino acids and the numerous inorganic ions (Na^+, K^+, Cl^-, Ca^{2+}, Mg^{2+}, H^+, HCO_3^-, etc.); and
(iii) many uncharged but polar substances (glucose, fructose, etc.) that also find it energetically unfavorable to cross the hydrophobic barrier presented by the lipid tails. Some small polar molecules, such as carbon dioxide (CO_2) and ammonia (NH_3), can cross lipid bilayers without great difficulty, as can small non-polar molecules (O_2, steroids, triglycerides, etc.)

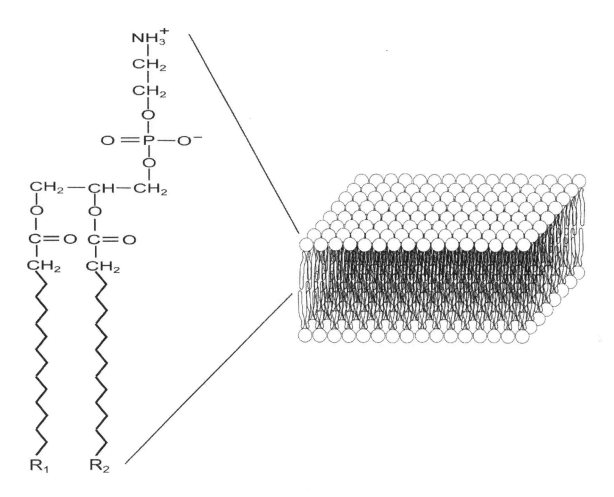

Figure 1.5 Left: structure of a single phospholipid molecule, in this case a phosphatidyl-ethanolamine molecule (with hydrocarbon tails shown as zig-zag lines). Right: schematic view of a lipid bilayer (thickness, 3-4 nm), made up of many phospholipid molecules arranged in two layers, with facing hydrocarbon tail groups. [After Boron and Boulpaep (2009).]

The protein molecules of the cell membrane reside within, and interface with, the lipid bilayer (Fig. 1.6). They can be divided into two types: (i) integral membrane proteins, which usually have one or more long chains of amino acids, such as alpha (α) helices, that penetrate and/or cross the membrane and which can be separated from the membrane only with difficulty, e.g., by solubilizing the membrane with detergents; and (ii) the remainder -- the peripheral membrane proteins -- which are loosely associated with the membrane (e.g., they may be non-covalently bound to integral membrane proteins) and can be separated from the membrane relatively easily.

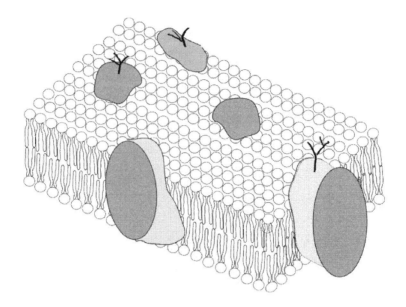

Figure 1.6 Schematic of a portion of a cell membrane, showing the lipid bilayer and membrane proteins. [After Singer and Nicholson (1972).]

Classification of these proteins includes the following:
- transport proteins (e.g., ion channels, pumps, and carriers), whose function is to control the traffic of polar molecules across the membrane and also carry out important electrical signaling functions, including generation of APs;
- receptor proteins (e.g., G-protein-coupled receptors), whose function is to receive signals from circulating molecules, such as hormones and growth factors, and pass along a signal to other membrane proteins and/or to the cell interior for an appropriate response;
- structural proteins (e.g., sarcoglycans, integrins), which help maintain the structural integrity of the membrane and, in some cases, have receptor functions;
- enzymes (e.g., membrane-bound kinases, phosphatases, and cyclases), which facilitate biochemical reactions at or near the membrane and may also have receptor and transport functions;
- identification proteins, with antigenic determinants, that make the cell recognizable to other cells, including the immune system.

The cell membrane is sometimes described by the term "fluid-mosaic model" (first used by Singer and Nicolson, 1972), which implies that the lipids and proteins are free to diffuse within the two-dimensional structure of the membrane. This idea is only approximate, as it ignores important organized domains within the overall membrane structure that limit diffusion, including arrays of protein, specialized lipid domains (e.g., lipid 'rafts'), and structural restraints imposed by the cytoskeleton.

In later chapters, the function of a number of key membrane transport proteins will be considered in some depth. Here, we mention the all-important sodium-potassium ATPase -- sometimes called 'the Na/K pump', or just 'the sodium pump'. The principal component of this ion-translocating enzyme is its α sub-unit (Fig. 1.7), which is an integral membrane protein of molecular mass ~100 kDaltons (kDa).

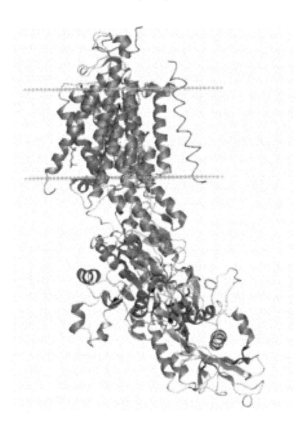

Figure 1.7 Ribbon structure of the α subunit of the Na^+/K^+ ATPase, the principal subunit of the membrane protein that is sometimes just called the 'sodium pump'. The horizontal lines mark the boundaries of the cell membrane; the outside of the cell is at the top. The various spiral-shaped structures are α helices. The protein has two smaller auxiliary subunits, the beta (β) and gamma (γ) subunits. [Credit: Andrei Lomize, University of Michigan (Wikipedia).]

The sodium pump is found in various isoforms in the surface membrane of nearly all animal cells. It uses the energy of ATP to expel the Na^+ ions that are constantly leaking into cells through other integral membrane proteins and to retrieve the K^+ ions that are constantly leaking out of the cell. To do so, the pump cycles between two main conformational states: one in which it binds three Na^+ ions on the inside of the membrane and the other in which it binds two K^+ ions on the outside of the membrane. As the Na^+/K^+ pump cycles between these states by a mechanism that depends on the hydrolysis of ATP, the bound ions are sequestered in a hydrophilic pathway within the protein's interior and then given access to the solution on the other side of the membrane. If this protein is rendered non-functional, cells will swell and die, so the Na^+/K^+ pump is of central importance in maintaining the integrity of nearly all cells (considered in more detail in Chapter 6).

1.5 CELL MEMBRANE POTENTIAL (V_m)

An essential, and sometimes unappreciated, component of cell homeostasis is the electrical voltage difference across the cell's surface membrane. This voltage difference is usually called the cell's 'membrane potential' (denoted 'V_m'). According to the modern convention, V_m is the inside electrical potential relative to the outside electrical potential, i.e., $V_{in} - V_{out}$. At rest, animal cells have negative values of V_m (Fig. 1.8) that vary between, say, the -10 mV found in red blood cells and the -70 to -90 mV found in nerve and muscle cells.

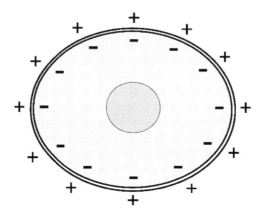

Figure 1.8 Animal cells at rest have a negative membrane potential. The **very** small excess of negative charges over positive charges inside the cell is balanced by an equally-small excess of positive charges over negative charges outside the cell. As suggested by the diagram, the excess charges move as close to each other as the membrane allows so as to minimize the electrical energy (potential energy) inherent in their separation.

In most cells at rest, V_m is primarily set as a K^+-ion 'diffusion potential' (described more fully in Chapter 5), with a minor influence from Na^+ ions and sometimes a minor influence from Cl^- and HCO_3^- ions. In non-resting circumstances, V_m can be very different from the resting potential due to strong influences from Na^+ and Ca^{2+}. There is also an intimate relation between the resting value of V_m, the internal ionic concentrations, and cell volume. For example, the cell swelling mentioned above that occurs with uptake of Na^+, Cl^-, and water is typically accompanied by a "run-down" of V_m (meaning V_m becomes less negative, i.e., moves toward 0 mV). Several exercises in a later chapter explore the relation between cell volume, the activity of the Na^+/K^+ pump, V_m, and other factors.

1.6 THE CONCENTRATION OF FREE Ca^{2+} IONS

The divalent ions Ca^{2+} and Mg^{2+} are unusually important to many cellular functions, especially the Ca^{2+} ion. Because of their highly-localized double-charge, these ions, when bound to a receptor site on a protein, can have a strong influence on the protein's conformation and, thus, on the protein's activity. 'Free calcium' refers to the calcium ions that are dissolved in the water solution inside or outside the cell and are not bound to other entities such as proteins and phosphates. The other calcium ions are referred to as 'bound' calcium ions.

In most situations that we will discuss, the concentration of bound Ca^{2+} is much higher than that of free Ca^{2+}. The concentration of free calcium ions in the ECF ($[Ca^{2+}]_o$; where the subscript 'o' refers to outside the cell) is smaller than the concentration of the univalent ions discussed above. The concentration of free calcium ions inside the cell ($[Ca^{2+}]_i$) is **much** smaller than that of the other ions mentioned above. Specifically, $[Ca^{2+}]_o$ is 1-2 mM, whereas $[Ca^{2+}]_i$ in a cell at rest is estimated to be between 0.00002 and 0.0001 mM (0.02 to 0.1 µM). The latter range, which is so low as to render difficult the precise measurement of resting $[Ca^{2+}]_i$, is between 10,000 and 100,000 times lower than $[Ca^{2+}]_o$. As might be expected, this large difference between $[Ca^{2+}]_o$ and $[Ca^{2+}]_i$ sets the stage for many important effects involving control of cell functions by a change in $[Ca^{2+}]_i$. Cells at rest (with those in bone being an exception) need to maintain a low value of $[Ca^{2+}]_i$ in order to avoid the formation of rock-hard precipitates with phosphate ions, which are found in the mmolar range inside cells. Thus, mechanisms designed to keep $[Ca^{2+}]_i$ low are an important part of cellular homeostasis.

1.7 INTRODUCTION TO SIGNALING MECHANISMS

The cells and tissues of the body are in constant communication with one another. Three general methods are used to send information ('signals') from one place to another.

1) Diffusion, which occurs because of the temperature-dependent random jittery movement of molecules ("Brownian motion"). Diffusion (discussed more in Chapters 2-4) causes the net movement of molecules from a region of higher concentration to a region of lower concentration. Diffusion, however, is only useful as a signaling mechanism when distances are short -- for example, at a chemical synapse between two cells such as a nerve and muscle cell. In the latter case, when the membrane electrical signal known as an 'action potential' arrives in the nerve terminal that is in contact with a skeletal muscle fiber, a small amount of the neurotransmitter acetylcholine is released from the nerve terminal into the ~0.1 µm-wide 'synaptic cleft' between the nerve and muscle cell. Because of the small width of the cleft, acetylcholine can quickly reach the muscle membrane by diffusion, thereby raising its concentration in a fraction of a ms from essentially zero into the micromolar (µM) range. In consequence, acetylcholine binds to protein receptors on the muscle membrane, which causes an electrical response in the muscle cell (described in Chapter 11). As a rough rule of thumb, for a small molecule like acetylcholine (molecular mass, 146 Daltons), the time for a diffusive signal to spread 1 µm is roughly 1 ms; however, the time required varies with the square of the distance -- so, for example, if distance is 3 times longer, the time required is 9 times longer. By this rule, it would take a diffusive chemical signal more than a day to travel 1 cm, and many years to travel 1 meter.

2) Bulk flow, for example as driven by the pressure differences that occur within the vasculature during the circulation of the blood. Compared with diffusion, bulk flow can dramatically shorten communication time. In humans at rest, blood from the heart reaches all parts of the body within about 1 minute, as can oxygen and the various signaling molecules carried by the blood. By means of both diffusion and bulk flow, the concentration of signaling molecules can rise locally to 'activating' levels, i.e., levels that result in substantial physiological effects -- in this case due to the binding of the signaling molecules to receptor sites on cellular targets. Once the signaling molecules bind to their targets, important cellular activities can be activated or inhibited.

3) Electrical signals, such as action potentials (discussed in Chapter 8). In the nervous system, propagation of action potentials over distance is very fast, requiring only 10 ms

per meter in a large nerve fiber and 1 s per meter in a small one. As described in a later chapter, the three major types of muscle cells -- skeletal muscle (voluntary muscle), heart muscle (cardiac muscle), and smooth muscle (e.g., the muscle cells at surround blood vessels and hollow organs) -- also utilize propagating electrical signals to control their function, although the typical propagation velocities in these cells and tissues are slower.

In addition to these mechanisms, cells contain motor proteins, which can move cargo and, potentially, information -- the latter in the form of signaling molecules -- from one location to another along long filamentous structures within the cell. For example, the motor protein myosin uses ATP to move cargo such as lipid vesicles along actin filaments. Similarly, the motor proteins kinesin and dynein use ATP to move cargo along microtubules. Movements by these motor mechanisms proceed on the order of 1 mm per s, with the time requirement increasing with the first power of the distance.

1.8 CELL SIGNALING VIA VOLTAGE AND CALCIUM

As noted above, complex signaling pathways, both within one cell and among many cells, are a hallmark of animal cells. These pathways evolved from single-celled organisms, where it was also of great benefit to be able to sense changes in the local environment and transmit this information to other locations or organelles in the cell to evoke a response useful for nutrition, movement, osmotic regulation, or reproduction.

An illustrative example is the avoidance response of a ciliated paramecium (Fig. 1.9). Normally, this protozoan (a one-celled animal) swims on 'auto-pilot', moving steadily forward in a slow wandering path driven by the forward beat of its cilia. If the organism collides with an object, however, a stereotyped response ensues -- it backs up briefly and then swims forward in a different direction.

This response (Naitoh and Eckert, 1969) happens to be mediated by two signaling pathways that are also used in many multi-cellular organisms:

(1) A change in membrane potential of the surface membrane (ΔV_m). The ΔV_m in this case is an initial depolarization (i.e., a rise of V_m towards 0 mV) followed by an action potential.

16 CHAPTER 1

(2) A change in intracellular free Ca^{2+} concentration ($\Delta[Ca^{2+}]_i$). The $\Delta[Ca^{2+}]_i$ in this case is an increase from the nanomolar (10^{-9} molar) level to the micromolar (10^{-6} molar) level, followed by a decrease.

During the paramecium's action potential, Ca^{2+} enters the cell from the ECF, where $[Ca^{2+}]_o$ is several mM. Because $[Ca^{2+}]_i$ is very low at rest (perhaps ~50 nM) and the relevant distances within the cell are short, a relatively small amount of entering Ca^{2+} can quickly raise the local $[Ca^{2+}]_i$ many-fold above the resting level. This $\Delta[Ca^{2+}]_i$ serves as the signal for the cilia to reverse their beat and move the organism backward.

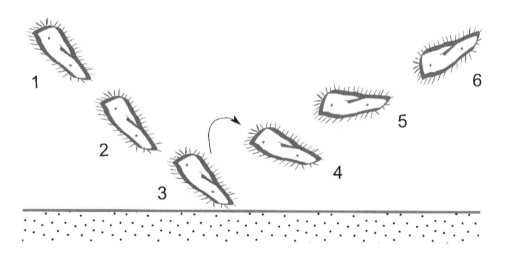

Figure 1.9 The avoidance response of a paramecium. Upon encountering an object, the beat of the paramecium's cilia reverses briefly to allow a change of course. [After Hille (2001)].

The mechanism involves the binding of Ca^{2+} ions to Ca^{2+}-sensitive regulatory molecules on motor proteins; with Ca^{2+} bound, the regulatory molecules change conformation and cause a larger-scale change -- in this case, a change in the direction of the beating of the cilia on the surface membrane. The normal forward beat resumes after reversal of these signaling events, i.e., after V_m and $[Ca^{2+}]_i$ return to near their resting levels.

1.9 WHAT HAPPENS WHEN A HEALTHY CELL MEMBRANE IS DAMAGED?

Of the myriad different signaling pathways in use in animals, it is remarkable how many utilize as building blocks a ΔV_m and/or a $\Delta[Ca^{2+}]_i$. It is instructive to imagine how evolutionary forces might have directed this to happen. For example, imagine the hypothetical case of a primitive one-celled organism with a long cytoplasmic process that is used to explore the environment (Fig. 1.10A). If damage occurred to the 'cell body' (defined here as the bulbous part of the cell containing the nucleus) -- e.g., due to a major tear of its cell membrane -- the death of the cell might be the most likely outcome. If the damage were smaller, however, and occurred on the cell process (Fig. 1.10B), the consequences, while serious, might not be fatal. Near the damage site, there would be, among other things, (i) a local decrease in the absolute value of membrane potential (i.e., V_m would rise toward 0 mV) and (ii) a large increase in $[Ca^{2+}]_i$, approaching the mM level at the site of damage, due to the diffusion of Ca^{2+} from outside the cell to inside the cell.

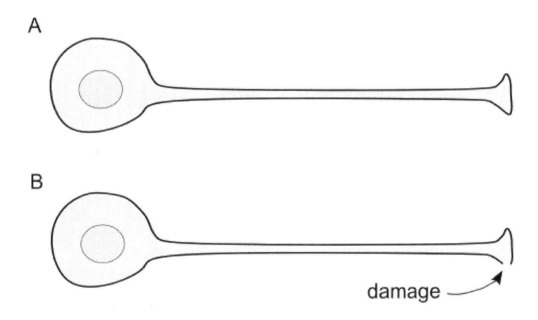

Figure 1.10 Hypothetical single-celled organism with a long cell process for exploring the environment. A. Undamaged cell. B. Cell with a tear at its end.

It would be very useful if the cell could sense these local changes (ΔV_m and $\Delta[Ca^{2+}]_i$) and initiate appropriate survival responses. For example, if the cell membrane contained voltage-dependent ion channels, these could sense the local ΔV_m, respond by changing their conformation, and quickly send an electrical signal along the cell membrane to the cell body to notify it of the damage. The cell body could then respond in various ways, including directing an increased synthesis of proteins. If the cytoplasm near the site of damage had appropriate Ca^{2+}-dependent enzymes and other metabolic machinery, organized molecular responses could take place to address both the immediate threat and the longer-term aftermath. For example:

(i) motor proteins acting on internal filaments could retract the cell process to avoid further insult;

(ii) lipid vesicles, stored internally, could be moved to the surface membrane to fuse to the damaged membrane and plug the leak;

(iii) internal organelles such as the endoplasmic reticulum could take up the excess Ca^{2+} on a temporary basis and return the Ca^{2+} to the ECF at a later time;

(iv) energy stored in the form of glycogen could be broken down to glucose to help maintain the immediate energy sources (e.g., ATP);

(v) the mitochondria could also take up a fraction of the Ca^{2+} and use the rise in mitochondrial $[Ca^{2+}]$ as a signal to increase production of ATP, whose need would likely be large over the next minutes and hours to restore the resting state of the cell.

Signaling pathways that depend on ΔV_m and/or $\Delta[Ca^{2+}]_i$ of the type imagined here are, in fact, commonplace in cells. A number of these will be considered in later chapters.

1.10 EXERCISES

Exercise 1.1 Given that ~40% of the total water in the body is found in the extracellular fluids and ~60% in intracellular fluids, use the information in Fig. 1 to estimate whether total body water contains more Na^+ ions or more K^+ ions.

Exercise 1.2 The Na^+/K^+ pump (the function of which will be discussed in detail in Chapter 6) uses the energy in the hydrolysis of one ATP molecule to move 3 Na^+ ions from the ICF to the ECF and 2 K^+ ions from the ECF to the ICF. Does this activity, considered in isolation, cause V_m to become more negative, more positive, or remain unchanged? Alternately stated, if all Na^+/K^+ pump activity in a cell at steady-state were to suddenly cease, would the immediate effect on V_m be for it to become more positive, more negative, or remain unchanged? [Note: if the reader is uncertain about the answer to this question, the material in Chapter 6 will make the answer clear.]

CHAPTER 2

DIFFUSION, OSMOSIS, AND MEMBRANE PERMEABILITY

Diffusion and osmosis are physical processes that occur throughout the natural world. Not surprisingly, many physiological mechanisms depend on diffusion and osmosis, including the permeability of membranes to many constituents. This chapter considers the laws that govern these processes. Many applications of these laws arise in later chapters.

2.1 SIMPLE DIFFUSION

Atoms and molecules, whether in gases, liquids, or solids, are always in motion. If a particular atom or molecule is not constrained, it will move randomly in three dimensions. Thus, its location at some later time cannot be predicted from its location at an earlier time. Collections of such molecules, however, behave in statistically predictable ways.

Fick's First Law. Eqn. 2.1 gives a basic law of diffusion in one dimension, as stated by Adolf Fick. It states that the rate at which an uncharged substance moves by diffusion along a direction x perpendicular to a planar boundary is a function of three variables:
- dC/dx, the concentration gradient of the substance at the boundary;
- A, the area of the boundary;
- D, a proportionality factor known as the 'diffusion coefficient' (sometimes called 'diffusion constant').

$$\frac{\text{Quantity of substance}}{\text{unit time}} = \frac{dQ}{dt} = -D\,A\,\frac{dC}{dx} \,. \tag{2.1}$$

The rate of movement of the substance per unit area A is called the 'flux' (usually denoted 'J'). Thus, another way of writing Fick's first law is:

$$J = -D\,\frac{dC}{dx} \,. \tag{2.2}$$

The minus sign in Eqns. 2.1 and 2.2 means that the net movement of the substance is from the region of higher concentration to the region of lower concentration. Typical units of dQ/dt and D are moles/s and cm²/s, respectively. Note that dQ/dt is proportional to the first power of each of the three variables in Eqn. 2.1. If, for instance, dC/dx should become twice as large while A and D remained unchanged, the rate at which the substance would move across the boundary per unit time would double. Appendix B gives a derivation of Fick's first law based on the assumption that the movement of each molecule (or particle) is a sequence of random steps in either the -x or +x direction.

Fig. 2.1 considers a hypothetical example. A barrier consisting of a uniform permeable material is located between the dotted vertical lines at 6 and 9 arbitrary distance units on the x axis. The concentration C of a permeant substance (continuous line) is assumed to be constant at the indicated values in the solutions on either side of the material but decrease linearly within the material from left to right (thus dC/dx < 0 in this region).

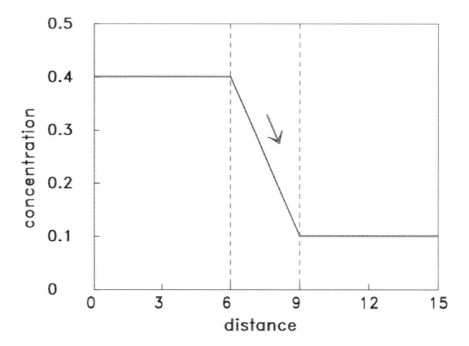

Figure 2.1 Hypothetical example of the diffusive movement of a substance down a concentration gradient through a permeable material located between the dashed vertical lines on the x axis. The units on both axes are arbitrary.

Fick's first law says that there will be net diffusion of the substance from left to right, i.e., down the concentration gradient, as indicated by the arrow in Fig. 2.1. The rate at which the substance diffuses across any area A that is within the material and is perpendicular to the x axis will be the same because the diffusion coefficient of the substance within the material is constant (since the material is uniform) and the concentration gradient, equal to the slope of the line, is constant. Thus, there will be a steady movement of the substance from left to right down the concentration gradient.

It should be noted that the movement of the substance from left to right in Fig. 2.1 is actually made up of independent movements of the substance from both left to right and right to left. For example, the concentration profile in Fig. 2.1 can be thought of as the sum of the two concentration profiles in Fig. 2.2. According to Fick's first law, the net movement associated with the concentration profile in Fig. 2.2A is from left to right whereas that in Fig. 2.2B is from right to left. The latter will be smaller, however, because the associated concentration gradient is smaller. The net movement in Fig. 2.1 is proportional to the net gradient, which is the sum of the two gradients shown in Fig. 2.2.

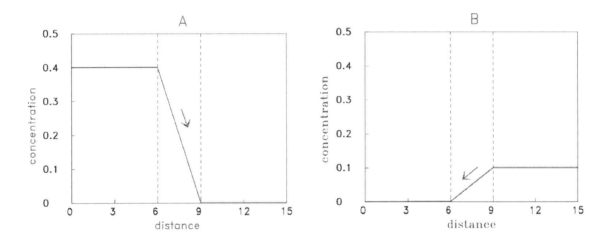

Figure 2.2 Deconstruction of the net diffusive movement in Fig. 2.1 into a sum of two unidirectional movements in opposite directions: A, left to right; B, right to left.

In the example of Figs. 2.1-2.2, the concentration profile is assumed to be static. Over time, however, the profile would be expected to change due to the movement of the molecules that make up the profile. Qualitatively, the concentration in the solution near the left side of the material would decline and that near the right side of the material would rise; consequently, the concentration gradient within the material would become less steep and the net flux would decrease. A *Python* program illustrating these features is considered at the end of Chapter 4.

Fick's Second Law. This law predicts how a concentration profile is expected to change with time. The second law follows from the first law and the assumption that the substance is neither created nor destroyed. If diffusion takes place only in the x dimension, the applicable equation is (see Appendix B for a derivation):

$$\left(\frac{\partial C}{\partial t}\right) = D\left(\frac{\partial^2 C}{\partial x^2}\right). \tag{2.3}$$

That is, the rate of change of concentration at any location x equals the diffusion coefficient times the second derivative of the concentration at location x with respect to distance.

This equation can be understood as follows. If $\partial^2 C/\partial x^2 \neq 0$, $\partial C/\partial x$ is not constant around x. Thus, according to Fick's first law, the net diffusion of the substance just to the left of point x differs from that just to the right of point x. If $\partial^2 C/\partial x^2 > 0$, the concentration profile is concave upward at x and the diffusion gradient that is causing the substance to arrive at x from one direction is greater than that which is causing the substance to leave from x in the other direction; thus, C(x) will be increasing with time. If $\partial^2 C/\partial x^2 < 0$ (i.e., the concentration profile is concave downward at x), the reverse will be true and C(x) will be decreasing with time.

For diffusion in three dimensions (x, y, and z) in an isotropic medium, the analogous equation is:

$$\left(\frac{\partial C}{\partial t}\right) = D\left(\frac{\partial^2 C}{\partial x^2} + \frac{\partial^2 C}{\partial y^2} + \frac{\partial^2 C}{\partial z^2}\right), \tag{2.4}$$

where $\partial/\partial x$ denotes the partial derivative of C(x,y,z,t) with respect to x, and so forth.

For an application of Eqn. 2.3, consider a cell with a long cell process of small diameter (e.g., as in Fig. 1.10 of Chapter 1). Suppose that, somewhere in the middle of the long process, a bolus of a diffusible substance is introduced into the cytoplasm at time t = 0. During each small time interval Δt thereafter, each molecule of the substance is free to move randomly a small distance "left" or "right" relative to its current location; some molecules, of course, will move to the left and some to the right. Over time, the concentration profile will spread out as an ever-widening distribution in the form of a bell-shaped curve (a "Gaussian" curve) centered at the initial location (see Exercises 2.1 and 2.2).

Suppose at time t = 1 (arbitrary time units), the concentration profile looks that in Fig. 2.3A. In this example, the horizontal dashed line in A, which is drawn at the half-height of the bell shape, happens to be of length 3.33 (arbitrary distance units). Fick's second law predicts what the concentration profile will look like at, say, t = 9, i.e., a nine-fold later time. The main portion of this profile is the bell shape shown in Fig. 2.3B.

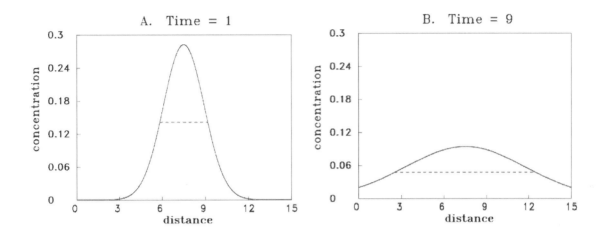

Figure 2.3 Fick's second law applied to a case of one-dimensional diffusion. The plots show theoretical concentration profiles (in arbitrary concentration and distance units) at two times, 1 and 9 (in arbitrary time units), after a bolus of the substance was introduced at time t = 0 at point 7.5 on the distance axis.

The length of the half-height line in B is 10.0, which is three times that in A, whereas the maximum concentration in B is one-third that in A. The total area under the profile, which is proportional to the total amount of the substance, is the same in both cases. (The assumption has been made that the molecules are not altered by metabolism nor can they leave the cell by crossing the cell membrane.) Note that, for distances < 3 or > 12, the concentration is negligible in A but substantial in B.

In summary, with diffusion, the concentration of a substance that was initially negligible at a particular location can, with time, become substantial. This increase comes about because the concentration at other locations decreases with time. Because the time required for the increase in the width of the bell-shaped curve at half-height depends on the square of the distance (see also Exercise 2.2 and the *Python* program Example4_1.py in Chapter

4), diffusion is a very slow process if long distances are considered. This is illustrated in Table 2.1, which is roughly applicable to small molecules diffusing in the body.

Table 2.1 Distances and Times for Small-molecule Diffusion in Example Structures

Distance	Time Required	Example
0.1 µm	10 µsec	synaptic cleft
1 µm	1 ms	air/blood barrier in lung
10 µm	0.1 sec	a small cell
100 µm	10 sec	a large cell
1 cm	1 day	subcutaneous fat
1 m	30 years	a leg

2.2 MEMBRANE PERMEABILITY

We now consider some examples related to the important subject of how molecules move across cell membranes. Our focus will be a thin lipid bilayer that separates two solutions of different composition. Consider an uncharged substance C, whose concentrations in the solutions on the outside and inside of the membrane are denoted C_o and C_i, respectively. (For convenience, we omit the usual concentration brackets ([…]) when referencing concentrations.) To simplify, we treat the bilayer as a uniform phase of thickness w, e.g., w ≈ 3 nm (= 3×10^{-9} m). The concentration of the substance within the membrane phase itself, denoted C^m, is related to that in the aqueous phase by β, the lipid-water partition coefficient for the substance:

$$\beta = \frac{C_o^m}{C_o} = \frac{C_i^m}{C_i} . \qquad (2.5)$$

C_o^m and C_i^m denote the substance concentrations in the membrane immediately adjacent to the outside and inside solutions, respectively. β, which is substance specific, is a number that states how much more (or less) soluble the substance is in lipid relative to water.

Fig. 2.4 considers an example in which the concentration within the membrane is higher than that in the immediately adjacent solution because β is >1 (≈ 1.25). Then, according to Eqn. 2.5, C_o^m will be β times higher than C_o, i.e., $C_o^m = \beta C_o$; similarly, $C_i^m = \beta C_i$.

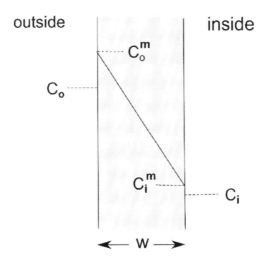

Figure 2.4 Hypothetical concentration profile of a substance on either side of, and within, a lipid membrane of thickness w. C_o and C_i denote the concentrations outside and inside the membrane respectively; superscript m denotes a concentration within the membrane itself.

Given that the membrane phase is uniform, we assume that the concentration gradient within the membrane is constant. It follows that: $dC^m/dx = (C_i^m - C_o^m)/w = \beta (C_i - C_o)/w$.

Then, according to Fick's first law, the (net) rate at which the substance diffuses across the membrane from outside to inside is given by:

$$\frac{\text{Quantity}}{\text{unit time}} = \frac{dQ}{dt} = D \, A \, \beta \, \frac{C_o - C_i}{w} \, . \qquad (2.6)$$

In Eqn. 2.6, D (the diffusion coefficient of substance C in lipid), w (the thickness of the lipid bilayer), and β (the solubility of C in lipid relative to that in water) depend on properties of the lipid phase. These three variables can be lumped together to define a new variable P, the membrane's permeability (or permeability coefficient) for C, which has units of speed (distance per unit time, e.g., cm/s):

$$P = \frac{D\beta}{w}. \tag{2.7}$$

After substitution of Eqn. 2.7 into Eqn. 2.6, the (net) quantity of C that diffuses per unit time from outside to inside across a membrane region of area A is given by:

$$\frac{\text{Quantity}}{\text{unit time}} = \frac{dQ}{dt} = A\,P\,(C_o - C_i). \tag{2.8}$$

Because, as noted, flux is the quantity of the substance moving per unit time per unit area:

$$\text{Flux} = \frac{(dQ/dt)}{A} = P\,(C_o - C_i). \tag{2.9}$$

Eqn. 2.9 has a simple form, which says that the (net) diffusive flux of an uncharged substance C across the membrane is proportional to the difference in the concentrations of C on the two sides of the membrane, with the proportionality factor being the permeability of the compound. As we saw in connection with Fig. 2.2, the net flux is the difference between two uni-directional fluxes, $P \cdot C_o$ (from outside to inside) and $P \cdot C_i$ (from inside to outside). Since P has units of speed, it is as if the molecules adjacent to the outside of the membrane are drifting (diffusing) from outside to inside with speed P, and vice-versa for the molecules adjacent to the inside of the membrane. The speed (i.e., P), of course, differs for different substances because, in general, D and β will vary with the substance.

Membrane permeability is usually determined operationally with Eqn. 2.9. Given (i) a known concentration difference on the two sides of the membrane and (ii) a measurement of the flux, then, by Eqn. 2.9, a measurement of the permeability of that compound is obtained. In the rare case that one had an estimate of the partition coefficient of a compound in the lipid bilayer and the compound's diffusion coefficient in the lipid and the thickness of the bilayer, one could estimate, a priori, the membrane's permeability for that compound with Eqn. 2.7.

In the case of a charged substance, the membrane permeability is most easily determined as the proportionality factor between flux and concentration in the absence of a membrane potential. If an electrical potential exists across a membrane, the flux of a charged molecule across the membrane will depend on the membrane potential as well as the permeability. For example, cells at rest have negative membrane potentials, so the influx of cations for a given extracellular concentration will be enhanced, whereas the influx of anions will be retarded (and, conversely, for the efflux). Chapter 6 considers examples and equations (Eqns. 6.7 – 6.9) regarding how the flux of an ion species across the membrane is expected to vary as a function of the ion's permeability and the membrane potential.

Examples of permeability values determined operationally at room temperature for three important substances and real cell membranes (e.g., frog muscle) are given in Table 2.2.

Table 2.2 Example Membrane Permeabilities of Three Important Molecules

Substance	Permeability (cm/s)
H_2O	10^{-3} to 10^{-2}
K^+	10^{-6}
Na^+	10^{-8}

Note that the permeability of water is several orders of magnitude higher than that of typical small ions. As a rule, cell membranes are highly permeable to water, so much so that, for all practical purposes, water will always be distributed at equilibrium across cell membranes. The exception is the membrane of epithelial cells that face the "outside world" -- e.g., in the intestine, bladder, and parts of the kidney. This so-called 'apical' membrane (which contrasts with the 'baso-lateral' membrane on the other side of the epithelial cell and faces the body) generally has a low water permeability. In some cases the water permeability of these membranes can be regulated upward by hormones. In general, permeabilities of small uncharged molecules will fall between those for water and for K^+.

2.3 RELATION BETWEEN LIPID SOLUBILITY AND MEMBRANE PERMEABILITY

As shown in Fig. 2.5, when cell membranes are tested for their permeability to uncharged molecules of various sizes, in many cases the oil/water partition coefficient (equivalently, lipid solubility) of a substance is a good predictor of its relative membrane permeability (denoted 'p' on the ordinate of Fig. 2.5). For each compound, the ordinate shows p scaled by the 3/2 power of the compound's molecular weight (M), which corrects for the effect of molecular size on the diffusion coefficient (since a larger molecule would be expected to have a smaller diffusion coefficient and thus lower permeability).

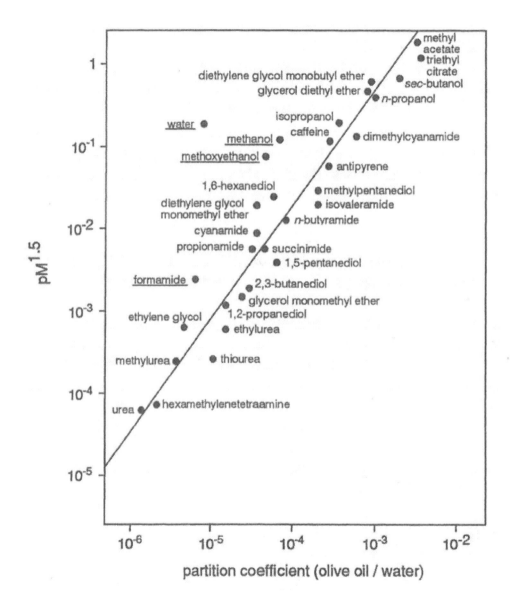

Figure 2.5 Relation between the relative permeability p of various uncharged molecules across the cell membrane of the giant alga *Nitella* (a convenient experimental cell) and the oil/water partition coefficient of these molecules. [Credit: Hall and Baker (1977); after Collander (1954).]

Generally, the experimental values of the permeabilities in Fig. 2.5 correspond quite well to those that would be predicted for permeation through a 3 nm layer of lipid. These findings are in agreement with the lipid bilayer model of a membrane and the idea that the movement of many uncharged molecules across the bilayer occurs by simple diffusion through the lipid.

2.4 EXCEPTIONS TO THE LIPID SOLUBILITY RULE

At least two important exceptions exist to the idea that, for uncharged molecules, relative lipid solubility is a good predictor of relative membrane permeability. The exceptions are all in the direction of a higher-than-expected permeability. The general explanation is that these molecules do not, in fact, cross the membrane primarily by dissolving in and diffusing through the lipid phase; rather, the molecules cross through specialized membrane proteins, generically called 'transport proteins'.

1) The permeability of cell membranes to several small hydrophilic molecules, including glycerol, methanol, ethanol, formamide, and especially H_2O, is higher than would be expected on the basis of their oil/water partition coefficients. (Note in Fig. 2.5 the vertical displacement of the points for formamide, methanol and, particularly, water relative to the straight line). The permeation of H_2O and these other small hydrophilic molecules must rely on a mechanism mediated by membrane transport proteins. In the case of H_2O, the transport is mediated by 'aquaporins', i.e., water-pore proteins.

Aquaporins are a special type of membrane transport protein. A complete aquaporin molecule consists of 4 identical (or similar) subunits, each of molecular mass ~30 kDa, arranged within a roughly square boundary if looked at from above or below the membrane. Each subunit (see structural diagram in Fig. 2.6) contains an internal hydrophilic pathway in which a number of H_2O molecules (a dozen or more) reside at any one time. A narrow constriction towards the middle of the pathway limits passage to a single file of diffusing H_2O molecules while excluding most other molecules. Aquaporins likely also provide a permeability pathway for some other small uncharged polar molecules that have a size similar to water, such as CO_2. Eleven different aquaporin genes are known to be expressed in humans, and several clinical disorders have been associated with mutations in these genes.

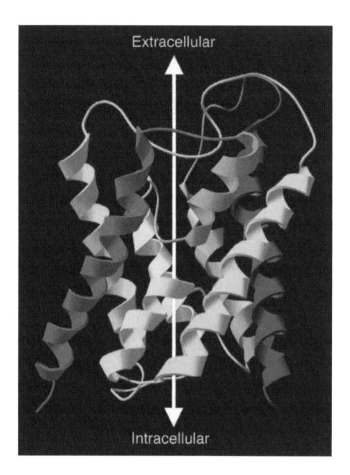

Figure 2.6 Diagram ('ribbon structure') of one subunit of the tetrameric aquaporin 1 protein (AQP1) from human red blood cells. In each subunit, six membrane-spanning α helices surround two hemi-pores (demarcated by the loops connected to the shorter helices) that meet in the center of the bilayer. The core of the subunit thereby supplies a hydrophilic pathway (arrow) through which water, possibly other small uncharged hydrophilic molecules, and perhaps some small ions can diffuse across the membrane. [Credit: Kozono et al. (2002).]

2) Some larger molecules with low lipid solubility (e.g., glucose) can cross the membranes of some cell types quite readily and, in some cases, their permeability can be regulated dynamically. Such permeabilities can often be blocked by specific poisons -- e.g., in the case of glucose, by phlorizin, which is a toxic 'glycoside' made by some plants. (A glycoside is a compound with a sugar molecule bound to another chemical group.) This anomalously high permeability is explained by the existence of another type of transport protein, sometimes called by the somewhat misleading name of 'carrier protein'. In the

case of glucose, these transporters are known as 'GLUT' proteins (short for 'glucose transport' proteins); they are found in all phyla and, in vertebrates, exist in a number of different isoforms.

A carrier protein (also called a 'carrier' or 'transporter') operates by a mechanism called facilitated diffusion (Fig. 2.7). The protein switches by thermal motion between three major states -- one, in which a molecule of a specific chemical type (e.g., a monosaccharide such as glucose) can bind to and dissociate from the transporter on one side of the membrane; another, in which the transported molecule is sequestered within the interior of the protein, having access to neither the outside nor inside of the membrane; and a third, in which the transported molecule can bind to and dissociate from the transporter on the other side of the membrane.

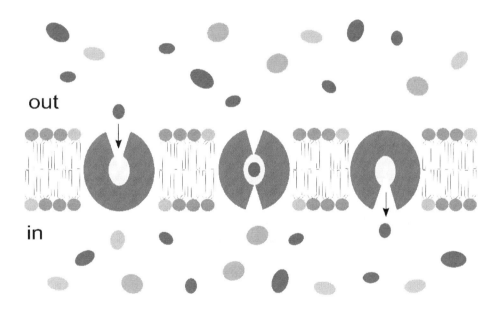

Figure 2.7 Postulated mechanism of facilitated diffusion by a membrane carrier protein. The protein switches by thermal motion between three states, as shown. Each type of carrier protein binds only molecules of similar chemical structure. The binding can take place from the outside or the inside of the membrane. [After Boron and Boulpaep (2009).]

The kinetics of facilitated diffusion differs from that of simple diffusion (Fig. 2.8). With facilitated diffusion, the overall rate of transport of substrate by the carrier protein depends on the rates at which the substrate C binds to and dissociates from the carrier, as well as on the time it takes the carrier to switch between its different states. As the concentration of the substrate increases, it is more likely that a carrier molecule will have a substrate molecule already bound to it; thus, some of the carrier molecules will not be immediately available to bind another substrate molecule. Therefore, kinetic studies of carrier-mediated transport typically reveal 'saturation' kinetics -- meaning that, while the rate of transport of substrate (denoted 'J_C' in Fig. 2.8) increases as substrate concentration increases, the slope relating J_C and [C] becomes progressively smaller (Fig. 2.8A). In contrast, with simple diffusion, the slope relating J_C and [C] remains constant over a large range of substrate concentrations (Fig. 2.8B).

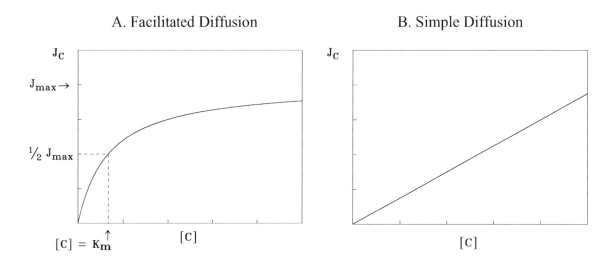

Figure 2.8 Hypothetical comparison of the kinetics of facilitated diffusion (or 'carrier-mediated transport') (A) and simple diffusion (B). For simplicity, it is assumed that the concentration of the transported molecule on the other side of the membrane is zero and that the rate of transport is measured as a uni-directional flux. The ordinate, J_C, shows the transport rate (equivalently, flux) as a function of the concentration [C] of the transported substance on the side of the membrane from which the transport starts.

Facilitated diffusion does not require the input of external energy; it simply provides a pathway for the net movement of a particular molecular species from a higher to a lower concentration. As with simple diffusion, the net transport is made up of opposing uni-directional movements. Should the concentration gradient become reversed, net transport of the molecules across the membrane would occur in the opposite direction.

In Fig. 2.8A, the curve satisfies the equation: $J_C = J_{max} [C]/([C] + K_m)$. This equation (which will be revisited in detail in Chapter 9) has the same form as the Michaelis-Menten equation used in the analysis of enzyme kinetics. As [C] increases, J_C approaches its maximum value, J_{max}. In analogy with the Michaelis-Menten equation, the value of [C] when transport is $J_{max}/2$ is called the 'K_m' (pronounced "k m"). The lower the value of K_m, the higher is the binding affinity between C and the transporter (see also Chapter 9.)

It should be noted that the name "carrier" is not an accurate description of the mechanism of facilitated diffusion, as the protein does not bind the substrate on one side of the membrane and ferry it across to the other by diffusing through lipid. Rather the protein itself spans the membrane and the cargo moves within the protein, as occurs with water in aquaporins (although aquaporins are not thought to change between states in the manner diagrammed in Fig. 2.8).

2.5 OSMOSIS (THE DIFFUSION OF WATER)

As mentioned above, the permeability of cell membranes to water is unusually high. Consequently, any differences in water concentration between the outside and the inside of the cell, or between the cytoplasm and a membrane-delimited organelle, will almost immediately be dissipated by the movement of water across the membrane. For most animal cells, the time required to re-establish water equilibrium following a perturbation is roughly a second or less. Thus, for all practical purposes, animal cells can be considered to always be in "water equilibrium" with their surroundings. An important exception is epithelial cells, which are generally not in water equilibrium with respect to the outside world -- e.g., the kidney can produce concentrated or dilute urine.

'Water concentration' is not a common scientific term; rather, 'osmotic pressure' is. The two terms reflect the same physical reality. Consider a vessel divided into two compartments by an inflexible membrane that is permeable to water but not to solutes (Fig. 2.9). If the compartments are filled to the same level with pure water, no net movement of water takes place.

Now suppose part of the water in the right-hand compartment is replaced with solute, e.g., sucrose. This, in effect, dilutes the water concentration. We know from Fick's first law that net movement of water will occur by diffusion down its concentration gradient -- in this case, from left to right. This type of water movement has historically been called 'osmosis'. Application of physical pressure P onto the sucrose solution (downward arrow, right side of Fig. 2.9) will slow the entry of water. A sufficiently high pressure can even reverse the flow. Such movement of water against its concentration gradient, under the effect of physical pressure, is called 'ultrafiltration'. For a given dilution of water (that is, a given concentration of solute), a well-defined pressure exerted on that solution will exactly stall the influx of water from the left-hand compartment. This pressure, by definition, is called the 'osmotic pressure' of that solution.

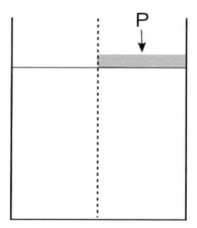

Figure 2.9 Two-compartment vessel illustrating an apparatus for the measurement of osmotic pressure. The dashed vertical line denotes an inflexible membrane that is permeable to water but not to solutes. A variable pressure, P, can be applied to the solution in the right-hand compartment.

Osmotic pressure is sometimes misunderstood. Any solution has a positive osmotic pressure since, if it were placed in the right-hand side of our vessel, pressure would be needed to prevent net entry of water if the compartment on the left contained pure water. The solution itself, however, exerts no physical pressure. It might then be asked: why use 'osmotic pressure' when we mean the concentration of water (low water concentration = high osmotic pressure)? Two reasons apply:

1) A fundamental thermodynamic equivalence exists between a physical pressure that can potentially be exerted on a solution and the presence of a solute in that solution -- for example, Fig. 2.9. On the one hand, the presence of solute, which dilutes the water, causes

water to flow from one compartment to the other. (Note that the water flows from the low osmotic-pressure compartment to the high-osmotic-pressure compartment.) On the other hand, we know that physical pressure itself can cause water to flow. As far as the flow is concerned, the operations of adding solute to one compartment or applying pressure on the other are equivalent and interchangeable. If pressure is applied to the compartment with solute, the flow into it is slowed. If the applied pressure exactly matches the difference in osmotic pressure between the two compartments, no water will flow. If the pressure is applied to the low-osmotic-pressure compartment, the driving force for water flow will be the sum of both forces and the flow will increase.

2) It is customary to use the term 'osmotic pressure'. Suppose a cell has a low water concentration inside. It is equivalent to say that water will flow into the cell until "the inside and outside concentrations are equal" or until "the osmotic pressures of the two sides are equal". In casual discussion of osmotic pressure, pressure dimensions may not even be used. Instead of "the osmotic pressure of solution A is x atmospheres" (or "x mm of Hg"), it might be said that "the osmotic pressure of solution A is x osmoles per liter". Taken literally, the latter expression is incorrect, yet custom has made it an acceptable shorthand.

In most systems, including biological systems, water movements are usually determined by both an osmotic pressure difference and a conventional physical pressure difference. Examples in physiology include the formation of lymph in the capillary beds (see Exercise 2.5) and the filtration of glomerular fluid in the kidney. In both cases the "physical" pressure is the blood pressure, which results from contraction of the heart.

The osmotic pressure of a solution is usually denoted 'Π' (Greek capital π), and, as noted, Π is inversely related to the water (= solvent) concentration. It follows that Π must also be a measure of the amount of solute in that solution. The relationship between osmotic pressure and solute concentration was formulated by J. H. van't Hoff:

$$\Pi = \frac{n}{V} R T = C R T, \qquad (2.10)$$

where n is the number of moles of osmotically-active particles ('osmoles') present, V is the solution volume, C is the concentration of solute, R is the gas constant, and T is absolute temperature. Eqn. 2.10 is closely related to the general gas equation ('ideal gas law'). A common feature of both, which took physical chemists some time to appreciate, is that the macroscopic properties of molecules in solution and of molecules in gases both arise from the random movements of a large but finite number of molecules contained within a confined space.

If we express Π in atmospheres and C in osmoles/liter, then, neglecting non-ideality:
- at 37 °C, a 1 M solution of, say, sucrose will have an osmotic pressure of 25.4 atmospheres (atm) (note that this is a **high** pressure);

- for the same 1 M solution at 22 °C (typical room temperature), Π would be 24.8 atm; at 0 °C (freezing point of pure H_2O), Π would be 22.4 atm.

Reminder: because salts dissociate, a 1 M solution of NaCl is a 2 osmolar solution, so Π would be 50.8 atmospheres at body temperature; a 1 M solution of Na_2SO_4 would be 3 osmolar; and so forth.

2.6 APPLICATION OF OSMOTIC PRESSURE LAWS TO LIVING CELLS

As noted above, the osmotic pressure of the intracellular fluid of most animal cells will quickly become equal to the osmotic pressure of the bathing fluid (i.e., the concentration of water in the two solutions will become equal). Applying the van't Hoff formula (and ignoring non-ideality) we have:

$$\Pi V = n R T, \qquad (2.11)$$

where Π is the osmotic pressure (of either the cell or its bathing medium, which have become equal), V is the volume of the cell, n is the number of osmoles present inside the cell, and R and T have their usual meaning.

Now consider a simple experiment that can be carried out in a few minutes. Because the water permeability of most biological membranes is very high, water will equilibrate on a time scale of a second or so in response to an osmotic perturbation of the extracellular solution. On this time scale, the flux of the solutes present inside or outside the cell can be ignored when compared with the flux of water. Thus, we will assume that no solutes are entering or leaving the cell, i.e., n can be taken to be constant. And, because R and T are also constant, Π V = constant, or:

$$V = \frac{\text{constant}}{\Pi} . \qquad (2.12)$$

Thus, if the cell behaved osmotically in an ideal way (as an 'ideal osmometer'), its volume would vary inversely with the osmotic pressure of the bathing fluid. The impossible extreme predicts a vanishing volume at very high osmolarities. In reality, however, not all the volume of the cell is water. The non-solvent volume is made up of proteins, lipids, and other cell constituents. Thus, the volume of the cell that will actually respond to an osmotic perturbation is (V - b), where b is the non-solvent (also called 'non-osmotic') volume. Hence:

$$V - b = \frac{\text{constant}}{\Pi} . \qquad (2.13)$$

Fig. 2.10 shows the graphical version of Eqn. 2.13. The intersection of the line with the y-axis corresponds to the non-osmotic volume.

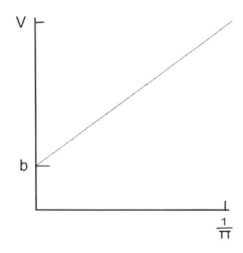

Figure 2.10 The volume of a cell (V) is expected to vary inversely with the osmotic pressure of the bathing solution (Π), with an offset b (= the non-osmotic volume).

In the case of red blood cells, b is about 0.20 - 0.25 of the normal volume. The normal volume is set by the osmolarity of human plasma, which is about 300 mosmol/liter. Any solution with that osmolarity (e.g., 150 mM NaCl) is said to be 'isotonic'. Solutions of higher and lower osmolarity are said to be 'hypertonic' and 'hypotonic', respectively.

Animal cells placed in a hypertonic solution (e.g., sea water) will shrink; maximal shrinking is to about 0.20-0.25 of the resting volume. Cells placed in hypotonic solutions will swell, and, when they exceed a maximum volume, they burst. Erythrocytes burst at about 1.6 times their normal volume.

2.7 EXERCISES

Exercise 2.1 The curves in Fig. 2.3 are plots of the following equation at 2 time points:

$$C(x,t) = \frac{M e^{\frac{-x \cdot x}{4Dt}}}{2\sqrt{\pi Dt}}, \qquad (2.14)$$

where x is distance, t is time, M is a scaling factor (proportional to the total amount of the substance per cross-sectional area of the long cell process), D is the diffusion coefficient, and '·' denotes multiplication.

a) Show that this equation satisfies Fick's second law, i.e., Eqn. 2.3. (This equation, with experimental examples, will be considered further in Chapter 3.)

b) Suppose in Eqn. 2.14 that t is a constant and $D \cdot t = 0.5$ (in distance units squared). At what positive value of x does $(d^2/dx^2) C(x,t) = 0$, i.e., what is the value of $x > 0$ at which $C(x,t)$ changes between convex downward and convex upward?

c) Again suppose that t is a constant and $D \cdot t = 0.5$ and let x_o be your answer to part b). How does $C(x_o,t)$ compare with the maximum value of $C(x,t)$?

Exercise 2.2 Given Eqn. 2.14:

a) How does the amplitude of the concentration profile at $x = 0$ depend on t?

b) If the amplitude of the concentration profile times the width of the profile at half-height is constant as a function of t, how does the width of the profile at half-height vary with t? Conversely, how does t vary with the width of the profile?

Exercise 2.3 Suppose that a cell, in a medium with given osmotic pressure Π_1, has a volume of 120 µm³, of which 20 µm³ is non-osmotic. When placed in a new solution of osmotic pressure Π_2, this cell acquires a new volume of 170 µm³. What is Π_1 / Π_2 ?

Exercise 2.4 Suppose a red blood cell has a volume of 100 µm³ when bathed in isotonic (150 mM) NaCl solution. It is known that the non-osmotic volume of the cell is 30 µm³

(= the volume of the cell that is insensitive to osmotic changes). For the short duration (seconds) of the following experiments, assume that no solutes enter or leave the cell. What volume will the cell acquire when plunged into large volumes of (a) 300 mM sucrose, (b) 100 mM NaCl, or (c) 150 mM NaCl + 300 mM sucrose?

Exercise 2.5 The blood capillaries, the smallest vessels in the vascular system, permit exchange of nutrients and waste between the blood and the tissues via the movement of fluid between the capillaries and the tissues. This fluid, which consists of water and small-molecular-weight solutes, moves primarily through capillary openings of diameter ~5 nm (so-called 'vascular pores '), which are located between the cells that make up the capillary walls. The movement of this fluid is determined primarily by the following diffusive and hydrostatic forces, which are known as the 'Starling forces':

- An osmotic pressure difference of about 20 to 25 mm of Hg that exists between the blood and the tissues (higher in the blood), which is primarily due to the presence of blood proteins that are too big to move through the capillary pores. This osmotic pressure, which goes by the name 'oncotic pressure', favors the movement of fluid from the tissues to the blood.

- A hydrostatic pressure in the tissues (tissue 'turgor pressure') of about 1 mm Hg. This pressure also favors the movement of fluid from the tissues to the blood.

- A hydrostatic pressure within the capillaries due to the blood pressure. This pressure, which is perhaps 30-35 mm of Hg at the arteriolar end of the capillary and 15-20 mm of Hg at the venular end, favors the movement of fluid from the blood to the tissues.

Draw a graph of these various pressures as a function of distance (in arbitrary units) along a capillary between its arteriolar and venular ends and use it to interpret where along the capillary the net force will cause fluid to move into or out of the vascular system. Assume that blood pressure declines linearly from the arteriolar to the venular ends of the capillary.

Note: Under normal circumstances, more capillary fluid moves from blood to tissue than vice-versa. The excess fluid moving into the tissues is returned to the vascular system through drainage via the lymphatic system.

CHAPTER 3

INTRODUCTION TO PYTHON

The introduction to the *Python* programming language in this chapter should enable the reader to start to make useful calculations that are relevant to the study of cell physiology. Chapter 4 gives a more systematic presentation of the elements of *Python* as a programming language.

3.1 A PROGRAM THAT PLOTS A ONE-DIMENSIONAL DIFFUSION PROFILE

We begin with an example of a short *Python* program that produces some graphical output. The reader is encouraged to type this program into the Editor of the *Spyder* IDE or equivalent setup and run it. (From here on, we will simply say 'IDE' and assume that the reader is using *Spyder* or its equivalent on a Windows platform; see Appendix A. Similar features should also apply on a Mac and other environments.)

The reader is not expected to fully understand this first program. Rather, the example has been selected to illustrate how just a few lines of *Python* code can produce a useful calculation and plot. The line numbers are produced by the Editor and are not part of the program itself. The first four lines of the program are comments (flagged by the # sign). Other comments (also flagged by # signs) are included in later lines. The reader can omit typing the comments if he/she wishes. To save space, indented coding lines below use only 2 spaces rather than the usual 4.

```
1 #-*- coding: utf-8 -*-
2 # First example: Example3_1.py
3 # Description: calculate and plot a Gaussian profile in one-dimension
4 #blank lines and "white space" within lines are ignored in Python
5  import numpy as np                  #this makes available all functions in the numpy library
6  import matplotlib.pyplot as plt     #make available some functions in the matplotlib library
7
8  def my_Gaussian(x):                 #the colon in this function-definition statement is important
9    return A*np.exp(-x*x/B)           #the indentation of several spaces in this line is important
```

```
10                         #the end of the indented lines ends the function definition
11 A,B = 1,1               #for the present we will set both A and B to 1
12 X=np.linspace(-4.,4.,200)    #X is an array of 200 values of the independent variable
13 Y=my_Gaussian(X)        #calculate values on X with the my_Gaussian function
14
15 #get_ipython().run_line_magic('matplotlib', 'qt')  #for plot to appear in its own window
16 plt.plot(X,Y, 'k')      #make an x-y plot in black ('k') using the values in arrays X and Y
17 plt.xlim(-4.0,4.0)      #this sets a specific plot range for the x axis
18 plt.ylim(0.,1.05)       #this sets a specific plot range for the y axis
19 plt.xlabel('distance')  #these 3 lines add labels to the axes and a title to the plot
20 plt.ylabel('concentration')
21 plt.title('Example3_1: one-dimensional Gaussian profile')
22 plt.savefig('example3_1.png', dpi=200)   #save as png image at a resolution of 200 dpi
23 plt.show()              #show the plot on the computer screen
```

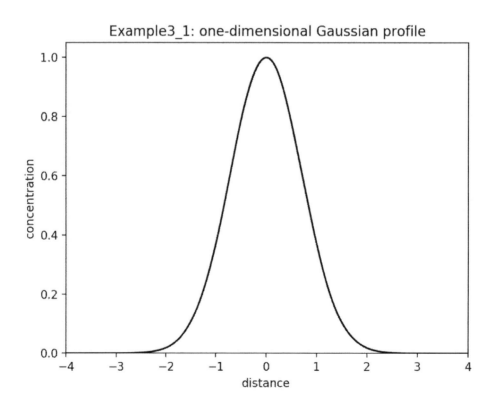

Figure 3.1 Plot of a one-dimensional diffusion profile, obtained as output from Exampe3_1.py.

Program Notes
- Line 1 is supplied by the Editor. After the remaining lines have been typed, the simplest way to run the program is to click the green right-facing triangle button (the 'play' button), which is on the tool bar in the Editor panel (located just to the right of the icon to save all open files). You can also run the program with the F5 function key. In either case, the program file will be saved in the working directory before program execution starts. (If you haven't yet set your working directory, do so now; see Appendix A. If you haven't given a name to your program, do so now.) If your program has been saved in the working directory, a third way to run it is to use the Console panel and type 'run example3_1' on the input line of the Console. In this case, the program will **not** be re-saved automatically from the Editor into the working directory. In all of these cases, the program name should now appear in the list of file names in your working directory. A program file of this type is often called a 'script' file.

- When the program is run, the *Python* Interpreter reads the first executable line of code, which, in this case, is line 5. Under the assumption that the interpreter does not detect a typing or other error, it executes that line of code. If an error is detected, program execution stops at that point, an error is reported to the Console, and the error must be fixed. The interpreter then reads the second line of executable code (line 6) and executes that. It continues in this fashion until the last line of executable code has been processed (line 23). In this example, each line of executable code is specified by a single line in the program file; however, this is not a requirement. A long line of executable code may need the information specified in several sequential lines of coding. In this case, the backslash character ('\'), which serves as the line-continuation character, should be the last character in all but the last line in that series of program lines. This allows *Python* to read several lines from the file before it concatenates the result and attempts to execute the combination as a single line of code. Examples of this feature will be seen in later programs.

- If the entered coding lines are error-free, the output of the program should look like the plot in Fig. 3.1. The plot shows a standard bell-shaped curve (a Gaussian profile) that is centered at 0 on the x-axis. On a Windows platform, the color of the curve is, by default, blue, but, in line 16, it has been set to black by means of the argument in quotes ('k'; see below).

- The curve, which is a special case of Eqn. 2.14, is calculated by means of the function my_Gaussian (lines 8-9). Among other things, this curve has the functional form of a "diffusion profile" in one dimension for certain starting conditions. Specifically, if a bolus of a substance is introduced at time t=0 within an infinitely narrow location centered at x=0 and the substance is free to diffuse in the +x and -x directions only, the curve describes the relative concentration of the substance vs. distance at some later time. Equivalently, if a single molecule of the substance is introduced at x=0 and t=0, the curve shows the relative probability of finding the molecule at location x at a later time. The reason for use of the factors A and B in the function (for convenience, here set to 1) will be explained below. A calibration of the x-axis in specific distance units would depend on two factors: the elapsed time after introduction of the substance at zero time and the diffusion coefficient of the substance. For simplicity, these values have been left out of this particular calculation. The calibration of the y-axis in concentration or other units would depend on the amount of substance in the bolus (also omitted for simplicity). If all the values for a real calculation had been specified, a plot of this type would typically give x in units of cm and y in moles per cm^3 of solution (or perhaps in molar units = moles per liter of solution, abbreviated M). The units of the diffusion coefficient are often given in $cm^2 \, s^{-1}$.

- The .py extension at the end of the file name (line 2) identifies this file as a *Python* program. The Interpreter expects this extension and may complain if it is not there when you try to run your program under the name of the saved script file.

- Any sequence of characters that starts with the number-sign character (#) and fits on a single line of the file -- whether the # sign begins at the start of the line or later in the line -- is treated as a comment and therefore ignored by the Interpreter. A common coding practice is to have a line in the program file begin with an executable statement, then be followed later on the same line with a short comment that starts with #. The reader is encouraged to make liberal comments throughout all of his/her programs to specify the intended effect of the coding lines. This helps avoid the common problem that a line of code that has an "obvious" meaning at the time of writing may be almost indecipherable when the program is examined at a later time.

- Although not shown in Example3_1.py, any block of code that starts and ends with three double-quotation marks in a row (""" ... """) is treated as a comment. Use of this feature allows you to enter long comments in your program, such as many consecutive comment lines, without starting each line with the # sign. This feature also provides a simple way to disable entire sections of executable lines of code in a program, e.g., during the debugging process.

- The blank lines in the program have no effect on program execution; they are included to isolate logical segments of code to increase readability.

- In line 5, the Interpreter is asked to import into computer memory a specific collection of functions called 'numpy' and make these available during execution. Importing numpy with the phrase 'as np' allows for use of a short-cut in syntax when calling the associated functions (e.g., lines 9 and 12). [Note: a collection of external functions that is imported into a program is commonly called a 'library'. In *Python*, a library is often referred to as a 'package', and large packages are sometimes divided into smaller units called 'modules'. We will often refer to these external collections of functions simply as 'libraries'.]

- Line 6 asks the Interpreter to import the pyplot module that is part of the matplotlib package so that its functions are available and can be referred to with their own short-cut syntax.

- Lines 8-9 define the function my_Gaussian that will carry out the major calculation needed in the program. (1) The use of the keyword 'def' marks the start of a user-defined function; (2) the function name 'my_Gaussian' is chosen so as to convey some meaning about what the function does, in this case to calculate a Gaussian-shaped curve; (3) when the function is called by the main program, the dummy argument x, which is enclosed in parentheses and is expected to appear somewhere in the body of the function, has its value passed from the main program; (4) the presence of the colon after the specification of the parenthesized function argument(s) marks the end of the function declaration; (5) the indentation, which is normally 4 spaces (not a tab), that starts line 9 marks the beginning of the body of the function definition, and the lack of an indentation in line 11 marks the end of the function definition; (6) the use of the keyword 'return' in front of the value in line 9 means that this value will be made available to the main program at the location that called the function. These features apply generally to any user-defined function.

- The term 'A*np.exp(-x*x/B)' in line 9 does the function's main work. This term uses the 'np' function 'exp' to calculate the result of exponentiating e (the base of the natural logarithms) to whatever value is specified by the expression in parentheses. Note that, to access a specific function in the np library, the syntax starts with the library name (np) followed by a dot (.) and then the function name; as is common practice, variables passed to the function are enclosed in parentheses. These are features of many function calls in *Python*. In this case, the function takes the argument x (whose value is passed from the main program) multiplies x by itself, divides the result by B (which happens to be defined outside the function), takes the negative of that result, and exponentiates e to this value. The result is then multiplied by the variable A (also defined outside the function) and that product is returned to the main program.

- Line 11 is a double 'assignment' statement that sets to 1 the values of A and B, which are 'global' variables whose values are set in the main program (not in 'my_Gaussian' proper). Because the variables are global, their values are available to the function as long as their values have been specified prior to the first function call (which occurs in line 13).

- Line 12 invokes 'linspace', another function in the np library. This very useful function will be encountered often. Its effect here is to create an array of floating-point numbers whose values can be referred to all at once by the name X. X has 200 equally-spaced numbers between -4. and 4., inclusive. If necessary, its values can be accessed by standard array-index notation. This means that the first number of X is referred to as X[0] (which, in this case, equals -4.0) and the last number of X is referred to as X[199] (which equals 4.0). *Python*, like most other computer languages, finds it convenient to index arrays beginning with 0 rather than 1; hence the last number in the 200-element array has an index of 199 rather than 200. These indices and values can be seen in the Variable Explorer panel of the IDE after double-clicking on the right-hand side of the line for variable X in Variable Explorer. A new window is then displayed that lists the values in array X.

- Line 13 passes an array X to the my_Gaussian function and assigns to Y the value returned by the function. This type of calculation is an example of a 'vector calculation' (or a 'vectorization'). It is a very powerful feature of *Python*. If the argument passed to the function had been just a single value, my_Gaussian would have used its internal formula to calculate and return just one value. But, because the function argument X is an array of numbers (a 'vector'), the function returns an array of the same dimension as X, the values of which are calculated by sequential application of the formula within the function to the individual elements of X. This feature works similarly for multi-dimensional arguments.

- Line 15 calls a strange-looking function, get_ipython().run_line_magic, with the string variables 'matplotlib' and 'qt' as arguments. This function call is not required to make and save the plot but, in some cases, does bring up a bit of magic. (Note: this call is **not** needed if the 'Graphics backend option' described under '2.' in Appendix A has changed 'inline' to 'Automatic'. If so, the 'get_ipython…' line can be omitted.) If active, this function enables Figure 3.1 to be viewed in its own window, in which a toolbar is displayed that permits examination of some features of the plot in greater detail without the need to re-run the program with different values of its variables. For example, one can use the zoom-to-rectangle tool to see blow-ups of different regions of the plot.

- Line 16 tells *Python* to use the function 'plot' in the pyplot module to create a plot of y values vs. x values in black ('k' is the abbreviation for black). As it happens, the names of the two sets of values used in the function call are Y and X, respectively. Notice that line 13 could be skipped if line 16 were changed to 'plot(X,my_Gaussian(X))'.

- Lines 17-18 set specific ranges for the x and y axes of the plot; without these statements the plt.plot function would select reasonable default values for the plotting range.

- The effect of lines 19-21 is obvious -- they provide labels and a title for the plot by means of calls to other functions in matplotlib.pyplot. Note that the argument passed to each of these functions is a string variable (i.e., a sequence of characters), as indicated by their enclosure in single quotes. If preferred, an enclosing pair of double quotes can be used.

- Line 22 calls the function 'plt.save()' to save the figure in the working directory under the name specified in parentheses (which, again, is a string variable surrounded by quotation marks). In this case, the extension 'png' causes the figure to be saved in the format of a png image file and the resolution is set to 200 dpi. Other resolutions and other formats for the saved figure can also be specified, such as jpg, eps, and pdf. The phrase 'dpi=200' within the function call specifies what is called a 'keyword argument'. A keyword argument supplies an optional addition to a function call. (If it is omitted, a default value for the variable 'dpi' is supplied by the interpreter.) Many standard functions in *Python* have keyword arguments. If the console is selected and the phrase 'help(plt.savefig)' is typed followed by the 'enter' key, information about the function 'plt.savefig', including information about the allowed keyword arguments, will be printed to the console -- and similarly for other functions known to the interpreter.

- In line 23, the call to the function 'show()' in matplotlib.pyplot may be required for some environments to make the plot appear in the IDE Console or in a separate window in the Anaconda Navigator (where it is labeled 'Figure 1').

Also of Note

- In general, *Python* ignores blank lines and 'white space' within lines. For example, statements such as 'y= float(x)' and 'y =   float(x)' are treated the same. White space is important, however, in the case of statements that are part of a function definition (e.g., line 9) or that control the logical flow of a program (such as the lines immediately after the 'if' and 'while' statements that occur in Example3_3.py below); in these cases, indentations are required. The common standard is to use 4 spaces for an indentation, not a tab. If the user enters a tab, the Editor will replace it with 4 spaces. These indentations substitute for the brackets and related features that are required in other languages, such as C++, to set off logical sections of code. A line with an unexpected indentation may generate an error.

- *Python* distinguishes between lowercase and uppercase letters. If, for example, line 11 said "a,b=1,1" and the definition of 'my_Gaussian' were left unchanged, the Interpreter would stop program execution at line 13 due to the error detected when my_Gaussian is called and would report an error to the Console. The user would then have to edit the names for consistency before proceeding to run the revised program.

- As noted, values of the variables created by this program can be examined in the Variable Explorer tab of the upper right-hand panel of the IDE. They include A and B, whose values are both the integer 1 (not the floating value of 1.0) and two 200-member arrays of floating-point numbers, X and Y. (Chapter 4 reviews the most-common variable types that we will use in *Python*.) Also used implicitly is the built-in number e (the base of the natural logs), which is used in the function np.exp within the function my_Gaussian. This number does not appear in Variable Explorer because it is a constant not a variable. Note that, in calculating the return value of my_Gaussian in line 9, *Python* does automatic type conversions as needed. In this case the values of A and B as used in the function will be converted to floating point numbers (in this case, 1.0 and 1.0) that can be multiplied by the floating-point number returned by the np.exp function. (The values of A and B as integers in the main program are not affected by these conversions.) The final value returned by the function is thus also a floating-point number. The latter number does not appear in Variable Explorer for two reasons: it does not have a name, and it is calculated within a function, whose internal values cease to be available once the function call is completed.

- Once the plot is displayed in the figure window, you can place the tip of the cursor arrow anywhere within the plot proper -- for example, somewhere on the curve itself -- and the corresponding x and y values will be shown in the lower left-hand corner of the figure panel. This is a very useful capability of *Python* that comes 'for free' in the matplotlib library.

- If the user types 'help(plt.plot)' into the Console, the 'help' function is called and information about the plt.plot function is printed out for the user to see. Scanning this information will give an idea of the full capabilities of this function and how other features might be used by modifying the call to plt.plot. Similarly, the help function can be used to gain information about the functions plt.xlabel, plt.ylabel, plt.title, etc. It can even be used to get information about entire libraries and sub-libraries such as numpy and matplotlib.pyplot. In the latter cases, much more information will be printed out to the Console than the user is likely to be interested in at present. As you become more familiar with *Python*, you will find yourself using the help function more and more -- e.g., to expand your understanding of the various functions that appear in your programs and to help in recovering from programming errors.

- If the program is terminated by the Interpreter because of a programming error, information about the coding error will be printed out, including the line number of the error and some information about what the error is due to. One can then use the Editor to make a correction in the program file and re-run the program. Sometimes unexpected things can happen with this approach because the variables in the program retain the values that they had when the program terminated (and, of course, their current values can be examined with the Variable Explorer). To be on the safe side, before re-running a newly-edited program, you may want to type '%reset' (or, in some systems, you can type either 'reset' or '%reset') into the Console, which will then delete all the current variables once you have responded 'y'. Alternatively, to start anew with a clean slate, you can click on the small 'Options' box at the top right of the Console menu bar and select "Restart kernel". A third, more-drastic, option is to close the IDE and restart it.

3.2 A PROGRAM THAT PLOTS A TWO-DIMENSIONAL DIFFUSION PROFILE

We now consider a second example of a short *Python* program. This program produces a somewhat more complicated graphical output, namely, a surface plot of a two-dimensional Gaussian concentration profile. Fig. 3.2 shows, on the z-axis, the calculated function values for many pairs of x,y values. The reader is encouraged to type Example3_2.py into the Editor and run it. As before, it is not expected that the reader will fully understand all lines of code; again, the example is chosen to illustrate the power of just a few lines of *Python* code. New comments are given only for the coding lines that are different from those already discussed in Example3_1.py.

```
1  # -*- coding: utf-8 -*-
2  # Second example: Example3_2.py
3  # Description: calculation and surface plot of a 2D Gaussian profile
4
5  import numpy as np
6  import matplotlib.pyplot as plt
7  from mpl_toolkits.mplot3d import Axes3D  #get the surface-plotting function Axes3D
8
9  def my_Gaussian(x):
10     return A*np.exp(-x*x/B)
11
12 A,B = 1,1
13 coords = np.linspace(-3.,3.,100)         #coords holds 100 floating-points between -3. and 3.
14 X,Y = np.meshgrid(coords,coords)         #and define an x,y grid of 10,000 point-pairs
15 R = np.sqrt(X**2+Y**2)                   #R is an x,y point grid; sqrt is the np square-root function
16 Z = my_Gaussian(R)                       #apply the my_Gaussian function to the point-pairs in R
17
18 #get_ipython().run_line_magic('matplotlib', 'qt')  #not needed with 'automatic' graphics
19 ax=Axes3D(plt.figure())                  #Axes3D will return a name for the surface plot-to-be
20 ax.plot_surface(X,Y,Z,color='gray',rstride=1,cstride=1)  #create the surface plot
21 ax.set_xlabel('x distance')
22 ax.set_ylabel('y distance')
23 ax.set_zlabel('concentration')
24 ax.set_title('Example3_2: surface plot of a two-dimensional diffusion profile')
25 plt.show()
26
27 plt.savefig('Example3_2.png', dpi=200)
```

The z-axis in the plot shows concentration as a function of the x,y point pairs. This plot would apply, for example, at some time $t > 0$ if (a) a bolus of a substance were introduced at time $t = 0$ and location 0,0 in the x,y-plane and (b) the substance could diffuse equally well in both the x and y dimensions (i.e., the same diffusion coefficient applied to both dimensions). Again, a calibration of the axes of the plot would depend on the amount of the substance introduced at zero time, on the elapsed time after introduction of the substance, and on the value of the diffusion coefficient.

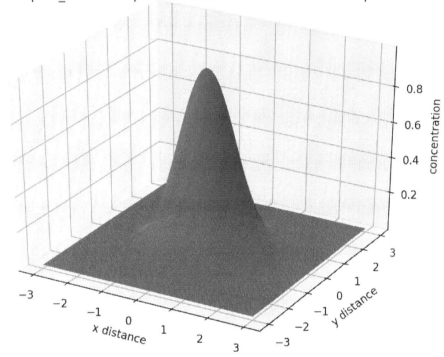

Figure 3.2 Plot of a two-dimensional diffusion profile, obtained as output from Example3_2.py.

Program Notes
- Apart from the new name, the only change from Example3_1.py in the first part of the program is the statement to import the single function 'Axes3D' from the 'mplot3d' module of the mpl_toolkits package, i.e., the function needed to make the surface plot. Instead of asking the Intepreter to bring all the functions in the library into computer memory, the syntax 'from ... import ...' gives the program access to just the one-needed function.

- Line 13 again uses the np.linspace function to create an array variable 'coords' (short for coordinates), with 100 evenly-spaced values between -3. and 3.

- Line 14 uses coords in the np.meshgrid function to define two arrays (X and Y) of x,y point pairs that will be used as the independent variables in the surface plot.

- Line 15 uses *Python's* vectorization capability to create another two-dimensional array of the same size as X and Y that holds the Cartesian distance from the origin of each x,y point pair.

- Line 16 uses the same user-defined function that appeared in Example3_1.py to calculate the value of concentration as a function of distance from the origin (in this case, the two-dimensional Cartesian distance).

- Line 19 "gets control" of the axes of the surface plot by calling Axes3D; the name 'ax' is assigned to the function's return value (which is used in Line 19).

- To make the surface plot, line 20 calls the function 'plot_surface', which is available to the object 'ax' returned by Axes3D. The call is made with arguments X, Y, and Z, along with several keyword arguments of the function; that they are keyword arguments, not standard function arguments, is indicated by the use of equal signs in the function call. The values selected for these keyword arguments specify the color of the surface (color='gray') and two values of stride ('rstride' for row-stride, 'cstride' for column-stride), where a stride of 1 means that all points are to be plotted.

Also of Note
- As before, if the user types 'help(Axes3D)' or 'help(ax.plot_surface)' into the Console, information about these functions is printed out for the user to see.

- The execution time of program Example3_2.py is inherently longer than that of Example3_1.py because Example3_2.py uses a two-dimensional vector in the call to my_Gaussian, which entails a larger number of values for the function to process. Because of this, only 100 elements are used in the definition of coords rather than the 200 elements used for x in Example3_1.py. With this change, my_Gaussian calculates values for only 10,000 (=100^2) x,y-point pairs rather than the 40,000 (=200^2) that would otherwise have been calculated, thus shortening the run-time by about a factor of 4.

- We could have specified a user-defined function to calculate the distance R; however this is a simple calculation, so one line of ordinary code suffices. Also, because the calculation done by the function my_Gaussian is quite simple, we could have done its work with a single line of ordinary code. The way it is done, however, illustrates how user-defined functions are implemented in *Python*. Also, re-use of user-defined functions in different programs is a habit worth cultivating, as it will often save time in the long run. As one might expect, it is easy to create one's own library/package of user-defined functions in *Python* and call them into a program when needed -- e.g., by means of the syntax illustrated in Example3_1.py (lines 5-6) and Example3_2.py (lines 5-7).

- The surface plot is displayed in the plot window (as usual, called 'Figure 1'). Because of the function call in line 18 (or, in the absence of this call, because the 'Graphics backend option' has been set to 'Automatic' in 'Preferences'), the user can click on the plot and rotate the surface in any way desired. This remarkable capability is enabled by functions in the mpl_toolkits library.

3.3 A PROGRAM THAT PERMITS INPUT AND OUTPUT OF TEXT AND NUMBERS

The next example illustrates a *Python* program that accepts user-input from the Console and prints out results to the Console. These elementary capabilities are useful in many programs.

```
1   # -*- coding: utf-8 -*-
2   # Third example: Example3_3.py
3   # Description: example of simple i/o to and from the Console
4
5   import numpy as np             #np not used here but useful for almost all programs
6   import matplotlib.pyplot as plt   #plt not used here but useful for almost all programs
7
8   x=input('Enter a number to be squared (or zero to exit): ')   #example of input() fct
9   print('The character string you entered is',x)                #example of print() fct
10  y=float(x)                     #convert the string variable x to a floating-point number
11
12  if y != 0: print('The square of your number is', y*y)   #example of an 'if' statement
13
14  while y!=0:                                             #example of a 'while' statement
```

```
15    x=input('Enter another number to be squared (or zero to exit): ')
16    y=float(x)
17    if y!=0:                        #example of alternative syntax for an 'if' statement
18        print('The square of {:.5} is {:.10}.'.format(y, y*y))
19
20 print('Your entry of zero ends this program.')
```

Program Notes

- Line 8 passes a string variable (recognized as a string because it is enclosed in quotes) to the input function, which then prints out the string as a message to the Console. The message asks the user to enter a number to be squared. In addition to printing the message, the input function waits for a response from the user, which will be passed as a string to the variable x.

- Line 9 prints the string entered by the user back to the Console, in this case by means of the print function (which, in contrast to the input function, does not wait for input from the user).

- Line 10 attempts to convert the entered string to a floating-point number. If this conversion is successful (for example, the user entered a character string like '10.0' rather than something unrecognized as a number, like 'ten'), the result is stored in variable y.

- Line 12 begins with a condition to be tested, namely, whether y is different from 0; the characters '!=' in this context mean 'not equal'. The colon in line 12 marks the end of the test condition. If the condition is true, the remainder of line 12 is executed, whereas, if false, the remainder of the line is skipped. Important: if the test condition had been to determine whether y equals 0, the condition would have been written 'if y==0', i.e., with two equal signs, not one. (The single equal sign is what is used in assignment statements -- for example, in line 10.)

- The second half of Line 12 uses the print function to print the square of the entered number to the Console. This executable statement could also have been written on the next line (line 13) but, in that case, it would require an indentation.

- Lines 14 to 18 constitute a 'while loop'. This section of code is executed repeatedly as long as the condition that begins the loop of code remains true -- in this case, as long as the variable y in line 14 remains different from 0. These lines allow the user to enter a number to be squared; if the number is not zero, the number and its square are then printed out. Because the value of the variable y can be changed within the while loop, the loop has the possibility of terminating, i.e., the conditional test in line 14 might fail the next time the loop is executed. Note that line 17 sets up a conditional test itself (an 'inner' condition within an 'outer' condition). This type of nesting of program-control statements is very common. The double-level of indentation in line 18 reflects its logical subservience to the while loop that starts with line 14. The net effect is: if the new value of y that results from the assignment in line 16 is not equal to 0, the condition in line 17 will be true and line 18 will print y and its square to the Console. If, however, y should equal 0, the Interpreter will skip line 18 and return to the test condition in line 14. This condition would also fail if y equals 0, in which case line 20, the last line of the program, is executed.

- The output produced by the print statement in line 18 is similar to that in line 12 except that, for purposes of illustration, line 18 uses the 'format' function that can be invoked as part of a print statement. This function permits considerable flexibility in printing -- for example, here it allows printing both the number and its square on the same line and specifies how the numbers appear when printed. The syntax in this case involves a character string within which the formatted values of the variables in question will be imbedded during output. The format for each value is determined by characters that begin and end with open- and closed-brackets ({...}). Here, we wish to print out two values within the formatted string, namely, y and y*y. To do so, the format function within the print function uses parentheses within which the values to be printed are listed in order. Because two values are to be printed, the string proper requires two sets of brackets ({...}), each at the location where the corresponding value to be printed will be inserted. The information within each pair of brackets specifies the printing format. The colon (:) is a proxy for the value itself. The characters '.5' after the first colon indicate that the first value (y) should be printed out as a floating-point number with no more than 5 characters (less will be used if not all 5 are needed); similarly, the characters '.10' following the second colon indicate that the second value (y*y) should be printed out as a floating-point number with no more than 10 characters. Use of this formatting facility avoids awkward many-character printouts such as is observed if the user should enter '1.1' in response to the question posed when the program is first run (cf. lines 8-9).

Also of Note

- In the process of writing a new program with the Editor, it is a good idea to test the effect of each new statement or small block of statements as you proceed. This is especially important if you are not 100% sure that these statements do exactly what you expect them to. Mistakes in writing a new program, both in typing and logic, are extremely common. Achieving a successful final product becomes much simpler if each statement and small segment of a program are tested as you go. As a minimum, this approach can test whether a newly-added block of statements is syntactically correct, i.e., does not immediately generate an error at run time.

- You do not have to use the Editor to write your program. Instead, you can enter the executable coding lines of your program one at a time directly into the Console, where each line of code will be processed immediately after it is entered. Similarly, single lines of code can be entered and executed after a script file (run in the usual way) terminates and before all the variables have been reset. However, it is generally **much better practice** to enter the program and its incremental improvements into the Editor, where it can be saved and re-run from the beginning -- a process that can avoid much retyping. In some cases, execution of one or more single lines of code entered into the Console can be very useful.

3.4 FURTHER EXAMPLES WITH A ONE-DIMENSIONAL DIFFUSION PROFILE

We expand our knowledge of *Python* with a useful general equation with which to calculate a one-dimensional diffusion profile (Gaussian profile) of a substance S following its introduction as a bolus at location x=0 and time t=0. The equation is (see also Exercise 2.1):

$$S(x,t) = \frac{M \, e^{\frac{-x \cdot x}{4Dt}}}{2\sqrt{\pi Dt}}. \tag{3.1}$$

Here, x is distance, t is time, M is the amount of the introduced substance per cross-sectional area, D is the diffusion coefficient of the diffusing substance, and S(x,t) is the concentration of the substance at distance x and time t ('•' denotes multiplication). Typical units for these 5 quantities are cm, seconds, moles cm^{-2}, cm^2 s^{-1}, and moles cm^{-3} (or sometimes, molar units), respectively.

In Example3_4.py below, we use Eqn. 3.1 to calculate and plot several curves of S(x) for different values of D but with constant values of M and t. The first time you run this program, the Interpreter might print a strange message: 'MatplotlibDeprecationWarning: Using default event loop ...'. If so, this message can be safely ignored.

```
1  # -*- coding: utf-8 -*-
2  # Fourth example: Example3_4.py
3  # Description: using i/o to calculate multiple 1-D diffusion profiles
4  import numpy as np
5  import matplotlib.pyplot as plt
6
7  #we define a new fct, which uses different global variables than my_Gaussian()
8  def my_1D_Gaussian(x):
9      return M*np.exp(-x*x/(4*D*t))/(np.sqrt(4*np.pi*D*t))  #np.pi is the constant π
10
11 M=1.0         #arbitrary units
12 t=6270        #units of seconds
13 D=2.5e-7      #starting value of D; units of cm*cm/s
14
15 X=np.linspace(-0.5,0.5,500)
16
17 Y=my_1D_Gaussian(X)
18 plt.plot([], [], ' ', label="D values")      # plot nothing but include a header label in the inset
19 plt.plot(X,Y,label=D)           #plot the current curve and add the value of D to the inset list
20
21 while D!=0:
22    plt.pause(0.1)               #this allows user to see curves as they are added
23    x = input('D={:.8}; enter a new value for D (or zero to exit): '\
24       .format(D))
25    D = float(x)
26    if D==0: break               #if D is zero, 'break' will cause an exit from the while loop
27    Y=my_1D_Gaussian(X)
28    plt.plot(X,Y,label=D)
29
30 plt.xlabel('distance (cm)')
```

```
31  plt.ylabel('concentration (a.u.)')
32  plt.title('Example3_4: 1D-diffusion profile at {:d} seconds'.format(t))
33  plt.legend()
34  plt.show()
35
36  plt.savefig("example3_4.png", dpi=200)
```

Program Notes

- The program begins by setting the values of M, t, and a first value of D and plots the curve of S(x) that is calculated with these values. The program then uses the logic illustrated in Example3_3.py to allow the user to enter as many new values of D as desired. (It would be reasonable to limit the number of values to 3 or 4.) For each new value of D, the corresponding curve for S(x) is added to the figure. The user can see the plot as the curves accumulate by hovering and/or clicking the mouse over the appropriate panel on the task bar. If this doesn't work, all the calculated curves can be seen in the figure after the program finishes and also in the plot file 'Example3_4.png' that is written to disk.

- Because the program did not use the calls to 'plt.xlim()' and 'plt.ylim()' that were used in Example3-1.py, *Python* uses default values to set the plotting ranges for the x and y axes.

3.5 COMPARISON OF A ONE-DIMENSIONAL DIFFUSION PROFILE WITH AN EXPERIMENTAL DATA SET

Example3_5.py extends the ideas in Example3_4.py with a program that permits a comparison between calculated one-dimensional diffusion profiles and an experimental data set. The goal is to estimate the diffusion coefficient of a foreign substance introduced into the cytoplasm of a living cell. If the substance is well-chosen, it can give information about the properties of the cytoplasm, such as its viscosity.

Lines 8-9 of Example3_5.py give the experimental data set, which was obtained at 16 °C from a singly-dissected frog skeletal muscle cell. (This preparation, described more fully in Chapter 12, is commonly called an 'intact single fiber' and is a cell that is in essentially normal physiological condition.) Skeletal muscle fibers are among the largest cells in an animal, and frog single fibers, like the one used in this experiment, typically have a cylindrical shape that can be as long as several cm, yet the cross-sectional diameter is small, only about 0.05 mm. Early in this experiment, defined as time t = 0, phenol red, a colored non-toxic diffusible substance that is commonly used as a pH indicator dye, was micro-injected into the fiber at one location in its middle (defined as x = 0). Within a short time after injection, the dye reached diffusional equilibrium throughout the fiber cross-section close to the injection site, and thereafter net diffusion of the dye took place only in one dimension, namely, along the fiber axis (x-direction). Late in the experiment (average time, 100 min = 6000 s after injection; line 19), the concentration of this substance was estimated at different distances from the injection site along the fiber axis (line 8). To do so, the absorbance of phenol red was measured at each location by means of a small beam of light of an appropriate wavelength that trans-illuminated the fiber in a direction perpendicular to the fiber axis. Beer's Law was used to convert the absorbance measurements to the concentration values (line 9), which happen to be given in mmolar units (abbreviated mM).

```
1  # -*- coding: utf-8 -*-
2  # Fifth example: Example3_5.py
3  # Description: using i/o to calculate multiple 1-D diffusion profiles
4
5  import numpy as np
6  import matplotlib.pyplot as plt
7
8  x1=np.array([-0.090,-0.039,0,0.036,0.092,0.136,0.183])        #distance (cm)
9  y1=np.array([0.2810, 0.5965, 0.7184, 0.6138, 0.2939, 0.0778, 0.0259])  #conc. (mM)
10 plt.plot(x1,y1,'s')
11
12 def my_1D_Gaussian(x):
13     """
14     Example of a Docstring in a user-defined function definition
15     This Gaussian function uses different variables than my_Gaussian
16     """
17     return M*np.exp(-x*x/(4*D*T))/(np.sqrt(4*np.pi*D*T))
18
19 T=6000      #time of the phenol red measurements (units of seconds)
20 D=1e-6      #diffusion coefficient (units of cm*cm/s)
21 M=0.1       #initial guesstimate of M (arbitary units)
```

```
22
23  X=np.linspace(-0.35,0.35,500)  #for phenol red
24  Y=my_1D_Gaussian(X)
25  plt.plot(X,Y)
26
27  Y=my_1D_Gaussian(X)
28  plt.plot([], [], ' ', label="D values")    #header label for the inset list
29  plt.plot(X,Y,label=D)          #add current value of D to the inset list
30
31  while D!=0:
32     plt.pause(0.1)              #this allows user to see curves as they are added
33     x = input('D={:.8}; enter a new value for D (or zero to exit): '\
34        .format(D))
35     D = float(x)
36     if D==0: break              #if D is zero, exit from the while loop
37     x = input('M={:.8}; enter a new value for M (or zero to exit): '\
38        .format(M))
39     M = float(x)
40     if M==0:
41        break                    #if D is zero, exit from the while loop
42     Y=my_1D_Gaussian(X)
43     plt.plot(X,Y,label=D)
44
45  plt.xlabel('distance (cm)')
46  plt.ylabel('concentration (mM)')
47  plt.title('Example3_5: 1D-diffusion profiles at {:d} seconds'.format(T))
48  plt.legend()
49  plt.show()
50
51  plt.savefig("example3_5.png", dpi=200)
```

Program Notes

- Line 10 plots the experimental data given in lines 8-9 as filled squares (plot not shown below), and lines 12-17 define a function, my_1D_Gaussian, that is based on Eqn. 3.1.

- Lines 13-16 of the function my_1D_Gaussian constitute what is called a 'Docstring' (documentation string) which is a commented block of lines within a function definition that begins and ends with three double quotes ("""). The Docstring begins on the line of the function definition immediately following the colon. In addition to providing documentation about the use and purpose of the function in the script file, the commented lines are available to the user at runtime. If the user enters 'help(my_1D_Gaussian)' on a new line on the Console after Example3_5.py has been run, the block of text located between the pairs of three double quotes will be printed out on the Console. A carefully-constructed Docstring can be extremely helpful in allowing the original author and later users to take best advantage of a user-defined function.

- Lines 20-21 provide initial values (guesses) for the two remaining parameters required for calculations with Eqn. 3.1, namely, D (the diffusion coefficient) and M (a quantity proportional to the total amount of phenol red injected into the muscle fiber), and lines 23-24 calculate and plot the one-dimensional diffusion profile that corresponds to these initial choices of D and M.

- The second part of the program allows the user to enter different values of D and M and plot, on the same figure, the associated curves calculated with Eqn. 3.1. By trial and error (perhaps starting the program anew when the number of calculated curves becomes unwieldy), the user can find values of D and M that, visually, yield a curve that agrees well with the experimental data. Once such a curve is found, it is reasonable to conclude that the corresponding value of D gives a reasonable estimate of the diffusion coefficient of phenol red inside the muscle fiber. This idea is explored further in the exercises at the end of this chapter.

Experimental Note: It has been found that, with phenol red and other small compounds of similar molecular weight, the diffusion coefficient that is estimated for these compounds in the cytoplasm of single muscle cells can be as large as, but not larger than, about half that measured at the same temperature when the compounds are dissolved in a simple salt solution that mimics the ECF. Thisstatement applies for compounds that do not bind to or interact strongly with cytoplasmic constituents (e.g., Kushmerick and Podolsky, 1969). For compounds that do bind to or interact strongly with cytoplasmic constituents, the estimated cytoplasmic diffusion coefficients can be much smaller than 0.5 times that expected in a simple salt solution. Thus, from experimental data of the type presented in

Example3_5.py, it has been concluded that the viscosity of cytoplasm may be about twice that of the ECF. This follows because the diffusion coefficient of a substance is inversely proportional to the viscosity of the medium in which it is diffusing.

The higher viscosity of cytoplasm compared with that of a simple salt solution is likely due to the substantial concentrations of soluble proteins, amino acids, and other organic constituents that are found in the cytoplasm but not in a simple salt solution. Additionally, a 'tortuosity' factor may influence the results. The cytoplasm of most cells, including muscle fibers, contains internal filaments and fixed structures that could interfere with the free diffusion of dissolved substances and thus contribute to the lower measured diffusion coefficients when compared with those in free solution.

A Note on Quantitative Modeling. As a first approach, it is reasonable to use a visual assessment to estimate the parameters of a model to explain a data set (e.g., as in the example above, to find values of D and M for which the calculation of concentrations at different distances with Eqn. 3.1 provides acceptable agreement with the data in Example3_5.py). The preferred means of assessment, however, is to use a quantitative approach, such as the method of least-squares. This method, as applied to the example above, would begin with initial guesses of D and M. Then, for each measurement location, the square of the difference between the measured phenol-red concentration and that predicted by Eqn. 3.1 would be calculated, and the squared differences would be summed over all measurement points -- 7 in this case. (The differences are squared in order that model deviations above and below the measurements can be accounted for without regard to the sign of the differences.) The procedure is then repeated with different values of D and M in an attempt to reduce the sum-of-squares deviations. Once values of D and M are found that minimize the sum-of-squares deviations, these values are accepted as the "best" estimates of the parameters of the model.

Appendix D gives an example of a *Python* program that implements this least-squares fitting procedure. The example can be modified in obvious ways to fit other models to other data sets. The reader may wish to defer examination of Appendix D until after additional *Python* programs and statements are explained -- e.g., until after Chapter 4 or after Chapter 6.

3.6 EXERCISES

Exercise 3.1 Given the phenol red concentrations at different distances from the injection site in Example3_5.py, follow the suggestion in the preceding section to use this program to estimate the cytoplasmic values of D and M for this substance in this experiment.

Exercise 3.2 A data set is given here for another experiment of the type described in connection with Example3_5.py, this time with a colored absorbent substance named Azo1, which has been used in muscle cells as a calcium indicator dye.

Distance data (cm): [-0.045, -0.030, -0.0150, 0, 0.0150, 0.030, 0.045]
Concentration data (mM): [0.0, 0.0283, 0.1226, 0.2083, 0.1483, 0.0492, 0.0]
Time: 24.5 min = 1470 s

Use a program like that in Example3_5.py to estimate the values of D and M in this experiment. Given the fact that that the molecular size of Azo1 is similar to that of phenol red, propose an explanation for why the value of D is quite different from that of phenol red.

Exercise 3.3 Write a *Python* program that begins like Example3_4 but include a function to calculate S(x) at different times T for fixed values of D and M. Then:

a) Use your program to calculate S(x) for a number of different values of T; in each case, estimate the peak amplitude of the curve. Now make a plot of peak amplitude vs. the time values that you chose -- e.g., on a piece of graph paper or perhaps by writing another *Python* program. Can you explain the form of your plot in terms of Eqn. 3.1? [**Note**: to estimate the amplitude of each curve, you could print out the value by means of your program or you might use *Python's* ability to read out values on a curve by letting the cursor hover over the peak value in the plot. A particularly convenient way to obtain the maximum value of any np array is to use the function 'max()' that is available to it. For example, if your program has an array named Y, type 'Y.max()' into the Console or add a line 'print(Y.max())' to your program and see what happens. The explanation for this behavior is that, because Y is an 'object' of type 'np array', it has access to the 'methods' (i.e. functions) associated with an np-array object. The syntax 'Y.max()' invokes the method/function to return the maximum value that is a member of Y.]

b) Repeat part a) except, instead of estimating the peak amplitude of each curve, estimate by eye the x-locations of the two inflection points on the bell shape of each curve. The difference between the x-locations of the inflection points of a Gaussian curve is a measure of the width, i.e., spread, of the curve, so your plot here will show how a diffusion profile spreads out with time. (The inflection points are found at symmetric locations on either side of the curve, where the curve switches from concave downward to concave upward or vice-versa. In this case, there is no single method that is available to an np-array variable to estimate the inflection points. A more accurate way to estimate the inflection points of a plotted curve will be discussed in one of the exercises at the end of the next chapter.)

c) Based on your analyses in parts a) and b), how would you expect the product of the amplitude and width of a Gaussian profile to vary with time? Does this agree with the intuitive interpretation that the area under a time-varying Gaussian profile of the type considered here should remain constant, since the total amount of the diffusing substance is not changing?

Exercise 3.4 In several places in this chapter, the text implied that the diffusion coefficient of a dissolved substance will depend on both the temperature and molecular size of the compound. Qualitatively, in what way would you expect the diffusion coefficient to depend on these factors?

Exercise 3.5 The text related to the discussion of the surface plot in Fig. 3.2 states that diffusion in two-dimensions (2-D) is described by the 2-D Gaussian function of Example3_2.py. If this were true, one would expect that the 2-D Gaussian surface integrated with respect to y (equivalently, projected onto the x-axis) would yield a 1-D Gaussian profile in x. Is this true? [Note: if you are unsure of the analytic answer to this question, a numerical way to answer it will be addressed in one of the exercises at the end of the next chapter.]

CHAPTER 4

ELEMENTS OF PYTHON

This chapter surveys *Python* as a programming language and gives a summary of the basic information needed to start writing complete programs in *Python*. It emphasizes the features that are most relevant to the examples and exercises discussed in this book.

Notes. The reader is encouraged to use the Console and/or the Editor to try out the executable statements discussed below, which are all short. The user should observe how the values of the variables created by these statements appear in the Variable Explorer, including when the statements are first executed and, later, if the user modifies the variables. To avoid unexpected results when using the Editor, the Console, and the Variable Explorer, the user should click in the appropriate panel before proceeding (this ensures that the cursor is active in that panel). *Python* has a very useful feature that applies to any entity known to the Interpreter, whether it be a built-in entity or one defined previously by the user. If that entity's name or an expression for its value is entered as a new line on the Console (i.e., if the name or expression is typed and the 'Enter' key is pressed), the value of the entity will be printed immediately on the Console.

4.1 DATA TYPES

Information within *Python* programs is encoded in a number of different structures and formats (commonly referred to as 'data types'), such as character strings, individual numbers, arrays of numbers, lists, dictionaries, and so forth. In principle, all such *Python* entities are examples of a general class called an 'object'. Objects have attributes (commonly referred to as 'data'), such as a specific character string, number, or sequence of numbers. Objects also have associated methods (commonly referred to as 'functions'), which provide ways of manipulating or analyzing the attributes (data).

An example of a method was encountered in Chapter 3 with variables of the type 'np-array'. If Y is the name of such an array, then 'Y.max()' is an expression that returns the maximum value of the numbers in Y. The standard syntax for invoking a method of this type starts with the name of the variable, then a dot ('.'), then the name of the desired method, and then a pair of parentheses. The parentheses are used to enclose any arguments that might be needed by the method for the task at hand.

If Y is an np array and 'help(Y)' is entered as a new line on the Console, a large list of information is printed out about the np-array data type, including information about the 'max()' method and the other methods that are available to this object. Further examples of the use of such methods are given below.

4.1.1 CONSTANTS AND VARIABLES

Suppose a *Python* program contains the following assignment statement: 'A = 2.0'. After execution, A is the name of a variable that has access to a place in memory that contains 2.0, which is a floating-point number (also called a 'float'). A has the type float because the object assigned to it, 2.0, is a float. The number 2.0 itself is a constant (not a variable like A), so it can never be anything other than 2.0. The value of A, however, is easily changed; for example, the statement 'A = A*A' would change the value of A to another float, the square of its previous value. The data type of A is also easily changed; for example, the statement 'A = 2' would change its type from a float to an integer (an 'int') with a value of 2 (not 2.0). With the Variable Explorer, you can see the types and values of the currently-active variables, i.e., those known to the Interpreter. In contrast, values such as 2.0 and 2 do not appear as primary entries in the Variable Explorer because they are constants, not variables. As expected, *Python* has a number of built-in constants such as the number np.pi (i.e., the geometric constant π = 3.14159 ..., which is known to *Python* to 16 significant figures) and np.e (i.e., the base of the natural logarithms = 2.781828 ..., which is also known to *Python* to 16 significant figures).

4.1.2 STRINGS

A string is an ordered sequence of characters. A string variable (whose type is 'str') is created by a statement such as 'S="hello world"', where the string's attribute is enclosed in quotes. (If preferred, one also use a pair of single quotes to enclose a character string). We encountered a number of examples of strings in Chapter 3, along with several methods for printing strings to the Console and reading strings from the console. If one enters 'help(str)' into a new line in the Console, one can survey the large number of methods that are available for manipulating strings, including how to combine them, break them apart, extract sub-strings, etc.

4.1.3 LISTS

A list is a data structure whose attribute (i.e., data) consists of members of the same or different data type, for example, strings and/or floats and/or ints arranged in a specific order. If a list is created in an assignment statement, or if the contents of an existing list is printed on the Console without formatting, the members of the list appears as a sequence of items that are enclosed by brackets and separated by commas. An example is 'L = ["one", 1.0, "two", 2.0, "three", 3.0]'. This list consists of 6 members -- three strings and three floats -- in the specified order. The lists that we will encounter will consist primarily of one data type, e.g., 'L = [1.0, 4.0, 9.0]', which happens to be a list of 3 floats. The individual members of a list can be accessed by standard index notation; for example, in the second case, L[0] equals 1.0, L[1] equals 4.0, and L[2] equals 9.0. A reference to L[3], however, would generate an error, since this member does not exist.

A list is a variable data structure; both the number of members in the list can change as can the individual members in the list. (In contrast, a tuple -- next paragraph -- is a constant, not variable, data structure.) Lists have their own specific methods. For example, if the statement 'L.append(16.)' is executed, the number 16.0 will be added to L at its end, i.e., L of the preceding paragraph would now equal [1.0, 4.0, 9.0, 16.0]. Note that the last action could not have been carried out with the statement 'L[3] = 16.0'. Thus, while the latter syntax can be used to change the contents of an existing element of a list (e.g., 'L[2] = -L[2]', which here could be equivalently expressed as 'L[2] = -9.0'), it is not an allowed method for adding a new element to a list. Other examples of methods that can be used with lists include the following:
- If the statement 'L.reverse()' is executed, L now equals [16.0, 9.0, 4.0, 1.0].
- If the expression 'L.__len__()' is entered as a new line on the Console, '4' (which is the number of members in L, i.e., its length) will be printed on the Console.
- If the statement 'L = []' is executed, L becomes the empty list.
- If the expression 'L.__len__()' is now entered as a new line in the Console, '0' will be printed on the Console (since L now has no members).

- If the user enters 'help(L)' on the Console, information about L, including a summary of the methods available to it, will be printed on the Console.

A list is an adaptable type of data structure. For example, one can create a list of lists. Suppose that the next 3 statements are executed:
- 'L1 = [1]',
- 'L2 = [2]',
- 'LL = [L1, L2]'.

If one now enters 'LL' as a new line on the Console, '[[1], [2]]' will be printed out. The complexity and allowed-number of members of a list is only limited by the memory available in the machine. Lists will have some important uses in later programs in this book.

4.1.4 TUPLES

A tuple is data structure something like a list except, as noted above, it is a constant data structure. The members of a tuple can be of different type (e.g., strings, ints, floats, etc.) but, once defined, the members cannot be changed. A simple statement creating a tuple T is: 'T = (1, 2, 3)'. Note that parentheses are (typically) used to specify the contents of a tuple, whereas brackets are used to specify the contents of a list. In the case of tuples, the parentheses can be omitted, however; so 'T = 1, 2, 3' creates the same tuple as above.

If the contents of a tuple are printed to the Console without formatting, the members of the tuple will appear enclosed by parentheses and separated by commas. Perhaps surprisingly, to access the members of a tuple, brackets (not parentheses) are used. For example, entering 'T[0]' as a new line on the Console will return '1', and entering 'T[1]' will return '2'. In contrast, 'T(0)' or 'T(1)' would generate an error.

A tuple is an example of a so-called 'immutable' object. For example, the statement 'T[0] = 0' applied to the tuple (1, 2, 3) is not allowed and would generate an error. To make such a change to T, one would have to start over with a complete redefinition of T by the statement 'T = (0, 2, 3)'. Tuples can contain nothing; for example, the statement 'T=()' defines T to be the empty tuple. Again, the complexity and allowed-number of members in a tuple is only limited by the available memory in the machine. Tuples will be used only occasionally in this book.

4.1.5 NUMBERS

Python is well-suited for calculations of all types and makes available to the user a variety of appropriate number types. One reason different number types exist is that they use different amounts of memory in the computer -- for example, ints use less memory than floats, which use less memory than complex numbers. In the case of numbers of all types, two or more can be combined using standard arithmetic operations (+, addition; -, subtraction; *, multiplication; /, division). The type of the resulting number may, however, differ from that of the numbers used in the initial operation; for example, the expression '1/3' involves two ints but the result is a float. If two or more numbers of different type are combined by one or more operations, any needed values will be automatically "upgraded" so that all numbers have the same type -- e.g., ints may be converted to floats, and floats may be converted to complex numbers. If one is uncertain about whether a conversion will take place automatically, it can be forced. For example, if the variable I is of type int, the statement 'I = float(I)' will convert I to a float.

4.1.5.1 INTEGERS

The statement 'A = 1' creates a variable A of type int. Ints are used primarily for counting and doing basic arithmetic. Two or more ints combined with addition, subtraction and/or multiplication will yield another int. (As noted above, with division, a float may result, not an int.) If the user wants to do 'integer division' (i.e., discard any fractional part, so that the result is an int), the '//' operator can be used -- e.g., 9//5 yields a value of 1. The 'modulo' operator (%) applied to two integers will give the integer remainder after division -- e.g., 9%5 yields a value of 4. The // and modulo operators can also be applied to floats, yielding appropriate results.

4.1.5.2 FLOATING-POINT NUMBERS

Floating-point numbers are numbers that are commonly thought of as containing a decimal point when written (e.g., 1.0, 0.666666, etc.) or, if expressed as a ratio of integers, does not equal an integer (e.g., 1/3). This description requires some qualification, however. For example, '1e2' is scientific notation for 10 raised to the power of 2, which, in *Python*, is a float. (That '1e2' is a float can be checked in two ways. If '1e2' is entered as a new line on the Console, the Console responds by printing out '100.0'. Also, if 'type(1e2)' is entered as a new line on the Console, the Console's response tells us that the number is a float.) In contrast 10*10 or 10**2 (where ** is the exponentiation operator in *Python*) returns a value of 100, which is an int. The great majority of the calculations carried out in this book are done either with (a) floating-point numbers or (b) arrays of floating-point numbers created with the numpy library (see below).

4.1.5.3 COMPLEX NUMBERS

In *Python*, the square-root of minus 1 is denoted j. This follows the notation used by engineers rather than that of mathematicians, who use i. If you start the Console anew and enter 'j' on a new line, you will get an error. (Note: use of j by itself in the context of complex numbers will almost always generate an error.) However, if you enter '1j' on the Console, it will respond '1j', which indicates that the Interpreter recognizes the entry. That 1j is, in fact, a complex number can be demonstrated in two ways. If 'type(1j)' is entered as a new line on the Console, the Console's response is 'complex'. Also, if 'help(1j)' is entered on the Console, the response, while lengthy, begins with 'class complex(object)'. So, the type of 1j is complex. If you enter '(2+1j)*(2-1j)' on a new line in the Console, the Console will respond '5+0j', thus showing that the Interpreter knows how to do basic arithmetic operations with complex numbers. In fact, the Interpreter knows that the last number, even though of complex type, is equivalent to 5 (the latter number being of type 'int'), as can be checked by entering this conditional expression as a new line on the Console: '5 == 5+0j'. (The double equal sign here flags a conditional test, asking whether the two expressions on either side are equal; the value returned is either True or False.) The Console responds 'True' (note the capital 'T'). Conditional tests will be discussed in more detail below, but the point here is that the Interpreter does the sensible thing. Rather than generating an error because the two numbers on the two sides of the conditional expression are of different type, it converts both numbers to the same type -- in this case, by "upgrading" the number with the type 'int' to one with the type 'complex' -- so that it can carry out the requested test by its standard method.

While *Python* has the ability to do basic calculations with complex numbers, more extensive calculations can be aided by use of the complex number package called 'cmath'. In this case, the user should import this package by including the line 'import cmath', preferably at the beginning of the program. Complex numbers will rarely be used in this book.

4.1.6 ARRAYS OF NUMBERS

Python's numerical abilities are demonstrated most obviously by its facility for doing calculations with arrays of numbers, particularly arrays of floats created with the numpy library ('numpy' is short for 'numerical *Python*'), including its ability to do 'vector calculations'. A vector calculation is one that can be carried out on an entire array of numbers with one expression or statement. (The program examples in Chapter 3 included several simple examples of vector calculations.) For these and other types of numerical calculations, the user will usually want to begin a program by importing the numpy library, e.g., with the statement 'import numpy as np'. The use of the 'np' abbreviation allows for a more compact syntax when invoking the numpy methods and thus can save much typing.

As noted, *Python* has the ability to create lists of numbers, e.g., with statements like 'A = [1,2,3]' and 'B = [4,5,6]'; however, the methods to combine and manipulate lists are not usually what one wants for calculations. For example, if the two statements above had been executed, and the statement 'A+B' is entered into the Console, the Console would respond by printing '[1, 2, 3, 4, 5, 6]' rather than '[5, 7, 9]'. Thus, even though the individual members in these lists are of type 'int' (as one can check by invoking the 'type' method with statements like 'type(A[0])' entered as a new line to the Console), the '+' operator/method applied to a list results in concatenation of the individual members of the lists rather than addition of the individual members. The problem here is that a list is too general an object. What is needed is something suited specifically to numbers -- hence, the reason for the numpy library. Basic *Python* itself (i.e., in the absence of imported libraries) does not have an 'array' data type.

Next we consider short examples of statements or expressions that illustrate some of the very useful array methods that are available in numpy (more are considered later in this chapter). We assume here that the user has previously executed the statement 'import numpy as np' and that the examples below are entered as new lines on the Console.

- 'A = np.zeros(100)'. A is now a floating array containing 100 members, all of which are 0.0.

- 'B = np.ones(100)'. B is now a floating array containing 100 members, all of which are 1.0.

- 'C = A+B'. C is now an array whose values have been obtained by the 'vector addition' capability of np arrays. (Note: if the number of members in the two numpy arrays were not the same, an error would be generated.) C, in fact, has exactly the same values as array B because A is an array of all zeroes. An identical C could also have been created with the statement 'C = A+1'. Although in the latter case, A is an array of 100 floats and 1 is an integer constant, *Python* does the sensible thing and adds 1 to each member of A. The fact that C (generated by either of the preceding statements) has the same contents as B can be demonstrated by entering the conditional expression 'B == C' as a new line on the Console. The Console will respond with a 100-element array whose values are all 'True'. If, instead, the user had entered the statement 'D = (B == C)' on the Console, a new np array of 100 members would have been created, all of whose members are 'True'. (This can be confirmed by entering 'D' as a new line on the Console and seeing the Console's response.) If one enters 'type(D[0])' as a new line on the Console, the Console will respond 'numpy.bool_'. This demonstrates the existence of a data type called 'bool_' that is known to numpy. This data type encodes a Boolean variable, i.e., a variable that can have exactly one of two values: True or False (again, note the capital T and capital F). If the statement 'b1 = np.bool_('True')' is entered as a new line on the Console, b1 becomes a Boolean variable whose value is True. Boolean variables are also available in basic *Python*, i.e., without the need to import numpy. If one enters 'b2=True' as a new line on the Console followed by 'help(b2)', the Console responds with a lot of information starting with 'class bool(int)'. As expected, if 'b1==b2' is entered as a new line on the Console, the Console responds 'True'.

4.2 EXPRESSIONS AND STATEMENTS

An expression in *Python* is a phrase that has a value. We have encountered many examples already, such as 'A+B', '[1.0, 4.0, 9.0]', '(2+1j)*(2-1j)', 9%5, '(B==C)', 'np.e', and 'L.__len__()'. A statement, in contrast, while it often contains one or more expressions, causes something to happen, for example, names a new variable and assigns it a value in memory or modifies the value of an existing variable. Examples are 'C = A+B' and 'L.reverse()'.

4.3 THE ASSIGNMENT STATEMENT

Assignment statements such as 'C = A + B' tell the Interpreter to create a new variable C or redefine the value of an existing variable. The name that is on the left-hand side of the equal sign becomes 'bound to' (i.e., given the value of) the expression or variable on the right-hand side. A variable name in *Python* is required to follow a few rules.
- It must start with a letter or the underline character (_).
- The remaining characters in the name can be can be letters, numbers, or underlines.
- The length of the variable name can, in principle, be as long as one likes, but a limit of 79 characters is recommended.
- Uppercase letters are distinguished from lowercase letters -- so, for example, 'c' and 'C' refer to different variables.

The value assigned to the variable is that on the right-hand side of the equal sign, but exactly how this is done can be a source of confusion. Suppose the Console is reset by typing '%reset' (or just 'reset' on some systems) as a new line on the Console and the following statements are executed:
- 'import numpy as np'
- 'r = 0.0'
- 's = r'
- 'r = 1.0'.

As one might expect, the value of s is still 0.0, which can be checked by entering 's' as a new line on the Console. The Console's response is '0.0'.

Suppose now that these statements are executed:
- 'R = np.zeros(3)'
- 'S = R'
- 'R[0] = 1.0'.

Somewhat surprisingly, the value of S is now [1.0, 0.0, 0.0]. The reason is that assignment statements like 'r = 0.0' and 's = r', which involve simple numbers (not lists or arrays of number), do not bind the second name to the same data location in memory as the first. So, r has one data location in memory, which contains the number 0.0, and s is given its own data location, which is also filled with the number 0.0. In contrast, in the case of np arrays, the statement 'S = R' binds the two names to the same data location in memory. The reason is that the R array might, in principle, be a very large array and it is conservative of

execution time and memory space to have the one data location serve both variables if it can. (This feature of using a common data location in memory is not limited to array variables created with the numpy library; it also applies to lists, which are a part of basic *Python*.) If the user wants to ensure that R and S have separate locations in memory, each with its own data, and thereby avoid this potential source of confusion, the following approach is one way to make this happen:
 - 'R = np.zeros(3)'
 - 'S = 1*R'
 - 'R[0] = 1.0'.

In this situation, S[0] retains its original value, 0.0. The reason is that '1*R' is an expression whose value happens to be the value of R, but it is not R itself. So the request to *Python* to assign the value of R to S causes a copy of the data of R to be written to a new location in memory and bound to S.

A single line of code can contain more than one statement but, if so, the statements need to be separated by semi-colons.

4.4 CONTROL STATEMENTS

In Chapter 3, we saw several examples of statements that began by testing whether a condition is true or false (e.g., the 'if' and 'while' statements in Example3_3.py, Example3_4.py, and Example3_5.py) and, by this means, determined whether the subsequent statement(s) that were logically-dependent on the condition being true are executed or not. In each case, a colon marked the end of the test condition. The dependent statements, which come immediately after, can follow either of two formats. As noted above, a single statement or several short statements can appear on the same line as the condition; if two or more statements appear, they need to be separated by semi-colons. More typically, the dependent statements that fall under the condition will appear on separate lines, each with an indentation of 2 or more spaces (4 is the usual number). A second conditional statement can, of course, occur within the first block of dependent statements. If so, the statement or block of statements to be executed under control of the second condition must follow the same rules, including the requirement that, if the second block of dependent statements appears on separate lines, each statement must begin with its own added degree of indentation (usually another 2-4 spaces). And so forth.

The condition that identifies the start of one of these control sequences can follow various formats. Examples of these expressions include the following:
- 'if A < B:'   ('<' means 'less than')
- 'if A == (B+1):'   ('==' means 'is equal to')
- 'while A != B:'   ('!=' means 'is not equal to')
- 'for i in r:'   ('r' here is a range variable -- see the 'for' statement described below).

4.4.1 THE WHILE STATEMENT

The 'while' statement, controls the number of times that a single dependent statement, or a block of dependent statements, that follows the colon is executed. The statement or block is executed repeatedly as long as the conditional test that immediately follows the 'while' keyword equals 'True'. Examples of the use of a 'while' loop to control execution of a block of statements are given in the last 3 program examples in Chapter 3. Another way to end the execution of the block of statements in a 'while' loop is by a 'break' statement, which, if executed, causes program control to immediately exit from the 'while' loop and pass to the first statement after the 'while' loop. If a 'while' loop is found within a 'while' loop, a 'break' statement within the second loop will cause program control to exit from the second loop but not from the first loop.

The 'continue' statement within a 'while' loop is something like a 'break' statement; it causes the remaining statements in the loop to be bypassed. However, in contrast to the 'break' statement, which causes control to pass to the first statement after the 'while' loop, the 'continue' statement causes control to go back to the beginning of the 'while' loop, with the dependent statements being executed all over again if the value of the conditional test is still 'True'.

4.4.2 THE IF STATEMENT -- AND THE ELIF AND ELSE STATEMENTS

Several examples of the use of an 'if' statement controlling program execution are given in Chapter 3, including lines 36 and 40 of Example3_5.py. In both of these lines, only one dependent statement follows the test condition and, in both case, it happens to be a 'break' statement. As with a 'while' loop, the 'break' statement, if executed, causes program control to exit from the block of statements that is dependent on the 'if' condition.

The next example illustrates how the 'if' statement can be used in conjunction with the 'elif' (short for 'else if') and 'else' statements to control program execution. It assumes that y has previously been defined as an int or a float.
- 'if y > 0:'
- '   print ("y is a positive number")'
- 'elif y == 0:'
- '   print ("y is zero")'
- 'else:'
- '   print ("y is a negative number")'

This type of control structure allows use of as many 'elif' statements as is logically needed in the sequence of conditions being tested within one overall block. The final 'else' statement (which, like an 'elif' statement, is reached only if none of the preceding conditions equals 'True') is not required to be present. In that case, program control would simply pass to the next statement in the program without any of the preceding dependent statements being executed.

4.4.3 THE FOR STATEMENT

The 'for' statement, like the 'while' statement, controls the number of times that a single dependent statement, or a block of dependent statements, that follows the colon is executed. In practice, the 'for' statement is more likely to be used than the 'while' statement. An example of the 'for' statement controlling an iterable block of statements is:
- 'r = range(-1,5,2)'
- 'for i in r:'
-'   print(i)'
-'   print(i*i)'

This 'for' loop could also be written: 'for i in r: print(i); print(i*i)'. When it is executed, the output to the Console would be;
-1
1
1
1

The explanation is as follows. The variable 'r' is defined to be of type 'range', which is a data type with which an iteration can be controlled in conjunction with another variable -- in this case, with the variable 'i'. The range of values for the iteration is specified by (up to) three integers that are enclosed in parentheses in the range expression. The first value is the starting value of the range, the second value is the end value of the range, and the third value is the increment to be added repeatedly (if necessary) to the starting value until the end value is reached or exceeded. In cases when fewer than three integers are specified, default values are set by the Interpreter for the missing integers (next paragraph). In the case above, the iteration variable i is set initially to -1, and, since -1 does not equal or exceed 5 (the end value of the range), the body of the 'for' loop (in this case, the two 'print' statements) is executed. Then, i is incremented by 2 and control returns to the top of the loop. Since i (now 1) is still less than the end value of the range, the body of the loop is executed again. And so forth. When i is finally found to equal or exceed the end of the range, execution bypasses the body of the loop and moves to the next statement in the program. Note that negative increments can be used in the range of an iteration, for example, 'r = range(5, -5, -3)'. Here the value of i would start at 5, would increment by -3 to 2 for the next iteration, then to -1, then to -4, and the body of the loop would be executed in all 4 cases. However, once i incremented to -7, the execution of the loop would cease, since -7 equals or "exceeds" the end of the range, -5.

A range statement with just two integers such as 'r = range(2,5)' is allowed. This statement is equivalent to 'r = range(2,5,1)', i.e., if the third integer is omitted, an increment of 1 is used by default. Note that the statement 'r = range(5,2)' would not allow any statements in the body of the loop to be executed, since, with a positive increment (in this case, 1, by default), the starting value of the range (=5) already exceeds the end value (=2). A range statement such as 'r = range(5)' is also allowed; by default, this is equivalent to 'r = range(0,5,1)'.

Another example of an iterable range is a numpy array defined with the 'np.linspace()' expression (explained further below). For example the phrase 'xx=np.linspace(0,2,0.5)' defines a numpy array containing the numbers '0., 0.5, 1., 1.5, 2.' which can be used to control an iteration.

The 'continue' and 'break' statements can be used within a 'for' loop, with the same logical effects described above for the 'while' loop.

4.5 USER-DEFINED FUNCTIONS

User-defined functions represent a powerful tool for both clarifying and simplifying the logic of a program. These functions can also save time in the long run because, once a good user-defined function has been written, it has the potential to be re-used in many other programs. Examples of several user-defined functions were given in the preceding chapter.

A user-defined function is required to have a number of elements, which usually appear in the following order:
- the keyword 'def', which alerts the Interpreter that a user-defined function follows.
- the name of the function (which must follow *Python's* naming conventions).
- a pair of parentheses followed by a colon. The parentheses enclose dummy names for the arguments of the function, the actual values of which will be passed from the main program when the function is called. (The function call by the main program will start with the function's name followed, in parentheses, with the actual arguments to be used by the function.)
- an optional 'Docstring' (see next paragraph).
- the body of the function, which, like an 'if', 'for', or 'while' loop, will usually consist of a series of indented statements that follow the usual rules for indentation. As for an 'if', 'for', or 'while' control, if the body of the function consists of only one or a few short statements, those statements can follow on the same line as the function name, separated by semi-colons if more than one statement appears.
- the 'return' statement. The body of the function will usually have a statement that begins with the keyword 'return' and is immediately followed by a value to be returned to the location in the main program at which the function call was made. The 'return' statement is typically the last statement in the function definition but is not required to be last. A return value is not even required. If a return value is not specified, *Python* will return a special object called 'None' to the main program.

If desired, a user-defined function can contain a 'Docstring', which, if present, is a block of commented text that begins on the second line of the function definition (see, for example, the user-defined function, 'my_1D_Gaussian' in Example3_5.py in Chapter 3). The first line of the Docstring must begin with three double-quotes ("""), and the last line of the Docstring must end with three double-quotes ("""). The text between the quotes is treated as a comment, and this comment can be accessed by the user at runtime. For example, after Example3_5.py is run, if the user enters 'help(my_1D_Gaussian)' on a new line on the Console, the block of text located between the pairs of three double quotes will be printed out. Well-constructed Docstrings permit new (and old) users to acquire detailed information (and reminders) about how to take full advantage of a user-defined function. This can be especially important when the user does not have access to the actual code that determines the function's behavior.

4.6 MORE ON ARRAYS

The creation and use of numpy arrays will be central to most computational examples in this book. The usual reason to create a numpy array is to have a single- or multi-dimensional series of floating-point numbers that can then be manipulated in various ways with one or a few commands. (As pointed out above, the 'list' data type that is available in basic *Python* is not suited for many calculations.) All of the examples considered in this section will assume that the statement 'import numpy as np' has already been executed.

4.6.1 CREATING ONE-DIMENSIONAL ARRAYS

The user can create arrays "manually", e.g., by statements such as 'A = np.array([1, 2, 3, 4, 5])'. If 'A' is entered as a new line on the Console, the Console will responds 'array([1, 2, 3, 4, 5])'. The lack of a decimal point in the array members suggests that this is an 'int' array. This can be tested by entering 'type(A[0])' as a new line into the Console. The response is 'numpy.int32'. So, A is indeed an integer array, with each member represented with 32 bits. However, if A is defined with the statement 'A = np.array([1., 2, 3, 4, 5])', the type of the array is 'np.float64', i.e., all numbers in this array are 64-bit floating point numbers because a decimal point has been included on one or more of the numbers. (Note: a frequent mistake in statements creating numpy arrays is omission of the brackets; for example, the statement 'A = np.array(1, 2, 3, 4, 5)' will generate an error.)

Another useful statement for creating numpy arrays is 'A = np.arange(0.,5,1)'. The np.arange function, with its three numerical arguments, mimics the logic of the range function described above, which is part of standard *Python*. In this case, A is a floating-point array, since at least one of the 3 numbers within parentheses is a float. The first member of the array A is set to 0.0 (which is specified by the first argument in np.arange); an increment of 1 (which is specified by the third argument in np.arange) is then used to specify the next member of the array (= 1.0); and so forth. The last member of the array is 4.0, which is the last number in the sequence that remains less than the end value in the range, which, in this case, is 5.0 (specified by the second value in the call to np.arange). So, the result is that A = [0.0, 1.0, 2.0, 3.0, 4.0]. If less than 3 numbers are specified as arguments to np.arange, default values will be used that follow the same rules described above for the range function.

The following statements are examples of useful ways to create arrays pre-loaded with specific floating-point numbers:
- 'A = np.zeros(100)' ; this A is a 100-element array filled with 0.0.
- 'A = np.ones(100)' ; this A is a 100-element array filled with 1.0.
- 'A = np.linspace(0,10,11)'; this A is an array containing 11 floats between 0 and 10 that are equally-spaced on a linear scale, i.e., [0.0, 1.0, 2.0, …, 10.0]. (Note that the second number in the 'linspace' function is included in the array, i.e., the range limits in this case are inclusive.)
- 'A = np.logspace(0, 4, 5)'; this A is an array containing 5 floats between $10^{**}0$ (=1) and $10^{**}4$ (= 10,000) that are equally-spaced on a logarithmic scale (i.e., the ratio of any two successive numbers in the array is the same). In this case, the numbers are [1, 10.0, 100, 1000.0, 10000.0] = [1e0, 1e1, 1e2, 1e3, 1e4].

4.6.2 CREATING MULTI-DIMENSIONAL ARRAYS

Multi-dimensional arrays are used in many types of calculations, and, like one-dimensional arrays, are easily created by means of the numpy library. Again, the examples here will assume that the statement 'import numpy as np' has already been executed.

An example of a two-dimensional array created manually is 'A=np.array([[0.,2,4,6,8], [1.,3,5,7,9]])'. The result is an array with 10 members, consisting of 2 rows, each with 5 members (this can also be thought of as 2 rows each with 5 columns). Note the use of parentheses to contain the individual rows in the array, which are enclosed in brackets and separated by a comma. As before, this A is a floating-point array because a decimal point was included on at least one member.

If 'A' is now entered as a new line on the Console, the Console gives a two-line response (note how parentheses and brackets are used in the response):
- 'array([[0., 2., 4., 6., 8.],'
- '   [1., 3., 5., 7., 9.]])'.

The response to 'A[0][0]' is '0.0', as is the response to 'A[0,0]'. These examples illustrate two ways to access the individual array members by standard index methods.

Interestingly, the response to 'A[0][:]') is 'array([0., 2., 4., 6., 8.])', so this demonstrates a method for listing all members of row 0 by using the ':' character as a proxy for 'all members'. An even shorter method for listing all members of row 0 of A is just 'A[0]'. Similarly, the response to 'A[1]' is 'array([1., 3., 5., 7., 9.])'.

Following this same logic, the response to 'A[:,0]' (which is shorthand for all row members of column 0) is 'array([0.,1.])'. Similarly, the response to 'A[:,4]' is 'array([8.,9.])'.

As expected, two-dimensional arrays are easily pre-loaded with some specific numbers. Try out 'A=np.array(np.zeros(10), np.zeros(10))'. Then, enter 'A' as a new line on the Console and see if the Console responds in the expected way.

Creation of arrays of higher dimensions follows a straightforward extension of the rules described here for two-dimensional arrays.

4.6.3 RESHAPING ARRAYS

Arrays are easily reshaped as long as the number of elements is taken into account correctly. Suppose A is the two-dimensional array defined above as 'A=np.array([[0., 2, 4, 6, 8], [1., 3, 5, 7, 9]])'. Next, define B as 'B=np.reshape(A, 10, 1)'. If 'B' is entered as a new line into the Console, the console responds 'array([0., 1., 2., 3., 4., 5., 6., 7., 8., 9.])'. So, the members of the two rows were combined by interleaving rather than by 'stacking' them back-to-back (see next section).

4.6.4 STACKING ARRAYS

Suppose A and B are defined as follows: 'A=np.array([0., 2, 4, 6, 8])' and 'B=np.array([1., 3, 5, 7, 9])'. Then, a one-dimensional "horizontally-stacked" array can be created by 'C=np.hstack([A, B])', which is equivalent to 'C = np.array ([0., 2., 4., 6., 8., 1., 3., 5., 7., 9.])'. Similarly, a two-dimensional "vertically-stacked" array D can be created by 'D=np.vstack([A, B])', which is equivalent to 'D = np.array([[0., 2., 4., 6., 8.], [1., 3., 5., 7., 9.]])'. An equivalent array D can be created with the statement 'D=np.row_stack([A,B]). On the other hand, the statement 'E=np.column_stack([A,B])' is equivalent to 'E=np.array([[0.,1.], [2.,3.], [4.,5.], [6.,7.], [8.,9.]]).

4.6.5 FLATTENING ARRAYS

Suppose D is a two-dimensional array defined as follows: 'D = np.array([[0., 2., 4., 6., 8.], [1., 3., 5., 7., 9.]])' and A is defined by 'A=D.flatten()'. The result is equivalent to 'A = np.array([0., 2., 4., 6., 8., 1., 3., 5., 7., 9.])'. Thus, all the values of D have been repackaged into a one-dimensional array. 'flatten' will do a similar repackaging of arrays of any order into a one-dimensional array.

4.6.6 SLICING ARRAYS

'Slicing' is a very useful array method for extracting a sub-array out of a larger array. Suppose we have a two-dimensional array given by 'A=np.array([[0., 2, 4, 6, 8], [1., 3, 5, 7, 9]])'. Then the following methods work to extract sub-arrays of various compositions:
- 'A[0,:]' will be a one-dimensional array consisting of all column members of the first row, i.e., the equivalent of 'np.array([0., 2., 4., 6., 8.])'.
- 'A[:,0]' will be a one-dimensional array consisting of all row members of the first column, i.e., the equivalent of 'np.array([0., 1.])'.
- 'A[0,0:3]' will be a one-dimensional consisting of the first 3 column members of the first row, i.e., the equivalent of 'np.array([0., 2., 4.])'
- 'A[:,:]' is the equivalent of the entire array, as is 'A[:]'.
- 'A[:, 0:4:2]' asks for all rows and, in each row, for every column member between 0 and 4 with a stride of 2. The result is a two-dimensional that is the equivalent of 'np.array([[0., 4.], [1., 5.]]). The syntax '0:4:2' says to start with the first member, go up to but do not

include the fourth member, and select every second member as you go. This approach also works in the 'reverse' direction, i.e., 'A[:, 4:0:-2]' yields the equivalent of 'np. array([[8., 4.], [9., 5.]])'. The syntax asks for all rows and, in each row, start with the fifth member (remember, 0 is the index of the first member), go down to but do not include the first member, and select every second member as you go.

As one might suspect, a great many more methods exist for manipulating numpy arrays and analyzing the data therein than is given here in this brief survey. Use of the help function as well as other resources, including on-line resources, should facilitate the user's ability to take advantage of these many other methods should the need arise. The on-line resource 'stackoverflow.com' is particularly recommended for having helpful information about features of *Python* that seem puzzling or are missing an obvious path forward.

4.7 ORDER OF OPERATIONS

Python evaluates an expression involving more than one arithmetic operator in the usual way. The exponentiation operator (**) has precedence over multiplication (*) and division (/), which have equal precedence; multiplication and division have precedence over addition (+) and subtraction (-), which have equal precedence. Expressions are evaluated from left to right. Thus, for example, 2/5*4 is equal to 1.6, not 0.1. Because expressions within parentheses are evaluated before the other orders of precedence are applied, if in doubt, one should use parentheses to ensure that an expression is evaluated as intended.

Python also has the ability to combine integers expressed in binary form by means of bitwise operators ('and', 'or', and 'exclusive or'), which we will not have occasion to use.

4.8 PYTHON SHORTCUTS

Python has a number of shortcuts that allow for a compressed syntax and thus for less typing. Some examples are:

- 'A += 1' is a shortcut for 'A = A + 1'. Similar shortcuts apply to the other arithmetic operators (-, *, /) as well as the exponentiation operator (**), the modulo operator (%), and the operator to obtain the integer part that results from division (//).

- Multiple statements can appear on the same line if they are separated by semi-colons, e.g., 'A=1; B=2'.

- Multiple assignments can appear on the same line if they are separated by commas, e.g., 'A,B = 1,2' is equivalent to 'A=1; B=2'.

- 'A,B = B,A' is a simple way to exchange the values of A and B. The equivalent in most other programming languages would be something like: 'temp = A', 'A = B', 'B = temp'.

4.9 PROGRAMMING STYLE

As programs grow and change, it is very easy for them to become hard to read. Even to the person who wrote the program, what once seemed obvious can later be mystifying. Good programming style can help this problem as well as make the program easier to read by others. The following approaches should be adopted when possible:
- Import libraries and other external modules as the earliest executable statements in the program.
- Define user-defined functions early in the program and use them, where possible, for repetitive tasks.
- Give meaningful names to program variables and user-defined functions. A statement such as 'def my_Gaussian()' is better than 'def my_function()'. Usually, the more specific, the better.
- Assign variable names to important constants in your program, even to physical constants (e.g., Avogadro's number, Faraday's constant, the gas constant, etc.), and use these names thereafter rather than the constants. This approach can be valuable if something that you initially think will be a fixed value in your program changes in later versions of the program, especially when multiple instances of other 'constants' that depend on the first value also change. For example, if, at an early development stage, a program uses a 100-member array that begins with all zeros, it is better to say 'A_len = 100' and 'A = np.zeros(A_len)' than 'A=np.zeros(100)'. At a later stage, the length of the array and all related values can then be changed with one statement.
- Use appropriate data types for the variables in a program. Ints will usually be appropriate for counting or controlling iterations, floats will usually be required for simple calculations, and numpy floating arrays will usually be required for more elaborate calculations.

- Include comments to explain the effect of both individual lines and separate sections of a program. Good comments can aid clear thinking and help avoid errors. Comments that are very brief at the time of initial writing are often difficult to decipher at a later time, so err on the side of comments with more information rather than less. Avoid, however, commenting on something that is truly obvious.

Also of Note
- When a program stops, examine the Variable Explorer, which likely contains a wealth of information about the state of the program that can be very useful during debugging.
- Make liberal use of the 'print()' function to track the progress of your programs during debugging and, if appropriate, during normal execution of long programs.
- If you are uncertain about the effect or correct syntax of a statement, try it out on the Console if possible. If not, write a separate small program to test the statement.
- *Python* has many other capabilities besides those discussed in this book. Hopefully, the reader will be motivated by the information supplied here to learn about, and make use of, those capabilities as needs arise. Some additional features of *Python* will be introduced and explained in later sections and chapters in the appropriate context.

4.10 SIMULATED DIFFUSION USING A RANDOM-NUMBER GENERATOR

The goal of this section is to present a more-advanced example of a *Python* program -- one that uses a number of *Python's* features discussed previously and also that introduces some new features. This program follows up material in Chapters 2 and 3 on one-dimensional diffusion.

Recall Fig. 2.2A in Chapter 2, which shows a hypothetical one-dimensional diffusion profile with a non-zero concentration of a diffusible substance to the left of a barrier and a zero concentration of the substance to the right of the barrier. From Fick's first law it was concluded that the substance would diffuse at a steady rate from left to right down the concentration gradient. It was also noted that, realistically, the concentration profile of the substance would not remain fixed as a function of time. Rather, unless special precautions were taken, the concentration to the left of the barrier would progressively decline, the concentration to the right of the barrier would progressively rise, and the concentration gradient within the barrier would become progressively less steep. The program example below (Example4_1.py) illustrates these points.

It is assumed that a conceptual (not actual) barrier separates two solutions. The 'distance' variable in the program is defined by 700 Δx units, 350 to the left of the barrier and 350 to the right. The initial condition for the calculations sets the "concentration" (i.e., the number of particles per small distance unit) to 1000 in each of the Δx units to the left of the barrier and to 0 in each of Δx units to the right of the barrier. It is also assumed that, in each time interval Δt, each particle located in each Δx unit can move randomly (i.e., can "diffuse") either to the left or to the right by one Δx unit. So, for example, a particle immediately to the left of the barrier can, in any Δt interval, move either slightly further from the barrier (then being two Δx units to the left of the barrier) or can cross the barrier (then being one Δx unit to the right of the barrier). And similarly for each particle at all other Δx locations (expect for the left-most and right-most locations; see Program Notes below).

The program calculates how the number of particles in all the Δx locations changes with time. The program listing is given next, followed by the two plots generated by the program, the printed output of the program, and the Program Notes.

```
1  # -*- coding: utf-8 -*-)
2  #Simulation of random particle steps to left or right: Example4_1.py
3  #Description: diffusion in one-dimension starting from a square-wave distribution
4
5  import numpy as np
6  import matplotlib.pyplot as plt
7  from numpy.random import random as rng  #import a psuedo-random-number generator
8  from numpy.random import seed       #seeding permits calculation reproducibility
9  import datetime                     #we will track how long the calculation takes
10
11 X_locs=2*350     #use an even total number of particle locations on x-axis (0 to X_loc-1)
12 Max_points=1000  #starting number of particles at each left-side x-location
13 Min_points=0     #starting number of particles at each right-side x-location
14 N_frames=10000   #number of frames (= times to re-calculate the particle profiles)
15
16 X=np.linspace(0,X_locs-1,X_locs,dtype=int)        #the integer array of x-locations
17 YA=Max_points*np.ones(int(X_locs/2),dtype=int) #particles in first-half of x-locs
18 YB=Min_points*np.ones(int(X_locs/2),dtype=int)   #particles in second half of x-locs
19 Y=np.hstack([YA,YB])     #array specifying number of particles in all x-locations
20 #Y will also hold the number of particles in the x-profile of the 'current' frame
```

```
21  Y0=1*Y                       #Y0 remembers the initial particle distribution
22  Spread=np.zeros(N_frames, dtype=int)   #track the spread of the profile in each frame
23
24  seed(1)         #seed(1) will start the random number generator in a reproducible way
25  print("Total number of particles at start = {} ".format(np.sum(Y)))
26  NN=4            #number of times to print out how the calculation is progressing
27  now0 = datetime.datetime.now()    #get the date & time at the start of the calculation
28
29  #Calculate the particle profiles for a total number of iterations/frames = N_frames
30  for i in range(0,N_frames):
31      Z=0*Y                    #Z, the 'next' particle profile, starts with all zeros
32      if (i!=0 and i%(N_frames/NN)==0):
33          #print out the progress of calculation every 100/NN percent of the way
34          now1 = datetime.datetime.now()    #get the current time and print elapsed time
35          print("{} out of {} frames; elapsed minutes = {:.2f}".format(i,N_frames,60*\
36              (now1.hour-now0.hour)+(now1.minute-now0.minute)+(now1.second\
37              -now0.second)/60))
38      for j in range(X_locs):          #run through all the x-locations in the profile
39          if j == 0:                    #treat the first x-location as a special case
40              for k in range(Y[j]):     #decide whether to move each particle at first loc
41                  if rng() < 0.5: Z[j] += 1 #no, keep the particle at first loc
42                  else: Z[j+1] += 1        #yes, move the particle right one loc
43          elif j == X_locs-1:              #also treat the last x-location as a special case
44              for k in range(Y[j]):        #decide whether to move each particle at last loc
45                  if rng() > 0.5: Z[j] += 1   #no, keep the particle at last loc
46                  else: Z[j-1] += 1           #yes, move the particle left one loc
47          else:
48              for k in range(Y[j]):        #decide how to move each particle at location j
49                  if rng() < 0.5: Z[j-1] += 1  #move the particle left one loc
50                  else: Z[j+1] += 1            #move the particle right one loc
51      Y=1*Z               #Y now becomes the profile for the 'current' frame
52      #get some statistics related to the particle spread of the current profile
53      index_1=0;index_2=0
54      for j in range(X_locs):
55          if index_1==0 and Z[j]<(0.75*Max_points): index_1=j
56          if index_2==0 and Z[j]<(0.25*Max_points): index_2=j
```

CHAPTER 4

```
57     Spread[i] = index_2-index_1    #record points for 3/4 to 1/4 fall of the Z profile
58
59  now2 = datetime.datetime.now()      #get the time at the end of the calculation
60  print('{} out of {} frames; minutes of calculation = {:.2f} '.format(N_frames,\
61     N_frames,60*(now2.hour-now0.hour)+(now2.minute-now0.minute)+\
62     (now2.second-now0.second)/60))
63
64  #get some statistics related to the profile calculated in the last frame
65  print("Total number of particles at end = {} ".format(np.sum(Y)))
66  print("Number of particles in first half = {} ".format(np.sum(Y[0:int(X_locs/2)])))
67  print("Number of particles in second half = {} ".format(np.sum(Y[int(X_locs/2):X_locs])))
68  print("Spread of final profile (3/4 to 1/4) = {} ".format(index_2-index_1))
69
70  #plot the first and last particle profiles
71  plt.figure()
72  plt.plot(X,Y0,'gray')              #this is the first profile; plot as connected curve in gray
73  plt.plot(X,Y,'.k',markersize=4)    #this is the last profile; plot as small black dots
74  plt.xlim(0,X_locs)                 #range of x-locations to view
75  plt.ylim(0,1.2*Max_points)         #vertical scale for number of particles
76  plt.xlabel('x-location')
77  plt.ylabel('Number of Particles')
78  plt.title("Simulation of 1-D Diffusion Starting from a Square Wave")
79  #plt.savefig("Example4_1a.png", dpi=200)
80
81  #also plot the frame-by-frame spread of the profiles
82  plt.figure()
83  plt.plot(range(N_frames),Spread,'.k',markersize=1)
84  plt.xlim(0,N_frames)
85  plt.ylim(0,1.6*np.sqrt(N_frames))
86  plt.xlabel('Frame Number')
87  plt.ylabel('Spread of Profile (3/4-way to 1/4-way down)')
88  plt.title("Simulation of 1-D Diffusion Starting from a Square Wave")
89  #plt.savefig("Example4_1b.png", dpi=200)
```

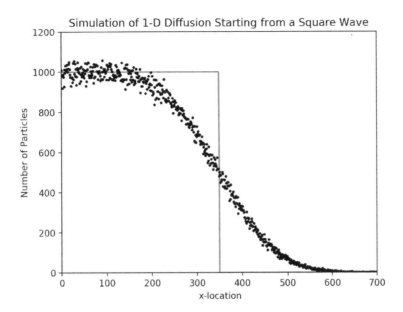

Figure 4.1 Distribution of the 350,000 particles in Example_4.1.py after 10,000 iterations to simulate the diffusion of the particles among 700 locations in the x dimension. The gray right-angle waveform shows the starting particle distribution.

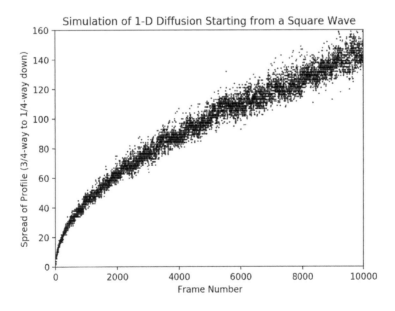

Figure 4.2 Spread of the particle profiles calculated in Example_4.1.py during 10,000 iterations of simulated diffusion. Profile spread is measured as the number of x-locations between the decline of the profile from 3/4's of its maximum value (= 3/4 x 1,000; see Fig. 4.1) to 1/4 of its maximum value (= 1/4 x 1,000).

Total number of particles at start = 350000
2500 out of 10000 frames; elapsed minutes = 13.65
5000 out of 10000 frames; elapsed minutes = 26.78
7500 out of 10000 frames; elapsed minutes = 39.90
10000 out of 10000 frames; minutes of calculation = 52.87
Total number of particles at end = 350000
Number of particles in first half = 310207
Number of particles in second half = 39793
Spread of final profile (3/4 to 1/4) = 133

Program Notes. *Python* features that were explained previously or that are obvious from comments in the program itself are not discussed.

- The program relies on *Python's* pseudo-random number generator, which is imported from the 'numpy.random' module and can be called within a program statement with the expression 'rng()'. Each call to rng() returns a floating-point number that is distributed evenly in the interval [0,1). The program also uses the function 'seed' from the same module. The expression 'seed()' (with nothing inside the parentheses) starts the random number generator based on the current time and date; thus, if the program is re-run at a later time, the sequence of random numbers generated in the program will not be the same. This feature can be a disadvantage during debugging, since the program will never repeat itself in exactly the same way. To overcome this disadvantage, seed can be called with a specific number (e.g., seed(0), seed(1), seed(2), etc.), which will start the random number generator in a way unique to each number. Thus, if a seed number is specified within the parentheses, the generated sequence of random numbers will be the same each time the program is run.

- Lines 11-14 of the program define several parameter values needed for the initial conditions of the simulation. The factor 2 in the statement 'X_locs=2*350' is used as a reminder that, of the total Δx units in the particle distribution (700, in this case), half will be to the left of the hypothetical barrier and half to the right. 'Max_points=1000' gives the number of particles that, at the outset, will reside in each Δx unit to the left of the barrier; 'Min_points=0' gives the number of particles that, at the outset, will reside in each Δx unit to the right of the barrier. 'N_frames' is the number of times to calculate the particle distribution; in each new frame, each particle (except those at location 0 and location 699;

see below) is required to move randomly either one Δx unit to the left or one Δx unit to the right of its x-location in the current frame.

- Lines 16-22 define the numpy arrays that hold the results of the simulation. The X array holds the sequence of the 700 Δx locations (numbered from 0 to X_locs-1, i.e., from 0 to 699). The Y array keeps track of the number of particles in each Δx location. YA and YB define the particle arrays to the left and right, respectively, of the hypothetical barrier (which occurs between locations 349 and 350, i.e., half way along the x axis). Y is obtained by concatenating (i.e., horizontally stacking) the YA and YB arrays. These arrays have been defined as int arrays by use of the keyword argument 'dtype=int'. (As noted: a keyword argument allows the user to override the default setting of a function argument; in this instance, without the keyword argument, the data type would default to a numpy floating array.) 'Spread' is another int array that, for each frame of the simulation, will hold a measure of the spread of the calculated particle profile. Each number in Spread is calculated based on how steeply the particle distribution in that profile declines from left to right; specifically it calculates how many Δx locations separate the profile from 3/4's of Max_points (= 0.75*1000) to 1/4 of Max_points (= 0.25*1000) (see lines 54-57 in the listing).

- Lines 24-27 start the random number generator in a reproducible manner ('seed(1)') and provide outputs to the console as a way for the user to monitor the progress of the program during the time of the 10,000 simulations of the particle profiles (which is expected to take tens of minutes or more, depending on the speed of the computer).

- The body of the calculation, lines 29-57, is repeated for a total of N_frames (=10000). Each iteration begins by setting the number of particles in array Z to zero at all X_locs locations (= 700). Then, at each of the x-locations that are neither 0 nor 699 (i.e., not the left-most or right-most locations), the random number generator is called to decide whether to move each particle at that location (the current number of which is stored in the Y array) either one Δx unit to the left (if rng() is between 0 and 0.5) or one unit to the right (if rng() is between 0.5 and 1). Array Z keeps track of the number of particles that are moved to each x-location as the new particle profile is calculated.

- Two special cases arise in the calculation of the Z array, which correspond to the starting and ending x-locations (0 and 699, respectively). Since particles at location 0 cannot move to the left (since there is no location = -1) and particles at location 699 cannot move right (since there is no location = 700), particles that might have moved left from location 0 or right from location 699 are kept at location 0 or 699, respectively. These special cases would eventually compromise the accuracy of the simulated diffusion if N_frames were continued to a number substantially larger than 10,000; however, for the calculation as carried out in Example_4, any impact of these special cases has a negligible effect on the program's results.

- Following completion of the body of the calculation, lines 65-68 print out information about the total time of the calculation and the final x-distribution of the 350,000 particles in the simulation.

- Lines 71-89 generate the two figures produced by the program. The first figure plots the initial and final particle distributions. Adding 'gray' to the call to plt.plot in line 72 specifies that the initial distribution is drawn in gray. Adding '.k' to the call to plt.plot in line 73 specifies individual dots ('.') in black ('k') rather than connected lines in the plot of these data. Adding 'markersize=4' specifies that a relatively small dot be used (markersize is a keyword argument that can be invoked within plt.plot to set the size of the dot). A smaller value of markersize (namely, 1) is specified in the second figure, which plots the spread of the profile distribution calculated in each iteration.

Physiological Significance

The starting particle distribution, shown by the right-angle gray line in Fig. 4.1, if considered as a limiting case of a continuous curve, is concave downward to the left of the barrier and concave upward to the right of the barrier. Let the position of this barrier be thought of as 'location 349.5'. Fick's second law says that, with time, the particle number (a proxy for concentration) will decline to the left of location 349.5 and rise to the right of location 349.5, and the slope at 349.5 will become less steep. Indeed, this is what happens during the simulation. Moreover, in each simulation frame, the original concavities (downward on the left, upward on the right) continue to hold qualitatively, so that the net effect from frame-to-frame (i.e., from one Δt to the next) is for the number of particles, on average, to continue to decline to the left of location 349.5 and to rise to the right of location 349.5. The average rate at which particles move during each Δt from the left of 349.5 to the right of 349.5 is given by Fick's first law, which states that the net particle movement is proportional to (Y[350]-Y[349]). Given that the maximum number of particles per Δx location is only 1000, it is possible (even likely) that, because of random variation, the net movement of particles during a particular frame might occasionally be from right to left rather than from left to right at location 349.5. Overall, however, the inevitability of Fick's laws will apply; thus, the particle distribution will continue to drift in the direction of fewer particles to the left of location 349.5, more particles to the right of location 349.5, and a smaller (negative) slope at location 349.5. [Note: Exercise E.5 in Appendix E discusses the curve defined by the dotted points in Fig. 4.1, if averaged at each x location.]

Fig. 4.2 shows the relation between the spread of the particle distribution and the frame number, which, apart from the noise in the relation, is also of interest. In the simulation, the frame number is a proxy for time. Recall that Exercise 2.2 of Chapter 2 and Exercise 3.3 of Chapter 3 explored the relation between the width (equivalently, spread) of a Gaussian diffusion profile and time. It is left to the reader in Exercise 4.4 to explore this relation in the context of the diffusion profile assumed in Example4_1.

4.11 EXERCISES

Exercise 4.1 Example3_2.py in the previous chapter creates a surface plot that shows a two-dimensional Gaussian function plotted at a large number of point pairs in the x-y plane. It starts by defining a variable 'coords', which is a one-dimensional np.array. It then uses this variable to create the independent variables X and Y, which are two-dimensional np.arrays containing point pairs in the x-y plane.

a) Use the Variable Explorer to see in what ways arrays X and Y are similar and different.

b) The dependent-variable Z, which is another two-dimensional np.array, contains values that are proportional to concentration at the different x,y point pairs. Modify Example3_2.py to take slices of Z at several locations on either the x or y axis and use the 'plt.plot()' function in 'matplotlib' to make a standard x-y plot of these slices on one graph. In these plots, let 'coords' play the role of x and the slice in Z play the role of y.

c) Analyze the curves that you plotted in b) to decide whether they have the same shape (i.e., differ only by a y-scaling factor) or whether they have different shapes.

Exercise 4.2 Suppose in Exercise 4.1 that the surface defined by variable Z is integrated with respect to y at each value of x to obtain a new function f(x). Based on either your analysis in part c) of Exercise 4.1 or on an analytical analysis of the equation specifying the surface plot, do you think a plot of f(x) vs. x would have a Gaussian shape?

Exercise 4.3 In Exercise 3.3 of Chapter 3, part b) asks the reader to calculate several one-dimensional Gaussian curves and, for each curve, estimate the inflection points on the curves by eye. A more accurate way to obtain a numerical estimate of the inflection points on one of these curves is as follows.

- Let X and Y denote, respectively, the numpy arrays that contain the independent and dependent variables that define the Gaussian curve. It would be helpful to plot the first differences of Y vs. X, since this plot, apart from a scaling factor, approximates the derivative of the original curve.

- The derivative of the original curve will reach a maximum (or minimum) when the convexity of the original curve changes from concave upward to concave downward (or concave downward to concave upward), so the first-difference curve can be analyzed to determine the point on the x-axis where it reaches a maximum or minimum.

- The numpy method 'np.diff(Y)' applied to the numpy array Y returns an array that contains the first differences of Y. Call this array 'diff_Y' (e.g., with the statement 'diff_Y = np.diff(Y)' and use it to plot the first differences of Y vs. X. Before doing so, however, note that, because it takes two members of Y to obtain one member of diff_Y, the size of the diff_Y array is one less than that of Y. (This can be checked with the 'size' method applied to a numpy array: the expressions 'Y.size' and 'diff_Y.size' will report the size of these arrays. Oddly, no parentheses are used in these function calls; e.g., the expression 'Y.size()' will generate an error.) So, to avoid generating an error, you will need to adjust the size of the independent array X in some reasonable way before you can plot diff_Y vs. X.

- Print out the maximum and minimum values of diff_Y by use of appropriate functions available to np.arrays [recall part a) of Exercise 3.3].

- Finally, to obtain the values of X that correspond to the maximum and minimum values of diff_Y, use function calls to 'np.argmax(diff_Y)' and 'np.argmin(diff_Y)' to obtain the indices of the array diff_Y where its values are maximal and minimal, respectively. These indices can then be used to find the values in the X array that correspond to the inflection points on the original curve. [Note: this overall approach is subject to a slight error because of the finite size of arrays X and Y. An increase in the size of the arrays would reduce the size of this error to an inconsequential value.]

Exercise 4.4 Make a plot of the function $y = \sqrt{t}$ for integer values of t between 1 and 10,000 and compare the result with the plot of the data points in Fig. 4.2. Do you expect these plots to be similar (apart from a scaling of the ordinate) or different?

Exercise 4.5 Modify program Example4_1.py to start with 175000 particles in location 349, another 175000 particles in location 350, and 0 particles elsewhere. This is approximately the case for a bolus of particles introduced at the mid-point location on the x-axis. Simulate the particle profiles for several choices of N_frames between, say, 100 and 10000 frames and view the plots that correspond to those in Fig. 4.1 and 4.2. To evaluate the spread of each profile, determine the distance between the x-locations that define the half-height of the profile on the left and the half-height on the right. To estimate the half-heights, you will first need to use some reasonable method to evaluate the height of the profile in each frame.

- Do you recognize the shapes of the particle profiles that result after a few iterations?

- Do you recognize the shape of the relation between the spread of the particle distributions and the frame number?

Exercise 4.6 This is a *Python* programming exercise in logic and counting. In Section 4.10, the first paragraph under Physiological Significance states that "Given that the maximum number of particles per Δx location is only 1000, it is possible (even likely) that, because of random variation, the net particle movement during a particular frame might occasionally be from right to left rather from left to right at location 349.5." Modify program Example4_1.py to determine for some N_frame number between 20 and 10000 how many of the frames have more particles crossing from right to left than from left to right at location 349.5. While you are debugging and making sure that your program is running correctly, be sure to start your counting with a small number of frames.

Exercise 4.7 This exercise illustrates use of the numpy 'shape' method to reveal the dimensions of several types of numpy arrays. As an example, enter into the Console the following statements: 'import numpy as np', 'A=np.array([0, 1, 2, 3])', 'B=np.array([[0, 1, 2, 3]])', and 'C=np.array([[0], [1], [2], [3]])'. Next enter into the Console the expressions 'A.shape', 'B.shape', and 'C.shape'. The Console responds with tuples that give the dimensions of the corresponding arrays. A is just a one-dimensional array; B and C, however, are special cases of two-dimensional arrays. Specifically, B is a two-dimensional array with just one column (a 'column vector') whereas C is a two-dimensional array with just one row (a 'row vector'). Next enter into the Console the expressions 'A.flatten()', 'B.flatten()', and 'C.flatten()'. The output indicates that the flattened arrays are all the same and equal to A. In some circumstances, *Python* may treat A, B, and C similarly, e.g., row and column vectors may suffice as input to a function that expects a simple one-dimensional array. Forgiving behavior of this type does not always apply, however. Thus, the reader should be aware of the dimensions of (i) the various np arrays that are assigned to the program variables and (ii) any np array(s) that are returned to the main program by its function calls. (Note: the 'Size' column in the Variable Explorer panel also provides information about the dimensions of the np arrays defined within a program.)

CHAPTER 5

INTRODUCTION TO ELECTROPHYSIOLOGY

At all times, a great variety of chemical and electrical events take place within the cells and tissues of the body. Chemical events usually follow the law of mass action and standard binding reactions involving the reaction participants (see Chapter 9). Electrical events can seem more mysterious. This chapter introduces basic ideas and terminology about how electricity is used in cells and tissues. The material draws on concepts from both college physics and biology courses and provides essential background for many topics considered in later chapters.

5.1 MEMBRANE VOLTAGE (V_m)

Voltage is electrical pressure. It is sometimes called 'electrical potential' or just 'potential'. A voltage implies the ability to make charged particles move and thereby release energy and do work. Voltage usually refers to a potential **difference** between 2 points in space and is defined as the work to move a unit charge from one point in space to another. Energy is released when a positive charge moves from a region of higher voltage to one of lower voltage or when a negative charge moves from a region of lower voltage to one of higher voltage. In solutions, voltages arise from either an excess of positive (cationic) charge over negative (anionic) charge, or the reverse.

All cells in the body have a membrane voltage (V_m), defined as the voltage inside the cell minus that outside the cell. Membrane voltages are used for a variety of important activities, including cell homeostasis and electrical signaling. Electrical signaling involves changes in V_m (ΔV_m) and is essential for the rapid coordination of a variety of activities in excitable cells. As noted in Chapter 1, the major advantage of electrical signaling over other signaling mechanisms is that it is fast. In the case of large nerve cells at 37° C, the action potential (AP) spreads along a meter's length of axon in about 10 ms, i.e., at about 100 m per s ($\approx$ 200 mph).

Cells undoubtedly began to develop and exploit electrical mechanisms very early in evolution. Plants and bacteria, as well as all animal cells, have membrane voltages and use V_m in a variety of ways:

- Bacteria use a negative V_m in combination with a proton gradient (high $[H^+]$ outside the cell, low $[H^+]$ inside the cell) to drive their flagella to initiate propulsive movement.

- Bacteria use the same two factors to make ATP.

- In higher organisms, the mitochondria, which are adaptations of ancient bacteria that took up a symbiotic relation within cells, also make ATP by using V_m and a proton gradient.

- Animal cells, which have fragile membranes, use V_m as a part of their mechanism for osmotic balance -- specifically to help prevent the cell from taking up large amounts of Na^+ and Cl^-. Because (most) cell membranes are quite permeable to water, uptake of salt would necessarily be accompanied by the uptake of water, which would cause swelling of the cell and risk cell death.

Our main interest will be in the transmembrane voltage, the difference in the electrical pressure on the two sides of a membrane. By convention, the voltage of the solution outside the cell is usually taken as zero, and the internal voltage is denoted 'V_m'. In cells at rest, V_m is nearly always negative, e.g., for a skeletal muscle fiber it is about -80 to -90 mV. During the brief (~ 1 ms) electrical event of an AP in a nerve or muscle cell, the voltage inside (V_m) goes transiently positive, to about +30 to +40 mV. In heart cells, V_m changes with each heartbeat and may spend a large fraction of the time at elevated levels (near zero mV or at positive levels).

Calling the voltage zero in the external solution is an approximation. If it were always exactly zero, there could be no current flow in the external solution because no electrical pressure would exist to drive current. In fact, there are very small extracellular voltages, measured in microvolts (μV), due to the ongoing electrical activity of the body's excitable cells, which are associated with current flow in the extracellular fluid.

These voltages are readily recorded in clinical tests such as the electrocardiogram (EKG), the electromyogram (EMG), or the electroencephalogram (EEG). Such recordings involve the placement of 2 (or more) recording electrodes on 2 (or more) places on the body, then measuring and amplifying the difference(s) in voltage between the electrodes. Membrane voltages, however, are so much larger that we can conveniently ignore the small μV differences in the extracellular fluid unless we are interested in recordings such as the EKG, EMG, or EEG.

5.2 THE ORIGIN OF MEMBRANE VOLTAGES

All body fluids contain ions, which have an electric charge. Whenever there is an excess of positive or negative charge in a volume of solution, that volume acquires electrical pressure. An excess of positive ions gives rise to a positive voltage, which repels positive ions and attracts negative ions. Conversely, an excess of negative ions gives rise to a negative voltage, which repels negative ions and attracts positive ones.

So-called 'diffusion potentials' can arise whenever there is a concentration difference of a dissolved salt, e.g., sodium chloride (NaCl). Imagine a sharp interface between two NaCl solutions, where the concentration is high at the left and low at the right (Fig. 5.1). The individual sodium and chloride ions will diffuse to the right, but Cl⁻ diffuses faster than Na⁺ because its diffusion coefficient is larger. This leaves a small excess of Na⁺ over Cl⁻ on the left, and introduces a small excess of Cl⁻ over Na⁺ on the right. Because of the charge separation, the solution develops a voltage that is positive at the left, negative at the right. As the diffusion potential develops, Cl⁻ movement to the right is inhibited; conversely, the movement of Na⁺ to the right is encouraged. Thus the charge separation never gets very large.

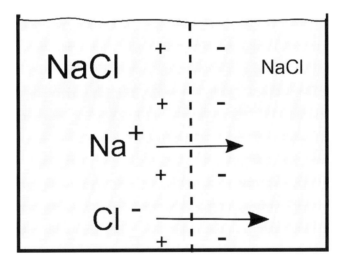

Figure 5.1 Schematic of a diffusion potential developing in solution of differing concentrations because the diffusion coefficient of Cl⁻ is greater than that of Na⁺.

There are at least two ways that the developing voltage might be made larger; both exaggerate the mobility differences between anions and cations.

1) Imagine, in the example above, that all of the Cl⁻ ions are fixed to a matrix that cannot move, so that only Na⁺ ions can diffuse. A larger voltage would develop, but, in this case, the voltage would be positive to the right.

2) Imagine that a membrane separates the two solutions, and suppose that the membrane is 'ion-selective', allowing only Na⁺ ions to pass through. Again, an excess of Na⁺ ions would accumulate on the right, making a positive voltage. After a time, the voltage would be large enough to prevent further net movement of Na⁺ to the right. This example is highly relevant to the way membrane potentials develop across cell membranes. If a difference in [Na⁺] exists on the two sides of the membrane, it is appropriate to speak of a **sodium battery**, because the concentration difference, like a battery, can cause the development of a predictable voltage and drive the movement of charges in a predictable direction (i.e. drive an electric current). The Nernst equation (see below) provides a formula to calculate the expected voltage of the sodium battery, i.e., the membrane voltage required to prevent net movement of Na⁺. The Nernst equation can be applied similarly to other ion species.

To summarize: voltages arise where there are concentration differences in the positively- and negatively-charged species found within a region in space. The main concentration differences of this type in the body occur on the inside vs. the outside of a cell's plasmalemma (surface membrane). The associated voltage difference across the membrane is an energy source (battery) that can power electrical activities in the body, such as action potentials. The main batteries that we will discuss arise from differences in concentration of Na^+, K^+, Cl^- and Ca^{2+} on the two sides of cell membranes. While the voltage differences across cell membranes, which are measured in mVs, are relatively small, they are much larger than the voltage differences that can be measured between, say, the chest and the feet when the EKG is recorded. Those voltages, measured in μVs, are about 1000-fold smaller and will be mostly ignored from here on.

5.3 CHARGE AND CURRENT

The <u>net</u> charge, Q, in a volume of solution equals the sum of cationic charge plus the sum of anionic charge (considered as a negative quantity). Two units are useful: *e*, the elementary charge, and the coulomb. One coulomb ≈ 6.24×10^{18} e. A calcium ion has a charge of $+2e$, and a chloride ion has a charge of $-1e$. If, in a small volume of solution, there are 2 Cl⁻ ions and 1 Ca²⁺ ion, Q is zero. Another very useful quantity to remember is that 1 mole of a <u>monovalent</u> ion contains approximately 10^5 coulombs; the exact value is given by Faraday's constant (F) ≈ 96,485 coulombs/mole of univalent charge. A mole of a divalent ion (e.g., Ca^{2+}) contains twice that amount, $\sim 2 \times 10^5$ coulombs.

Electric current, I, is the flow of charge. It has units of amperes (= coulombs/s) or e/s and a direction of flow. Current must always flow within a conductor. In the biological case, the most common conductor is a salt solution; there, the current will be carried by any mobile ion. An exception is found in select cells of the immune system where an oxidative bacteria-killing enzyme transports electrons to the extracellular fluid, thus generating currents carried by moving electrons. When current flows in solution, cations (positive ions) go one way and anions (negative ions) go the other. Following the convention developed by Benjamin Franklin, a (positive) current moves in the direction that positive charges flow. If the conductor is a wire, electrons are the only mobile charges available since the positive metal atoms are fixed in a lattice. In this case, since electrons are negatively-charged, the direction of current flow is opposite to that of the electron flow.

At Na⁺ concentrations and transmembrane voltages in the physiological range, the Na⁺ battery almost always causes the **inward** flow of Na⁺ ions -- and thus an inward current. Such a current, in the absence of other effects, causes V_m to become more positive (since V_m by definition is the electrical potential inside the cell relative to outside the cell and positive charge is added to the inside of the cell when Na⁺ ions flow inward). Under physiological conditions, the K⁺ battery of the cell membrane (which is due to the K⁺ concentration difference across the membrane, greater inside than outside) in most cases causes outward K⁺ current. An outward ionic current, in the absence of other effects, causes V_m to become more negative. The direction of Cl⁻ current is more variable but is often outward; if so, in the absence of other effects, such Cl⁻ current, like K⁺ current, causes V_m to become more negative. In this case, however, because the chloride ions are negatively charged, the flow of Cl⁻ ions is inward. Nevertheless, this flow constitutes an outward current, because, by convention, the direction of current flow is referred to the direction in which positive charge moves.

The lipid-bilayer construction of the cell membrane presents a large hydrophobic energy barrier that limits the transmembrane movement of the common ions found in physiological solutions (primarily Na^+, K^+, Cl^-, HCO_3^-, Ca^{2+}, and Mg^{2+}). Therefore these ions must seek a path across the membrane other than through the lipid per se. Most of these movements take place through *ion channels*, which are integral membrane proteins that contain a hydrophilic pathway within their core (Fig. 5.2),

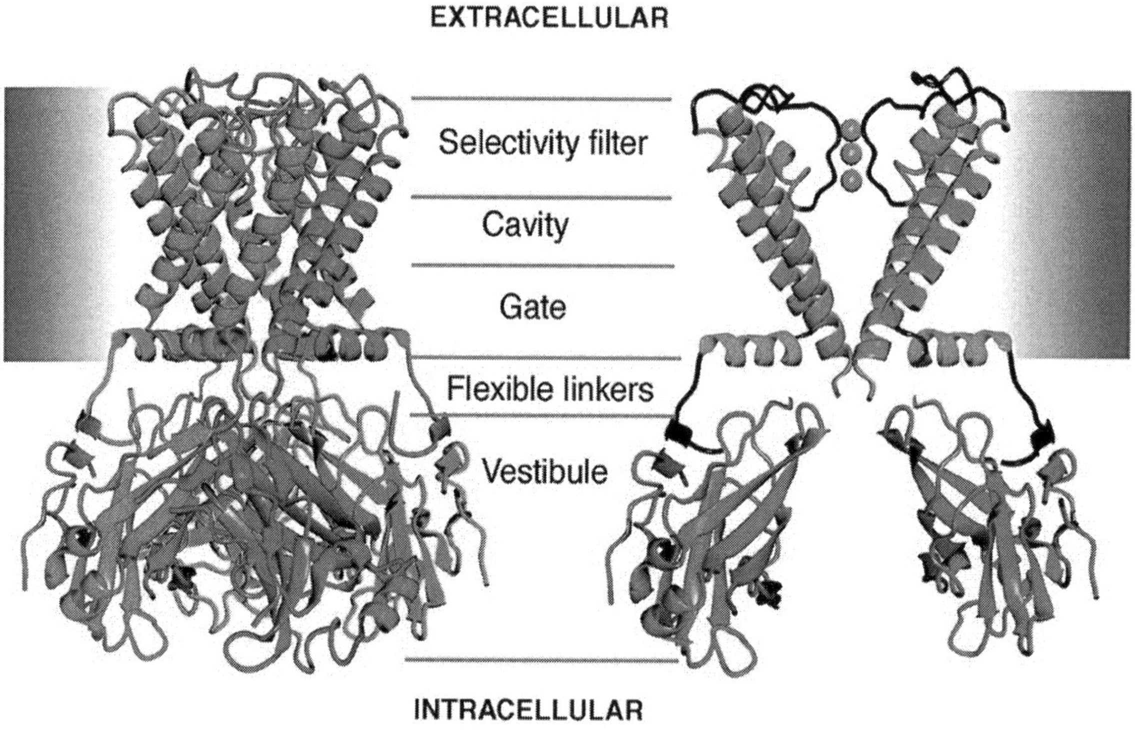

Figure 5.2 Ribbon structure of a K^+ channel in a cell membrane. The rectangular background at the top denotes the approximate extent of the cell membrane. The channel is a homo-tetramer. On the left, each of the 4 sub-units is shown in a slightly different gray scale. On the right, two subunits are shown with the same gray scale. The three small balls at the top right are K^+ ions; these mark the axis of the hydrophilic pathway by which K^+ ions move between the ICF and ECF through the inside of the protein. Under physiological conditions, K^+ ions usually, but not always, move from the ICF to the ECF. The Cavity contains a substantial number of water molecules (not shown). The helical structures surrounding the Cavity are α helices. The Gate in this channel is in the 'closed' configuration due to the close apposition of the ends of the α helices on the inner side of the membrane. [Credit: Kuo et al. (2003).]

Ion channels provide a pathway through which small ions can cross the membrane 'passively', i.e., without being linked to an external source of energy such as ATP. The defining functional characteristic of an ion channel is that it provides a pathway for ions to cross the membrane passively at a very high frequency. Typically, at room temperature, a particular ion species can cross the membrane through an ion channel at a rate of several million ions per s.

Ion channels come in many varieties and isoforms (see Chapter 10) and are often named for the ion that moves most easily through the channel -- e.g., K^+ channels, Na^+ channels, Cl^- channels, Ca^{2+} channels, etc. Many of these ion channels are 'gated' channels, that is, they can be in either the 'open state', allowing movement of ions through them, or in the 'closed state', not allowing ion movements. As described below, the unfailing rule for determining the direction of current flow of an ion species moving through an open ion channel comes from the concept of 'driving force'.

5.4 CAPACITORS AND CAPACITIVE CURRENT

A capacitor is formed by two conductors separated by an insulator. Cells have capacitance because an internal conductor, the cytoplasm (i.e., the ICF), is separated from an external conductor (the ECF) by the membrane, which is a good but not perfect insulator. Thus, all cell membranes have the important property called 'membrane capacitance' (Fig. 5.3).

A *capacitive current* (sometimes called 'capacity current') refers to the movement of charges of one sign onto one side (one 'plate') of the capacitor and, simultaneously, the movement of charges of the other sign onto the other plate, resulting in accumulation of positive charge on one side and negative charge on the other side. No current flows directly from conductor to conductor due to the insulator separating them. So, whenever current is said to flow "through" the capacitance, positive charges are accumulating on one plate and negative charges on the other plate. When this happens, the voltage difference between the two sides of the capacitor changes. Importantly, whenever a net ionic current is flowing into a cell, V_m is moving to a more positive value because charge is being added to the membrane capacitance; similarly, when net ionic current is flowing out of the cell, V_m is moving negative.

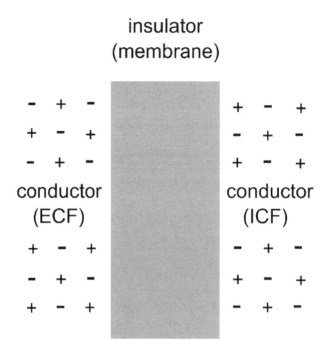

Figure 5.3 Schematic of the capacitance of the cell membrane.

As we shall see, capacitance is usually a shortcoming for electrical signaling because the larger the capacitance, the slower will an electrical signal move. A major protein in the nervous system, myelin basic protein, is present mainly to reduce membrane capacitance.

As a specific example, imagine that an open K^+-selective ion channel is inserted in the membrane of a cell, with $V_m = 0$ at the moment of insertion. If, as usual, $[K^+]$ is higher inside than out, K^+ then begins to diffuse out and there is an outward current (Fig. 5.4 left, arrow). Each K^+ that goes out leaves behind an unpaired anion, A^-. (We suppose that A^- cannot pass through the K^+ channel.) Because of the K^+ current, positive charge accumulates outside, negative charge accumulates inside at a 1:1 ratio, and V_m, the voltage inside, goes negative. The excess positive charges on the outside immediately crowd up to the membrane as closely as possible, attracted by the excess internal negativity on the inside as they try to minimize the overall electrical energy. Simultaneously, the excess negative charges inside try to get as close as possible to the positive charges outside. We call the movement of K^+ ions from inside the cell through the ion channel to the outside of the cell an 'outward ionic current' (Fig. 5.4, left).

In contrast, the movement of the excess positive charges on the outside of the membrane and the excess negative charges on the inside of the membrane to their minimally-separated positions at their respective membrane surfaces is called an 'inward capacity current'. The right part of Fig. 5.4 illustrates the final ion distribution (after both the outward ionic and inward capacitive movements are complete). It should be noted, however, that these 2 types of ion movements (currents) take place essentially simultaneously. The outward ionic and inward capacity currents considered simultaneously thus constitute a loop of current. In all cases, currents flow in closed loops.

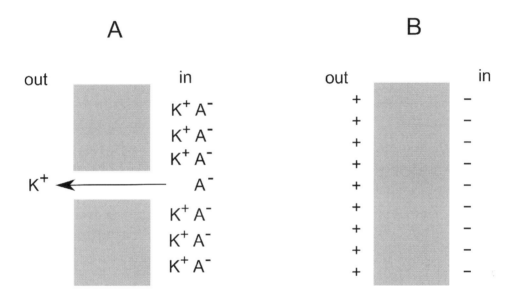

Figure 5.4 Schematic of how an outward K^+ current through a K^+-selective channel (A) leads to charge separation on the membrane capacitance (B).

As discussed, a negative voltage inside the cell is due to an excess of anionic (−) over cationic (+) charge. The amount of excess negative charge required for −70 mV depends on the area of the cell's surface membrane and how far away are the positive charges outside the cell (and another factor, the permittivity, which we will not discuss). In the case of most cells, the positive charges are just on the other side of the membrane, only ~30 Å (3×10^{-9} m) away, so they have a lot of influence on the voltage at the inner surface. As a result, quite a lot of negative charges must accumulate inside, approximately 4,370 elementary charges/μm^2, to give −70 mV. If the membrane were thicker, the voltage at the inner surface would be less influenced by the positive charges, and fewer negative charges would be required for -70 mV. Myelin, which coats the axons of many neurons, effectively thickens the membrane and thereby reduces its capacitance. The equation for this is:

$$Q = C \cdot V. \tag{5.1}$$

Eqn. 5.1 states that that the required charge Q is directly proportional to the voltage to be established. The proportionality constant C is called the 'capacitance'. C has units of coulomb $\cdot$ V^{-1}, or F (which is the abbreviation for farads, not to be confused with Faraday's constant, also abbreviated F -- see above). Other things being equal, C varies inversely with the distance separating the conductors. For a typical unit of unmyelinated membrane, $C \approx 10^{-6}$ F per cm^2 of membrane = 10^{-14} F per μm^2 of membrane.

5.5 THE NERNST EQUATION

The Nernst equation is one of the most useful and most cited equations in biology. When used in a calculation, it applies to a particular ion species, so there is a Nernst equation for Na$^+$, a Nernst equation for K$^+$, a Nernst equation for Cl$^-$, etc. The equation predicts what voltage would be established across a membrane by any particular set of concentrations of a particular ion species on the two sides of the membrane if the membrane were permeable to that ion alone. The general form of the equation can be written:

$$E_{ion} = \frac{RT}{zF} \ln\left(\frac{[ion]_o}{[ion]_i}\right) = 2.303 \frac{RT}{zF} \log_{10}\left(\frac{[ion]_o}{[ion]_i}\right). \tag{5.2}$$

E_{ion} is the ion's equilibrium potential, R is the universal gas constant ($\approx$ 8.314 Joules K^{-1} mole^{-1}), T is temperature in degrees Kelvin (K), F is Faraday's constant ($\approx$ 96,485 coulombs per mole), z is the charge on the ion species of interest (+1 for K$^+$, -1 for Cl, +2 for Ca^{2+}, etc.), and $[ion]_o$ and $[ion]_i$ are the ion's concentrations on the outside and inside of the membrane, respectively. Appendix C gives a proof of the Nernst equation.

At body temperature ($\approx$ 37 °C = 310 K), 2.303 $\cdot$ RT/F $\approx$ 61 mV. At room temperature ($\approx$ 20 °C = 293 K), 2.303 $\cdot$ RT/F $\approx$ 58 mV. Thus, for example, for an amphibian skeletal muscle fiber at room temperature for which $[K^+]_o$ = 2.5 mM and $[K^+]_i$ = 140 mM, $E_K \approx$ -101.4 mV. It follows that, if V_m = -101.4 mV, K$^+$ ions will be in *electrochemical equilibrium* across the cell membrane. In other words, the chemical force that favors the net diffusion of K^+ from inside to outside the cell (which is due to $[K^+]$ being higher inside than outside) is exactly balanced by the electrical force supplied by the V_m of -101.4 mV, which attracts cations to the inside of the cell. Thus, in this example, there would be no **net** movement of K^+ ions through an open ion channel of the type shown in Fig. 5.4. Unidirectional K^+ movements would still take place, but inward movements would equal outward movements.

An approximation of Eqn. 5.2 for an ion of valence z that is often used (which applies at 30 °C) is:

$$E_{ion} = \frac{60}{z} \log_{10}\left(\frac{[ion]_o}{[ion]_i}\right) \text{ mV} . \quad (5.3)$$

For example, if the concentration of Na^+ is 10-fold higher outside the cell than inside, E_{Na} = +60 mV. If the concentration of Cl^- is 10-fold higher outside the cell than inside, E_{Cl} = -60 mV. If the concentration of Ca^{2+} is 10,000-fold higher outside the cell than inside, E_{Ca} = +120 mV.

5.6 CONDUCTANCE

Some conductors are better than others, because they have more and/or more freely mobile charges to carry current. The conductance g of a current path is a measure of how much current it will carry per volt of driving pressure; thus, g has units of ampere $\cdot V^{-1}$, which defines a siemens (a man's name), denoted 'S'.

Two conductors are of interest:
1) The internal and external fluids of cells are conductors by virtue of the many small mobile ions that they contain (the higher the salt concentration, the better the conductor). In the ECF, conductivity is supplied mainly by the dominant ions, Na^+ and Cl^-. The Na^+ ions move one way and the Cl^- ions move the other whenever current flows. In the ICF, conductivity is mainly due to K^+ ions. Since the anionic charge inside a cell is mainly on proteins and larger molecules such as phosphates, these move more slowly (and, in some cases, not at all) and contribute only weakly to the conductance of the ICF.

2) Because cell membranes are penetrated by ion channels that permit the flow of ions, cell membranes qualify as conductors. Some ion channels are highly *selective* for specific ions,

e.g., Na$^+$ channels and K$^+$ channels, while others are not very selective. For an open K$^+$-selective channel, the potassium conductance, which varies with the type of K$^+$-channel, is typically 10 to 200 pS (picosiemens, 10^{-12} S); in such channels, the sodium conductance is close to zero, as is the conductance for anions (e.g., Cl$^-$).

It is convenient when speaking of individual ion channels to coin a new term, the single-channel conductance, denoted 'γ' (the Greek letter gamma); thus, the conductance of a single potassium channel in the open state is denoted 'γ_K'. g_K, the potassium conductance of a membrane with n open K$^+$ channels of the same type, is therefore given by: $g_K = n \cdot \gamma_K$. If p_K denotes the probability that any given K$^+$ channel is in the open state, then:

$$g_K = p_K \cdot N_K \cdot \gamma_K, \qquad (5.4)$$

where N_K is the total number of K$^+$ channels in the membrane, open or closed. (We make the simplifying assumption here that all of the K$^+$ channels are of one type.)

5.7 RESISTANCE

It is sometimes useful to emphasize the imperfection of a conductor and employ resistance, which is the reciprocal of conductance (R = 1/g). Electrical resistance has fundamental units of V amp^{-1}, i.e., ohms (recall Ohm's Law: V = I R). I_g, the current through a simple conductor is, by a rearrangement of Ohm's Law, $I_g = g\ V$. If, instead, we think of the conductor as a resistor, we can write: $I_R = V/R$.

Both equations imply a proportional relationship between current and voltage. As with the Nernst equation, Ohm's law (or slight modifications thereof, next section) will be central to the understanding of electrophysiology.

5.8 DRIVING FORCE

Consider an ideally-selective open K$^+$ channel in a membrane whose voltage, V_m, is initially 0 mV, with [K$^+$]$_o$ = 5 mM and [K$^+$]$_i$ = 150 mM at a temperature of 30 °C (Fig. 5.5). In this case, E_K (the K$^+$ equilibrium potential, given by the Nernst equation) is approximately -89 mV. If V_m could be made equal to -89 mV, the electrical force on K$^+$

ions would match the chemical force due to the difference in concentrations, and there would be no net movement of K$^+$ ions. That is, if $V_m = E_K$, the current through the channel would be zero. For other values of V_m, let us simplify and say that current is proportional to the driving force on K$^+$, defined as the difference between V_m and E_K.

This reasoning leads to the following relation (analogous to a rearrangement of Ohm's law):

$$i_K = \gamma_K (V_m - E_K). \qquad (5.5)$$

Here, i_K denotes the current through the single open K$^+$ channel. For a channel governed by this equation, we could, as suggested in Exercise 5.1 below, construct a so-called 'i-V curve' (current vs. voltage curve). The relationship in this case would be a straight slanted line that intersects the voltage axis at E_K.

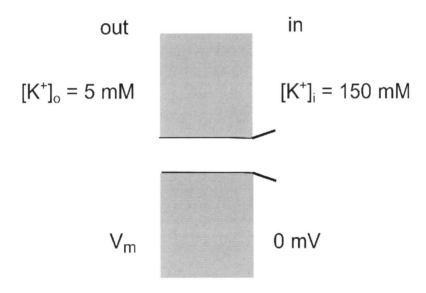

Figure 5.5 Schematic of a gated K$^+$-selective ion channel in a membrane at 0 mV. The channel gates, shown protruding on the inside of the membrane, are in the open state.

In reality, the i-V curve of a channel may not be a straight line. For example, in the case considered here, [K$^+$]$_o$ is much lower than [K$^+$]$_i$, so that, for an equivalent driving force, fewer ions are available for carrying inward current than for outward current. However, for values of V_m in the physiological range, which is usually between E_K and E_{Na} (with E_{Na}

≈ +60 mV), the simplification is often useful. Eqns. 6.7 – 6.9 in Chapter 6 consider examples of non-linear current-voltage curves.

5.9 THE TIME TO CHARGE A CAPACITOR

The time to charge (or discharge) a capacitor is particularly important in understanding the dynamics of electrical signaling -- for example, the propagating action potentials that control the activity of nerve, muscle, and endocrine cells.

To simplify, let us suppose we have a spherical cell, with a resting potential of -70 mV and with a surface area of 200 µm² (cell radius r of 4 µm, since surface area of a sphere = $4\pi r^2$). The capacitance of this cell is ~200 x 10^{-14} F (= 200 µm² x 10^{-14} F per µm²). At time zero, let us close all K^+ and Cl^- channels and open a single Na^+-selective channel that stays open indefinitely. In this ideal case, V_m would go from -70 mV to E_{Na}, since there are no other channels in the membrane. Suppose that E_{Na} is +60 mV. The voltage will thus change by 130 mV or 0.13V, and this will require the movement of about 1.6 million Na^+ ions:

$$Q = C\ \Delta V = (200\ \text{x}\ 10^{-14}\ \text{F}) \text{ x } (0.13\text{V}) = 26\ \text{x}\ 10^{-14}\ \text{coul} \approx 1.6\ \text{x}\ 10^6\ Na^+ \text{ ions.}$$

How long does it take for 1.6 million sodium ions to go through a sodium channel? As mentioned above, the current through the Na^+ channel will depend on the conductance and on the driving force. For Na^+, the relation we need is:

$$i_{Na} = \gamma_{Na}\ (V_m - E_{Na}) . \tag{5.6}$$

Here, the use of i_{Na} and γ_{Na} indicates that we are dealing with a single channel. Suppose γ_{Na} = 10 pS. Then, for a 130 mV driving force (which is the driving force on Na^+ when the channel first opens), the channel will pass 8.1 x 10^6 Na^+ ions s^{-1} (Note: 10 pS x 0.13 V = 1.3 pA = 8.1 x 10^6 ions s^{-1}). So V_m will initially change at a rate that appears that it will take ~0.2 s to get from -70 to +60 mV (since 1.6x$10^6 \approx$ 0.2x8.1x10^6). After a smaller time interval, however, V_m will have moved closer to E_{Na}, the current will be smaller because driving force, $V_m - E_{Na}$, is smaller, and V_m will change more slowly. Because the current is proportional to the driving force, the rate of change changes continuously and follows an exponential curve (curve in Fig. 5.6; the slanted line extends the initial change in V_m).

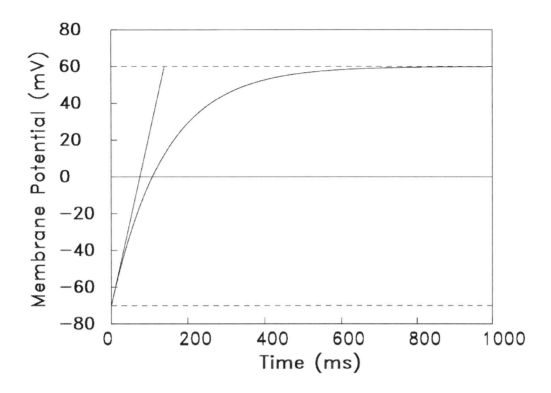

Figure 5.6 The curve shows the time course of V_m for the example considered in the text.

With an exponential time course, V_m goes halfway from -70 to +60 mV in one half time, goes half the remaining half in another half time, goes half the remaining quarter in another half time, etc. Because V_m and the current get smaller in parallel, both change exponentially with the same half time. The V_m half time for this example is about 0.14 s; more precisely, at time = 139 ms, V_m will be -5 mV. This time is undesirably long for many electrical signals used by excitable cells (i.e., nerve, muscle, and endocrine cells).

How could we shorten the half time and thus make electrical signaling faster? In two ways:

i) The first strategy would be to insert more Na^+ channels. If we had two instead of one, the half time would be cut in half; if we had 5 channels, the half time would be cut 5-fold.

ii) The amount of charge required for the change in V_m could be decreased if the capacitance were smaller. We could decrease the capacitance with myelin. If we doubled the thickness of the membrane, we would cut the capacitance in half, and thus cut the half time in half. Cells in fact use both approaches to increase the speed of electrical signals.

To put all of this into an equation, the half time is directly proportional to C (capacitance), and inversely proportional to g_{Na}, where g_{Na} is the combined conductance of all the Na^+ channels present; the proportionality constant turns out to be ln(2) (the natural log of 2) ≈ 0.693. So,

$$\text{half time} \approx 0.693 \, C/g_{Na} = 0.693 \, R_{Na} \, C \, . \tag{5.7}$$

In a case where there are channels other than Na^+ channels present, the total conductance of the membrane, g_m (where subscript 'm' is short for 'membrane'), determines the half time and, in that case, the value toward which V_m would be moving would differ from E_{Na}. In either case, under the assumption that current is proportional to driving force, the time course of V_m follows an exponential time course. If just Na^+ channels are present:

$$V_m(t) = E_{Na} - (130 \text{ mV} \times 2^{-t/\text{half time}}) \approx E_{Na} - (130 \text{ mV} \times e^{-0.693 t/\text{half time}}) \, , \tag{5.8}$$

where t is time and e is the base of the natural log system. Frequently the term 'time constant' or τ (the Greek letter tau) is used in this context. $t_{1/2}$ (half time) and τ are related by the equation:

$$t_{1/2} = \ln(2) \, \tau \approx 0.693 \, \tau \, . \tag{5.9}$$

Thus, $\tau = R_{Na} \cdot C = C/g_{Na}$. Using τ simplifies the appearance of the equation for V_m to:

$$V_m = E_{Na} - (130 \text{ mV}) \, e^{-t/\tau} \, . \tag{5.10}$$

For this reason, time courses are often given in time-constant units rather than half-time units.

Because C (in farads) divided by g (in siemens) has units of seconds, one can directly calculate that, for the example above, τ (= C/g) is 0.2 s and that half time (= ln 2 x τ) is 139 ms (as noted above). It is useful to remember that an exponential "signal" -- in this case, the change in V_m -- achieves ~63% (i.e., 1 - 1/e ≈ 63.21%) of its full size when t = τ.

5.10 EXERCISES

Exercise 5.1 Section 5.8 discussed Eqn. 5.5 [$i_K = \gamma_K (V_m - E_K)$] in the context of the current that flows through a single ion channel that is perfectly selective for K^+.

a) Assume that γ_K is 50 pS and that E_K is -89 mV. Write a program in *Python* that uses this equation to plot i_K vs. V_m for values of V_m between -100 mV and +100 mV. This plot shows what is called the I-V relation for this K^+ channel.

b) Repeat part a) for a single ion channel that is perfectly selective for Na^+; assume that γ_{Na} is 10 pS and that E_{Na} is 60 mV. Plot this I-V relation on the same graph as in part a). Estimate by eye at what value of V_m the sum of the currents (i.e., the net current) through both channels is zero.

c) Add a third plot to your graph in b) that represents the net current through the two channels and use an appropriate method in *Python* to determine exactly at what value of V_m the net current is zero.

Note: Some ion channel types are not highly selective for a particular ion species; rather, they pass two or more ion species with approximately equal facility. One channel of this type, the 'nicotinic' acetylcholine receptor (discussed in Chapters 10 and 11), has approximately the same conductance for Na^+ as for K^+. In this situation, the I-V relation of the channel is related to that calculated in c). The value of V_m for which the net current through the channel is zero is then called the 'reversal potential' of the channel (denoted 'E_R') rather than the 'equilibrium potential'. The term 'equilibrium potential' is not used since E_R is not equal to the equilibrium potential of either of the conducted ions, in spite of the fact that the net current through channel is zero when $V_m = E_R$. The name 'reversal potential' is used in cases like this because the direction of the current through the channel reverses from minus to plus if V_m is changed from a value less than E_R to one greater than E_R.

Exercise 5.2 The last section of this chapter discussed the ideas that underlie Fig. 5.6.

a) Write a program in *Python* that uses these ideas to reproduce the plot in Fig. 5.6.

b) Allow your program to show, on the same plot, the time course of V_m for different values of g_{Na} and for different values of C. Do the relations among the curves agree with the statements in the text about how changes in these variables affect the time it takes for V_m to change during an electrical signaling event?

Exercise 5.3 Modify your last program so that it restores the original values of C and g_{Na} and includes a new variable g_K with an initial value of zero. Plot the time course of V_m until it reaches ~40 mV. At that time point, change the value of g_{Na} in your program to 0 and change the value of g_K to 50 pS and see what effect this has on the overall time course of V_m (assume E_K = -70 mV). If done correctly, you now have a program that provides a crude simulation of an action potential in an excitable cell. (The action potential and its mechanism is discussed in detail in Chapter 8.)

CHAPTER 6

OSMOTIC BALANCE IN CELLS

Animal cells contain large concentrations of vital impermeant constituents, many of which are in the form of negatively-charged proteins and phosphates. Cells must therefore keep the concentrations of other internal constituents under careful control in order to keep available 'osmotic space' for the impermeant proteins and phosphates. This chapter examines the role of several key factors that enable an animal cell to achieve an osmotically-stable resting state. In doing so, the cell avoids the inherent tendency to take up water and swell due to the presence of the impermeant proteins, phosphates, and other essential internal constituents

6.1 A MODEL OF OSMOTIC BALANCE IN CELLS

The most important factor in the osmotic balance of a cell is the low permeability of the surface membrane to the osmotically-active particles found on either side of the membrane, particularly the dominant small ions, Na^+, K^+, and Cl^-. The low permeability by itself is not sufficient, however, and two other important factors come into play: (1) the Na/K pumps on the cell's surface membrane, which use the energy of ATP to reverse the constant leakage of Na^+ into the cell and K^+ out of the cell, and (2) a negative value of the cell's membrane potential (V_m), which keeps the intracellular concentration of Cl^- low without requiring that energy be expended to expel Cl^-. In the absence of these factors, the cell would take up large amounts of Na^+ and Cl^- and, hence, water -- thus swell and die.

Section 6.3 presents a computational model of osmotic balance in a generic animal cell. Here, we preview the elements of the model in its basic form. For simplicity, the generic cell is assumed to be spherical in shape, and the osmotically-important constituents in the intracellular and extracellular solutions are assumed to be either univalent cations or univalent anions.

The factors and variables that are included in the model, with their abbreviations and units used in the calculations, are:
- The cell radius (radius, in cm) and the related variables: membrane surface area (area, in cm^2) and cell volume (volume, in cm^3).

- The electrical capacitance of the surface membrane (C_m, in farads cm^{-2}).

- The membrane potential (V_m, in V or mV).

- The extracellular (= outside) and intracellular (= inside) concentrations of Na$^+$, K$^+$, and Cl$^-$ ([Na$^+$]$_o$, [K$^+$]$_o$, [Cl$^-$]$_o$ and [Na$^+$]$_i$, [K$^+$]$_i$, [Cl$^-$]$_i$, respectively; in moles cm^{-3}) and the intracellular concentration of impermeant anions ([A$^-$]$_i$, in moles cm^{-3}). A$^-$ is a proxy for impermeant intracellular negatively-charged proteins, phosphates, and related constituents. (In the *Python* program below, [Na$^+$]$_o$, [K$^+$]$_o$, and [Cl$^-$]$_o$ are called 'Naout', 'Kout' and 'Clout', respectively, and [Na$^+$]$_i$, [K$^+$]$_i$, [Cl$^-$]$_i$, and [A$^-$]$_i$ are called 'nain', 'kin', 'clin', and 'pin', respectively.)

- The permeability of the surface membrane to Na$^+$, K$^+$, and Cl$^-$ (P_{Na}, P_K, and P_{Cl}, respectively; in cm/s). Qualitatively, the membrane permeability of a substance is proportional to the ease with which the substance can cross the membrane in the presence of concentration and electrical forces. In the case of ions, the permeability pathways are primarily due to ion channels in the membrane. Quantitatively, the ion permeabilities, in combination with the ion concentrations and V_m, determine the passive fluxes of Na$^+$, K$^+$, and Cl$^-$ across the membrane (fluxNa, fluxK, and fluxCl, in moles cm^{-2} s^{-1}; see Eqns. 6.7-6.9 below).

- The active ion fluxes due to the Na$^+$/K$^+$ ATPase (Na/K pump), which uses the energy of ATP to expel Na$^+$ ions and take up K$^+$ ions (FNapump and FKpump, in moles cm^{-2} s^{-1}).

Some variables and factors that are ignored in the model include:

- The possibility of active transport of Cl$^-$ ions. (No chloride pumps are known for animal cells.)

- Osmotic and electrical effects due to other small permeant ions -- for example, Ca^{2+}, Mg^{2+} and HCO$_3^-$. (The concentrations of these ions are low compared to those of the dominant permeant ions Na$^+$, K$^+$, and Cl$^-$.)

- Changes in ion permeabilities due to opening and closing of gated ion channels. (This extensive subject was mentioned in Chapter 5 and will be taken up in detail in later chapters.)

In the basic model, $[Na^+]_o$, $[K^+]_o$, and $[Cl^-]_o$ are taken as constants, i.e., are time-independent. This is reasonable since the extracellular solution is large with respect to the small volume of any particular cell. The intracellular concentrations, however, can change with time (t, in s and ms), as can several other variables. The time-dependent variables in the model are the following:

- $[Na^+]_i(t)$, $[K^+]_i(t)$, $[Cl^-]_i(t)$, and $[A^-]_i(t)$.

- radius(t) (the variation of which reflects cell swelling or shrinking), along with the related variables area(t) ($= 4\pi$ radius^2(t)) and volume(t) ($= 4\pi$ radius^3(t)/3).

- $V_m(t)$.

- fluxNa(t), fluxK(t), and fluxCl(t), the net passive fluxes of Na^+, K^+, and Cl^+ across the surface membrane through the permeability pathways. The fluxes are time-dependent because of the time-dependence of $V_m(t)$, $[Na^+]_i(t)$, $[K^+]_i(t)$, and $[Cl^-]_i(t)$. A positive flux is taken in the direction from inside the cell to outside.

- FNapump(t) and FKpump(t), the fluxes of Na^+ ions and K^+ ions, respectively, across the surface membrane due to activity of the Na/K pumps. These active fluxes are assumed to be linked in a fixed stoichiometric ratio S. In the basic model, S is -3/2 (= -1.5) since each turnover of the pump is known to translocate 3 Na^+ ions out of the cell for every 2 K^+ ions translocated into the cell.

Because of the complex interactions among these various factors, the model seeks a numerical (not analytic) solution. The solution relies on two macroscopic constraints:

1) **The Law of Electroneutrality**. In practice, this law means that, within any significant extracellular or intracellular volume, the total charge on all cations plus that on all anions is equal to zero. As pointed out in Chapter 5, when the cell membrane is considered, a small discrepancy in charge is actually present due to the existence of the membrane potential. For example, a negative V_m means that there is a slight excess of anions over cations inside the cell, which is matched by a slight excess of cations over anions outside the cell. This slight charge imbalance is taken into account in the model and, apart from this imbalance, electroneutrality requires that, at all times:

$$[Na^+]_o + [K^+]_o = [Cl^-]_o, \text{ and } [Na^+]_i + [K^+]_i = [Cl^-]_i + [A^-]_i .$$

2) The Requirement that the Solutions outside and inside the Cell are in Osmotic Equilibrium. As noted in Chapter 2, cell membranes are generally permeable to water due to the presence of integral membrane proteins known as 'aquaporins', which function as water channels. It is therefore reasonable to assume that the osmotic pressure (a solution property determined by the total concentration of the osmotically-active particles) is the same outside and inside the cell. Indeed, if the osmotic pressures differed, the concentration of water would be higher on one side of the membrane than the other and water would move quickly by diffusion from the region of higher concentration to the region of lower concentration. So, the equality of osmotic pressures is equivalent to the statement that the total concentration of osmotically-active particles outside the cell equals that inside the cell. In the model, this means that, at all times, $[Na^+]_o + [K^+]_o + [Cl^-]_o = [Na^+]_i + [K^+]_i + [Cl^-]_i + [A^-]_i$. It should be noted that this requirement, by itself, does not mean that the cell is in an osmotically-stable state. As shown below without the activity of the Na/K pumps, Na^+, Cl^- and water will continuously enter the cell, and the cell volume will steadily increase.

It is instructive to consider also changes to several factors and variables that are treated as constants in the basic model. Changes of this type are considered in the last section of this chapter and in the Exercises. These include:
- a reduction in the activity of the Na/K pumps;
- a change in S (the stoichiometry ratio for the Na/K pump);
- a change in P_{Na}, P_K, and/or P_{Cl};
- a change in concentration of the extracellular constituents: $[Na^+]_o$, $[K^+]_o$, and/or $[Cl^-]_o$.

6.2 A DIGRESSION ON SYSTEMS OF ORDINARY DIFFERENTIAL EQUATIONS

The osmotic model summarized in the previous section is implemented in the program presented in the next section. The program relies on *Python's* ability to solve a system of differential equations ('deqs'). In the model, the deqs to be solved are those that specify the rates of change of $[Na^+]_i(t)$, $[K^+]_i(t)$, and $[Cl^-]_i(t)$, which are the primary time-dependent variables in the model. The other time-dependent variables are easily calculated if

$[Na^+]_i(t)$, $[K^+]_i(t)$, and $[Cl^-]_i(t)$ are known. We digress here to explain how to use *Python* to solve numerically a system of first-order deqs.

Suppose we have two time-dependent functions y0 and y1 that are defined as follows:

$$y0(t) = \sin(t) \tag{6.1}$$

$$\text{and} \quad y1(t) = \cos(t) . \tag{6.2}$$

Recall from calculus that:

$$(d/dt) \, y0(t) = \cos(t) \tag{6.3}$$

$$\text{and} \quad (d/dt) \, y1(t) = -\sin(t) . \tag{6.4}$$

It follows that:

$$(d/dt) \, y0(t) = y1(t) \tag{6.5}$$

$$\text{and} \quad (d/dt) \, y1(t) = -y0(t) . \tag{6.6}$$

Eqns. 6.5 and 6.6 considered together constitute a system of first-order differential equations in which the rates of change of the functions are known in terms of the current values of the functions. Let us suppose that we have forgotten that Eqns. 6.1 and 6.2 are the solution to this system but that we know that Eqns. 6.5 and 6.6 describe our system of interest. Let us also suppose that the values of y0 and y1 are known at an initial time, e.g., at t = 0. The last assumption means that y0(0) = 0 and y1(0) = 1. We seek to find the values of y0 and y1 on a grid of values of t between the initial time and some later time, say, 4π. Since we know the values of y0 and y1 at the initial time and, from Eqns. 6.5 and 6.6, we know the rates of change of y0 and y1 in terms of the current values of y0 and y1, we should be able to estimate the values of y0 and y1 at a series of later time points -- for example, at 0+dt, 0+2dt, 0+3dt ..., 4π, where dt is a small increment in time. In other words, we should be able to numerically integrate this system of equations and thus estimate y0 and y1 on the selected grid of time points.

The following *Python* program numerically integrates this system of deqs using the function odeint, which resides in the integrate module in the scipy library ('scipy' is short for scientific *Python*), and plots the result.

```
1  # -*- coding: utf-8 -*-
2  """
3  Python 3.7
4  Created on Thu Jan 31 18:42:41 2019
5  Example6_1.py -- using 'odeint' to solve a simple system of simultaneous first-order deqs
6  """
7
8  import numpy as np
9  import matplotlib.pyplot as plt
10 from scipy.integrate import odeint
11
12 #function F contains the formulas for dy1/dt and dy2/dt for our system of deqs
13 def F(y,t):      #F returns the dy/dt values when passed the current values of y
14     dy=[0,0]    #create a list to store the values of the derivatives dy/dt
15     dy[0]=y[1]  #value of the derivative of the first function goes in dy[0]
16     dy[1]=-y[0] #value of the derivative of the second function goes in dy[1]
17     return dy   #return the list of dy/dt values to the calling statement
18
19 t_start=0; t_end=4*np.pi; N_steps=1000     #define the arguments for np.linspace()
20 t=np.linspace(t_start, t_end, N_steps+1)   #t is the time domain of grid points
21 init0= 0.0                                 #y0 at t_start is 0.0 [= sin(0)]
22 init1=1.0                                  #y1 at t_start is 1.0 [= cos(0)]
23
24 y_init=[init0, init1]                      #y0 is a list with the initial conditions
25
26 #odeint will return the solutions for y0 and y1 on grid t
27 y=odeint(F,y_init,t)     #y is a numpy array whose columns contain y0 and y1 on grid t
28
29 plt.figure()
30 plt.plot(t, y[:,0], 'k', linewidth=2, label="y0")   #the slice y[:,0] contains y0
31 plt.plot(t, y[:,1], 'k--', label="y1")              #the slice y[:,1] contains y1
```

```
32  plt.legend()
33  plt.title("odeint solution of system of sin & cos deqs")
34  plt.xlabel('time (t)')
35  plt.ylabel('y0(t) and y1(t)')
36  plt.savefig("Example6_1.png")
```

The plot created by the program is shown in Fig. 6.1. As expected, for times between 0 and 4π, the continuous and dashed curves are excellent replicas of the functions sin(t) and cos(t), which we know are the analytically-correct solutions for y0 and y1.

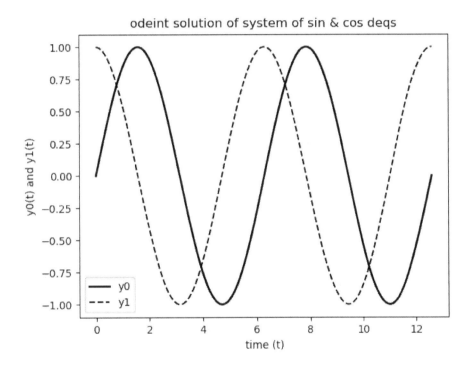

Figure 6.1 Solution of a system of two linked first-order differential equations, obtained as the output of Example6_1.py.

Program Notes
- Lines 1-10 of the program are of the type that have been explained in earlier programs, as are lines 29-35. The only new feature in the plotting part of the program occurs in lines 30-32, which are used to plot the legend in Fig. 6.1. The keyword arguments that are specified within the calls to 'plt.plot()', i.e., label="y0" and label="y1" (lines 30 and 31), specify the labels to be used for the two different types of curves. The call to 'plt.legend()'

in line 32 then causes samples of the two different curve types to be drawn in the legend and the corresponding labels printed next to them.

- Line 11 imports the function odeint. The call to this function (line 27) does the main work of the program, namely, integrating the system of first-order differential equations on the time domain t defined by lines 20-21. To do so, the call to odeint has to be properly setup. This is done in lines 13-17, which define the function F used by odeint, and in lines 21-22, which set the values of the initial conditions of the system.

The explanation of odeint and its setup is as follows.

- odeint can be invoked to solve either a single deq or a system of deqs. For the latter case, the system of deqs must be expressed as a system of first-order deqs. If the original system involves, say, a second-order deq (e.g., (d^2/dt^2) y = -y), then that deq must be recast into two first-order deqs (e.g., (d/dt)y = y1 and (d/dt)y1 = -y). Similarly, if the system has a third order deq, it must be recast into three first-order deqs, and so forth. Appendix F gives an example of a second-order equation recast into two first-order equations.

- Prior to the call to odeint, a function must be defined by the user that takes the form of F(y,t) in line 13. Argument y is a proxy variable for the current value of the solution to the system (one column for each deq to be solved) and argument t is a proxy variable for the grid of points on which the numerical solution is to be computed. Depending on how the body of F is defined, y can be either a scalar argument (i.e., one argument if there is only one deq to be solved) or a vector argument (i.e., multiple scalar arguments if there are multiple deqs to be solved). The value(s) of y passed by odeint to F will, in the first instance, be the values of the initial conditions.

- As odeint, in combination with F, proceeds to calculate the solution for the later values on the time-point grid, the current value(s) of the growing solution is/are used automatically to calculate the current rate(s) of change of y. If y is a vector argument (as in the program above), the first line of F will typically create a list 'dy' of zeros, the number of members of which matches the number of deqs to be solved. The function body will then have a statement that calculates the rate of change of each member of the list (dy[0], dy[1], etc.) from the current values of y0, y1, etc. The return value of F (i.e., dy) will then be either a single rate of change (if there is only one deq to be solved) or a vector list of n rates of change (if there are n deqs to be solved).

- The initial value(s) of y must be set, one for each deq to be solved. This is typically done with a list (called 'y_init' above, in line 24), but a tuple can also be used.

- After F has been defined and y_init has been setup, the call to odeint is made with a statement like that in line 27: 'y = odeint(F, y_init, t)'. Once odeint has finished its calculation, y in the main program will contain the result. If the solution involves just one deq, y will be a one-column array containing the solution on the grid t. If the solution involves more than one deq, y will be a multi-column vector array. This array can be unpacked with slicing expressions like 'y[:,0], y[:,1], ...' to extract the solutions for the first, second, ... deq in the system on the grid t.

Of Note. F returns the value(s) of dy/dt whereas odeint returns the value(s) of y.

Accuracy. As can be easily checked, for the solution calculated by odeint and stored in the vector array y in Example6_1.py, the maximum absolute error between any calculated value and the corresponding actual value of the sin(t) and cos(t) functions is less than 3e-7 in the interval 0 to 4π. The maximum absolute error gets larger, however, if the integration interval is made longer. For example, if the integration interval is increased to 40π, the maximum error is approximately 10 times larger, and if the integration interval is increased to 400π, the error is approximately 100 times larger. Depending on the calculation of interest, it will often be important to keep in mind some reasonable limits for the grid of points of the independent variable when a numerical solution for a system of deqs is sought with odeint.

Importantly, an optional keyword argument 'hmax' can be included in the call to odeint to increase the accuracy of the solution. If hmax is set to something other than 0.0, this argument overrides the default value of the step size that is used during the integration routine. For example, if the call to odeint above had taken the form ' y=odeint(F, y_init, t, hmax=1e-1)', the absolute errors mentioned above would be decreased by about a factor of 3. If hmax had been set to 1e-2, the errors would be decreased by more than a factor of 10. The ability to set the value of hmax in odeint to a small number is a feature that will be required in the osmotic program presented in the next section.

Also of Note. In Example6_1.py, the body of function F is quite simple. The statements that calculate the rates of change of y can, however, be complex -- for example, they might include other expressions involving the variable t (e.g., t - t*t/2 + np.exp(t)) and they might call other functions. And those functions might call other functions, and so forth. As an example, statements 13-17 in Example6_1.py could be replaced by the following:

```
13  def f1(x1,x2):    #f1 returns the rate of change for the first function to be solved
14      return x2
15
16  def f2(x1,x2):    #f2 returns the rate of change for the second function to be solved
17      return -x1
18
19  def F(y,t):       #F returns the values of dy/dt given the current values of y
20      dy=[0,0]
21      dy[0]=f1(y[0],y[1])
22      dy[1]=f2(y[0],y[1])
23      return dy     #return list of dy/dt values to the calling statement
```

This approach is used in the program Osmotic1.py in the next section.

6.3 A PYTHON MODEL OF OSMOTIC BALANCE IN CELLS

The program listed here, Osmotic1.py, implements the osmotic model described in Section 6.1. The printed output of the program is given after the listing, followed by the plotted output, which shows $V_m(t)$ (Fig. 6.2). Obviously, time-dependent variables other than $V_m(t)$ might also be unpacked and plotted, according to the user's wish (see Exercises).

```
1   # -*- coding: utf-8 -*-
2   """
3   Python 3.7
4   Osmotic1.py: implementation of basic osmotic model
5   start with reasonable guesses for Vm and for internal [Na], [K], and [Cl]
6   """
7
8   import numpy as np
9   import matplotlib.pyplot as plt
10  from scipy.integrate import odeint
11
12  #here we have the fct definitions needed for the model
13  def volume(nain,kin,clin):       #cell volume; cm^3
```

```
14      return (nain+kin+clin+pin0)/(Naout+Kout+Clout)
15
16  def radius(nain,kin,clin):          #cell radius; cm
17      return (0.75*volume(nain,kin,clin)/np.pi)^(1/3)
18
19  def area(nain,kin,clin):            #surface membrane area; cm^2
20      return 4*np.pi*radius(nain,kin,clin)^2
21
22  def FNapump(nain,kin,clin):         #active flux of Na due to Na/K pump; moles cm^-2 s^-1
23      return Pmax/(1+KD3/(nain/volume(nain,kin,clin))**3)
24
25  def FKpump(nain,kin,clin):          #active flux of K due to Na/K pump; moles cm^-2 s^-1
26      return FNapump(nain,kin,clin)/S
27
28  def Vnorm(nain,kin,clin):           #Vm in normalized units, VmF/RT; unitless
29      return (F/RToverF)*(nain+kin-clin-pin0)/(area(nain,kin,clin)*Cm)
30
31  def fluxNa(nain,kin,clin):          #passive flux of Na due to PNa; moles cm^-2 s^-1
32      return Vnorm(nain,kin,clin)*PNa*(nain/volume(nain,kin,clin)-Naout* \
33          np.exp(-Vnorm(nain,kin,clin)))/(1.-np.exp(-Vnorm(nain,kin,clin)))
34
35  def fluxK(nain,kin,clin):           #passive flux of K due to PK; moles cm^-2 s^-1
36      return Vnorm(nain,kin,clin)*PK*(kin/volume(nain,kin,clin)-Kout* \
37          np.exp(-Vnorm(nain,kin,clin)))/(1.-np.exp(-Vnorm(nain,kin,clin)))
38
39  def fluxCl(nain,kin,clin):          #passive flux of Cl due to PCl; moles cm^-2 s^-1
40      return Vnorm(nain,kin,clin)*PCl*((clin/volume(nain,kin,clin))* \
41          np.exp(-Vnorm(nain,kin,clin))-Clout/ \
42          (1.-np.exp(-Vnorm(nain,kin,clin)))
43
44  #G will be the function name required by odeint for the system of deqs
45  def G(y,t):
46      dy=[0,0,0]                      #set up a 3-member list to hold values of derivatives
47      dy[0]=-(fluxNa(y[0],y[1],y[2])+FNapump(y[0],y[1],y[2]))* \
48          area(y[0],y[1],y[2])
49      dy[1]=-(fluxK(y[0],y[1],y[2])+FKpump(y[0],y[1],y[2]))* \
```

```
50        area(y[0],y[1],y[2])
51    dy[2]=-fluxCl(y[0],y[1],y[2])*area(y[0],y[1],y[2])
52    return dy              #returns rates of change of inside Na, K, and Cl; moles/s
53
54 #here are the constants for the basic model
55 R=8.314                #gas constant (Joules per degree K per mole)
56 F=96485.               #Faraday's constant (coulombs/mole)
57 Temp=303.              #degrees K for calculation (= 30 degrees Centrigrade)
58 RToverF=R*Temp/F       #scaling constant (volts) for normalizing Vm
59 Pmax=1e-11             #max rate of Na pumping by Na/K pump (moles of Na cm^-2 s^-1)
60 S=-1.5                 #stoichiometry of Na/K pump (Na-out over K-out)
61 KD3=(1e-5)**3          #Hill Kd for Na pumping (moles cm^-3)^3 = (10 mM)^3
62 PK=1e-6                #K permeability of membrane (cm/s)
63 PNaratio=0.01          #PNa/PK permeability ratio
64 PNa=PNaratio*PK        #Na permeability of membrane (cm/s)
65 PClratio=2             #PCl/PK permeability ratio
66 PCl=PClratio*PK        #Cl permeability of membrane (cm/s)
67 Cm=1e-6                #membrane specific capacitance (farad/cm^-2)
68 Kout=5e-6              #[K]out (moles per cm^3) (= 5 mM)
69 Naout=140e-6           #[Na]out (moles per cm^3) (= 140 mM)
70 Clout=Naout+Kout       #[Cl]out (moles per cm^3 (= 145 mM)
71 radius0=5e-4           #initial cell radius (cm)
72 area0=4*np.pi*radius0**2    #initial membrane surface area (cm^2)
73 volume0=4*np.pi*radius0**3/3  #initial cell volume (cm^3)
74
75 V0 = -60.              #guess for starting value of membrane potential (in mV)
76 #guesses for stable values of internal concentrations of Na+, K+, Cl-, and P-
77 kin0=volume0*140e-6    #initial guess of inside [K] (=140 mM)
78 nain0=volume0*5e-6     #initial guess of inside [Na] (=5 mM)
79 clin0=volume0*14.5e-6  #initial guess of inside [Cl] (=14.5 mM)
80 pin0=(nain0+kin0-clin0) #uncorrected moles of (negative) inside P
81
82 deltac=Cm*V0*.001*area0/F #mole-correction amount based on charge needed for Vm
83 kin0=kin0+deltac/2     #corrected moles of (positive) inside K
84 pin0=pin0-deltac/2     #corrected moles of (negative) inside P
85 osmolein0=(nain0+kin0+clin0+pin0)/volume0 #initial osmolarity (M)
```

```
 86
 87  t_start=0.0; t_end=float(1000); N_steps=int(1000*t_end) #arguments for np.linspace()
 88  t=np.linspace(t_start, t_end, N_steps+1)  #t is the solution time domain
 89
 90  init0=nain0                    #initial inside Na (in moles)
 91  init1=kin0                     #initial inside K  (in moles)
 92  init2=clin0                    #initial inside Cl (in moles)
 93  y_init=[init0, init1, init2]   #initial-condition list for odeint
 94
 95  #y will contain solutions for Nain, Kin, and Clin
 96  y=odeint(G,y_init,t,hmax=1e-2)  #necessary to include small value for hmax!
 97
 98  v1=Vnorm(y[:,0],y[:,1],y[:,2])*RToverF*1000 #get unnormalized Vm in mV
 99  plt.ylim(-90.,-50.)            #set plot limits for Vm
100  plt.plot(t,v1,'k')             #plot Vm vs t in black
101  plt.xlabel("time (s)")
102  plt.ylabel("Vm (mV)")
103  plt.title("Osmotic Balance, Basic Model, Initial Vm = -60 mV")
104  plt.savefig("Osmotic1_1000s.png")
105
106  print("")                      #print out some useful final values from the model calculation
107  print("End time = {:.3} s with {:} time points".format(t_end, N_steps))
108  Final_Vm=1000*RToverF*Vnorm(y[N_steps,0],y[N_steps,1],y[N_steps,2])
109  print("Final Vm (mV) {:.4} ".format(Final_Vm))
110  Final_radius=radius(y[N_steps,0],y[N_steps,1],y[N_steps,2])
111  print("Final radius (cm) {:.6} ".format(Final_radius))
112  N_volume=volume(y[N_steps,0],y[N_steps,1],y[N_steps,2])/volume0
113  print("Final normalized volume {:.4} ".format(N_volume))
114  Final_Nain=1e6*y[N_steps,0]/volume(y[N_steps,0],y[N_steps,1],y[N_steps,2])
115  print("Final [Nain] (mM) {:.4} ".format(Final_Nain))
116  Final_Kin=1e6*y[N_steps,1]/volume(y[N_steps,0],y[N_steps,1],y[N_steps,2])
117  print("Final [Kin] (mM)  {:.4} ".format(Final_Kin))
118  Final_Clin=1e6*y[N_steps,2]/volume(y[N_steps,0],y[N_steps,1],y[N_steps,2])
119  print("Final [Clin] (mM) {:.4} ".format(Final_Clin))
120  Final_Pin=1e6*pin0/(volume0*N_volume)
121  print("Final [Pin] (mM) {:.4} ".format(Final_Pin))
```

```
122  Final_Osm=Final_Nain+Final_Kin+Final_Clin+Final_Pin
123  print("Final osmolarity (mM) {:.4} ".format(Final_Osm))
124  Final_ECl=-1000*RToverF*np.log(1e6*Clout/Final_Clin)
125  print("Final ECl (mV) {:.4} ".format(Final_ECl))
126  Vm_GHK=1000*RToverF*np.log(1e6*(Kout+PNaratio*Naout)/\
127          (Final_Kin+PNaratio*Final_Nain))
128  print("Final Vm calculated by GHK eqn. (no pump; mV) {:.4} ".format(Vm_GHK))
129
130  #print out some initial values for the calculation"
131  print("")
132  print("Initial radius (cm) {:.3}".format(radius0))
133  print("[Kin0] (mM) {:.5}".format(1e6*kin0/volume0))
134  print("[Nain0] (mM) {:.5} ".format(1e6*nain0/volume0))
135  print("[Clin0] (mM) {:.5} ".format(1e6*clin0/volume0))
136  print("[Pin0] (mM) {:.5} ".format(1e6*pin0/volume0))
137  print("inside osmolarity (mM) {:.5} ".format(1e6*osmolein0))
138  print("Starting Vm (mV) {:.5} ".format(V0))
```

End time 1e+03 s with 1000000 time points
Final Vm (mV) -81.69
Final radius (cm) 0.000489999
Final normalized volume 0.9412
Final [Nain] (mM) 9.403
Final [Kin] (mM) 135.6
Final [Clin] (mM) 6.346
Final [Pin] (mM) 138.7
Final osmolarity (mM) 290.0
Final ECl (mV) -81.69
Final Vm calculated by GHK eqn. (no pump; mV) -79.74

Initial radius (cm) 0.0005
[Kin0] (mM) 140.0
[Nain0] (mM) 5.0
[Clin0] (mM) 14.5
[Pin0] (mM) 130.5

inside osmolarity (mM) 290.0
Starting Vm (mV) -60.0

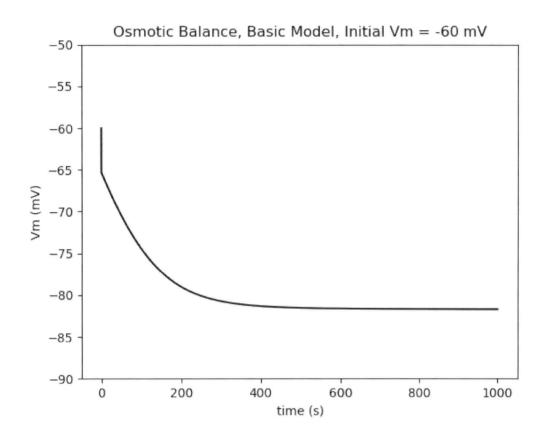

Figure 6.2 Solution of Osmotic1.py for the time-dependent variable V_m, given initial guesses for V_m (= -60 mV), $[K^+]_i$ (= 140 mM), $[Na^+]_i$ (= 5 mM), and $[Cl^-]_i$ (= 14.5 mM).

6.4 PROGRAM NOTES

A discussion of the physical meaning of the program's output is deferred to the next section of this chapter. Here, we focus on the structure of the program, which divides logically into the user-defined functions, the specification of the constants used in the calculations, the setup and call to odeint, the unpacking of the array of solutions returned by odeint, and the plotting and print sections.

Function Definitions

Function G(y,t) (lines 45-52) takes the place of function F(y,t) in Example6_1.py. (The name has been changed from F to G because F is the symbol usually reserved for Faraday's constant, which appears in the constants section of the program.) The three derivatives defined in the body of G are proxies for $(d/dt)[Na^+]_i$, $(d/dt)[K^+]_i$, and $(d/dt)[Cl^-]_i$. In actuality, the program keeps track of the number of moles of each ion species within the cell -- and, separately, cell volume -- rather than the concentrations per se (i.e., the number of moles per unit volume). The internal ion concentrations are easily calculated from the number of moles of each ion and the cell volume. With all three ions, the value of the rate of change of the number of moles in the cell volume is calculated from the ion's total flux across the cell membrane, which includes the active flux (if any) plus the passive flux. Since the units of flux in the program are calculated per cm^2 of surface membrane, it is necessary to multiply each flux by the area of the surface membrane to obtain the rate of change of the number of moles within the cell volume. As also noted in the preceding section, the area of the surface membrane and the cell radius are two other time-dependent variables that are included in the model; these are calculated from the cell volume based on the standard geometric formulas for a sphere.

The user-defined functions used by G(y,t) are given in lines 13-42. Most of these definitions, except for the radius and area functions, deserve some further explanation.

- 'def volume'. As mentioned in Section 6.1, because cells are generally permeable to water, it is reasonable to assume that the concentration of all osmotically-active particles inside the cell at all times matches that outside the cell. Given that the quantities of the internal constituents (Na^+, K^+, Cl^-, and P^-) are calculated in units of moles rather than moles cm^{-3} whereas those of the external constituents (Na^+, K^+, Cl) are given in moles cm^{-3}, dividing the sum of the former by the sum of the latter gives the cell volume.

- 'def FNapump'. The active flux of sodium is known to depend on the internal concentration of Na^+, the external concentration of K^+, and the internal concentration of ATP. In the basic model, $[K^+]_o$ is taken to be a constant at 5 mM, which is not rate-limiting for the activity of the Na/K pump. Similarly, $[ATP]_i$, while not explicitly included in the model, is not thought to be rate-limiting for pump activity at normal internal concentrations of ATP. The model therefore makes the simplifying assumption that the activity of the Na/K pumps depends only on $[Na^+]_i$. The value calculated by FNapump is given by the product of a value assumed for the maximum-possible pumping rate (Pmax) and a factor between 0 and 1 that reflects the degree to which the pumps are activated by $[Na^+]_i$. The degree of activation is assumed to be set by a binding reaction that depends on $[Na^+]_i$ raised to the third power (since the pump binds 3 Na^+ ions prior to translocating Na^+ out of the cell; binding reactions are discussed further in Chapter 9). The value chosen for KD3, the half-activating concentration of $[Na^+]_i$, is 10 mM. With this value of KD3 and with the initial value chosen for $[Na^+]_i$ (5 mM), it can be calculated that the Na/K pumps are working at 0.111 of their maximum rate (where $0.111 = ([Na^+]_i)^3 / (([Na^+]_i)^3 + KD3^3)$).

- 'def FKpump'. The statement in the body of this function follows from the fact that the active flux of potassium is known to be linked stoichiometrically to the active flux of sodium (2 K^+ ions moving into the cell for every 3 Na^+ ions that move out).

- 'def Vnorm'. 'Vnorm' stands for V_m normalized by the factor RT/F (where F denotes Faraday's constant). With T specified in the model at 303 K (= 30 °C), V_m is easily calculated from Vnorm and vice-versa. The reason to use Vnorm rather than V_m is that the formulas for the passive fluxes of Na^+, K^+, and Cl^- are more compactly expressed in terms of Vnorm rather than V_m (see next paragraph). V_m itself is calculated by the formula $V_m = Q/C$, which is a rearrangement of the usual equation for a capacitor (see Chapter 5). Q, the charge imbalance inside the cell required to explain V_m, is calculated as the total charge on the cations inside the cell minus that on the anions. The corresponding charge imbalance in the extracellular solution is ignored because the volume of the extracellular solution is large with respect to that of the intracellular solution. C, the total capacitance of the surface membrane, is calculated as the total surface area of the cell times C_m, the membrane capacitance per unit area of membrane.

- 'def fluxNa', 'def fluxK', and 'def fluxCl'. The net passive fluxes of Na^+, K^+, and Cl^- across the membrane are calculated from the well-known Goldman-Hodgkin-Katz (GHK) flux equations for univalent ions (e.g., Hodgkin and Katz, 1949). The net flux of each ion depends on the internal and external concentrations of the ion, the ion's membrane permeability, and Vnorm (denoted $\bar{v}$ in Eqns. 6.7-6.9 below). These equations express in a more-recognizable form the formulas for the passive fluxes calculated in Osmotic1.py. Because of the negative valence on Cl^-, the form of the equation for Cl^- differs from that of the equations for Na^+ and K^+.

$$\text{Flux}_{Na} = \frac{\bar{v} \, P_{Na}([Na]_i - [Na]_o \, e^{-\bar{v}})}{1 - e^{-\bar{v}}}, \tag{6.7}$$

$$\text{Flux}_K = \frac{\bar{v}\; P_K\left([K]_i - [K]_o\, e^{-\bar{v}}\right)}{1 - e^{-\bar{v}}}. \qquad (6.8)$$

$$\text{Flux}_{Cl} = \frac{\bar{v}\; P_{Cl}\left([Cl]_i\, e^{-\bar{v}} - [Cl]_o\right)}{1 - e^{-\bar{v}}}. \qquad (6.9)$$

The flux in each of these equations is a net flux, i.e., the difference between an efflux and an influx. The efflux term is proportional to the ion's permeability times its internal concentration and the influx term is proportional to the ion's permeability times its external concentration. If Vm = 0, that is all that comes into the equation, as the terms involving $\bar{v}$ drop out. If, however, Vm ≠ 0, an account must be made for the fact that, for a positive ion, a negative membrane potential will decrease the efflux and increase the influx and, conversely, for a negative ion, a negative membrane potential will increase the efflux and decrease the influx. Hence, each unidirectional flux is multiplied by a term involving $\bar{v}$ that either assists or impedes the flux. This multiplicative term behaves as one might expect if $\bar{v}$ becomes either large and positive or large and negative. For example, for a positive ion like Na$^+$, if $\bar{v}$ is large and positive, the efflux becomes proportional to $\bar{v} \cdot P_{Na} \cdot [Na]_i$ while the influx approaches zero; the converse holds for a large and negative value of $\bar{v}$. For a negative ion like Cl$^-$, if $\bar{v}$ is large and positive, the efflux approaches zero while the influx becomes proportional to $\bar{v} \cdot P_{Cl} \cdot [Cl]_o$, and conversely if $\bar{v}$ is large and negative.

Values of Constants
- Lines 55-73 set the values of the constants used in the program.

- In lines 55-57, R and F have standard values; the temperature variable Temp is set to the Kelvin equivalent of 30 °C.

- Pmax is the maximum rate at which Na$^+$ is transported per cm^2 of surface membrane by the Na/K pumps, i.e., if pumping is not limited by the availability of the Na$^+$ on the inside of the membrane, K$^+$ on the outside of the membrane, or ATP on the inside of the membrane. The value chosen for Pmax is a reasonable value for a generic cell at 30 °C.

- S, the stoichiometry ratio for Na$^+$ transport relative to K$^+$ transport, is -1.5, as noted previously.

- KD3 is a constant (a 'binding' constant; see Chapter 9) that expresses the fact that the actual rate of Na/K pumping depends on the internal concentration of Na^+. As noted above, the assumption is made that the rate of half-maximal pumping will occur when $[Na^+]_i$ is 10 mM and that the dependence of pumping on $[Na^+]_i$ follows a third-power relation (see definitions of FNapump and FKpump, lines 22-26).

- The value assigned to P_K is a reasonable value for a generic animal cell as are the values for P_{Na} and P_{Cl}, which are calculated from the permeability ratios PNaratio ($= P_{Na}/P_K$) and PClratio ($=P_{Cl}/P_K$). The ratio for Na^+ is much smaller than 1.0, as is the case for most cells in their resting state. The ratio for Cl^- is greater than 1.0, as is the case for many animal cells.

- Cm, membrane specific capacitance, is given a standard value for a generic cell.

- The values for $[K^+]_o$ (= 5 mM), $[Na^+]_o$ (= 140 mM), and $[Cl^-]_o$ (= 135 mM) are reasonable values for a generic cell.

- radius0, the initial radius of the cell, is set to 0.0005 cm (= 5 µm); the values of the initial cell surface membrane area (area0) and cell volume (volume0) are calculated accordingly.

- Since animal cells are known to have negative values of V_m, the program makes an initial guess of -60 mV for the V_m of the generic cell in the model (denoted V0, line75).

- Animal cells are known to have a low value of $[Na^+]_i$ and a high value of $[K^+]_i$. Accordingly, the initial guesses for these variables are 5 mM and 140 mM, respectively; the values for the actual number of moles of internal Na^+ and K^+ are calculated from these assignments based on volume0, the value assumed for the initial cell volume.

- Because Cl^- is not an actively-transported ion, E_{Cl} is expected to be close to V_m. If, indeed, $E_{Cl} \approx -60$ mV (the starting value chosen for V_m) and $[Cl^-]_o$ is 145 mM, then $[Cl^-]_i$ should be close to $[Cl^-]_o/10$, i.e., 14.5 mM. Hence the initial guess for $[Cl^-]_i$ is 14.5 mM; clin0, which is the corresponding number of moles, is calculated based on the value of volume0.

- Initially, pin0, the number of moles of the impermeant anion, is set without any adjustment for the excess negative charges inside the cell due to the negative V_m, i.e., pin0 is set by the law of electroneutrality (line 80). Lines 82-84 then adjust the internal concentrations of pin0 and kin0 for the negative value of membrane potential by taking into account Cm and the surface area of the cell. The variable deltac (which has a negative value because V_m has a negative value) gives the corresponding number of moles that is required for this adjustment. Adding deltac/2 to kin0 and subtracting deltac/2 from pin0 thus gives the required total excess of deltac negative charges inside the cell, the value required for the assumed value of V_m at t = 0. A similar adjustment is not made to the charges in the extracellular solution as the volume of this solution is assumed to be large with respect to the solution volume of the model cell.

The Setup and Call to Odeint
- Lines 87-88 define the grid of time-point for the solution: 0 to 1000 s, with one time point for every ms in between.

- The call to odeint (line 96) asks that nain, kin, and clin (the number of moles of Na^+, K^+, and Cl^- contained within the volume of the cell) be calculated at every time point on the grid t. Thus, lines 90-93 need to specify initial values for these variables. These are then used to set the list y_init, which appears in the call to odeint.

- The call to odeint must include the name of the function that has the formulas for calculating the rates of change of nain, kin, and clin -- in this case, G. Importantly, the keyword argument hmax is set to 0.01 to insure that a small step size is used during the integration process (see Section 6.2 above). Without the inclusion of a small value for hmax, odeint will not return an accurate solution. (Note: the solution returned by Osmotic1.py has been checked for accuracy by an independent mathematical-modeling software package.)

Unraveling the Solution; Plotting and Printing
Lines 98-140 use standard function calls, in combination with appropriate slices of the vector y and/or with appropriate indexing to select individual members of y, to obtain the plot and printed values shown above. Recall that Chapter 4 explains how to obtain subsets of np.arrays by means of the slicing and indexing facilities in *Python* and that Chapter 3 explains how to use the format facility within the print function to control the appearance of the printed output.

6.5 PHYSICAL INTERPRETATION OF THE MODEL

1) The principal feature of the time course of V_m in Fig. 6.2 is that an adjustment period of several hundred s is required for the cell to reach a stable state. This occurs because the initial values chosen for V_m, $[K^+]_i$, $[Na^+]_i$, and $[Cl^-]_i$ are not steady-state values that are fully consistent with the values chosen for $[K^+]_o$, $[Na^+]_o$, and $[Cl^-]_o$. They would, however, likely be close to the steady-state values for some choices of $[K^+]_o$, $[Na^+]_o$, and $[Cl^-]_o$ that are not markedly different from the ones in this example. Thus, the readjustments in V_m, $[K^+]_i$, $[Na^+]_i$, $[Cl^-]_i$, and $[A^-]_i$ that occur during the 1000 s time period illustrated in Fig. 6.2 can be thought of as being representative of the type of changes that would occur in a cell as it sought to re-achieve a stable steady-state following a sudden modest perturbation in the extracellular conditions (see also Exercise 6.8). The time for the adjustment in Fig. 6.2 is affected by the size of the cell and the magnitude of the associated ion fluxes. The fluxes are small because of the low membrane permeabilities of the ions and the relatively modest value used for the maximum rate of Na/K pumping in the model (see Exercise 6.9). When a stable state is finally reached, the value of V_m is -81.7 mV, and the internal ion concentrations, rounded to the nearest 0.1 mM, are 135.6 for $[K^+]_i$, 9.4 for $[Na^+]_i$, 6.3 for $[Cl^-]_i$, and 138.7 for $[A^-]_i$. The final cell volume is 0.9412 times the initial volume and, as expected, the internal osmolarity (290 mM, which is calculated as the total concentration of all constituents inside the cell) matches the external osmolarity. Because all of the constituents in the model are univalent, half of the osmolarity of each solution is accounted for by cations and half by anions, except for the small excess of internal negative charges that are required in order that $V_m = -81.7$ mV.

2) According to the Nernst equation, at the final inside and outside concentrations of Na^+ and K^+, the value of E_{Na} is +70.4 mV and that of E_K is -86.0 mV. The steady-state value of V_m, -81.7 mV, is close to E_K and far from E_{Na}. This situation arises because the membrane is 100 times more permeable to K^+ than to Na^+ (see also Eqn. 6.10 below). With V_m at -81.7 mV, the driving force on Na^+ is large and inward and that on K^+ is small and outward. Thus, there is a net passive influx of Na^+ and a net passive efflux of K^+. These passive fluxes of Na^+ and K^+ are balanced by the active fluxes of the Na/K pump. This steady-state balance of passive and active fluxes is sometimes referred to as the 'pump-leak model' of the osmotic stability of a cell.

3) In contrast to the passive fluxes of Na^+ and K^+, the passive flux of Cl^- is zero because E_{Cl} is -81.7 mV, the same as V_m. Cl^- has thus reached electrochemical equilibrium. Even

though the highest membrane permeability in the model is to Cl^-, Cl^- does not affect the value of V_m at steady-state; rather, V_m determines the value of $[Cl^-]_i$ at steady-state (see also Exercise 6.3).

4) Another noticeable feature of the time course of V_m in Fig. 6.2 is that there is an early fast decline of V_m from -60 to -65 mV. The time course of this fast phase, which is completed within ~10 ms, cannot be accurately judged from Fig. 6.2 itself, but it can be seen by sequential use of the 'magnifying-glass' feature in the plot displayed by *Python* at run time. (It can, of course, also be seen in a separate plot with an appropriately selected time base.) The fast phase of V_m reflects the fact that the membrane time constant of a cell (discussed in Chapter 5) is typically in the ms time range. In the model, the properties of the fast phase of V_m depend on the values assumed for P_{Na}, P_K, and P_{Cl} in combination with the values of the extracellular and intracellular concentrations of the permeant ions ($[K^+]_o$, $[Na^+]_o$, $[Cl^-]_o$ and $[K^+]_i$, $[Na^+]_i$, $[Cl^-]_i$, respectively). Given the values in the model, the cell membrane potential would prefer to be at -65 mV rather than the initial estimate of -60 mV; in consequence, V_m moves on a ms time scale to -65 mV, where it lingers in a quasi-stable (but not actually-stable) state. The decline of V_m that follows on a s time scale occurs during the slow time course in which $[K^+]_i$, $[Na^+]_i$, $[Cl^-]_i$, and cell volume are being readjusted according to the constraints of the model. After many s of calculation, these and the other time-dependent values in the model finally reach a stable state.

5) **The Goldman Equation**. Eqn. 6.10, which is sometimes called the 'GHK voltage equation' but often just 'the Goldman equation', is commonly used to predict the resting potential of a cell from the concentrations of the univalent ions on either side of the membrane and the ions' membrane permeabilities. The equation assumes that the only significant ion permeabilities are to Na^+, K^+, and Cl^-.

$$V_m = \frac{RT}{F} \ln \left(\frac{P_K[K]_o + P_{Na}[Na]_o + P_{Cl}[Cl]_i}{P_K[K]_i + P_{Na}[Na]_i + P_{Cl}[Cl]_o} \right). \quad (6.10)$$

Note that, because Cl^- is an anion, it enters into the equation differently from Na^+ and K^+, which are cations. Eqn. 6.10 might have been used to make a more accurate initial guess for V_m in the model. If this equation had been used, the calculated value is -65 mV, and, indeed, this is the value to which V_m settles within the first few ms after start of the calculation. The model V_m then continuously adjusts itself, approximately as predicted by Eqn. 6.10, as the internal concentrations of Na^+, K^+, and Cl^- change with time. It should be noted, however, that the value of V_m in the model is not at any time directly related to Eqn. 6.10; rather, V_m is determined by the constraints of the model as embodied in the user-defined functions and the values assumed for the various constants in the model.

6) The question might be asked if it is reasonable to assume that the surface membrane of a cell can actually contract or expand as the cell volume changes. For example, if the cell membrane is fragile, why would it not tear as soon as the cell volume increased by even a small amount? In fact, cell membranes have regions of infolding and, in addition, they contain 'caveolae' (little caves), which are small pinched-off invaginations of exterior membrane that are distributed periodically over the membrane surface. The caveolae thus supply a source of lipid and protein that can fuse with the surface membrane if the tension on the surface membrane increases to a problematic level. These and other features allow the cell to sustain some increase in cell volume without incurring damage to its membrane. In the model, the membrane properties per unit area of membrane (P_{max}, P_{Na}, P_K, P_{Cl} and C_m) are assumed to be constant as the surface area of the cell changes. In terms of the caveolae or infolded membrane, this assumption means that the properties of these membranes, if expressed per cm^2 of membrane, match those of the surface membrane.

7) In Osmotic1.py, the activity of the Na/K pumps is an essential feature that permits the cell to reach an osmotically-stable state. At least one animal cell type, the red blood cells of dogs, is known that lacks Na/K pumps yet are osmotically stable. How can this stability be achieved without Na/K pumps? Interestingly, the plasmalemma of these cells rely on other membrane-transport proteins that, together, accomplish the work that the Na/K pump does by itself in most other cells. For example, to expel Na^+, these red blood cells have (i) a passive-transport protein known as 'the sodium-calcium exchanger' that allows counter-transport of Na^+ and Ca^{2+} ions across the surface membrane, i.e., an influx of Na^+ is coupled to the efflux of Ca^{2+} or an efflux of Na^+ is coupled to the influx of Ca^{2+}, with the net movements constrained by the electrochemical driving forces established by $[Na^+]_o$, $[Ca^{2+}]_o$, $[Na^+]_i$, $[Ca^{2+}]_i$ and V_m; and (ii) a primary ion ATPase that uses ATP to expel Ca^{2+} (i.e., a Ca^{2+} pump). So, in these cells, the constant leak of Na^+ into the cells is reversed by an energy-dependent transport mechanism, but the link is indirect. It is the Ca^{2+} pumps that use ATP to lower $[Ca^{2+}]_i$; then the passive influx of Ca^{2+} through the cell's sodium-calcium exchangers drives the efflux of Na^+.

8) Mechanisms in addition to the Na/K pumps also contribute to the volume assumed by various cell types (see, e.g., Hoffman et al., 2009). These mechanisms appear to provide a

secondary means to fine tune the final cell volume, with the primary mechanism affecting cell volume due to the Na/K pumps. These mechanisms are ignored in the model.

9) The importance of Na/K pumping to the economy of animal cells is indicated by the amount of energy consumed by the Na/K pumps. It is estimated that, on average, ~20% of the metabolic energy consumed by animal cells is due to Na/K pumping (Rolfe and Brown, 1997).

6.6 OTHER TIME-DEPENDENT RESPONSES IN THE MODEL

In Osmotic1.py, $V_m(t)$ responds with a fast phase (time scale of ms) because of the inaccurate initial guess for V0. For the same reason, a noticeable fast phase is also found on the time courses of the passive fluxes (which depend directly on $V_m(t)$), i.e., fluxNa(t), fluxK(t), fluxCl(t), but not the other time-dependent variables, i.e., $[K^+]_i(t)$, $[Na^+]_i(t)$, $[Cl^-]_i(t)$, $[A^-]_i(t)$, volume(t), radius(t), area(t), and the active fluxes. These latter variables change from their initial to final values along a time course that approximately matches the slow phase of $V_m(t)$ in Fig. 6.2. It is left to the reader to confirm these statements (see Exercise 6.4).

6.7 RESPONSE OF THE MODEL IN THE ABSENCE OF NA/K PUMPING

As noted above, once the cell reaches an osmotically-stable state (e.g., at the 1000 s time point in Fig. 6.2), Na^+ and K^+ are not at electrochemical equilibrium. Rather, the net passive fluxes of these ions across the cell membrane are balanced by the active fluxes of the Na/K pumps. Without the active fluxes, it would be expected that the cell would gain Na^+ and lose K^+, V_m would rise toward 0 mV, the cell would accumulate Cl^- ions, and the cell volume would increase. These predictions can be tested in a modified version of Osmotic1.py in which Pmax (the maximum pumping capability of the Na/K pumps) is set to 0. The result of this calculation, which starts at the time point and values with which Oxmotic1.py ends in Fig. 6.2, is shown in Fig. 6.3; the time base is 10-fold longer than that in Fig. 6.2. (Note: because of the long time scale, the computer may take some minutes to finish this calculation.)

It is clear from Fig. 6.3 that the cell is not in a stable state; rather, it is heading for disaster. This calculation demonstrates the essential role of the Na/K pumps in maintaining osmotic balance. This situation can be mimicked experimentally by exposing cells to a chemical, such as ouabain or one of its many chemical congeners, that poisons the Na/K pumps. (Note: chemicals like ouabain that poison the Na/K pumps are sometimes used therapeutically in small quantities to treat some clinical conditions, e.g., heart failure.)

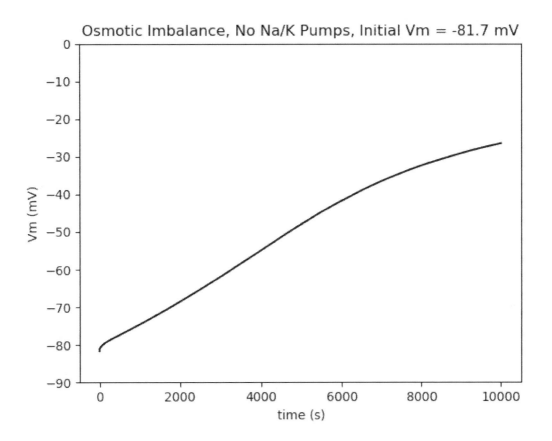

Figure 6.3 Calculation similar to that in Fig. 6.2 but on a ten-fold longer time scale and without Na/K pumping. The starting point of the calculation corresponds to the endpoint in Fig. 6.2.

6.8 EXERCISES

Exercise 6.1 Examine whether, for the final steady-state that is reached in Osmotic1.py (at the 1000 s time point), the net passive flux of Na^+ is inward and exactly -1.5 times the net passive flux of K^+ (which is therefore outward) and whether these fluxes equal minus the active fluxes of the two ions due to Na/K pumping.

Exercise 6.2 Once the final steady-state is reached in Osmotic1.py, is there any net flux of Cl^- ions? Is there any unidirectional flux of Cl^- ions? How do your answers to these questions relate to the final value of E_{Cl}?

Exercise 6.3 If $V_m = E_{Cl}$, show that Eqn. 6.10 can be re-written without the terms for Cl^-, i.e., with only the terms for Na^+ and K^+.

Exercise 6.4 Section 6.6 states that, in Osmotic1.py, the time courses of $[K^+]_i(t)$, $[Na^+]_i(t)$, $[Cl^-]_i(t)$, $[A^-]_i(t)$, volume(t), radius(t), area(t), and the active ion fluxes (but not the passive ion fluxes) are approximately the same as that of the slow phase of $V_m(t)$ in Fig. 6.2. Test the validity of this statement to your satisfaction by extracting and plotting some or all of these time courses with appropriate statements in *Python* added to the end of Osmotic1.py or entered directly on the Console. Why should the passive ion fluxes, like $V_m(t)$, but not the active ion fluxes, have a noticeable fast-phase in their responses?

Exercise 6.5 In the model, the permeability properties per unit area of membrane are the same whether the radius of the cell is small or large, as are the fluxes per unit area of membrane for given concentrations of the model's constituents outside and inside the cell. Given this fact, in what way would you expect the results of the model to vary if the radius were changed?

Exercise 6.6 Run the osmotic model with the change used in Fig. 6.3 (i.e., with removal of significant Na/K pumping from the model) and determine what are the values for $[K^+]_i$, $[Na^+]_i$, $[Cl^-]_i$, $[A^-]_i$, and cell volume at the 10,000 s time point. On what trajectory is the cell heading?

Exercise 6.7 Return to the osmotic model like that in Fig. 6.2, i.e., with Na/K pumping restored and with a time scale of 1000 s.

a) It is sometimes said that the large negative value of V_m that characterizes a normal resting cell at steady-state is due to the fact that the Na/K pumps have, if considered on a long time scale, expelled many more Na^+ ions than the K^+ ions that they have taken up, thus making the cell interior negative. To test this statement, change S (the pump stoichiometry value) from -1.5 to -1, recalculate, and plot whatever variables you think are most revealing of the result. Based on the result of your calculation, do you agree with this statement?

b) When the Na/K pump is working with its normal value of S (-1.5) and then is turned off completely, is there any immediate effect on the value of V_m? If so, explain why; if not, why not?

Exercise 6.8 With Na/K pumping restored in the model and with S at its normal value of -1.5, change V0 to -81.7 and set the initial values of $[K^+]_i$, $[Na^+]_i$, and $[Cl^-]_i$ to 135.6 mM, 9.403 mM, and 6.346 mM, respectively, i.e., set kin0, nain0, and clin0 to the values that apply at the end of the calculation in Fig. 6.2.

a) Now double the value of Kout (i.e., increase it from 5e-6 to 10e-6 = 1e-5), change the time scale of the calculation to 500 s, and recalculate. Can you explain why the time course of $V_m(t)$ has two distinct phases?

b) Restore Kout to its normal value (5e-6) and shorten the time scale of the calculation to 0.05 s. Now run this brief calculation with either V0 = -71.7 or with V0 = -91.7, plot the time course of $V_m(t)$, and calculate the initial rate at which $V_m(t)$ relaxes back toward -81.7. Divide minus the peak amplitude of ΔV_m (i.e., either -10 mV or 10 mV, respectively) by the initial rate of change of $V_m(t)$ to estimate the time constant with which $V_m(t)$ returns to -81.7. [Note: the ΔV_m in this calculation does not exactly follow a single-exponential time course but it is very close to one, so it is an acceptable approximation to speak of the time constant of this change.]

c) Now change P_K or P_{Cl}, re-run this brief calculation, and predict if/how the time constant will change. [Note: if your plot of $V_m(t)$ does not look like that of smooth exponential time course that relaxes back to a stable value, see what effect increasing N_steps and/or decreasing hmax has on the appearance of $V_m(t)$.]

Exercise 6.9 In Osmotic1.py, Pmax (the maximum rate of pumping Na$^+$ by the Na/K pumps) is set to 10^{-11} moles of Na$^+$ per cm^2 of surface membrane per s. This may well be a conservative value. For example, in some mammalian cells: (i) the density of sodium pumps may be about 1.2×10^{-12} moles per cm^2 of surface membrane, a number calculated from the average of the values reported for rabbit corneal cells (2.1×10^{-12} moles per cm^2; Geroski and Edelhauser, 1984) and dog tracheal cells (0.4×10^{-12} moles per cm^2; Widdicombe et al., , 1985), and (ii) the pump turnover number is about 55 per s at 36 °C (estimated for guinea pig ventricular cells; Nakao and Gadsby, 1989). Multiplying these numbers together, and taking into account that each turnover of the pump moves 3 Na$^+$ ions across the membrane, gives a Pmax of 2×10^{-10} moles of Na$^+$ per cm^2 per s. If this Pmax is adjusted to 30 °C (the temperature in Osmotic1.py), a value of about 1×10^{-10} moles of Na$^+$ per cm^2 per s would apply, which is 10-fold larger than the value used in Osmotic1.py.

Increase Pmax in Osmotic1.py by a factor of 10 and see what effect this has on (i) the time course to reach the final steady state and (ii) the final values of V_m, $[K^+]_i$, $[Na^+]_i$, $[Cl^-]_i$, $[A^-]_i$, and cell volume.

Exercise 6.10 In the paragraph in the text that discussed the Goldman equation (Eqn. 6.10), it was noted that a more accurate initial guess for the value of V_M in Osmotic1.py could have been made with Eqn. 6.10 when compared with the method actually used to set the initial value of V_M. This suggests that an alternate strategy for calculating V_M as a function of time during the model calculations might be to use Eqn. 6.10. Implement the osmotic model with this strategy and compare the results, both in accuracy and speed, with those obtained with the strategy used in Osmotic1.py to calculate V_M.

Exercise 6.11 Choose one of the equations 6.7 – 6.9 and write a *Python* program that plots the influx, the efflux, and the total flux predicted by the equation over a range of membrane potentials (e.g., -150 to +150 mV). For your selected equation, assume that the inside and outside concentrations are those that apply to a generic cell in the steady-state, e.g., as for the example simulated in Fig. 6.2 at the 1000 s time point.

CHAPTER 7

PASSIVE ELECTRICAL PROPERTIES OF CELLS

This chapter extends the material on bio-electricity in Chapters 5 and 6 in two ways. It discusses how the electrical properties of cells can be modeled with circuit diagrams (also called 'equivalent circuits') and it applies these ideas to what is known as 'one-dimensional cable theory'. This chapter also describes several electrophysiological techniques that are commonly used to study the function of many cell types. Two *Python* programs are presented that illustrate a number of basic concepts.

7.1 A SIMPLE CIRCUIT MODEL OF A CELL AT REST

Circuit diagrams containing batteries, resistors, capacitors, and related elements can be used in combination with Kirchhoff's laws (Section 7.2) to provide a valuable tool with which to analyze and understand the electrical properties of cells and tissues.

Fig. 7.1 shows two equivalent circuits for a generic cell at rest; one will be preferred in this book. Both circuits follow the convention that the outside of the cell is shown at the top and the inside of the cell is shown at the bottom. Both also follow the modern convention that V_m, the membrane potential of the cell, is defined as $V_{in} - V_{out}$. That V_{out} is the reference location for voltage is indicated by the 'ground' symbol labeled 'V_{out}' (= zero voltage). (Note: most of the electrophysiological literature of the 1940's and 1950's used the reverse convention, in which V_m was defined as $V_{out} - V_{in}$.) These circuits also assume implicitly that V_m has the same value at all locations in the cell; for example, the cell geometry might be that of a small spherical cell.

Each circuit diagram in Fig. 7.1 has two limbs between the inside and outside, one for each of the pathways by which current can flow relative to the membrane. These are (recall Chapter 5): (i) the pathway by which ions can accumulate on either side of the membrane, thereby changing the charge on the membrane capacitance (see capacitor symbol C_m), and (ii) the pathway by which ions can cross the membrane, typically through ion channels (see resistor symbol R_m), governed by a battery (see battery symbol E) and an associated electro-chemical driving force. Exercise 7.1 reviews the reason that R_m and E are shown "in series" for the latter pathway.

Both circuits have one loop around which current might flow in the absence of an external source. The possibilities are a clockwise flow, a counter-clockwise flow, and no flow (i.e., zero current). In the first case, if one starts from the lower left, the current can flow through the capacitance C_m, then the resistance R_m, then the battery E, and then return to the point of origin (the lower left), which completes the circuit. In the second case, the flow involves the same elements but in the opposite direction.

Circuit layouts A and B differ only in how the battery appears in the circuit. Two differences apply to this element: (i) the orientation of the long and short arms of the battery symbol, and (ii) the value assigned to E, the battery voltage. If we take the case of no current flow in the circuit (i.e., the circuit is at steady-state), we would like to confirm that both circuit layouts are consistent with a resting V_m of -80 mV.

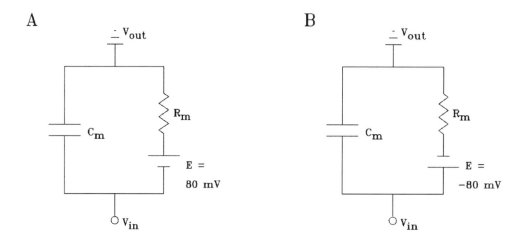

Figure 7.1 Two circuits to model the electrical properties of a generic cell at rest. C_m denotes the membrane capacitance, R_m denotes the membrane resistance, and E denotes an electromotive force (i.e., a battery) that, in combination with V_m (= V_{in} - V_{out}), governs the flow of ions through R_m. Parts A and B differ in the convention chosen to indicate the properties of the battery (see text).

The circuit in Fig. 7.1A follows the convention in physics books for how a battery is represented in a circuit diagram. According to this convention, the voltage of the battery is a non-negative number (in this case, E = 80 mV), and the polarity of the battery is indicated by the position of the long and short arms of the battery symbol, which denote the positive and negative poles of the battery, respectively. The advantage of this convention is that one can tell at a glance how this battery, if acting alone, would affect the circuit. In this case, the battery acts to make the potential inside the cell lower than that outside, i.e., to make V_m negative. With this convention, if one traces the voltage changes around a circuit and a battery is encountered, the voltage increases by the amount E when one moves from the short arm to the long arm of the battery symbol; conversely, it changes by the amount -E if one moves from the long arm to the short arm. Because we have assumed that there is no current flow in this circuit, the voltage change across the resistor R_m is zero (recall that, for a resister, $V = I \cdot R$ and, since $I = 0$, $V = 0$). It follows that V_{in} is 80 mV lower than V_{out} -- hence, indeed, V_m is -80 mV.

In tracing the voltage from inside to outside along the left limb of the circuit, we only encounter the capacitor. Since, the voltage change between two points in a circuit is independent of the path between the points (see Kirchhoff's second law below), the voltage change across the capacitor, as measured on the inside plate of the capacitor relative to the outside plate, must also be -80 mV. We know that, physically, this means that a small excess of negative charges has accumulated on the inside of the membrane and an equal small excess of positive charges has accumulated on the outside of the membrane, driven at an earlier time by the ionic current through the right limb of the circuit. Q, the (absolute) amount of charge that has accumulated on either plate of the capacitor, can be calculated with the formula $Q = C \cdot V$. In this case, $Q = C_m \cdot E$.

The circuit shown in Fig. 7.1B uses a different convention. The long arm of the battery is oriented toward the inside of the cell and the short arm toward the outside; the polarity of the battery is indicated by the sign of E, which can be **either** plus or minus. This convention is consistent with the modern conventions that (i) V_m is defined as inside potential relative to outside potential and (ii) electro-physiological batteries are calculated with the Nernst equation, with the polarity defined as inside potential relative to outside (see Eqn. 5.2 of Chapter 5), and can be either positive or negative. With this convention, the rule is retained that the battery of voltage E (a positive or negative number) is the potential at the long arm of the battery minus that at the short arm. For the circuit in Fig. 7.1B, we see that, in the absence of current flow, V_m, as expected, is -80 mV since E is -80 mV.

Some sources mix the two conventions, allowing, as in Fig. 7.1A, the orientation of the arms of the battery symbol in the circuit to indicate at a glance which side of the battery is at the higher potential (namely, the long arm) while also allowing E, the battery voltage, to have its sign changed to minus when the voltage is substituted into the associated current equation. Thus, in the standard equation for ionic current flow from inside to outside the cell, namely, $I = (V_m - E)/R_m$, the positive number E might be changed to a negative number (e.g., E = - 80 mV) when substituted into this equation. This awkward situation involving a possible sign change of some battery voltages is avoided by the convention in Fig. 7.1B, which is the one that we will adopt.

7.2 KIRCHHOFF'S LAWS FOR ELECTRICAL CIRCUITS

An analysis of electrical circuits depends on two important laws, which are attributed to the physicist Gustave Kirchhoff. These are:
-- Kirchhoff's current law: the sum of the currents entering or leaving any point in a circuit must equal zero.
-- Kirchhoff's voltage law: the sum of the voltage changes around any closed loop in a circuit must be zero. This law has already been referred to implicitly above, since it implies that the voltage difference between two points in a circuit does not depend on the path that is followed.

Also of Note: in tracing voltage changes in a circuit, a voltage change may occur across each element of the circuit, but no voltage change occurs along the thin lines that connect the circuit elements, as these lines denote paths with negligible resistance to current flow.

7.3 TECHNIQUES USED TO STUDY THE ELECTRICAL PROPERTIES OF CELLS

When studying the electrical properties of cells, electrophysiologists use a variety of techniques to measure and/or manipulate V_m and I_m (the current across the cell membrane). Given the convention that V_m is inside potential relative to outside, the natural convention for I_m is that a positive I_m denotes the flow of positive charges from inside to outside the cell (or negative charges from outside to inside). If, in either a circuit analysis or in an actual measurement, I_m turns out to be a negative number, positive charges must be crossing the membrane from outside to inside or negative charges from inside to outside.

Fig. 7.2 illustrates two experimental techniques that are commonly used to measure and/or manipulate V_m and I_m of cells. Both techniques use a tubular-shaped glass pipette that is hollow along its length, patent at both ends, and filled with a conductive salt solution, e.g., 3 M KCl. An electrical connection is made between the solution in the pipette and an electronic apparatus (denoted by the triangular-shaped amplifier symbols in the figure) by means of a wire -- typically, a silver/silver-chloride wire -- that is inserted into the back of the pipette. In Fig. 7.2, the tip of the pipette is in contact with the cell's interior (A) or with a small area of membrane on the surface of the cell (B).

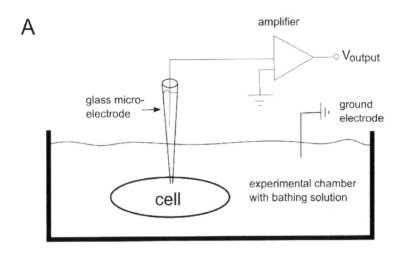

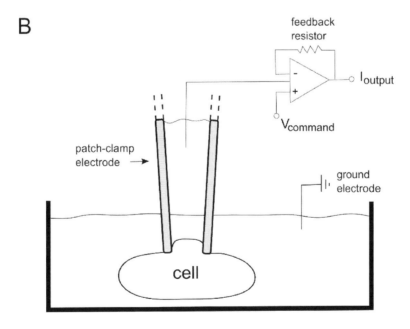

Figure 7.2 Two techniques commonly used to study the electrical properties of cells. A. The intracellular glass micro-electrode technique. B. The patch-clamp technique. The $V_{command}$ input to the amplifier is a voltage waveform for the cell's membrane potential to follow (see section 7.5).

1) With the intracellular glass micro-electrode technique (Fig. 7.2A), one end of the glass pipette is drawn to an extremely fine point by briefly melting a short segment of the glass and pulling it quickly. The tip of the pipette is patent and its outside diameter is usually less than one µm (< 1 cm^{-4}), often < 0.5 µm. The pipette is mounted in a stable mechanical device that permits finely-controlled movements of the tip in multiple dimensions. Because the tip is small and sharp, if care is taken, it can be inserted across the cell membrane into the cytoplasm of the cell with little or no damage to the membrane or leakage of ions across the membrane at the site of impalement. The result is that good electrical contact can be established between the cell cytoplasm and the electronic apparatus via the open tip of the pipette and the wire inserted into the back of the pipette. V_{in} can then be measured relative to the potential recorded by another electrode ('ground electrode') placed in the external solution. Also, membrane currents of chosen amplitude and time course can be passed between the two electrodes and the effects on V_m can be recorded. To increase accuracy in measurements of the latter type, two similar glass micro-electrodes are often inserted into the cell -- one to measure V_m and one to manipulate I_m.

2) With the patch-clamp technique (Fig. 7.2B), the tip of the glass pipette contacting the cell is usually larger than that used in Fig. 7.2A, typically 1-3 µm, and is usually fire-polished to removed jagged edges. Because it is important that the entire glass perimeter of the pipette tip make good contact with the membrane, the membrane is often pre-treated with proteolytic enzymes to remove most of the fibrous extracellular matrix that surrounds the cell membrane. Then, to make a good seal between the pipette tip and the membrane (a so-called 'tight seal' or 'gigohm seal'), suction is applied to the back of the pipette until the leakage of current around the tip of the electrode into the bath is negligible. Several different experimental configurations are possible with this technique (Hamill et al., 1981). All require that an extracellular bath electrode (ground electrode, i.e., as described in the previous paragraph) be used to complete the circuit for measurement of V_m and/or for collection of any current that flows across the membrane between the interior of the patch pipette and the extracellular solution.

- In the 'cell-attached' configuration, the glass perimeter of the pipette tip remains attached to the outside of the cell, and the patch of membrane that is in contact with the solution in the pipette tip is not disrupted (as shown in Fig. 7.2B). Any current that flows across the patch of membrane, either spontaneously or in response to a change of voltage imposed by the apparatus or in response to a chemical agent that is added to the pipette, can be collected by the pipette and measured by the apparatus.

- In the 'whole cell' configuration, the patch of membrane in contact with the pipette tip is either physically disrupted (for example, by strong suction) or by chemical permeabilization; as a result, the conductive salt solution inside the pipette comes into direct contact with the cytoplasm of the cell, as occurs with the technique in Fig. 7.2A. If a tight seal exists between the glass tip of the pipette and the surrounding region of membrane, the cell can function normally (or nearly-normally) for extended periods, while the electrical properties of the cell membrane can be measured and manipulated.

- In the 'membrane-patch' configuration, a small patch of membrane associated with the pipette tip and sealed to the glass at its perimeter is detached from the cell. This patch of membrane can then be studied in isolation, with one side of the patch facing the inside of the pipette and the other side facing the bathing solution in which the pipette tip is located. Again, any current that flows across the patch of membrane can be collected by the pipette and measured by the apparatus. Two versions of this configuration are possible depending on how the patch of membrane is detached from the cell. In one version -- the "inside-out" configuration -- the side of the membrane patch that originally faced the ICF faces the bathing solution; in the other -- the "outside-out" configuration -- the side of the membrane patch that originally faced the ECF faces the bathing solution.

With both the microelectrode technique and the patch-clamp technique, a typical goal of an experiment is either (i) to measure I_m across the cell membrane (or patch of cell membrane) while V_m is either held constant or changed in a controlled manner, or (ii) to measure V_m across the cell membrane (or patch of cell membrane) while I_m is held constant or changed in a controlled manner.

7.4 THEORETICAL RESPONSE OF A CELL MEMBRANE TO A CURRENT PULSE

We now suppose that a small spherical cell with a radius of 10 µm is studied by means of either the glass micro-electrode technique or the whole-cell patch-clamp technique; thus the cytoplasm of the cell is in contact with the electronic apparatus via the conducting solution and wire within the electrode. We also suppose that the equivalent circuit shown in Fig. 7.1B is a good model of the cell's membrane electrical properties and that a 200 picoamp pulse of current of 20 ms duration is passed from the apparatus, through the micro-electrode, and across the cell membrane to the reference electrode in the external solution.

This current will cause the membrane potential of the cell to change transiently in the positive direction, during which time V_m is monitored by the voltage-recording electrode.

The results of an experiment of this type are simulated with the *Python* program Example7_1.py. The program's listing is shown here, followed by the graphical output of the program (Fig. 7.3), and the information printed to the console. The values of the circuit parameters given in the legend of Fig. 7.3 are reasonable values for a generic cell.

```
1   # -*- coding: utf-8 -*-
2   """
3   Python 3.7
4   Created on Wed Feb 13 09:22:55 2019
5   Example7_1.py
6   Description: membrane equivalent-circuit for response of Vm to a chosen Im
7   """
8
9   import numpy as np
10  import matplotlib.pyplot as plt
11  from scipy.integrate import odeint
12
13  def G(Vm,t):    #function for use with odeint to solve the single deq for Vm
14      Im=0        #current Im is zero unless time t is between J_start and J_end
15      if t >= J_start and t < J_end:
16          Im=J    #J is the current amplitude when the pulse of current is "on"
17      dVm=(Im + (E-Vm)/Rm)/Cm  #formula for dVm/dt from the equivalent circuit
18      return dVm
19
20  def Im(t):      #function used to define the pulse function for Im for the plot
21      I=0.*t      #t is the array with the grid of time points
22      for i in range(len(t)):
23          if t[i] >= J_start and t[i] < J_end: I[i]=J
24      return I
25  #fct's G and Im cannot be combined because t cannot be both a scalar and vector in G
26
27  #constants for the membrane circuit elements
```

```
28  R=1e3                    #membrane specific resistance (ohm cm^2)
29  C=1e-6                   #membrane specific capacitance (farad cm^-2)
30  E=-80e-3                 #battery voltage (= resting Vm) (volts)
31  r=10e-4                  #radius of spherical cell (cm)
32  area=4*np.pi*r*r         #surface area of cell (cm^2)
33  Rm=R/area                #membrane resistance (ohms)
34  Cm=C*area                #membrane capacitance (farads)
35
36  J= 0.2e-9                #size of current pulse across the membrane (amps)
37  J_start, J_end = .01,.03 #J will be "on" between these time points (s)
38
39  t_start=0; t_end=0.05; N_steps=1000        #arguments for linspace()
40  t=np.linspace(t_start, t_end, N_steps+1)   #t is the grid of time points (s)
41  dt=(t_end-t_start)/N_steps  #dt is the step size for the time-point grid
42
43  Vm_init=E                                  #define initial condition for use in odeint
44
45  #odeint will return the solution for Vm on grid t
46  Vm=odeint(G,Vm_init,t,hmax=1e-1)     #Vm is a 1-col numpy array
47
48  #plot the result as two sub-plots -- one for Vm, one for Im
49  plt.figure()
50  plt.subplot(2,1,1)
51  plt.plot(t, 1e3*Vm, 'k', linewidth=2, label="Vm")
52  plt.ylim(-90.,-50.)
53  plt.title("Vm response to current pulse in a circuit with R, C, and E")
54  plt.ylabel('Vm(t) (mV)')
55  plt.subplot(2,1,2)
56  plt.plot(t, 1e12*Im(t), 'k', linewidth=2, label="Im")
57  plt.ylim(-300.,300.)
58  plt.xlabel('time (s)')
59  plt.ylabel('Im(t) (picoamps)')
60  plt.show()
61  plt.savefig('example7_1.png',dpi=200)
62
63  #calculate the membrane time constant based on initial dVm/dt
```

```
64  index_start=int(N_steps*J_start/t_end)
65  index_end=int(N_steps*J_end/t_end)
66  delta_Vm=Vm[index_end]-E
67  initial_slope=(Vm[index_start+1]-Vm[index_start])/dt
68
69  print("membrane time constant estimated from change of Vm(t) (ms): {:.4}"\
70      .format(1000*delta_Vm[0]/initial_slope[0]) )
71  print("membrane time constant calculated as Rm x Cm (ms): {:.4}".format(\
72      1000*Rm*Cm))
```

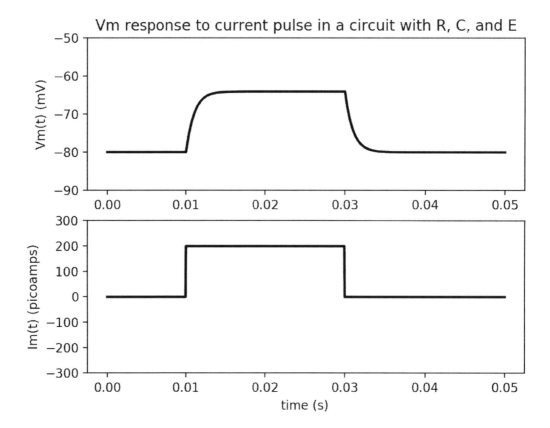

Figure 7.3 Simulated voltage response (upper) due to a 200-picoamp rectangular current pulse (lower) passed between the inside and outside of the equivalent circuit shown in Fig. 7.1B. A cell radius of 10 μm is assumed with a value of E = -80 mV and values of R_m and C_m calculated under that assumption that membrane specific resistance is 1000 ohm cm^2 and membrane specific capacitance is 10^{-6} farad cm^{-2}. If the amplitude of Im(t) had been -200 picoamps, the change in Vm(t) would have been minus that shown in the upper panel.

membrane time constant estimated from change of Vm(t) (ms): 1.051
membrane time constant calculated as Rm x Cm (ms): 1.0

Program Notes
- If a current I_m is passed across the circuit in Fig. 7.1B, it divides into two components: the capacitive current (I_c) and the resistive/ionic current (I_{ion}), i.e., $I_m = I_c + I_{ion}$. From the rule for a capacitor, we know that $I_c = C_m \cdot dV_m/dt$, and, from the rule for a resistor, we know that $I_{ion} = (V_m - E)/R_m$. Solving for dV_m/dt:

$$\frac{dV_m}{dt} = \frac{(I_m + \frac{E-V_m}{R_m})}{C_m}. \tag{7.1}$$

This first-order deq is solved numerically for V_m in the program Example7_1.py by means of the function odeint from the scipy.integrate module. The user-defined function G (lines 13-18) is set up to work in conjunction with odeint as described in Chapter 6. The value returned by G is the rate of change of V_m, which is calculated from V_m, I_m, and the circuit parameters according to Eqn. 7.1. After the call to odeint is executed, the program variable Vm contains the solution to V_m on the time-point grid t. The solution, of course, depends on I_m, which is calculated in the user-defined function Im (lines 20-24). The choice of a brief pulse of current like that in the lower panel of Fig. 7.3 is a waveform commonly used in experiments of this type.

If traces like those in Fig. 7.3 were recorded during an actual experiment, the effective value of R_m could be estimated with Ohm's law ($V = I \cdot R$). Specifically, the amplitude of the steady-state voltage change could be divided by the amplitude of the current pulse to yield R_m. Recall from Chapter 5 that the membrane time constant equals $R_m \times C_m$ and that the time constant can be estimated from the time course of the voltage change (either when V_m is rising to its new steady-state value, as done for the printout at the end of the program listing, or when it is returning to the resting potential). C_m can then be estimated by dividing the time constant by R_m. E equals the measured value of V_m when I_m is zero. Hence the values of all circuit elements are readily estimated in an experiment of this type.

- The constants section of the program calculates Rm (membrane resistance, in ohms), Cm (membrane capacitance in farads), and E (resting membrane potential, in volts). Given the surface area of this generic spherical cell (radius, 10×10^{-4} cm), Rm and Cm are calculated from commonly-used values of membrane specific resistance (R, in ohms cm^2) and membrane specific capacitance (C, in farads cm^{-2}).

- The effect of most of the remaining program statements should be clear from program notes discussed in connection with the *Python* program examples presented in earlier chapters. One new statement concerns the two-panel plot this is carried out in lines 48-61. The statement 'plt.subplot(2,1,1)' in line 50 does the setup for the plot. The first two function arguments (2 and 1) specify that this is a 2x1 plot, i.e., a two-panel plot organized vertically; the third argument (1) specifies that the plot in progress is the first of the two sub-plots (i.e., the top panel). The second sub-plot (i.e., the lower panel) is then generated after the statement 'plt.subplot(2,1,2)' in line 55.

- The final section of Example7_1.py prints out the estimate of the time constant of the circuit. To do so, it calculates the initial rate at which V_m is moving towards the steady-state value reached during the current pulse and divides that rate by the amplitude of the change in V_m; the result is 1.051 ms. This number can be compared with that calculated with the formula for the time constant ($R_m \times C_m = 1$ ms), which is also printed to the console. The time constant estimated from the rate of change of V_m is in error by 5%. This error can be reduced to a small value by increasing the size of the program variable N_steps. For example, if N_steps is increased by a factor of 10, the error is reduced to 0.5%; if N_steps is increased by a factor of 100, the error is reduced to 0.05%.

7.5 THEORETICAL RESPONSE OF A CELL MEMBRANE TO A CHANGE IN VOLTAGE

We now extend the approach in Section 7.4 and suppose that our same small spherical cell is being studied with the voltage-clamp technique. This technique has been extremely successful in elucidating many properties of excitable cells, including the mechanism of the action potential (discussed in Chapter 8), as well as many electrical and non-electrical phenomena in non-excitable cells. With this technique, instead of changing I_m in a controlled way and measuring V_m, the reverse is done, i.e., V_m is changed in a controlled way and the I_m required to do so is measured. While the example of this technique as considered here is very basic, its power will become apparent in Chapter 8, which describes how the voltage clamp technique was used to reveal the mechanism of the action potential.

In a common voltage-clamp experiment, V_m is held constant for some seconds or minutes at an initial value, which is often the cell's resting potential. The initial value of V_m could, however, be some other voltage -- selected, for example, by passing a steady current across the membrane -- in which case it is called the 'holding potential'. V_m is then rapidly changed in an almost step-wise fashion from the initial potential to a test potential, where it is held for a selected period of time, and then rapidly changed back to the initial potential. (More complicated waveforms for the change in V_m are also used.) One reason to control V_m and measure I_m is that V_m is a major factor that controls the gates on many types of ion channels, i.e., V_m controls whether the channels are passing ions or are electrically silent. The voltage-clamp technique thus permits investigating how V_m controls channel gating. Also, during the normal functioning of many cell types, the activity of the cell's ion channels has a strong effect on V_m and V_m has a strong effect on the activity of the channels. The voltage-clamp technique provides an experimental way to break the link between these two processes and study them separately.

To produce a step-like change in V_m across a membrane whose equivalent circuit is like that in Fig. 7.1B, it is necessary that I_m initially pass a brief surge of current to change the charge on the capacitor in the desired direction; once that is done, V_m will be at a new level. If V_m remains constant thereafter, dV_m/dt will be zero, so the remaining membrane current, if any, must move through the ionic pathway(s) in the membrane, with none of it moving through the capacitive pathway. Because both I_m and V_m are measured in an experiment of this type, a great deal can be learned about the pathways in the membrane for ion movements. For example, if the gates on the ion channels within the membrane should change from closed to open or from open to closed while V_m is being held constant, this change will be detected as a change in I_m (if the driving force on the relevant ion species is not zero).

For the circuit in Fig. 7.1B, the I_m waveform required to generate a step in voltage is, in principle, very simple. Let ΔV_m denote the size of the desired voltage step. A large, brief capacitive current that supplies an amount of charge equal to $C \cdot \Delta V_m$ will produce this step in voltage; thereafter V_m will remain constant if I_m equals $(V_m - E)/R_m$, which is the ionic current that flows at the new value of V_m.

In practice, generating the required I_m is not always straightforward. For example, the experimental apparatus often has limitations due to the resistance of the electrode through which I_m must flow, which can lengthen the time required to supply the capacitive charge for changing V_m. Also, the electrical properties of the membrane are not known ahead of time. In practice, the I_m waveform to produce the required V_m response is generated by the electronic apparatus in a clever way. The apparatus starts by generating a 'command' voltage waveform, i.e., one whose amplitude and time course are set by the experimentalist; this serves as a template for the desired amplitude and time course of V_m. For example, the command waveform might be a voltage step of amplitude ΔV that starts from the holding potential and lasts for a specific time. Then, by means of a feedback circuit in the apparatus that works on a fast time scale, the difference between the command waveform and the measured $V_m(t)$ waveform (this difference is sometimes called the 'error signal') is used to dynamically adjust the shape of the $I_m(t)$ waveform so that the $V_m(t)$ waveform closely matches the command waveform.

This approach is used in the next *Python* program (Example7_2.py), which simulates a voltage-clamp experiment applied to the circuit in Fig. 7.1B. The program is listed next, followed by the output printed to the console, and the plot produced by the program.

```
1  # -*- coding: utf-8 -*-
2  """
3  Python 3.7
4  Created on Wed Feb 13 09:22:55 2019
5  Example7_2.py
6  Description: equivalent-circuit simulation of the Im waveform required to produce a step
7     change in Vm
8  """
9
10 import numpy as np
11 import matplotlib.pyplot as plt
12
13 #define a voltage waveform for Vm to imitate as a function of time
14 def Vm_Command(E,V_step,t):
15     Vc=E       #command value is E unless time t is between V_start and V_end
16     if t >= V_start and t < V_end:
```

```
17      Vc=E+V_step
18      return Vc           #return the scalar value of the command voltage
19
20  def Vm_Error(i):    #voltage error: Vcommand minus Vm (both indexed by i)
21      return Vm_Command(E,V_step,t[i]) - Vm[i]   #return is a scalar (volts)
22
23  #constants for the membrane circuit elements
24  R=1e3               #membrane specific resistance (ohm cm^2)
25  C=1e-6              #membrane specific capacitance (farad cm^-2)
26  E=-80e-3            #battery voltage (= resting Vm) (volts)
27  r=10e-4             #radius of spherical cell
28  area=4*np.pi*r*r    #surface area of cell
29  Rm=R/area           #membrane resistance (ohms)
30  Cm=C*area           #membrane capacitance (farads)
31
32  V_step=15e-3            #size of command voltage step (volts)
33  V_start, V_end = .01,.03    #time range during which V_step is "on" (s)
34  Error=1e-5      #maximum allowed error between Vm_Command and Vm (volts)
35  Gain=0.25       #factor with which to temper the needed adjustment to Im
36  #if gain>1.0, the waveforms show instability
37
38  t_start=0; t_end=0.05; N_steps=int(1e4)    #set the arguments for linspace()
39  t=np.linspace(t_start, t_end, N_steps+1) #t is the grid of time points (s)
40  dt=(t_end-t_start)/N_steps      #dt is the step size for the time-point grid (s)
41
42  Im=0.*t             #initialize the Im waveform to zero (amps)
43  Vm=Im+E             #initialize the Vm waveform to E (volts)
44
45  #Calculate the change to Im needed to get the next Vm to move close to Vm_Command.
46  #Im and Vm cannot move in absolute synchrony (since they are defined on a grid of
47  #points separated by dt), so calculate Im[i] based partly on what Vm[i+1] will be.
48  for i in range(0,N_steps):
49      dIm=0.          #dIm is the amount by which we need to charge the capacitor
50      dVm=0.          #dVm is the amount by which Vm[i+1] will change due to the dIm
51      dE = Vm_Error(i)    #dE is the error in voltage at time t[i]
```

```
52    if abs(dE) > Error:    #if error is larger than allowed error, do something
53        dIm = Gain*Cm*dE/dt      #capacitor current to add to Im to change Vm
54        dVm = Gain*dE            #and Vm will change by this amount due to dIm
55        Vm[i+1] = Vm[i] + dVm    #attribute the effect of dIm on Vm to Vm[i+1]
56 #we must also add to Im[i] the ionic current required for Vm, which we estimate
57 #   as the average of that to maintain Vm[i] and Vm[i+1]
58        Im[i] = dIm + ((Vm[i+1]-E)/Rm + (Vm[i]-E)/Rm)/2
59
60 #plot the result as two sub-plots -- upper for Vm, lower for Im
61 plt.figure()
62 plt.subplot(2,1,1)              #do the upper plot first
63 plt.plot(t, 1e3*Vm, 'k', linewidth=2, label="Vm")     #show Vm in mV
64 plt.ylim(-100.,-50.)
65 plt.ylabel('Vm(t) (mV)')
66 plt.title("Vm and Im during a voltage step in a circuit with R, C, and E")
67 plt.subplot(2,1,2)              #do the lower plot second
68 plt.plot(t, 1e9*Im, 'k', linewidth=2, label="Im")  #show Im in picoamps
69 plt.ylim(-10.,10.)
70 plt.xlabel('time (s)')
71 plt.ylabel('Im(t) (nanoamps)')
72 plt.savefig('example7_2.png',dpi=200)
73 plt.show()
74
75 #get some statisitics for maximum changes in Im at on and off of voltage step
76 i_max = np.argmax(Im)
77 i_min = np.argmin(Im)
78 print("Im-max is {:.4} amps for dt = {:.4} s".format(Im[i_max],dt))
79 print("dVm for this step is {:.4} volts".format(Vm[i_max+1]-Vm[i_max]))
80 print("Im-min is {:.4} amps for dt = {:.4} s".format(Im[i_min],dt))
81 print("dVm for this step is {:.4} volts".format(Vm[i_min+1]-Vm[i_min]))
```

Im-max is 0.0002525 amps for dt = 1e-05 s
dVm for this step is 0.0025 volts
Im-min is -0.0002423 amps for dt = 1e-05 s
dVm for this step is -0.002498 volts

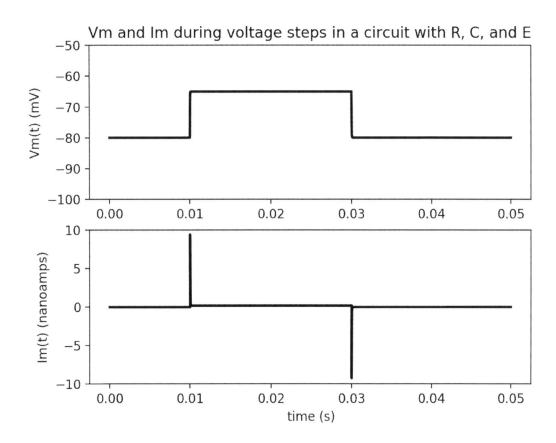

Figure 7.4 V_m and I_m waveforms for a simulated voltage-clamp experiment on the circuit in Fig. 7.1B. In contrast to Fig. 7.3, where I_m changes in a step-wise fashion, I_m here is chosen to make V_m change by +15 mV in a near step-wise fashion. The values of R_m, C_m, and E are the same as in Fig. 7.3.

Program Notes
- Eqn. 7.1 above cannot be rearranged to yield a deq for I_m in terms of V_m and I_m and the circuit parameters, analogous to the approach used in Example7_1.py (see line 17). The simulation of this experiment therefore cannot take advantage of the function odeint. Rather, the simulation mimics the logic of an actual voltage-clamp circuit. The program creates a command voltage waveform against which the V_m waveform is compared on a point-by-point basis as V_m and I_m are being constructed by the program. The error between the two voltage waveforms is used to adjust the construction of the I_m waveform. The result is that the constructed V_m waveform closely matches the command waveform, and the constructed I_m waveform matches that expected for the circuit in Fig. 7.1B. Two functions are defined in Example7_2.py for this purpose:

(i) Vm_command (lines 14-18) defines the time-varying command waveform, which starts at E and, between time points V_start and V_end, adds a constant voltage amount (V_step) to E.

(ii) Vm_Error (lines 20-21) returns the difference between the command waveform and the calculated value of the variable Vm for any specified time point on the grid of the solution time points.

- As in Example7_1.py, the program takes advantage of the fact that I_m is made up of two components: the capacitive current (I_c) and the ionic current (I_{ion}). If I_m is suddenly changed, I_{ion} cannot change until V_m changes because $I_{ion} = (V_m - E)/R_m$ and E and R_m are constants. So, at the moment that I_m first changes, the change in I_m initially equals the change in I_c. Once I_c has changed the charge on the capacitor, V_m will necessarily have changed and thereafter some of the change in I_m is due to a change in I_{ion}. These principles are used in Example7_2.py to construct I_m so as to get the required change in V_m due to I_c, and, thereafter, to hold V_m constant. Once V_m is constant, $I_c = 0$ and $I_m = I_{ion}$.

- After the user-defined functions are specified, the program sets the values of the equivalent circuit's electrical constants (R_m, C_m, and E) and defines the time grid on which the Im and Vm waveforms are to be solved. Lines 48-58 carry out the main work of the program. Line 48 starts a 'for' loop that is executed for each time step on the solution time grid. For each step in the loop, the error between the command waveform and Vm is determined and an amount dIm (which represents capacitive current; see preceding paragraph) is calculated for inclusion in the value of the Im waveform at that time point. The effect of this dIm by itself is to move Vm closer to the command waveform at the time of the next time point. Because Vm can differ from E, the ionic current required to sustain the value of Vm is also included in Im; this is calculated with the usual formula, i.e., (Vm – E)/Rm, but with a slight twist. Because (i) an interplay exists between the Im and Vm waveforms that are being constructed in the loop and (ii) the grid of time points is not continuous, the ionic component of Im that is set at the current time point is based on an average of the value of (Vm – E)/Rm at the current time point and at the next time point (the value of which is set before the value of Im is set for the current time point). This averaging improves the accuracy of the simulation when compared with an approach in which the ionic component of Im is calculated based only on either the current value of Vm or the next value of Vm.

- The program uses a variable called 'Gain' (the value of which is set to 0.25 in line 35) to modulate the actual value of I_c that is used to adjust V_m during the construction of the I_m and V_m waveforms in lines 48-58. If the value of Gain were made larger, the capacitive component of I_m would be larger, and V_m would rise to its intended level faster. However, as the value of Gain is increased, there is risk of introducing instability in the interplay between the I_m and V_m waveforms. This instability phenomenon, which can occur in an actual voltage-clamp circuit, is called 'ringing'. Exercise 7.4 asks the reader to investigate how the value of the Gain variable in Example7_2.py affects the I_m and V_m waveforms constructed in the simulation.

- In Fig. 7.4, the simulated waveforms for Vm(t) and Im(t) look very like the corresponding waveforms in an actual voltage-clamp experiment. Thus, the program successfully simulates a voltage-clamp experiment for the circuit in Fig. 7.1B. Exercise 7.2 leaves it to the reader to decompose the Im(t) waveform in Fig. 7.4 into its capacitive and ionic components. As in the simulation of the current-step experiment (Fig. 7.3), the values of the circuit elements (R_m, C_m, and E) can be readily estimated from the Im(t) and Vm(t) waveforms and from the value of V_m that corresponds to Im = 0 (see Exercise 7.2).

7.6 A MORE REALISTIC MEMBRANE EQUIVALENT CIRCUIT FOR A RESTING CELL

The circuit in Fig. 7.1B has just one pathway for ions to cross the membrane and thus it represents the simplest possible circuit of this type. In contrast, in Chapter 6, in which the osmotic balance of a generic cell was simulated, the analysis considered the passive movements of three ion species across the cell membrane: Na^+, K^+, and Cl^-. A more realistic equivalent circuit for the membrane of a generic cell at rest would allow pathways for the movement of several ion species across the membrane.

Fig. 7.5 shows an equivalent circuit like that in Fig. 7.1B, but modified in two ways: (i) it includes pathways for Na^+, K^+, and Cl^-, and (ii) the resistor symbols have been relabeled as conductances (recall that conductance G, in siemens, equals 1/R).

The relation between this circuit and that in Fig. 7.1B is not as complicated as might seem at first glance. The analysis of the circuit in Fig. 7.5 is simplified algebraically by use of G rather than R. The current flow across each pathway is given by the relation:

$I_i = G_i \cdot (V_m - E_i)$ (for i = Na, K, or Cl). It is left as an exercise (Exercise 7.6) for the reader to show that the circuit in Fig. 7.5 reduces to that in Fig. 7.1B if (i) $1/R_m$ (= G_m) = G_K + G_{Na} + G_{Cl}, and (ii) E = ($E_K \cdot G_K$ + $E_{Na} \cdot G_{Na}$ + $E_{Cl} \cdot G_{Cl}$) / (G_K + G_{Na} + G_{Cl}). That is, for the circuit in Fig. 7.5, the effective conductance of the entire membrane is equal to the sum of the conductances of each ion species, and (ii) E, the effective battery voltage of the entire membrane, is equal to the average value of the battery voltages of the individual ion species, each weighted by the fraction of the total membrane conductance that is due to that ion species.

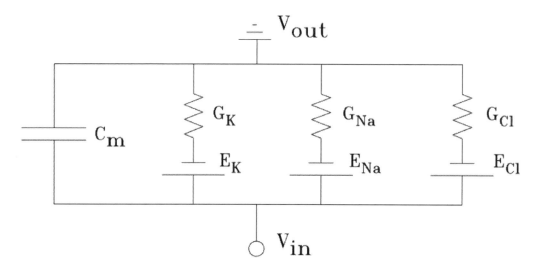

Figure 7.5 Membrane equivalent circuit for a cell with a membrane capacitance C_m and membrane conductances for K^+, Na^+, and Cl^-. The batteries are labeled according to the convention in Fig. 7.1B. Under normal physiological conditions, E_{Na} is positive and E_K and E_{Cl} are negative.

It can be concluded that experiments of the type presented in Sections 7.4 and 7.5 for a generic cell, if applied to the circuit in Fig. 7.5, give information about the more complex parameter set: C_m, $E_K \cdot G_K$ + $E_{Na} \cdot G_{Na}$ + $E_{Cl} \cdot G_{Cl}$, and G_K + G_{Na} + G_{Cl}. To gain information about the individual parameters (E_K, E_{Na}, E_{Cl}, G_K, G_{Na}, and G_{Cl}) for a particular cell or cell type, additional experiments would need to be carried out -- for example: (i) experiments like those discussed in Sections 7.4 and 7.5 could be repeated in the presence of pharmacological agents that blocked specific types of ion channels (which could set to zero one more of the values G_K, G_{Na}, and G_{Cl}), or (ii) measurements of the intracellular concentrations of Na^+, K^+, and/or Cl^- might be made (which would provide information about E_K, E_{Na}, and/or E_{Cl}), or (iii) experiments like those in Sections 7.4 and 7.5 could be repeated in the presence of different ion concentrations in the extracellular solution (which would change the values of E_K, E_{Na}, and E_{Cl} in known ways). In fact, approach (iii) was used in the experiments carried out on squid giant axons that first clearly elucidated the mechanism of the action potential in nerve cells (discussed in Chapter 8).

7.7 MEMBRANE CONDUCTANCE VS. MEMBRANE PERMEABILITY

The equivalent-circuit approach discussed above, and also discussed implicitly in Chapter 5, has focused on how the movement of ions across the membrane can be described in terms of the laws of capacitors, resistors (or their inverse, conductances), batteries, and driving forces. With this approach, the main equation for the membrane ionic current due to any particular ion is: $I_{ion} = G_{ion} \cdot (V_m - E_{ion})$, where E_{ion} is the ion's Nernst potential (Eqn. 5.2) and G_{ion} is its membrane conductance. A different approach was used in Chapter 6, in which Eqns. 6.7-6.9 were used calculate the passive flux of an ion across the membrane as a function of the ion's membrane permeability, the ion's concentrations on the two sides of the membrane, and V_m. The questions might be raised: what is the relation between these two approaches for describing ion movements across the membrane and what is the relative advantage of each?

To address these questions, we consider the net passive movements of Na^+, K^+, and Cl^- across the membrane. With both approaches, the net membrane current for each ion: (i) is zero if V_m equals E_{ion}, (ii) becomes increasingly outward as V_m is made increasingly greater than E_{ion}, and (iii) becomes increasingly inward as V_m is made increasingly less than E_{ion}. (Note that for a positive univalent ion, the current equals the flux times Faraday's constant whereas, for a negative univalent ion, the current equals minus the flux times Faraday's constant.)

Qualitatively, calculations with the conductance and permeability approaches are therefore expected to give similar results. With the conductance approach, the I-V relation (the current-voltage relation) of each ion is linear, and this linearity simplifies the associated calculations, especially when multiple ion movements are involved. For example, in Chapter 8, we will see that the analysis of the mechanism of the action potential was carried out with the simplifications inherent in the conductance approach. With the permeability approach, the I-V relations are non-linear, and the associated calculations are somewhat more complicated.

The permeability approach might be considered more realistic, however, since it explicitly takes into account expected differences in the uni-directional movements of an ion across the membrane as V_m becomes progressively different from E_{ion} (see discussion of Eqns. 6.7-6.9 in Chapter 6). Neither approach, however, takes into account the actual molecular details of how an ion crosses the membrane through an open ion channel.

To provide a concrete comparison between the two approaches, we extend here the calculations given in the *Python* program Osmotic1.py in Chapter 6, which used membrane permeabilities and the associated flux equations to calculate the passive movements of Na^+, K^+, or Cl^-. If Faraday's constant and the valence of the ions are taken into account, Eqns. 6.7-6.9 permit construction of the individual I-V relations for Na^+, K^+, and Cl^-. From these relations, the effective conductance of each ion species at any particular value of V_m is easily estimated as the slope of the I-V relation -- i.e., as dI/dV. For example, if V_m is chosen to be -81.7 mV (the steady-state value of resting potential of the hypothetical cell in Osmotic1.py), the calculated conductance values, in siemens cm^{-2}, are: 4.7×10^{-6} for Na^+, 68.7×10^{-6} for K^+, and 153.5×10^{-6} for Cl^-. The estimate for the total membrane conductance is therefore 226.9×10^{-6} siemens cm^{-2}.

Since $R=1/G$, the corresponding estimate of the membrane resistance is 4.41×10^3 ohms cm^2. The last value is several-fold larger than the 1×10^3 ohms cm^2 value for R_m that was assumed in the examples considered in Figs. 7.2 and 7.3 but is still a reasonable value for a generic cell. As one might expect, because of the non-linearities in Eqns. 6.7-6.9, the value estimated for membrane conductance from the dI/dV of the I-V relation depends on the value of V_m at which the estimate is made (see Exercise 7.7).

It may also be noted in this example that, with a membrane resistance of 4.41×10^3 ohms cm^2 and a membrane capacitance of 1×10^{-6} farads cm^{-2}, the calculated value of the membrane time constant based on the formula $R_m \times C_m$ is 4.41 ms. This value can be compared with the time constant with which V_m returns to -81.7 mV in Osmotic1.py if, at the 1000 s time point, V_m is suddenly perturbed by a small amount and allowed to relax back to -81.7 mV. If the perturbation is 5 mV in the positive direction, the estimate of the time constant is 4.2 ms; if the perturbation is 5 mV in the negative direction, the estimate is 4.6 ms. As expected, both values are in good agreement with the 4.41 ms value calculated with the formula $R_m \times C_m$.

7.8 ONE-DIMENSIONAL CABLE THEORY

Many cells do not have simple, nearly-spherical shapes. In such cases, it is often not appropriate to model the resting electrical properties of the cell with an equivalent circuit like that in Fig. 7.1B or Fig. 7.5, which assumes that V_m is the same in all regions of the cell. An extreme example of such a case is the long cylindrical shape that applies to many skeletal muscle fibers, some regions of cardiac tissue, some types of smooth muscle and, of course, a dendrite or the long axon of a nerve cell. For these cells and tissues, the equivalent circuit shown in Fig. 7.6 provides a useful circuit model with which to estimate how a voltage change in one region of the cell is related to voltage changes in adjacent regions of the cell.

The circuit in Fig. 7.6 shows a series of repeating elements organized in the longitudinal direction (x dimension), which resembles a long electrical cable. For this reason, the theory associated with the analysis of a circuit of this type is called 'one-dimensional cable theory'.

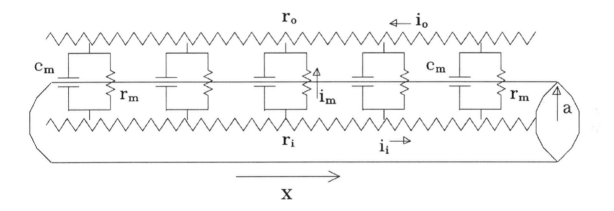

Figure 7.6 Equivalent circuit of the passive electrical properties of a long cylindrical cell or cell process (such as a nerve axon). The diagram shows repeating elements that extend in both the +x and –x directions, each assumed to occupy a small distance dx. The symbols are: membrane capacitance, c_m (in farads cm^{-1}); membrane resistance, r_m (in ohm cm); membrane current, i_m (in amps cm^{-1}); resistance of the inside solution, r_i (in ohm cm^{-1}); the internal longitudinal current, i_i (in amps); resistance of the outside solution, r_o (in ohm cm^{-1}) and the external longitudinal current, i_o (in amps). The tubular overlay of radius a represents the long cylindrical cell or cell process.

The elements in Fig. 7.6 include (i) a repeating series of capacitors and resistors, which represent the capacitive and resistive properties of the surface membrane as it extends in the +x and −x directions, and (ii) two long resistors, r_o and r_i, which represent the resistance to longitudinal current flow outside and inside the cell, respectively, in the +x and −x directions, due to the finite conductance of the external and internal solutions. For simplicity, the symbols E for the membrane ion batteries have been omitted from the circuit diagram since the batteries simply provide a voltage offset that sets the resting potential. If resting V_m is assumed to be the same at all values of x, the battery effects can be omitted in the equations below, the goal of which is to calculate what <u>changes</u> occur with respect to the resting potential at different locations in the cell in response to the flow of current in the cell.

In the analysis, we will initially ignore the extracellular resistance (i.e., r_o will be set to zero) and assume that all of the outside solution is at ground potential. The possibilities for current flow as a function of x in the circuit are then twofold: along the axis of the cylinder (i_i in the diagram) or across the membrane to ground (i_m in the diagram). We will use Kirchhoff's laws to derive a general equation for $V_m(x,t)$, i.e., how V_m varies with distance and time in response to current flow. Then we will solve this equation for $V_m(x)$ in the steady state if a long-lasting step of current is injected into the circuit (i.e., the cell) somewhere in its middle, which we will define as x = 0.

From Ohm's law in its differential form, i.e., applied to a small distance dx along the cable, we can write:

$$(\partial/\partial x) V_m = - i_i \cdot r_i , \qquad (7.2)$$

where $(\partial/\partial x)V_m$ denotes the partial derivative of $V_m(x,t)$ with respect to x. To account for any i_i that might leak out across the membrane to ground, we have:

$$i_m = -(\partial/\partial x) i_i . \qquad (7.3)$$

Combining the two equations gives:

$$(\partial^2/\partial x^2) V_m = r_i \cdot i_m . \qquad (7.4)$$

Since i_m is the sum of the membrane ionic and capacitive currents (i_{ion} and i_c, respectively), we can write:

$$(\partial^2/\partial x^2)\, V_m = r_i \cdot (i_{ion} + i_c). \tag{7.5}$$

And, since $i_{ion} = V_m/r_m$ and $i_c = c_m \cdot (\partial/\partial t)\, V_m$:

$$(\partial^2/\partial x^2)\, V_m = r_i \cdot (V_m/r_m) + r_i \cdot c_m \cdot (\partial/\partial t)\, V_m. \tag{7.6}$$

Dividing this equation by r_i, multiplying by r_m, and rearranging, we have:

$$(r_m/r_i) \cdot (\partial^2/\partial x^2)\, V_m - c_m \cdot r_m \cdot (\partial/\partial t)\, V_m - V_m = 0. \tag{7.7}$$

If we define $\lambda = \sqrt{(r_m/r_i)}$ (where λ is called the 'space constant' and has units of m or mm) and $\tau = c_m \cdot r_m$ (where τ is called the 'time constant' and has units of s or ms), we have:

$$\lambda^2 \cdot (\partial^2/\partial x^2) V_m - \tau \cdot (\partial/\partial t) V_m - V_m = 0. \tag{7.8}$$

[**Note**: because we have assumed that $r_o = 0$, no x-related change in potential occurs in the extracellular solution. If $r_o > 0$ and if $i_o \neq 0$, then $i_o \cdot r_o \neq 0$, in which case the potential in the extracellular solution does change with distance. Note, however, that $i_o = -i_i$ since currents flow in loops; thus, any current flowing along the intracellular solution at a point x must be balanced by a current of the same amplitude but of opposite sign flowing along the extracellular solution at x. Since $V_m(x)$ is the difference between the internal potential at x and the external potential at x, it follows that $(\partial/\partial x)\, V_m = - i_i \cdot (r_i + r_o)$ and thus that $\lambda = \sqrt{(r_m/(r_i + r_o))}$. For convenience, in the material that follows, we will continue to ignore r_o and assume that $\lambda = \sqrt{(r_m/r_i)}$.]

We define X as distance normalized by λ (i.e., $X = x/\lambda$) and T as t time normalized by τ (i.e., $T = t/\tau$). Substituting, we obtain:

$$(\partial^2/\partial X^2)\, V_m(X,T) - (\partial/\partial T)\, V_m(X,T) - V_m = 0. \tag{7.9}$$

Eqn. 7.9 is a general equation for a one-dimensional cable expressed in dimensionless form.

We now solve this equation for a special case. We imagine that a glass micro-electrode is used to impale the surface membrane of the long cell process somewhere in its middle (defined as x=0) and that this electrode is used to inject a long-lasting step of current into the cytoplasm. This current will divide into two components and spread equally in the +x and –x directions, which are assumed to be without bound. We suppose that we wait until the new steady-state is reached. In this case, V_m becomes a function of distance only; so Eqn. 7.9 simplifies to:

$$(d^2/dX^2)\, V_m(X) - V_m = 0 . \tag{7.10}$$

The general solution to Eqn. 7.10 is:

$$V_m(X) = C_1 \exp(-X) + C_2 \exp(X) . \tag{7.11}$$

We know that V_m must go to zero as X becomes either large and positive or large and negative and that $V_m(0)$ can have only one value. Thus, the particular solution to Eqn. 7.11 takes the form:

$$V_m(X) = C \exp(-X) \text{ if } X \geq 0$$

$$\text{and } V_m(X) = C \exp(X) \text{ if } X \leq 0 . \tag{7.12}$$

A plot of Eqn. 7.12, with $V_m(X)$ normalized by the constant C, is shown in Fig. 7.7. $V_m(X)$, the maintained voltage change (the "signal"), decays exponentially with distance in the +x and – x directions. For each space constant $\lambda = \sqrt{(r_m/r_i)}$ that X is moved further from the site of current injection, $V_m(X)$ declines by the factor 1/e. The particular dependence of λ on r_m and r_i makes qualitative sense, since if r_m were made larger, the current injected at X=0 would leak less easily across the membrane and thus spread further along the axis of the cylinder; therefore, the change in V_m would extend further from the site of injection and λ would be larger. Conversely, if r_i were made larger, the current injected at X=0 would spread longitudinally less easily and more current would cross the membrane nearer to the injection site; therefore, the change of V_m would be more localized to the injection site and λ would be smaller. Exercise 7.9 considers what information is needed to express a plot like that in Fig. 7.7 in absolute units (e.g., with cm on the x axis and volts on the y axis) rather than in normalized units.

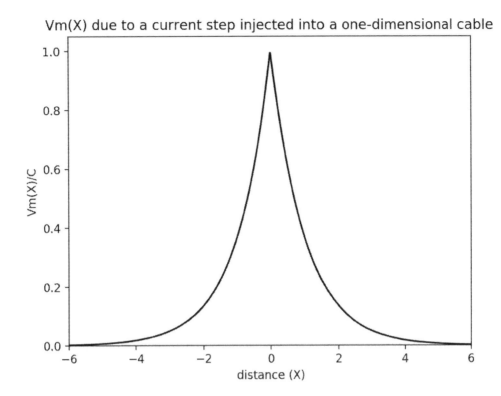

Figure 7.7 Steady-state solution of the one-dimensional cable equation in response to injection of a step of current at X = 0. Both axes are shown in normalized units.

The reader may be interested in the time-dependent solution to Eqn. 7.9 for this case of a step of current injected into the long cell process at X=0. The solution to this problem, which is given in Appendix E, involves a function called the 'error function', which is defined as the integral of a Gaussian function (recall the Gaussian functions mentioned in Chapter 3 in connection with the discussion of diffusion coefficients, e.g., Eqn. 3.1).

A final point of interest concerns another special case. Suppose that r_m is infinite and a bolus of charge Q is deposited instantaneously on the membrane capacitance at x = 0. What is $V_m(x,t)$ in this case? Clearly, none of the charge would be able to leak out of the cable to ground and its time-dependent spread down the cable would be inversely proportional to both c_m and r_i. Interestingly $1/(c_m \cdot r_i)$ has units of $cm^2 \; s^{-1}$, i.e., units of the diffusion coefficient. In fact, $V_m(x,t)$ obeys the diffusion equation (Eqn. 3.1 in Chapter 3) with M proportional to Q and $D = 1/(c_m \cdot r_i)$. Because c_m and r_i both vary with the radius of the cylinder but in different ways, this "electrical diffusion coefficient" varies with radius. Exercise 7.10 asks the reader to explore this dependence.

The Need for Action Potentials. Exercise 7.9 shows how to put an absolute distance scale on a plot like that in Fig. 7.7. The answer shows that, for cells at rest with typical electrical properties of the surface membrane, the space constant λ is a relatively small number. This means that a current-induced depolarization that is substantial at one location on a cell membrane can spread "passively" (i.e., according to the assumptions of cable theory) only to nearby regions of that cell's membrane before it declines to insignificance. If an electrical signal is required to carry information over a substantial distance, as is the case in nerve and muscle cells, some mechanism is needed to sense and regenerate the electrical change as a function of distance. The action potential (discussed in detail in Chapter 8) is the self-regenerating electrical signal invented by evolution to solve this problem.

7.9 EXERCISES

Exercise 7.1 In Fig. 7.1, the pathway for ionic current across the membrane is shown as a resistor Rm and a battery E joined 'in series', i.e., if current flows through either element it must flow through both. Write an equation for how much current must flow across this pathway as a function of V_m (= V_{in} - V_{out}). Now compare this equation with that derived in Section 5.8 of Chapter 5 (entitled 'Driving Force'). Are the equations essentially identical?

Exercise 7.2 This exercise explores further the calculations carried out in the program Example7_2.py.

a) Separate the $I_m(t)$ waveform in Fig. 7.3 into I_c and I_{ion}. (Hint: note that I_{ion} is proportional to V_m - E) and the $V_m(t)$ waveform is also calculated in Example7_2.py.

b) Calculate the total charge under I_c at either the 'on' or 'off' times of the voltage step. (I_c is also called the 'capacitive transient' or sometimes the 'capacity transient'.)

c) Calculate C_m in the underlying circuit based on your result in b) and on the associated change in V_m.

d) Calculate the value of R_m in the circuit from information in the $I_m(t)$ and $V_m(t)$ waveforms.

Exercise 7.3 Example7_2.py includes a negative feedback section that adjusts V_m to match a 'set-point' (recall Fig. 1.3 in Chapter 1). Which statements or variables in Example7_2.py would you point to as carrying out the functions of the 5 boxes/entities in Fig. 1.3?

Exercise 7.4 In program Example7_2.py, change the variable 'Gain' to both smaller and larger values and see what effect these changes have on the $I_m(t)$ and $V_m(t)$ waveforms. In doing so, use at least one value of gain that is substantially greater than 1.0 (e.g., a Gain = 1.99 yields an interesting result).

Exercise 7.5 Modify the user defined function 'Vm_Command' in Example7_2.py by adding the following statement ' if t ≥ 0.015 and t < 0.025t: Vc =Vc + V_step' just before the statement 'return Vc', and see if you can predict what effect this change to Vm_Command has on the plot produced by the program. The voltage paradigm illustrated with this version of Vm_Command is commonly used in the study of ion channels. It starts at a holding potential (which in this case is the resting potential, i.e., the zero-current potential), then moves to a 'conditioning' potential, and finally to a 'test' potential before returning back to the conditioning potential and then the holding potential.

Exercise 7.6 Confirm the statement in Section 7.6 that that the circuit in Fig. 7.5 is equivalent to that in Fig. 7.1B if $1/R_m (= G_m) = G_K + G_{Na} + G_{Cl}$, and $E = (E_K \cdot G_K + E_{Na} \cdot G_{Na} + E_{Cl} \cdot G_{Cl}) / (G_K + G_{Na} + G_{Cl})$.

Exercise 7.7 Section 7.7 stated that the *Python* program Osmotic1.py in Chapter 6 could be extended slightly to construct I-V relations for Na^+, K^+, and Cl^- by means of Eqns. 6.7-6.9 and, from these, the slopes (dI/dV) of the I-V relations at the cell's steady-state resting potential (-81.7 mV) could be calculated. Carry out these calculations to see if you agree with the value mentioned in Section 7.7 for the total membrane conductance of that hypothetical cell at the resting potential (226.9×10^{-6} siemens cm^{-2}). Repeat this calculation for several other values of V_m (e.g., -30 mV and +30 mV) to see how much the estimate of membrane conductance differs at different values of V_m. Can you propose a reason for the variation that is seen in these calculations?

Exercise 7.8 Consider two spherical cells at rest (denoted '1' and '2'), each with a cell radius of 10^{-3} cm (10 microns) and with a membrane equivalent circuit like that in Fig. 7.1B. Assume that membrane specific capacitance is 10^{-6} farads cm^{-2}, that membrane specific resistance is 1000 ohms cm^2, that $E_1 = -90$ mV and $E_2 = -60$ mV. Also suppose that the cells have an incipient anatomical connection between them though a short narrow strand of cytoplasm, and let R_S denote the resistance of this strand of cytoplasmic. To begin with, assume that this connection is not patent, i.e., that R_S is infinite. Thus, the resting membrane potential of cell #1 will be E_1 and that of cell #2 will be E_2. Now suppose that, at time t = 0, the cytoplasmic pathway suddenly becomes patent and R_s assumes a value of 80×10^6 ohms (80 megohms). (i) Write a *Python* program that calculates and plots the time course of $V_{m1}(t)$ and $V_{m2}(t)$, the membrane potential of the two cells (or, rather, now better described as two different regions of the same cell) as a function of time. Start your calculation at t = 0 and extend it sufficiently for V_{m1} and V_{m2} to reach a new steady-state. (ii) Redo this problem if membrane specific resistance of cell #2 is 3000 ohms cm^2.

Hint: The current I_S that flows from cell/location #2 to cell/location #1 is determined by Ohm's law: $I_S(t) = (V_2(t) - V_1(t))/ R_S$. At t = 0, this means that $I_S(0) = (E_2 - E_1)/ R_S$. Also note that I_S must flow in a loop, i.e., cross the membrane of both cells.]

Note: This type of electrical coupling, in which current flow is generated between two connected cells -- or, equivalently, two regions of the same cell -- that, by themselves, would prefer to have their own separate value of membrane potential, is called 'electrotonic coupling' or 'electrotonus'.

Exercise 7.9 This exercise addresses how to obtain a plot like that in Fig. 7.7 in unnormalized units. The first question is how large $V_m(X)$ would be at X=0 at a long time after a current step of amplitude I is injected at X=0. From symmetry, half of I would flow in the +X direction and half in the –X direction. Consider the half in the +X direction. From Ohm's law in its differential form (i.e., $(\partial/\partial x) V_m = - i_i \cdot r_i$; see above), we know that, at x=0, $(d/dx) V_m(x) = - r_i \cdot I/2$. We also know that $V_m(X) = C \exp(-X)$; so, $dV_m(X)$ at X = 0 is -C. Since $X = x/\lambda$, we have $C = (\lambda \cdot r_i \cdot I)/2$. Hence $V_m(0) = \sqrt{(r_m r_i)} \cdot I/2$. The input resistance of the cable, which is defined as $V_m(0)/I$, is therefore $\sqrt{(r_m r_i)}/2$. To calculate $V_m(0)$ from I we need to know r_m and r_i. These values will depend on R_i (= the specific resistivity of cytoplasm), R_m (= the specific membrane resistance), and the radius of the cylinder. Suppose that $R_i = 10^2$ ohm cm, $R_m = 10^3$ ohm cm^2, and the cylinder radius is 10^{-3} cm. Calculate the following:

a) What is the input resistance of this cable?

b) If I = 10 nanoamps (=1e-8 amps), calculate $V_m(0)$.

c) At what distance from the site of current injection will $V_m(x)$ have fallen to 1/e of its value at x=0, i.e., what is λ?

Note that, in an actual experiment, if the radius is known, R_i and R_m can be estimated from the measurements of λ and input resistance by use of the above relations.

Exercise 7.10 The penultimate paragraph of the text noted that, if r_m is infinite, a bolus of charge Q introduced instantaneously at x=0 will spread down the one-dimensional cable according to Eqn. 3.1 if $D = 1/(c_m \cdot r_i)$.

a) Determine the value of D if the radius of the cylinder is 10^{-3} cm and the values of R_i and R_m are as in Exercise 7.9.

b) Compare the value in a) with that of the diffusion coefficient discussed in Chapter 3 for a small molecule that appears to diffuse freely in the cytoplasmic (i.e., does not appear to bind heavily to cytoplasmic constituents). What does this comparison say about the speed of a passive electrical process vs. that of chemical diffusion?

c) The diffusion coefficient of a small molecule in the cytoplasm of a long cylindrically-shaped process does not vary with the radius of the cylinder in which it is diffusing. However, because c_m and r_i both vary with the radius of the cylinder but in different ways, the "electrical diffusion coefficient" (p. 172) does vary with the radius. What value of radius, if any, would give a value for $1/(c_m \cdot r_i)$ that is comparable to that of a chemical diffusion coefficient?

d) Show analytically that, if $V_m(x,t)$ equals the right-hand side of Eqn. 3.1, then: $(\partial^2/\partial x^2) V_m - (1/D) \cdot (\partial/\partial t) V_m = 0$, i.e., the diffusion equation is a solution to the one-dimensional cable equation for the case that r_m is infinite.

CHAPTER 8

THE ACTION POTENTIAL IN NERVE AXONS

Action potentials carry information over short or long distances and initiate important cell processes such as release of a neurotransmitter, contraction of a muscle cell, or secretion of a hormone. The mechanism of the action potential was first revealed in voltage-clamp experiments on giant axons of the squid (Hodgkin and Huxley, 1952a,b,c). The proposed mechanism was confirmed computationally in simulations of the action potential (Hodgkin and Huxley, 1952d). In this chapter we revisit this ground-breaking work. Two *Python* programs are included, one that reconstructs action potentials from Hodgkin and Huxley's theoretical model and another the results of their voltage-clamp experiments.

8.1 A BRIEF SURVEY OF ACTION POTENTIALS

An action potential is a quick rise in membrane potential (V_m), usually of 40 to 120 mVs, followed by a return of V_m close to the value at which it started. Fig. 8.1 illustrates some of the variation in action potential waveforms that is seen in different cell types.

An action potential typically starts from a V_m between -50 and -90 mV. In some cells, the rise in V_m starts from a stable resting potential, while in other cells, such as the rhythm-generating cells of the heart, the action potential starts from an unstable, slowly-rising V_m (a 'pacemaker potential'). In yet other cells, such as secretory cells, V_m may rise to a plateau level from which bursts of action potentials occur. At the peak of the action potential, V_m is usually between -20 and +40 mV. The return of V_m to the negative level also shows variation. In some cells V_m 'overshoots' the resting potential, i.e., pauses briefly at values positive to the resting level, and, in other cells, 'undershoots' the resting potential, i.e., pauses briefly at values negative to the resting level. As is revealed below, these variable features can be explained by the interplay between the properties of the ion channels in the membranes of the various cell types.

An action potential can be a spatially-limited event that involves the entire cell membrane at once, such as occurs in a spherically-shaped endocrine cell or a short oblong-shaped cardiac muscle cell. In these cases, all the cell's surface membrane undergoes the change in membrane potential essentially simultaneously.

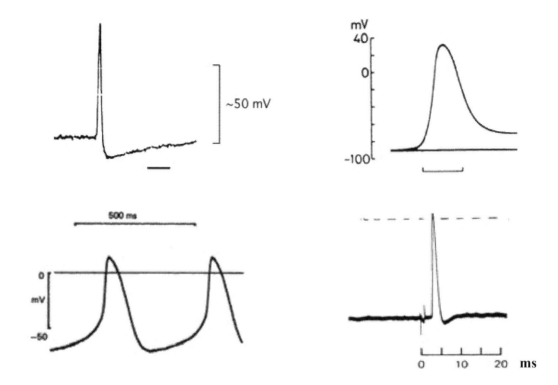

Figure 8.1 Action potentials in different cell types. Upper left: frog posterior pituitary; horizontal calibration bar, 50 ms [Credit: Brian Salzberg, University of Pennsylvania]. Upper right: frog skeletal muscle cell; horizontal calibration bar, ~2 ms. Lower left, sino-atrial cell of the rabbit heart, revealing rhythmicity [Credit: DiFrancesco et al. (1986)]. Lower right: turtle visual cell; dashed line = 0 mV; action potential height ≈ 60 mV [Credit: Baylor and Fettiplace (1979)].

Alternatively, an action potential can be an event that starts in one region of a cell and propagates (i.e., spreads over distance) to other regions of the same cell, as occurs in long cylindrically-shaped cells such as skeletal muscle fibers or in the long axons and dendrites of nerve cells. In these cases, the action potential starts at one location, then passes current electrotonically (see, e.g., Exercise 7.8 in Chapter 7) to raise the potential of a nearby region of the cell membrane to the value of membrane potential at which the action potential mechanism becomes self-sustaining (i.e., to 'threshold'; discussed below); then that active region of the cell membrane, while completing its action potential, passes current to raise the potential of an adjacent region of membrane to threshold, and so forth. By this means the action potential can spread steadily over a long distance with an essentially constant propagation velocity. As noted in Chapter 5, propagating electrical signals represent the fastest type of signaling mechanism available to the organism.

In some cell types, e.g., in the heart, action potential properties can vary substantially with the physiological conditions, such as the initiating stimulus or the hormone level in the blood stream. Experimentally, action potential properties can depend strongly on the temperature and ionic conditions of the solution in which the cell is studied.

8.2 THE ACTION POTENTIAL IN THE SQUID GIANT AXON

The work of Hodgkin and Huxley on nerve axons marks an historic milestone in the study of excitable cells. Squid giant axons were chosen for the experiments because of their large size, which allowed the use of experimental approaches that, at that time, could not easily be applied to other preparations. The success of the work is illustrated in Fig. 8.2.

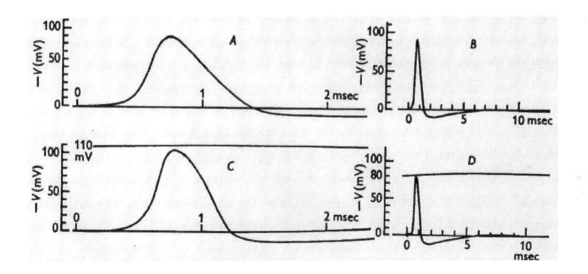

Figure 8.2 Comparison of computed (upper) and measured (lower) propagated action potentials in a squid giant axon at 18.5 °C [Credit: Hodgkin and Huxley (1952d)]. The calibration of the ordinate, -V (mV), refers to the change in V_m with respect to the resting potential, with V_m defined as $V_{out} - V_{in}$. The AP propagation velocity is 18.8 m/s in A and 21.2 m/s in C.

The lower traces show two propagating action potentials measured in a squid axon. The upper traces show a propagated action potential calculated with Hodgkin and Huxley's quantitative model and displayed on the same time scales as the measured action potentials. Good agreement is seen between the measured and calculated action potentials.

8.3 THE VOLTAGE-CLAMP TECHNIQUE APPLIED TO THE SQUID GIANT AXON

Use of the voltage clamp technique in squid axons permitted the first clear conclusions to be drawn about what currents flow across an excitable membrane during an action potential and why. Fig. 8.3 shows a schematic of the apparatus used by Hodgkin and Huxley.

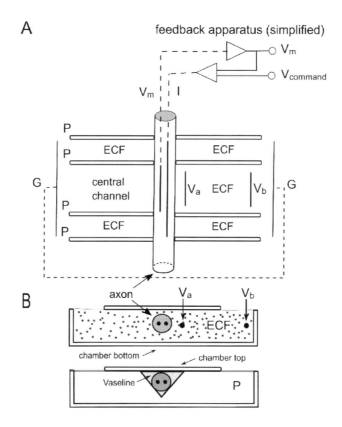

Figure 8.3 Apparatus to study the electrical properties of a squid giant axon (A, top view; B, end view). An axon is placed in an experimental chamber consisting of a flat plastic box with appropriately-spaced plastic partitions P. V-shaped notches in the partitions support the axon (lower B; not to scale) and contain Vaseline seals to ensure that the current that crosses the axon membrane within the central region of the chamber (length, ~7 mm) flows to the ground electrodes G through the ECF along the central channel. The current in the central channel is calculated from the specific resistance of the ECF and the measured potential difference between electrodes V_a and V_b. V_m, the membrane potential of the axon in the central region, is recorded via a silver wire that is uninsulated only in the central region. The V_m wire leads to an electronic feedback circuit that, when in voltage-clamp mode, compares V_m with a 'command' voltage waveform and passes current through the current wire I to force V_m in the central region to follow $V_{command}$.

THE ACTION POTENTIAL IN NERVE AXONS

The first step in the application of the technique was the careful dissection of a squid giant axon away from the mantle muscle to which it is attached. One end of the axon was tied off while the other end was left open so that two long wire electrodes, one for recording V_m and one for passing current, could be inserted into the axon's long core after the axon was mounted in the experimental chamber. These electrodes, as well as the presence of physical barriers (P in Fig. 8.3), which guided the flow of current outside the axon, insured that the internal potential within a long region of the core of the axon was 'isopotential' (i.e., at the same value) and that current flow across this region of membrane could be accurately measured. This arrangement and the associated electronic apparatus allowed the electrical properties of a uniform length of functioning axon membrane to be studied.

The electronic apparatus could be used in one of two modes (see Chapter 7): (i) current-passing mode, in which a specified current waveform could be passed between the internal current wire and the external solution while V_m was measured; (ii) voltage-clamp mode, in which the membrane potential was forced to follow a command voltage waveform selected by the experimentalist, while the membrane current required to do so was measured.

A key advantage of the voltage-clamp technique is that it can disrupt the strong positive feedback loop that normally controls the movement of Na^+ ions across the membrane during an action potential. In this feedback loop, which operates on a millisecond time scale, an increase in V_m causes an increase in Na^+ conductance, which allows increased movement of Na^+ ions across the membrane from outside to inside the cell, thus causing the membrane to depolarize further; this causes a further increase in Na^+ conductance and a further entry of Na^+, etc. By forcing the membrane potential to remain constant, the voltage clamp disrupts the feedback loop, thereby allowing the ion currents and conductance changes that underlie the action potential to be studied.

The measurements of Hodgkin and Huxley were analyzed with the equivalent circuit shown in Fig. 8.4. In this circuit, C_m, as usual, denotes the capacitance of the membrane. The conductances and batteries in the circuit have their usual significance, with the following exception. The arrows through the conductances for potassium ions (G_K) and sodium ions (G_{Na}) indicate that these conductances are variable, unlike the constant conductances in the equivalent circuits discussed in Chapter 7. The variable conductances and their associated batteries (plus for E_{Na}, minus for E_K; see legend) provide the mechanistic basis for how an axon membrane is able to generate action potentials.

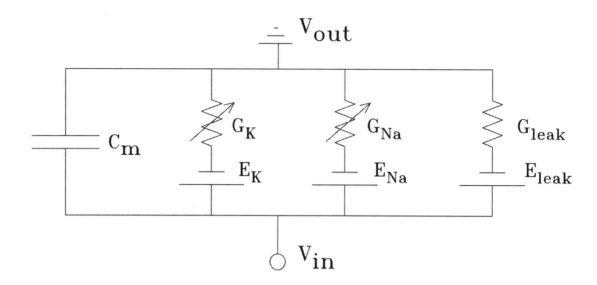

Figure 8.4 Equivalent electrical circuit used in the analysis of Hodgkin and Huxley to describe the electrical properties of the membrane of a squid axon. The approximate values of E_K, E_{Na}, and E_{leak} in the experiments, if expressed according to modern conventions, were -77 mV, +50 mV, and -54 mV, respectively; the value of resting V_m was about -65 mV. In the model, the values of C_m, G_K, G_{Na}, and G_{leak} are referred to 1 cm² of membrane.

Hodgkin and Huxley had strong evidence for the existence of separate pathways for the flow of sodium and potassium currents across the membrane, although they did not know the molecular nature of the conductances. It is now known that the G_K and G_{Na} in Fig. 8.4 represent separate populations of ion channels -- potassium-selective channels and sodium-selective channels, respectively. Both types of channels are gated, and the opening and closing of their gates varies with V_m and time.

G_{leak} and E_{leak} denote a constant conductance and electromotive force, respectively, that contribute a small background current across the membrane and help set the axon's resting V_m. The term 'leak' in this context was chosen because the ion species and its Nernst potential -- or combination of ion species, each with its own Nernst potential -- was not precisely known. It was known, however, that ions are slowly leaking across the axon membrane in the resting state. Thus, G_{leak} and E_{leak} represent the equivalent conductance and battery, respectively, of the unspecified ions that, in combination with a small contribution from the variable conductances G_K and G_{Na} and their batteries, set resting V_m.

8.4 THE MEMBRANE ACTION POTENTIAL

In their work, Hodgkin and Huxley sometimes studied "membrane" action potentials, which allow an experimental simplification. These APs do not propagate over the length of the axon, as occurs normally. Instead, they are generated experimentally by means of an electrical stimulus that is applied uniformly over the length of axon under study, thus avoiding the generation and flow of internal and external currents along the axon length. The lower trace in Fig. 8.5 is an example of a membrane action potential recorded from a squid axon at 20.5 °C. The upper trace shows a computational reconstruction of this action potential at a similar temperature (18.5 °C).

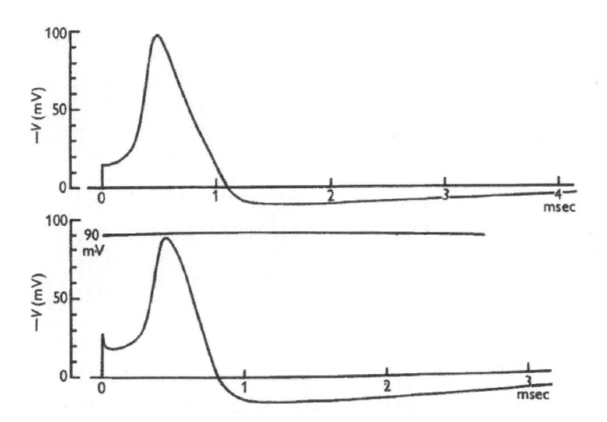

Figure 8.5 A membrane action potential in a squid axon at 20.5 °C (lower) and a computed membrane action potential at 18.5 °C (upper). The stimulus for both action potentials is a brief current pulse that rapidly raises V_m 15-25 mV above the resting potential [Credit: Hodgkin and Huxley (1952d)].

The principal difference between a membrane action potential (Fig. 8.5) and a propagating action potential (Fig. 8.2) is that the membrane action potential occurs simultaneously over a long length of axon membrane, whereas the propagating action potential starts at one end of the axon and moves at a constant speed toward the other. As mentioned, a membrane action potential can by initiated experimentally by passing a brief outward current across a length of axon membrane. If, as shown in Fig. 8.5, the current is of sufficient amplitude to cause V_m to depolarize by 15-25 mV within a small fraction of a ms, an action potential is generated.

The experimental paradigm of using a brief current pulse to stimulate a membrane action potential is a revealing one, as it demonstrates that there is reasonably well-defined 'threshold' value of V_m at which an action potential will be generated. That is, if V_m is raised quickly above the threshold, the value of which can vary somewhat from axon to axon, an action potential with its stereotyped shape occurs, whereas if V_m is raised somewhat but does not reach threshold, no action potential occurs. This phenomenon is referred to as the 'all-or-nothing' property of the action potential. In should be noted, however, that the time taken for the stimulus to raise V_m is also an important variable. The longer the time to raise V_m to the normal threshold, the less likely it is that the action potential will occur. Thus, there is actually no fixed threshold voltage for action potential generation. In fact, if V_m is raised sufficiently slowly, no action potential occurs, no matter how high V_m is raised above the resting level. In general, in a discussion of any voltage-dependent phenomenon related to either the action potential or the gating of the ion channels that underlie the action potential, both the value of V_m and the time required to reach that value are important.

8.5 THE HODGKIN-HUXLEY MODEL

The model of the action potential in a squid axon (Hodgkin and Huxley, 1952d; hereafter, referred to as 'the HH model') is based on the equivalent circuit of Fig. 8.4. At all times, I_m, the membrane current for this circuit, equals $I_C + I_K + I_{Na} + I_{leak}$, and the associated current equations for the 4 limbs of the circuit are:

$$I_c = C_m \cdot dV_m / dt , \qquad (8.1)$$

$$I_K = G_K \cdot (V_m - E_K) , \qquad (8.2)$$

$$(V_m - E_{Na}), \qquad (8.3)$$

$$I_{leak} = G_{leak} \cdot (V_m - E_{leak}). \qquad (8.4)$$

The model assumes that the variable conductances G_K and G_{Na} satisfy:

$$G_K = n^4 \cdot \overline{G}_K \qquad (8.5)$$

$$\text{and } G_{Na} = m^3 \, h \cdot \overline{G}_{Na}. \qquad (8.6)$$

$\overline{G}_K$ and $\overline{G}_{Na}$ are constants (with units of siemens cm^{-2} or msiemens cm^{-2}) that represent the maximal membrane conductance for currents carried by potassium and sodium ions, respectively. The entities n, m, and h are unitless probability variables whose values lie between 0 and 1. These variables, which depend on both voltage and time, are assumed to be independent of one another. Thus, G_K is governed by four n variables that act independently, and G_{Na} is governed by three m variables and one h variable, which also act independently. The closer the product of the probability variables is to 1 in Eqns. 8.5 and 8.6, the closer will be the conductances G_K and G_{Na} to their maxima.

To give the probability variables physical meaning, they can be thought of as charged 'gating particles' in the membrane that move between two states, governed by the value of V_m and their transition rate constants (next paragraph). The exact dependence of n, m, and h on voltage and time is of central importance in the model. Qualitatively, the steady-state values of n and m increase with increasing V_m, whereas the steady-state value of h decreases with increasing V_m. Also, the time-dependence of the variables differs. If V_m should suddenly change, m moves quickly from its present value towards its steady-state value at the new V_m, whereas n and h move more slowly toward their new steady-state values.

The kinetics of the n, m, and h variables are defined by reaction schemes 8.1-8.3. According to these schemes, each of the probability variables can be in one of two states: '1-x' or 'x' (where x = n, m, or h). When in state 1-x, the variable will move to state x according to the rate constant α_x; and, when in state x, the variable will move to state 1-x according to the rate constant β_x. The α_x and β_x (units of ms^{-1}) depend only on voltage.

$$(1-n) \underset{\beta_n}{\overset{\alpha_n}{\rightleftarrows}} n \qquad \text{Scheme 8.1}$$

$$(1-m) \underset{\beta_m}{\overset{\alpha_m}{\rightleftarrows}} m \qquad \text{Scheme 8.2}$$

$$(1-h) \underset{\beta_h}{\overset{\alpha_h}{\rightleftarrows}} h \qquad \text{Scheme 8.3}$$

From these reaction schemes, the equation for the rate of change of x (x = n, m, or h) is:

$$(d/dt)\, x = \alpha_x \cdot (1-x) - \beta_x \cdot x, \qquad (8.7)$$

which can be re-written as:

$$(d/dt)\, x = -(\alpha_x + \beta_x) \cdot x + \alpha_x. \qquad (8.8)$$

At steady-state, when $(d/dt)\, x = 0$:

$$x = \alpha_x / (\alpha_x + \beta_x). \qquad (8.9)$$

The steady-state value of x is usually referred to as 'x_∞' (x-infinity). According to Eqn. 8.8, x moves along an exponential time course, with rate constant $\alpha_x + \beta_x$, towards its steady-state value (see also Exercise 8.1). The associated time constant τ_x (units of ms) is therefore:

$$\tau_x = 1/(\alpha_x + \beta_x). \qquad (8.10)$$

The equations for the α_x and β_x, which are specified in the model for 6.3 °C, are:

$$\alpha_n = 0.01\,(-V_m + V_r + 10)/(\exp((-V_m + V_r + 10)/10) - 1) \qquad (8.11)$$

$$\beta_n = 0.125\,\exp((-V_m + V_r)/80) \qquad (8.12)$$

$$\alpha_m = (-V_m + V_r + 25)/(10\,(\exp((-V_m + V_r + 25)/10) - 1)) \qquad (8.13)$$

$$\beta_m = 4\,\exp((-V_m + V_r)/18) \qquad (8.14)$$

$$\alpha_h = 0.07 \exp((-V_m + V_r)/20) \tag{8.15}$$

$$\beta_h = 1/(\exp((-V_m + V_r + 30)/10) + 1). \tag{8.16}$$

In these equations, V_r denotes the resting potential. The equations have been transcribed from those in the original HH model with two changes:

(i) The voltages are defined according to the modern convention, i.e., with $V_m = V_{in} - V_{out}$. [Hodgkin and Huxley used the reverse convention, as was common at the time.]

(ii) The rate constants are specified with respect to absolute values of V_m under the assumption that V_r is -65 mV. [The equations in the original HH model are given in terms of membrane potential minus the resting potential rather than in absolute membrane-potential units. If referred to the modern convention, E_{Na} was reported to be about +50 mV and also about 115 mV above the resting potential (Hodgkin and Huxley, 1952a,d).]

The upper panels of Figs. 8.6 – 8.8 show plots of the α_x and β_x (x = n, m, or h) as a function of V_m at 6.3 °C, and the lower panels show the steady-state dependence of x on V_m.

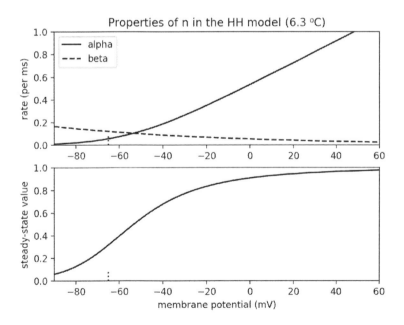

Figure 8.6 V_m-dependence of alpha-n and beta-n at 6.3 °C (upper panel) and n_∞, the steady-state value of n (lower panel).

188   CHAPTER 8

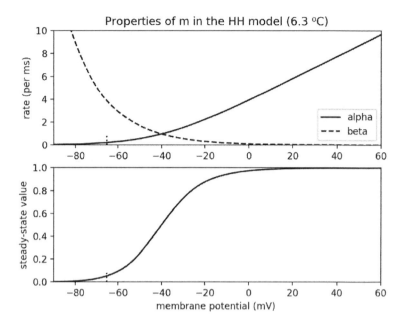

Figure 8.7 V_m-dependence of alpha-m and beta-m at 6.3 °C (upper panel) and m_∞, the steady-state value of m (lower panel).

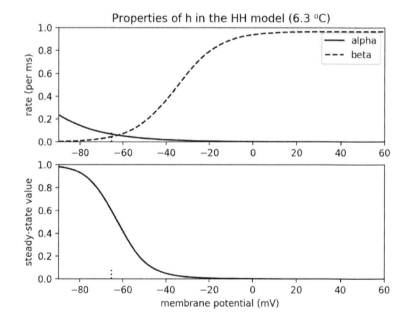

Figure 8.8 V_m-dependence of alpha-h and beta-h at 6.3 °C (upper panel) and h_∞, the steady-state value of h (lower panel).

In each of these plots, the short dotted vertical line at -65 mV on the x-axis marks the value assumed for the resting potential.

Many of the experiments that led to the HH model were carried out on axons bathed in a cold experimental solution, which is the reason the rate constants for the α_x and β_x are given for 6.3 °C. The rate constants at a different temperature T were calculated with a Q_{10} of 3, meaning that, if R(6.3) denotes a rate constant at 6.3 °C and R(T) denotes the corresponding rate constant at T, then $R(T) = R(6.3) \cdot 3^{(T-6.3)/10}$. Thus, R(16.3) is 3 times R(6.3), R(26.3) is 9 times R(6.3), and so forth.

Of special note in Figs. 8.6-8.8 is that the variable h depends on V_m in a manner that is qualitatively different from m (and also from n). Because m increases as V_m increases, m, if acting alone, would cause an increase in G_{Na} when V_m increases. However, because (i) h decreases with increasing V_m and (ii) the rate constants for m are approximately an order of magnitude faster than those for h, the combined effect of m and h on G_{Na} depends strongly on the time course of any change in V_m. Specifically, if V_m were to increase quickly, G_{Na} would increase (due to the quick increase in m) but soon after would decrease (due to the slower decrease in h). Before the effect of h became the dominant one, the increase in m would cause inward Na^+ current to flow due to the increase in G_{Na}; this would cause a further increase in V_m, which would cause more inward Na^+ current due to a further increase in G_{Na} -- and this, in turn, would cause a further increase in V_m, etc. This cycle would thus cause V_m to move quickly toward E_{Na}, thereby generating the rising phase of the action potential.

On a slower time scale, the fall in h would decrease G_{Na} and thus decrease the inward Na^+ current moving V_m toward E_{Na}. This change, coupled with the increase in n that would also take place on the slower time scale, would produce an increasing amount of outward K^+ current that would overtake the decreasing amount of inward Na^+ current. The onset of a net outward current would then drive V_m in the negative direction, generating the falling phase of the action potential.

As V_m returned to negative levels, h would slowly begin to increase again and n would slowly decrease again, while m would quickly move towards its new small steady-state value. Thus, the ability of the membrane to generate another action potential would, after a short delay, be restored.

8.6 SIMULATION OF ACTION POTENTIALS WITH THE HH MODEL

The next *Python* program, HHAP.py, uses the information given in the previous section to simulate a membrane action potential in a squid axon at two temperatures (6.3 °C and 18.5 °C). The program listing is shown next, followed by the plot produced by the program (Fig. 8.9) and the printed output from the program. Appendix F extends the approach used in HHAP.py to the calculation of the more-complicated propagated action potential.

```
1  # -*- coding: utf-8 -*-
2  # Hodgkin-Huxley model for membrane action potential: HHAP.py
3  # Description: calculate and plot two Vm responses to a quick 15 mV depolarization
4  # The basic units of the calculation are voltage in mV, time in ms, distance in cm,
5  # membrane conductance in msiemens/cm^2, and membrane capacitance in uFarad/cm^2
6
7  import numpy as np
8  import matplotlib.pyplot as plt
9  from scipy.integrate import odeint
10
11 #here are the user-defined functions that will be needed
12 def Near_0(x):            #to avoid 0/0 error need to check if x is near zero
13     if np.abs(x)<0.00002: return 1.
14     else: return x/(np.exp(x)-1.)
15
16 def alpha_n(Vm):          #calculate rate constant alpha-n at Vm (per ms)
17     vx=(-Vm+Vr+10.)/10.
18 #    return 0.1*(vx/10)/(np.exp(vx/10)-1.)  #if vx=0 gives an error due to 0/0
19 #other attempts to deal here with the case vx=0 also give an error and stop
20     g=np.vectorize(Near_0)   #this works as expected without error
21     return R_factor*0.1*g(vx)
22
23 def beta_n(Vm):           #calculate rate constant beta-n at Vm (per ms)
24     return R_factor*0.125*np.exp((-Vm+Vr)/80)
25
26 def alpha_m(Vm):          #calculate rate constant alpha-m at Vm (per ms)
27     vx=(-Vm+Vr+25.)/10.
28     g=np.vectorize(Near_0)   #this works as expected without error
```

```
29      return R_factor*g(vx)
30
31  def beta_m(Vm):           #calculate rate constant beta-m at Vm (per ms)
32      return R_factor*4.*np.exp((-Vm+Vr)/18)
33
34  def alpha_h(Vm):          #calculate rate constant alpha-h at Vm (per ms)
35      return R_factor*0.07*np.exp((-Vm+Vr)/20)
36
37  def beta_h(Vm):           #calculate rate constant beta-h at Vm (per ms)
38      return R_factor/(np.exp((-Vm+Vr+30)/10)+1.)
39
40  def n_infinity(Vm):       #calculate steady-state value of n at Vm (unitless)
41      return alpha_n(Vm)/(alpha_n(Vm)+beta_n(Vm))
42
43  def m_infinity(Vm):       #calculate steady-state value of m at Vm (unitless)
44      return alpha_m(Vm)/(alpha_m(Vm)+beta_m(Vm))
45
46  def h_infinity(Vm):       #calculate steady-state value of h at Vm (unitless)
47      return alpha_h(Vm)/(alpha_h(Vm)+beta_h(Vm))
48
49  def rate_factor(T):   #rate adjustment factor if temperature T differs from 6.3 C
50      return(Q10**((T-6.3)/10.))    #HH model uses a Q10 = 3.
51
52  def I_ionic(Vm,n,m,h):    #ionic current, a fct of Vm, n, m, and h (uamps/cm^2)
53      IK=GK_max*n**4*(Vm-EK)        #K current
54      INa=GNa_max*m**3*h*(Vm-ENa)   #Na current
55      Ileak=Gleak*(Vm-Eleak)        #leak current
56      return IK+INa+Ileak
57
58  #set up the initial conditions for Vm, n, m, and h as a function of temperature
59  def Set_conditions(Temp):
60      Vm_init=Vr
61      n_init=n_infinity(Vm_init)
62      m_init=m_infinity(Vm_init)
63      h_init=h_infinity(Vm_init)
64      return [Vm_init,n_init,m_init,h_init]
```

```
65
66  #specify basic constants to use in the calculation
67  Vr=-65.                    #resting membrane potential (mV)
68  ENa=Vr+115.                #ENa is 115 mV above resting Vm (mV)
69  EK=Vr-12.                  #EK is 12 mV below resting Vm (mV)
70  Eleak=Vr+10.613            #Eleak is 10.613 mV above resting Vm (mV)
71  GK_max=36.                 #maximum K conductance (msiemens cm^-2)
72  GNa_max=120.               #maximum Na conductance (msiemens cm^-2)
73  Gleak=0.3                  #leak conductance (msiemens cm^-2)
74  Q10=3.0                    #Q10 value to adjust rates of alphas and betas
75  Cm=1.0                     #membrane capacitance (10^-6 farads cm^-2)
76  #F contains the formulas for dVm, dn, dm, and dh in the call by odeint
77  def F(y,t):                #y is a 4-member list with the initial conditions in its call
78      dy=[0,0,0,0]           #create a list to hold the 4 derivatives of y to be returned
79      dy[0]=(I_stim(t) - I_ionic(y[0],y[1],y[2],y[3]))/Cm   #rate of change of Vm (mV/ms)
80      dy[1]=alpha_n(y[0])*(1-y[1])-beta_n(y[0])*y[1]        #rate of change of n (per ms)
81      dy[2]=alpha_m(y[0])*(1-y[2])-beta_m(y[0])*y[2]        #rate of change of m (per ms)
82      dy[3]=alpha_h(y[0])*(1-y[3])-beta_h(y[0])*y[3]        #rate of change of h (per ms)
83      return dy
84
85  def I_stim(t):             #set up a brief current step to stimulate an AP
86      if t>Stim_time: return 0   #stop the stimulus if time exceeds Stim_time
87      else: return Stim_size
88  #parameters for setting up time grid for the solution (ms)
89  t_start=0;t_end=10;N_steps=10000         #start and end times; N_steps
90  dt=(t_end-t_start)/float(N_steps)        #time increment per step
91  t=np.linspace(t_start,t_end,N_steps+1)   #time grid for solution
92
93  #parameters for shock stimulus; 15 nC per cm^2 will comfortably set off an AP
94  Stim_size=1500.            #stimulus strength (uamps cm^-2)
95  Stim_time=0.01             #stimulus duration (ms)
96
97  #set up an array with 2 x,y point-pairs with which to plot a dotted baseline at Vr
98  rx=np.zeros(2)
99  rx[1]=t_end
100 ry=Vr*np.ones(2)
```

```
101
102  plt.figure()
103  #set temp and initial conditions; then calc and plot first AP
104  Temp=6.3                         #reference temperature in the HH model is 6.3 degrees C
105  R_factor=rate_factor(Temp)       #adjust all rates according to R_factor
106  y_init=Set_conditions(Temp)      #set temperature (degrees C) and initial conditions
107  y=odeint(F,y_init,t)
108  plt.subplot(2,1,1)               #select first plot of two-panel plot
109  yy=y[:,0]                        #select the Vm trace from the solution
110  plt.ylim(-80., 50.)              #set the y-axis limits
111  plt.plot(t,yy,'k')
112  plt.plot(rx,ry,'k:')             #plot the Vm baseline in black dashes
113  plt.ylabel("Vm (mV)")
114  plt.text(8,20,"{:.3} \u1D52C".format(Temp), fontsize=12)    #add temperature label
115  plt.title("Membrane APs simulated with the HH model")
116  #print some info to the console about AP properties
117  print("Temp={:.4}, Vr={:.4}: AP height is {:.4} mV at {:.4} ms where Vm = {:.4} mV"\
118      .format(Temp,Vr,yy[np.argmax(yy)]-Vr,np.argmax(yy)*dt,yy[np.argmax(yy)]))
119  print("   AP undershoot is {:.4} mV below Vr at {:.4} ms where Vm = {:.4} mV"\
120      .format(yy[np.argmin(yy)]-Vr,np.argmin(yy)*dt,yy[np.argmin(yy)]))
121
122  #set temp and initial conditions; then calc and plot second AP
123  Temp=18.5                        #temperature for another AP computed by HH
124  R_factor=rate_factor(Temp)       #adjust all rates according to R_factor
125  y_init=Set_conditions(Temp)      #set temperature (degrees C) and initial conditions
126  y=odeint(F,y_init,t)
127  plt.subplot(2,1,2)               #select second plot of two-panel plot
128  yy=y[:,0]                        #select the Vm trace from the solution
129  plt.ylim(-80., 50.)              #set the y-axis limits
130  plt.plot(t,yy,'k')
131  plt.plot(rx,ry,'k:')             #plot the Vm baseline in black dashes
132  plt.xlabel("time (ms)")
133  plt.ylabel("Vm (mV)")
134  plt.text(8,20,"{:.3} \u1D52C".format(Temp), fontsize=12) #add label for temperature
135  #print some info to the console about AP properties
136  print("Temp={:.4}, Vr={:.4}: AP height is {:.4} mV at {:.4} ms where Vm = {:.4} mV"\
```

137   .format(Temp,Vr,yy[np.argmax(yy)]-Vr,np.argmax(yy)*dt,yy[np.argmax(yy)]))
138 print(" AP undershoot is {:.4} mV below Vr at {:.4} ms where Vm = {:.4} mV"\
139   .format(yy[np.argmin(yy)]-Vr,np.argmin(yy)*dt,yy[np.argmin(yy)]))
140 plt.show()
141 plt.savefig("hhap.png", dpi=200)

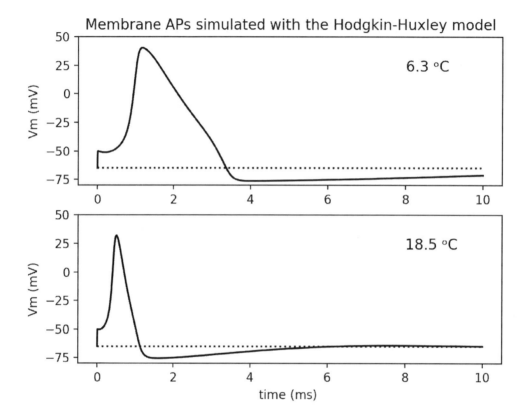

Figure 8.9 Simulated membrane action potentials at two temperatures. As in the original HH model, these action potentials are evoked by a brief current stimulus designed to quickly depolarize the axon by ~15 mV above the resting potential of -65 mV (indicated by the dotted lines).

Temp=6.3, Vr=-65.0: AP height is 105.4 mV at 1.165 ms where Vm = 40.42 mV
  AP undershoot is -11.18 mV below Vr at 4.033 ms where Vm = -76.18 mV
Temp=18.5, Vr=-65.0: AP height is 96.93 mV at 0.496 ms where Vm = 31.93 mV
  AP undershoot is -10.49 mV below Vr at 1.6 ms where Vm = -75.49 mV

The action potentials in Fig. 8.9 and the particular initiating stimulus to generate them were selected to match two of the action potentials calculated by Hodgkin and Huxley (Hodgkin and Huxley, 1952d) The program HHAP.py is easily modified to carry out many other simulated electrical responses of the axon membrane, for example, at other temperatures, with other types of current waveforms to stimulate either one action potential or a train of action potentials, or, indeed, with any other reasonable modification to the variables and parameters in the HH model (see Exercises 8.2 - 8.5 and 8.10 – 8.12).

Program Notes
- The user-defined functions in lines 10-47 specify the rate constants at 6.3 °C for α_x and β_x (x = n, m, and h) and their steady-state values. The function Near_0(x) is used to avoid the possibility of a *Python* error that otherwise could be caused by the functions alpha_n(Vm) and alpha_m(Vm) if they were called with variable Vm exactly equal to 0. The limit for both functions as Vm approaches 0 is 1, which is the value the Near_0 returns if Vm is very small, rather than the undefined error value 0/0 that would otherwise be returned if Vm = 0. This check by Near_0 for Vm = 0 cannot be carried out directly in alpha_n or alpha_m because the latter functions are used in 'vectorization' calls from the main program (i.e., entire arrays of numbers are processed by means of one statement; see Chapters 3 and 4). A straightforward vectorization call would result in a *Python* error if the 'if' statement and its associated logic in Near_0 had been directly incorporated into alpha_n and alpha_m. To circumvent this issue, alpha_n and alpha_m contain the statement 'g = np.vectorize(Near_0)'. This statement allows the vectorization process to proceed seamlessly in the calls to alpha_n and alpha_m because the statement with the logic check for the possibility that Vm = 0 has been moved to Near_0.

- The function 'I_ionic(Vm,n,m,h)' in lines 52-56 is called with arguments Vm and the probability variables n, m, and h. It uses the relations in Eqns. 8.1-8.6 in combination with the parameter values specified in lines 67-75 to calculate the membrane ionic current. I_ionic(Vm,n,m,h) is used by the function odeint (see below) at the series of time points specified on the solution time-point grid.

- The function 'Set_conditions(Temp)' in lines 59-64, where 'Temp' stands for temperature, is used to calculate the initial values of Vm, n, m, and h, which must be set before the call to odeint. Set_conditions makes the assumption that Vm has been at the resting potential for a long time and therefore that the initial values of n, m, and h can be calculated with calls to the functions n_infinity, m_infinity, and h_infinity with Vm = Vm_init (= Vr).

- The constants section of the program (lines 67-75) is straightforward, given that voltages are calculated in mV units and the other units are referred to one cm^2 of axon membrane. This section would normally be put after all user-defined functions but, by placing it where it is, the first 75 lines in this program become identical to the program HHVC.py described in the next section, thus saving space in the listing in the next section.

- The function 'F(y,t)' in lines 77-83 is set up in the usual way for use with the calls to odeint. These calls occur twice -- once in line 107 for the calculation of the action potential at 6.3 °C and once in line 126 for the calculation at 18.5 °C. As discussed in connection with previous programs, odeint can be used to obtain a numerical solution to a system of first-order differential equations if (i) the initial values are specified for the variables in the system and (ii) formulas are given to calculate the rates of change of the variables in terms of the present values of the variables. The initial conditions are set up just before each call to odeint (lines 104-106 for the call at 6.3 °C and lines 123-125 for the call at 18.5 °C). As is usual, F begins by creating the variable 'dy', which, in this case, will be a 4-member list that will hold the formulas to calculate the rates of change of the 4 functions whose simultaneous solutions are sought, namely, Vm, n, m, and h. Line 79 gives the formula for (d/dt)Vm. This formula involves the difference between the stimulating current (I_Stim(t); lines 85-87) and the membrane ionic current. The formula mimics that given in Eqn. 7.1 of Chapter 7 (and is explained in connection with line 17 in Example7_1.py), although, in the case of HHAP.py, the calculations are referred to one cm^2 of membrane.

- The function 'I_Stim(t)' (lines 85-87) defines the waveform that is used to stimulate the axon, i.e., the simulated current that crosses the axon membrane to change Vm.

- Lines 89-91 specify the time grid (denoted 't') on which the values of Vm, n, m, and h are to be calculated. In this program, the calls to odeint do not require use of the 'hmax' keyword argument (discussed in Chapter 6), as the accuracy of the numerical solution for the HH model is high with the specified time grid and the standard step size used by odeint.

- Lines 94-95 set the current strength to be used in I_stim. In this case, a total of 15 nC of charge per cm^2 of membrane is added to the membrane capacitance in a small fraction of a ms. This is the same stimulus used by Hodgkin and Huxley in several of their simulations, including a membrane action potential at 6.3 °C and another at 18.5 °C (Hodgkin and Huxley, 1952d). The upper trace in Fig. 8.4 shows the one at 18.5 °C.

- Lines 98-100 are used to define an array of two x,y point-pairs, which is used to draw a dotted baseline on the action-potential plots at the value of Vm equal to the resting potential.

- The only other plotting feature not seen in previous programs is the use of the 'plt.text' function (lines 114 and 134). This function allows printing text on plots at a location that can be specified in coordinate units of the plot. To make the printed temperature on the plot look acceptable, a superscript 'o' character, set by the 'Unicode' value of u1D52 (which is flagged as being Unicode by the leading 'u'), is printed after the numerical value of the temperature but before the letter 'C'.

Physiological Conclusions from the Action Potential Simulations
Hodgkin and Huxley developed their model based on several types of experiments. The most important of these were their extensive voltage-clamp experiments. By using a variety of voltage-command protocols and by changing the ionic composition of the external solution, which changed the value of E_K or E_{Na} (see Exercises 8.8 and 8.9), they were able to estimate the Na^+ and K^+ currents separately and determine the time- and voltage-dependence of the Na^+ and K^+ conductances individually. The work left no doubt that the mechanism of the action potential is explained by the two variable conductances, one selective for Na^+ and one selective for K^+, which behave independently of one another except through their common dependence on membrane potential and time.

Some of the details of the HH model are now known to be false -- for example, the idea that the h variable (also called the sodium 'inactivation' variable) behaves independently of the m variable (also called the sodium 'activation' variable). Nevertheless, the following ideas as specified in the model and the circuit diagram in Fig. 8.4 are now accepted fact: (i) the presence of two different conductances in the membrane, one for G_{Na} and one for G_K, controlled by voltage and time, (ii) the approximate kinetic and steady-state description of how G_{Na} and G_K depend on voltage and time, (iii) the central importance of an inactivation process for G_{Na}, and (iv) the combined effects of an electrical equivalent circuit involving membrane capacitance, membrane conductance, ion batteries, and membrane current in determining the amplitude and time course of V_m.

More-recent studies -- physiological, biochemical, structural, and genetic -- have revealed much about the voltage-dependent Na^+ and K^+ channels in axons and other excitable membranes (see also Chapter 10). Remarkably, the gating variables for G_{Na} and G_K in the HH model have found structural counterparts. The Na^+ and K^+ channels are now known to have either 4 sub-units or 4 homologous domains, each with a mobile chain of positively-charged amino acids. K^+ channels have 4 identical sub-units, coded by the same gene. Na^+ channels, in contrast, have 4 homologous domains (akin to 4 distinct sub-units) in one large protein, coded by a gene that is approximately four times the size of the K^+-channel gene. Numerous ongoing studies are exploring the structure-function relations in these proteins and in other closely-related ion channels, such as voltage-dependent Ca^{2+} channels.

8.7 SIMULATION OF VOLTAGE-CLAMP EXPERIMENTS WITH THE HH MODEL

We next consider the *Python* program HHVC.py, which simulates the membrane currents that, according to the HH model, would be measured on a squid axon in response to a user-specified voltage-clamp protocol. Since (i) experimentally, the details of the HH model were based on voltage-clamp experiments, and (ii) computationally, the HH model successfully simulates the action potential responses of the axon, it can be expected that this program can satisfactorily simulate the voltage-clamp experiments on squid axon membranes that led to the understanding of the action potential.

The program listing for HHVC.py, which uses a +55 mV voltage step from the resting potential at 6.3 °C, is given next, after which the plot produced by the program is shown (Fig. 8.10). Because the first 75 lines of the listing are identical to those in HHAP.py above, the listing begins with line 76.

```
76  #define a voltage waveform (mV) for Vm to imitate as a function of time
77  def Vm_Command(E,V_step,t):
78      Vc=E        #command value is E unless time t is between V_start and V_end
79      if t >= V_start and t < V_end:
80          Vc=E+V_step
81  #   if t>=V_end:return E-2*V_step  #uncommenting this line is a way to change the result
82      return Vc                      #return the scalar value of the command voltage
83
84  def Vm_Error(i):                   #voltage error: Vcommand minus Vm (both indexed by i)
85      return Vm_Command(Vr,V_step,t[i]) - Vm[i]    #return is a scalar (mV)
```

```
86
87  V_step=55.                         #size of command voltage step (mV)
88  V_start, V_end = 10., 30.          #time range during which V_step is "on" (ms)
89  Error=1e-2                         #maximum allowed error between Vm_Command and Vm (mV)
90  Gain=0.225                         #factor with which to temper the needed adjustment to Im
91  #if Gain>1.0, the waveforms show instability
92
93  t_start=0.; t_end=50.; N_steps=int(1e4)     #set the arguments for linspace()
94  t=np.linspace(t_start, t_end, N_steps+1)    #t is the grid of time points (ms)
95  dt=(t_end-t_start)/N_steps                  #dt is the step size for the time-point grid (ms)
96
97  Im=0.*t                            #initialize the Im waveform to zero (uamps per cm^2)
98  Vm=Im+Vr                           #initialize the V waveform to Vr (mV)
99
100 Temp=6.3                           #reference temperature in the HH model is 6.3 degrees C
101 R_factor=rate_factor(Temp)         #adjust all rates according to R_factor
102 y_init=Set_conditions(Temp)        #set temperature (degrees C) and initial conditions
103
104 #start n, m, and h at their steady-state values for Vr
105 n0=y_init[1];m0=y_init[2];h0=y_init[3]
106 n=0.*t+y_init[1]
107 m=0.*t+y_init[2]
108 h=0.*t+y_init[3]
109
110 #Calculate the change to Im needed to get the next Vm to move close to Vm_Command.
111 #Im and Vm cannot move in absolute synchrony (since they are defined on a grid of
112 #points separated by dt), so calculate Im[i] based partly on what Vm[i+1] will be.
113 for i in range(0,N_steps):
114     dIm=0.                         #dIm is the amount by which we need to charge the capacitor
115     dVm=0.                         #dVm is the amount by which Vm[i+1] will change due to the dIm
116     dE = Vm_Error(i)               #dE is the error in voltage at time t[i]
117     if abs(dE) > Error:            #if error is larger than allowed error, do something
118         dIm = Gain*Cm*dE/dt        #capacitor current (uamps/cm^2); add to Im to change Vm
119         dVm = Gain*dE              #and Vm will change by this amount due to dIm
120     Vm[i+1] = Vm[i] + dVm          #attribute the effect of dIm on Vm to Vm[i+1]
```

```python
121 #we must also add to Im[i] the ionic current required for Vm, which we estimate
122 #  as the average of that to maintain Vm[i] and Vm[i+1]
123     n[i+1]=n[i]+dt*(alpha_n(Vm[i])*(1-n[i])-beta_n(Vm[i])*n[i]) #n+(dn/dt)
124     m[i+1]=m[i]+dt*(alpha_m(Vm[i])*(1-m[i])-beta_m(Vm[i])*m[i]) #n+(dm/dt)
125     h[i+1]=h[i]+dt*(alpha_h(Vm[i])*(1-h[i])-beta_h(Vm[i])*h[i]) #n+(dh/dt)
126     Im[i] = dIm + (I_ionic(Vm[i],n[i],m[i],h[i]) + \
127            I_ionic(Vm[i+1],n[i+1],m[i+1],h[i+1]))/2.      #uamps/cm^2
128     if i==(N_steps-1): Im[i+1]=Im[i]                #need to account for last value of Im
129
130 #set up an array with 2 x,y point-pairs with which to plot a  dotted baselines
131 rx=np.zeros(2)
132 rx[1]=t_end
133 ry=Vr*np.ones(2)
134
135 #plot the result as two sub-plots -- upper for Vm, lower for Im
136 plt.figure()
137 plt.subplot(2,1,1)                          #do the upper plot first
138 plt.plot(t, Vm, 'k', linewidth=2, label="Vm")    #show Vm in mV
139 plt.ylim(-100.,40.)
140 plt.plot(rx,ry,'k:')                        # dotted baseline in upper panel
141 plt.ylabel('Vm(t) (mV)')
142 plt.title("Vm and Im during a voltage step in a circuit with R, C, and E")
143 plt.subplot(2,1,2)                          #do the lower plot second
144 plt.plot(t, 1e-3*Im, 'k', linewidth=2, label="Im") #show Im in mamps/cm^2
145 ry=1e-3*Im[0]*np.ones(2)
146 plt.plot(rx,ry,'k:')                        # dotted baseline in lower panel
147 plt.ylim(-2.8,2.8)                          #y-axis in uAmps
148 plt.xlabel('time (ms)')
149 plt.ylabel('Im(t) (mamps/cm^2)')
150 plt.savefig("hhvc.png", dpi=200)
151 plt.show()
```

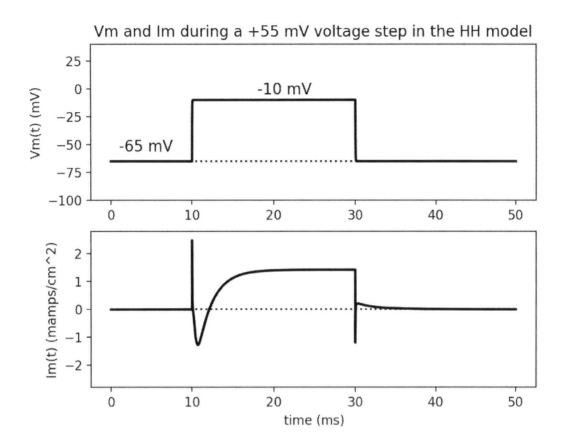

Figure 8.10 Simulation of a voltage-clamp experiment in a squid axon with the HH model. Membrane current (lower) is shown in response to step in voltage (upper) from a resting potential of -65 mV to -10 mV for 20 ms (6.3 °C).

Program Notes
- Lines 77-90 set up the user-defined functions and constants that specify the functions with which to calculate the voltage-command waveform and the "error signal", as described previously in connection with Example7_2.py in Chapter 7.

- Lines 93-108 define the time grid on which the current and voltage waveforms will be calculated and set the initial conditions that correspond to the selected temperature (= 6.3 °C).

- The 'for' loop in lines 113-128 does the main work of the program. The logic follows that in Example7_2.py of Chapter 7 except, here, the calculation of the membrane current is also accompanied by calculation of the probability variables n, m, and h on the solution time-point grid.

Physiological Interpretation of the Current Waveform, Im(t), in Fig. 8.10

The current trace in the simulated voltage-clamp experiment of Fig. 8.10 reveals 5 distinct phases. Qualitatively, these are:

1) At 10 ms, there is a large surge of outward capacitive current. This supplies the charge required to change V_m within a small fraction of a ms to the command voltage level of -10 mV (= 55 mV above the resting potential), which is approximately midway between E_K (= -77 mV) and E_{Na} (= +50 mV) and also midway between the positive and negative voltage extremes of the action potential. Thus, both the active sodium and potassium currents are expected to be visible at later times in the trace and perhaps to be of roughly similar peak amplitudes (but of opposite sign).

2) Very soon after completion of the capacitive transient, a large inward ionic current flows across the membrane, which reaches a negative peak of more than 1 mamp cm^{-2} at about 1.8 ms after the voltage step to -10 mV. This inward current, which is carried by Na$^+$, results from the increase in the m variable that controls G_{Na}. This increase happens quickly in response to the increase in V_m; in contrast, h (the inactivation variable that controls G_{Na}), which has a relatively high value at the resting potential (~0.6), moves more slowly towards a new steady-state value close to zero. Thus, for at least a brief time, G_{Na} increases (Eqn. 8.6) and so does I_{Na}.

3) The inward Na$^+$ current is then overtaken by an outward K$^+$ current, which grows to more than 1 mamp cm^{-2}. This change occurs for two reasons: (i) the declining value of h in response to the rise in V_m causes G_{Na} to decline/inactivate and thus I_{Na} to decrease, and (ii) the steady increase in the value of n, whose steady-state value at -10 mV is almost 0.9 (see lower panel of Fig. 8.6), causes a large increase in G_K and thus I_K.

4) At 30 ms, a large inward capacitive transient occurs, which supplies the charge required to change V_m within a small fraction of a ms back to the command voltage level of -65 mV (= V_r). This transient is analogous to that of the initial capacitive transient but of opposite sign.

5) From 30 to 40 ms, a declining "tail" of potassium current is observed as the K$^+$ conductance that was activated during the voltage-step to -10 mV returns back to a low level. This time-dependent change is due to the decrease in n in response to the more negative value of V_m. The fact that the amplitude of I_K immediately after the negative step in V_m back to -65 mV is much smaller than that immediately before the step (when V_m = -10 mV) is due to the sudden change in driving force on K$^+$ ions (= $V_m - E_K$, which is equal to 67 mV before the step and 12 mV after the step).

Fig. 8.11 shows a separation of the membrane current trace in Fig. 8.10 into its component parts.

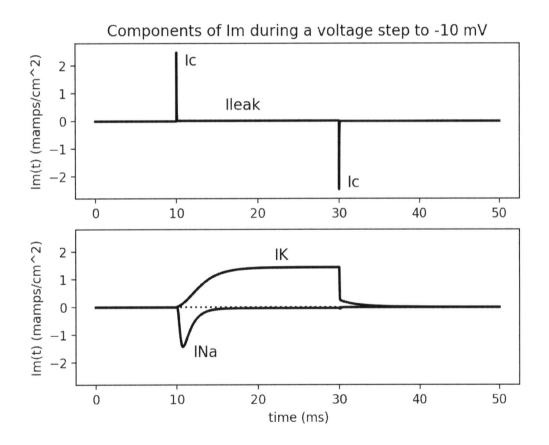

Figure 8.11 Components of the Im(t) trace in the calculation in Figure 8.10 (ΔV_m = +55 mV; 6.3 °C). Upper panel, linear components; lower panel, non-linear components.

The upper part of Fig. 8.11 shows the "linear" components of the current, namely, the current I_C through the left-most limb of the circuit in Fig. 8.4 and the small steady current I_{leak} (barely-discernible) through the right-most limb of the circuit. Because the values of C_m, G_{leak}, and E_{leak} are constants, these currents scale in proportion to either the change in V_m (in the case of I_C) or the change in $V_m - E_{leak}$ (in the case of I_{leak}).

The lower part of Fig. 8.11 shows the "non-linear" components of the total membrane current, i.e., I_{Na} and I_K. The properties of these traces confirm the qualitative conclusions stated in the preceding paragraph about I_{Na} and I_K.

There are several ways to make minor modifications to HHVC.py to obtain the plots in Fig. 8.11. These plots were obtained as follows by use of the np.load() and np.save() functions (which allow loading and saving np arrays from and to the disc):

- To obtain the I_C and I_{leak} trace, HHVC was re-run with GK_max and GNa_max set to 0. The statement "np.save('HHVC_Ilinear.npy',Im)" was then used to save the resulting Im trace to disk. This makes the trace available for later use, including for the plot in the upper panel of Fig. 8.11.

- To obtain the I_{Na} trace, HHVC was re-run with GNa_max at its normal value and with GK_max set to 0. The I_C and I_{leak} trace previously saved in the file 'HHVC_Ilinear.npy' was loaded into memory with the statement "Ilinear=np.load('HHVC_Ilinear.npy')", and Ilinear was subtracted from Im to yield I_{Na}.

- To obtain the I_K trace, the procedure to obtain the I_{Na} trace was followed except that HHVC was re-run with GK_max at is normal value and with GNa_max set to 0.

With such modifications to HHVC.py, it is easy to calculate the individual components of the membrane current in a simulated voltage-clamp experiment with the HH model.

The More Important Issue
How did Hodgkin and Huxley extract the components of I_{Na} and I_K from their measured I_m traces? After all, it was the good estimates of I_{Na} and I_K -- and also of I_C and I_{leak} -- obtained in their voltage-clamp experiments that allowed Hodgkin and Huxley to take the inductive step from their experimental data to their successful model.

To examine this question, Exercises 8.8 and 8.9 ask the reader to modify HHVC by altering E_{Na}, which simulates one of the approaches used by Hodgkin and Huxley to estimate the individual I_{Na} and I_K components of the measured I_m traces in a voltage-clamp experiment.

8.8 VOLTAGE-DEPENDENCE OF GNa AND GK

As noted in Section 8.5, each of the gating variables n, m, and h in the Hodgkin-Huxley model can be thought of as a charged particle located physically within the membrane that moves between two states according to the transition rate constants α_x and β_x (x = n, m, and h), which are set by the value of V_m. A property of both G_{Na} (proportional to m^3h) and G_K (proportional to n^4) is the remarkable 'steepness' of their voltage dependence, meaning that a relatively small increase in V_m can cause a substantial increase in conductance. One way to quantify this steepness is to plot the conductance on a logarithmic scale vs. membrane potential and determine the steepest slope of the relation. For a conductance that increases with increasing values of V_m, as is the case for G_{Na} if measured early after a step increase in V_m and for G_K if measured later after a step increase in V_m, the steepest slope in such a plot occurs at negative values of membrane potential. It is customary to express this steepest slope (also called the 'limiting slope' or 'limiting steepness') as the number of mVs required for the conductance to change e-fold in value. In the measurements of Hodgkin and Huxley, the limiting steepness for G_{Na} corresponds to an e-fold change for ~4 mV and that for G_K to an e-fold change for ~5 mV (Figs. 9 and 10 of Hodgkin and Huxley, 1952a). In the HH model itself, the limiting slopes are somewhat steeper, with an e-fold change for ~2.2 mV for G_{Na} and ~2.3 mV for G_K (see Exercise 8.13).

For a simple ion channel gated by a particle with one electronic charge that moves across the full membrane electrical field in response to a change in V_m, the expected limiting steepness of the conductance vs. voltage relation at 6.3 °C is e-fold for 24 mV (see Exercise 8.14). If gating is controlled by the movement of two such charges, the expected limiting steepness is e-fold for 12 mV (=24 mV/2), and so forth. For G_{Na} and G_K in a squid axon, the limiting-steepness measurements of Hodgkin and Huxley (1952a) imply that multiple gating charges control these conductances. The calculated number of charges is ~6 for G_{Na} (= 24/4) and ~4.8 for G_K (= 24/5); in the HH model, the corresponding values are ~10.9 (= 24/2.2) and ~10.4 (= 24/2.3), respectively. More recently, limiting-steepness measurements have been made for a voltage-dependent potassium channel from mammalian cardiac muscle and give an estimate of 6.4 for the number of gating charges (Zhang et al., 2004). In work on cloned voltage-dependent channels from flies and mammals, experimental measurement of 'gating currents' (a type of measurement that differs from the measurements of the limiting steepness of the conductance; see next section) gives estimates of 10 to 14 charges for potassium channels (Schoppa et al., 1992; Ishida et al., 2015; Aggarwal and MacKinnon, 1996; Noceti et al., 1996, Islas and Sigworth, 1999) and 12 for sodium channels (Hirschberg et al., 1995). All of this work implies that a substantial number of gating charges controls the voltage-dependent conductances that underlie action potentials in excitable membranes (see also Chapter 10).

8.9 FIRST MEASUREMENTS OF CHANNEL GATING CURRENTS IN SQUID AXONS

In 1973, a major experimental step forward was taken in elucidating the mechanism of gating of voltage-dependent ion channels (Armstrong and Bezanilla, 1973). The goal of these experiments was to measure the charges that move within the cell membrane and control the opening and closing of the voltage-dependent Na^+ channels. To do so, squid axons were studied with a voltage-clamp technique that was similar to that used by Hodgkin and Huxley but linked to a computer data-taking system with data-processing and signal-averaging capabilities. The axons were exposed to two pharmacological agents, tetrodotoxin and cesium ions (Cs^+), which, respectively, block the large Na^+ and K^+ currents that normally occur with voltage-clamp steps into the voltage range where G_{Na} and G_K are activated. The remaining currents that were measured were corrected by subtraction for the presence of the linear components of the currents (i.e., the capacitive and leakage currents; Section 8.7 and Fig. 8.11), which occur in response to voltage-clamp steps involving any voltage range. After the subtraction, small non-linear currents remained that moved outward on depolarization and inward on repolarization. The currents had the properties expected, including their approximate time- and voltage-dependence, to be movement of charges within the membrane controlling activation and deactivation of G_{Na}. The interpretation of Armstrong and Bezanilla -- that these currents do, in fact, monitor the movement of such charges -- has been confirmed in many subsequent studies.

An example of Na^+ channel gating currents recorded in the experiments of Armstrong and Bezanilla is shown in Fig. 8.12. Five superimposed current traces are shown, all recorded in response to a voltage-clamp step (not shown) from -70 mV to +50 mV and back to -70 mV. The duration of the steps to +50 mV varied between 0.3 and 5 ms (see labels in Fig. 8.12). The outward current that was observed during each positive voltage step was similar in all traces up to the time point at which the negative voltage step was initiated. For very brief step durations (≤ 0.3 ms), the total charge that moved -- i.e., the absolute value of the integrated time course of the current -- was approximately the same during depolarization and repolarization. This result would be expected if the currents were due to charges confined to the membrane that moved reversibly in response to changes in the electric field.

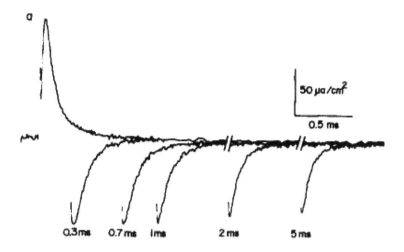

Figure 8.12 Gating currents measured in squid axons in response to voltage-clamp steps from -70 to +50 mV of various durations and back to -70 mV (8 °C). Currents during positive voltage-clamp steps are outward and those during negative steps are inward. The vertical calibration bar is 50 µamps per cm^2 of axon membrane. The two pairs of slanted lines mark time breaks in the plotted records. [Credit: Armstrong and Bezanilla (1977).]

As the duration of the step was increased beyond 0.3 ms, however, the total charge that was detected with repolarization became progressively smaller than that detected with depolarization. Armstrong and Bezanilla concluded that some of the gating charges that control Na^+ channel activation become 'immobilized' as a function of time in response to depolarization. Importantly, (i) the time course of charge immobilization was very similar to that of Na^+ channel inactivation, and (ii) no component of gating current was detected that itself had the time course of inactivation, in contrast to that which would have been expected from the HH model. These results are therefore not consistent with the HH model, which assumes that the inactivation process is independent of the activation process. The detection of charge immobilization was one of the first experimental findings that indicated that the HH model cannot be fully correct -- indeed, that Na^+ channel inactivation is not independent of activation but, rather, linked to it, a conclusion that has now been well established by a variety of experiments.

For additional information on the measurement and interpretation of gating currents in voltage-dependent ion channels, the reader is referred to the review by Bezanilla (2018). For additional information on inactivation in voltage-dependent ion channels, the reader is referred to the review by Armstrong and Hollingworth (2017).

8.10 EXERCISES

Exercise 8.1 Eqns. 8.9 and 8.10 apply to a probability variable x that satisfies the equation: $(d/dt) x = - (\alpha_x + \beta_x) \cdot x + \alpha_x$, where α_x and β_x are rate constants that depend on V_m. The text stated that the movement of x towards its steady state value of $\alpha_x / (\alpha_x + \beta_x)$ follows an exponential time course with a time constant τ_x equal to $1 / (\alpha_x + \beta_x)$.

a) Confirm this statement analytically. Alternatively, write a *Python* program to confirm this statement in a calculation and a plot. For the latter approach, it may be of help to use the function odeint from the scipy library.

b) Suppose V_m is at a steady-state value V_0 and, at t = 0, V_m suddenly changes to a new steady-state value V_1. Let x_0 denote the initial steady-state value of x and x_1 the final steady-state value. True or False: $x(t) = x_1 + (x_0 - x_1) \cdot \exp(-t/\tau_x)$.

c) Use *Python* to make a plot of the time constants τ_n, τ_m, and τ_h as a function of membrane potential. Compare the shapes and amplitudes of the three curves and note in what range of membrane potentials the time constants have their largest values.

Exercise 8.2 Choose one of the APs calculated with HHAP.py in Fig. 8.9 and plot the time course of the variables n, m, h and n^4 and m^3h. Do these time courses look qualitatively as you expect? For example, does the difference in the time courses of n and n^4 make sense?

Exercise 8.3 Again, choose one of the APs calculated with HHAP.py in Fig. 8.9 and this time plot the time course of the 3 ionic currents during the AP: INa, IK, and Ileak. Do these time courses look qualitatively as you expect? What is the explanation for INa having two negative peaks? (Hint: recall that ionic current depends on two factors: conductance and driving force.)

Exercise 8.4 Modify the stimulus in HHAP.py with the statements: 't_end=100.', 'Stim_size = 8.0' and 'Stim_time=t_end' and see how the model's response differs from the original stimulus. Can you explain this response?

Exercise 8.5 Modify the stimulus in HHAP.py with the statements: 't_end=100.', 'Stim_size = -2000.', and 'Stim_time=0.01' and see how the model responds. Can you explain this somewhat surprising result? (Note: to understand this phenomenon, which is called 'anode break excitation', examine how the stimulus affects the n, m, and h variables in the time period before the generation of the action potential, and recall that the kinetics of m is substantially faster than the kinetics of n and h.)

Exercise 8.6 Use HHVC.py in Section 8.7 to examine the time course of the variables n, m, h, n^4 and m^3h in response to a 20 ms voltage-clamp step to -10 mV. To plot these variables, begin by adding the statement 'plt.figure()' after line 151. This will open a new figure window in which you can plot these time courses using the appropriate 'plt.plot()' command. Explain the difference in time courses, including the difference between the time course of n and n^4.

Exercise 8.7 Fig. 8.11 shows a decomposition of the current record in Fig. 8.10 into the currents through the 4 limbs of the circuit in Fig. 8.4. Modify the program HHAP.py to make a plot of the 3 ionic components of membrane current (Na, K, and leak) during a simulated action potential at 6.3 °C. Note that the approach used in Fig. 8.11 to obtain the current components in the voltage-clamp simulation of Fig. 8.10 cannot be used for this exercise, so another approach must be used.

Exercise 8.8 This exercise concerns what experimental method would be helpful to separate ionic current traces of the type shown in Fig. 8.10 into the individual contributions of I_{Na} and I_K. Unfortunately, Hodgkin and Huxley did not have available specific blockers of the sodium conductance or the potassium conduction to help them do this. The concentration of Na^+ in 'artificial seawater' (the name for the standard external solution used in the experiments of Hodgkin and Huxley) was approximately 460 mM, and E_{Na} in the axons under study was approximately +50 mV. At 6.3 °C, 2.303·RT/F (see Eqn. 5.2 in Chapter 5) is approximately 55 mV. Suppose that some of the Na^+ in artificial seawater is replaced with choline (an impermeant univalent positive ion) such that E_{Na} in this sodium-choline-seawater solution is changed to -10 mV.

a) Calculate the sodium concentration in this solution to give E_{Na} = -10 mV.

b) Change E_{Na} in HHVC.py to -10 mV and re-run HHVC.py with a voltage-clamp step to -10 mV. How do you expect Im(t) to change and how has it changed? Does having this new Im(t) trace available help to separate the contributions of $I_{Na}(t)$ and I_K (t) to the Im(t) trace in Fig. 8.10?

c) With E_{Na} in HHVC.py at -10 mV, re-run HHVC.py with a voltage step to +20 mV instead of -10 mV. Explain how $I_m(t)$ has changed and why.

d) Can you think of a way that the linear components of $I_m(t)$ (i.e., that due to I_c and I_{leak}) might be obtained once and then manipulated in some way to remove the linear components in any $I_m(t)$ waveform obtained in a voltage-clamp experiment? Test your idea with HHVC.py using several different voltage-clamp protocols.

Exercise 8.9 This exercise concerns experimental methods to learn more about how the h variable controls G_{Na} in the HH model. Repeat part c) of Exercise 8.8 but, instead of one voltage-clamp step, change HHVC.py so that it can generate two voltage-clamp steps. Let the first step change V_m to -80 mV for 15 ms and let the second step change V_m to -10 mV for 20 ms before V_m is returned to -65 mV. Explain how $I_m(t)$ has changed and why.

Exercise 8.10 Modify HHAP.py so that the stimulating current consists of two pulses, each like the brief pulse in HHAP.py, and let the time between the pulses, Δt, be a variable. How long does Δt have to be before the second plus is able to set off an action potential?

Exercise 8.11 Modify HHAP.py so that the stimulating current is a slowly increasing positive current. Can you confirm the statement in the text that, if V_m is raised sufficiently slowly, no action potential occurs, no matter how high V_m is raised?

Exercise 8.12 This exercise concerns the innate tendency of an excitable membrane to generate repetitive activity. Run HHAP.py with the following changes:
- reduce GK_max from 36. to 13.;
- reduce Gleak from 0.3 to 0.03;
- increase t_end from 10. to at least 200.;
- reduce Stim_size from 1500. to 0.

Do you expect an action potential to occur? Can you explain why there is a difference between what happens at 6.3 °C vs. 18.5 °C?

Exercise 8.13 In the HH model, the limiting steepness of the relation between the probability variable n and V_m can be determined as the limiting slope of a plot of $\ln(n_\infty)$ vs. V_m at negative values of V_m. The limiting steepness of the relation between G_K (which is proportional to n^4) is then the limiting steepness for n_∞ divided by 4. Write a *Python* program that plots $\ln(n_\infty)$ vs. V_m and use this plot to determine the limiting steepness of the

n_∞ vs. V_m relation. Does this confirm the statement in the text that the limiting steepness for G_K is e-fold for ~2.3 mV? Alternatively, write a *Python* program that plots $\ln((n_\infty)^4)$ vs. V_m and use this plot to determine directly the limiting steepness of the G_K vs. V_m relation.

Exercise 8.14 The text states that, for a voltage-dependent conductance that is controlled by a gating particle with one electronic charge that moves from one side of the membrane electrical field to the other in response to a change in V_m, the expected limiting steepness of the conductance-voltage relation at 6.3 °C is e-fold for 24 mV. This can be understood as follows. The Boltzmann distribution of statistical mechanics states that the equilibrium probability of finding a particle in state 2 (probability P_2) vs. state 1 (probability P_1) is related to the energy difference between the two states, $\Delta E = E_2 - E_1$, according to:

$$P_2/P_1 = \exp(-\Delta E/kT), \qquad (8.17)$$

where k is the Boltzmann constant and T is the Kelvin temperature. If the energy units are given for a mole of such charges, k is replaced by R (the gas constant).

Consider a charged particle of valence +1 that can move across the membrane electrical field between the inside (state 2) and outside (state 1) of a membrane whose potential is $V_m = V_2 - V_1$. Then, per mole of such charges, ΔE between the two states is equal to $F \cdot V_m$. At 6.3 °C and with V_m expressed in mVs, Eqn. 8.17, after substitution, becomes:

$$P_2/P_1 = \exp(-V_m/(RT/F)) = \exp(-V_m/24). \qquad (8.18)$$

Since $P_1 + P_2 = 1$, substitution and rearrangement yields:

$$P_1 = 1/(1 + \exp(-V_m/24)). \qquad (8.19)$$

a) Determine analytically whether the limiting steepness for P_1 in Eqn. 8.19 is e-fold for 24 mV. Alternatively, adapt your *Python* program of Ex. 8.13 to use Eqn. 8.19 to plot $\ln(P1)$ vs. V_m and determine the limiting steepness of this curve at negative V_m.

b) Write a *Python* program that uses Eqn. 8.19 to plot P_1 vs. V_m. What is the steepest value of the slope on this curve and at what value of V_m does it occur? Alternatively, determine the steepest slope of Eqn. 8.19 analytically and determine at what value of V_m this occurs.

Note 1: The equilibrium distribution of a hypothetical gating charge that moves between the inside and the outside of the membrane might be affected by energy terms other than V_m, for example, terms due to chemical interactions with other membrane constituents that are in the vicinity of the charge. To account empirically for such energy terms, Eqn. 8.19 can be rewritten with an extra parameter V' that expresses the combined effect of such energy terms in units of voltage:

$$P_1 = 1/(1 + \exp(-(V_m - V')/24)) \,. \tag{8.20}$$

In Eqn. 8.19, the value of V_m at which half the particles are in state 1 and half in state 2 is 0 mV; in Eqn. 8.20, this value is offset to V'. Note that the Hodgkin and Huxley equations for the α_x and β_x (x = n, m, and h; Eqns. 8.11 – 8.16) all contain a voltage-offset term that is the equivalent of the V' term in Eqn. 8.20.

Note 2. Eqn. 8.18 can be applied in a different way. Instead of V_m being the independent variable that sets the ratio P_2/P_1 at equilibrium, suppose P_2 is the probability that, say, a K^+ ion is present in the ICF and P_1 is the probability that a K^+ ion is present in the ECF. Then $P_2/P_1 = [K^+]_{in}/[K^+]_{out}$ and Eqn. 8.18 can be rearranged to yield:

$$V_m = (RT/F) \ln ([K^+]_{out}/[K^+]_{in}) \,. \tag{8.21}$$

The right-hand side of Eqn. 8.21 gives the value of V_m at which the concentration and electrical energy terms related to the movement of a K^+ ion between the ICF and ECF are in equilibrium. As discussed in Chapter 5, (i) this value is usually called the 'K^+ equilibrium potential' and is denoted 'E_K', and (ii) Eqn. 8.21, with E_K substituted for V_m, gives the Nernst equation for K^+ (Eqn. 5.2). (See also Appendix C, which gives a different way to derive the Nernst equation.)

Exercise 8.15 Following your approach in Exercise 8.6, modify HHVC.py to examine the time course of m^3h and its rate of change in response to a 0.3 ms and a 0.7 ms voltage-clamp step from -70 mV to +50 mV and back to -70 mV (protocols like that used for the two briefest experimental measurements in Fig. 8.12). Change the temperature of your simulation to 8 °C to match that in Fig. 8.12 and adjust the amplitude and time course of the simulated voltage-clamp steps appropriately. How do the time courses of $(m^3h)(t)$ and $(d/dt)(m^3h)(t)$ compare with that of the corresponding gating-current measurements in Fig. 8.12? (For simplicity, estimate the time course of $(d/dt)(m^3h)(t)$ as the first difference of the $(m^3h)(t)$ waveform.) Would you expect that any differences between $(d/dt)(m^3h)(t)$ and the time course of the corresponding measurements in Fig. 8.12 contain clues regarding how the actual kinetics of activation and deactivation of voltage-dependent Na$^+$ channels differs from that assumed in the HH model?

Exercise 8.16 Choose one of the APs calculated with HHAP.py in Fig. 8.9 and examine the time courses of the sodium conductance and the potassium conductance.
(a) What are the times of peak of these conductances and how do they compare with the time of peak of the action potential itself?
(b) What is the ratio of the peak sodium conductance to that of the resting sodium conductance and what is the ratio of the peak potassium conductance to that of the resting potassium conductance (assume V_r = -65 mV).

Exercise 8.17 Make the following changes to HHAP.py: set Stim_size = 0 and, in lines 110 and 129, substitute the statement 'plt.ylim(-65.01, -64.99)' for the ones that are there. After running this revised program, notice that, in the absence of an external stimulus, the Vm trace at this high gain is not really stable at -65 mV; rather, it increases slightly and then settles to a membrane potential that is close to -64.996 mV. If you wished to do calculations with the Hodgkin-Huxley model and a stable resting potential of -65.000 mV, which of the constants in lines 67-75 would you adjust and by how much?

Exercise 8.18 (a) Estimate the density of voltage-dependent Na$^+$ channels in the membrane of a squid giant axon from the following information: (i) your estimate of the integrated area (in coulombs/cm^2) under the positive portion of the gating-current measurements in Fig. 8.12 (where V_r = -70 mV); (ii) the assumption that the activation gates on each Na$^+$ channel are controlled by 6 mobile charges confined within the membrane, the movement of which gives rise to the gating-current measurements (see Sections 8.8 and 8.9); and (iii) the estimate that about 75% of the Na$^+$ channels are in the closed and non-inactivated state when V_r = -70 mV (see lower panels of Figs. 8.7 and 8.8).

(b) Estimate the single-channel conductance of a squid-axon Na$^+$ channel from your estimate of channel density and from the peak value of the Na$^+$ current in a simulated voltage-clamp measurement of the type shown in Figs. 8.11 (but use V_r = -70 mV).

(c) How do your estimates in (a) and (b) differ if the number of gating charges controlling each Na$^+$ channel is 12 rather than 6 (cf. Section 8.8)?

CHAPTER 9

REACTION SCHEMES AND KINETIC EQUATIONS

The work of Hodgkin and Huxley discussed in Chapter 8 illustrates the use of a quantitative model to help understand an important process in cell physiology. In this chapter we delve further into reaction schemes and kinetic equations, which are basic elements for many types of physiological and biochemical analyses.

9.1 THE LAW OF MASS ACTION

A great variety of chemical reactions take place at all times within cells, both in the cytoplasm and within intracellular compartments. The reactions often begin with the reversible binding of two constituents to form a complex, as indicated in the following reaction scheme:

$$A + B \underset{k_r}{\overset{k_f}{\rightleftharpoons}} AB \qquad \text{Scheme 9.1}$$

A and B denote the reactants and AB the reaction complex; k_f and k_r are the forward and reverse rate constants, respectively, for the reaction pathways, which are denoted by arrows. Let brackets ([ ]) denote the concentrations of the reaction constituents in moles per liter of solution (molar, M). The kinetic equation associated with Scheme 9.1 is:

$$(d/dt)[AB] = k_f[A][B] - k_r[AB]. \qquad (9.1)$$

The first term on the right-hand side of Eqn. 9.1 expresses the law of mass action applied to the forward reaction in Scheme 9.1, namely, that the rate of formation of complex AB is proportional to the concentration of A times the concentration of B, with the proportionality constant being k_f. Stated qualitatively, (i) the likelihood that a molecule of A and a molecule of B will be in close contact at any moment in time is proportional to the concentration of A times the concentration of B, and (ii) the likelihood that the reaction complex will form when A and B are in close contact is proportional to k_f. The second term on the right-hand side of Eqn. 9.1 accounts for the reversibility of the reaction, i.e., the dissociation of complex AB into A and B. The more stable the complex, the smaller will be k_r. The usual units for k_f, k_r, and (d/dt) [AB] are $M^{-1} s^{-1}$, s^{-1}, and $M s^{-1}$, respectively.

Kd (pronounced "k d"), the dissociation constant of the reaction (units of M), is defined as:

$$Kd = k_r / k_f . \qquad (9.2)$$

Ka (pronounced "k a"), the association constant of the reaction (also called the 'affinity constant'), is the inverse of Kd (units of M^{-1}) and defined as:

$$Ka = k_f / k_r . \qquad (9.3)$$

In reactions of this type, we will usually focus on Kd rather than Ka.

At steady-state (or equilibrium), (d/dt) [AB] = 0 and:

$$[A][B] = Kd [AB] . \qquad (9.4)$$

The larger the value of Kd (equivalently, the smaller the value of Ka), the lower will be the concentration of AB for given values of [A] and [B], and conversely. When Kd is large (equivalently, when Ka is small), the binding reaction is said to be of 'low affinity'; conversely, when Kd is small (equivalently, when Ka is large), the reaction is said to be of 'high affinity'.

9.2 AN EXAMPLE WITH Ca^{2+} AS A REACTANT

We illustrate Scheme 9.1 with an example of a commonly-occurring intracellular binding reaction of physiological importance. In Scheme 9.1, we replace A with the calcium ion (Ca^{2+}) and assume that B is a Ca^{2+}-binding site, denoted S, on an unspecified Ca^{2+}-binding protein. In this circumstance, Ca^{2+} is often referred to as the reaction 'ligand'. Eqns. 9.1 and 9.4 can be re-written as:

$$(d/dt) [CaS] = k_f [Ca^{2+}][S] - k_r [CaS] , \qquad (9.5)$$

$$\text{and} \quad [Ca^{2+}][S] = Kd [CaS] . \qquad (9.6)$$

[Ca^{2+}] denotes the concentration of free Ca^{2+} ions, i.e., those in solution but not complexed with other reactants. For notational convenience, Eqns. 9.5 and 9.6 ignore the charge on Ca^{2+} when bound to S.

The formation of CaS is often a first step in the control of the activity of a Ca^{2+}-sensitive protein by Ca^{2+}. Many such proteins are found in cells, including:
- calmodulin, which controls the activity of a number of metabolic enzymes (e.g., phosphorylase kinase, which breaks down glycogen to glucose);
- troponin, which, when bound with Ca^{2+}, activates contraction in skeletal and cardiac muscle cells;
- recoverin, which helps regulate the light sensitivity of photoreceptor cells in the retina;
- synaptotagmin, a protein that serves as a Ca^{2+}-sensor for vesicle-based secretion from neurons and other secretory cells;
- the 'Ca^{2+} pump' (two main types exist), which is a membrane-bound enzyme, analogous to the Na$^+$ pump (Na/K ATPase) discussed in earlier chapters, that helps lower the cytosolic free Ca^{2+} concentration.

As discussed below, it is often the case that a Ca^{2+}-sensitive protein has more than one site capable of binding Ca^{2+}.

We next consider the binding of Ca^{2+} in the steady-state to site S on our generic Ca^{2+}-binding protein. The Ca^{2+} ions that are in solution and not bound to S (nor bound to any other Ca^{2+}-binding constituents) will be referred to as the 'free' Ca^{2+} ions and those that are bound as the 'bound' Ca^{2+} ions. Let f_{CaS} denote the fraction of the S sites that are bound with Ca^{2+}, i.e., f_{CaS} = [CaS]/([S] + [CaS]). f_{CaS} may also be thought of as the probability that any particular S site is bound with Ca^{2+} at any moment in time. We ask the questions:
1) How does f_{CaS} depend on the free Ca^{2+} concentration in the solution?
2) How does f_{CaS} depend on the total Ca^{2+} concentration in the solution?

f_{CaS} versus [Ca^{2+}]. From the definition of f_{CaS} and Eqn. 9.6, it follows that:

$$f_{CaS} = \frac{[Ca^{2+}]}{[Ca^{2+}] + K_d} . \tag{9.7}$$

The functional form of Eqn. 9.7 is the same as that of a Langmuir binding isotherm (first used to describe adsorption of gas molecules onto a solid surface) and it is also closely related to the Michaelis-Menten equation (Chapter 2), used to quantify enzyme kinetics.

Let us assume that Kd is 10^{-5} M (= 10 µM), which, for a Ca^{2+}-binding site on a cytoplasmic protein is considered to be of moderate affinity, i.e., not particularly high or low. Fig. 9.1 shows a plot of Eqn. 9.7 for $[Ca^{2+}]$ between 0 and 100 µM for the case that Kd = 10 µM.

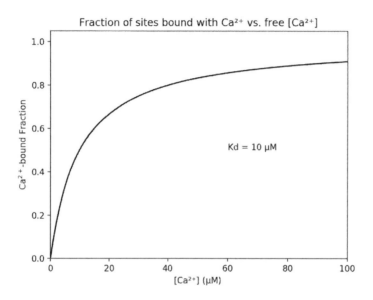

Figure 9.1 The fractional occupancy of a Ca^{2+}-binding site with Ca^{2+} vs. free $[Ca^{2+}]$ if Kd = 10 µM; theoretical plot with free $[Ca^{2+}]$ expressed on a linear scale.

Of note in Fig. 9.3:
- the slope of the curve is steepest at $[Ca^{2+}]$ = 0, where the slope equals 1/Kd;
- f_{CaS} = 0.5 when $[Ca^{2+}]$ = 10 µM, i.e., when $[Ca^{2+}]$ = Kd;
- the approach of the curve to 1.0 is shallow; for example f_{CaS} = 0.909 when $[Ca^{2+}]$ = 100 µM and (not shown) f_{CaS} = 0.990 when $[Ca^{2+}]$ = 1000 µM.

Physiologically, cytoplasmic $[Ca^{2+}]$ can vary over several orders of magnitude during activation of a Ca^{2+}-dependent process, and this variation can be associated with almost no activation to almost full activation of the process. A plot like that in Fig. 9.1, which shows $[Ca^{2+}]$ on a linear scale, does not reveal the complete Ca^{2+}-binding dependence for such a process. To better reveal this dependence -- and to allow for ready comparisons with other Ca^{2+}-binding curves -- f_{CaS} is often plotted as a function of $[Ca^{2+}]$ expressed on a logarithmic scale, specifically, a pCa scale. This scale is analogous to a pH scale for $[H^+]$.

pCa is defined as the negative of the common logarithm of the free Ca^{2+} concentration, i.e., pCa = - $\log_{10}$([Ca^{2+}]), with [Ca^{2+}] expressed in molar units. Thus, if [Ca^{2+}] = 10^{-3} M, pCa is 3; if [Ca^{2+}] = 10^{-6} M pCa is 6; and so on. When the dissociation constant of the reaction is expressed on this scale, it is referred to as 'pKd' (pronounced "p k d") (= - $\log_{10}$(Kd)).

It should be noted that an important distinction exists between a pH scale and a pCa scale. pH is defined as the negative logarithm of the H^+ **activity** whereas pCa is the negative logarithm of the free Ca^{2+} **concentration**. In a dilute solution, activity is the same as the free concentration, but, in a concentrated solution, activity (the 'effective' free concentration) is less than the actual free concentration.

Fig. 9.2 replots the theoretical curve of Fig. 9.1 with [Ca^{2+}] shown on a pCa scale.

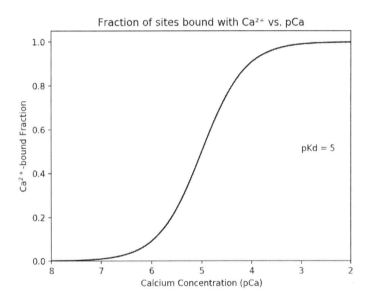

Figure 9.2 The fractional occupancy of a Ca^{2+}-binding site with Ca^{2+} vs. free [Ca^{2+}] if Kd = 10 µM; theoretical plot with free [Ca^{2+}] expressed on a pCa scale.

Of note in Fig 9.2:
- the full range of the binding curve is readily seen, with 98% of the change in the Ca^{2+}-bound fraction occurring between pCa = 7 and pCa = 3 (i.e., ±2 orders of magnitude relative to pKd);
- the steepest slope occurs at pCa = pKd (where f_{CaS} = 0.5);
- the shape of the curve is symmetric about pKd.

Exercise 9.2 leaves it to the reader to determine the slope of the curve at pCa = pKd.

f_{CaS} versus Total [Ca^{2+}]. To address this problem, we make the simplifying assumption that S is the only Ca^{2+}-binding site to be considered in the solution of interest. Let [Ca$_T$] and [S$_T$] denote the total concentration of Ca^{2+} and S sites, respectively. Then:

$$[Ca_T] = [Ca^{2+}] + [CaS], \tag{9.8}$$

$$\text{and} \quad [S_T] = [S] + [CaS]. \tag{9.9}$$

It is left to the reader (Exercise 9.3) to show that Eqns. 9.6, 9.8, and 9.9 can be used to calculate [CaS], [S], and [Ca^{2+}] for given values of [Ca$_T$], [S$_T$], and Kd.

As above, we let f_{CaS} denote the fraction of the total S sites that are bound with Ca^{2+}, i.e., f_{CaS} = [CaS]/[S$_T$], and we assume that Kd = 10 µM. Fig. 9.3 plots f_{CaS} vs. [Ca$_T$] for two values of [S$_T$]: 1 µM (dotted curve) and 100 µM (continuous curve).

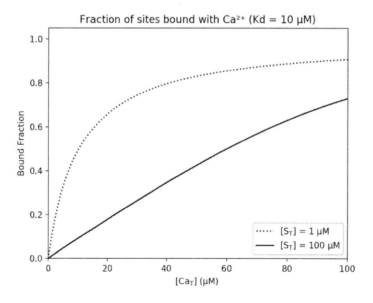

Figure 9.3 The fractional occupancy of Ca^{2+}-binding sites with Ca^{2+} vs. [Ca$_T$] if Kd = 10 µM and the total concentration of sites is either 1 µM (dotted curve) or 100 µM (continuous curve).

If [S$_T$] = 1 µM, [CaS] is necessarily low and therefore free [Ca^{2+}] ≈ [Ca$_T$]; hence the dotted curve in Fig. 9.3 is virtually indistinguishable from the binding curve in Fig. 9.1. On the other hand, if $[S_T] = 100$ µM, [CaS] can be a substantial fraction of $[Ca_T]$, and free $[Ca^{2+}]$ can be quite different from $[Ca_T]$. This is the case in Fig. 9.3 for the continuous curve, which is quite different from the dotted curve.

Further examples of the relation between $[Ca_T]$, $[Ca^{2+}]$, and the fractional occupancy of cytoplasmic Ca^{2+}-binding sites with Ca^{2+} will be considered in Chapter 13.

9.3 THE KINETICS OF Ca^{2+} BINDING IN RESPONSE TO A CHANGE IN $[Ca^{2+}]$

The previous section focused on Ca^{2+} as a reactant when steady-state conditions apply. Here we consider the kinetics of Ca^{2+} binding to, and dissociation from, a hypothetical Ca^{2+}-binding site S in response to a change in free $[Ca^{2+}]$. In this example, we use Eqn. 9.5 with Kd set to 10 µM and analyze the response to a step change in $[Ca^{2+}]$. Many pairs of choices exist for k_r and k_f such that Kd (= k_r / k_f) = 10 µM. We will assume that $k_f = 10^8$ M^{-1} s^{-1}, a value commonly assumed to apply to Ca^{2+}- binding sites on proteins under intracellular conditions at ~20 °C if the main kinetic limitation is the rate at which Ca^{2+} can diffuse to the site S. In such a case, k_f is referred to as a 'diffusion-limited' rate constant.

If $k_f = 10^8$ M^{-1} s^{-1}, then, from Eqn. 9.2, $k_r = k_f \cdot$ Kd $= 1000$ s^{-1}. From Eqn. 9.5, it follows that the rate constant for the change in f_{CaS} (the fraction of sites S in the Ca^{2+}-bound form) in response to a new level of free $[Ca^{2+}]$ is $k_f [Ca^{2+}] + k_r$ (see also Exercise 9.4). Fig. 9.4 shows the time course of this change if free $[Ca^{2+}]$ changes in a step-wise manner from 0.1 µM to 10 µM for 10 ms and then returns to 0.1 µM.

The value of f_{CaS} before the change in $[Ca^{2+}]$ is 0.0099 (= $[Ca^{2+}]/([Ca^{2+}] +$ Kd)). Following the step increase in $[Ca^{2+}]$ to 10 µM, f_{CaS} rises to 0.5 with a time constant of 0.5 ms (equivalently, a rate constant of 2 ms^{-1}). When $[Ca^{2+}]$ returns to 0.1 µM, f_{CaS} falls to its initial value with a ~2-fold longer time constant, 0.99 ms. (Exercise 9.4 asks the reader to confirm these statements.) Overall, at any instant, f_{CaS}, whether it is rising or falling, is moving along an exponential time course toward the steady-state level appropriate to the current value of $[Ca^{2+}]$ with time constant $1/(k_f [Ca^{2+}] + k_r)$ (equivalently, with rate constant $k_f [Ca^{2+}] + k_r$).

The kinetic case of the Ca^{2+} occupancy of binding sites S in response to a change in total $[Ca^{2+}]$ is considered in Exercise 9.11 (see also Exercise 13.4).

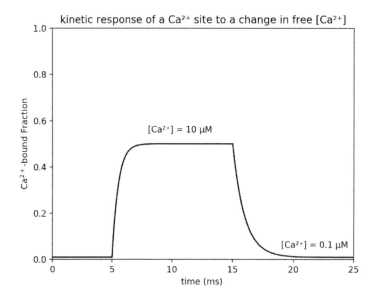

Figure 9.4 Time course of the change in the fractional occupancy of a Ca^{2+}-binding site with Ca^{2+} in response to a step change in free $[Ca^{2+}]$ from 0.1 to 10 μM and back if the forward and reverse rate constants of the reaction are 10^8 M^{-1} s^{-1} and 1000 s^{-1}, respectively (K_d = 10 μM).

9.4 COMPETITIVE BINDING: STEADY-STATE

Many binding sites are not specific for one ligand. For example, a site on a protein that is capable of binding Ca^{2+} can usually also bind other divalent ions, of which Mg^{2+} is usually the most relevant physiologically. We therefore examine the case of a hypothetical site S that can bind either Ca^{2+} or Mg^{2+}. The affinity of such a site for Mg^{2+} is usually several orders of magnitude lower than that for Ca^{2+}. Under a cell's resting conditions, however, the cytoplasmic concentration of free Mg^{2+} is typically more than 4 orders of magnitude higher than that of Ca^{2+} (~1 mM vs. ~0.05 μM, respectively). According to the law of mass action, the higher the free $[Ca^{2+}]$, the more likely it is that site S will be occupied by Ca^{2+}; conversely, the higher the free $[Mg^{2+}]$, the more likely that site S will be occupied by Mg^{2+}. Thus, the usual situation is a competition between Ca^{2+} and Mg^{2+} for occupancy of site S. This situation is referred to as 'competitive binding'.

An example of a protein that can bind Ca^{2+} or Mg^{2+} is parvalbumin (a name that translates as 'small albumin'). Parvalbumin is found in the cytoplasm of many cells and is found at particularly high concentrations in some cell types in the brain and in some types of skeletal muscle fibers. Parvalbumin, like its namesake albumin (the most abundant protein in blood plasma), is a globular-shaped protein. Its molecular mass is ~11 kDaltons, which is about one-sixth that of albumin (~67 kDaltons). Interestingly, each parvalbumin molecule has 2 similar divalent-ion binding sites, and each site appears to bind Ca^{2+} or Mg^{2+} independently of the other site.

A reaction scheme to describe the competitive binding of Ca^{2+} and Mg^{2+} to either of the divalent-ion binding sites S on parvalbumin is:

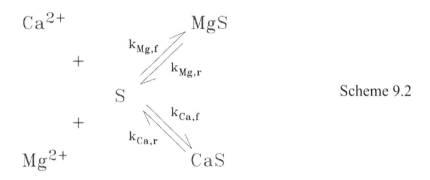

Scheme 9.2

S, CaS, and MgS denote unbound sites, Ca^{2+}-bound sites, and Mg^{2+}-bound sites, respectively; the forward and reverse rate constants of the reactions for the two different ions are labeled accordingly. Analogous to Eqn. 9.2, the dissociation constant for Ca^{2+} in the absence of Mg^{2+} is denoted Kd_{Ca} and defined as:

$$Kd_{Ca} = k_{Ca,r} / k_{Ca,f} . \qquad (9.10)$$

Similarly, the dissociation constant for Mg^{2+} in the absence of Ca^{2+} is denoted Kd_{Mg} and defined as:

$$Kd_{Mg} = k_{Mg,r} / k_{Mg,f} . \qquad (9.11)$$

With parvalbumin, Kd_{Ca} is ~10 nM (equivalently, $pKd_{Ca} \approx 8$) and Kd_{Mg} is ~100 μM (equivalently, $pKd_{Mg} \approx 4$); thus, S has a high affinity for Ca^{2+} and a relatively low affinity for Mg^{2+}.

Analogous to Eqn. 9.6, we also have:

$$[Ca^{2+}] [S] = Kd_{Ca} [CaS] , \qquad (9.12)$$

$$\text{and} \quad [Mg^{2+}] [S] = Kd_{Mg} [MgS] . \qquad (9.13)$$

In this case, we define f_{CaS}, the fraction of the total S sites in the Ca^{2+}-bound form, as $[CaS]/([S]+[CaS]+[MgS])$. Substituting from Eqns. 9.12 and 9.13 and rearranging, we obtain:

$$f_{CaS} = \frac{[Ca^{2+}]}{[Ca^{2+}] + Kd_{Ca}(1+[Mg^{2+}]/Kd_{Mg})} . \qquad (9.14)$$

Eqn. 9.14 reduces to Eqn. 9.7 if $[Mg^{2+}] = 0$. If $[Mg^{2+}] > 0$, however, the effective Ca^{2+}-dissociation constant for Ca^{2+} binding, which, in this case, is called the 'apparent' Ca^{2+}-dissociation constant (denoted Kd'_{Ca}), is larger than the actual Ca^{2+}-dissociation constant by the factor $(1 + Mg^{2+}]/Kd_{Mg})$, i.e., $Kd'_{Ca} = Kd_{Ca}(1 + [Mg^{2+}]/Kd_{Mg})$. If Kd'_{Ca} is substituted into Eqn. 9.12, Eqn. 9.14 becomes formally identical to Eqn. 9.7.

Similarly, we define f_{MgS}, the fraction of the total S sites in the Mg^{2+}-bound form, as $[MgS]/([S]+[CaS]+[MgS])$. By symmetry:

$$f_{MgS} = \frac{[Mg^{2+}]}{[Mg^{2+}] + Kd_{Mg}(1+[Ca^{2+}]/Kd_{Ca})} , \qquad (9.15)$$

and the apparent Mg^{2+}-dissociation constant, Kd'_{Mg}, equals $Kd_{Mg}(1 + [Ca^{2+}]/Kd_{Ca})$.

In summary, a second ligand at a non-zero concentration appears to increase the dissociation constant of the site for the first ligand, but the functional form of the binding curve remains unchanged. If stated in terms of ligand affinity, the presence of the second ligand appears to lower the affinity of site S for the first ligand (and vice-versa). If viewed in terms of Scheme 9.2, the presence of the second ligand promotes complexation of S with the second ligand, thus making some of the S sites unavailable to react with the first ligand (and vice versa). Therefore, a higher concentration of the first ligand is required to achieve the level of binding with the first ligand that would otherwise occur in the absence of the second ligand.

Given the assumptions above, Fig. 9.5 plots the steady-state relations for Ca^{2+} binding to parvalbumin with and without Mg^{2+}. Each panel shows two curves of f_{CaS} vs. $[Ca^{2+}]$ for the case that $Kd_{Ca} = 10$ nM and $Kd_{Mg} = 100$ μM ($pKd_{Ca} = 8$ and $pKd_{Mg} = 4$); the continuous and dotted curves correspond to free $[Mg^{2+}] = 0$ and 1 mM, respectively. [Note: under resting conditions, cytoplasmic free $[Mg^{2+}] \approx 1$ mM in many cell types, similar to that of extracellular free $[Mg^{2+}]$.]

From Eqn. 9.14, the apparent dissociation constant of the S sites for Ca^{2+} is increased by a factor of 11 when $[Mg^{2+}]$ is increased from 0 to 1 mM. This lowering of the affinity of S for Ca^{2+} by Mg^{2+} is obvious in both panels of Fig. 9.5, where the dotted curve is right-shifted with respect to the continuous curve. The overall effect, however, is more readily appreciated in the right-hand panel, which expresses Ca^{2+} on a pCa scale and the full extent of both curves can be seen. In this plot, both curves have the same shape apart from the fact that the dashed curve is right-shifted by 1.041 log units ($= \log_{10}(11)$).

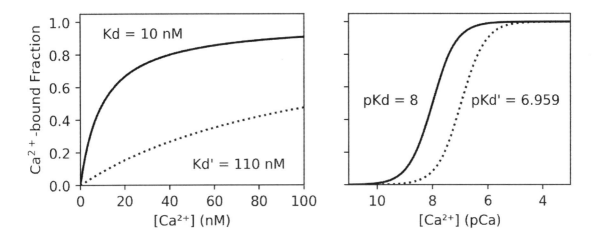

Figure 9.5 Theoretical plots of the fractional occupancy of a Ca^{2+}-binding site with Ca^{2+} vs. free $[Ca^{2+}]$ if $Kd_{Ca} = 10$ nM ($pKd_{Ca} = 8$) and $Kd_{Mg} = 100$ μM ($pKd_{Mg} = 4$) and the free $[Mg^{2+}]$ is either 0 mM (continuous curves) or 1 mM (dotted curves). The plot on the left shows free $[Ca^{2+}]$ on a linear scale and, on the right, on a pCa scale.

9.5 A STEADY-STATE EQUIVALENCE BETWEEN Ca^{2+} AND Mg^{2+} EFFECTS ON BINDING

We return to Eqn. 9.7 and the particular example in Fig. 9.1, where the free Ca^{2+} concentration is expressed in µM units and Kd is 10 µM. Suppose, for example, that the S sites are in a solution in which $[Ca^{2+}]$ is set to an initial value of 15 µM. In this case, f_{CaS} is 15/25 = 0.6. Suppose now that the solution $[Ca^{2+}]$ is progressively increased above 15 µM until f_{CaS} approaches 1. How does the remaining fraction of the f_{CaS} binding curve (i.e., the f_{CaS} values between 0.6 and 1) depend on $[Ca^{2+}] > 15$ µM if the remaining fraction of the binding curve is translated so that its leftmost point is at the origin of the plot and the amplitude of the remaining curve is re-scaled to 1.0?

Fig. 9.6 explores this example graphically. In the left panel, the dotted curve shows f_{CaS}, and the continuous overlay on this curve shows the part of f_{CaS} for $[Ca^{2+}] > 15$ µM. In the right panel, the continuous curve from the left panel has been replotted with its left-most point translated to the origin and with the amplitude of the remaining curve scaled to be 1.0 at saturating $[Ca^{2+}]$. That is, the continuous curve on the right shows the function $F_{CaS} = (f_{CaS}([Ca^{2+}]+15) - 0.6)/(0.4)$.

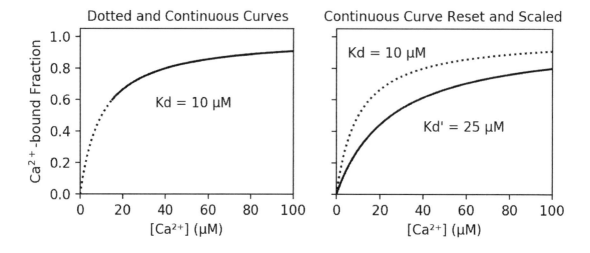

Figure 9.6 (Left) Two plots of the binding curve in Fig. 9.1: full curve (dotted) and the portion for $[Ca^{2+}] > 15$ µM (continuous). (Right) Plots as on the left except that the continuous curve on the left has been replotted after translation of its left-most point to the origin and with its amplitude scaled to 1.0 at saturating $[Ca^{2+}]$ (not evident on the scale shown).

After substitution of f_{CaS} from Eqn. 9.7 into F_{CaS}, it follows that $F_{CaS} = [Ca^{2+}]/([Ca^{2+}] + 25)$, the right-hand side of which can be rewritten as $[Ca^{2+}]/([Ca^{2+}] + Kd + 15) = [Ca^{2+}]/([Ca^{2+}] + Kd(1+15/Kd))$. Interestingly, F_{CaS} has the same functional form as f_{CaS} except that F_{CaS} is right-shifted with respect to f_{CaS} due to its larger apparent Kd (25 rather than 10 µM).

This example can be generalized by supposing that $[Ca^{2+}]$ is set to an initial value denoted $[Ca^{2+}]_0$, and that the function F_{CaS} is defined as $(f_{CaS}([Ca^{2+}]+[Ca^{2+}]_0) - f_{CaS}(Ca^{2+}]_0) / (1 - f_{CaS}(Ca^{2+}]_0)$. Then, after simplification:

$$F_{CaS} = \frac{[Ca^{2+}]}{[Ca^{2+}] + Kd(1+[Ca^{2+}]_0/Kd)} . \tag{9.16}$$

Eqn. 9.16 is formally similar to Eqn. 9.14, except that $[Ca^{2+}]_0$ now substitutes for $[Mg^{2+}]$. The second term in the denominator of Eqn. 9.16, if expanded, yields $Kd + [Ca^{2+}]_0$, whereas the second term in the denominator of Eqn. 9.14, if expanded, yields $Kd_{Ca} + [Mg^{2+}] \cdot Kd_{Ca}/Kd_{Mg}$. Thus, the right-shifting effect that $[Ca^{2+}]_0$ has on the shape of the remaining portion of the f_{CaS} binding curve is analogous to the right-shifting effect that $[Mg^{2+}]$ has on the competitive f_{CaS} binding curve except that the denominator term involving $[Ca^{2+}]_0$ in Eqn. 9.16 is unscaled whereas the term involving $[Mg^{2+}]$ in Eqn. 9.14 is scaled by the factor Kd_{Ca}/Kd_{Mg}. Not surprisingly, the larger is Kd_{Mg} compared with Kd_{Ca}, the less effective is Mg^{2+} compared with Ca^{2+} in right-shifting the f_{CaS} binding curve.

9.6 COMPETITIVE BINDING: KINETICS

We now consider the kinetics of the change in Ca^{2+} and Mg^{2+} binding to, and dissociation from, a competitive divalent-ion binding site S in response to a change in free $[Ca^{2+}]$. We use Scheme 9.2 with rate constants $k_{Ca,f}$, $k_{Ca,r}$, $k_{Mg,f}$, and $k_{Mg,r}$.

The associated kinetic equations are:

$$(d/dt)[CaS] = k_{Ca,f}[Ca^{2+}][S] - k_{Ca,r}[CaS], \tag{9.17}$$

and $$(d/dt)[MgS] = k_{Mg,f}[Mg^{2+}][S] - k_{Mg,r}[MgS]. \tag{9.18}$$

For a specific example, we again consider the case of parvalbumin, and assume that Kd_{Ca} and Kd_{Mg} are 0.01 μM and 100 μM, respectively. As for the example in Section 9.3, we assume that $k_{Ca,f} = 10^8$ M^{-1} s^{-1}, which approximates a diffusion-limited rate constant for Ca^{2+} binding at room temperature. It follows that $k_{Ca,r} = k_{Ca,f} \cdot Kd_{Ca} = 1.0$ s^{-1}. With Mg^{2+}, we assume that $k_{Mg,f}$ is 10^5 M^{-1} s^{-1}; consequently, $k_{Mg,r} = k_{Mg,f} \cdot Kd_{Mg} = 10$ s^{-1}. The reason that $k_{Mg,f}$ is so much smaller than $k_{Ca,f}$ is that the Mg^{2+} ion is smaller than the Ca^{2+} ion and therefore is more strongly hydrated in solution than Ca^{2+}. Mg^{2+}, like Ca^{2+}, must lose bound water molecules before it can bind to site S on parvalbumin. Because loss of these water molecules is energetically unfavorable for the small Mg^{2+} ion, Mg^{2+} has a much smaller forward rate constant than Ca^{2+}. As before, we define [S$_T$] = [S]+[CaS]+[MgS], f_{CaS} = [CaS]/[S$_T$], and f_{MgS} = [MgS]/[S$_T$].

Fig. 9.7 shows plots of f_{CaS} (continuous curve) and f_{MgS} (dotted curve) in response to a step change in free [Ca^{2+}] from 0.05 μM to 1 μM for 1200 ms and then a step-change back to 0.05 μM. The plot on the left is on a fast time base (500 ms) and that on the right on a slow time base (5000 ms). The calculations are based on Eqns. 9.17 and 9.18 and assume that free [Mg^{2+}] is 1 mM and remains constant during the change in [Ca^{2+}] (thus, Mg^{2+} is assumed to be "well-buffered").

The values of f_{CaS} and f_{MgS} before the change are calculated from Eqns. 9.14 and 9.15; these are: f_{CaS} = 0.3125 (= 0.05/(0.05 + Kd_{Ca}(1 + 1000/Kd_{Mg}))) and f_{MgS} = 0.6250 (= 1000/(1000 + Kd_{Mg}(1 + 0.05/Kd_{Ca}))) [where concentration units are shown in μM].

Following the step increase in [Ca^{2+}], f_{CaS} rises to a final value ≈ 0.90, but the time course of the rise is not a single-exponential (as it was in Fig. 9.4); rather, as shown on the left, it proceeds in two phases. The first phase, which is barely discernable, involves a small, quick rise in f_{CaS} of ~0.03; this is explained by the binding of Ca^{2+} to the parvalbumin sites that are free of both Ca^{2+} and Mg^{2+} prior to the increase in [Ca^{2+}]. The second phase involves a larger, slower rise in f_{CaS} from ~0.35 to ~0.90. This phase reflects Ca^{2+} binding to parvalbumin sites that were bound with Mg^{2+} prior to the increase in [Ca^{2+}] but become free to bind Ca^{2+} as Mg^{2+} dissociates from MgS in response to the mass-action perturbation caused by the rise in [Ca^{2+}] (see Scheme 9.2).

Following the step decrease in [Ca^{2+}] back to 0.05 μM, f_{CaS} and f_{MgS} return to their original values with similar time courses. As Ca^{2+} dissociates from CaS in response to the fall in [Ca^{2+}], Mg^{2+} rebinds to the available divalent-free S sites.

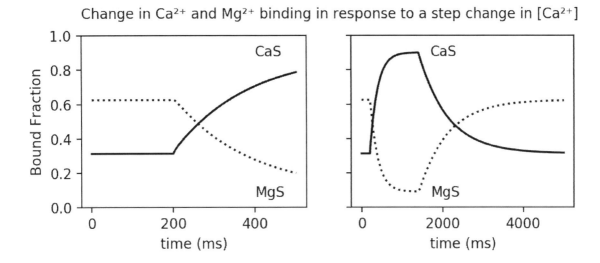

Figure 9.7 Changes in the fraction of a hypothetical site S bound with Ca^{2+} (continuous curves) or with Mg^{2+} (dotted curves) in response to a step rise in $[Ca^{2+}]$ from 0.05 µM to 1 µM beginning at 200 ms and lasting 1200 ms, followed by a step fall in $[Ca^{2+}]$ to 0.05 µM. The kinetics of Ca^{2+} and Mg^{2+} binding to site S (see text) are similar to that of binding to the divalent-ion binding sites on parvalbumin. Left: fast time base; right: slow time base.

An example of this type will be explored further in Chapter 13, where the role that parvalbumin plays in speeding the relaxation of skeletal muscle fibers will be discussed.

9.7 COOPERATIVE BINDING AND THE HILL EQUATION

Many proteins have more than one binding site for their ligand(s). For example, as discussed in the previous section, parvalbumin has two binding sites that, under physiological conditions, can bind either Ca^{2+} or Mg^{2+}. Parvalbumin's reactions with its ligands might be considered atypical, however, as ligand binding to one site appears to be independent of ligand binding to the other site. In contrast, with many proteins that have multiple binding sites for its ligand(s), binding does not behave independently.

We explore this issue here. We again use the example of Ca^{2+} as a ligand. To further simplify, we consider a generic protein P with two Ca^{2+}-specific binding sites -- that is, we ignore the possibility that the sites can bind another ligand such as Mg^{2+}.

Scheme 9.3 shows a reaction that is sometimes used to describe a type of multiple-ligand binding that is referred to as 'cooperative' binding. Again, for notational convenience, we ignore the charge on Ca^{2+} when it is bound to P. According to this scheme, two Ca^{2+} ions react with the two binding sites on P in a single reaction step. Thus, at the free Ca^{2+} concentrations of interest, the probability that only one Ca^{2+} ion is bound to the sites on P is sufficiently low that it can be ignored.

$$Ca^{2+} + P + Ca^{2+} \underset{k_r}{\overset{k_f}{\rightleftharpoons}} Ca_2P \qquad \text{Scheme 9.3}$$

In Scheme 9.3, k_r, the reverse rate constant, has units of s^{-1} (as in Scheme 9.1); k_f, the forward rate constant, however, has units of $M^{-2} s^{-1}$, since two ligands are involved in the forward reaction. As usual, we define $Kd = k_r / k_f$, which has units of M^2.

The steady-state binding equation associated with Scheme 9.3 (analogous to Eqn. 9.4) is:

$$[Ca^{2+}] [Ca^{2+}] [P] = Kd [Ca_2P] . \qquad (9.19)$$

We define f_{CaP} as the fraction of all P sites that are bound with Ca^{2+}. Because each molecule P has 2 Ca^{2+}-binding sites, $f_{CaP} = 2 [Ca_2P] / (2 [Ca_2P] + 2 [P]) = [Ca_2P] / ([Ca_2P] + [P])$. After substitution from Eqn. 9.19, it follows that:

$$f_{CaP} = \frac{[Ca^{2+}]^2}{[Ca^{2+}]^2 + Kd} . \qquad (9.20)$$

Eqn. 9.20 can be generalized by replacing the integer 2 with the integer N as the exponent of the ligand concentration on the right-hand side of the equation. Eqn. 9.20 so generalized, with ligand L replacing Ca^{2+}, is called 'the Hill equation', Eqn. 9.21 (named after Archibald Hill who studied the cooperative binding of oxygen to hemoglobin). In this case, N ligands bind in one step to form the complex and the units of Kd are M^N.

$$f_{LP} = \frac{[L]^N}{[L]^N + Kd}. \qquad (9.21)$$

We now consider a specific example with two Ca^{2+} ions as the ligand, and with $k_r = 20\ s^{-1}$ and $k_f = 20\ (\mu M)^{-2}\ s^{-1}$; thus, $Kd = 1\ (\mu M)^2$. The continuous curve in the left-hand panel of Fig. 9.8 is a plot of f_{CaP} vs. $[Ca^{2+}]$ based on Eqn. 9.20 with $Kd = 1\ (\mu M)^2$. For comparison, the dotted curve in the left-hand panel shows a standard binding curve with $Kd = 1\ \mu M$ (one-site binding, Eqn. 9.7). The dotted curve also describes the case that protein P has two identical sites, each with a Kd of $1\ \mu M$, that bind Ca^{2+} independently.

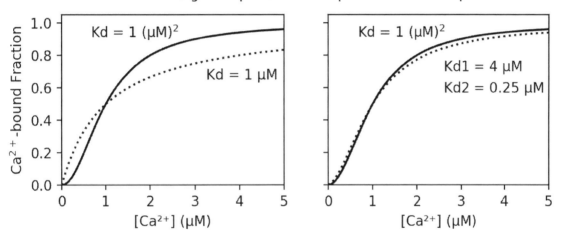

Figure 9.8 Left: the fraction of the sites on protein P bound with Ca^{2+} for a fully-cooperative two-site binding scheme (Scheme 9.3, continuous curve) and an independent (i.e., non-cooperative scheme) (Scheme 9.1, dotted curve). Right: the fraction of the sites on protein P bound with Ca^{2+} for the fully-cooperative binding scheme (Scheme 9.3, continuous curve) and a partially-cooperative scheme (Scheme 9.4, dotted curve) for which $Kd1 \cdot Kd2 = 1\ (\mu M)^2$.

Of note regarding the curves in the left-hand panel of Fig. 9.8:
- at $[Ca^{2+}] = 0$, the slope of the dotted curve has its maximum value, whereas the slope of the continuous curve is zero;
- the maximum slope of the continuous curve occurs between $[Ca^{2+}] = 0$ and $[Ca^{2+}] = \sqrt{Kd}$ (see Exercise 9.6);
- f_{CaP} is 0.5 when $[Ca^{2+}] = Kd$ (dotted curve) or $[Ca^{2+}] = \sqrt{Kd}$ (continuous curve)

- the continuous curve reaches values close to 1.0 at substantially lower values of $[Ca^{2+}]$ than the dotted curve.

These properties of the continuous curve in the left-hand panel of Fig. 9.8 show that the cooperative binding scheme (Scheme 9.3) has important differences -- often, advantages -- over a non-cooperative scheme (Scheme 9.1) as a means of controlling the activity of a Ca^{2+}-dependent protein. Two such proteins that are activated cooperatively by $[Ca^{2+}]$ levels in the µM range were mentioned in Section 9.2: troponin, a structural protein in the cytoplasm of skeletal muscle cells, which activates muscle contraction when it binds two Ca^{2+} ions, and the enzyme phosphorylase kinase, which breaks down glycogen to glucose (and is activated when its sub-unit calmodulin binds several Ca^{2+} ions). Note that, with a cooperative binding scheme like Scheme 9.3 as the basis of Ca^{2+}'s control of a protein's activity, the slope of the binding curve is small when $[Ca^{2+}]$ is low; thus, the protein would not be significantly activated at normal levels of resting $[Ca^{2+}]$, which, in most cells, is in the nM range, e.g., ~50 nM. Furthermore, $[Ca^{2+}]$ needs to rise to only to 2-3 times $\sqrt{K_d}$ for the protein to achieve nearly full activation. Mechanistically, this type of control can be achieved if a significant conformational change in the protein, from resting to active, occurs only when Ca^{2+} ions are bound to both control sites (assuming N = 2). As N becomes progressively larger in the Hill equation, the binding curve becomes progressively more 'switch-like', i.e., rising from 0 to 1 in an almost step-wise fashion (see Exercise 9.6).

Reaction Scheme 9.3 might be considered unlikely, as it shows two ligands binding to the two binding sites on protein P in one step. Scheme 9.4 shows another two-ligand scheme for Ca^{2+} binding to a hypothetical protein P that is mechanistically more likely than Scheme 9.3.

$$P \underset{k_{r1}}{\overset{Ca^{2+}, k_{f1}}{\rightleftharpoons}} CaP \underset{k_{r2}}{\overset{Ca^{2+}, k_{f2}}{\rightleftharpoons}} Ca_2P \qquad \text{Scheme 9.4}$$

In Scheme 9.4, as in Scheme 9.1, the reverse rate constants, k_{r1} and k_{r2}, have units of s^{-1}, and the forward rate constants, k_{f1} and k_{f2}, have units of $M^{-1} s^{-1}$ (since one ligand is involved in each reaction). As usual, we define Kd1 = k_{r1}/k_{f1} and Kd2 = k_{r2}/k_{f2}, the units of which are M.

The steady-state binding equations are:

$$[Ca^{2+}] [P] = Kd1 [CaP], \qquad (9.22)$$

$$\text{and} \quad [Ca^{2+}] [CaP] = Kd2 [Ca_2P]. \qquad (9.23)$$

Again, we define f_{CaP} as the fraction of all P sites that are bound with Ca^{2+}. Because each P molecule has 2 Ca^{2+}-binding sites, f_{CaP} = ([CaP] + 2 [Ca$_2$P]) / 2 ([CaP] + [Ca$_2$P] + [P]). After substitution from Eqns. 9.22 and 9.23, it follows that:

$$f_{CaP} = \frac{[Ca^{2+}]^2 + 0.5 [Ca^{2+}] Kd2}{[Ca^{2+}]^2 + [Ca^{2+}] Kd2 + Kd1\, Kd2}. \qquad (9.24)$$

With appropriate values of Kd1 and Kd2, Scheme 9.4 also yields a binding curve with cooperative properties that are similar to those of Scheme 9.3. For example, suppose that (i) when the protein in its Ca^{2+}-free state, either P binding site can bind Ca^{2+} and does so with a relatively low affinity, and (ii) once CaP has formed, a conformational change takes place such that the remaining binding site binds Ca^{2+} with a relatively high affinity. In this case, Kd2 is small relative to Kd1 and the right-hand side of Eqn. 9.24 will approximate the right-hand side of Eqn. 9.20 if the term Kd1· Kd2 is substituted for Kd. In this circumstance, a plot of Eqn. 9.24 is expected to resemble a plot of Eqn. 9.20.

As an example of Scheme 9.4 and Eqn. 9.24, we consider the case that Kd1 = 4 µM and Kd2 = 0.25 µM. Then, Kd1 · Kd2 = 1 (µM)^2, i.e., the same value of Kd as for the plot of the continuous curve in the left-hand panel of Fig. 9.8. The right-hand panel of Fig. 9.8 shows the latter curve replotted, and, for comparison, the dotted curve shows a plot of Eqn. 9.24 with Kd1 = 4 µM and Kd2 = 0.25 µM. The two curves in the right-hand panel are barely distinguishable. The slope of the dotted curve at [Ca^{2+}] = 0 is non-zero, so it is larger than that of the continuous curve (which, as mentioned above, is zero) but not markedly so. For high values of [Ca^{2+}], the continuous curve is closer to 1.0 than the dotted curve but, again, not markedly so. It may be concluded that Scheme 9.4 and Eqn. 9.24

yield a good approximation of the binding behavior described by the Hill equation for the case that N=2 if the ratio Kd1/Kd2 in Eqn. 9.24 is a moderately large number, e.g., >15.

9.8 A KINETIC SCHEME FOR THE Ca^{2+} PUMP OF THE SARCOPLASMIC RETICULUM

We now consider a more complicated kinetic scheme and its associated equations. This scheme has been used to estimate Ca^{2+} transport by the Ca^{2+} ATPase (the 'Ca^{2+} pump') that is found in high density in the membranes of the sarcoplasmic reticulum (SR) and endoplasmic reticulum (ER) and helps maintain cytoplasmic $[Ca^{2+}]$ at a low value. (The SR, which is found in muscle cells, is analogous to the ER, which is found in non-muscle cells). This Ca^{2+} pump, whose principal subunit is a 110 KDalton protein, sometimes goes by the acronym 'SERCA' pump (<u>s</u>arco-<u>e</u>ndoplasmic <u>r</u>eticulum <u>c</u>alcium <u>A</u>TPase). A related Ca^{2+} pump is found in the surface membrane of many cells and also functions to lower cytoplasmic $[Ca^{2+}]$. The SR/ER Ca^{2+} pump uses one ATP molecule for each pump cycle, during which two Ca^{2+} ions are transported from the cytoplasm to the lumen of the SR/ER in exchange for (probably) two protons (H^+) transported in the other direction. As discussed in Chapters 12 and 13, Ca^{2+} transport by the SR Ca^{2+} pump is important for the relaxation of skeletal muscle cells following their activation by Ca^{2+}.

Scheme 9.5 shows a reaction mechanism for the binding and pumping of Ca^{2+} by the SR Ca^{2+} pump, which is based on the work of Peinelt and Apell (2002):

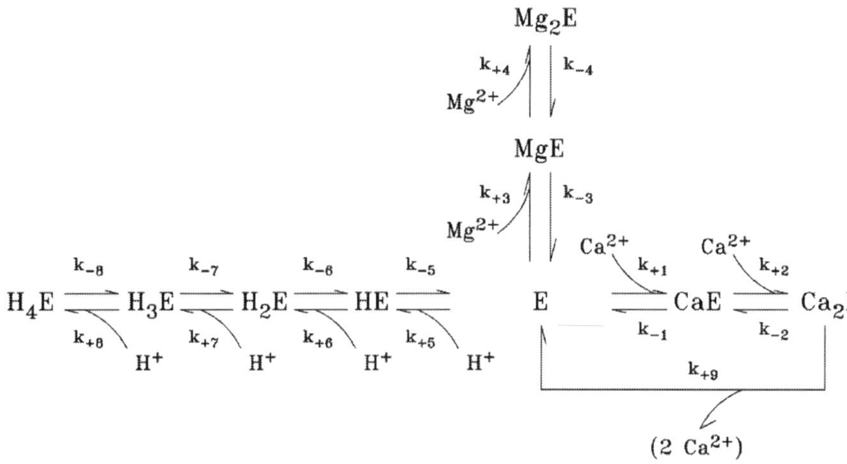

Scheme 9.5

In this scheme, E (which is short for 'Enzyme') denotes a Ca^{2+} pump molecule; k_{+n} and k_{-n} denote the forward and reverse rate constants for reaction steps 1 to 8, respectively. Reaction step 9 (the Ca^{2+} translocation step, described below) is considered irreversible at normal values of resting $[Ca^{2+}]$ for normally-energized cells; therefore, only a forward rate, k_{+9}, is shown for step 9. Again, for notational convenience, the charges on Ca^{2+}, Mg^{2+}, and H^+, when bound to E, are not shown.

According to this scheme, if the enzyme is free of Ca^{2+}, Mg^{2+}, and H^+, it is able to bind two Ca^{2+} ions on the cytoplasmic side of the SR membrane in a two-step sequential reaction and translocate these ions to the lumen of the SR membrane. The translocated Ca^{2+} ions are shown in parentheses at the bottom of the scheme (labeled '(2 Ca^{2+})'). In exchange, protons are translocated from the lumen of the SR to the cytoplasm (not shown). Because the movement of Ca^{2+} ions from the cytoplasm to the lumen of the SR is energetically unfavorable, it requires input of energy from another source. As noted, this energy is supplied by ATP (not shown), one molecule of which is hydrolyzed during each cycle of the enzyme, i.e., for every 2 Ca^{2+} ions pumped from the cytoplasm to the SR.

According to Scheme 9.5, of the pump molecules that are not in the Ca_2E state, only those in the E and CaE states are immediately available to bind Ca^{2+}. The remaining molecules are bound either with Mg^{2+} (MgE and Mg_2E) or with H^+ (HE, H_2E, H_3E and H_4E) and, when so bound, are unable to bind Ca^{2+} because they are competitively-inhibited. This competitive inhibition by Mg^{2+} and H^+ has physiological significance. When the cell is in its resting state (with the free $[Ca^{2+}]$ level low), the fact that a large fraction of the pump molecules are bound with Mg^{2+} or H^+ means that these molecules are unavailable to (immediately) bind Ca^{2+}. If $[Ca^{2+}]$ should suddenly rise (e.g., as occurs during muscle activation), Ca^{2+} will then have a chance to bind to sites on other proteins, such as on troponin, and activate them before Ca^{2+} can bind to the SR Ca^{2+} pump in significant amounts. Thus, Ca^{2+} can be used more efficiently to activate these other proteins on a priority basis before the SR Ca^{2+} pump begins to work near its full activity to remove Ca^{2+} from the cytoplasm and return $[Ca^{2+}]$ back to the resting level.

Table 9.1 gives the values of the rate constants (k_{+n} and k_{-n}) and dissociation constants ($Kd_n = k_{-n} / k_{+n}$) in Scheme 9.5 that have been used to estimate the pumping of Ca^{2+} by the SR Ca^{2+} pump in skeletal muscle cells at 18 °C (Hollingworth et al., 2006). For the reactions with H^+, the dissociation constants are given in units of pK (= $-\log_{10}(Kd)$). The rate constants for the H^+ reactions are listed as instantaneous because reaction rates of H^+ with binding sites on proteins are expected to be much faster than those of Ca^{2+} or Mg^{2+}.

Table 9.1 Rate Constants Associated with Scheme 9.5 (18 °C)

Number and Reaction	Forward Rate (k_{+n})	Reverse Rate (k_{-n})	Ratio (k_{-n}/k_{+n})
1. $Ca^{2+} + E \leftrightarrow CaE$	2×10^8 M^{-1} s^{-1}	8 s^{-1}	$Kd_1 = 0.04$ μM
2. $Ca^{2+} + CaE \leftrightarrow Ca_2E$	2×10^8 M^{-1} s^{-1}	10 s^{-1}	$Kd_2 = 0.05$ μM
3. $Mg^{2+} + E \leftrightarrow MgE$	10^5 M^{-1} s^{-1}	5 s^{-1}	$Kd_3 = 50.0$ μM
4. $Mg^{2+} + MgE \leftrightarrow Mg_2E$	10^5 M^{-1} s^{-1}	100 s^{-1}	$Kd_4 = 1000$ μM
5. $H^+ + E \leftrightarrow HE$	instantaneous	instantaneous	$pK_5 = 8$
6. $H^+ + HE \leftrightarrow H_2E$	instantaneous	instantaneous	$pK_6 = 8$
7. $H^+ + H_2E \leftrightarrow H_3E$	instantaneous	instantaneous	$pK_7 = 6$
8. $H^+ + H_3E \leftrightarrow H_4E$	instantaneous	instantaneous	$pK_8 = 5$
9. $Ca_2E \leftrightarrow E + (2\ Ca^{2+})$	4 s^{-1}	0	$Kd_9 = 0$

These rate constants and the information in Scheme 9.5 are used in the next *Python* program, CaPump.py, to estimate the Ca^{2+} pumping activity of the SR Ca^{2+} pump. The particular example calculates the steady-state turnover rate of the pump as a function of $[Ca^{2+}]$. To simplify the calculation, $[Mg^{2+}]$ and pH are assumed to be constant (i.e., to be "well buffered") at 1 mM and 7, respectively. The program listing is shown next, followed by the plot (Fig. 9.9) and printed output of the program.

```
1  # -*- coding: utf-8 -*-
2  # Example for Scheme 9.5 and Fig. 9.9 in Ch.9: CaPump.py
3  # Description: calculate and plot the turnover rate of SR Ca-pump vs [Ca]
4
5  #the units for the reaction rates will be in uM and ms
6  #the notation for the states of the Ca-pump will involve E (for Enzyme)
7  #the total amount of enzyme will be 1.0 and we will deal in fractional units
8  #CaE and MgE denote the fraction of enzyme bound with one Ca or Mg ion, respectively
9  #Ca2E and Mg2 denote the fraction of enzyme bound with two Ca or Mg ions, respectively
10 #HE,H2E, H3E and H4E denote the fraction of enzyme bound with 1, ..., 4 H ions
11 #E by itself will denote the enzyme fraction not bound with Ca, Mg, or H
12 #E_and_H denotes the fraction of total enzyme not bound with Ca or Mg, i.e.,
13 #   E_and_H = E + HE + H2E + H3E + H4E
14
```

```python
15  import numpy as np
16  import matplotlib.pyplot as plt
17
18  def f_E(H):        #H is the value of [H+] (a constant)
19  #f_E returns the fraction of the non-Ca, non-Mg enzymes states that is H-free
20  #the 5 addends in the sum give the relative amounts of E, HE, H2E, H3E, and H4E
21      sum=(1+H/Kd5+H**2/(Kd5*Kd6)+H**3/(Kd5*Kd6*Kd7)+H**4/(Kd5*Kd6*Kd7*Kd8))
22      return 1/sum
23
24  def Factor_Ca2E(CaR):        #CaR is the value of [Ca2+] (a constant)
25  #Factor_Ca2E returns the factor by which to multiply fE_and_H to get fCa2E
26      return kp1*kp2*CaR*CaR/(kp9*kp2*CaR+(kp9+km2)*km1)
27
28  def Factor_CaE(CaR):        #CaR is the value of [Ca2+] (a constant)
29  #Factor_CaE returns the factor by which to multiply fE_and_H to get fCaE
30      return Factor_Ca2E(CaR)*(kp9+km2)/(kp2*CaR)
31
32  def f_E_and_H(CaR):        #CaR is the value of [Ca2+] (a constant)
33  #f_E_and_H returns the fraction of all states in state E plus the H-bound states
34      MgE=MgR/Kd3          #this factor times E plus the H-bound states gives MgE
35      Mg2E=(MgR/Kd4)*MgE   #this factor times E plus the H-bound states gives Mg2E
36      CaE=Factor_CaE(CaR)  #this factor times E plus the H-bound states gives CaE
37      Ca2E=Factor_Ca2E(CaR)#this factor times E plus the H-bound states gives Ca2E
38      return 1/(1+MgE+Mg2E+CaE+Ca2E)
39
40  def Ca_Turnover_Rate(CaR):
41  #the turnover rate equals kp9 times the fraction of the total enzyme in the Ca2E state
42      return kp9*f_E_and_H(CaR)*Factor_Ca2E(CaR)
43
44  def rate_to_console(CaR):  #function for outputting rates to the console
45      temp=1000*Ca_Turnover_Rate(CaR)
46      print("Turnover rate (per s) = {:.4} for CaR = {:}".format(temp,CaR))
47
48  #this section gives rate constants for non-instantaneous reactions
49  kp1=2e-1   #per uM per ms
50  km1=8e-3   #per ms
```

```
51  kp2=2e-1        #per uM per ms
52  km2=1e-2        #per ms
53  kp3=1e-4        #per uM per ms
54  km3=5e-3        #per ms
55  kp4=1e-4        #per uM per ms
56  km4=100e-3      #per ms
57  kp9=4e-3        #per ms
58
59  Kd5=1e-2        #H in uM if pK for step 5 = 8
60  Kd6=1e-2        #H in uM if pK for step 6 = 8
61  Kd7=1e0         #H in uM if pK for step 7 = 6
62  Kd8=1e1         #H in uM if pK for step 8 = 5
63
64  MgR=1000.       #resting [Mg2+] (assumed to be 1 mM and constant)
65  pH=7            # resting pH (assumed to be 7 and constant)
66
67  #fE must be set before the call to the other user-defined functions
68  fE=f_E(10**(-pH+6)) #10**(-pH+6) gives [H] in uM, converted from pH units
69  #fE is the fraction of non-Ca, non_Mg states able to react with Ca (step 1) or Mg (step 3)
70  kp1=kp1*fE      #then this is the effective value of kp1 for step 1
71  kp3=kp3*fE      #and this is the effective value of kp3 for step 3
72
73  #these are the actual (Kd2 and Kd4) or effective (Kd1 and Kd3) Kd's for steps 1 to 4
74  Kd1=km1/kp1     #uM
75  Kd2=km2/kp2     #uM
76  Kd3=km3/kp3     #uM
77  Kd4=km4/kp4     #uM
78
79  plt.figure()
80  plt.subplot(2,1,1)
81  X1=np.linspace(.01,100,1000)
82  Y1=1000*Ca_Turnover_Rate(X1)  #convert turnover rate from ms to s
83  plt.plot(X1,Y1,'k')
84  plt.xlim(0,100)
85  plt.ylim(0,4)
86  plt.ylabel("Turnover Rate (s$^{-1}$)")
```

```
87  plt.title('Turnover Rate of the SR Ca\u00B2\u207A Pump vs. Free [Ca\u00B2\u207A]')
88
89  plt.subplot(2,1,2)
90  X2=np.linspace(.01,.20,100)
91  Y2=1000*Ca_Turnover_Rate(X2)  #convert the turnover rate from ms to s
92  plt.plot(X2,Y2,'k')
93  plt.xlim(0,.2)
94  plt.ylim(0,.15)
95  plt.xlabel("[Ca$^{2+}$] \u03BCM")
96  plt.ylabel("Turnover Rate (s$^{-1}$)")
97  plt.savefig("CaPumping.png", dpi=200) #this looks fine at 55KB
98
99  rate_to_console(0.05)
100 rate_to_console(0.1)
101 rate_to_console(3.425)
102 rate_to_console(1e5)
```

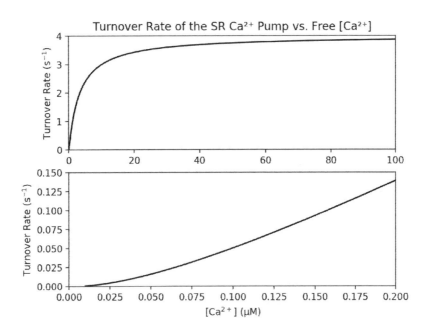

Figure. 9.9 The curves show the steady-state turnover rate of the SR Ca^{2+} pump (ordinate) at different levels of free [Ca^{2+}] (abscissa) as calculated with Scheme 9.5 and the reaction rates in Table 9.1. The lower plot shows points from the upper plot near the origin, with expanded vertical and horizontal scales.

Turnover rate (per s) = 0.01618 for CaR = 0.05
Turnover rate (per s) = 0.05061 for CaR = 0.1
Turnover rate (per s) = 2.0 for CaR = 3.425
Turnover rate (per s) = 4.0 for CaR = 100000.0

Program Notes

- The statements for the constants and plotting sections of the program are either obvious or have been discussed in previous program notes.

- The units of the calculations are ms for time, μM for $[Ca^{2+}]$, $[Mg^{2+}]$, $[H^+]$, and fractional units for the enzyme, i.e., the calculations consider the different states of one unit of the enzyme in Scheme 9.5. Thus, the sum of the 'concentrations' of the different states of the enzyme, i.e., $[E]+[HE]+[H_2E]+[H_3E]+[H_4E]+[MgE]+[Mg_2E]+[CaE]+[Ca_2E]$, is 1.0. The program omits brackets and subscripts when referencing these states. $[H^+]$ and $[Mg^{2+}]$ are constant at 0.1 μM (i.e., pH = 7) and 1,000 μM, respectively. For any given calculation of the pump's steady-state turnover rate, $[Ca^{2+}]$ (denoted 'CaR' in the program -- short for 'Resting $[Ca^{2+}]$') is also a constant. Given CaR, the program needs only to calculate Ca_2E (the fraction of the enzyme in the Ca_2E state), since the enzyme turnover rate will then be $k_{+9} \cdot Ca2E$.

- The strategy of the program is to use the various reaction equations that, in Scheme 9.5, correspond to the 8 forward and reverse reaction steps and the forward reaction step 9. Calculation of Ca2E then follows after substitutions in, and simplification of, these equations for use in the relevant functions defined in the program.

- It is important to note that, because the example considers a steady-state calculation, the concentrations of all 9 species in the reaction must be constant, i.e., $(d/dt)E = 0$, $(d/dt)CaE =0$, $(d/dt)MgE = 0$, … . Also, for the reactions involving the states MgE, Mg$_2$E, HE, H$_2$E, H$_3$E, and H$_4$E, the 'forward fluxes' associated with these reactions must equal the 'reverse' fluxes, i.e., $k_{+3} [Mg^{2+}] [E] = k_{-3} [MgE]$, $k_{+4} [Mg^{2+}] [MgE] = k_{-4} [Mg_2E]$, etc. (If there were net fluxes associated with these reactions, the reaction species would not be constant.) However, for the reaction of E with Ca^{2+}, the forward and reverse fluxes are not equal, i.e., $k_{+1} [Ca^{2+}] [E] \neq k_{-1} [CaE]$; and, similarly, $k_{+2} [Ca^{2+}] [CaE] \neq k_{-2} [Ca_2E]$. This follows because there must be a net flux of Ca^{2+} through states CaE and Ca_2E because there is a net flux of Ca^{2+} through reaction 9 (from state Ca_2E to E). Thus, while the equilibrium equations can be applied to simplifications involving states MgE, Mg_2E, HE, H_2E, H_3E, and H_4E, they cannot be applied to states CaE and Ca_2E.

- To take into account the states of the enzyme in the H^+-bound form (HE, H_2E, H_3E, H_4E), the four equilibrium binding equations are used, i.e., $[H^+][E] = Kd5\,[HE]$; …; $[H^+][H_3E] = Kd8\,[H_4E]$. After substitutions and simplification, the relation involving 'sum' in function 'f_E(H)' in the program is obtained, which permits calculation of the fraction of the non-Ca^{2+} and non-Mg^{2+} states of the enzyme that is in the E form, i.e., not bound with any H. Line 68 does the call to this function, with the return value assigned to variable fE. The effect of the H-bound states on making some of E (actually, most of E) unavailable to react with Ca^{2+} and Mg^{2+} can then be accounted for simply by multiplying the forward rates k_{+1} and k_{+3} (denoted kp1 and kp3 in the program) by fE (lines 70-71). This reduction in the effective values of kp1 and kp3 is transmitted to the steady-state condition, i.e., to Kd1 and Kd2, by lines 74 and 76.

- To account for the states of the enzyme in the Mg^{2+}-bound and Ca^{2+}-bound forms, two approaches are used in function 'f_E_and_H'. For Mg^{2+}, the equilibrium equations apply; thus, $[Mg^{2+}][E] = Kd3[MgE]$ and $[Mg^{2+}][MgE] = Kd4[Mg_2E]$. For Ca^{2+}, the kinetic equations must be used because, as noted above, there is flux of Ca^{2+} through reactions 1, 2, and 9. After substitutions and simplification, four factors are obtained for use in the body of function f_E_and_H that, when multiplied by the sum of all non-Ca^{2+}- and non-Mg^{2+}-bound states (i.e., by E+HE+H2E+H3E+H4E), yield the relevant fractional values for CaE, Ca2E, MgE, and Mg2E. The function f_E_and_H returns the summed fraction of the enzyme in the 5 states that involve E and the various H_nE, i.e., it returns E+HE+H2E+H3E+H4E. Because function f_E_and_H has accounted for the Mg^{2+}-bound states (MgE, and Mg2E), it also permits accounting for the competitive inhibition of the enzyme due to Mg^{2+}.

- The function 'Factor_Ca2E' returns the factor by which to multiply the return value of f_E_and_H to obtain Ca2E; similarly, the function 'Factor_CaE' returns the factor by which to multiply the return value of f_E_and_H to obtain CaE. These functions use formulas obtained from the kinetic equations that apply to the flux of Ca^{2+} through reactions 1, 2, and 9 involving the composite 'state' E+HE+H2E+H3E+H4E (the fractional value of which is returned by function f_E_and_H) and states CaE and Ca2E. Note that E+HE+H2E+H3E+H4E is a proxy for a composite state E' that can react with Ca^{2+} to give state CaE via the forward reaction rate constant kp1. However, kp1 has been modified from its original value in line 49 by multiplication in line 70 by the factor fE, i.e., the value returned by function f_E, which takes into account the effects of protons in reactions 5 through 8.

- With the above functions in place, the function 'Ca_Turnover_Rate' can then report the enzyme turnover rate, which is kp9*f_E_and_H(CaR)*Factor_Ca2E(CaR).

Physiological Interpretation
Based on the program's printed output to the console and Fig. 9.9, it follows that:
- A maximal pump turnover rate of 4.0 s^{-1} (= k$_{+9}$) applies at saturating [Ca^{2+}].
- The half-maximal turnover rate, 2.0 s^{-1}, occurs at free [Ca^{2+}] = 3.425 µM.
- At [Ca^{2+}] = 0.05 µM (the approximate resting [Ca^{2+}] level in many cells), the turnover rate is 0.0162 s^{-1}, i.e., only 0.0041 of the maximum possible rate.
- The shape of the curve near [Ca^{2+}] = 0.05 µM in the lower panel of Fig. 9.9 is concave upward. For example, the ordinate value of the curve at [Ca^{2+}] = 0.1 µM is 0.0506 s^{-1}, which is 3.1 times that for [Ca^{2+}] = 0.05 µM. Thus, near the resting level, if [Ca^{2+}] rises above its normal level, the activity of the Ca^{2+} pump is expected to increase more than linearly as it works to restore [Ca^{2+}] to the normal resting level.
- If the total concentration of Ca^{2+} pumps, if referred to the cytoplasmic water volume, is 120 µM (as is thought to be the case in some skeletal muscle fiber types; see Chapter 13), the maximal rate at which the Ca^{2+} pumps could remove Ca^{2+} ions from the cytoplasm is given by the pump concentration (120 µM) times the maximal pump turnover rate (4 s^{-1}) times the number of Ca^{2+} ions translocated per pump turnover (2), i.e., 960 µM Ca^{2+} ions per s. At the normal level of resting free [Ca^{2+}] (= 0.05 µM), the rate of Ca^{2+} removal would be 3.9 µM Ca^{2+} ions per s. For the SR to be in a steady-state at a resting [Ca^{2+}] level of 0.05 µM, the leakage of Ca^{2+} out of the SR would necessarily equal the uptake rate, i.e., be 3.9 µM per s.

9.9 STRUCTURE OF EF-HAND Ca^{2+} BINDING SITES WITHIN PROTEINS

The previous sections of this chapter mentioned several Ca^{2+}-binding proteins whose activity is important or essential for the functioning of many cell types. Many such Ca^{2+}-binding proteins are known and these fall into two broad classes: (i) Ca^{2+} buffers, such as parvalbumin, which bind Ca^{2+} on a temporary basis, eventually releasing the bound Ca^{2+}

for handling by other pathways, such as those that pump Ca^{2+} into the SR or ER by the SERCA Ca^{2+} pump or out of the cell by a surface-membrane Ca^{2+} transport protein; and (ii) Ca^{2+} sensors, such as troponin, calmodulin, and recoverin, which, when bound with Ca^{2+}, change their conformational state and thereby alter the activities of associated enzymes to which they are bound, such as acto-myosin, phosphorylase kinase, and rhodopsin kinase, respectively.

Interestingly, many of the Ca^{2+}-binding domains on these various proteins have a similar structure, which is referred to as an 'EF hand' binding domain. This protein motif, which is found, for example, on parvalbumin, troponin, calmodulin, and recoverin, consists of ~30 amino acids that provide the structural basis for Ca^{2+}-binding. Fig. 9.10 (left side) diagrams the structure of this motif. It consists of two alpha-helices that are oriented approximately at right angles to each other and a flexible loop of 9 amino acids that connects the two helices. A sequence of 12 amino acids defines the binding pocket for Ca^{2+}, 9 from the flexible loop plus the first 3 amino acids in the following helix (Gifford et al., 2007).

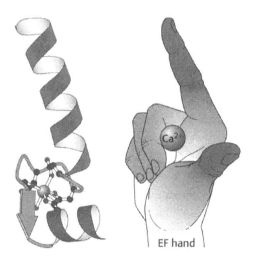

Figure 9.10 Structure of the helix-loop-helix Ca^{2+}-binding motif that is found in many Ca^{2+}-binding proteins and is referred to generically by the name 'EF hand'. Left: two alpha helices are shown, disposed approximately at right angles. A flexible amino-acid loop connects the helices, within which is a binding site for Ca^{2+}. The bound Ca^{2+} ion, which is shown as a sphere in the middle of the binding loop, is coordinated by amino-acid oxygen atoms within the loop surrounding the Ca^{2+} ion. Right: see text. [Credit: *Biochemistry* by Berg et al. (2002).]

The name 'EF hand' was given to this helix-loop-helix motif because of its characteristics as revealed in the crystal structure of the protein parvalbumin, the first protein in which this type of Ca^{2+}-binding site was identified (Kretsinger and Nockolds, 1973). The parvalbumin in this first study was obtained from fish muscle; related isoforms of parvalbumin are found in many other cell types in substantial concentrations, including skeletal muscle fibers of mammals and fast-firing neurons in the brain. The following characteristics were observed for this fish parvalbumin. (i) The two alpha helices that surrounded the loop of amino acids in which the bound Ca^{2+} ion was identified are the fifth and sixth such helices in the protein (counting from the N terminus). Because this series of helices was named for their order of appearance beginning with the letter 'A', the helices on either side of the bound Ca^{2+} ion are the 'E' and 'F' helices. (ii) The relative length and orientation of the E and F helices, with the intervening loop and the bound Ca^{2+} ion, are reminiscent of the thumb, index, and middle fingers of a human right hand if positioned to hold a small round ball (a proxy for a spherical Ca^{2+} ion) within a curled middle finger (Fig. 9.10, right side).

Under the parvalbumin-crystallization conditions of Kretsinger and Nockolds, only one Ca^{2+} ion and one Ca^{2+} binding site were identified in the protein. Subsequent work revealed that parvalbumin has a second functional Ca^{2+}-binding site at the site of the C and D helices and its connecting loop, the structural arrangements of which are similar to those of the E and F helices and its connecting loop. (The A-B helix with its connecting loop is also a potential Ca^{2+}-binding site but it appears to be non-functional.) Ca^{2+}-binding proteins with similar structural motifs have been identified subsequently in many other Ca^{2+}-binding proteins, including those mentioned above. Often, the EF-hand sites come in functional pairs that may influence each other's binding reaction with Ca^{2+} in a cooperative fashion. Thus, Ca^{2+}-binding proteins with EF-hand motifs often have two or four functional Ca^{2+}-binding domains.

Subsequent crystal structures of parvalbumin and other Ca^{2+}-binding proteins have revealed additional details about the EF-hand binding motif, including the following:

- Typically, the bound Ca^{2+} ion is stabilized in the Ca^{2+}-binding pocket by 7 coordinating oxygen atoms, which usually include 6 on the residues in the 12 amino-acid loop (if the first 3 residues on the second helix are included in the loop count) plus an oxygen on a water molecule. The protein oxygens are usually contributed by residues 1, 3, 5, 7, 9, and 12 (counting from the end of the E helix) and are mostly side-chain oxygens. In general, the double-positive charge on a Ca^{2+} ion needs to be heavily shielded, hence the 6-7 coordinating oxygen atoms for a Ca^{2+} ion bound to a protein. This compares with the 8-9 coordinating oxygen atoms from the water ions that surround and shield a Ca^{2+} ion in solution.

- With the EF-hand motif, five of the oxygens on the loop residues are often arranged in a roughly planar configuration, thereby defining a pentagon, with a sixth oxygen above the plane and a seventh below. This configuration, with 7 oxygen atoms coordinating the bound Ca^{2+} ion, is referred to as a 'pentagonal bi-pyramid'.

9.10 EXERCISES

Exercise 9.1 Write a *Python* program to make a plot like that in Fig. 9.1. Compare the slope of the curve at $[Ca^{2+}] = 0$ with that at $[Ca^{2+}] = K_d$. Generalize this difference qualitatively in terms of a statement regarding how the incremental binding of Ca^{2+} by site S varies with $[Ca^{2+}]$.

Exercise 9.2 Write a *Python* program to make a plot like that in Fig. 9.2. Determine the maximum slope of the curve in your figure and verify that this occurs at pCa – pKd. Formulate a qualitative statement regarding at what pCa the maximal incremental binding of Ca^{2+} to site S occurs for a given fractional change in $[Ca^{2+}]$.

Exercise 9.3 Write a *Python* program that uses Eqns. 9.6, 9.8, and 9.9 to calculate [CaS], [S], and $[Ca^{2+}]$ for given values of $[Ca_T]$, $[S_T]$, and Kd and make a plot like that in Fig. 9.3 for several different values of $[S_T]$.

Exercise 9.4 Given Eqn. 9.5:
a) Show that the rate constant at which f_{CaS} changes in response to a new level of $[Ca^{2+}]$ is $k_f [Ca^{2+}] + k_r$. (The rate constant will be the coefficient of $(d/dt)f_{CaS}$ in the appropriately-expressed equation.)

b) Write a *Python* program that (i) makes a plot like that in Fig. 9.4 in response to a step change in $[Ca^{2+}]$ from 0.1 to 10 µM and back again, and (ii) include statements in your program to estimate the time constant of the change both during the rising and falling phases of f_{CaS}.

Exercise 9.5
a) Confirm that the function $F_{CaS}([Ca^{2+}])$, if defined as $(f_{CaS}([Ca^{2+}]+[Ca^{2+}]_0) - f_{CaS}(Ca^{2+}]_0))/(1 - f_{CaS}(Ca^{2+}]_0))$, satisfies Eqn. 9.16.

b) Interpret the effect of $[Ca^{2+}]_0$ in Eqn. 9.16 and the effect of $[Mg^{2+}]$ in Eqn. 9.14 in terms of Scheme 2.

c) Suppose that a divalent-ion binding site on a cytoplasmic protein can bind either $[Ca^{2+}]$ or $[Mg^{2+}]$ and that the resting free $[Ca^{2+}]$ and resting free $[Mg^{2+}]$ levels in the cytoplasm are $[Ca^{2+}]_0$ and $[Mg^{2+}]_0$, respectively. Let S denote the fraction of these sites that are not bound with either Ca^{2+} or Mg^{2+} at rest and let $F_{CaS}([Ca^{2+}])$ denote the fraction of these sites that are Ca^{2+}-bound in the steady-state at some $[Ca^{2+}]$ level $> [Ca^{2+}]_0$. Derive a formula for $F_{CaS}([Ca^{2+}])$.

Exercise 9.6
a) Determine where the slope of the continuous curve in the left-hand panel of Fig. 9.8 (the cooperative Ca^{2+}-binding curve, with N=2) has its maximum value. Express the result in terms of $[Ca^{2+}]$ relative to Kd.

b) What is the value of the maximum slope and how does it compare with the maximum slope of the dotted curve in Fig. 9.8?

c) Compare several plots of the Hill equation (e.g., for N=1, N=2, N=4, N=8) on the same graph; do this for the independent variable expressed both on a linear scale and a $\log_{10}$ scale.

Exercise 9.7 Determine the derivative of Eqn. 9.24 with respect to $[Ca^{2+}]$. What is its value at $[Ca^{2+}] = 0$? How does its maximum value compare with that of the fully-cooperative Ca^{2+}-binding curve (Eqn. 9.20)?

Exercise 9.8 Fig. 9.8 shows 4 Ca^{2+}-binding curves, 3 of which are different. Write a *Pyhon* program that plots these 3 curves on a pCa scale.

Exercise 9.9 The 3 different curves in Fig. 9.8 and their underlying schemes (independent binding, fully-cooperative binding, and partially-cooperative binding) have relative advantages and disadvantages as a basis for controlling the steady-state activity of a Ca^{2+}-dependent enzyme or process. (Some of these advantages and disadvantages were discussed in Section 9.7.) Two other schemes are described below in which two Ca^{2+} ions can bind to two sites on a Ca^{2+}-dependent protein and thereby control its activity. With each scheme, assume that each site on P binds Ca^{2+} with a Kd of 1 µM and does so independently of the other site. For each of the schemes: (a) write a *Python* program that plots the associated Ca^{2+} binding curve vs. free $[Ca^{2+}]$ between, say, 0 to 5 µM (i.e., plot a curve analogous to the curves in Fig. 9.8), and (b) discuss the advantages and disadvantages of the binding curve as a control mechanism relative to the curves in Fig. 9.8.

(i) Suppose that P is a Ca^{2+}-activated protein that is active only when both of its Ca^{2+} binding sites have bound a Ca^{2+} ion. (Hint: note that the probability of the occurrence of two independent events is the product of the probabilities of occurrence of each event.)

(ii) Suppose that P is a Ca^{2+}-activated protein that is active when either or both of its Ca^{2+} binding sites contain a bound Ca^{2+} ion. (Hint: note that this situation is the complement of both sites not having a bound Ca^{2+} ion.)

Exercise 9.10 Table 9.1 and Scheme 9.5 in the text define one reaction that has been used to model Ca^{2+} transport by the SR/ER Ca^{2+} pump. Another reaction for this transport is shown below in Table 9.2 and Scheme 9.6 (Baylor et al., 2002). As before, 'E' denotes the enzyme and '(2 Ca^{2+})' denotes the two Ca^{2+} ions released on the luminal side of the SR/ER membrane.

In this scheme, the first Ca^{2+} ion binds to the pump with relatively low affinity. In response to this binding, the pump switches to a new conformation, CaE', to which the second Ca^{2+} ion binds with relatively high affinity. Overall, the two Ca^{2+} ions thus bind to the enzyme in a cooperative manner.

Given Scheme 9.6, write a *Python* program that calculates the steady-state turnover rate of the enzyme at different values of $[Ca^{2+}]$ and compare the turnover properties with those in Fig. 9.9.

(i) Note any differences related to the maximum turnover rate, the value of $[Ca^{2+}]$ that corresponds to the half-maximal turnover rate, and how the turnover rate varies with $[Ca^{2+}]$ near the resting level.

(ii) Also note the qualitative kinetic difference between this pump scheme and that of Scheme 9.5. In Scheme 9.6, the first Ca^{2+} ion binds with a rate constant of 10^8 M^{-1} s^{-1} whereas in Scheme 9.5 the first Ca^{2+} ion binds with a much smaller effective rate constant due to the competitive binding of Mg^{2+} and H^+ to the enzyme at low $[Ca^{2+}]$. Thus, if $[Ca^{2+}]$ should rise suddenly, Scheme 9.5 has a built-in kinetic delay before its full Ca^{2+}-pumping activity is in effect. (See text for discussion of the physiological advantage that this kinetic difference gives to Scheme 9.5 compared with Scheme 9.6.)

REACTION SCHEMES AND KINETIC EQUATIONS   249

Table 9.2 Rate Constants Associated with Scheme 9.6 (18 °C)

Number and Reaction	Forward Rate (k_{+n})	Reverse Rate (k_{-n})	Ratio (k_{-n}/k_{+n})
1. $Ca^{2+} + E \leftrightarrow CaE$	10^8 M^{-1} s^{-1}	1000 s^{-1}	$Kd1 = 10$ μM
2. $CaE \leftrightarrow CaE'$	500 s^{-1}	1200 s^{-1}	$Kd2 = 2.4$
3. $Ca^{2+} + CaE' \leftrightarrow Ca_2E'$	10^8 M^{-1} s^{-1}	10 s^{-1}	$Kd3 = 0.1$ μM
4. $Ca_2E' \leftrightarrow E + (2\ Ca^{2+})$	20 s^{-1}	0	$Kd4 = 0$

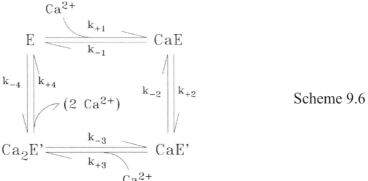

Scheme 9.6

Exercise 9.11 This exercise asks the reader to simulate the kinetic response of a Ca^{2+}-binding site S to a sudden increase in total $[Ca^{2+}]$ ($[Ca_T]$). The simulation mimics the results of a 'stopped-flow' experiment in which a solution of known volume containing a known amount of total Ca^{2+} is rapidly mixed with another solution of known volume containing a known amount of total S. The mixing, which produces a step increase in $[Ca_T]$ within the combined volume, drives a time-dependent increase in the concentration of CaS ($[CaS](t)$), rising from zero at the moment of mixing ($[CaS](0) = 0$) to a final steady-state level ($[CaS](\infty)$). $[CaS](t)$ depends on the forward (k_f) and reverse (k_r) rate constants of the underlying Ca^{2+}-binding reaction, which is assumed to be like that in Scheme 9.1.

a) To simulate this stopped-flow experiment, write a *Python* program that calculates and plots $[CaS](t)$ and free $[Ca^{2+}](t)$ ($= [Ca_T] - [CaS](t)$) in response to a step increase in $[Ca_T]$. The partial program listed below part (c) may help with this exercise.

b) For several values of $[S_T]$ (the total concentration of S) and $[Ca_T]$, characterize the kinetics of $[CaS](t)$ in terms of the rate constant of a fitted single-exponential waveform. Note, however, that $[CaS](t)$ may not exactly follow a single-exponential waveform. Use of *Python*'s curve_fit function, described in Appendix D, may help with this exercise.

c) Investigate how the rate constants of your exponential fits depend on k_f and k_r.

Partial program
```
import numpy as np
import matplotlib.pyplot as plt
from scipy.integrate import odeint
from scipy.optimize import curve_fit  #not in the snippet below but required for 'curve_fit'
#function F below contains the formula for (d/dt)[CaS] in the call by odeint
#CaT-CaSite gives free [Ca]; ST-CaSite gives free [S]; work in units of uM and ms
def F(CaSite,t):
    return kf*(CaT-CaSite)*(ST-CaSite)-kr*CaSite
ST=100.     #example value of total site concentration (uM)
CaT=100.    #example value of total Ca concentration (uM)
Kd=10.      #example value of the dissociation constant of S for Ca
kf = 1e-1   #assumed on-rate constant of the Ca-S reaction (per uM per ms)
kr = kf*Kd  #calculated off-rate constant of the Ca-S reaction (per ms)
#parameters for setting up time grid for the kinetic response (ms)
t_start=0.; t_end=4.; N_steps=1000     #start and end times; number of steps in between
t=np.linspace(t_start,t_end,N_steps+1)   #time grid for the calculation
y_init=0.          #y will contain the time course of CaS
y=odeint(F,y_init,t)  #y is a column vector (a type of 2-dimensional array)
#y=y.flatten()     #if needed, this would make y a 1-dimensional array
plt.figure()              #make a plot of the kinetic response
ymax=max(ST,CaT)    #find the maximum of ST and CaT
plt.ylim(0., ymax)        #set the y-axis limits for the plot
plt.xlim(0., t_end)       #set the x-axis limits for the plot
plt.plot(t,y,'k', label="CaS")              #the [CaS] curve will be continuous
Ca=CaT-y
plt.plot(t,Ca,'k--', label="Ca\u00B2\u207A")  #the free [Ca2+] curve will be dashed
```

Exercise 9.12 For notational convenience, redefine Kd in Eqn. 9.21 as k^N. Write a *Python* program that tests, for several values of N>1, whether the maximal rate of change of f_{LP} is given by the expression: $(N-1)^{(N-1)/N} \cdot (N+1)^{(N+1)/N} / (4 N k)$. If so, can you show analytically that this formula is correct (e.g., Burdyga and Kosterin, 1991)?

CHAPTER 10

MORE ON ION CHANNELS

Ion channels are ubiquitous components of cells. Previous chapters have discussed basic properties of ion-channel function, including equilibrium potential, driving force, single-channel currents, and channel gating. In this chapter we examine further the structure, function, and physiological roles of ion channels. A particular focus is how the gating and permeation properties of individual ion channels are revealed in electrical recordings of the activity of single channels. Some important historical examples are included.

10.1 ION-CHANNEL FAMILIES

Bacteria contain ion channels. It is therefore likely that ion channels appeared very early in evolution. As organismal complexity evolved, so did the number and types of ion channels.

In vertebrates, ion channels are required for functions such as (i) establishing a stable resting state of cells, (ii) controlling the movement of salts and water into and out of cells, (iii) modulating the activity of individual cells according to the local metabolic conditions and hormonal environment, (iv) coding information about the internal and external world in the language of electrical signals, (v) sending electrical signals over distances, such as to integrating centers in the central nervous system or throughout the heart during the contractile cycle, (vi) processing information for higher brain functions such as perception, memory, thought, and consciousness, and (vii) initiating or modifying the output of effector cells, including the contractions of muscle cells and the secretions of endocrine and exocrine cells.

In mammals, more than 400 genes code for ion channels or their subunits (e.g., Cochet-Bisseul et al., 2014). Moreover, the number of different channel structures is likely to be substantially more than the number of channel genes because of alternative splicing of genes and the fact that ion channels complexes can be assembled in different ways from different subunits. Thus, the number of different channel types within any organism is very large.

In all cases, understanding channel functions begins with a characterization of two important properties: channel gating and channel permeation. Gating concerns what factors make the channel open or close and with what kinetics. Permeation concerns what ion species are able to move through the open channel (i.e., the selectivity of the channel) and with what rates (i.e., the permeability or the conductance of the channel).

A number of methods are used to classify ion channels into groups. The classifications are usually based on a commonality of either functional or structural properties. Such channel classifications often do not identify unique structural entities. Typically, several genes will code for different versions of any particular named channel type and, even if there is just one gene, splice variants can give rise to channels with somewhat different functional properties.

Functionally, the simplest distinction is based on whether a channel is selective for cations or anions. Commonly-recognized cation channels include Na^+ channels, K^+ channels, Ca^{2+} channels, and non-selective cation channels (which pass Na^+ and K^+ ions with approximately equal facility and sometimes also readily pass Ca^{2+} ions). Anion channels usually pass Cl^- (the most commonly-occurring anion), and several types of Cl^- channels are well-recognized (Jentsch et al., 2002). Cl^- channels, however, are usually not highly-selective for Cl^-; they often pass other anions, such as nitrate (NO_3^-), thiocyanate (SCN^-), and bicarbonate (HCO_3^-).

A second functional classification is based on the channel's gating properties, for example, whether it is voltage-dependent (opens or closes in response to a change in membrane potential), ligand-dependent (opens or closes in response to the binding of a chemical ligand such as acetylcholine, glycine, Ca^{2+}, or a cyclic nucleotide), stretch-dependent (opens or closes in response to a mechanical force applied to the channel), or temperature-dependent (shows a large change in opening or closing kinetics in response to a small change in temperature).

Often, the first and second methods of channel classification are used together to specify a particular family of channels -- for example, the family of voltage-dependent Na^+ channels, the family of glycine-activated Cl^- channels, and so forth.

Ligand-dependent channels, especially if activated by a ligand acting on the extracellular side of the channel, are often referred to as 'receptors' rather than 'channels' and are named for the 'agonist' (i.e., ligand) that controls the channel gating. Thus, acetylcholine-gated channels are commonly called 'acetylcholine receptors' (abbreviated 'AChRs'); glycine-gated channels are called 'glycine receptors'; and so forth.

It should also be noted that **not** all so-named receptors are ion channels. For example, among acetylcholine receptors, the nicotinic subtypes (denoted 'nAChR') are ion channels but the muscarinic subtypes (denoted 'mAChR') are not. The naming of a particular type of an AChR as nAChR or mAChR was initially made based on whether the cellular response of the receptor was more sensitive to activation by nicotine or muscarine -- two pharmacological agents used in studies of acetylcholine-activated membrane proteins. nAChRs belong to a diverse family of cation channels, whereas mAChRs are now known to be part of a membrane complex whose activity depends on a 'G protein' (short for 'guanine-nucleotide binding protein'), a type of GTPase.

G proteins are localized to the cytoplasmic side of the plasmalemma or the cytoplasmic side of an intracellular membrane and, by means of their ability to bind and hydrolyze guanosine triphosphate, help transmit signals from the ECF or from within an intracellular compartment or its membrane to other membrane proteins or to the cytoplasm of the cell. G proteins are typically controlled by G-protein-coupled receptors (GPCRs), which are integral membrane proteins that extend across the membrane.

Most frequently, a G protein is activated when its associated GPCR binds a signaling molecule such as a hormone or a neurotransmitter in the ECF. A change in the conformation of the GPCR then activates the associated G protein. While neither GPCRs nor their associated G proteins are ion channels, some G proteins that are activated by GPCRs have important effects on ion channels, such as occurs after activation of mAChRs in heart muscle cells. This book will not consider further the large number of signal-transduction pathways that are controlled by GPCRs and G proteins.

Sometimes families of ion channels, such as the family of voltage-dependent Na^+ channels and the family of voltage-dependent K^+ channels, etc., are referenced together as a 'superfamily'. In general, superfamilies are channel groups that have a common genetic history, such as all voltage-dependent channels, or all anion channels, or all ligand-gated channels, or, even more specifically, all pentameric ligand-gated ion channels. The last grouping includes nAChRs and serotonin receptors, which are cation channels, as well as glycine receptors and γ-aminobutyric acid (GABA) receptors, which are anion channels.

All four of these channel types have five principal sub-units, i.e., 'pore-forming' subunits; these surround and define the water-filled pore within the protein complex that provides the hydrophilic pathway for ion flow across the membrane. The binding sites for the agonists are located on the outside of the extracellular surface of the receptors.

Channel families are sometimes classified into sub-families. For example, the family of voltage-dependent K^+ channels identified in flies has been divided into four sub-families called 'Shaker', 'Shab', 'Shaw', and 'Shal', which have distinguishing structural and functional features. Originally, four fly genes were identified that coded for the principal subunits of the four channel types. In humans, many more genes (~40) code for the pore-forming subunits of voltage-dependent K^+ channels. Yet, based on similarities in amino-acid sequences and functional properties, a number of these types can be grouped into the same four sub-families that were identified in flies.

Another important family of ion channels gated by an extracellular ligand is the family of glutamate receptors (GluRs). Glutamate is an important excitatory transmitter and is thought to be involved in much of the information processing that takes place in the central nervous system and spinal cord. In glutamate channels, the hydrophilic pathway within the protein complex is made up of four sub-units. This contrasts with the other ligand-gated channels mentioned above that are activated extracellularly, in which the hydrophilic pathway is made up of five sub-units.

Three sub-families of glutamate ion-channel receptors have been identified, distinguished according to their responses to pharmacological analogues of glutamate. One responds with specificity to n-methyl-d-aspartate (NMDA), another to α-amino-3-hydroxy-5-methyl-4-isoxazole propionic acid (AMPA), and the third to kainate. Multiple receptor types within each of these sub-families are recognized. When open, these channels, like nAChRs, function as non-selective cation channels, passing Na^+, K^+, and, in some cases, Ca^{2+}. In general, the electrical responses of AMPA and kainate receptors are somewhat faster than those of NMDA receptors, whereas the permeability of NMDA receptors to Ca^{2+} is usually functionally significant and of special importance in eliciting cellular responses that depend on a rise in the intracellular Ca^{2+} concentration. Two other glutamate receptor sub-families have been identified but do not function as ion channels. One is the so-called 'metabotropic glutamate receptors' (mGluRs), which are G-protein-coupled receptors. The other is the 'delta' sub-family, identified because of its structural homologies with the NMDA, AMPA, and kainate sub-types.

An important ion-channel family that is gated by ligands acting on the cytoplasmic side of the membrane is the family of cyclic nucleotide-gated (CNG) channels. CNG channels are also non-selective cation channels; they are centrally important in sensory transduction, including vision and olfaction. CNG channels open in response to the binding of cyclic nucleotides, such as cyclic adenosine monophosphate (cAMP) or cyclic guanosine monophosphate (cGMP), in the cytoplasm. Although these are ligand-gated channels, they are not called 'receptors' because the ligand binding takes place intracellularly, not extracellularly. In CNG channels, the hydrophilic pathway within the protein complex is made up of four sub-units.

Another classification of ion channels is based on whether a particular pharmacological agent is capable of activating or blocking the channel's activity with 'specificity' (i.e., with the ability to affect one channel type but not others) or with 'sensitivity' (i.e., with the ability to affect a channel type with a high affinity). Thus, channels may be classified as those that are sensitive to tetrodotoxin (TTX), which blocks most voltage-dependent Na^+ channels with high sensitivity and specificity, or tetraethylammonium (TEA), which blocks many types of K^+ channels but does so with variable sensitivity.

An ion channel type that binds a specific pharmacological agent with high specificity or sensitivity is sometimes referred to as 'receptor' for that agent even though the agent is not a physiological ligand for the channel. For example, ryanodine is an insect toxin isolated from certain plants in Central and South America that binds with high specificity and sensitivity to the Ca^{2+} release channels of the sarcoplasmic reticulum (SR) of skeletal and cardiac muscle cells. Because ryanodine was used to isolate this channel biochemically (Imigawa et al., 1987; Inue et al., 1987; Lai et al., 1988), this channel is often referred to as the 'ryanodine receptor', which is now known to exist in vertebrates in 3 major isoforms.

In a few cases, channels are classified according to how they are **not** gated, e.g., the cation channel known colloquially as the 'sodium leak channel' (NALCN). This voltage-insensitive channel is a non-selective cation channel whose formal name is '$Na_{Vi}2.1$' (where 'Na' denotes sodium and the 'Vi' subscript denotes voltage-insensitivity). Structurally, this cation channel belongs to the family of voltage-dependent Na^+ channels. It is found in cardiac cells and some types of neurons, and may be regulated by G proteins. These channels can be open in cells at rest and continuously allow Na^+ to enter the cell and K^+ to leave the cell -- hence the name 'leak channel'. These channels can therefore contribute importantly to setting or modifying the cell's resting V_m or, in the case of cells like heart cells and some neurons that have an unstable membrane potential, to determining the frequency of initiation of action potentials by the cell.

A number of other families of ion channels have been identified but are not discussed here.

10.2 STRUCTURAL MOTIFS OF ION CHANNELS

As noted previously, an ion channel's principal subunit (or complex of principal subunits) (i) extends across the membrane and (ii) contains a hydrophilic pathway within its interior through which ions can traverse the membrane at a high rate. In addition, other protein subunits that do not directly contribute to the formation of the hydrophilic pathway may be bound to the principal subunit(s) and modify their functions. These other subunits are called 'auxiliary' or 'accessory' subunits.

Several types of diagrams are commonly used to represent the structural features of ion channels and their subunits. One such is the ribbon diagram, an example of which is shown in Fig. 5.2 of Chapter 5. That diagram shows a relatively simple K^+ channel (a non-voltage-dependent one) that consists of four subunits, each with two transmembrane crossings. In ribbon diagrams such as Fig. 5.2, the pathway for ion movement through the channel is often clear, as are the transmembrane crossings, which take the form of α-helices (see also Fig. 2.6 of Chapter 2).

Another common method for representing structural features of ion-channels is a topological diagram. For each relevant protein or protein sub-unit, these diagrams extend from N-terminus to C-terminus, which are usually identified, and show general features related to the number of transmembrane crossings and the folding architecture. The pathway for ion movement through the channel may not be as clear in a topological diagram as in a ribbon structure. Fig. 10.1 shows two examples of such topological diagrams, on the left for one of the four principal subunits of a voltage-dependent K^+ channel and on the right for the principal subunit of a voltage-dependent Na^+ channel or a voltage-dependent Ca^{2+} channel.

As suggested by Fig. 10.1, Na^+ and Ca^{2+} channels likely evolved from K^+ channels by gene duplication. The pore-forming subunit of a K^+ channel (the α subunit) is made up of four identical subunits that come together in the membrane to surround the hydrophilic pathway.

With a Na⁺ or a Ca²⁺ channel, a single gene that is approximately four times the size of a K⁺-channel α-subunit gene codes the pore-forming part of the channel. In these channels, the protein has four distinguishable regions (called 'domains', or sometimes 'membrane-bound repeats'), which are structurally similar and are typically numbered I, II, III, and IV from the N- to the C- terminus. Together, these surround the hydrophilic pathway in a manner that mimics the structural arrangement of the four α subunits of a voltage-dependent K⁺ channel. As is the case for the α subunit of K⁺ channels, humans have multiple genes that code for different α subunits of voltage-dependent Na⁺ channels (at least 9) and for different α_1 subunits of voltage-dependent Ca²⁺ channels (at least 10).

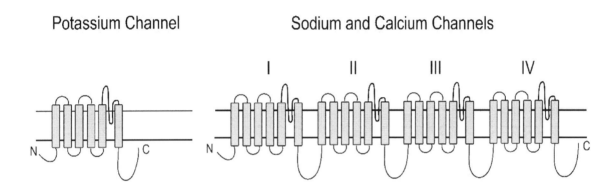

Figure 10.1 Topological diagrams showing structural features of the α subunit of a voltage-dependent K⁺ channel (left) and the α subunit of a voltage-dependent Na⁺ channel or the α_1 subunit of a voltage-dependent Ca²⁺ channel (right). The horizontal lines denote the width of the lipid bilayer. The N- and C-termini of the proteins, which are on the intracellular side the membrane, are labeled. The vertically-oriented rectangles denote membrane-crossing α helices; curved lines denote intracellular and extracellular protein loops. The hairpin loops that dip into the membrane from the extracellular side mark the location of the hydrophilic pore region of the channel; these loops have one or two short helices (not shown).

Fig. 10.2 shows a more detailed topological diagram of the two subunits that make up a voltage-dependent K⁺ channel: the α subunit (Doyle et al., 1998), the same subunit diagrammed on the left-side of Fig. 10.1, and the β subunit, which is an auxiliary protein that is found in some voltage-dependent K⁺ channels. The β subunit binds to the α subunit on its cytoplasmic side and can modify the channel's gating properties as well as affect the number of such K⁺ channels that are expressed in the membrane. The α subunit has six α-helical transmembrane crossings. These are sometimes called transmembrane 'Segments' and are labeled 'S1' through 'S6' in Fig. 10.2

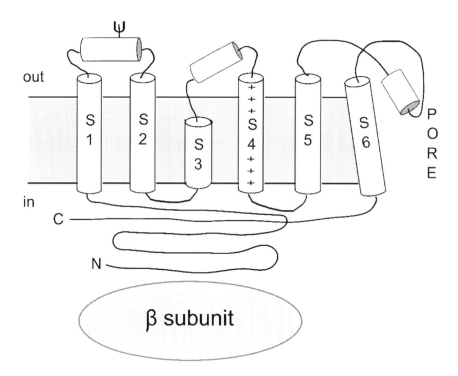

Figure 10.2 A more-detailed topological diagram of the α subunit of a voltage-dependent K⁺ channel; also diagrammed is the β subunit, which is bound to the intracellular side of the alpha subunit. A full channel has four copies of both subunits. The cylindrically-shaped structures that penetrate the membrane, labeled S1 through S6, are α helices. See text for discussion of the plus signs on S4 and the short helix and loop adjacent to the 'PORE' label. [After Hille (2001).]

In Fig. 10.2, the plus signs on the S4 crossing indicates the presence of a series of positively-charged amino acids. These are most frequently arginines but in some cases lysines. They appear as every third amino acid within each S4, and some S4s have a series of 5, 6, or even 7 such arginines and lysines. A similar series of arginines and lysines is found in the S4 of each of the four domains of voltage-dependent Na⁺ channels and voltage-dependent Ca^{2+} channels. In all of these voltage-dependent channels, when membrane potential is changed appropriately, the change in the electric field across the membrane causes the S4 helix to move relative to the membrane and the other regions of the protein. This electrically-driven movement is part of the sequence of conformational changes within the protein that leads to the opening of the channel. For example, in response to depolarization, the S4 helices move outward. In voltage-clamp experiments, the movement of the positively-charged amino acids within the S4 helix can be detected as channel gating currents (see discussion in Sections 8.8 and 8.9 of Chapter 8).

As shown in Fig. 10.2, several shorter α helices are also found on the extracellular side of the α subunit. The helix located topologically between S5 and S6 is shown dipping into the protein and pointing at an angle toward the middle of the membrane. This short helix is called the 'pore helix' (P helix; Doyle et al., 1998) and the protein loop between the C-terminal end of the P helix and the start of the S6 helix is an important structural region of all voltage-dependent ion channels. This protein loop contains the so-called 'pore loop domain'. It forms the outer part of the hydrophilic pathway for ion movement within the channel and provides the structural basis for the ion selectivity of each particular channel type (see the region labeled 'PORE' in Fig. 10.2; see also the pore loops in Fig. 5.2, which show bound potassium ions in the outer region of the channel). This channel region is also known as the 'selectivity filter'. It has a specific amino-acid sequence that, depending on channel-type, preferentially binds a K^+ ion, a Na^+ ion, or a Ca^{2+} ion with an appropriate affinity, letting it pass through this channel region while rejecting (or limiting) the binding and passage of other ion species.

The S5 and S6 helices within each of the four subunits of a voltage-dependent K^+ channel -- or within the four domains of a voltage-dependent Na^+ channel or Ca^{2+} channel -- surround the hydrophilic pathway within the channel. As suggested in Fig. 10.2, the S6 helices overall are closer to the axis of the pathway for ion flow than the S5 helices. As shown in Fig. 5.2, each subunit of a voltage independent K^+ channel has two membrane helices that correspond to the S5 and S6 helices found in voltage-dependent channels. When the cytoplasmic ends of the second of these helices in each subunit (or, in the case of a voltage-dependent Na^+ channel or Ca^{2+} channel, the last helix in each domain) are close to each other, the flow of ions along the hydrophilic pathway is blocked; thus, the channel is in a non-conducting/closed state (as suggested in Fig. 5.2). When the S4 helices in voltage-dependent channels move outward in response to membrane depolarization, a conformational rearrangement is conveyed to the ends of the S6 helices that allows (or forces) their ends to separate from one another. When this happens, the channel switches to open, thus permitting ions to transit from the ICF to the ECF or the ECF to the ICF. Subsequent conformational changes, such as those that allow the ends of the S6 helices to come together again -- or those that produce the inactivated state (which involves a different type of conformational change) -- cause the channel to revert to closed.

Typically, voltage-dependent Na^+ channels have one or two β subunits, which bind to the extracellular side of the α subunit. The β subunits of Na^+ channels come in subtypes that are coded by different genes. Voltage-dependent Ca^{2+} channels have four types of auxiliary subunits, denoted $α_2$, β, γ, and δ, which also come in various subtypes. The β and γ subunits are coded by separate genes, whereas the $α_2$ and δ subunits are synthesized as one protein but are cleaved post-translationally into separate subunits. The $α_2$ and δ subunits then usually remain in close contact, linked together by disulfide bonds.

Two sub-families of voltage-dependent Ca^{2+} channels will come up in later chapters, termed 'Ca_V1' and 'Ca_V2'. Cav1 channels are also known as 'L-type Ca^{2+} channels', as 'dihydropyridine-sensitive Ca^{2+} channels', or simply as 'dihydropyridine receptors' (DHPRs); they are important in excitation-contraction coupling in skeletal muscle (see Chapter 12) and in cardiac muscle. Ca_V2 channels include the Ca^{2+}-channel subtypes known as 'P-/Q-type', 'N-type', and 'R-type'; these are important in synaptic transmission (e.g., Turner et al. (1992); see also Chapter 11). Because voltage-dependent Ca^{2+} channels control the activity of many intracellular processes, they are often regulated by a variety of intracellular signaling pathways, including ones that involve G proteins, kinases, phosphatases, and cyclases. In consequence, most voltage-dependent Ca^{2+} channels have intracellular binding sites for such proteins and other signaling molecules, the binding of which can dynamically change the channel's activity.

Another feature that is sometimes shown in topological diagrams of ion channels are sites of extracellular glycosylation, which is a type of post-translational modification of membrane and secretory proteins. One such site is shown in Fig. 10.2 (see the 'ψ' symbol). Such glycosylation involves a branched chain of carbohydrate molecules linked to an amino acid on the extracellular side of the channel. In some channels, glycosylation can be extensive and account for a substantial fraction of the mass of the channel. Glycosylation can alter channel gating and may contribute to the recognition of the protein by the immune system.

10.3 SINGLE-CHANNEL RECORDING FROM ARTIFICIAL LIPID BILAYERS

The patch-clamp technique (described in Chapter 7) has permitted the study of the activity of single ion channels from a large number of ion channel families. Prior to the invention of the patch-clamp technique, the first electrical recordings of the movement of ions through individual protein complexes that behaved like ion channels were made with the artificial lipid-bilayer technique. In this technique, a thin plastic barrier with a hole of small diameter, e.g., 10-200 µm, in its middle separates two chambers. Then, a solution with a monolayer of lipid molecules on its surface is added to both chambers (Montal and Mueller, 1972). Alternatively, a solution of lipid in a hydrocarbon solvent is painted over the hole in the plastic barrier. In the first case, when the level of the solutions on both sides of the plastic barrier is raised higher than the location of the small hole, the two lipid monolayers fuse across the hole. In the second case, the hydrocarbon solvent is squeezed out. In both cases, a lipid bilayer results that is an experimental model of a membrane separating the solutions on the inside and outside of a cell. With electrical contacts in place between the solutions in the two chambers and an appropriate electronic apparatus, it is possible to measure the conductance and capacitance of the lipid bilayer as well as changes in these properties when molecules such as candidate ion channels are added to the bilayer.

Fig. 10.3 shows results from a study in which single-channel currents were recorded in an artificial bilayer system to which gramicidin A, a soil-bacterium protein and a candidate ion channel at the time, had been added (Hladky and Haydon, 1970). The lowest current level corresponds to the baseline state without gramicidin activity. Channel activity is seen as stepwise upward deflections of approximately constant amplitude. The presence of gramicidin thus causes the appearance of quantized current levels. The currents have been calibrated in conductance units, inverse ohms (Ω^{-1}); the vertical calibration bar of $4 \cdot 10^{-11}$ Ω^{-1} is equivalent to 40 pS in modern units. The individual current deflections last a fraction of a second to a few seconds. Overall, the recording reveals the activity of individual ion channels, occasionally the coincident activity of two channels, and, during one brief period in the middle of the record, the coincident activity of up to 4 channels. Since the potential difference between the two chambers was 100 mV, the vertical calibration bar corresponds to a current of 4 pA. Thus, the amplitudes of the unitary currents in this experiment are ~4 pA and the corresponding conductance amplitudes are ~40 pS.

In 1970, when this study was done, little was known about (1) the density of ion channels that are found in cell membranes, (2) the conductance of an individual open channel, and

(3) apart from the ion channels in a few excitable cells, the gating properties of ion channels. This study with gramicidin was one of the first to clearly resolve step changes in membrane current of the type that would be expected for at least some types of ion channels -- in this case, a monovalent cation channel -- when the channel switches between its closed and open states.

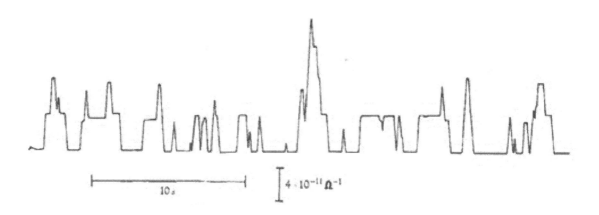

Figure 10.3 Recording of unitary currents vs. time from an artificial bilayer system that contained gramicidin A molecules. The current axis (vertical) has been calibrated in conductance units (inverse ohms, Ω^{-1}) based on a voltage difference across the lipid bilayer of 100 mV. The lowest current level corresponds to the baseline level in the absence of gramicidin activity. The solution in the two chambers was 1 M KCl; room temperature. [Credit: Hladky and Haydon (1970).]

In these gramicidin experiments, current amplitudes were linearly proportional to the potential across the bilayer (up to ~200 mV) and showed some saturation when the concentration of the solutions in the two chambers was increased (up to ~2 M). At 150 mM NaCl (the approximate tonicity of mammalian cells), the unit conductance was ~10 pS. It is now known that 10 pS is in the range of values commonly observed for the single-channel conductance of many types of ion-channels, 1 to 300 pS (see next sections; see also the single-channel conductance example discussed in Section 5.9 of Chapter 5). On the other hand, the gating behavior of gramicidin in Fig. 10.3 -- for which the open-time of the channel events, and the time between open events, is a fraction of a second to a few seconds -- is probably not relevant to mechanisms of ion-channel gating in most cells. With gramicidin A, a unitary current event likely arises when, due to thermal energy, two individual gramicidin molecules, each extending about half way across the bilayer, randomly associate to form a helical dimer, linked by hydrogen bonds, that extends all the way across the bilayer. The result is a hydrophilic pathway within the dimer that permits ion movements across the membrane. The associated current event disappears when, again due to thermal energy, the dimer dissociates into monomers.

10.4 SINGLE-CHANNEL RECORDING WITH THE PATCH-CLAMP TECHNIQUE

The first recordings of single-channel activity from a cell preparation were reported in 1976 by Neher and Sakmann in experiments on denervated frog skeletal 'muscle fibers' (i.e., muscle cells), which contain a large number of nAChRs on their surface membrane. Membrane current through nAChRs was measured with the cell-attached version of the patch-clamp technique, which collects and measures ionic currents that move through the small patch of membrane under the patch electrode (see Chapter 7).

Indirect estimates of the current and associated conductance of single nAChRs activated by acetylcholine had been made previously on non-denervated (normal) frog muscle fibers with a conventional two-micro-electrode voltage-clamp technique (Anderson and Stevens, 1973). The estimated single-channel conductance was 32 pS and reported to be independent of membrane potential (-140 to +60 mV) and temperature (8-18 °C). This work relied on an analysis of the current fluctuations (also called 'current noise' or 'membrane noise') that can be observed in electrical recordings from muscle cells when a number of nAChRs are active at the same time. The analysis assumed that the observed fluctuations were due to the random opening and closing of individual nAChRs in the membrane region under study, i.e., to 'stochastic' gating of the channels.

Neher and Sakmann used denervated frog muscle fibers in their experiments because denervation was known to greatly increase the number of nAChRs expressed outside their normal location at the muscle 'endplate', a highly-localized site in the middle of the muscle cell onto which a motorneuron makes a synapse (see Chapter 11). Thus, after denervation, a much larger area of the muscle cell's surface membrane was available for study. Additionally, it was known that the mean open-time of AChRs expressed in denervated fibers is 3- to 5-fold longer than that of the AChRs found at the normal synaptic location. Furthermore, the muscle fibers were cooled to 6-8 °C, which also increases the channel open-time. Finally, suberyldicholine (SubCh), a chemical analogue of acetylcholine that is known to produce longer channel open-times than acetylcholine itself, was used to activate the nAChRs in some experiments. These various maneuvers increased the likelihood that single-channel currents through individual nAChRs could be resolved.

Fig. 10.4 summarizes several results from the experiments of Neher and Sakmann. Part *a* shows a current trace recorded in the presence of SubCh by a patch-clamp electrode attached to the surface of a muscle fiber whose membrane potential was held at -120 mV by means of a conventional two-micro-electrode voltage-clamp.

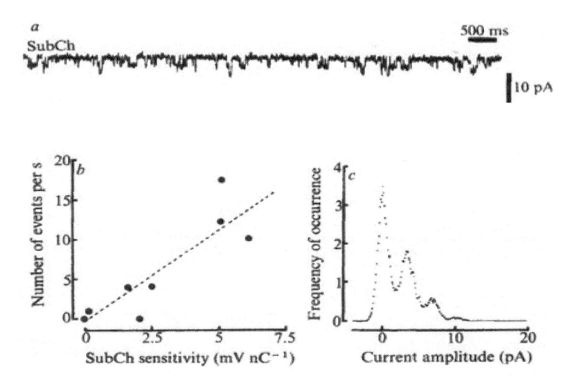

Figure 10.4 Single-channel data and analysis of nAChR activity in denervated frog skeletal muscle fibers, the surface of which had been cleaned by treatment with proteolytic enzymes. a) Sample current recording showing quantized currents recorded with a cell-attached patch pipette in which channels were activated by suberyldicholine (SubCh), which was present in the pipette at a concentration of 0.2 µM. The baseline current is the uppermost level on the trace and the single-channel currents correspond to stepwise downward deflections. The membrane potential at the recording site was -120 mV. b) Number of current steps per second plotted vs. the sensitivity of the membrane to SubCh. c) Amplitude histogram of (minus) the SubCh-activated membrane currents at -120 mV, i.e., the frequency (in arbitrary units) of the indicated current levels relative to baseline collected and plotted from traces like those in part *a*. [Credit: Neher and Sakmann (1976).]

In trace *a*, the baseline current level is at the top of the recording and channel activity is seen as downward deflections, which corresponds to inward membrane currents. This is the expected direction for activation currents through nAChRs, a non-selective cation channel whose reversal potential (E_R) is approximately -7 mV, i.e., close to the average of E_K and E_{Na} (see Exercise 5.1 in Chapter 5 for a discussion of E_R).

In spite of the high-frequency noise present in the current trace in Fig. 10.4*a*, individual step-wise deflections of -3 to -3.5 pA can be resolved. The duration of some of these quantized events is very brief, whereas others persist for periods of several hundred ms; on average, the duration of the events was 45 ms. The current amplitudes occasionally reach -6 to -7 pA, consistent with the interpretation that these larger currents arise from the coincident activity of two channels, each with an individual current amplitude of -3 to -3.5 pA. From these and other results, it was concluded that these quantized current events arise from the brief openings of single AChRs. At $V_m = -120$ mV, a single-channel conductance of 28 pS can be calculated from the average quantized current level of -3.2 pA and a driving force of -113 mV (= -120 - E_R). In 27 similar experiments, an average single-channel conductance of 22.4 pS (± 0.3 pS, standard error of the mean) was estimated. The latter value is similar to, but slightly smaller than, the value of 28.6 pS estimated from fluctuation analysis for the conductance change of single nAChRs in frog muscle activated by SubCh (Colquhoun et al., 1975).

Part *b* of Fig. 10.4 shows that the frequency of occurrence of quantized current events like those in part *a* was correlated with the overall SubCh sensitivity of the membrane region under investigation. Sensitivity was evaluated by application of a known quantity of SubCh onto the surface of the muscle fiber near the membrane region under study, followed by estimation of the change in membrane potential (in mV) per amount of SubCh applied. SubCh, a molecule whose charge is +2, was applied locally by the passage of current through a near-by electrode containing SubCh, and the amount was calibrated in integrated current-passing units, nanocoulombs (nC). Sensitivity is thus expected to be proportional to the number of AChRs in the membrane region. The approximately linear relation observed in Fig. 10.4*b* between the frequency of the quantized current events and the sensitivity of the preparation to SubCh supports the conclusion that the events were indeed due to the activation of AChRs by SubCh.

Part *c* of Fig. 10.4 shows an amplitude histogram, which tabulates the frequency with which different time points on currents traces like those in part *a* have particular amplitudes. The largest peak is centered at 0 pA, i.e., the baseline level; thus, the most frequent observation was the absence of channel activity. Three additional peaks in the histogram occur at approximate x-axis locations of (minus) 3.4, 6.8, and 10.2 pA. As discussed in Sections 10.6 and 10.7 below, the relative amplitudes of these peaks is approximately that expected if the mean amplitude of the elementary current event is 3.0-3.5 pA and the probability of occurrence of an event (i.e., the probability of a channel being in the open state) is distributed randomly according to the Poisson probability distribution (next section).

In part *c*, the variation in current amplitudes about the peaks at 3.4, 6.8, and 10.2 pA is thought to be largely, but not entirely, due to the high-frequency noise that accounts for the variation in current amplitudes about the histogram peak at 0 pA. The additional factor that is thought to contribute to the amplitude variation at the three non-zero peaks is non-uniformity in the single-channel current amplitudes. The authors noted that it is not clear whether this non-uniformity is a genuine feature of the open-channel currents or a measurement artifact. The latter might arise, for example, if currents from channels that are peripherally located within the patch of membrane under study (i.e., at or near the glass rim of the patch-clamp electrode) are not fully measured.

10.5 A DIGRESSION ON THE POISSON PROBABILITY DISTRIBUTION

The Poisson probability distribution, named after French mathematician S. D. Poisson, is often used to estimate how many times a repeatable but rarely-observed event is likely to occur within a specified time period T (e.g., a year, a day, a s, etc.). Suppose that (i) data are tabulated on the number of occurrences of such an event for many different fixed time periods T, and (ii) the mean number of such occurrences is found to be M, where M>0. Then, if P(n) denotes the probability of observing n occurrences of the event in time T (n = 0, 1, 2, …), the expected probability distribution is, according to the Poisson probability equation, given by:

$$P(n) = \frac{e^{-M} M^n}{n!}. \tag{10.1}$$

Thus, the probability of observing 0 events is e^{-M} (since M^0 is 1 and, by definition, 0! is 1); the probability of observing 1 event is $e^{-M} \cdot M$; 2 events is $e^{-M} \cdot M^2/2$; 3 events is $e^{-M} \cdot M^3/6$;

etc. As expected, the sum of P(n) for all n is 1, since, for any M, the infinite series $1 + M + M^2/2! + M^3/3! + \ldots$ converges to e^M.

A commonly-quoted application of the Poisson probability equation concerns radioactive decay. Suppose that the radioactivity of a substance is monitored with a Geiger counter and each decay event is recorded as a 'blip'. The underlying mechanism is that the substance contains a very large number of radioactive atoms, each of which has a very small probability of radioactive decay within a specified time period. Suppose further that the number of blips is recorded during 1 s intervals for a number of seconds and that, on average, they occur at a rate of 1 per s. The left-hand side of Fig. 10.5 shows the expected probability of observing 0, 1, 2, … blips within any 1 s interval (which is denoted 'T' in the figure), as calculated with Eqn. 10.1. On the other hand, if the mean number of blips were 4.5 times larger, the right-hand side of Fig. 10.5 shows the corresponding probabilities.

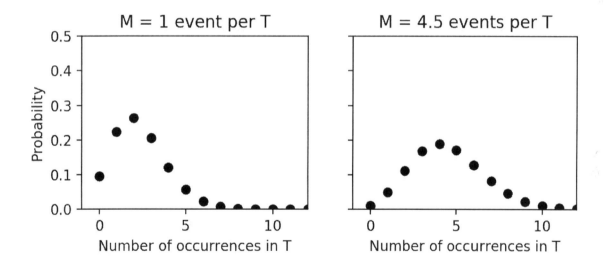

Figure 10.5 Two calculations of a Poisson probability distribution. The mean number of expected events in time interval T is 1 (left) and 4.5 (right).

As suggested by the plot on the right side of Fig. 10.5, as M becomes large, the shape of the probability distribution calculated with Eqn. 10.1 becomes indistinguishable from a symmetric 'bell shape', i.e., from a Gaussian curve (see, e.g., Eqn. 3.1 in Chapter 3). Note, however, that the Poisson distribution is defined only at integer values on the x axis whereas a Gaussian curve is defined continuously, i.e., at integer and non-integer values.

The Poisson distribution is sometimes used to approximate probability calculations for an underlying variable that has a 'binomial' distribution, which has only two possibilities -- one with probability p and the other with probability q, where p + q = 1. The approximation works well if one of the two probabilities is much small than the other. For example, suppose that p = 0.05 and q = 0.95, and suppose also that the number of times possibility #1 is observed out of 20 trials is recorded again and again. The average number expected per 20 trials is 1 (= 20 x 0.05). The exact distribution of probabilities can be calculated with the formula for binomial probabilities (see Exercise 10.4), but the Poisson distribution shown on the left side of Fig. 10.5 yields a good approximation.

10.6 FIRST SIMULATION OF THE RESULTS IN FIGURE 10.4c

In Fig. 10.4c, identifiable peaks occur in the frequency plot at current amplitudes approximately equal to 0, 3.4, 6.8. and 10.2 pA, and these peaks occur with approximate relative frequencies of 3.47, 1.85, 0.56, and 0.09. This plot is likely to represent the quantized activity of individual nAChRs within the patched area of membrane (number unknown), each having a single-channel current of 3 to 3.5 pA and an unknown, but small, probability of being open during any one of the series of small time periods T (duration unspecified) that were used to compile the data for the plot. In this case, the frequency of occurrence of the 4 quantized currents peaks is expected to scale approximately in proportion to the sequence of probabilities P(0), P(1), P(2), P(3), as calculated with Eqn. 10.1 for an appropriately chosen value of M.

To test these assumptions, Fig. 10.6 was generated by the next program, 'Achr_Poisson.py'. This program compares the peaks of the frequency data in Fig. 10.4c with appropriately-scaled Poisson probabilities, calculated with Eqn. 10.1 under the assumption that the single-channel current is 3.4 pA, and with an appropriately-selected value of M in Eqn. 10.1

```
1  # -*- coding: utf-8 -*-
2  #Achr_Poisson.py
3  #Description: simulate AChR current frequencies with the Poisson distribution
4
5  import numpy as np
6  import matplotlib.pyplot as plt
```

```
7  import math
8
9  def my_factorial(X):              #vectorizing the math-package factorial function
10     return math.factorial(X)
11
12 #math.factorial(X) expects X to be a single integer, so use it in vectorized form
13 def Poisson(mean,X):
14     return np.exp(-mean)*mean**X/np.vectorize(my_factorial)(X)
15
16 Mean=0.55  #mean value for calculations with the Poisson probability equation
17 N_last=5   #last integer value for calculation in the Poisson equation
18
19 x=np.linspace(0,N_last,N_last+1)    #quantized integer values for Poisson calculation
20 y=Poisson(Mean,x)                   #Poisson probabilities for the selected integer values
21 x_scale=3.4      #scaling factor to setup current axis for quantized current events of 3.4 pA
22 x*=x_scale       #scale current axis by appropriate scaling factor
23
24 plt.figure()
25 data=np.array([3.47, 1.85, 0.56, 0.09,0.,0.])       #estimated frequency peaks in Fig. 4c
26 plt.plot(x,data,'xk', markersize=10, label='data')  #plot data as black x's of size = 10
27 y*=data.sum()     #scale Poisson probabilities to match shape of frequency data
28 plt.plot(x,y,'ok',label='Poisson')  #plot scaled Poisson probabilities to compare with data
29 plt.xlim(-3,20)      #set x-limit of plot
30 plt.ylim(0.,4)       #set y-limit of plot
31 plt.xlabel('Curent amplitude (pA)')
32 plt.ylabel('Frequency of occurrence')
33 plt.legend()
34 plt.title("Current frequencies vs. prediction from Poisson's equation")
35 plt.savefig("Fig10_6.png", dpi=200)
```

The good agreement in Fig. 10.6 between the data and calculation supports the assumptions of the calculation. The 0.55 value of M, which was selected by trial-and-error during several runs of the program, appears to be reasonable based on the current trace in Fig. 10.4a. This trace appears to be close to the zero current level a little more than half the time, which is consistent with the value exp(-0.55) = 0.577, the Poisson probability prediction for 0 channels being open during a time interval T.

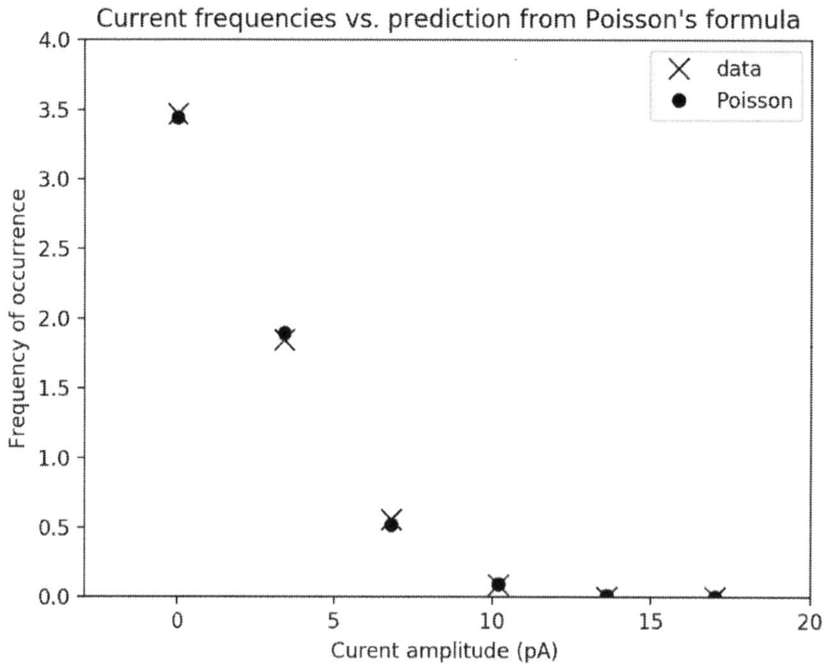

[Figure: scatter plot titled "Current frequencies vs. prediction from Poisson's formula" with x-axis "Curent amplitude (pA)" from 0 to 20, y-axis "Frequency of occurrence" from 0.0 to 4.0, showing data (X) and Poisson (●) markers nearly overlapping at approximately (0, 3.5), (3.5, 1.85), (7, 0.55), (10.5, 0.1), (14, 0), (17, 0).]

Figure 10.6 Frequency of occurrence of the quantized peak currents in Fig. 10.*4c* (X) and Poisson probabilities calculated with Eqn. 10.1 with mean = 0.55 (●). The scaling of the ordinate is in arbitrary units to match that in Fig. 10.*4c*.

Program notes. Most of the program lines are straightforward uses of statements that have appeared in earlier programs.

- Line 7 imports the 'math' module library to carry out the factorial calculations required in the Poisson equation (Eqn. 10.1). Unfortunately, 'math.factorial()' expects to be passed single integers, so it cannot work directly with np arrays without generation of an error. As was described for several functions encountered in Chapter 8, this type of error can be circumvented if a 'vectorized' version of the relevant function is defined and called. This vectorization is done via line 14 and the function 'my_factorial' defined in lines 9-10.

- Lines 22 and 27 carry out the appropriate scaling of the calculations with the Poisson equation (x and y values, respectively), so that they can be compared with the data. Line 27 uses the numpy 'sum' function to calculate the y-value scaling factor. This function can be applied to any numpy array, whether it be single- or multi-dimensional, to get the sum of all of its elements. Its use in this case is to obtain a scaling factor that provides a good overall fit to the data. In line 26, 'xk', which is a type of optional argument called a 'format string', specifies that the points to be plotted are x-shaped symbols ('x') in black color ('k'). Similarly, the 'ok' in line 28 specifies that the points to be plotted are filled circles ('o') in black color ('k').

- Lines 31-34 are the statements needed to create the legend in the plot (see also the program for Fig. 6.1 of Chapter 6, which uses similar statements to create a plot legend).

10.7 A MORE COMPLETE SIMULATION OF THE RESULTS IN FIGURE 10.4c

The analysis in the previous section makes the assumption that the estimated values of the single-channel current level (3.4 pA) and of M in Eqn. 10.1 (0.55) are not affected by the two sources of variation in Fig. 10.4a mentioned by the authors, i.e., the high-frequency current noise and the likely non-uniformity in the single-channel current amplitudes. To test this assumption, it is of interest to simulate the amplitude histogram in Fig. 10.4c by inclusion of these factors. Fig. 10.7 shows such a simulation.

The plot in Fig. 10.7 is in good agreement with that in Fig. 10.4c, with relative peak amplitudes in the histogram of approximately 3.49, 1.87, 0.56, and 0.09 at current values of 0, 3.4, 6.8, and 10.2 pA, respectively. In this simulation, (i) the parameter values used for the mean single-channel current and for M were 3.4 pA and 0.54, respectively (which are essentially the same as those in Fig. 10.6), (ii) the variation in the single-channel current amplitude about 3.4 pA was assumed to be that of a standard normal distribution with a mean of 0 and a standard deviation of 0.68, scaled by a factor of 0.5, and (iii) high-frequency noise, the amplitude of which is similar to that in Fig. 10.4a, was included in the simulated current trace (not shown).

Exercise 10.8 encourages the reader to write a *Python* program to carry out a simulation of this type; the suggestions on how to proceed depend on the background information presented in Sections 10.8 and 10.9 below.

Both simulation methods support the conclusion that current traces of the type shown in Fig. 10.4a are due to the activity of single channels whose simultaneous open probabilities are consistent with a Poisson distribution (Neher et al., 1978) and whose quantized current level is 3-3.5 pA. Specifically, it is thought that (i) the patch of membrane contains a substantial but unknown number of AChR channels and (ii) each channel has a similar small probability of being open at any moment, independent of that of the other channels.

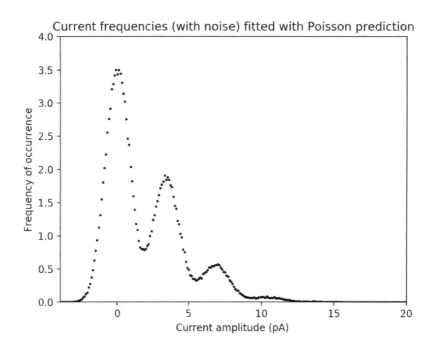

Figure 10.7 Simulation of the amplitude histogram in Fig. 10.4c with inclusion of high-frequency current noise and a modest variation in the single-channel current amplitude. The values assumed for M in Eqn. 10.1 and the mean single-channel current are 0.54 and 3.4 pA, respectively. The mean open time of an AChR activated by SubCh is assumed to be 45 ms (Neher and Sakmann, 1976); the open-time distribution is assumed to be exponentially distributed (see Sections 10.8 and 10.9 below).

10.8 A DIGRESSION ON A POISSON PROCESS

The term 'Poisson process' is sometimes used to describe a specific type of model or calculation related to the Poisson probability distribution. Consider again the example of a variable that has a binomial distribution, in which possibility #1 occurs with probability p and possibility #2 with probability q, where p + q = 1. One might ask: if a long series of trials is recorded for this variable and possibility #1 has just occurred, what is the probability that the next occurrence of possibility #1 is seen in exactly m more trials (m = 1, 2, 3, ...). Similarly, with the radioactive decay example, one might ask: given that the mean number of blips per s is M and given that a blip has just occurred, what is the distribution of waiting times before the next blip occurs.

These examples are a type of time-series or waiting-time calculation in which probabilities of occurrence do not depend on the outcomes that have already happened, i.e., the process is 'memoryless'. (A memoryless random process is also called a 'homogeneous Markov process'). The Poisson equation can assist in this calculation, hence the name 'Poisson process'.

Consider again the example of radioactive decay, in which, in contrast to the binomial example, the waiting time is a continuous (not discrete) variable. To analyze this case, let x denote the waiting time until the next blip. Then, the probability that $x > t$ (where $t \geq 0$) is the probability that there are no blips in time t. Since, according to Poisson's equation (Eqn. 10.1), M·t is the mean number of blips in time t, the probability of no blips in time t is exp(-M·t). Thus, exp(-M·t) is the probability that $x > t$ and 1- exp(-M·t) is the probability that $x \leq t$. If f(t) denotes the derivative of the latter function with respect to t, then:

$$f(t) = M\, e^{-M\,t}. \qquad (10.2)$$

This decaying-exponential function is known as the 'negative exponential distribution' and gives the probability density function of the waiting time.

Fig. 10.8 plots this function for the case that M = 4.5 per s. The area under the curve is 1, as required for a probability density function.

Qualitatively, the curve in Fig. 10.8 indicates that a short waiting time is more likely than a long waiting time. Quantitatively, the curve indicates that (i) if t1 and t2 are two times, with t1<t2, and (ii) if dt is a small increment of time, it is more likely by the factor exp(-M·t1)/exp(-M·t2) that the waiting time will occur in the interval t1-dt/2 to t1+dt/2 than in the interval t2-dt/2 to t2+dt/2. The average waiting time, calculated as the integral from 0 to ∞ of t · M · exp(-M·t) with respect to t, is 1/M. Also, if no blip has occurred after some time interval T, the probability density function for the waiting time until the next blip still applies but with time reset to the present time, i.e., the new 'time 0' corresponds to time T of 'old time'. This follows from the basic assumption of a Poisson process that probabilities do not depend on outcomes that have already happened.

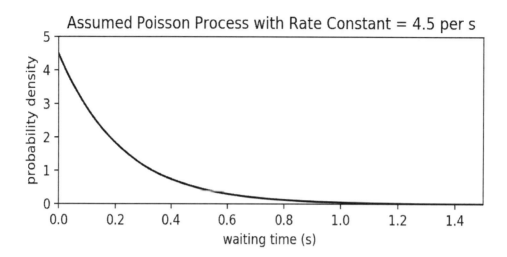

Figure 10.8 Probability density function of the waiting time for the occurrence of the next event in a Poisson process for which the rate constant is 4.5 per s.

10.9 MODELS OF CHANNEL GATING

Another example of a Poisson process to be considered is that of a randomly-occurring biophysical event such as the gating of an ion channel. It might be asked: given that a particular type of ion channel stays open, on average, for 45 ms (e.g., as reported by Neher and Sakmann for nAChRs activated by SubCh under the experimental conditions of Fig. 10.4), does the probability density function for the channel open-time (i.e., the waiting time before the channel closes) behave as in Fig. 10.8 except that $M = 22.2$ per s $= (45$ ms$)^{-1}$? If so, the data would be consistent with the hypothesis that the channel has a single open state whose transition to the closed state is governed by a rate constant that is independent of its history in prior states. Conversely, if the channel open-time distribution did not obey a single exponential, a more complicated kinetic scheme than just a single, memoryless open-state of the channel would be required to explain the data.

As reported in a later study (Sakmann et al., 1980), analysis of the gating kinetics of open nAChRs under the experimental conditions in Fig. 10.4 is not straightforward because nAChRs expressed in denervated frog fibers away from the endplate region are heterogeneous. A minority have a mean open time of ~10 ms, which is similar to that found for nAChRs normally expressed at the endplate, whereas the majority have a mean open-time that is 3- to 5-fold longer, as noted in the third paragraph of Section 10.4.

Fig. 10.9 shows results from another patch-clamp study of single nAChRs in which the kinetics of channel gating, at least for the particular experimental conditions, revealed a simple interpretation in terms of the assumptions that underlie Fig. 10.8.

Membrane currents from regions of a denervated frog muscle fiber were again studied with the cell-attached patch-clamp technique (Sakmann et al., 1980). The experimental conditions were similar to those in Fig. 10.4, but with two modifications: (i) the nAChRs were activated by acetylcholine (ACh), which is the normal physiological agonist for these channels, rather than by SubCh; and (ii) only channels whose properties were thought to be the same as those found at the normal end-plate region of non-denervated fibers were studied (see below).

Part *a* of Fig. 10.9 shows a sample current recording in these experiments. The trace starts in the absence of channel activity, then reveals a 'burst' of openings and closings that last ~1.5 s, during which time the current level fluctuates between the baseline level and a negative level of about -4 pA. In this case, only one channel in the patch was thought to be active. Parts *b* and *c* of Fig. 10.9 show two histograms that summarize the kinetic behavior of such channel events during active periods like that in part *a*.

Part *b* shows the distribution of channel open-times (i.e., the waiting time for a current level that had just started at ~-4pA to revert to baseline), and part *c* shows a corresponding histogram for channel closed-times (i.e., the waiting time for a current level that had just started at the baseline to jump back to ~-4pA). In both cases, the distributions are fitted satisfactorily with a decaying single-exponential function. τ_o, the time constant of the first exponential function, is 10.6 ms, and τ_c, the time constant of the second, is 18 ms.

Thus, during the periods of a current burst, the channel appears to switch states according to the scheme:

$$\text{closed} \underset{k_c}{\overset{k_o}{\rightleftarrows}} \text{open} \qquad \text{Scheme 10.1}$$

where k_o is the rate constant for transition from the closed to open state of the channel, and k_c is the rate constant for transition from the open to closed state (both having units of s^{-1}). The fitted values of τ_o and τ_c in parts b and c of Fig. 10.9, gave the following estimates for the rate constants: $k_c = 94.3\ s^{-1}$ (= $1/\tau_o$ = $(10.6\ ms)^{-1}$) and $k_o = 55.6\ s^{-1}$ (= $1/\tau_c$ = $(18\ ms)^{-1}$).

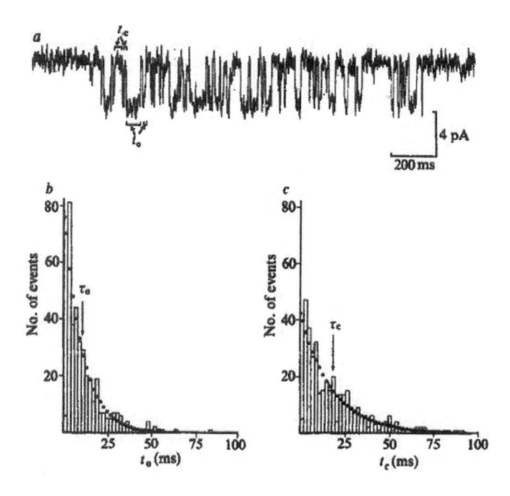

Figure 10.9 Single-channel data and analysis of nAChR activity in denervated frog skeletal muscle fibers. *a*) Sample current recording showing a burst of quantized current events of ~-4 pA recorded with a cell-attached patch pipette in which channels were activated by acetylcholine, which was present in the pipette at a concentration of 10 μM. The baseline current is the uppermost level on the trace and the single-channel currents correspond to downward deflections (inward currents). Brackets with the labels 't_c' and 't_o' indicate how individual channel closed-times and open-times, respectively, were measured. Membrane potential, -130 mV; temperature, 12 °C. *b, c*) Histograms of the distribution of channel open-times (t_o) and closed-times (t_c), each fitted with a decaying single-exponential function, which is shown as a dotted line. The fitted time constants, τ_o and τ_c, are 10.6 ms and 18 ms (parts *b* and *c*, respectively). [Credit: Sakmann et al. (1980).]

Part *a* of Fig. 10.9 also shows that before and after its bursting activity, the nAChR appeared to be in another state, called the 'desensitized' state, in which channel activity is suppressed by ACh and the channel is non-conducting. The existence of the desensitized state was well-known at the time from other types of experiments; it arises when nAChRs are exposed for a substantial period of time to ACh (or to other channel agonists). It was this property of the nAChRs that the authors were able to take advantage of in their experiments. With a substantial concentration of ACh included in the patch pipette, it was expected that most, perhaps all, of the channels within the patched area of membrane would rapidly become desensitized; then, only occasionally, would one of the channels revert to a non-desensitized state, thereby allowing individual bursts of agonist-induced current activity from a single channel to be studied, as in Fig. 10.9a.

The full pattern of current activity in nAChR single-channel recordings that lasted a number of seconds, such as in Fig. 10.9a, revealed kinetic evidence for at least two, rather than just one, desensitized states (Sakmann et al., 1980). This finding illustrates that the analysis of the kinetic states of ion channels is, generally, not straightforward.

It is a rare that an ion channel is reported to have just one closed and one open state, with waiting times between states that follow single-exponential kinetics. A K^+ channel of this type, isolated from the membranes of the sarcoplasmic reticulum of mammalian skeletal muscle cells is discussed in Fig. 10.10 below (Labarca et al., 1980; Miller, 1983).

It is not surprising that the analysis of single-channel currents of ion channels should reveal the existence of multiple closed and open states, sometimes including 'sub-conductance' states, i.e., open states whose conductance is smaller than the protein's usual 'full' conductance state. Because of thermal motion, under any particular condition, protein molecules of the size of ion channels would be expected to fluctuate among multiple reasonably-stable conformations. The goal of experiments and analyses such as those in Fig. 10.9 is to identify major functional sub-classes of the ion-channel's conformational states and thereby allow useful analyses of its gating and permeation properties to be made.

10.10 OTHER EXAMPLES OF SINGLE-CHANNEL RECORDINGS

In recent decades, a great variety of ion channels from many different cell types have been studied with the artificial-bilayer and patch-clamp techniques. The studies have been carried out under many different experimental conditions, including with physiological and pharmacological agents known to have important effects on ion-channel function. Concurrently, technical improvements have increased the signal-to-noise ratio of the measurements, and new analytical tools have increased understanding of the different functional states of ion channels. The result of this work is that the study of ion channels has deepened our understanding of how cells and tissues carry out their normal functions. To give a flavor of the accomplishments, five examples of experiments carried out with the artificial-bilayer and patch-clamp techniques are considered next.

A. An Example from an Artificial-bilayer Experiment. Fig. 10.10 shows a sample recording (part A), with analysis (part B), of results obtained in a study of a type of K^+ channel that is found in the sarcoplasmic reticulum (SR) of vertebrate skeletal muscle cells.

In these experiments, vesicles of SR membrane were isolated biochemically and added in small quantity to one chamber of an artificial-bilayer apparatus after the bilayer had been formed. In Fig. 10.10A, ~20 s after the start of the current recording, it is thought that one vesicle, which contained perhaps 6 potassium channels, all in the open state, suddenly fused with the bilayer. This caused a sudden increase in outward current of ~30 pA (indicated by the large upward deflection).

Subsequently, as the channels randomly closed and reopened, the current record oscillated between 6 quantized current levels (numbered 0 to 5 on the graph in Fig. 10.10A) separated by ~4.7 pA. Thus, ~4.7 pA is thought to be the amplitude of the single-channel current under the conditions of the experiment. Since, in Fig. 10.1A, the potential difference across the bilayer was 50 mV, the single-channel conductance is calculated to be ~93 pS.

Part B of Fig. 10.10 shows the results of a probability analysis carried out for an experiment similar to that in part A except that, in this experiment, several vesicles fused with the bilayer, which, together, added somewhat more channels to the bilayer. The open circles in the plot show a relative frequency histogram, analogous to that in Fig. 10.6, with the ordinate calibrated in probabilities (rather than frequencies) and the abscissa in the number of open channels.

In Fig. 10B, the most common current level in the recordings, which was seen about 23% of the time, corresponds to the simultaneous opening of 4 channels. The curve in Fig. 10.10B is based on the prediction of the binomial probability distribution in which it was assumed that 18 individual channels were present, each with a probability of being open 25% of the time, independent of the state of the other 17 channels.

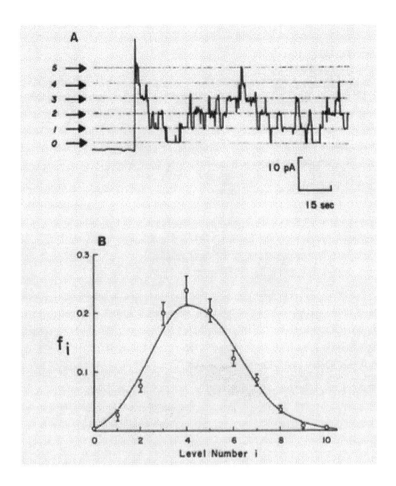

Figure 10.10 Single-channel data and analysis for a type of K^+ channel found in the SR membranes of rabbit skeletal muscle fibers. A) Sample current recording from an artificial-bilayer system in which one SR vesicle, which is thought to have contained ~6 identical K^+ channels, fused to the bilayer at approximately 20 s after the start of the recording. Six quantized current levels (number 0 to 5), each separated by ~4.7 pA, are indicated by the dotted lines. The concentration of K^+ in the chambers on the two sides of the bilayer was 100 mM. B) Statistical analysis of results from an experiment like that in part A in which perhaps 3 vesicles, collectively containing a larger number of K^+ channels than in A, fused to the bilayer. The open circles show the experimentally observed relative frequencies (ordinate; expressed as probabilities) for the indicated number of current levels that were open simultaneously at different times during the recordings (abscissa). The curve connects the (discrete) probability values predicted by the binomial distribution for the different levels under the assumption that the bilayer contained 18 channels, each with a probability of 0.25 of being open, independent of that of the other channels. [Credit: Miller et al. (1984).]

Exercise 10.4 asks the reader to write a *Python* program to compare the analysis of the data in Fig. 10.10B with two approaches: one based on the binomial distribution (as in Fig. 10.10B) and the other on the Poisson distribution (as in Fig. 10.6 but adapted appropriately to the relative frequencies plotted in Fig. 10.10B).

B. A Second Example from an Artificial-bilayer Experiment. Fig. 10.11 shows currents recorded from an artificial-bilayer that contained an unusual Cl^- channel, which was isolated from the electric organ of an electric ray fish, *Torpedo californica* (Hanke and Miller, 1983). The activity of this anion channel is unusual in that it appears as if two channels of equal conductance are either both active (but gating independently) or both not active. This channel has sometimes been referred to as a 'double-barreled' Cl^- channel, meaning a channel with two separate hydrophilic pathways across the membrane.

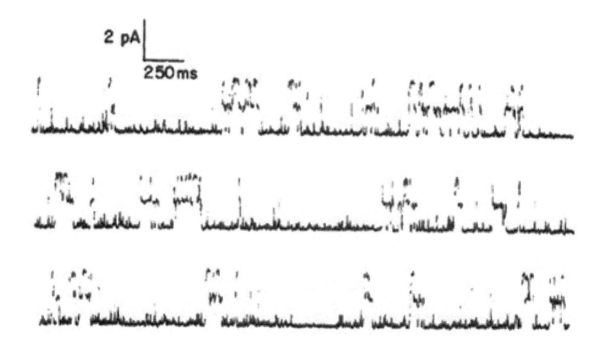

Figure 10.11 Single-channel activity of the dimeric Cl^- channel isolated from the plasmalemma of the electric organ of *Torpedo californica*. An upward deflection corresponds to channel opening (and an outward current if referred to the cell membrane). Both chambers of the artificial-bilayer system contained 200 mM NaCl (holding potential, -120 mV; pH, 7.5; room temperature). [Credit: Hanke and Miller (1983).]

The gating activity of this channel appears to have two modes: a slow mode, which takes place on a time scale of s or many ms, when the channels are either both closed or both open (but, if open, are gating independently); and a fast mode, which takes place on a time scale of ms, when individual channel openings and closings are seen. During these latter periods, 3 current levels are revealed -- referred to by the authors as 'U' for up, 'M' for middle, and 'D' for down -- during which time it is thought that two channels within the one dimeric protein complex open and close independently.

Thus, three well-defined conductance states of 0, 20, and 40 pS (in 200 mM NaCl solution) are revealed. In the recording in Fig. 10.11, the gaps between the active periods, when the channels are closed, tend to last somewhat longer than the active periods themselves.

The authors report that the gating of the two conductances during the active periods occurs independently with binomial probabilities. At -100 mV and pH=7.5, the open and closed probabilities were estimated to be 0.38 and 0.62, respectively, and the opening and closing rate constants were estimated to be 36 to 40 s^{-1} and 63 to 67 s^{-1}, respectively.

C. An Example from a Patch-clamp Experiment. Fig. 10.12 shows recordings of single-channel activity of voltage-dependent Na^+ channels in a patch-clamp experiment on an inside-out patch of membrane from a rat skeletal muscle 'myotube' (a type of immature muscle cell) that was grown in tissue culture (Patlak and Horn, 1982).

The membrane patch in this experiment evidently contained at least two voltage-dependent Na^+ channels. Currents from other potentially-active channels, such as voltage-dependent K^+ channels, were blocked by the presence of Cs^+ in the bathing solution (which substituted for the intracellular solution). The patch pipette itself contained a solution that mimicked a normal extracellular solution and included 150 mM NaCl.

Because the voltage-dependent Na^+ channels in this study were from muscle cells, the kinetics of their opening and closing was expected to be noticeably slower than that of voltage-dependent Na^+ channels from neuronal preparations (see also Chapter 12), thus making the detection of single-channel activity somewhat easier.

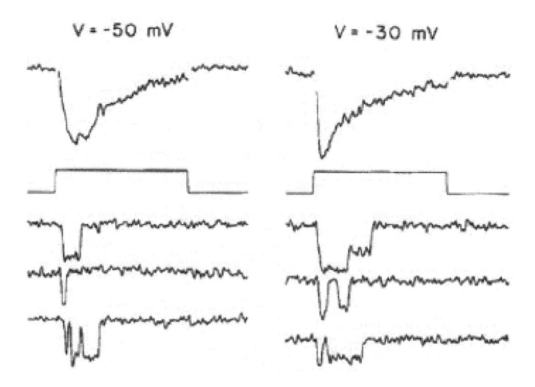

Figure 10.12 Multi-channel and single-channel activity of voltage-dependent Na$^+$ channels from an excised inside-out patch from the surface membrane of a developing rat skeletal muscle fiber. A downward deflection corresponds to channel opening (and an inward current across the membrane of an intact cell). The patch electrode contained a nominal extracellular solution whose primary constituent was 150 mM NaCl. The bathing solution contained 160 mM CsF and 5 mM of a pH buffer (pH=7.3; holding potential, -110 mV; 10 °C). The noise-free trace is a template voltage pulse, the duration of which was 65 ms; the amplitude of the template gives the current calibration, which is 1 pA. The membrane potential during the pulse is indicated at the top (-50 mV, left; -30 mV, right). The current traces above the templates are averages of 144 individual sweeps similar to those below the templates, collected at a rate of 1 per s. These averaged traces have been scaled arbitrarily to have about the same amplitude. Capacitive transients and linear leak currents were removed electronically or by digital subtraction. [Credit: Patlak and Horn (1982).]

D. A Second Example from a Patch-clamp Experiment. Fig. 10.13 shows recordings of single-channel activity of voltage-dependent K$^+$ channels in a patch-clamp experiment on an outside-out membrane patch from a cell from a type of tumor of the adrenal gland known as a 'pheochromocytoma'. These tumor cells, which are also known as 'PC12' cells, secrete various molecules and hormones, including norepinephrine and epinephrine.

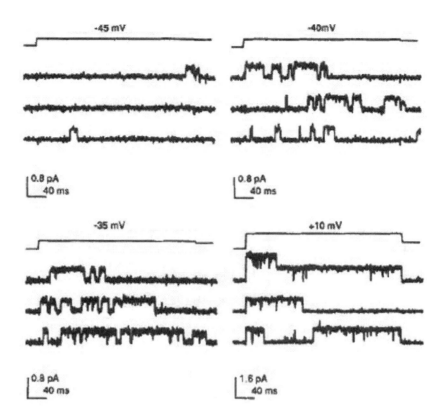

Figure 10.13 Single-channel activity of voltage-dependent K$^+$ channels (of type 'K$_Z$') from an excised outside-out patch from the surface membrane of a PC-12 tumor cell of the adrenal gland. Responses are shown for 3 different trials at each of the 4 indicated voltages. The patch electrode contained a nominal intracellular solution whose primary constituent was 150 mM K$^+$ aspartate (pH=7.2). The principal constituent of the bathing solution was 145 n-methylglucamine aspartate (pH=7.2). Holding potential, -90 mV; room temperature. The linear leak and capacitive currents were removed by subtraction. An upward deflection corresponds to channel opening (and an outward current across the membrane of an intact cell). [Credit: Hoshi and Aldrich (1988).]

In each current record, single-channel outward currents can be clearly resolved. The current amplitudes are ~0.3 pA at -45, ~0.4 pA at -40, ~0.5 pA at -35 mV, and ~1.0 pA at +10 mV. As expected, an increased frequency of openings of these voltage-dependent K$^+$ channels is seen in response to larger depolarizations. (The increase in current activity is more clearly seen in an average of the single-channel traces; not shown).

The complement of voltage-dependent K$^+$ channels in pheochromocytoma cells is complex, with at least 5 different types identified. One of these, of large conductance, is activated by both membrane potential and intracellular [Ca^{2+}]. The other 4, termed 'K$_W$', 'K$_X$', 'K$_Y$', and 'K$_Z$', are related to the type shown in Fig. 10. Interestingly, some of these channel types, including the K$_Z$ channel, show inactivation if the voltage-clamp step is maintained for a period of a second or more. Thus, inactivation is a mechanism that can be observed in voltage-dependent K$^+$ channels as well voltage-dependent Na$^+$ channels.

E. A Third Example from a Patch-clamp Experiment. Fig. 10.14 shows recordings from a patch-clamp experiment on an excised outside-out membrane patch from a neuron in the rat brain. Single-channel activity, with quantized current levels of ~2.8 pA, is clearly seen due to activity of glutamate receptors on this cell's surface membrane. The conductance of an open channel is stated to be ~50 pS.

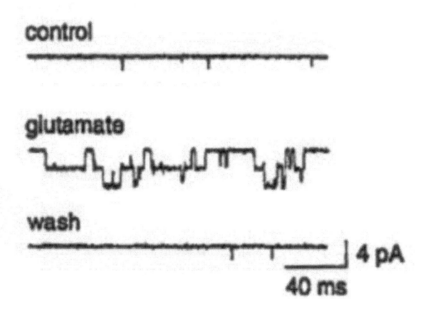

Figure 10.14 Single-channel activity from glutamate receptors of the NMDA-sub-type on an outside-out patch of membrane from the dendritic portion of a pyramidal neuron in the rat brain. Responses are shown before, during, and after the outside of the patch was exposed to 1 µM glutamate. A downward deflection corresponds to channel opening (and an inward current if referred to the membrane as normally attached to the cell). Holding potential, -60 mV; room temperature. The primary cation in the bath solution was Na$^+$ (125 mM NaCl and 25 mM NaHCO$_3$). The patch electrode contained a nominal intracellular solution whose primary constituent was K$^+$ gluconate. [Credit: Stuart et al. (1993).]

The signal-to-noise ratio of the single-channel recording in Fig. 10.14 is high (see also Fig. 10.13) when compared with that of the first single-channel patch-clamp recordings (Fig. 10.4a), which were carried out two decades earlier by one of the same authors. This increase in signal-to-noise ratio illustrates some of the technical improvements in single-channel measurements that have taken place over time.

Recommended Reading

For additional information on ion channels, including examples of the different types of single-channel studies that have been carried out, the techniques used, and the methods of analysis employed in this large and active field, the reader is referred to the many scholarly reviews in the literature on ion-channels and to two books:

Hille, B. (2001). *Ion Channels of Excitable Membranes* (3rd edition; Sinauer Associates; Sunderland, MA);

Sakmann, B. and Neher, E. (1995). *Single Channel Recording* (2nd edition, Springer; New York).

10.11 EXERCISES

Exercise 10.1 If the current in a single channel is 4 pA and carried by a monovalent cation (e.g., see Fig. 10.3), how many ions per s cross the membrane? (Recall that Faraday's constant $\approx$ 96,485 coulombs per mole of a univalent ion.)

Exercise 10.2
a) The text states that the single-channel current amplitude of the voltage-dependent K^+ channel that is shown in Fig. 10.13 (which is of type 'K_Z') is ~0.3 pA at -45 and ~1.0 pA at +10 mV. Under the assumption that current amplitude is proportional to driving force, calculate the single-channel conductance of the K_Z channels in this experiment.

b) The text states that the single-channel conductance of the glutamate-activated channels in Fig. 10.14 is 50 pS. Given that the membrane potential of the patch was -60 mV and that the single-channel current level was approximately -2.8 pA, what is the approximate reversal potential for this channel?

Exercise 10.3 Write a *Python* program to compare the shape of the Poisson probability distribution (Eqn. 10.1) with that of a Gaussian curve (e.g., Eqn. 3.1 in Chapter 3). How large does M need to be in Eqn. 10.10 for there to be good agreement between the Poisson equation and a Gaussian equation? Ignore the fact that the Poisson probability distribution is defined at discrete values only whereas a Gaussian curve is a continuous function.

Exercise 10.4 Part B of the legend of Fig. 10.10 states that the curve that connects the normalized frequencies (= probabilities) of the quantized current levels that were observed in that experiment were calculated based on a binomial distribution. The assumption was made that the artificial bilayer contained 18 channels, each with a probability of 0.25 of being open, independent of the state of the other channels. Let p denote the probability of a channel being open and q (= 1 - p) denote the probability of a channel being closed.

a) Confirm algebraically that if the bilayer had contained 2 such channels rather than 18, the probability distribution for 0, 1, and 2 channels being active simultaneously and independently would be q^2, 2qp, and p^2, respectively.

b) Confirm algebraically that if the bilayer had contained 3 channels, the probability distribution for 0, 1, 2, and 3 channels being active simultaneously and independently would be q^3, $3q^2p$, $3qp^2$, and p^3, respectively.

c) Confirm (or accept the fact) that if the bilayer had contained n channels, the probability distribution for 0, 1, 2, ..., n channels being active simultaneously and independently is given by the n+1 addends in the binomial formula:

$$(q+p)^n = \sum_{k=0}^{n} \binom{n}{k} q^{n-k} p^k , \tag{10.3}$$

where the symbol $\binom{n}{k}$ means n!/(k!(n-k)!).

d) Write a *Python* program to calculate the binomial probability distribution for the case of 18 channels, each of whose probabilities of being open and closed is 0.25 and 0.75, respectively. Does your calculation agree with Fig. 10.10B?

e) Repeat part d) for the case of 10 channels, each of whose probabilities of being open and closed is 0.45 and 0.55, respectively. Is the agreement with the data in Fig. 10.10B noticeably better or worse than for your calculation in d)?

f) Write a *Python* program that compares an appropriately-chosen Poisson probability distribution (Eqn. 10.1) with that of the binomial probability distribution calculated in d). Does either the binomial distribution or the Poisson distribution agree with the data in Fig. 10.10B better than the other, and, if so, how do you interpret this observation?

g) Now repeat your calculations in f) for the 18 channels but use a smaller value of p and ignore whether the results agree or disagree with the data in Fig. 10.10B. How small does p have to be for an appropriately-selected Poisson distribution to be in very good agreement with the binomial distribution?

h) Perhaps using the program in Appendix D as a sample, write a *Python* program that does a least-squares fit of the binomial distribution to the data in Fig. 10.10B, i.e., find the parameters n and p that minimize the sum-of-squares deviation between calculated binomial probabilities and the probability data in Fig. 10.10B at integer values 0, 1, ..., 10.

Hint: *Python's* curve_fit function is easier to use if the variables to be adjusted are real values (not integer values). Thus, the factorial function (Eqn. 10.3, which uses integer values of k and n) is better replaced with the gamma function from the scipy.special module, which takes real values as its argument (e.g., use the statement 'from scipy.special import gamma'). Note, however, that, for integer values n, factorial(n) = gamma(n+1).

Exercise 10.5 Write a *Python* program that produces a figure similar to Fig. 10.8.

a) What is the slope of the curve at t = 0 and where does this slope intersect the x-axis? How is the intersection point related to the rate constant?

b) Confirm for this distribution that the mean waiting time (also known as the 'expected' waiting) time is 1/M, as stated in the text.

c) Modify your program but plot the ordinate on a log scale. Does this plot look as you expect?

Exercise 10.6 Write a *Python* program that produces a simulation result like that in Fig. 10.7. To do so, you will need to simulate a current trace like that in Fig. 10.4*a* prior to generating the histogram analysis of that trace. The following steps may be helpful in your approach:

- You will need a random number generator to simulate various random processes that affect your simulated current trace, so import the random number generator from the numpy module (see, e.g., lines 7-8 from Example4_1.py in Chapter 4). Include an argument with the seed statement (e.g., 'seed(0)') so that the randomness in your calculations will be reproducible during the debugging process.

- You may also find it helpful to use the function 'np.random.normal(0,std_dev)', which, once the value of std_dev is set, allows random numbers to be generated that have a normal distribution with mean = 0 and standard deviation = std_dev. This type of randomness is usefully introduced into the program at several points.

- You will need to decide how frequent the time points will be in your simulated current trace (e.g., one per ms, might be a good start) and for how many ms (e.g., 2000 or more).

- You will need a variable to specify the mean single-channel current.

- You will need a variable to keep track of the total channel current at each of your time points.

- You will need to use Poisson's equation (Eqn. 10.1) and set the value of M as a way to select how much channel activity will be included in the program.

- For each time period in your simulation, you will need to decide (i) how many channels have just opened (use the Poisson distribution to decide this in random fashion), (ii) how much current is carried by each channel (to do so, randomly vary the amplitude about the mean single-channel current, e.g., by appropriately using the random normal distribution, although you may wish to start with 0 variation and add this in only later to mimic that in the trace in Fig. 10.4a; when you add in this variation, start conservatively and increase the amplitude of the variation until it appears to be appropriate), and (iii) how long each channel stays open (the duration needs to be chosen in a specific random way -- for example, if the average lifetime of an open channel is 45 ms, you will need to employ a random number from a probability density distribution like that in Fig. 10.8 to select the number of intervals on your time grid that the channel activity needs to continue).

To do (iii), think about how to transform a number that is distributed on the interval [0,1) with a uniform probability density to one that is distributed on the interval [0, ∞) with a probability density like that in Fig. 10.8. Alternatively, do a search to see if *Python* has a function that will randomly select a random number from a negative exponential distribution.

- Your current trace should now consist of random stepwise increments, both up and down, as a function of the time points on your time grid -- but with some variation in the amplitude of the steps due to the variation introduced above.

- To make the current record look similar to that in Fig. 10.4a, it will need to have some high-frequency noise. It would help to subdivide each of your basic time periods (e.g., 1 per ms) into 4 or 8 sub-intervals and, to begin with, set the value of the current for each sub-interval to that of the existing value for that time period; now you can add the high-frequency noise to your expanded grid of time-points (i.e., including the sub-intervals). Again, do this in a random fashion, e.g., using the random normal distribution, starting conservatively and increasing the noise until it is similar to that in Fig. 10.4a.

- To make a histogram plot like that in Fig. 10.7, you will have to tabulate how many of your time points have current amplitudes that, after appropriate rounding, correspond to the different allowed amplitudes in your histogram. You may find it useful to use *Python*'s 'round' and 'int' functions to do this.

- Make appropriate plots, including one of your current trace (which is expected to resemble that in Fig. 10.4a) and ones like those in Figs. 10.6 and 10.7.

- Now repeat your simulation with a different value of n in the statement 'seed(n)' to get a feel for how the presence of the various sources of random variation in your program influences your final plots.

- Consider modifying your simulation so as to take into account the fact that AChRs expressed in denervated muscle fibers are not homogeneous, i.e., do not all follow a single exponential probability distribution with the same mean open time. For example, assume that a minor fraction of your active channels has an average open time of 10 ms and the majority have an average open time of 45 ms (as reported by Sakmann et al., 1980). Then examine how this affects your plots.

Exercise 10.7 Given your program in Exercise 10.6, increase the number of active channels by increasing M (the parameter in the Poisson equation) so as to produce a current trace that appears to simulate that of a membrane with channel 'noise' but without clearly-resolved single channel activity. Compare this with literature recordings of acetylcholine-induced 'membrane noise' -- e.g., Fig. 2 of Anderson and Stevens (1973).

CHAPTER 11

SYNAPTIC TRANSMISSION AT THE NEUROMUSCULAR JUNCTION

When an action potential in the axon of a spinal motorneuron propagates to the axon's terminals, the surface membrane of the terminals depolarizes by ~100 mV. The concentration of free Ca^{2+} within the terminals then rises and initiates the release of the neurotransmitter acetylcholine (ACh) into the extracellular space. The ACh molecules diffuse to the underlying muscle cells, where they bind to, and open, ion channels in the muscle membranes, depolarizing the muscle cells. This chapter discusses these events and includes some important historical examples.

11.1 CHEMICAL VS. ELECTRICAL SYNAPSES

A chemical synapse is a junction between two cells at which an activation signal can be transferred in a directed fashion by means of diffusion of a chemical transmitter. The first cell (the 'presynaptic cell') releases the transmitter, and the second cell (the 'postsynaptic cell') is acted upon by the transmitter. The presynaptic cell is usually a nerve cell; the postsynaptic cell can be either a nerve cell, a muscle cell, or a secretory cell. The ubiquitous biological processes of exocytosis and endocytosis play central roles in the functioning of chemical synapses.

The neuromuscular junction (abbreviated 'nmj') is the site at which a motorneuron makes a chemical synapse on a skeletal muscle cell (also called a muscle 'fiber'). Although the vast majority of chemical synapses are found in the central nervous system (CNS), the nmj is large, experimentally-accessible, and one for which extensive structural and functional information is available. The nmj is therefore the main focus of this chapter.

The other major type of synapse is the electrical synapse, which will be mentioned only briefly here. Examples include the specialized contacts between adjacent cells in various tissues and organs, including epithelia, smooth muscle, the heart, and, in some cases, the brain. In contrast to chemical synapses, electrical synapses involve direct contact between proteins in the membranes of the two cells. These proteins form specialized channels, called 'gap junction channels', that provide a pathway for current to flow from the cytoplasm of one cell to the cytoplasm of the next. A gap-junction channel consists of two hemi-channels, one in each membrane of the two adjacent cells. Each hemi-channel contains a hydrophilic pathway that extends across that cell's membrane. Because the extracellular facets of the two hemi-channels are aligned and bound to each other, direct communication is established between the cytoplasm of the cells. The functional result is that electric current and molecules of molecular mass up to about 1 kD are able to pass through the gap-junction channels in both directions, as dictated by the relevant electrical and chemical driving forces. In some electrical synapses, current flows equally-well in both directions. In other electrical synapses, the current flow 'rectifies', i.e., is favored in one direction over the other (Furshpan and Potter, 1959; Gutierrez and Marder, 2013). In both cases, electrical synapses lack the absolute directionality of signal transmission that is characteristic of chemical synapses.

11.2 COMPONENTS OF A CHEMICAL SYNAPSE

Chemical synapses share a number of anatomical and functional features, several of which are shown in Fig. 11.1, which assumes that the presynaptic cell is a nerve cell. The surface membrane of the presynaptic-cell terminus (hereafter, called the 'terminal membrane') faces the membrane of the postsynaptic cell across a synaptic cleft ~0.1 μm wide.

The chemical transmitter is synthesized in the presynaptic cell and stored in many small membrane-bound vesicles. The largest pool of vesicles (the 'reserve vesicles') is located throughout the nerve terminal; a minor pool (the 'docked and primed vesicles') is positioned adjacent to the terminal membrane facing the synaptic cleft, where the vesicles are ready to be released. The docked vesicles are in contact with specialized regions of the terminal membrane called 'active zones'. There, a complex of proteins, including the 'SNARE' and 'SM' proteins (next paragraphs), are positioned to initiate fusion of the docked vesicles with the terminal membrane. Whenever the cytoplasmic concentration of free Ca^{2+} ($[Ca^{2+}]$) rises within the terminal, Ca^{2+} binds to sites on one or more of the fusogenic proteins (i.e., those comprising the exocytotic machinery) and exocytosis ensues. During this process, the membrane of the docked vesicles fuses with the terminal membrane, and the space inside the docked vesicles becomes continuous with the extracellular space. The vesicle contents can then diffuse to the postsynaptic cell.

Under physiological conditions, the rise in $[Ca^{2+}]$ within the nerve terminal results from the opening of voltage-dependent Ca^{2+} channels of type Ca_V2 (see Chapter 10), which are located in the terminal membrane close to the active zones. In summary, when the terminal is depolarized, the Ca$_V$2 channels open, Ca^{2+} enters the terminal from the ECF, Ca^{2+} binds to sites on one or more of the fusogenic proteins, and exocytosis takes place.

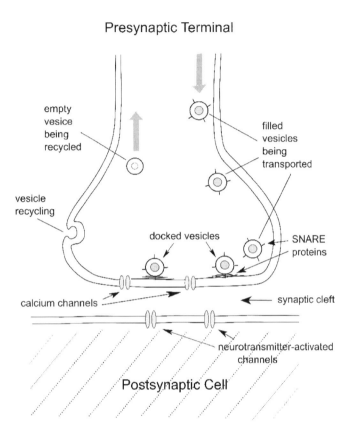

Figure 11.1 Schematic of a chemical synapse. The presynaptic cell (upper) is separated from the postsynaptic cell (lower) by the synaptic cleft, a small region of extracellular space. The terminal of the presynaptic cell contains (i) voltage-dependent Ca^{2+} channels in the part of its plasmalemma that faces the postsynaptic cell, (ii) synaptic vesicles in its interior, and (iii) SNARE and other proteins (see text) that mediate the fusion of the docked vesicles with the cell membrane. Synaptic vesicles containing the chemical transmitter are transported (down arrow) to the terminal membrane, to which they fuse during exocytosis. The vesicle membrane is recycled by endocytosis and sent to be repackaged with transmitter (up arrow). The membrane of the postsynaptic cell contains ligand-gated ion channels that open upon binding the chemical transmitter.

The exocytotic machinery consists of a complex set of proteins (Sudhof and Rothman, 2009). Some are anchored within the membrane of the vesicle, including synaptotagmin (which is reported to be the principal Ca^{2+}-sensitive protein for exocytosis), synaptophysin (which also binds Ca^{2+}), and synaptobrevin. These belong to a family of <u>v</u>esicle-<u>a</u>ssociated <u>m</u>embrane <u>p</u>roteins called the 'VAMP' family. Others, with acronyms such as 'SNAP' (soluble N-ethylmaleimide-sensitive factor attachment protein), 'SNARE' (soluble N-ethylmaleimide-sensitive factor attachment protein receptor), 'SM' (Sec1/Munc18-like protein), and 'RIM' (RAB3A-interacting molecule), are proteins that are closely associated with the terminal membrane and, in some cases, the vesicular membrane.

When $[Ca^{2+}]$ rises in the presynaptic terminal, these various proteins cooperate to catalyze the fusion of the vesicle membrane with the terminal membrane. Once the transmitter molecules are released into the ECF, they reach the membrane of the postsynaptic cell quickly, in ~10 µs, because the diffusion distance is small, ~0.1 µm (see Chapter 2). At the postsynaptic membrane, the transmitter molecules bind to, and open, ligand-gated ion channels, thus producing an increase in the conductance of the postsynaptic membrane. If the synapse is an excitatory synapse, the membrane potential of the postsynaptic cell depolarizes towards or above the threshold of its action potential. At an inhibitory synapse, the membrane potential might hyperpolarize slightly, depolarize slightly, or remain essentially unchanged. The common feature of the latter three cases is that the increase in membrane conductance holds the membrane potential of the postsynaptic cell more strongly at or near the resting potential. This makes the membrane resistant to any excitatory influence that might otherwise raise the membrane potential to threshold.

Once the docked vesicles undergo exocytosis, reserve vesicles move into position at the active zones, to be released in their turn. Concomitantly, the vesicle membrane that has fused with the surface membrane is retrieved by the process of endocytosis. Transmitter molecules (or their breakdown products) may be recaptured from the ECF, either by endocytosis or by movement of individual molecules through membrane transport proteins located in the nerve terminal. New transmitter molecules are synthesized within the nerve terminal and re-packaged in the recycled membrane. Because nerve terminals are metabolically active regions, they often contain substantial numbers of mitochondria.

11.3 ANATOMY OF THE NEUROMUSCULAR JUNCTION

The axon of a spinal motorneuron is myelinated over most of its length (see also Chapter 14). Near the muscle that it innervates, it becomes unmyelinated and branches to make a chemical synapse on each of the muscle cells that it controls, i.e., those in its 'motor unit'. Each synapse is located about half-way between the two tendon ends of the long muscle fiber. At the synapse, the nerve terminal forms a cluster of small endings that spread over and contact a number of μm² of the surface of the muscle cell.

Fig. 11.2 shows a schematic of the components of the nmj. The presynaptic components are similar to those diagrammed in Fig. 11.1. ACh is the transmitter stored in these synaptic vesicles.

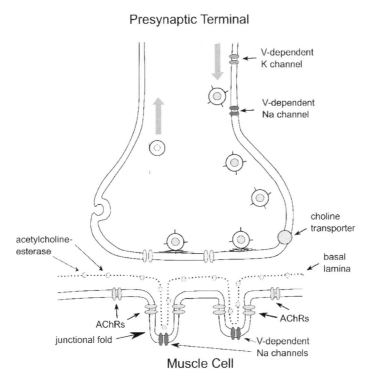

Figure 11.2 Schematic of the neuromuscular junction. The presynaptic terminal is shown as in Fig. 11.1 except for the addition of voltage-dependent Na⁺ and K⁺ channels and a membrane transporter protein for the uptake and reuse of choline. The synaptic cleft contains basement membrane with its basal lamina, to which molecules of the enzyme acetylcholinesterase are attached. The muscle membrane at the nmj is folded into crests and valleys. The crests contain a high density of AChRs and the valleys a high density of voltage-dependent Na⁺ channels.

Several additional components that are specific for the nmj, including the enzyme acetylcholinesterase, are shown in Fig. 11.2. Acetylcholinesterase is localized in the synaptic cleft on the extracellular connective tissue that surrounds the muscle cell. The enzyme appears to be attached to the basal lamina, which is part of the connective tissue layer (the 'basement membrane') that protects and provides mechanical support for the plasmalemma of the muscle cell.

The function of the acetylcholinesterase is to bind ACh and hydrolyze it into its components, acetate and choline, which are almost inactive as neurotransmitters, thereby terminating the action of ACh on the muscle cell. Because acetylcholinesterase is located between the terminal membrane and the muscle cell membrane, ACh molecules must "run the gauntlet" to reach the muscle membrane, i.e., to be effective, they must diffuse past the acetylcholinesterase. Obviously, some of the ACh molecules will be bound and hydrolyzed by the acetylcholinesterase as they make their random journey within the cleft. How many will depend, among other things, on the concentration of the ACh molecules, on the concentration of the acetylcholinesterase molecules, and on the enzyme's kinetics, including the rates of binding and dissociation of ACh. Some ACh molecules will diffuse out of the synaptic cleft before reaching the muscle membrane and thus also have no effect on the muscle cell.

The region of the muscle cell at the nmj is called the muscle 'endplate'. As diagrammed in Fig. 11.2, the surface membrane at the endplate has a high degree of folding. The crests in the folds contain a high density of AChRs; the valleys contain a high density of voltage-dependent Na^+ channels (the muscle isoform of this channel, which is different from the nerve isoform). This arrangement favors generation of an action potential in the muscle cell in response to the usual amounts of ACh that are released at the nerve terminal by an action potential (see next section). As discussed in Chapter 12, the remainder of the muscle membrane has a substantial density of voltage-dependent Na^+ channels and voltage-dependent K^+ channels. Under normal circumstances, once a muscle action potential is initiated at the endplate, it propagates to both tendon ends of the muscle cell in the usual manner, i.e., by electrotonic spread to depolarize adjacent regions of the cell membrane in combination with regeneration of the action potential waveform along the way by the voltage-dependent Na^+ and voltage-dependent K^+ channels.

Fig. 11.3 shows an electron micrograph of the ultrastructure of the nmj of a frog skeletal muscle cell. The nerve terminal is packed with synaptic vesicles, whose average diameter is 50-60 nm. A minor fraction of the vesicles is docked at the active zones, which, at the nmj, typically face the valleys of the folded muscle membrane. The protein machinery required for exocytosis is concentrated at the active zones, ready to be called into action when $[Ca^{2+}]$ rises. Each vesicle contains a large number of ACh molecules, estimated to be in the range of 6,000 to 10,000 (Kuffler and Yoshikami, 1975) or possibly more (see Exercise 11.13). A vesicle's worth of transmitter is commonly referred to as a 'quantum' and the number of vesicles of transmitter released under any particular circumstance -- e.g., in response to a nerve action potential -- is referred to as the 'quantal content' (note that the latter does not mean the number of molecules in a quantum).

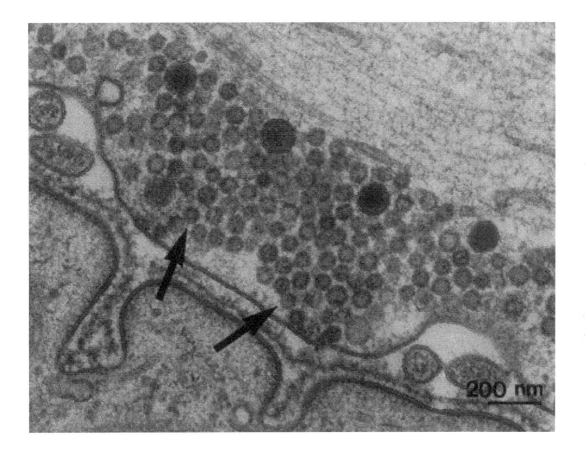

Figure 11.3 Electron micrograph of a frog neuromuscular junction. The nerve terminal (upper and to the right) contains many synaptic vesicles (arrows). The muscle cell (lower left) has a folded surface membrane, revealing crests and valleys. A synaptic cleft of ~0.1 μm separates the nerve and muscle cells. The basement membrane, which surrounds the outside of the muscle cell, is visible in the synaptic cleft. 'Fingers' (i.e., tubular extensions) of nearby Schwann cells, which are neuronal support cells that surround the nerve terminals, are also visible in the cleft. Note the scale bar of 200 nm at the lower right. [Credit: John Heuser and Joyce Evans, UCSF.]

11.4 FUNCTIONAL DETAILS OF THE NEUROMUSCULAR JUNCTION

To understand the function of the nmj, it is helpful to examine how the muscle cell responds to events in the nerve terminal. The earliest readily-detectable influence of the nerve cell on the muscle cell is a depolarization of the muscle membrane, which is referred to as the 'endplate potential' (abbreviation, 'epp'). The epp results from the binding of ACh to the AChRs (two ACh per AChR), which then open and function as non-selective cation channels, allowing primarily Na^+ and K^+ ions to move through the open channels according to the driving forces on each. Since, at the resting potential of the muscle cell, the inward driving force on Na^+ is much greater than the outward driving force on K^+, the muscle cell membrane depolarizes.

Not surprisingly, the epp is largest at the endplate, the location of the synapse. It is difficult, however, to resolve the properties of the epp under physiological conditions, because, as noted above, the epp normally triggers a muscle action potential at the endplate. Due to its regenerative nature and large peak amplitude, the action potential obscures the epp.

Unlike the action potential, the epp is not an all-or-nothing response; rather, it can be graded. This property is readily revealed in pharmacological experiments with curare, a mixture of poisonous plant alkaloids used historically by Central and South American Indians to subdue prey during hunting. The primary mechanism of action of curare is to reduce the size of the epp by binding to the AChRs. The result is that curare competitively inhibits the effect of ACh on AChRs; for example, curare reduces the depolarizing effect of exogenously applied ACh at the endplate in the same way that it reduces the epp. A highly-active component of curare is d-tubocurarine, which, at a concentration of a few µM, strongly reduces the amplitude of the epp.

Under normal circumstances, an action potential in the motorneuron releases many vesicles of ACh (i.e., many quanta), approximately 100-300 per muscle fiber. By itself, this amount of ACh would depolarize the endplate membrane of the muscle cell by some 60 to 80 mV. Because this depolarization would be well above the threshold for an action potential, which, in frog fibers, is 30-40 mV above the resting potential, a muscle action potential would ensue. Thus, under normal circumstances, the nmj functions as a reliable relay mechanism: the action potential in the nerve cell is followed with a small delay by an action potential in the muscle cell, which is followed by a muscle contraction (described in Chapter 12).

If curare is applied to a frog muscle preparation in an amount sufficient to reduce the size of the epp to ~20 mV, no action potential is generated because V_m remains below threshold. In this circumstance, the residual effect of ACh on the muscle cell can be recorded by an intracellular microelectrode without the obscuring effects of the muscle action potential, and the properties of the epp can be studied.

Fig. 11.4 shows results of an experiment in which intracellular recordings of the epp in a curarized frog muscle fiber were made at various locations along the cell. The recordings have been aligned in the figure on a common time and voltage axis.

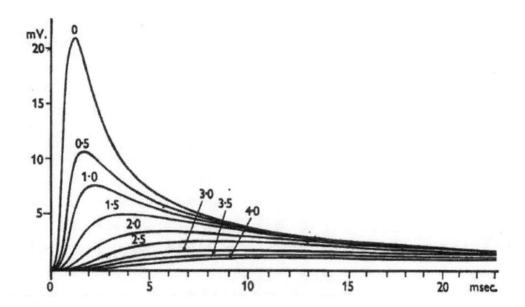

Figure 11.4. Intracellular recoding of epps at different distances from the endplate of a muscle cell in a curarized frog sartorius muscle in response to a (repeated) brief shock applied to the axon of the motorneuron that innervated the muscle cell. The numbers next to the traces give the recording distances in mm x 0.97 from the location of the endplate. Room temperature. [Credit: Fatt and Katz (1951).]

As expected, the largest and fastest epp occurs at the endplate (trace labeled '0'). At the other locations, the epp develops more slowly and reaches a smaller peak. On the time base in Fig. 11.4, 0 ms corresponds to about 3 ms after the axon was stimulated and about 1 ms after the action potential arrived at the nerve terminal. Thus, in a frog nmj at room temperature, the steps involving exocytosis of transmitter, diffusion of transmitter to the muscle cell, and opening of the AChRs in the muscle membrane occur within ~1 ms after the nerve terminal depolarizes. In the absence of curare, another 0.5 ms or so would be required for the membrane potential of the muscle cell to rise above the threshold for action potential generation.

Given that a frog muscle fiber is a long cylindrically-shaped cell, with a membrane space constant of ~2 mm and a time constant of ~20 ms (Fatt and Katz, 1951), the amplitudes and time courses of the waveforms in Fig. 11.4 are approximately those expected from one-dimensional cable theory (see Chapter 7). That is, the set of responses in Fig. 11.4 are similar to those that would be recorded in the muscle fiber at different distances from the nmj if a current-passing electrode had been inserted into the cell at the endplate and a small depolarizing current lasting ~2 ms had been injected.

If a higher concentration of curare had been used in the experiment of Fig. 11.4, the epps would all have been of smaller amplitude but their time courses would have been almost the same. Curare itself has no effect on the action potential machinery of the muscle membrane. For example, in the presence of a paralyzing concentration of curare, a muscle action potential can be elicited at the muscle endplate by a brief depolarizing stimulus that raises V_m above the threshold for action potential generation.

The size of the epp in a partially curarized preparation can be increased by drugs that act to inhibit acetylcholinesterase – so-called 'anticholinesterase drugs' -- such as eserine, prostigmine, and tensilon. This increase is to be expected since the enzyme that hydrolyzes ACh is inhibited. Such drugs have clinical uses in diseases such as myasthenia gravis, in which the number of functional AChRs is reduced.

11.5 MINIATURE ENDPLATE POTENTIALS

As noted in the previous section, under normal physiological conditions an action potential in a motorneuron releases perhaps 100-300 quanta of ACh, which causes a large depolarization of the muscle cell membrane. Interestingly, in the absence of a nerve impulse, the nerve terminals release individual quanta in an ongoing random series. The small depolarizations initiated by these quanta can be detected by an intracellular microelectrode located at the muscle endplate. These events are called 'miniature endplate potentials' (abbreviated 'mepps'; also called 'minis'). The upper traces on the left-hand side of Fig. 11.5 show examples of mepps in a frog muscle cell.

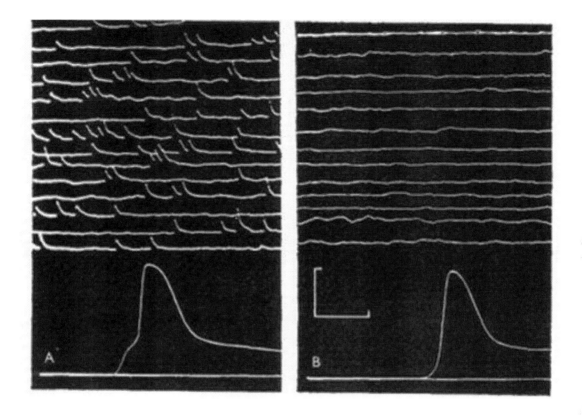

Figure 11.5 Intracellular recordings from a toe muscle cell of the frog (extensor digitorum longus IV). Upper left (14 traces): miniature endplate potentials recorded at the muscle endplate; the vertical and horizontal calibration bars for these traces are 3.6 mV and 46 ms, respectively (slow speed, high amplification). Bottom left: the muscle action potential recorded at the same location in response to a nerve impulse; the vertical and horizontal calibrations bars for this trace are 50 mV and 2 ms, respectively (high speed, low amplification). The traces on the right side are like those on the left except the recordings were made 2 mm from the endplate in the same muscle fiber. Room temperature; standard Ringer's solution. [Credit: Fatt and Katz (1950).]

The mepps in Fig. 11.5 (left) appear to occur randomly in time, rise abruptly to a peak amplitude of ~0.5 to 1 mV, and then decay to baseline approximately as expected based on the passive electrical properties of the muscle membrane. Mepps are thought to originate randomly at locations within the various points of synaptic contact of the nerve terminal with the muscle endplate. In Fig. 11.5 (left), these contact points are all located within a fraction of a space constant from the location of the intracellular microelectrode. If the microelectrode is located a distance of 2 mm or more from the endplate, the mepps are almost unrecognizable (Fig 11.5, right). The action potential recordings in Fig. 11.5 (lowermost traces) reveal that a large epp of 40-50 mV precedes the regenerative portion of the action potential at the endplate but not 2 mm from the endplate. Thus, the spatial dependence of the mepps is like that of the epp itself.

The frequency of mepps in frog muscle can vary widely from fiber to fiber; on average, the mean frequency is ~1 per s at room temperature. Because (i) the amplitude of mepps can be gradedly reduced by curare and (ii) mepp amplitude and time course can be markedly increased by acetylcholinesterase inhibitors, a mepp cannot be due to the binding of two ACh molecules to a single ACh receptor. Instead, it is triggered by the release of the thousands of molecules of ACh in a single quantum and involves the activation of many acetylcholine receptors.

Mepps give valuable information about the chemical-transmission process at synapses. For example, the frequency of mepps increases with increasing depolarization of the nerve terminal (del Castillo and Katz, 1954) and with increasing $[Ca^{2+}]$ in the extracellular fluid (Gage and Quastel, 1966), with little or no effect on the properties of individual mepps (see below). The normal epp that is observed in response to a nerve action potential is undoubtedly due to the summed action of many quanta of ACh, all released within a brief time. Thus, the nerve action potential does not appear to activate a novel exocytotic process but, rather, to increase, for a brief period -- and by a large factor -- the probability of release of individual quanta (see also next section and Exercise 11.13).

Mepps have been detected at the nmj of all vertebrates examined, including humans. Analogous quantal events likely occur at all types of chemical synapses, with involvement of a similar Ca^{2+}-dependent mechanism (Section 11.7).

11.6 STATISTICS OF MEPPS AND EPPS

Boyd and Martin (1956a,b) studied the statistical properties of mepps and epps in the tenuissimus muscle of the cat. As in frog muscle, mepps in cat muscle can be readily recorded by an intracellular microelectrode if it is located near an endplate. At room temperature, the properties of individual mepps are similar to those in frog fibers. The average values of rise time, peak amplitude, and half-decay time are 2.0 ms, 0.74 mV, and 3.4 ms, respectively. Under the hypothesis that a mepp is due to the random release of one vesicle at a time out of many possible vesicles that might be released, it is reasonable to propose that the waiting time between mepps behaves as a Poisson process (see Section 10.8 of Chapter 10). The rate constant of the associated negative-exponential distribution would then correspond to the inverse of the mean waiting time between events (see Eqn. 10.2 and related discussion).

Fig. 11.6 shows a histogram of the measured waiting times between mepps in an experiment on a tenuissimus muscle fiber at 37 °C. This histogram is the equivalent of a discrete probability distribution if the values on the ordinate are divided by the total number of mepps (= 143).

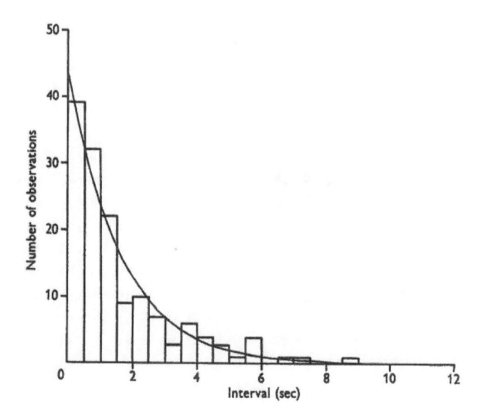

Figure 11.6 Histogram of waiting times between mepps in a series of 143 mepps that were recorded intracellularly at the endplate region of a fiber in the cat tenuissimus muscle. Waiting times were grouped in bins of duration 0.5 s; 37 °C. [Credit: Boyd and Martin (1956a).]

The data in the histogram are well-fitted by a decaying exponential function (curve) whose rate constant is 0.6 s^{-1}. Eqn. 10.2 with this rate constant then estimates the probability density function of the waiting time. The expected value of the waiting time between events, ~1.7 s (= (0.6 s^{-1})$^{-1}$), is close to the measured value of 1.6 s. In 72 such fibers, the mean frequency of mepps varied rather widely, 0.5 to 5 s^{-1}, with an average value of 1.43 s^{-1}. At 20 °C, the mean frequency of mepps was smaller, 0.35 s^{-1}, implying a mean waiting time of 2.9 s. For comparison, the mean frequency of mepps in frog muscle at 20 °C is ~1 s^{-1}.

These experiments on cat muscle fibers were carried out on muscles bathed in a Krebs solution, a standard extracellular solution for experiments on mammalian tissue. This solution includes NaCl and KCl at concentrations of 115 and 4.6 mM, respectively, and divalent ions at concentrations of 2.46 mM for Ca^{2+} and 1.15 mM for Mg^{2+}. Interestingly, if free [Mg^{2+}] in the Krebs solution is increased to 10-20 mM, the amplitude of the epp triggered by a nerve action potential (AP) is much smaller than normal. In general, Mg^{2+} antagonizes Ca^{2+} movements across membranes and, in this particular case, Mg^{2+} interferes with the ability of Ca^{2+} to permeate through Ca$_V$2-type Ca^{2+} channels.

A second factor that reduces the amplitude of the epps is that an increase in the extracellular concentration of divalent cations decreases the probability that these voltage-dependent channels will open at a given depolarized value of membrane potential. Thus, at elevated [Mg^{2+}], when an AP in the axon invades the nerve terminal, fewer Ca^{2+} channels open and, of the ones that do, less Ca^{2+} enters the nerve terminal through the open channels. The increase in cytoplasmic [Ca^{2+}] near the active zones is therefore smaller than usual and thus the quantal content of the epp is smaller.

Fig. 11.7 shows examples of three different epps recorded in a tenuissimus muscle fiber when the free [Mg^{2+}] in the bathing solution was 12.8 mM (11 times higher than normal) and the free [Ca^{2+}] was 2.46 mM (the normal value). The amplitude of the first epp is ~0.5 mV, which is similar to that of a mepp in normal Krebs solution. The amplitude of the second epp is about twice that of the first epp, and the amplitude of the third epp is zero.

The tentative conclusion is that the elevated level of free [Mg^{2+}] has greatly reduced the probability of presynaptic vesicle release such that, in response to a nerve AP, the number of released vesicles is very small -- e.g., sometimes one or a few, and sometimes none.

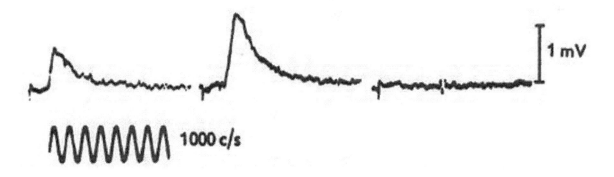

Figure 11.7 Upper: end-plate potentials in a fiber from cat tenuissimus muscle recorded with an intracellular microelectrode in response to 3 different stimulated nerve action potentials. Free $[Mg^{2+}]$ = 12.8 mM; free $[Ca^{2+}]$ = 2.46 mM; 37 °C. Lower: sinusoidal waveform at 1000 cycles per s provides a calibrated time base for the upper traces. [Credit: Boyd and Martin (1956b).]

Fig. 11.8 shows two amplitude histograms that provide additional understanding of the statistical nature of mepps and epps in cat tenuissimus fibers. The large histogram shows the distribution of amplitudes of 199 epps recorded in one experiment in which $[Mg^{2+}]$ was 12.5 mM -- and therefore the epp amplitude was greatly reduced. Eighteen trials revealed no response. Of the 181 trials in which there was a response, epp amplitudes ranged from 0.3 to 3 mV. The epp amplitudes in the histogram cluster around integer multiples of 0.4 mV, namely, 0.4, 0.8, 1.2, 1.6, ... mV. The small histogram in Fig. 11.8 shows the amplitude histogram for ~78 mepps in the same fiber exposed to the same solution. For these, the mean amplitude is ~0.4 mV, with some variation. The continuous curve in this histogram is a Gaussian curve centered at 0.4 mV, with a standard deviation of ~0.1 mV, which provides a good fit to these data.

Taken together, the two histograms in Fig. 11.8 suggest that, in 12.5 mM $[Mg^{2+}]$, epps greater than zero arise from a sum of one or more quantal events like those that give rise to mepps. The curve fitted to the data in the large histogram in Fig. 11.8 tests this hypothesis. The curve is based on the assumptions that, in 12.5 mM $[Mg^{2+}]$, (i) the quantal content of the epps obeys the Poisson probability distribution, with each quantal event having a small probability of occurrence (see Eqn. 10.1 in Chapter 10); (ii) epps due to a single quantal event have an amplitude distribution like that of the Gaussian curve in the smaller histogram in Fig. 11.8; (iii) epps due to n quantal events (n = 2, 3, 4, ...) have a mean amplitude that is n times that of a single quantal event and a variance that is n times that of the variance of the single quantal event [note: for any random variable, the variance of a sum of independent variables is the sum of their variances]; and (iv) the large histogram in Fig. 11.8 reflects all the quantal possibilities, including n = 0, with M, the mean number of quantal events per trial, ≈ 2.33 in this experiment. Because the curve fitted to this histogram provides a good fit to the data, the analysis supports the hypothesis that epps are composed of the same quantal events that produce mepps. Exercise 11.17 (with hints included) asks the reader to simulate this curve and its component parts.

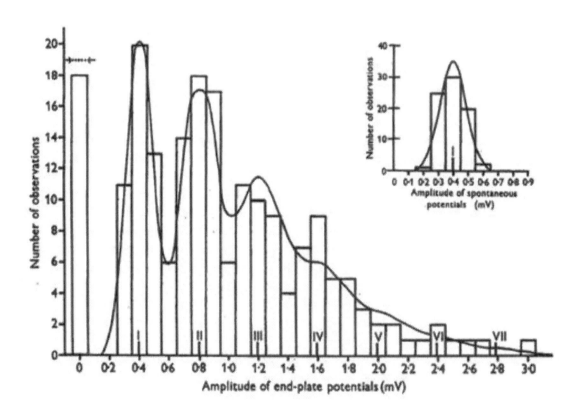

Figure 11.8 Amplitude histograms for 199 epps and ~78 mepps (i.e., 'spontaneous potentials') in a cat tenuissimus fiber in which neuromuscular transmission was inhibited by elevated [Mg^{2+}] (= 12.5 mM) in the Krebs solution bathing the muscle. The Gaussian curve superimposed on the mepp histogram was used in combination with Poisson's formula to calculate the multi-peaked continuous curve fitted to the epp histogram (see text). The horizontal arrows at location 0 on the abscissa of the epp histogram indicate the expected number of epp 'failures', i.e., epp responses whose amplitude is 0 mV; 37 °C. [Credit: Boyd and Martin (1956b); see experiment 4 of their Table 4]

In summary, this analysis of epp amplitudes strongly supports the hypothesis that epps are due to the summed action of individual quanta of ACh, all released at approximately the same time. From the properties of the epps measured in Krebs solutions containing [Mg^{2+}] at the normal value (1.15 mM), the quantal content elicited by a nerve action potential under physiological conditions was estimated to be 200-300 (37 °C; Boyd and Martin, 1956b). This value is similar to that estimated for frog fibers at room temperature (see also Exercise 11.13). It should be noted that, under physiological conditions, i.e., when the quantal content is large, the probability of release of any particular docked vesicle in response to the nerve AP may not be small. In this circumstance, an amplitude histogram analogous to that in Fig. 11.8 would be expected to be better fitted if based on a binomial, rather than a Poisson, distribution (see Eqn. 10.3 in Exercise 10.4).

11.7 Ca^{2+}-DEPENDENCE OF NEUROTRANSMITTER RELEASE

Under physiological conditions, a rise in free [Ca^{2+}] within the nerve terminal is the signal that initiates the vesicular release of neurotransmitters. As noted in section 11.2, the activation sequence is thought to involve the binding of Ca^{2+} to sites on one or more of the VAMP, SNARE, and related proteins; these then act to greatly increase the probability that a vesicle docked at an active zone will fuse with the terminal membrane. If action potentials continue in the presynaptic neuron, the pool of docked and readily-releasable vesicles will be depleted and replenishment of such vesicles from the reserve pool will be required. A second effect of the rise in [Ca^{2+}] in the nerve terminal is to speed the replenishment process (Bittner and Holz, 1992; von Ruden and Neher, 1993; Dittman and Regehr, 1998; Stevens and Wesseling, 1998; Wang and Kaczmarek, 1998). The discussion below focuses on the first action of [Ca^{2+}], i.e., on activation of the exocytotic machinery.

As noted, the concentration of divalent cations in the ECF has important effects on the release of neurotransmitters at chemical synapses. Typically, an increase in extracellular [Mg^{2+}] and/or a decrease in extracellular [Ca^{2+}] inhibits release and, conversely, an increase in extracellular [Ca^{2+}] and/or a decrease in extracellular [Mg^{2+}] enhances release (Douglas and Rubin, 1963; Douglas, 1968). These actions of external divalent cations were explored quantitatively in measurements of epps at the nmj of the frog's sartorius muscle (Dodge and Rahamimoff, 1967). To keep the amplitude of the epps in these experiments below the threshold for action potential generation, [Ca^{2+}] in the ECF was reduced from its normal value of 1.8 mM to values between 0.15 and 0.7 mM, and Mg^{2+} (which is normally not included in frog Ringer's solution) was included in the Ringer's solution at one of three concentrations, 0.5, 2, and 4 mM.

Fig. 11.9 shows that the amplitude of epps in frog muscle depends strongly on extracellular $[Ca^{2+}]$. When plotted on linear coordinates (part A), the relation between epp amplitude and $[Ca^{2+}]$ is highly non-linear, being convex upward for $[Ca^{2+}]$ between 0.15 and 0.7 mM. This dependence is seen at all three levels of $[Mg^{2+}]$. As expected, when $[Mg^{2+}]$ is increased, the epp amplitude vs. $[Ca^{2+}]$ relation is shifted to the right, i.e., at a higher $[Mg^{2+}]$, any particular value of $[Ca^{2+}]$ is less effective at enhancing release.

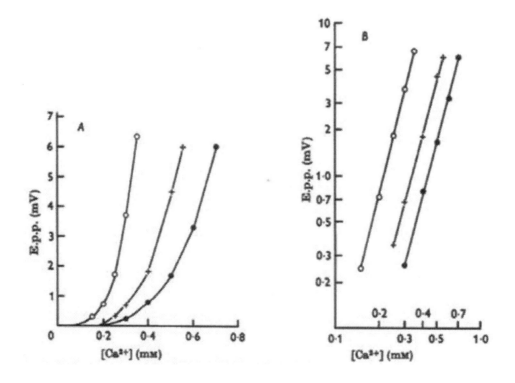

Figure 11.9 Amplitude of epps in frog sartorius muscle cells as a function of $[Ca^{2+}]$ in the Ringer's solution bathing the preparation. Results are shown at three different extracellular $[Mg^{2+}]$: 0.5 mM (open circles); 2.0 mM (+); 4.5 mM (filled circles). The plotting axes are shown on a linear scale in A and on a double-logarithmic scale in B. Epps were measured with a conventional intracellular microelectrode located at the endplate; temperature, 19-24 °C. [Credit: Dodge and Rahamimoff (1967).]

Interestingly, when the relation between epp amplitude and [Ca^{2+}] is plotted on double-logarithmic coordinates (Fig. 11.9B), a linear dependence is observed. At all three [Mg^{2+}] levels, the slopes of the lines are similar, almost 4. Thus, the epp amplitude almost follows the 4th power of [Ca^{2+}] -- for example, a doubling of [Ca^{2+}] increases epp amplitude by a factor of almost 16.

In 28 measurements like those in Fig. 11.9B, the average slope of the lines in double-logarithmic plots was 3.8 (with a standard deviation of 0.2). These results point to a highly-cooperative effect of Ca^{2+} on vesicle release; for example, 3-4 Ca^{2+} ions may bind cooperatively to the activation sites on the exocytotic machinery. The effect of Mg^{2+} is to competitively inhibit Ca^{2+}'s activating effect. Mg^{2+}'s effect, however, appears to be due to the binding of only one Mg^{2+} ion, with the effective dissociation constant of the inhibitory site for Mg^{2+} estimated to be ~3 mM (Dodge and Rahamimoff, 1967). Overall, these results are consistent with the idea that Ca^{2+} binds in a cooperative fashion to 3-4 sites on one or more proteins within the nerve terminal to activate transmitter release, while Mg^{2+} acts at a single site to inhibit release. Because Mg^{2+} is known to inhibit Ca^{2+} entry through voltage-dependent Ca^{2+} channels (e.g., Hagiwara and Byerly, 1981; Lansman et al., 1986), it is reasonable to suppose that Mg^{2+}'s main effect in these experiments is to block the entry of Ca^{2+} into the nerve terminal through the Ca_V2 Ca^{2+} channels.

Other experiments relevant to Ca^{2+}'s action on transmitter release examined how depolarization of the nerve terminal affects the frequency of mepps (del Castillo and Katz, 1954; Liley, 1956). In these experiments, the terminal membrane was depolarized by either passing a depolarizing current across the terminal membrane or by raising the concentration of K^+ in the physiological saline solution bathing the terminal. Both of these procedures increased the frequency of mepps. In rat diaphragm muscle, the limiting steepness of the relation between V_m and transmitter release was estimated to be e-fold for 6-7 mV (Liley, 1956). This voltage dependence is likely related primarily to the voltage-dependent activation of Ca_V2 Ca^{2+} channels, which, as noted above, are found in the terminal membrane located very close to the active zones and mediate the entry of Ca^{2+} into the nerve terminal. A recent report estimates the number of Ca^{2+} channels per active zone to be ~36 at the frog nmj (Luo et al., 2011).

Some debate exists in the literature regarding how cooperative is the effect of Ca^{2+} ions on the exocytotic machinery (e.g., Simon and Llinas, 1985). Experiments that have used the 'caged calcium' technique provide important information on this question (Millar et al.,

2005). In this technique, a Ca^{2+} buffer such as DMNPE-4 (Ellis-Davies, 2003), which binds Ca^{2+} with a high-affinity, is introduced with Ca^{2+} into the nerve terminal. This buffer is designed chemically to break down upon exposure to ultra-violet (UV) radiation; once broken down, the buffer has a low-affinity for Ca^{2+}. At the beginning of an experiment, with Ca^{2+} bound to the buffer in its high-affinity form in the nerve terminal, free $[Ca^{2+}]$ in the terminal is near its normal resting level, ~0.05 µM; consequently, the measured rate of vesicle exocytosis is, as expected, small. However, if the nerve terminal is exposed to a brief, high-intensity flash of UV radiation, some buffer is cleaved into its chemical components and Ca^{2+} is released from the buffer. Thus, free $[Ca^{2+}]$ in the terminal suddenly rises to a higher level. By calibration of the amount of caged calcium introduced into the terminal in combination with the strength of the UV flash of light, free $[Ca^{2+}]$ can be caused to jump to various estimated levels and the effect on vesicle release can be monitored with postsynaptic recordings.

Experiments of this type indicate that the rate of exocytosis varies with $[Ca^{2+}]$ raised to a power between 3 and 4 (Millar et al., 2005). This result is in agreement with the experiments of Dodge and Rahamimoff (1967) and supports the idea that multiple Ca^{2+} ions bind in a cooperative manner to sites on the exocytotic machinery within the terminal to activate transmitter release.

11.8 WHY ARE NOT ALL SYNAPSES ELECTRICAL?

Electrical synapses are anatomically and biochemically simpler than chemical synapses -- for example, they do not require the molecular machinery for the synthesis of transmitter molecules nor for vesicle release, retrieval, and transport. Instead, once gap junction channels have been synthesized and inserted into the appropriate membranes and the membranes brought into apposition, the process of communication between the pre- and postsynaptic cells becomes automatic. What, then, is the advantage of chemical synapses?

A principal advantage of a chemical synapse over an electrical synapse is its ability to amplify the communication signal. In the case of the neuromuscular junction, a small axon (e.g., of diameter ~10 µm) often needs to excite 50 to 100 large muscle cells (each of diameter, say, 50 µm). The axon simply is not able to generate sufficient current through an electrical synapse to reliably raise the membrane potential of even one of the muscle cells to the threshold for an action potential. This electrical problem is often summarized by the statement that a large 'impedance mismatch' exists between the nerve cell and the muscle cells. An analogous mismatch would apply if, say, one car battery and a number of small-diameter branching wires were used to try to simultaneously start the engines of 50-100 large vehicles.

In contrast, at the neuromuscular junction, two transmitter molecules of ACh are able to open one 28-pS ion channel in the muscle membrane. If the channel stays open for 2.5 ms and the average driving force is 50 mV on the permeant ions, then approximately 22,000 univalent ions move across the muscle membrane, the balance of which contributes to raising the membrane potential to threshold. Thus, the action of two transmitter molecules from the nerve cell on the muscle cell causes the movement of ~22,000 ions across the muscle membrane, giving an amplification factor of ~10^4 (22000/2).

A second advantage of a chemical synapse is that it permits flexibility in the response of the postsynaptic cell. In the case of neurons in the CNS, where the vast majority of chemical synapses are found, postsynaptic cells are typically under the influence of both excitatory and inhibitory transmitters from the terminals of several types of nerve cells. In such cases, the postsynaptic cell weighs the amplitude of both types of inputs before the decision is made whether to initiate an action potential. Often, repeated inputs from one presynaptic cell in close succession ('summation in time') and/or inputs from several different presynaptic cells ('summation in space') are required for the excitatory signal in the postsynaptic cell to reach action-potential threshold. This type of integration of signals from excitatory and inhibitory synapses, which may themselves be modulated on a rapid time scale by chemical synapses, confers flexibility.

A third advantage of chemical synapses (noted in section 11.1) is that they are inherently unidirectional. For complicated neuronal circuits, instability and other problematic effects might occur if the components making up the signal pathways were bidirectional.

A disadvantage of chemical synapses compared with electrical synapses is that they are slower. Indeed, time is required for exocytosis, for diffusion of transmitter to the postsynaptic membrane, for binding of transmitter to the ion channels in the postsynaptic membrane, and for opening of the channels. On the other hand, as shown by events at the nmj, if the transmitter vesicles are docked and ready to be released, if the synaptic cleft is narrow, and if the binding and opening kinetics of the ion channel are fast, the overall delay is acceptably small, ~1 ms at room temperature.

Regarding chemical transmission at the nmj, a final point is worth reemphasizing. When an excitatory signal is passed from the motorneuron to the muscle cell, the muscle endplate does not weigh messages of various types prior to carrying out its action. Rather, the nmj behaves simply as a powerful relay and, under normal circumstances, does so in an unfailing manner.

11.9 EXOCYTOSIS

Previous topics in this chapter have largely focused on the vesicular release of ACh at the nmj and subsequent effects on the muscle cell. This section briefly examines exocytosis more generally. Virtually all cells use exocytosis to move vesicle-stored cargo to an intended destination. In some cases, the important cargo is the interior contents of the vesicle -- e.g., neurotransmitter molecules to be released at a chemical synapse -- and the destination is the ECF. In other cases, the important cargo is part of the vesicular membrane -- for example, integral membrane proteins that were recently synthesized in the endoplasmic reticulum -- and the destination is the cell's plasmalemma. In both cases, fusion of the vesicle with the plasmalemma achieves the useful result.

While the immediate trigger for release of transmitters at chemical synapses is a rise in cytoplasmic $[Ca^{2+}]$, exocytosis in some cell types may not always depend on a rise in $[Ca^{2+}]$. In these cases, $[Ca^{2+}]$ may act as a co-factor and other intracellular changes may serve to initiate exocytosis. Possible changes of the this type include activation of a G protein (Fernandez et al., 1984; Penner and Neher, 1988) or phosphorylation or de-phosphorylation of a regulatory protein. Regarding the latter possibility, exocytosis is favored if the concentration of intracellular ATP is increased.

In other cells, exocytosis is thought to be 'constitutive', i.e., to be an unregulated process that, under resting cell conditions, takes place routinely about the time a vesicle arrives at a docking site near the plasmalemma. Exocytosis also occurs on very different time scales in different cells -- e.g., the fast response at the nmj, where transmitter release occurs within a ms after the arrival of the action potential in the nerve terminal, or the slow response in mast cells (see below), where stimulated release of its large secretory vesicles can take tens of seconds.

The study of exocytosis has been advanced considerably by use of the patch-clamp technique. In the first study of this type (Neher and Marty, 1982), a patch-clamp electrode was attached to a secretory cell in whole-cell mode and the capacitance of the cell membrane was measured at rest and during stimulated exocytosis. Subsequent studies of exocytosis have also applied the patch-clamp technique in the cell-attached mode (Lollike et al., 1995, Albillos et al., 1997). The principle of either application is that, if a secretory vesicle suddenly fuses with the surface membrane, the capacitance of the surface membrane is expected to increase in proportion to the amount of membrane area added by the fused vesicle. Furthermore, when the patch-clamp is used in whole-cell mode, it is possible to dialyze the cell's soluble contents, i.e., achieve diffusive exchange of the intracellular fluid with the fluid in the patch pipette. By this means, the concentrations of the cell's soluble cytosolic constituents can be manipulated experimentally.

Fig. 11.10 shows an example of the use of the whole-cell patch-clamp technique to study exocytosis in a rat mast cell, which is a type of white blood cell, found also in mucosal and epithelial tissue, that mediates allergic and other immunologic reactions. The two microscope images (left side of Fig. 11.10) show the morphology of the mast cell before and after 'degranulation', i.e., before and after the cell's many large internal vesicles (which contain histamine, heparin, various amines and peptides, and other inflammatory mediators) fuse with the surface membrane. As part of this dramatic event, the area of the surface membrane increases substantially, sometimes several-fold. During this increase, a similarly-large increase in the capacitance of the surface membrane can be recorded (not shown in Fig. 11.10).

The right side of Fig. 11.10 shows an example of the time course of a small fraction of the total increase in membrane capacitance that was recorded by the patch-clamp technique during degranulation of a mast cell. Strikingly, membrane capacitance increases in a stepwise fashion. The average increase per step, 15-20 fF, is approximately that expected from the fusion of individual vesicles, as calculated from (i) the average surface area of a mast cell vesicle and (ii) a membrane specific capacitance of 1 µF per cm^2 (see Exercise 11.19).

Another important observation in the experiments of Fernandez et al. (1984) is that the patch-clamp technique can also be used to monitor endocytosis. Under some circumstances, stepwise decreases in membrane capacitance were observed that had approximately the same size as the stepwise increases illustrated in Fig. 11.10. These changes were seen in situations when mast-cell degranulation had already occurred and further exocytotic events were unlikely to happen.

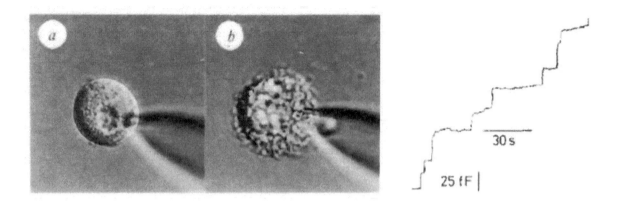

Figure 11.10 Exocytosis in rat mast cells studied with the patch-clamp technique. Left: a normal mast cell and an out-of-focus patch pipette after a whole-cell tight seal onto the surface membrane of the cell was made (viewed with Nomarski optics). (*a*) Before exocytosis was triggered, a prominent nucleus and many densely-packed secretory 'granules' (i.e., vesicles) are visible; cell diameter, ~13 μm. (*b*) The same cell after degranulation, i.e., after nearly-complete exocytosis of its granules. The image reveals puckering and folding of the surface membrane due to addition of the membrane of the fused granules; matrix material released from the granules can be seen floating near the surface of the cell. Right: stepwise increases in cell capacitance during degranulation of a mast cell, recorded with the patch-clamp technique used in the whole-cell mode. Each increase in capacitance is thought to be due to an incremental increase in the area of the cell's surface membrane accompanying the fusion of an individual granule. Vertical calibration bar, 25 fF (= 25×10^{-15} farads). [Credit: Fernandez et al. (1984).]

A final observation in the experiments of Fernandez et al. (1984) was that, under some circumstances, mast cell degranulation did not appear to require an increase in cytoplasmic [Ca^{2+}]. Instead, the process could be triggered by activation of an (unidentified) intracellular G-protein-dependent signal pathway. This conclusion followed from the observation that degranulation of mast cells could be triggered reliably if the solution bathing the cell did not include Ca^{2+} and the patch pipette itself contained both (i) a high-affinity Ca^{2+} buffer (which would keep the cytoplasmic free [Ca^{2+}] at or below its resting level) and (ii) GTP-γ-S, a long-acting analogue of GTP (which is expected to provide a maintained stimulus to intracellular G-protein-dependent signal pathways). These experiments demonstrated that, even if, under physiological conditions, a rise in $[Ca^{2+}]$ is the proximate trigger for exocytosis in mast cells, other pathways can have important effects on the control of exocytosis in this, and probably other, cell types.

11.10 EXERCISES

Exercise 11.1 Draw a picture of a presynaptic vesicle docked at the nerve terminal membrane; include the bilipid leaflet of both membranes in your drawing and, for each membrane, label the leaflet that faces the cytoplasm. Now redraw your picture (i) while the vesicle is in the process of fusing with the terminal membrane and (ii) after the vesicle has fused with the membrane. Which leaflet of the original vesicle membrane is facing the cytoplasm after fusion has taken place?

Exercise 11.2 If ACh is applied locally via pressure injection from a micropipette to the extracellular side of the endplate region of the muscle membrane, it produces a depolarization. If, in a similar experiment, the pipette first impaled the muscle cell near the endplate and ACh was pressure-injected into the cell, would this be expected to cause a depolarization, hyperpolarization, or no change in V_m?

Exercise 11.3 If an action potential (AP) in a frog muscle cell is evoked by direct stimulation of the cell by an external electric shock (thus no ACh is released onto the muscle cell), would you expect the shape of the AP to change as it propagated past the location of the nmj?

Exercise 11.4 In Section 11.4, the text mentioned that the depolarizing responses shown in Fig. 11.4 are similar to those that would be expected if a current-passing electrode were inserted into the muscle cell at the endplate and a small pulse of depolarizing current lasting a couple of ms were injected into the cell. If the direction of this hypothetical current is referred to its direction as it crosses the muscle cell membrane after leaving or entering the electrode, would this be an inward or an outward current?

Exercise 11.5 A current pulse is passed across the membrane of a resting muscle cell near the nmj and found to produce a ~15 mV change in V_m. The same current passed during the peak of an AP that was initiated by electrically stimulating the muscle cell is found to produce a change of ~1 mV.

a) What does this finding say about the relative conductance of the muscle membrane in the two situations?

b) If the muscle AP at the nmj were elicited by stimulating an AP in the motorneuron, explain whether the same current pulse at the peak of the synaptically-evoked muscle AP would be expected to elicit a response that is bigger or smaller than 1 mV.

Exercise 11.6 The legend of Fig. 11.5 states that the two recordings of the muscle AP (lowermost traces) were made 2 mm apart. Since the time at which the stimulation of the nerve that generated these recordings was the same relative to the recordings (namely, at the beginning of the displayed traces), the time delay between the two action potentials reflects a delay due to the propagation of the muscle AP along the muscle membrane.

a) Estimate the action potential's propagation velocity in the muscle cell and explain your method for doing so.

b) Explain the origin of the large initial hump in the action-potential recording at the muscle endplate and explain why this hump is absent in the recording 2 mm from the muscle endplate.

Exercise 11.7 The AChRs at the nmj are ligand-gated cation channels. Devise an experiment to decide if these channels are also voltage-gated for voltages between, say, -120 and -60 mV (i.e., for voltages below the threshold for generation of an action potential).

Exercise 11.8 If the action potential in the axon of a spinal motorneuron were prolonged by an agent such as tetraethylammonium (which has a blocking effect on voltage-dependent K^+ channels), would the quantal content elicited by an AP be expected to change?

Exercise 11.9 If the membrane potential of the nerve terminal were changed by doubling the $[K^+]$ in the ECF, would the frequency of mepps be expected to change and, if so, in what direction?

Exercise 11.10 A muscle fiber of small diameter is noted to have a larger input resistance than that of a large-diameter muscle fiber nearby (recall from cable theory in Chapter 7 that this is expected). If all vesicles in a presynaptic nerve terminal had the same content of ACh, how would the mepps in the small-diameter fiber compare in amplitude with the mepps in the large-diameter fiber?

Exercise 11.11 Would the amplitude of mepps be expected to be larger, smaller, or unchanged in the presence of a drug like eserine (also known as physostigmine), which inhibits acetylcholinesterase? What about the frequency of mepps?

Exercise 11.12 Suppose the frequency of mepps is measured at a mammalian nmj in a physiological Krebs solution with the usual concentration of free Mg^{2+} (1.15 mM). Would you expect the frequency of mepps to change if $[Mg^{2+}]$ in the Krebs solution was increased to 2.3 mM?

Exercise 11.13 In frog muscle, the conductance of a single open AChR at the nmj is estimated to be ~28 pS (2.8×10^{-11} S) (Lewis, 1979; see also Chapter 10).

a) If a single mepp produces a conductance change of ~1.47×10^{-7} S in the membrane of a frog muscle cell (Takeuchi and Takeuchi, 1960), how many open AChRs are required to explain this conductance change?

b) Two ACh molecules must bind to an AChR to cause it to open. What is the minimum number of ACh molecules in a quantum required to explain the conductance change of 1.47×10^{-7} S?

c) If 30% of the released ACh molecules in a quantum are wasted, either because they diffuse out of the synaptic cleft or are bound and hydrolyzed by acetylcholinesterase before they reach the AChRs, what is your revised minimum number of ACh molecules in a quantum?

d) An AP in a frog motorneuron is reported to release enough ACh that the conductance change in the membrane of the muscle cell due to the open AChRs is ~4×10^{-5} S (Fatt and Katz, 1951). How many open AChRs are required to explain this conductance change?

e) Use the relevant results in (a) to (d) to estimate the quantal content elicited by a single AP in a frog motorneuron.

f) Suppose that the release of this quantal content by the nerve terminal takes place during a 1 ms period after arrival of the nerve AP. If the frequency of mepps in a frog muscle cell at rest is 1 per s (Katz, 1970), by what factor does the nerve AP increase the probability of vesicle release from the nerve terminal during the time of peak release?

Exercise 11.14 The text states that, if an ion channel with a conductance of 28 pS stays open for 2.5 ms during which time the driving force is 50 mV, approximately 22,000 univalent ions move across the membrane. Check the accuracy of this calculation.

Exercise 11.15 In the experiment of Fig. 11.7, in which elevated $[Mg^{2+}]$ was used to reduce the amplitude of epps, the mean epp amplitude is ~1 mV but shows substantial variation from trial to trial. Suppose d-tubocurarine instead of elevated $[Mg^{2+}]$ had been used to reduce the mean epp amplitude to ~1 mV. Would you expect variations in the epp amplitude from trial to trial to be more, less, or similar to that observed in Fig. 11.7?

Exercise 11.16 The text that discussed the large histogram in Fig. 11.8 stated that the theoretical curve reflects the quantal content of all-possible epps under the assumption of a Poisson probability distribution for which M (the mean number of quantal events per trial) ≈ 2.33.

a) Use Poisson's formula (Eqn. 10.1) and the information in the histogram that P(0) (the probability that n = 0) is ~0.095 (= 19/199) to calculate M for the theoretical distribution.

b) A second way to estimate M uses the fact that M is the average quantal content observed for many epp measurements in one experiment (since a Poisson distribution with parameter M has a mean value of M). The average quantal content can be obtained by dividing the mean amplitude of the epps by the mean amplitude of the mepps measured in the same fiber. If M in the experiments of Fig. 11.8 is 2.33 and if the mean amplitude of the spontaneous potentials for the experiment in Fig. 11.8 is 0.4 (see small histogram), what is the mean amplitude of the epps in this experiment?

The graph below, from ten experiments (Boyd and Martin, 1956b), plots the estimates of M obtained by the two methods described in a) and b). The ordinate shows M based on the log of the number of trials divided by the number of failures (method a); the abscissa shows M based on the ratio of the mean amplitude of the epps divided by the mean amplitude of the mepps (method b). If the agreement between the two methods is perfect, all points would lie on the line (the slope of which is 1). Obviously, the agreement between methods is good, which supports the assumptions of the analysis.

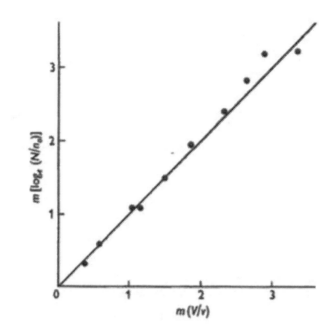

Exercise 11.17 Write a *Python* program that reproduces the curve in the large histogram of Fig. 11.8 based on the assumptions stated in the paragraph in Section 11.6 that discusses Fig. 11.8. See if your analysis supports that statement that $M \approx 2.33$ is the best choice for this parameter?

Hints:
- Given your choice of M, calculate and plot the Poisson probabilities for, say, $n = 0$ to 8. For your choice of M, P(0) (the probability that $n = 0$) should be consistent with the arrowed level (≈ 19) on the ordinate in Fig. 11.8 at 0 mV on the abscissa. Do you notice a disparity between the value of n where your probability plot has its maximum value and the equivalent value of n for the epp amplitude at which the curve in Fig. 11.8 has its maximum value? (Note: both calculations are correct; after you have completed the calculation of your curve, you should be able to explain this disparity.)

- You will probably find it useful to have *Python* code that calculates a normal probability-density distribution, which is a type of Gaussian curve, the area under which integrates to 1. You can use this distribution in several ways, including to help you decide on the standard deviation of the Gaussian curve that Boyd and Martin used to fit the histogram for the mepp measurements (see curve in the small histogram of Fig. 11.8, for which the value of the standard deviation is not stated by Boyd and Martin). Selection of the appropriate standard deviation will be critical in reproducing the curve in Fig. 11.8. You may be able to find *Python* code for a normal probability-density function on-line that meets your needs, but the statements below will probably suffice:

```
def normalpdf(x,mean,stddev):  #define a normal probability density function
    var=(stddev)**2
    denom=(2*np.pi*var)**0.5
    num=np.exp(-(x-mean)**2/(2*var))
    return num/denom
```

- Use your code for the normal probability distribution to help reproduce the curve in the large histogram of Fig. 11.8. First, reproduce the part of the curve that applies to a quantal content of 1 (i.e., epp amplitudes around 0.4 mV). You will need to choose an appropriate density of points on the x-axis for your plot and also scale your selected Gaussian curve in a logical way to match the number of observations (~20) at 0.4 mV on the x-axis. Note that the following factors are relevant for this scaling:

(i) the Poisson probability for $n = 1$;

(ii) the total number of observations in this experiment (199);

(iii) the fact that the curve in the figure is a continuous curve but it has been scaled to fit a histogram for which the x-increments are 0.1 mV (i.e., although the curve is continuous, the histogram data are discrete, based on the grouping of the data into bins of width 0.1 mV).

- Once you have calculated a curve to fit the histogram for a quantal content of 1, it should be straightforward to extend the logic of your program and your plot to include the remaining values of quantal content (i.e., 2, 3, …, 7).

Exercise 11.18 Several experiments discussed in the text (e.g., those in Figs. 11.4-11.9) used an intracellular micro-electrode at the muscle endplate to study mepps and epps. Would there be an advantage in the use of the voltage-clamp technique for carrying out such experiments -- for example, a two micro-electrode voltage-clamp located at the endplate, one for holding the membrane potential constant and one for measuring the current required to do so? [Note: (i) with the voltage-clamp technique, V_m is held constant; (ii) when mepps and epps are measured, V_m changes -- sometimes substantially; (iii) when V_m changes, a change occurs in the driving force on the currents responsible for the change in V_m.]

Exercise 11.19 Assume that, in a mast cell, the average diameter of a granule (= exocytotic vesicle) is 0.4 µm (cf. Fig. 11.10) and that the specific capacitance of the granule membrane is, like that of the plasmalemma, 1 µF per cm^2. Calculate the expected increase in the capacitance of the surface membrane due to exocytosis of an average-sized granule. Compare your answer with the average size of the step increases in capacitance on the right side of Fig. 11.10.

CHAPTER 12

EXCITATION-CONTRACTION COUPLING IN SKELETAL MUSCLE

Movement is a hallmark of life. In the case of animals, the movement is produced by the skeletal muscles. This chapter discusses the mechanisms within a skeletal muscle cell that underlie a muscle twitch, the simplest normal contraction of a muscle cell and the elemental basis of animal movement. The twitch is a rapid and reproducible mechanical event that involves the entire cell volume.

12.1 INTRODUCTION TO SKELETAL MUSCLE

The muscles of vertebrates are divided into three main categories: skeletal muscles, which are connected to the skeleton or cartilage through tendons; cardiac muscle, the type of muscle found in the heart; and smooth muscle, the type that surrounds blood vessels and hollow organs such as in the gastrointestinal and genito-urinary systems. Skeletal muscles are innervated by the somatic nervous system and are under voluntary control. Cardiac and smooth muscles are innervated by the autonomic nervous system and are not under voluntary control. Skeletal and cardiac muscle cells are termed 'striated' because, in the light microscope, anatomic stripes oriented transversely to the long axis of the cell are readily visible. Smooth muscle cells, in contrast, are not striated.

The skeletal muscles of vertebrates account for 40-50% of body weight. Each muscle is composed of tens to thousands of individual muscle cells. These cells, which are usually called 'fibers', have a long, cylindrical shape and are among the largest cells in the body. Because skeletal fibers are separated anatomically from one another by connective tissue and extracellular space, with careful dissection it is possible to isolate healthy single muscle fibers for physiological study. Such single-fiber studies have contributed importantly to the understanding of EC coupling.

The skeletal fibers of vertebrates are composed of different types, including slow-twitch, fast-twitch, and superfast-twitch; some vertebrates also have a non-twitch fiber type, termed 'tonic' fibers. The various fiber types express different isoforms of key muscle proteins, which allows them to perform contractile tasks at different speeds and levels of force. For example, slow-twitch fibers work at low frequencies (e.g., 10 Hz at 25 °C) and produce relatively high forces whereas superfast fibers work at high-frequencies (e.g., 200 Hz) and produce relatively low forces.

Voluntary contractions are initiated in the brain's motor cortex. The signal pathway from the spinal cord to the muscle is through large nerve cells, called 'alpha motorneurons' (α-motorneurons), whose cell bodies reside in the ventral horn of the spinal cord (Fig. 12.1). A single α-motorneuron and the muscle fibers it innervates work as a functional unit, called a 'motor unit'. Under normal circumstances, each action potential in an α-motorneuron initiates an action potential and twitch in each of the muscle fibers in that motor unit.

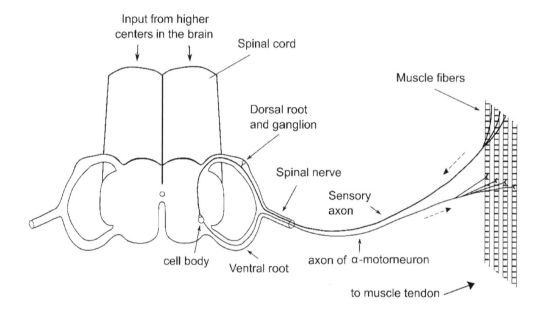

Figure 12.1 Information flow (dashed arrows) between the spinal cord and skeletal muscle fibers. The cell body of an α-motorneuron, located in the ventral horn of the spinal cord, sends its axon peripherally out the ventral nerve root. The axon divides near the muscle to contact the fibers in its motor unit (in this case, a small motor unit, with only a portion of 4 fibers, is shown). Axons of sensory neurons from the motor unit, which enter the spinal cord through the dorsal nerve root, carry information about muscle length and muscle force (see Chapter 14).

As discussed in Chapter 11, communication between the nerve and each muscle cell is mediated by a chemical synapse at the neuromuscular junction. At each nmj, depolarization of the nerve terminal causes the release of acetylcholine, which diffuses a short distance to the muscle cell. When acetylcholine activates the AChR channels in the muscle membrane, Na⁺ enters the fiber and initiates a muscle action potential and twitch (described below). At a given fiber length, the twitch generates a stereotyped amount of force with a stereotyped time course. It follows that the strength and duration of a fiber's contraction is primarily graded by varying the rate of firing of the α-motorneuron.

Motor units are recruited into activity as needed for the action at hand. For weak contractions, few motor units are active, the smallest units are used, and the rate of activation (action potentials per second) is low. In stronger contractions, the rate of activation increases, and more and larger units are recruited.

Overall, the force and velocity of voluntary movements are controlled rapidly and accurately for the intended movement. In addition to conscious input, a number of local feedback mechanisms help control the parameters of movement (described in Chapter 14). Twitches in skeletal fibers depend little on extrinsic hormonal and ionic conditions; this contrasts with the contractions of cardiac and smooth muscle, which can vary strongly with these factors.

12.2 INTRODUCTION TO EXCITATION-CONTRACTION COUPLING

Excitation-contraction coupling (EC coupling) is the name given to the sequence of steps that leads to contraction of a muscle cell following depolarization of its surface membrane. It involves an unusual voltage-dependent process (described in detail in section 12.6).

Historically, the understanding of EC coupling took an important step forward in the late 1700s, the time of the anatomical studies of Luigi Galvani, an Italian physician at the University of Bologna. In experiments on sacrificed frogs, Galvani noticed that the leg muscles would sometimes twitch if dissecting instruments made from two dissimilar metals were brought into contact with the muscles and touched together. A circuit involving two dissimilar metals was known to be a source of electricity and Galvani correctly surmised that the contraction of the muscles involved a bio-electric effect. He called this effect 'animal electricity'. It is now known that animal electricity is no different from ordinary electricity, which involves the separation and flow of charged particles, including ions. Since Galvani's time, the study of how electricity triggers muscle contraction has been one of the most intriguing subjects in all of physiology (reviewed by Franzini-Armstrong, 2018).

Much of the remaining material in this chapter discusses experiments on isolated fibers -- or short fiber segments -- of frog muscle, which are hardy cells that provide an accessible experimental preparation for physiological studies.

The experiment of Fig. 12.2 shows results from a modern version of Galvani's experiment. A single muscle fiber is held at fixed length, a condition under which a so-called 'isometric' contraction occurs. The muscle force is low in the relaxed state. The muscle action potential is triggered by a shock from a wire in the bathing solution extending along the entire length of the muscle fiber. This generates a membrane action potential (cf. Chapter 8), i.e., one that is initiated simultaneously over the entire fiber length. The main portion of the action potential is quite brief and returns close to, but pauses somewhat above, the resting potential before mechanical force begins to rise. The change in force, recorded by a tension transducer attached to one of the fiber's tendons, reaches a peak with some delay (~25 ms at room temperature) and then declines.

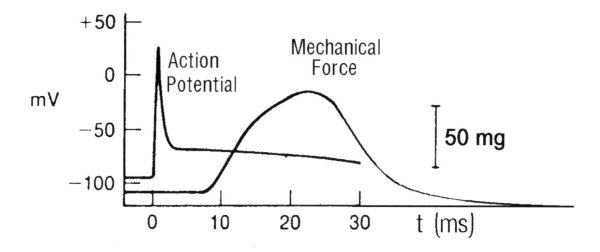

Figure 12.2 Relation between the muscle action potential (AP) and force during an isometric twitch of a frog single muscle fiber. The AP is calibrated on the left, the force on the right. (See Exercise 12.1 for the modern calibration of force transients.)

If a second stimulus is given before the first contraction has fully relaxed, the peak of force with the second twitch is usually higher than with the first (so-called 'summation'). If a number of stimuli are given in rapid succession, the force responses increase and fuse together since there is not enough time for relaxation between twitches. Completely fused twitches are called a 'tetanus' (or a 'fused tetanus').

12.3 A QUICK TOUR OF THE STEPS IN EC COUPLING

As noted, EC coupling normally begins with fiber depolarization at the muscle end-plate, where the density of voltage-gated Na^+ channels is especially high. Voltage-gated Na^+ channels and voltage-gated K^+ channels are present there and at a substantial density over the remaining surface membrane of the fiber; they generate a muscle action potential much like that in nerve axons. The gates on the voltage-dependent Na^+ and K^+ channels in the muscle membrane, however, open and close somewhat more slowly in response to changes in membrane potential. The following events then take place:

- longitudinal propagation of the action potential away from the endplate region to both tendon ends of the cylindrically-shaped muscle fiber;

- concomitant propagation of the action potential into the interior of the fiber along a system of tubular membranes (the 'T-tubular' membranes or the 'T-system'), which are oriented transversely to the long axis of the fiber and are connected electrically to the surface membrane; these membranes extend throughout the fiber cross section at regular intervals along the fiber length and also contain voltage-gated Na^+ channels and voltage-gated K^+ channels;

- activation of dihydropyridine receptors (DHPRs), a voltage-dependent protein complex found in the T-system at specialized locations where the T-tubular membranes meet the membranes of the sarcoplasmic reticulum (dihydropyridines are a class of compounds that bind with high-affinity to the DHPRs); the specialized sites where the T-tubular membranes meet the membranes of the sarcoplasmic reticulum (SR) are called 'triadic junctions' or 'triads';

- transmission of an activation signal from the DHPRs to Ca^{2+}-conducting cation channels in the membranes of the SR; these channels are known as the 'Ca^{2+}-release channels of the SR' and are also called 'ryanodine receptors' or 'RyRs', named after the toxin ryanodine, which binds with high affinity to these channels and allowed their isolation biochemically;

- opening of the gates on the SR Ca^{2+}-release channels and flux of Ca^{2+} ions through these channels down a steep Ca^{2+} concentration gradient from the lumen of the SR into the cytoplasm (in the case of muscle cells, the cytoplasm is also called the 'myoplasm');

- a quick local rise in myoplasmic free $[Ca^{2+}]$ near the triadic junctions, from a resting level of ~0.05 µM to, briefly, a peak level that is >100 µM;

- longitudinal diffusion of Ca^{2+} away from the triads and throughout the myoplasm;

- binding of Ca^{2+} to Ca^{2+}-regulatory sites on troponin, a protein located at regular intervals on the thin filaments of the interdigitating lattice of thick and thin filaments; this lattice is found throughout the cell volume and is organized longitudinally into sarcomeres and radially into myofibrils (the thin filaments are made up largely of actin);

- movement of tropomyosin (another thin-filament regulatory protein) away from its blocking position in the resting state to expose sites on actin that can bind myosin 'cross-bridges' (myosin is the main protein of the thick filament; the cross-bridges can be seen in the electron microscope as periodic projections on the sides of the thick filaments);

- binding, detachment, and rebinding of the myosin cross-bridges on the thick filament to receptor sites on actin on the thin filament, with associated conversion of the chemical energy of ATP into mechanical work by the myofilaments during each cycle of cross-bridge binding and detachment (these work-generating cycles by the cross-bridges are called 'power strokes');

- relative sliding (increased interdigitation) of the thick and thin filaments driven by the repeated power strokes of the attached cross-bridges; the macroscopic result is a shortening of the muscle fiber and/or development of tension all along the fiber length.

12.4 OVERVIEW OF THE STRUCTURE OF SKELETAL MUSCLE FIBERS

Skeletal muscle fibers are large, long cylindrically-shaped cells with obvious striations (Fig. 12.3). They have multiple nuclei along their length due to the fusion of many myoblasts to form myotubes during development. In most fiber types, each fiber has one neuromuscular junction, which is located approximately midway between its tendon ends.

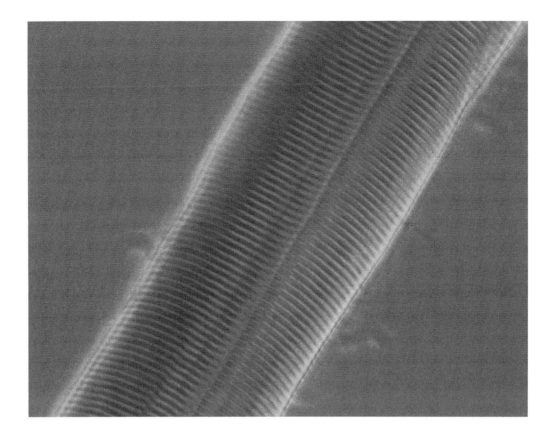

Figure 12.3 Light micrograph of two skeletal fibers from a leg muscle of the mouse; fiber diameters, ~30 μm. [Credit: Clara Franzini-Armstrong, University of Pennsylvania.]

The contractile, signaling, and energetic systems of a fiber are identifiable at the ultrastructural level (Fig. 12.4). The myofibrils are cylindrical or wedge-shaped protein assemblies, approximately 1 μm in diameter, organized in the transverse direction. The regular alignment of the proteins in these transverse assemblies leads to the banding pattern (striations) of the cells, as seen in Fig. 12.3.

The membrane systems controlling the muscle twitch are the surface membrane, the T-tubular membranes, and the sarcoplasmic reticulum. Depending on the fiber type, variable numbers of mitochondria (upper periphery of Fig. 12.4) are present. The transverse tubules consist of extensive invaginations of the surface membrane. Amphibian fibers have one T-tubular network per sarcomere located at the z-lines. Mammals, in contrast, have two T-tubular networks per sarcomere, which are offset slightly from the z-lines toward the middle of the sarcomere.

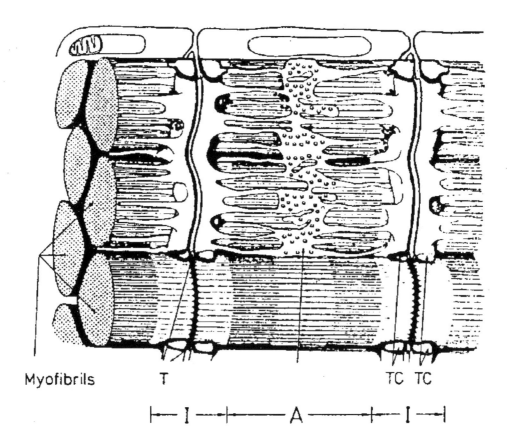

Figure 12.4 A. Schematic of the membranes and myofilaments of a frog skeletal muscle fiber. T, transverse tubular membranes; TC, terminal cisternae of the sarcoplasmic reticulum (SR); I, I-band; A, A-band. The short dense band in the middle of the I-band is the z-line. In the transverse direction, the contractile filaments are organized into bundles of thick and thin filaments called 'myofibrils'. Sarcomere length (z-line to z-line) is 2-3 μm. [After Peachey (1965).]

The lumen of the T-tubules is continuous with the extracellular space. T-tubular membranes are excitable membranes and propagate action potentials (APs) into the cell interior to carry the excitation signal throughout the fiber cross section (described further below; see also the interesting historical account of T-system discoveries by Rall, 2020).

The sarcoplasmic reticulum, a specialized form of endoplasmic reticulum, is a completely internal membrane system, i.e., its lumen is not continuous with the T-tubules or extracellular space. SR membranes do not have an action potential. The potential across the SR membranes is thought to be close to 0 mV at rest and probably changes transiently by at most a few mVs during the release of Ca^{2+}. The SR membranes meet the T-membranes at the triadic junctions where an activation signal during EC coupling is communicated between the proteins in the two membrane systems (described in Section 12.6). Two terminal cisternae (TC) of the SR flank each T-tubule (Fig. 12.4); this group of three membrane regions defines the triadic junction. The TC store the Ca^{2+} that is released into the myoplasm to activate the myofilaments.

Fig. 12.5 shows a reconstruction of the T-system of a frog skeletal muscle fiber in a cross section at a z-line. A similar mesh of T membranes is found at the z-line of every sarcomere along the fiber length. The T-system is thus a remarkable network of internal excitable membranes.

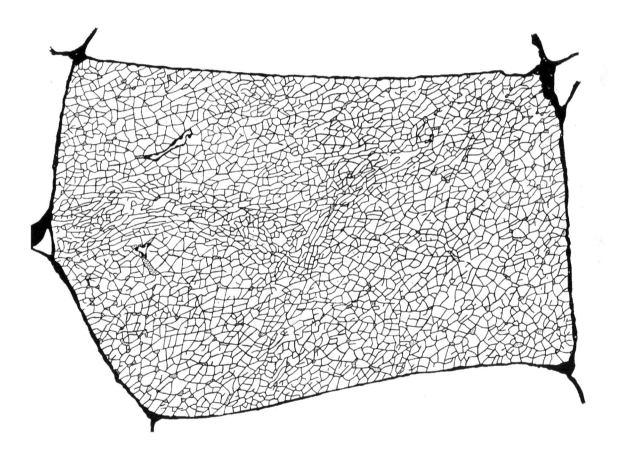

Figure 12.5 Reconstruction of the T-system at one z-line of a frog twitch fiber from high-voltage electron micrographs. The dark lines within the fiber are tracings of individual T-tubules based on a peroxidase staining method. The white spaces between the dark lines marks the location of the myofibrils. [Credit: Eisenberg and Peachey (1978).]

12.5 ELECTROPHYSIOLOGY OF SKELETAL MUSCLE

Resting Potential. Table 12.1 lists, for amphibian muscle, the approximate intracellular and extracellular concentrations of the ionic species most important for setting the fiber's resting potential and for electrical activity during EC coupling. K^+, Na^+, Cl^-, and Ca^{2+} concentration gradients are similar to those in many other cell types (see Chapters 6 - 8). Myoplasmic $[Ca^{2+}]$ is very low at rest, ~50 nM, which leads to the high Nernst potential for Ca^{2+}, +132 mV.

Table 12.1 Ion Concentrations and Nernst Potentials in Frog Muscle

Ion species	Extracellular concentration (mM)	Myoplasmic concentration (mM)	E_{ion} at 20 °C (mV)
K^+	2.5	140	-101
Cl^-	121	3.4	-90
Na^+	120	10	+63
Ca^{2+}	1.8	~0.00005	+132

The resting potential can be calculated from the Goldman-Hodgkin-Katz (GHK) voltage equation (Eqn. 6.10). Because $E_{Cl} \approx V_m$, it can be simplified to yield (at 20 °C):

$$V_m = 58 \text{ mV} \log_{10}\left(\frac{[K]_o + (P_{Na}/P_K)[Na]_o}{[K]_i + (P_{Na}/P_K)[Na]_i}\right). \tag{12.1}$$

As usual, Ca^{2+} can be ignored in calculating V_m because the calcium permeability in the resting muscle cell is very low.

The relative permeabilities of the resting muscle membrane to Na^+, K^+ and Cl^- are:

$$P_{Cl} \approx 2 > P_K = 1 > P_{Na} \approx 0.01 \text{ (muscle).}$$

Eqn. 12.1 thus yields: $V_m = -91.5$ mV, which is approximately the value measured in healthy amphibian fibers, -90 to -95 mV. Note that the relative permeabilities differ from the order of permeabilities in nerve cells at rest, where P_{Cl} is much lower than P_K:

$$P_K = 1 > P_{Cl} \approx 0.1 > P_{Na} \approx 0.01 \quad \text{(nerve)}.$$

The significance of the large resting P_{Cl}/P_K ratio in muscle is discussed in Exercise 12.8.

As in nerve cells, the resting V_m is due primarily to the resting potassium permeability. The relative permeabilities to sodium and potassium can be determined most directly after chloride ions have been removed from the external solution and replaced with an impermeant negatively-charged substitute.

Fig. 12.6 shows collected results of experiments in which resting V_m was measured while $[K^+]_o$ was varied systematically in the absence of Cl^-. As $[K^+]_o$ was increased or decreased, $[Na^+]_o$ was decreased or increased, respectively, so as to maintain constant tonicity and ionic strength in the test solution. The straight line is calculated from the Nernst equation for K^+, the relation expected if the membrane is permeable only to K^+. The curve, which provides a much better fit than the straight line to the data at lower values of $[K^+]_o$, is calculated from a simplified form of Eqn. 12.1, which (i) assumes that the ratio P_{Na}/P_K is 0.01 and (ii) ignores the small contribution of $[Na^+]_i$ to the denominator of Eqn. 12.1.

Although Cl^- does not contribute to setting the resting potential, V_m will change transiently if either extracellular or intracellular $[Cl^-]$ should suddenly change. For example, an artificial reduction in extracellular $[Cl^-]$ (replaced by an impermeant anion) will transiently depolarize V_m because the resulting net movement of Cl^- ions out of the cell leaves behind positivity. After a few minutes in a Cl^--free solution, V_m gradually returns to the normal resting potential (which is still determined by P_K/P_{Na}). During this time, Cl^- leaves the fiber in mmolar amounts, largely accompanied by K^+ to supply charge balance, and, thereafter, with no chloride inside or outside the fiber, chloride can have no further influence on V_m (see Chapter 6).

Minor Point
In Fig. 12.6, the data points at $[K^+] < 5$ mM lie slightly above the curved line. This deviation is due to a property of the muscle K^+ channels that are responsible for setting resting V_m termed 'inward rectification'. Inward rectification means that, for a given magnitude driving force, K^+ ions flow through these channels more easily if the driving force is inward than if it is outward. Because the outward driving force on K^+ progressively increases as $[K^+]$ is reduced, the effective P_K/P_{Na} ratio is also progressively reduced. See also Exercise 12.8.

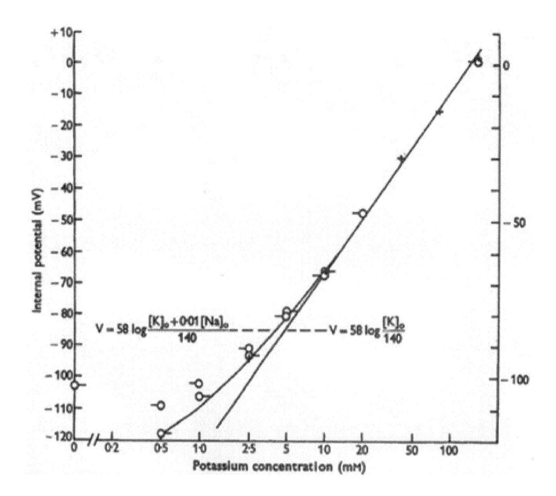

Figure 12.6 Relation between membrane potential of isolated frog single muscle fibers (ordinate) and external [K⁺] (abscissa, plotted logarithmically). The external solutions were chloride-free, the principal anion being sulfate, which is impermeant. [Credit: Hodgkin and Horowicz (1959).]

The Muscle Action Potential. Two propagating APs recorded from frog skeletal muscle fibers are shown in Fig. 12.7 (cf. the membrane action potential in Fig. 12.2). These APs have many features in common with a nerve AP:
- depolarization causes opening of the gates on voltage-dependent Na⁺ channels;
- Na⁺ flows in through the Na⁺ channels, which causes further (regenerative) depolarization and also passes current electrotonically to depolarize neighboring regions;
- V_m approaches E_{Na};
- the gates on the Na⁺ channels close because of inactivation;
- the depolarization causes opening of the gates on voltage-dependent K⁺ channels but more

slowly than opening of the gates on the voltage-dependent Na^+ channels;
- K^+ flows out to cause repolarization.

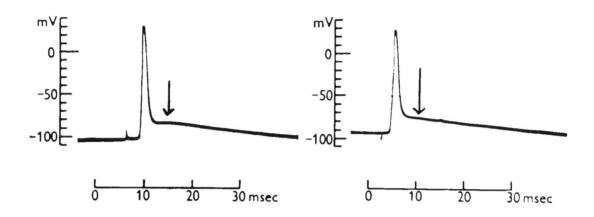

Figure 12.7 Propagating action potentials in two frog muscle fibers evoked by a brief shock from a localized pair of external electrodes (marked by the small artifacts that are visible preceding the rise of the action potential). The arrows point to the depolarized after-potential, during which time the T-tubular action potential reaches its peak.

The AP in skeletal muscle differs somewhat from that in a nerve axon. It has an early after-potential that is positive to the resting potential (arrows in Fig. 12.7) and a slower conduction velocity. Also, because P_{Cl} is relatively high in muscle membranes (Table 12.1) and E_{Cl} is near the resting potential ($\approx$ -90 mV), outward Cl^- current contributes somewhat to membrane repolarization.

As pointed out in Chapter 8, the AP in a squid giant axon has a small Cl^- conductance and a negative after-potential due to E_K and the voltage-dependent K^+ conductance. Muscles have positive after-potentials due to the electrical coupling (sometimes called 'electrotonic coupling'; see Exercise 7.8 of Chapter 7) between the surface and T-system membranes and, perhaps, due to a lower selectivity of K^+ over Na^+ in their voltage-dependent K^+ channels. (Recall that electrotonic coupling means that if two membrane regions are connected to one another, with one region trying to set V_m to V_1 and the other trying to set V_m to V_2, a loop of current is set up between the two regions so as to move V_m to a value that is between V_1 and V_2.)

12.6 T-TUBULAR DEPOLARIZATION TO SR Ca^{2+} RELEASE

Because the AP spreads into the T-system, the T-membranes throughout the fiber volume, including the membrane regions at the triadic junctions where the DHPR proteins (the voltage sensors of EC coupling) are located, transiently reach a membrane potential of ~+30 mV. This depolarization activates the DHPRs, which then initiate Ca^{2+} release from the SR (next paragraphs). The DHPRs are a type of voltage-dependent Ca^{2+} channel (type Ca$_V$1; see Chapter 10). However, these channels pass very little Ca^{2+} current during an action potential in the T-system, and the Ca^{2+} current that they do pass is not involved in initiating SR Ca^{2+} release.

How does activation of the DHPRs in the T-tubular membranes initiate SR Ca^{2+} release? At the triad, electron-dense proteins, called 'feet', span the T-SR space (Fig. 12.8).

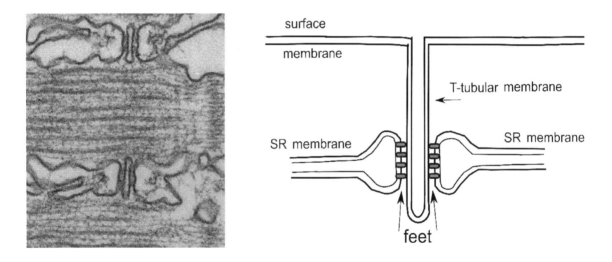

Figure 12.8 Left: electron-micrograph of two triads of a toadfish swimbladder fiber, each revealing two double rows of foot particles in the gaps between the T-tubular and SR membranes. Magnification, ~100,000x. [Credit: Clara Franzini-Armstrong, University of Pennsylvania.] Right: schematic of one triad, with the location of the foot proteins labeled as 'feet'. The view on the left is transverse to the T-tubule whereas that on the right is along the T-tubule. The foot protein, which is the Ca^{2+} release channel itself, is anchored in the SR membrane. The DHPRs in the T-membrane are not visible (left) or shown (right).

The foot protein has been identified as the receptor for the high-affinity plant alkaloid ryanodine, which can release Ca^{2+} pharmacologically from the SR. Thus, the ryanodine receptor (RyR), the foot protein, and the SR Ca^{2+} release channel all identify the same entity.

A Physical Coupling between the DHPR and RyR Proteins in Skeletal Muscle. The ionic content of the T-tubular lumen is like that of the extracellular fluid because it is continuous with the ECF. Free $[Ca^{2+}]$ in the ECF is 1-2 mM, which is similar to that within the lumen of the SR. In principle, Ca^{2+} within the lumen of the T-system could enter the fiber and supply some of the Ca^{2+} for triggering contraction, adding to the Ca^{2+} that is released from the SR in response to the T-tubular action potential. In fact, almost all of the Ca^{2+} for contraction is released from the SR at the terminal cisternae. The evidence for this includes the following: (i) a skeletal muscle cell in a Ringer's solution (extracellular solution) devoid of Ca^{2+} will give hundreds of twitches of normal amplitude (Armstrong et al., 1972) -- thus the major source of Ca^{2+} must be within the fiber; and (ii) the sarcomeric location where myoplasmic $[Ca^{2+}]$ first rises can be resolved with a confocal microscope and $[Ca^{2+}]$ goes up first near the terminal cisternae (described in section 12.10).

The DHPRs are arranged in close physical contact with the RyRs. Fig. 12.9 shows how these proteins are arranged at the triadic junctions of amphibians (left) and mammals (right). In both, the DHPRs are found in the T-membranes in clusters of 4, called 'tetrads'. Each DHPR is a complex of 5 subunits. The principal subunit (α_1 subunit) is a voltage-dependent membrane protein of ~125 kDa, with 4 domains (numbered I to IV) and 6 transmembrane segments (numbered S1 to S6), as found in other voltage-dependent ion channels (see Chapter 10).

Each ryanodine receptor is a gigantic (>2 MDalton) tetrameric protein with a membrane spanning region that is anchored in the SR and with a large extra-membrane portion that extends into the myoplasm. Each monomer of the RyR is about 540 kDa. Depolarization of the T-tubule changes the conformation of the DHPRs within the tetrad, enabling the tetrad to activate the RyR located just opposite it, thereby releasing Ca^{2+} from the SR into the myoplasm. The foot region of the RyR presumably changes conformation and relays a signal to a gate guarding the ion channel within the RyR. When the gate opens, Ca^{2+} moves down a large chemical gradient from the SR lumen into the myoplasm. This signaling mechanism, which involves a physical coupling (protein-protein interaction) between the DHPRs and RyRs, is sometimes referred to as 'mechanical coupling'.

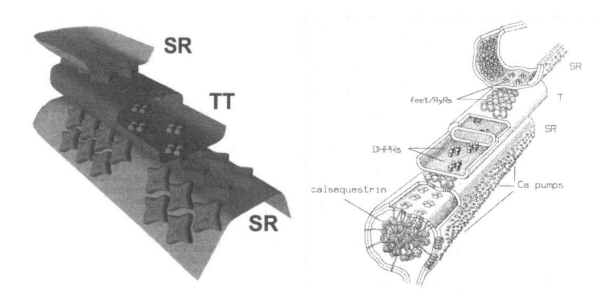

Figure 12.9 Ultrastructural schematics of vertebrate triadic junctions. Left: amphibian and fish fibers, which have 'parajunctional' RyRs (lighter squares, off to the side of the triad); right, mammalian and reptilian fibers, which do not. Within the junction proper, the DHPRs and RyRs are arranged in double rows in the T and SR membranes, respectively. Calsequestrin is a Ca^{2+}-storage protein located within the SR; the Ca^{2+} bound to this protein ensures that the SR contains sufficient Ca^{2+} for most contractile conditions. Away from the junction, the SR contains Ca^{2+} pump molecules at a high density. [Credits: left, Felder and Franzini-Armstrong (2002), with copyright (2002) and permission by the National Academy of Sciences, U.S.A.; right, Block et al. (1988).]

Fig. 12.10 diagrams how a voltage-dependent gating signal might be transmitted from the DHPRs to the RyRs by means of mechanical coupling. The voltage-sensor in Fig. 12.10 (the DHPR) is depicted as containing a mobile moiety with a net positive charge whose location depends on V_m. Thus, this moiety can move closer to the inside (resting and repolarized states) or the outside (depolarized state) of the membrane, as dictated by the T-tubular membrane potential. This movement is thought to control the gate on the RyR Ca^{2+} channel by a direct structural interaction, with no diffusible messenger being involved.

A large number of elegant studies on these triadic components of EC coupling have been carried out on mammalian and fish muscle with molecular-biological and ultra-structural techniques (e.g., Tanabe et al., 1987; Tanabe et al., 1988, 1990; Adams et al., 1990; Takekura et al., 1994, 2004; Nakai et al., 1996; Grabner et al., 1999; Proenza et al., 2002; Protasi et al., 2002; Kugler et al., 2004; Schredelseker et al., 2005, 2009; Nelson et al.,

2013). These studies reveal that the conformational signal from the DHPRs to the RyRs that initiates SR Ca^{2+} release depends critically on: (i) the assembly of DPHRs into tetrads in the T-tubular membrane and (ii) a structural interaction between the RyR and the amino-acid loop that connects domains II and III of the α_1-subunit of the DHPR.

A structural interaction between the RyR and the II-III loop of the DHPR also appears to be a requirement for the normal functioning of DHPRs as voltage-dependent Ca^{2+} channels in the T-tubular membrane (Grabner et al., 1999). The amount of Ca^{2+} that enters the myoplasm through these Ca^{2+} channels is normally small and not part of the chain of events that initiates the release of Ca^{2+} from the SR. Nevertheless, this entry is likely to be important for ensuring that the supply of Ca^{2+} to be released from the SR during EC coupling is sufficient under normal conditions for full activation of the myofilaments in response to the T-tubular action potential (see also Exercise 12.4).

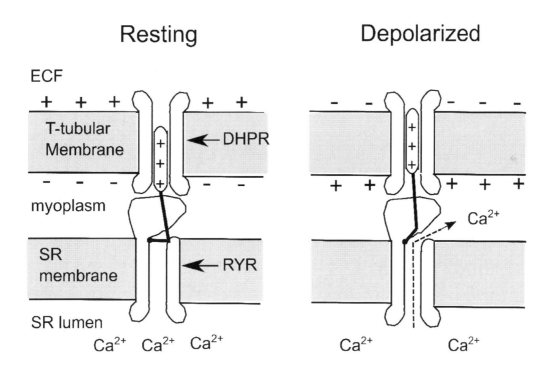

Figure 12.10 Schematic of how a charged protein moiety within the DHPR (the voltage sensor of EC coupling) moves outward in response to a positive membrane potential across the T-tubular membrane and opens a gate on the RyR, thus permitting the release of Ca^{2+} into the myoplasm. The model shows only one DHPR interacting with one RyR; in reality, a tetrad of DHPRs interacts with one RyR. [After Chandler et al. (1976).]

Similarities and Differences between Amphibian and Mammalian Fibers. Amphibian and mammalian fibers share many similarities in their EC coupling mechanism, including a primary reliance on the mechanical-coupling mechanism to initiate SR Ca^{2+} release in response to membrane depolarization (Fig. 12.10) and many similarities in the structure of their triadic junctions (Fig. 12.9, left vs. right).

Differences in the EC coupling mechanism have also been found. Both amphibians and mammals -- as for all animal classes -- have 3 types of RyRs, referred to as isoforms RyR1, RyR2, and RyR3. (RyR1 and RyR3 in non-mammalian classes are sometimes referred to as RyRα and RyRβ, respectively.) RyR2 is found in heart muscle but not in skeletal muscle, whereas RyR1 and RyR3 are found in skeletal fibers. Quite different relative amounts of RyR1 and RyR3, however, are found in different animal species and fiber types. Adult amphibian fibers express comparable amounts of RyR3 and RyR1 in all fibers, whereas adult mammalian fibers typically express RyR1 almost exclusively (Giannini et al., 1995). This difference correlates with the presence of parajunctional RyRs in amphibians and its absence in mammals (see Fig. 12.9).

The parajunctional RyRs found in amphibians appear to be mainly if not exclusively of type RyR3, whereas the junctional RyRs, which are found in all vertebrate species, appear to be mainly if not exclusively of type RyR1. Evidence suggests that the RyR3s release some SR Ca^{2+} secondarily in response to the primary release of Ca^{2+} through the RyR1s (see section 12.10 below). If so, a likely mechanism to mediate this secondary release is 'Ca^{2+}-induced Ca^{2+} release' -- meaning that some of the SR Ca^{2+} that is initially released through some of the RyRs (e.g., RyR1) binds to and activates the release of Ca^{2+} through other RyRs (e.g., RyR3). Section 12.10 considers some further functional differences between SR Ca^{2+} release in amphibian and mammalian fibers that correlate with the presence or absence of parajunctional RyRs.

12.7 THE RISE IN MYOPLASMIC FREE $[Ca^{2+}]$

The experimental approach of Fig. 12.2 can be readily extended to allow recording of the time course of the spatially-averaged myoplasmic free Ca^{2+} transient ($\Delta[Ca^{2+}]$) during a twitch. Fig. 12.11 shows a setup for stimulation of a frog single muscle fiber by a brief shock from a pair of electrodes positioned locally near the fiber. Because $\Delta[Ca^{2+}]$ is the immediate myoplasmic event that triggers muscle contraction, the fiber has been micro-injected with a fluorescent Ca^{2+} indicator dye at the location where $\Delta[Ca^{2+}]$ is to be recorded. A typical Ca^{2+} indicator used for an experiment of this type is furaptra (Raju et al., 1991) whose fluorescence signal is capable of reliably monitoring large and rapid changes in cytoplasmic $[Ca^{2+}]$. Under intracellular conditions, furaptra's dissociation constant for Ca^{2+} is estimated to be between 75 and 100 µM (Konishi et al. 1991, 1993).

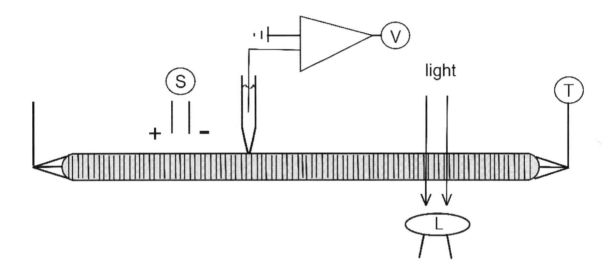

Figure 12.11 Apparatus for recording the muscle AP, Ca^{2+} transient, and twitch. S: stimulus electrodes (initiate membrane depolarization); V: intracellular micro-electrode connected to a voltage-recording circuit (records V_m); L: light-recording system (monitors changes in myoplasmic $[Ca^{2+}]$ by means of a Ca^{2+}-sensitive fluorescent indicator introduced into the fiber); T: mechanical transducer attached to one tendon (records muscle force/tension generated at the end of the fiber).

The results of the experiment diagrammed in Fig. 12.11 are shown in Fig. 12.12.

S shows the time course of the shock that activates the initially quiescent and relaxed fiber; the dashed line indicates the threshold for initiation of an AP. V shows the membrane potential; the propagating muscle AP arrives at the recording micro-electrode with a short delay (~1 ms) after the stimulus shock. The light signal (L) records the spatially-averaged $\Delta[Ca^{2+}]$ signal at the site of the optical recording. $\Delta[Ca^{2+}]$ begins to increase after another short delay and reaches almost 20 µM before decreasing. A short time after $\Delta[Ca^{2+}]$ begins to rise, the generation of the fiber's twitch response (T) begins.

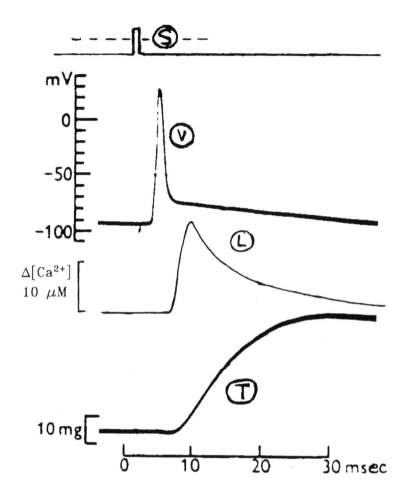

Figure 12.12 Time course of 3 major events in EC coupling in response to a brief electrical shock. The fiber is initially resting and relaxed. The stimulus S initiates a sequence of events: action potential, V; Ca^{2+} transient, L; and tension/contraction, T. Composite results from 2 experiments.

Technical aside. Ca^{2+} indicators work analogously to colorimetric pH indicators, which are commonly used to measure pH. At elevated free Ca^{2+} concentrations, the Ca^{2+} indicator will bind some of the Ca^{2+} and thereby change its optical properties -- e.g. its absorbance or its fluorescence -- which can be measured experimentally. Furaptra was used to measure $\Delta[Ca^{2+}]$ in the experiment of Fig. 12.12, and the fluorescence signal from this indicator is due to a reaction between Ca^{2+} and indicator having one-to-one stoichiometry and rapid kinetics. To convert the fluorescence signal to units of $\Delta[Ca^{2+}]$, a calibration curve is required. Fig. 12.13 shows a hypothetical calibration curve based on a 1:1 reaction between Ca^{2+} and indicator in which K_D (the dissociation constant of the reaction) is 10 μM.

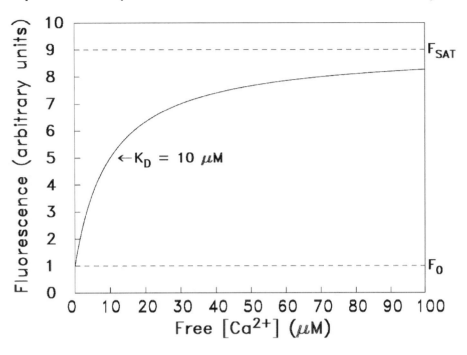

Figure 12.13 Example of a steady-state calibration of a fluorescent Ca^{2+} indicator. Fluorescence intensity (ordinate) vs. free $[Ca^{2+}]$ (abscissa) is determined in *in vitro* calibration solutions. The curve is based on a 1:1 binding between indicator and Ca^{2+} in which K_D is 10 μM. Curves like these are used to estimate intracellular free $[Ca^{2+}]$ levels in cells from measurements of indicator fluorescence intensity. See also Figure 9.1.

If free $[Ca^{2+}]$ in the calibration solution is systematically varied between, say, 0 and 100 μM, the fluorescence level goes from an initial level (F_0), which corresponds to none of the indicator molecules being bound with Ca^{2+}, toward a saturating level (F_{SAT}), at which all of the indicator molecules would be bound with Ca^{2+}. If the actual peak fluorescence level recorded in an experiment happened to be 5 of the units on the ordinate in Fig. 12.13, the calibration curve indicates that the associated $[Ca^{2+}]$ level is about 10 μM. As discussed in Chapter 9, with a 1:1 binding reaction, the slope of the curve -- and thus the sensitivity of the indicator's fluorescence response -- is largest at $[Ca^{2+}] < K_D$ and declines progressively at higher $[Ca^{2+}]$. [For more information on furaptra and related Ca^{2+} indicators, including a discussion of calibration issues that can arise when indicator molecules are used in the intracellular environment, see Baylor and Hollingworth (2011).]

Electrical vs. Chemical Signaling. The $\Delta[Ca^{2+}]$ signal in Fig. 12.12 monitors a change that takes place almost simultaneously throughout the fiber cross section. This signal is initiated by the AP that propagates into the T-tubules at every sarcomere along the fiber length. A fast activation of the entire fiber cross section could not be achieved by a chemical message that started at the surface membrane and spread into the cell interior by diffusion. Any such diffusive message would spread far too slowly into the depths of the fiber to achieve activation in a few ms (cf. Table 2.1 in Chapter 2). Because the T-tubular network branches many times, forming a chicken-wire mesh when viewed in cross section (Fig. 12.5), the fast-moving T-tubular action-potential is able to quickly activate SR Ca^{2+} release near every myofibril in the fiber cross section in a nearly-synchronous manner. Thus, $[Ca^{2+}]$ rises nearly simultaneously in all myofibrils throughout the fiber volume.

Summary. The schematic in Fig. 12.14 summarizes the temporal relations among 7 key events in the EC coupling process during a twitch. The amplitude of all traces is shown at the same height in order to reveal the timing sequence. Events that are readily recorded experimentally (cf. Fig. 12.12) are shown as continuous traces. Events whose timing has been inferred from experimental measurements but have not been directly recorded during a twitch are shown as dashed traces.

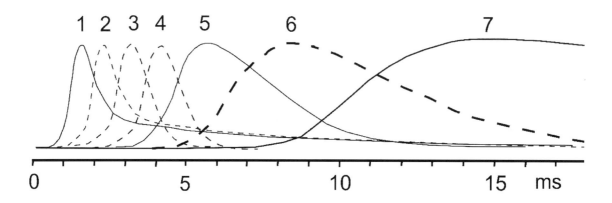

Figure 12.14 Schematic of the timing sequence of EC coupling events in a frog twitch fiber at 16 °C. Surface membrane AP (1); T-tubular AP (2); activation of DHPRs (3); flux of Ca^{2+} from the SR to the myoplasm (4; this is also the approximate open time of the RyRs); increase in spatially-averaged myoplasmic free $[Ca^{2+}]$ (5); increase in Ca^{2+} bound to the regulatory sites on troponin (6); development of muscle force (7).

When fibers are activated by an action potential, Ca^{2+} release from the SR is transient, lasting only a couple of ms (trace 4 in Fig. 12.14). Two processes limit the duration and amount of SR Ca^{2+} release. First, the action potential repolarizes, which deactivates the DHPR tetrads (i.e., they return to their normal resting state). Second, a strong negative feedback mechanism, termed 'Ca^{2+} inactivation of Ca^{2+} release', exists between elevated levels of myoplasmic $[Ca^{2+}]$ and the gating of the SR Ca^{2+}-release channels. It is thought that some of the released Ca^{2+} rapidly binds to an inactivation site(s) on the RyRs, thereby closing the channels. The degree of inactivation appears to be tuned to allow myoplasmic $[Ca^{2+}]$ to rise to a level that permits almost full Ca^{2+} occupancy of the Ca^{2+}-regulatory sites on troponin but not substantially higher.

This inactivation mechanism is very important physiologically, as it (i) conserves energy by preventing the release of wasteful amounts of SR Ca^{2+}, (ii) avoids unusually high levels of $[Ca^{2+}]$, which can be toxic to the fiber -- e.g., by adversely affecting the mitochondria or by activating Ca^{2+}-dependent proteases, and (iii) avoids prolonging $\Delta[Ca^{2+}]$ and thus prolonged activation of troponin, which would slow the mechanical relaxation of the fiber during the later phase of the twitch. Chapter 13 will explore some of these points in more detail with a *Python* program that uses the information in the measurement of $\Delta[Ca^{2+}]$ to estimate SR Ca^{2+} release and the movement of Ca^{2+} onto and off of the myoplasmic Ca^{2+} binding sites during a twitch.

12.8 RECOVERY PROCESSES AFTER A TWITCH

Soon after SR Ca^{2+} release ceases, the removal of Ca^{2+} from the myoplasm begins as Ca^{2+} is captured by the Ca^{2+} pump of the SR membrane (the kinetics of which was discussed in Chapter 9). This SR Ca^{2+} pump, which returns two Ca^{2+} ions to the lumen of the SR for each ATP consumed, is present within the fiber at a very high density, ~20,000 pumps per μm^2 of SR membrane, thus constituting ~75% or more of the total protein of the SR membrane. As discussed in Chapter 9, the myoplasm of some skeletal muscle fiber types contains substantial concentrations of parvalbumin, a soluble Ca^{2+} binding protein that assists in lowering $\Delta[Ca^{2+}]$ by temporarily binding Ca^{2+} before it is finally re-sequestered by the SR Ca^{2+} pump. As myoplasmic $[Ca^{2+}]$ declines toward the resting level due to the actions of parvalbumin and the SR Ca^{2+} pump, Ca^{2+} dissociates from troponin, tropomyosin returns to its blocking position on the thin filaments, and the fiber relaxes.

During and after a twitch, the ATP consumption can be allotted as follows. The myosin cross-bridges on the contractile filaments uses the majority of the ATP (~80%), the SR Ca^{2+} pumps use ~20%, and the surface membrane ion transporters, including the Na^+-K^+ ATPase, use perhaps 1-2%. After the contraction, the energetic and ionic state of the muscle must recover to pre-contraction values. Ion gradients are restored by Ca^{2+} pumping across the SR membrane and by Na^+/K^+ pumping across the surface and T-system membranes. This ion pumping continues for a number of seconds after relaxation of the twitch (see Chapter 13). The energy debts, including replenishment of ATP, are repaid by aerobic and anaerobic metabolism.

12.9 VOLTAGE-CLAMP STUDIES OF EC COUPLING

Because EC coupling is a voltage-dependent process, voltage-clamp studies of EC coupling in skeletal muscle cells have been carried out in many laboratories to elucidate this process. The brief discussion here focuses on two important topics.

Muscle Charge Movement. In 1973, a major step forward in the study of EC coupling in skeletal muscle was taken when the first measurements of an electrical signal termed 'muscle charge movements' were reported in experiments on frog twitch fibers (Schneider and Chandler, 1973). The measurements were made with a 3-micro-electrode voltage-clamp technique applied to a region at one end of an intact frog fiber in which essentially all of the ion-channel conductances of the surface and T-system membranes had been blocked pharmacologically. This technique permitted a reliable voltage-clamp study of the surface and T-system membranes in the end region of the fiber in the absence of ionic currents. Fig. 12.15 shows some of the results.

When V_m was changed from a negative holding potential into the voltage range where SR Ca^{2+} release is normally activated, small non-linear capacitive currents (i.e., the charge-movement currents) were detected that moved outward on depolarization and inward on repolarization (Fig. 12.15A). To detect these currents (which have a direct analogy with the Na^+-channel gating currents described in Chapter 8), the usual linear capacitive currents that are measured with voltage-clamp steps involving any voltage range were removed by subtraction. The kinetics of the outward current differs from that of the inward current -- and both kinetics are substantially slower than that of Na^+-channel gating currents – but the integrated amount of the outward and inward currents is the same (Fig. 12.15B). It was proposed that the outward current that is measured during depolarization is due to activation of the voltage sensors of EC coupling (which are located in the surface and T-system membranes), and that the inward current measured during repolarization monitors the return of the voltage sensors to their resting state (cf. Fig. 12.10).

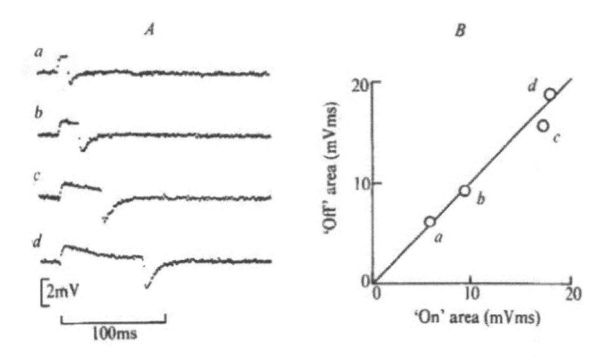

Figure 12.15 Properties of muscle charge movement in a frog skeletal muscle fiber whose exterior membrane (surface plus T-system) was studied with voltage-clamp steps from -80 to -33 mV (2 °C). A. Charge-movement currents measured in response to steps of various durations (a, 10; b, 20; c, 40; d, 80 ms). The currents are calibrated in mVs, as their measurement involved the recording of a voltage change due to the flow of current between 2 locations along the axis of the fiber. B. Integrated area (proportional to total membrane charge) of the 'off' currents in A (i.e., those measured in response to the return of V_m to -80 mV) plotted vs. that of the 'on' currents (i.e., those measured in response to the step of V_m to -33 mV). The straight line corresponds to equality of areas. To calculate the 'on' areas, the final level of trace d in A was subtracted from all records. The kinetics of the current traces in A is consistent with a signal that would initiate the EC coupling process at the temperature of the experiments. [Credit: Schneider and Chandler (1973).]

A large body of work since 1973 has confirmed the prescient interpretation of Schneider and Chandler about muscle charge movements, namely, that they are due to the reversible movement of charged moieties within the muscle cell's exterior membranes (primarily the T-system membranes) -- and about their physiological significance, namely, that they reflect activation and deactivation of the voltage sensors of EC coupling. Indeed, these currents are now known to reflect conformational changes in the DHPRs during their activation and deactivation (Rios and Brum, 1987; Tanabe et al., 1988).

The Voltage Steepness of SR Ca^{2+} Release. Under physiological conditions, SR Ca^{2+} release is initiated by activation of the voltage-sensors of EC coupling by depolarization. As discussed in Section 8.8 of Chapter 8, important quantitative information about any voltage-dependent process is revealed by studies of the limiting steepness of the process, i.e., how steeply the amplitude of the process increases with changes in membrane potential at negative values of V_m.

The first successful measurements of the steepness of SR Ca^{2+} release in the appropriate voltage range were made in intact skeletal fibers micro-injected with Ca^{2+} indicators and studied optically with a two micro-electrode voltage clamp. Ca^{2+} release at the detection threshold, monitored with the indicator, was observed to increase e-fold for 3-5 mV in both amphibian and mammalian fibers (Baylor et al., 1979; Hollingworth et al., 1993).

Fig. 12.16 shows results from an elegant experiment in which the limiting steepness of Ca^{2+} release in amphibian fibers was determined optically. A cut segment of a frog twitch fiber (a 'cut fiber'; Hille and Campbell, 1976) was isolated in a Ringer's solution that contained a high concentration of EGTA (ethylene glycol-bis(β-aminoethyl ether)-N,N,N',N'-tetraacetic acid). EGTA, which is a high-affinity Ca^{2+} buffer, was included in the experimental solution because it would diffuse into the myoplasm through the cut ends of the fiber segment and bind Ca^{2+} ions, thus keeping myoplasmic [Ca^{2+}] low and enabling SR Ca^{2+} release to be studied in the absence of fiber contractile activity.

In addition to EGTA, the experimental solution contained phenol red, a pH indicator, which also diffused into the myoplasm through the cut ends. Phenol red was used to monitor SR Ca^{2+} release optically during the depolarizing voltage-clamp steps. Because EGTA releases two protons when it binds Ca^{2+}, some of the released protons are bound by phenol red. With appropriate calibrations, the amount of Ca^{2+} bound by EGTA during Ca^{2+} release, which is a lower limit of the actual amount of Ca^{2+} release, can be estimated from the measurement of the absorbance change from phenol red that occurs when it binds protons. In fact, in these experiments, a sufficiently high EGTA concentration was used that almost all of the released Ca^{2+} was bound by the EGTA.

As confirmed in Fig. 12.16, the limiting steepness of Ca^{2+} release in amphibian muscle fibers is e-fold for ~4 mV. This indicates that at least 6 intramembranous charges are involved in the control of this process (and probably more; see Section 8.8 of Chapter 8).

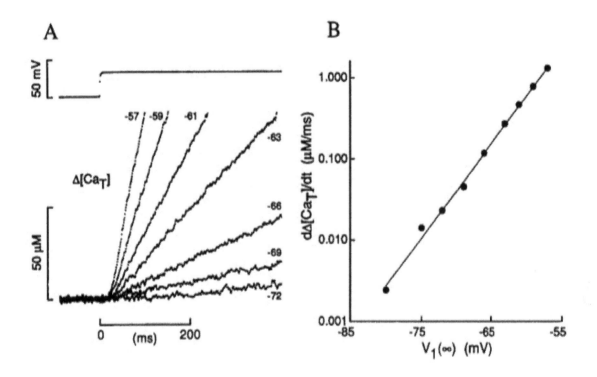

Figure 12.16 Measurement of the limiting steepness of SR Ca^{2+} release in a frog cut fiber. A) The top trace shows a representative voltage record during a 500 ms depolarization of the surface and T-tubular membranes from a holding potential of -90 mV. The lower traces show changes in total myoplasmic Ca^{2+} concentration ($\Delta[Ca_T]$) at the indicated values of V_m during the voltage step, as calibrated from absorbance changes measured with phenol red. B) The filled circles show values of $(d/dt)\Delta[Ca_T]$ (proportional to the rate of Ca^{2+} release), which were determined from the best-fitted straight lines to the traces in A, plotted semi-logarithmically. The line in B corresponds to an e-fold increase in the Ca^{2+} release rate for every 3.7 mV (14.5 °C). [Credit: Pape et al. (1995).]

12.10 CALCIUM SPARKS

A specialized optical technique can be used to detect elementary SR Ca^{2+} release events during EC coupling. These events, termed 'Ca^{2+} sparks', reveal new information about the gating and permeation of RyRs and the diffusion and binding of Ca^{2+} within the myoplasm. In this technique, which was first applied to studies of rat cardiac muscle cells (Cheng et al., 1993), a laser-scanning confocal microscope is used to view a single muscle cell that contains a high-affinity Ca^{2+} indicator dye such as fluo-3. The confocal microscope has the ability to record thin optical sections with sub-micron resolution; fluo-3 has the unusual property that its fluorescence is low when it is in its Ca^{2+}-free form but ~100-fold higher when in its Ca^{2+}-bound form. It thereby becomes possible to resolve the time and location of Ca^{2+} release within single sarcomeres of one myofibril in a living muscle cell.

To do so, a small length of a fiber is studied with 'x-t' confocal imaging while the fiber's membrane potential is held near the value at which SR Ca^{2+} release begins to be significant. To record the x-t image, a laser spot is moved along a line in the x direction of the fiber (the direction parallel to the fiber's long axis) by means of a rotating mirror so that the spot quickly crosses 10-20 adjacent sarcomeres. The fluo-3 fluorescence intensity is recorded at many locations along the way (e.g., every 0.1-0.2 µm), thereby producing a so-called 'line scan' of fluorescence intensity. Scanning is then repeated every 1-2 ms for several hundred such scans. Side-to-side alignment of the scans gives the x-t image, which is a picture of possible changes in [Ca^{2+}] within the sarcomeres as a function of time.

Fig. 12.17 shows two x-t images obtained with this technique from a frog intact single muscle fiber that had been micro-injected with fluo-3. The image on the left was recorded with the fiber in a normal Ringer's solution, which contained 2.5 mM [K^+]. In this solution, the fiber's membrane potential is expected to be about -90 mV (Fig. 12.6) and the voltage sensors on the DHPRs are expected to be in the resting position (Fig. 12.10, left-hand side). Thus, little or no SR Ca^{2+} release is expected, and, indeed, no regions of high fluorescence are seen within the 14 sarcomeres viewed in this image. [Note: if one looks along the image, one can see that the fluorescence intensity changes slightly as a function of distance; the spatial period of this variation matches the sarcomere length of the fiber, ~3.0 µm. This observation is unexpected and indicates that some of the fluo-3 molecules are probably bound to sarcomeric proteins such as actin or myosin.]

The image on the right of Fig. 12.17 was recorded from this fiber while bathed in 13 mM [K$^+$] Ringer's (achieved by addition of K$_2$SO$_4$ to normal Ringer's), in which the expected value of V$_m$ is about -65 mV (see Fig. 12.6). At this V$_m$, most of the voltage-sensing moieties on the DHPRs will still be in the resting position but small numbers are likely to switch randomly to the active position (Fig. 12.10, right-hand side; also Fig. 12.16) due to the extra electrical force on the positively-charged amino acids within the S4 transmembrane segments of the DHPRs. In this image, at least eight Ca^{2+} sparks (the punctate spots of bright fluorescence) can be seen. Each is thought to be controlled by one active tetrad; exactly which tetrads are active at any particular moment is a random process.

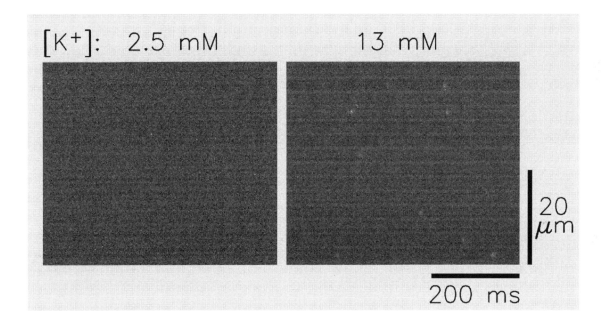

Figure 12.17 x-t fluorescence images taken at similar locations on a frog intact muscle fiber containing fluo-3 (18 °C). In both images, distance runs vertically and time runs horizontally. In the image on the left, which was taken in normal Ringer's ([K$^+$] = 2.5 mM), no Ca^{2+} sparks are seen. In the image on the right, which was taken in 13 mM [K$^+$] Ringer's, at least eight bright punctate spots are seen. These are Ca^{2+} sparks, which identify myoplasmic regions in which [Ca^{2+}] is transiently high (indicated by lighter tones in the image). [Credit: Hollingworth et al. (2001).]

Each spark is centered about half-way between two long narrow bands of slightly elevated fluorescence, the intensity of which does not change with time. It is known from other experiments that these bands of higher fluorescence mark m-lines; thus each spark is centered on a z-line, which is the location of the triadic junctions in frog fibers. The brief localized increases in fluorescence (i.e., the Ca^{2+} sparks) are due to the transient release of Ca^{2+} through RyRs. When Ca^{2+} is released, some of it binds to fluo-3, thus making these myoplasmic fluo-3 molecules highly fluorescent, which permits their detection with the confocal microscope.

The processes that determine the amplitude, time course, and spatial spread of a Ca^{2+} spark include: (i) the amplitude and time course of SR Ca^{2+} release, (ii) the amount and kinetics of Ca^{2+} binding to the various myoplasmic Ca^{2+} binding sites (including the indicator, fluo-3), (iii) the diffusion of Ca^{2+} and the mobile Ca^{2+} binding sites (including fluo-3) within the myoplasm, and (iv) the imaging properties of the confocal microscope. These processes have been modeled numerically with computer simulations, from which it has been estimated that an average Ca^{2+} spark arises from the release into the myoplasm of ~6,500 Ca^{2+} ions per ms for a period of 4-5 ms (Baylor et al., 2002; Hollingworth et al., 2006). Of the total of ~30,000 released Ca^{2+} ions, 4,000 to 5,000 are bound to fluo-3 at the peak of the spark. The peak rate of Ca^{2+} release (6,500 Ca^{2+} ions per ms) corresponds to a Ca^{2+} flux of ~2 pA (units of current, i.e., 2×10^{-12} amps).

Because electrical measurements from single RyRs studied in lipid bilayers indicate that, at physiological ion concentrations, the Ca^{2+} current through a single open RyR is 0.5-1 pA (Kettlun et al., 2003), it follows that a typical Ca^{2+} spark under physiological conditions is probably generated by the synchronous activity of several active RyRs. If so, some form of local communication is required to explain how a small cluster of RyRs can open and close in near synchrony. Possibilities include: (i) the Ca^{2+} ion itself serves as the coordinating message via Ca^{2+}-induced Ca^{2+} release; (ii) the open protein conformation of one active RyR in the array of RyRs physically induces a neighboring RyR to open by a protein-protein interaction (termed 'coupled gating'; Marx et al, 1998). In either case, the strong inhibitory mechanism mentioned above, namely, Ca^{2+} inactivation of Ca^{2+} release, ensures that, under physiological conditions, random activation of a few SR Ca^{2+} release channels does not lead to an extensive, self-propagating release of SR Ca^{2+}.

Fig. 12.18 shows the temporal and spatial properties of an averaged Ca^{2+} spark, obtained from measurements of many individual noisy sparks in frog fibers. The averaged Ca^{2+} spark rises to its peak in 4-5 ms and its spatial spread at time of peak is ~1.0 μm.

EXCITATION-CONTRACTION COUPLING IN SKELETAL MUSCLE 353

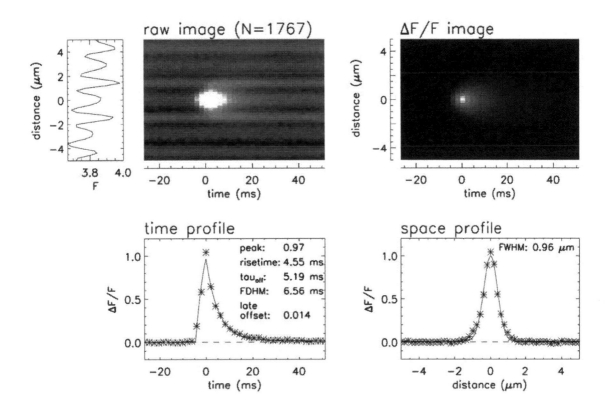

Figure 12.18 Averaged Ca^{2+}-spark properties in frog muscle estimated from 1,767 sparks aligned in time and space. Upper left: fluorescence intensity F at high gain averaged from many x-t images (the central pixels of the spark are in saturation because of the high gain); the inset at the left gives the spatial profile of F prior to spark onset. Upper right: $\Delta F/F$ image (change in fluorescence divided by resting fluorescence) of the averaged spark at low gain. Lower: time profile of the averaged $\Delta F/F$ waveform at the spark center (left) and space profile at the time of peak of the spark (right); both profiles have been fitted with empirical curves. FDHM = full duration at half maximum; FWHM = full width at half maximum. [After Hollingworth et al. (2001).]

A number of studies of Ca^{2+} sparks have been carried out on the frog cut-fiber preparation, including those that first successfully detected Ca^{2+} sparks in skeletal muscle (Tsugorka et al., 1995; Klein et al., 1996). These studies have revealed important spark properties, including how spark morphology and spark frequency depend on membrane potential. Spark frequency increases with V_m up to about +20 mV, at which point the frequency reaches saturation, and this increase occurs without a significant change in the morphological properties of sparks (Shtifman et al., 2000). Because the rise time of a spark is closely related to the open time of the active RyRs that underlie the spark, the finding that the spark rise time is approximately independent of V_m suggests that the mechanism responsible for the closing of the RyRs that give rise to a spark is largely voltage-independent. At negative values of V_m, spark frequency increases e-fold for ~4 mV (Klein et al., 1996). This finding is consistent with the macroscopic measurements of the voltage-dependence of Ca^{2+} release described in Section 12.9.

Relation of Ca^{2+} Sparks to the Twitch of a Frog Muscle Fiber. During a muscle action potential, V_m of the surface and T-system membranes rises and falls by more than 100 mV. This large transient depolarization briefly activates the DHPR tetrads at every triadic junction within the fiber. The activated tetrads will initiate spark-like events at every triadic junction. These events, on average, are likely to be substantially briefer than those described in connection with Fig. 12.18 because the occurrence of many such events at once in the same vicinity will cause a large, local, rapid increase in myoplasmic free $[Ca^{2+}]$. This, in turn, would be expected to abbreviate the time course of the elementary release events at each triadic junction due to the process of Ca^{2+} inactivation of Ca^{2+} release.

The rise in $\Delta[Ca^{2+}]$ near the junctions will drive diffusion of Ca^{2+} throughout the sarcomere. The resulting spatially-averaged Ca^{2+} transient is easily measured with standard optical-recording techniques and the more commonly-employed Ca^{2+} indicators (cf. Fig. 12.12). The increase in myoplasmic $[Ca^{2+}]$ is sufficient to saturate nearly all troponin regulatory sites with Ca^{2+}, which are mostly devoid of Ca^{2+} in the resting state (see Chapter 13). The result is a near-synchronous activation of the myofilaments throughout the fiber volume and a strong twitch. The spark-like activity is expected to cease soon after the action potential repolarizes, thus allowing the Ca^{2+} removal systems, in combination with the kinetic properties of the myofilament proteins, to control the duration of the twitch.

Differences in Ca^{2+} Sparks and Ca^{2+} Transients in Amphibians and Mammals. As noted in Section 12.6, the parajunctional RyRs found in amphibians (and also in some other vertebrate classes) appear to be mainly if not exclusively of type RyR3, whereas the junctional RyRs, which are found in all vertebrate species, appear to be mainly if not exclusively of type RyR1. Interestingly, Ca^{2+} sparks have not been detected in mammalian fibers under the conditions in which Ca^{2+} sparks in frog fibers are readily detected (Shirokova et al., 1998). This difference appears to be due to the fact that parajunctional RyR3s are present in amphibians but lacking in mammals.

In fish, as in amphibians, most skeletal muscles (i) express RyR3 at comparable levels as RyR1, (ii) have parajunctional RyRs, and (iii) have readily-detectable Ca^{2+} sparks. When the expression of RyR3 in fish fibers was reduced almost to zero by an RNA-silencing method, parajunctional RyRs and Ca^{2+} sparks became almost undetectable (Perni et al., 2015). The few sparks that remained were substantially smaller in size than those measured with RyR3 present and may have arisen from Ca^{2+} released through RyR1s only. These results provide strong corroborating evidence for the conclusions that (i) Ca^{2+} sparks, as normally detected (e.g., in frog fibers), depend on Ca^{2+} release by the RyR3 isoform; and (ii) the RyR3s provide, for some species, a distinct functional role during EC coupling, namely, to give a secondary amplification to the Ca^{2+} release process that takes place initially through RyR1s, which are activated by the mechanical-coupling mechanism described in Section 12.6.

It has also been observed that the spatially-averaged myoplasmic Ca^{2+} transient during a twitch differs somewhat in frog twitch fibers and mouse fast-twitch fibers if measured under otherwise identical experimental conditions. While the time of peak $\Delta[Ca^{2+}]$ and the peak amplitude of $\Delta[Ca^{2+}]$ are very similar in the two fibers types, the falling phase of $\Delta[Ca^{2+}]$ is slightly prolonged in frog fibers (Hollingworth and Baylor, 2013).

Computational modeling indicates that this difference in time courses can be explained if the two fiber types have a very similar primary component of SR Ca^{2+} release but that frog fibers have a secondary component of Ca^{2+} release that is not present in mouse fibers. The secondary component of release in frog fibers, which is hypothesized to be due to activity of RyR3s, appears soon after the primary component and is estimated to account for about 20% of the total Ca^{2+} release. The secondary component appears to ensure that the Ca^{2+} regulatory sites on troponin become well occupied with Ca^{2+} all along the length of the thin filament.

In summary, these various lines of evidence support the idea that the role of the parajunctional RyRs during a twitch is to provide a modest amplification of the primary release of SR Ca^{2+} that takes place through the junctional RyRs. Interestingly, a strong correlation has also been found between fiber types that have parajunctional RyRs and those that have their T-systems positioned at the z-line, as occurs in amphibian fibers and most fish fibers. In contrast, fiber types that have two T-systems per sarcomere offset slightly on each side of the z-line, including mammalian fibers and the superfast fibers of the toadfish swimbladder, appear to lack parajunctional RyRs. The T-system location in the latter fibers is in a more-favorable anatomic position to ensure that the Ca^{2+} ions that are released from the SR can diffuse quickly throughout the sarcomere and thereby activate troponin molecules along the entire length of the thin filament. Fibers whose T-systems are located at the z-line appear to make up for this disadvantageous anatomic location by expressing parajunctional RyRs. The latter give the SR the capability to modestly increase the total amount of Ca^{2+} that it releases during the EC coupling process when activated by an action potential and thereby increase the occupancy of troponin with Ca^{2+}.

12.11 EXERCISES

Exercise 12.1 The tension calibration bar in Fig. 12.2 is given in mg units. In modern units, tension (or force) is expressed in newtons. Recall that there are 9.80665 newtons of force per kilogram of mass (based on the force of gravity at sea level on Earth).

a) How many newtons does the calibration bar in Fig. 12 correspond to?

b) If the diameter of the fiber in Fig. 12.2 is 60 µm, how many newtons per square cm of fiber cross section does the calibration bar in Fig. 12 correspond to?

Exercise 12.2 The text states that Eqn. 6.10 simplifies to Eqn. 12.1 if $V_m = E_{Cl}$. Show that this is the case.

Exercise 12.3 Section 12.5 of the text states that, if a frog muscle fiber is placed in a Cl⁻-free solution, V_m will depolarize transiently by some mV, then repolarize back to about -90 mV as internal Cl⁻ leaves the fiber in mmolar amounts accompanied by K⁺. Modify the program Osmotic1.py in Chapter 6 to confirm this statement. In doing so, first check that the program ratio of P_{Cl} to P_K matches that found in skeletal muscle fibers (see p. 332).

Exercise 12.4 The metabolism of skeletal muscle accounts for ~20% of the metabolic rate in humans at rest and this percent can increase to as high as 80-90% during physical activity. Thus, skeletal muscle is probably the tissue mass in the body that is responsible for the largest time-averaged consumption of energy. The text mentions that the SR Ca^{2+} pump uses ~20% of the ATP consumed by a skeletal muscle fiber during a twitch. The efficiency with which Ca^{2+} ions are removed from the myoplasm during and after fiber activity is therefore of some importance. In fact, it is highly advantageous to the organism that (i) Ca^{2+} is released from the SR during activity and (ii) the SR Ca^{2+} pump returns Ca^{2+} to the SR by transporting two Ca^{2+} ions per ATP rather than one. As an alternative, consider the possibility that the Ca^{2+} ions required to activate contraction enter the myoplasm from the ECF by crossing the surface and T-system membranes and that this Ca^{2+} has to be returned to the ECF by the Ca^{2+} pump that is expressed on the fiber's surface and T-system membranes, which pumps only one Ca^{2+} ion per ATP hydrolysis. In that case, the energy required for Ca^{2+} pumping would be doubled. The reason for the difference in pump stoichiometry is the following. In general, the energy of pumping ions requires that work must be done against both chemical and electrical gradients. The chemical gradients for pumping Ca^{2+} from the myoplasm to the ECF and from the myoplasm to the lumen of the SR are similar. The electrical gradients, however, are very different because the resting potential across the SR membranes is ~0 mV whereas that across the exterior membranes is ~-90 mV. Thus, pumping Ca^{2+} ions out of the cell is energetically more costly because it has associated electrical work.

a) Calculate how much energy, in joules, is required to move a mole of Ca^{2+} ions uphill electrically against a resting potential of -90 mV. (Recall that there are ~2 x 96,485 coulombs per mole of Ca^{2+} ions and that 1 volt x 1 coulomb = 1 joule.)

b) Compare your answer in a) with the amount of energy available from the hydrolysis of ATP under intracellular conditions. [Note: the amount of energy available from the hydrolysis of a mole of ATP under 'standard' chemical conditions is reported to be ~30 kjoules per mole; however, a figure about twice as large is thought to apply under intracellular conditions, where, for example, the ADP concentration is much lower than that for standard chemical conditions.]

c) Based on your answers in a) and b), does it seem reasonable that the Ca^{2+} pump of the exterior membranes is able to pump one (but not two) Ca^{2+} ions per ATP hydrolysis?

Exercise 12.5 The last half of Section 12.3 described in words the structure and function of the thick and thin filaments, including several important filament proteins. Make a drawing of these filaments and proteins at rest and during activity and compare your drawing with some of the many that can be found with an appropriate literature search.

Exercise 12.6 The straight line in Fig. 12.16 indicates that the limiting steepness of SR Ca^{2+} release at negative values of V_m is e-fold for 3.7 mV.

a) How does this steepness compare with that measured for G_{Na} and G_K in squid axons?

b) What is the minimum number of electronic charges that must move across the membrane electric field per DHPR tetrad to explain this steepness (recall Section 8.8 of Chapter 8)?

Exercise 12.7 Explain the unifying feature of the following two properties of calcium sparks in skeletal muscle fibers (noted in Section 12.10):

a) The increase in spark frequency with increasing values of membrane potential is expected to saturate at about +20 mV.

b) Spark activity evoked by an action potential is expected to cease in response to action potential repolarization.

Exercise 12.8 The text in Section 12.5 states that the resting chloride permeability in skeletal muscle cells is several-fold higher than the resting potassium permeability; thus, resting P_{Cl}/P_K is much higher in muscle cells than in nerve cells. The reason for the high P_{Cl}/P_K in muscle appears to be related to the role of the T-tubules in EC coupling. Specifically, the rapid activation of the fiber cross section of a muscle fiber during a twitch depends on the action potential from the surface membrane spreading quickly throughout the T-tubules (an internal membrane system open to the ECF). During each action potential, V_m of the surface and T-tubular membranes depolarizes by ~100 mV due to the movement of Na^+ ions into the fiber and repolarizes by ~100 mV due (primarily) to the movement of K^+ ions out of the fiber.

a) Assume that the specific capacitance of a T-tubular membrane is 10^{-6} F/cm² (the usual value for a cell membrane). Calculate how many moles of a univalent ion per cm² of membrane are required to change V_m of the T-tubular membrane by 100 mV. (Recall that Faraday's constant is ~96,485 coulombs/mole).

b) Use Fig. 12.8 (left) to confirm that the surface to volume ratio of a T-tubule is approximately 1.6×10^6/cm.

c) Use the information in a) and b) to estimate the increase in $[K^+]$ that occurs within the lumen of a T-tubule due to action-potential repolarization.

d) Use your answer in c) and any other relative information to calculate by how much E_K of the T-system would move in the positive direction (i.e., depolarize) due to the increased $[K^+]$ in the T-system (call this value 'ΔV_m').

e) Assume that V_r, the resting potential of the muscle fiber, is -90 mV (= E_{Cl}). Recall that, under the assumptions of the osmotic model in Chapter 6: (i) the (net) resting flux of Cl^- at V_r is zero; (ii) the resting flux of K^+ is outward (due to P_K and the outward driving force on K^+), and the resting flux of Na^+ is inward (due to P_{Na} and the inward driving force on

Na$^+$); and (iii) the latter two passive fluxes are small and balanced by the active fluxes due to Na/K pumping (extrusion of Na$^+$ and uptake of K$^+$). To simplify the analysis, ignore the effects of Na/K pumping and the resting sodium permeability on V_r; instead, assume that resting $E_K = V_r$ and that the resting cation fluxes are zero. Then, just after repolarization of the T-tubular action potential, Cl$^-$ ions are trying to set V_m in the T-system to -90 mV (= E_{Cl}) and K$^+$ ions are trying to set V_m in the T-system to -90 mV + ΔV_m. If $P_{Cl} = 2 \cdot P_K$, the approximate value of V_m in the T-system just after the action potential is -90 mV + $\Delta V_m/3$. At this time, in what direction is the driving force on K$^+$ ions in the T-system and in what direction is the driving force on Cl$^-$ ions?

f) Over time, how would these driving forces affect the concentrations of K$^+$ and Cl$^-$ within the T-system and therefore the values of E_K, E_{Cl}, and V_m within the T-system?

g) In Section 12.5, the text before Fig. 12.6 mentioned that the resting K$^+$ channels in muscle have a property called 'inward rectification'. Given your answers to e) and f), does the inward-rectification property of these K$^+$ channels function to aid or impede the clearance of K$^+$ ions from the T-system and the return of resting V_m to its normal value?

Significance. Suppose that, say, 5 muscle action potentials occurred in close succession (e.g., in response to some intentional voluntary movement) and that the T-tubular membranes did not have the substantial P_{Cl} that they do. Then, immediately after these action potentials, resting V_m of the T-tubular membrane (i) would be elevated by some tens of mVs due to the elevated [K$^+$] in the T-system and (ii) might be above the threshold for action potential initiation. If (ii), the T-system would start generating action potentials on its own, i.e., in the absence of input from the motorneurons. Such action potentials would also spread to the surface membrane because of the electrical coupling between the two membrane systems. The presence of the high muscle P_{Cl}, however, blunts this potential electrical instability that arises when K$^+$ ions accumulate in the T-system in response to the normal action-potential activity. The high P_{Cl} is thus a compensatory adjustment for the instability inherent in an anatomic design with a large area of excitable membrane sequestered within the fiber.

Note. In the disease called 'myotonia congenita' (also known as "Thomsen's disease", named after a physician who described, and also had, this disease), a genetic mutation causes a large reduction in P_{Cl} in skeletal muscle fibers. Can you predict what some of the symptoms of this condition might be?

CHAPTER 13

CALCIUM DYNAMICS IN SKELETAL MUSCLE

The previous chapter described the participation of intracellular Ca^{2+} in EC coupling in skeletal muscle, including its release from the sarcoplasmic reticulum (SR), its binding to the Ca^{2+}-regulatory sites on troponin and to other divalent-ion binding sites in myoplasm, and its re-sequestration into the SR by the SR Ca^{2+} pump. This chapter describes a model of these intracellular movements and actions of Ca^{2+}, which will be referred to as myoplasmic 'calcium dynamics'.

13.1 MODEL PREVIEW

Section 13.2 presents a *Python* program that models the myoplasmic calcium dynamics of a frog twitch fiber activated by an action potential. The goal of this undertaking is to illustrate how information from a variety of physiological, anatomical, and biochemical studies can be integrated into a computational model whose aim is to achieve a quantitative understanding of an important cellular process. Because the calculations in this program are somewhat more detailed than those considered in the preceding chapters, the *Python* program in Section 13.2 is longer than the program examples in the other chapters.

In the discussion that follows, the concentration of myoplasmic free Ca^{2+} and the change in this concentration during activity are denoted '$[Ca^{2+}]$' and '$\Delta[Ca^{2+}]$', respectively. The model is a spatially-averaged one; thus, gradients in $\Delta[Ca^{2+}]$ during EC coupling are ignored (for relaxation of this assumption, see Exercise 13.4). The experimental arrangement to make the measurements of $\Delta[Ca^{2+}]$ that are employed in the model is diagrammed in Fig. 12.11 of Chapter 12.

Table 13.1 lists the concentrations of the myoplasmic constituents included in the model and the concentrations of the divalent-ion binding sites on these constituents; these will be referred to as 'Ca^{2+} buffers' and 'Ca^{2+} buffer sites', respectively. The concentrations are spatially-averaged and referred to the myoplasmic water volume (Baylor et al., 1983). Except for the resting levels of free $[Ca^{2+}]$ and free $[Mg^{2+}]$, total concentrations are given. Note that troponin, the SR Ca^{2+} pump, and parvalbumin have two Ca^{2+} buffer sites per molecule.

The model assumes that the concentration of myoplasmic free Mg^{2+} (denoted '$[Mg^{2+}]$') is 1 mM and constant and that the myoplasmic pH is 7 and constant. Furaptra, the Ca^{2+} indicator dye used to make the measurements of $\Delta[Ca^{2+}]$, is also a Ca^{2+}-binding molecule (although one that has been introduced exogenously into the myoplasm) and is therefore included in the model.

Table 13.1 Myoplasmic Concentrations of the Model Constituents

Constituent	Concentration (µM)	Concentration of Sites (µM)
Resting $[Ca^{2+}]$	0.050	--
Resting $[Mg^{2+}]$	1000	--
Troponin	120	240 (Ca^{2+}-regulatory sites)
SR Ca^{2+} Pump	120	240 (Ca^{2+}-transport sites)
Parvalbumin	750	1500 (Ca^{2+}/Mg^{2+} sites)
ATP	8000	8000 (Ca^{2+}/Mg^{2+} sites)
Furaptra	75	75 (Ca^{2+}/Mg^{2+} sites)

Fig. 13.1, which shows a schematic of the model, diagrams a half-sarcomere of a frog twitch fiber and includes the relevant membranes and myoplasmic constituents. A half-sarcomere suffices in this schematic because (i) the volume of a frog fiber is filled throughout with sarcomeres, the repeating organizational unit of the myofilaments, and (ii) the sarcomere itself is symmetric about the m-line, which is located in the middle of the sarcomere, i.e., half-way between one z-line and the next.

The model considers the release and reuptake of Ca^{2+} by the SR, the increase in $[Ca^{2+}]$ that results from Ca^{2+}'s release, and the binding of Ca^{2+} to the major myoplasmic Ca^{2+} buffers, i.e., troponin, ATP, parvalbumin, the SR Ca^{2+} pump, and furaptra.

From the $\Delta[Ca^{2+}]$ that is estimated from the optical change of furaptra upon binding Ca^{2+}, the other Ca^{2+} dynamics can be calculated based on information from the literature about (i) the concentration of the various Ca^{2+} buffer sites, (ii) the rates at which Ca^{2+} reacts with these sites, and (iii) the rate at which Ca^{2+} is returned to the SR by the SR Ca^{2+} pump.

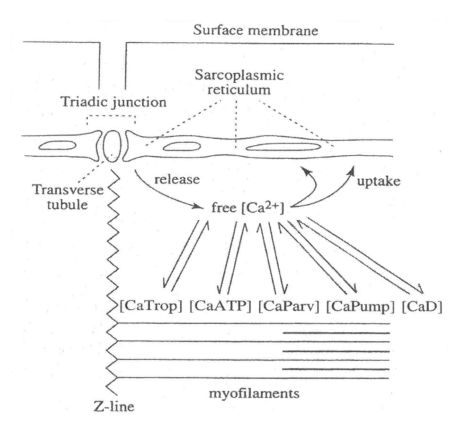

Figure 13.1 Schematic of calcium dynamics in a frog skeletal muscle fiber. Curved arrows denote the release of Ca^{2+} from the SR at the triadic junction and the reuptake of Ca^{2+} by the SR Ca^{2+} pump molecules; the latter are located at a high density throughout the non-junctional SR membrane. Straight arrows denote the binding reactions between Ca^{2+} and the myoplasmic Ca^{2+} buffers: troponin (Trop), ATP, parvalbumin (Parv), the SR Ca^{2+} pump (Pump), and the Ca^{2+} indicator dye (D).

Table 13.2 lists the reaction rate constants in the model. The reaction rates of protons (H^+) with the Ca^{2+} pump and of Ca^{2+} with furaptra are considered to be instantaneous because they are fast relative to the other kinetic changes in the model. The competitive reactions of Ca^{2+} and Mg^{2+} with parvalbumin and of Ca^{2+}, Mg^{2+}, and H^+ with the SR Ca^{2+} pump were discussed in Chapter 9. Statements from the *Python* program in Chapter 9 that calculate the binding and pumping of Ca^{2+} by the SR Ca^{2+} pump are used in the program in the next section.

Table 13.2 Rate Constants for the Binding Reactions Shown in Figure 13.1 (16 °C)

Buffers and Reactions	Forward Rate (k_{+n}) (10^8 M^{-1} s^{-1})	Reverse Rate (k_{-n}) (s^{-1})	Ratio (k_{-n}/k_{+n}) (μM)
1. Troponin (Trop)			
Ca^{2+} + Trop ↔ CaTrop	1.77	1544	Kd = 8.723
Ca^{2+} + CaTrop ↔ Ca$_2$Trop	0.885	17.15	Kd = 0.194
2. ATP			
Ca^{2+} + ATP ↔ CaATP	*0.1364	30,000	Kd = 2,200
3. Parvalbumin (Parv)			
Ca^{2+} + Parv ↔ CaParv	0.417	0.5	Kd = 0.012
Mg^{2+} + Parv ↔ MgParv	3.3 x10^{-4}	3	Kd = 90.9
4. Ca^{2+} pump (E)			
Ca^{2+} + E ↔ CaE	1.74	6.96	Kd = 0.04
Ca^{2+} + CaE ↔ Ca$_2$E	1.74	8.70	Kd = 0.05
Mg^{2+} + E ↔ MgE	8.70x10^{-4}	4.35	Kd = 50.0
Mg^{2+} + MgE ↔ Mg$_2$E	8.70x10^{-4}	87	Kd = 1000
H$^+$ + E ↔ HE	instantaneous	instantaneous	(pK = 8)
H$^+$ + HE ↔ H$_2$E	instantaneous	instantaneous	(pK = 8)
H$^+$ + H$_2$E ↔ H$_3$E	instantaneous	instantaneous	(pK = 6)
H$^+$ + H$_3$E ↔ H$_4$E	instantaneous	instantaneous	(pK = 5)
Ca$_2$E ↔ E + (2 Ca^{2+})	3.48 s^{-1}	0	Kd = 0
5. Furaptra (Dye)			
Ca^{2+} + Dye ↔ CaDye	instantaneous	instantaneous	Kd = 96

*The forward rate for the reaction of Ca^{2+} with ATP denotes an apparent rate under conditions appropriate to myoplasm, namely, [Mg^{2+}] = 1 mM, pH = 7, [K$^+$] = 150 mM, and viscosity = 2 centipoise. For the Ca^{2+} pump reactions, a Q_{10} of 2 has been used to adjust the rate constants given in Table 9.1 of Chapter 9 from 18 °C to 16 °C.

The on- and off-rate constants for the Ca^{2+}-troponin reactions in Table 13.2 deserve some comment. The values of these constants, while not known with certainty, are supported, at least approximately, by a number of experimental observations. (i) The on-rate constant for Ca^{2+} binding to EF-hand protein sites under intracellular conditions is typically $\sim 10^8$ M^{-1} s^{-1} at room temperature. (ii) Troponin has two EF-hand Ca^{2+}-regulatory sites that bind Ca^{2+} with positive cooperativity. (iii) Half-activation of the myofilaments occurs when free [Ca^{2+}] is ~1.3 µM. (iv) The apparent rate at which Ca^{2+} dissociates from troponin molecules reconstituted on thin filaments is estimated to be ~17 s^{-1} at 16 °C (Davis et al., 2004). The choice of the troponin rate constants in the model assumes that (1) the reaction between Ca^{2+} and troponin involves the binding of a first Ca^{2+} ion with low-affinity and a second Ca^{2+} ion with high-affinity (see the discussion of cooperative binding in Chapter 9), (2) the steady-state [Ca^{2+}] concentration at which half of troponin's regulatory sites are bound with Ca^{2+} is 1.3 µM, and (3) the first step of the association reaction between Ca^{2+} and the Ca^{2+}-free regulatory sites on troponin is the binding of Ca^{2+} to either of the two sites, which are assumed to be identical, and the first step of the dissociation reaction between Ca^{2+} and the doubly-occupied Ca^{2+}-regulatory sites is the dissociation of Ca^{2+} from either of the two sites.

Assumption (3) means that the forward rate constant of the first reaction in Table 13.2 and the reverse rate constant of the second reaction in Table 13.2 are twice those that apply to each site if they were to be considered individually. This follows because two Ca^{2+}-free sites are available to participate in the first forward reaction and two Ca^{2+}-bound sites are available to participate in the second reverse reaction. As noted in Chapter 9 (Eqn. 9.20, Scheme 9.4, and Eqn. 9.24), for a two-step reaction with positive cooperativity, which applies to the troponin reactions in Table 13.2, the square-root of the product of the reaction dissociation constants is equal to the steady-state value of [Ca^{2+}] at which half the sites are bound with Ca^{2+}. The choice of rate constants in Table 13.2 is consistent with (2) above since $\sqrt{(8.723 \mu M \times 0.194 \mu M}$ equals 1.3 µM. Other experimental information is also consistent with the troponin rate constants in Table 13.2. For example, the degree to which the Ca^{2+}-spark model mentioned in Chapter 12 agrees with the Ca^{2+} spark measurements discussed in that chapter is sensitive to the choice of the rate constants used to model the Ca^{2+}-troponin reaction, and the rate constants in Table 13.2 give good agreement between the spark model and the spark measurements.

ATP is present in most cells at millimolar concentrations. In frog twitch fibers the estimated concentration, if referred to the myoplasmic water volume, is 8 mM (Table 13.1; Baylor and Hollingworth, 1998). Each ATP molecule has a divalent-ion site that can bind either Ca^{2+} or Mg^{2+}. With resting [Mg^{2+}] = 1 mM, ATP is largely bound with Mg^{2+} in the resting state. The rate constants listed in Table 13.1 for the reaction of Ca^{2+} with ATP are effective rates that apply in myoplasm, i.e., they have been adjusted to take into account that ATP is largely bound with Mg^{2+} at rest.

The values of the reaction rate constants for parvalbumin in Table 13.2 differ slightly from those in Chapter 9. The values used in Chapter 9 were approximate ones, selected to illustrate general features of kinetic calculations with parvalbumin.

Furaptra (Raju et al., 1991) is a fluorescent Ca^{2+} indicator that reacts with Ca^{2+} with 1:1 stoichiometry and does so with rapid kinetics relative to the kinetics of $\Delta[Ca^{2+}]$ in the myoplasmic environment (Konishi et al., 1991; Baylor and Hollingworth, 2011). Furaptra, like ATP, can bind both Mg^{2+} and Ca^{2+}; however, furaptra's affinity for Mg^{2+} is in the mmolar, not µmolar, range. Thus, when furaptra is in the myoplasm of a frog twitch fiber, a relatively small fraction, ~0.09, of the indicator is in the Mg^{2+}-bound form at rest (Konishi et al., 1993). The model assumes that the effective myoplasmic dissociation constant of furaptra for Ca^{2+} under the conditions of the experiments is 96 µM (Konishi et al., 1991).

13.2 A PYTHON PROGRAM TO MODEL Ca^{2+} DYNAMICS DURING EC COUPLING

As diagrammed in Fig. 13.1, if a Ca^{2+} indicator is present in myoplasm and Ca^{2+} is released from the SR, $[Ca^{2+}]$ will rise and some of the released Ca^{2+} will be bound by the indicator. At typical myoplasmic concentrations of furaptra (50-100 µM), the indicator's fluorescence change upon binding Ca^{2+} (ΔF) is proportional to $\Delta[CaDye]$, the concentration of Ca^{2+} bound by the indicator. If furaptra's resting fluorescence in the fiber (F, proportional to the indicator concentration) and the fiber diameter are also known, $\Delta[CaDye]$, $\Delta[Ca^{2+}]$, and the indicator concentration ([Dye]) can be estimated from F and ΔF (next paragraphs). Given $\Delta[Ca^{2+}]$ and the information in Tables 13.1 and 13.2, the rates at which Ca^{2+} binds to and dissociates from the other myoplasmic Ca^{2+} binding sites can be calculated, as can the amount of Ca^{2+} returned to the SR by the SR Ca^{2+} pump (cf. Sections 9.6 and 9.8 of Chapter 9).

Because furaptra's reaction with myoplasmic Ca^{2+} is rapid, it can be assumed that f_{CaDye}, the fraction of the indicator that is bound with Ca^{2+}, is related to $[Ca^{2+}]$ through the usual steady-state equation (Eqn. 9.7), where Kd denotes the indicator's dissociation constant for Ca^{2+}:

$$f_{CaDye} = \frac{[Ca^{2+}]}{[Ca^{2+}] + K_d}. \tag{13.1}$$

Δf_{CaDye}, the change in the fraction of the indicator in the Ca^{2+}-bound form, can be calculated from the measurement of the indicator's $\Delta F/F$ (change in fluorescence divided by resting fluorescence). At the fluorescence excitation wavelength of the measurements (400-430 nm), the relation is (Konishi et al., 1991; Baylor and Hollingworth, 2003):

$$\Delta f_{CaDye} = -1.07 \cdot \Delta F/F. \tag{13.2}$$

Because furaptra's myoplasmic K_d is large with respect to resting $[Ca^{2+}]$ (96 µM vs. ~0.05 µM), the value of f_{CaDye} in the fiber at rest is essentially zero and it follows from Eqn. 13.1 that:

$$\Delta[Ca^{2+}] = K_d \cdot \Delta f_{CaDye} / (1 - \Delta f_{CaDye}). \tag{13.3}$$

$\Delta[CaTotal]$, the total amount of Ca^{2+} released from the SR into the myoplasm during fiber activity, can, at any time, then be calculated as the sum of (i) $\Delta[Ca^{2+}]$, (ii) the changes in concentration of Ca^{2+} bound to the various Ca^{2+} buffer sites, including the Ca^{2+} indicator, and (iii) the amount of Ca^{2+} returned to the SR by the SR Ca^{2+} pump ($\Delta[CaPumped]$). $(d/dt)\Delta[CaTotal]$, the rate of change of $\Delta[CaTotal]$, then gives an estimate of the rate at which Ca^{2+} is released from the SR during activity. It is expected that this time course closely approximates the open time course of the SR Ca^{2+}-release channels during activity.

The next *Python* program, Ca_dynamics.py, implements this model. The program listing is given next, followed by the plots produced by the program, and the program's printed output.

```
1  # -*- coding: utf-8 -*-
2  # Ca_Dynamics.py: a spatially-averaged model for Ca dynamics in frog fibers.
3  # Description: given furaptra's dFF signal, calculate and plot the Ca dynamics.
4  # The units of the calculation are in uM and ms; the temperature is 16 oC.
5
6  import numpy as np
```

```python
7  import matplotlib.pyplot as plt
8  from scipy.integrate import odeint
9
10 def Ca(t):   #Ca(t) equals resting [Ca2+] (=Ca0) plus the interpolated dCa,
11 #where dCa is the active [Ca] measurement (which is read in from disc; see below).
12 #Ca(t) is used in the various calls to odeint to solve the time-dependent changes
13    return Ca0+np.interp(t,time,dCa)   #see text for discussion of 'interp'
14
15 #The next 4 functions are used for calculating the resting states of the Ca Pump.
16 #They deal in fractional enzyme units, later multiplied by Pump (= total [enzyme])
17 def Factor_Ca2E(CaR):   #CaR is the value of resting [Ca2+]
18 #Factor_Ca2E returns the factor by which to multiply fE_and_H(CaR) to get fCa2E
19    return kp1*kp2*CaR*CaR/(kp9*kp2*CaR+(kp9+km2)*km1)
20
21 def Factor_CaE(CaR):   #CaR is the value of resting [Ca2+]
22 #Factor_CaE returns the factor by which to multiply fE_and_H(CaR) to get fCaE
23    return Factor_Ca2E(CaR)*(kp9+km2)/(kp2*CaR)
24
25 def f_E(H):     #H is the value of resting [H+] (a constant)
26 #f_E returns the fraction of the non-Ca, non-Mg enzymes states that is H-free
27 #The 5 addends in Sum give the relative amounts of E, HE, H2E, H3E, and H4E
28    Sum=
       (1+H/Kd5+H**2/(Kd5*Kd6)+H**3/(Kd5*Kd6*Kd7)+H**4/(Kd5*Kd6*Kd7*Kd8))
29    return 1/Sum
30
31 def f_E_and_H(CaR):     #CaR is the value of resting [Ca2+]
32 #f_E_and_H returns the fraction of the enzyme in state E plus the H-bound states
33    MgE=Mg0/Kd3             #this factor times E plus the H-bound states gives MgE
34    Mg2E=(Mg0/Kd4)*MgE  #this factor times E plus the H-bound states gives Mg2E
35    CaE=Factor_CaE(CaR)    #this factor times E plus the H-bound states gives CaE
36    Ca2E=Factor_Ca2E(CaR) #this factor times E plus the H-bound states gives Ca2E
37    return 1/(1+MgE+Mg2E+CaE+Ca2E)
38
39 #F_Pump has formulas for pump changes during activity (called by odeint)
```

```
40  def F_Pump(y,t):
41      dy=[0,0,0,0,0]  #create a list to hold the 5 derivatives of interest, which,
42  #in order, are (d/dt)CaE, (d/dt)Ca2E, (d/dt)MgE, (d/dt)Mg2E, and the pumping rate
43      dy[0]= kp1*Ca(t)*(1-y[0]-y[1]-y[2]-y[3])+km2*y[1]-(km1+kp2*Ca(t))*y[0]
44      dy[1]= kp2*Ca(t)*y[0]-(km2+kp9)*y[1]
45      dy[2]= kp3*Mg0*(1-y[0]-y[1]-y[2]-y[3])+km4*y[3]-(km3+kp4*Mg0)*y[2]
46      dy[3]= kp4*Mg0*y[2]-km4*y[3]
47      dy[4]= 2*kp9*(y[1]-fCa2Pump0)         # = (d/dt)[CaPumped]
48      return dy
49
50  #F_ATP has the formula for ATP changes during activity (called by odeint)
51  def F_ATP(y,t):
52      dy=[0]  #create a list to hold the derivative of interest
53      dy[0]= kCaf_ATP*Ca(t)*(1-y[0])-kCar_ATP*y[0]
54      return dy
55
56  #F_Trop has the formulas for Trop changes during activity (called by odeint)
57  def F_Trop(y,t):
58      dy=[0,0]  #create a list to hold (d/dt)CaTrop and (d/dt)Ca2Trop
59      dy[0]= kCaf1_Trop*Ca(t)*(1-y[0]-y[1])-kCar1_Trop*y[0]\
60          +kCar2_Trop*y[1]-kCaf2_Trop*Ca(t)*y[0]
61      dy[1]= kCaf2_Trop*Ca(t)*y[0]-kCar2_Trop*y[1]
62      return dy
63
64  #F_Parv has the formulas for Parv changes during activity (called by odeint)
65  def F_Parv(y,t):
66      dy=[0,0]  #create a list to hold (d/dt)CaParv and (d/dt)MgParv
67      dy[0]= kCaf_Parv*Ca(t)*(1-y[0]-y[1])-kCar_Parv*y[0]
68      dy[1]= kMgf_Parv*Mg0*(1-y[0]-y[1])-kMgr_Parv*y[1]
69      return dy
70
71  #-------------------------------------------------------------------------------
72  #set resting Ca, Mg, pH and [H]
73  Ca0=0.05           #resting [Ca2+] (assumed to be 0.05 uM)
```

```
74  Mg0=1000.           #resting [Mg2+] (assumed to be 1 mM and constant)
75  pH=7                #resting pH (assumed to be 7 and constant)
76  H0=10**(-pH+6)      #this gives resting [H+] in uM
77
78  #set [Pump] and reaction rate constants and get resting states for the pump
79  Pump=120.     #the total Pump concentration (uM)
80  kp1=1.74e-1   #per uM per ms (the numbering system for these rates is given in Chapter 9)
81  km1=6.96e-3   #per ms
82  kp2=1.74e-1   #per uM per ms
83  km2=8.7e-3    #per ms
84  kp3=8.7e-5    #per uM per ms
85  km3=4.35e-3   #per ms
86  kp4=8.7e-5    #per uM per ms
87  km4=87e-3     #per ms
88  kp9=3.48e-3   #per ms
89  #this section gives the Kds for the instantaneous pump reactions
90  Kd5=1e-2      #H in uM if pK for step 5 = 8
91  Kd6=1e-2      #H in uM if pK for step 6 = 8
92  Kd7=1e0       #H in uM if pK for step 7 = 6
93  Kd8=1e1       #H in uM if pK for step 8 = 5
94  #set the remaining pump reaction rate constants, including revisions to kp1 and kp3
95  #f_E returns the fraction of the non-Ca, non-Mg enzymes states that is H-free,
96  #thus the fraction of those states ready to react with Ca (step 1) or Mg (step 3)
97  fE=f_E(H0)   #fE applies both at rest and (implicitly) during activity
98  print("fE = {:.5f}".format(fE))
99  kp1=kp1*fE        #the modified kp1 is the effective forward rate value for step 1
100 kp3=kp3*fE        #and the modified kp3 is the effective forward for step 3
101 #and these are the Kd's for steps 1 to 4
102 Kd1=km1/kp1       #uM (effective Kd, given the modified kp1)
103 Kd2=km2/kp2       #uM (actual Kd)
104 Kd3=km3/kp3       #uM (effective Kd, given the modified kp3)
105 Kd4=km4/kp4       #uM (actual Kd)
106 EH=f_E_and_H(Ca0) #this is the pump fraction in state E plus the H-bound states
107 #now we can get the resting fractions of pump in Ca-bound and Mg-bound states
```

CALCIUM DYNAMICS IN SKELETAL MUSCLE

```
108  fCa2Pump0=EH*kp1*kp2*Ca0*Ca0/(kp9*kp2*Ca0+(kp9+km2)*km1)
109  fCaPump0=fCa2Pump0*(kp9+km2)/(kp2*Ca0)
110  fMgPump0=EH*Mg0/Kd3
111  fMg2Pump0=fMgPump0*Mg0/Kd4
112  print("f_E_and_H(CaR) = {:.5f}".format(f_E_and_H(Ca0)))
113  print("fCaPump0 = {:.5f}".format(fCaPump0))
114  print("fCa2Pump0 = {:.5f}".format(fCa2Pump0))
115  print("fMgPump0 = {:.5f}".format(fMgPump0))
116  print("fMg2Pump0 = {:.5f}".format(fMg2Pump0))
117  print("sum of pump states =
     {:.5f}".format(EH+fCaPump0+fCa2Pump0+fMgPump0+fMg2Pump0))
118
119  #set [ATP] and the reaction rate constants and get resting state for ATP
120  ATP=8000.                #total ATP concentration (uM)
121  KdCa_ATP=2200.           #Ca dissociation constant for site S (uM)
122  kCaf_ATP = 0.1364e-1     #forward rate constant for Ca binding to S (per uM per ms)
123  kCar_ATP = kCaf_ATP*KdCa_ATP   #reverse rate constant for Ca binding to S (per ms)
124  fCaATP0=Ca0/(Ca0+KdCa_ATP)     #fraction of ATP bound with Ca at rest
125  print("\n"+"fCaATP0 = {:.5f}".format(fCaATP0))
126
127  #set [Trop] and the reaction rate constants and get resting states for Trop
128  Trop=120.                #total Troponin concentration (uM)
129  KdCa1_Trop=8.723         #dissociation constant for binding of 1st Ca (uM)
130  kCaf1_Trop = 1.77e-1     #forward rate constant for binding of 1st Ca (per uM per ms)
131  kCar1_Trop = kCaf1_Trop*KdCa1_Trop   #reverse rate constant for 1st bound (per ms)
132  KdCa2_Trop=0.194         #dissociation constant for binding of 2nd Ca (uM)
133  kCaf2_Trop = 0.885e-1    #forward rate constant for binding of 2nd Ca (per uM per ms)
134  kCar2_Trop =
     kCaf2_Trop*KdCa2_Trop #reverse rate constant for 2nd bound Ca (per ms)
135  #now calculate the fractional states of trop at rest
136  fTrop0=
     KdCa1_Trop*KdCa2_Trop/(Ca0*Ca0+Ca0*KdCa2_Trop+KdCa1_Trop*KdCa2_Trop)
137  fCaTrop0=fTrop0*Ca0/KdCa1_Trop
138  fCa2Trop0=fCaTrop0*Ca0/KdCa2_Trop
```

```
139  print("fCaTrop0 = {:.5f}".format(fCaTrop0))
140  print("fCa2Trop0 = {:.5f}".format(fCa2Trop0))
141
142  #set [Parv] and the reaction rate constants and get resting states for Parv
143  Parv=1500.              #total Parvalbumin concentration (uM)
144  KdCa_Parv=0.012         #Ca dissociation constant for site S (uM)
145  kCaf_Parv = 0.417e-1    #forward rate constant for Ca binding to S (per uM per ms)
146  kCar_Parv = kCaf_Parv*KdCa_Parv   #reverse rate constant for Ca binding to S (per ms)
147  KdMg_Parv=90.9          #Mg dissociation constant for site S (uM)
148  kMgf_Parv = 3.3e-5      #forward rate constant for Mg binding to S (per uM per ms)
149  kMgr_Parv = kMgf_Parv*KdMg_Parv   #reverse rate constant for Ca binding to S (per ms)
150  #next calculate the fractional states of parvalbumin at rest
151  fCaParv0=Ca0/(Ca0+KdCa_Parv*(1+Mg0/KdMg_Parv))  #Ca-binding to Parv (resting)
152  fMgParv0=Mg0/(Mg0+KdMg_Parv*(1+Ca0/KdCa_Parv))  #Mg-binding to Parv (resting)
153  print("fCaParv0 = {:.5f}".format(fCaParv0))
154  print("fMgParv0 = {:.5f}".format(fMgParv0))
155
156  #--------------------------------------------------------------------------------
157  #read in the averaged furaptra measurement in frog fibers activated by one AP
158  data=np.load('frog_dff.npy')     #load the averaged dF/F measurement into 'data'
159  t_start=50;t_end=500             #select time points 50 to 500 for the analysis
160  time=data[t_start:t_end,0]       #the time base goes from -25.0 to 199.5 ms
161  dFF=data[t_start:t_end,1]        #get the dF/F values for the selected time base
162  dfCaDye=-1.07*dFF                #get the dfCaDye trace from the dF/F trace
163
164  Dye=75.                 #average furaptra concentration in the experiments
165  CaDye=Dye*dfCaDye       #get the [CaDye] transient from the dfCaDye trace
166  dCa=96.*dfCaDye/(1.-dfCaDye)  #get the Ca transient from the dfCaDye trace
167
168  #--------------------------------------------------------------------------------
169  #next calculate the active responses of ATP, Trop, Parv and Pump to the dCa signal;
170  #to get the changes during activity need to subtract the resting-state values
171
172  #set initial conditions and call odeint for ATP; then correct for resting state
173  y_init=[fCaATP0]                 #set initial conditions for odeint call for ATP
```

```
174  y=odeint(F_ATP,y_init,time)         #call to solve the deq
175  CaATP=(y[:,0]-fCaATP0)*ATP          #first column contains the solution for fCaATP
176
177  #set initial conditions and call odeint for Trop; then correct for resting state
178  y_init=[fCaTrop0,fCa2Trop0]         #set initial conditions for odeint call for Trop
179  y=odeint(F_Trop,y_init,time)        #call to solve the deq's
180  CaTrop=(y[:,0]-fCaTrop0)*Trop       #first column contains the solution for fCaTrop
181  Ca2Trop=(y[:,1]-fCa2Trop0)*Trop     #second column contains the solution for fCa2Trop
182
183  #set initial conditions and call odeint for Parv; then correct for resting state
184  y_init=[fCaParv0,fMgParv0]          #set initial conditions for odeint call for Parv
185  y=odeint(F_Parv,y_init,time)        #call to solve the deq's
186  CaParv=(y[:,0]-fCaParv0)*Parv       #first column contains the solution for fCaParv
187  MgParv=(y[:,1]-fMgParv0)*Parv       #second column contains the solution for fMgParv
188
189  #set initial conditions and call odeint for Pump; then correct for resting state
190  y_init=[fCaPump0,fCa2Pump0,fMgPump0,fMg2Pump0,0.]
191  y=odeint(F_Pump,y_init,time)        #call to solve the deq's
192  CaPump=(y[:,0]-fCaPump0)*Pump       #first column contains the solution for fCaPump
193  Ca2Pump=(y[:,1]-fCa2Pump0)*Pump     #2nd column contains the solution for fCa2Pump
194  CaPumped=y[:,4]*Pump                #4th column contains the (cumulative) amount pumped
195
196  #d[CaTotal] is the sum of d[Ca] plus all d[CaSite] plus the Ca removed by pumping
197  #Thus d[CaTotal] is the amount of Ca released into the myoplasm during activity
198  CaTotal=
         dCa+CaATP+CaTrop+2*Ca2Trop+CaParv+CaPump+2*Ca2Pump+CaDye+CaPumped
199
200  #--------------------------------------------------------------------------------
201  #now do the plotting; all plotted traces will have a dotted baseline
202  base_x=np.array([time[0],time[-1]]) #get x-values of a baseline for all plots
203  base_y=np.zeros(2)                   #get y-values of a baseline for all plots
204
205  #plot the dF/F and dfCaDye traces in a 2-panel figure and label accordingly
206  plt.figure()
207  plt.subplot(2,1,1)
```

```
208  plt.plot(time,dFF,'k')
209  plt.plot(base_x,base_y,':k')
210  plt.ylabel('\u0394F/F')
211  plt.title('\u0394F/F and \u0394fCaDye  (One AP)')
212  plt.subplot(2,1,2)
213  plt.plot(time,dfCaDye,'k')           #plot dfCaDye vs time as a continuous black curve
214  plt.plot(base_x,base_y,':k')
215  plt.xlabel('time (ms)')
216  plt.ylabel('\u0394fCaDye (\u03BCM)')
217  plt.savefig("Ca_Dynamics_1",dpi=200)
218
219  #plot the dCa and dCaATP traces in a 2-panel figure and label accordingly
220  plt.figure()
221  plt.subplot(2,1,1)
222  plt.plot(time,dCa,'k')
223  plt.plot(base_x,base_y,':k')
224  Ymax=20              #set the scale for the y-axis
225  plt.ylim(-.1*Ymax,Ymax)
226  plt.ylabel('\u0394[Ca] (\u03BCM)')
227  plt.title('\u0394[Ca] and \u0394[CaATP]  (One AP)')
228  plt.subplot(2,1,2)
229  plt.plot(time,CaATP,'k')
230  plt.plot(base_x,base_y,':k')
231  Ymax=75              #set the scale for the y-axis
232  plt.ylim(-0.1*Ymax,Ymax)  #set the y-axis limits
233  plt.xlabel('time (ms)')
234  plt.ylabel('\u0394[CaATP] (\u03BCM)')
235  plt.savefig("Ca_Dynamics_2",dpi=200)
236
237  #plot the Trop and Parv traces in a 2-panel figure and label accordingly
238  plt.figure()
239  plt.subplot(2,1,1)                #plotting the CaTrop and Ca2Trop traces
240  plt.plot(time,CaTrop,'k--')       #plot CaTrop vs time as a continuous black curve
241  plt.plot(time,2*Ca2Trop,'k')      #plot 2xCa2Trop vs time as a dotted black curve
242  plt.plot(base_x,base_y,':k')
243  Ymax=250                          #set the scale for the y-axis
```

```
244  plt.ylim(-0.1*Ymax, Ymax)        #set the y-axis limits
245  plt.ylabel('\u0394[Ca] bound to Trop (\u03BCM)')
246  plt.text(25,19,'\u0394[CaTrop]')
247  plt.text(100,107,'2x\u0394[Ca2Trop]')
248  plt.title
     ('\u0394[CaTrop], 2x\u0394[Ca2Trop], \u0394[CaParv], \u0394[MgParv]  (One AP)')
249  plt.subplot(2,1,2)               #plotting the CaParv and MgParv traces
250  plt.plot(time,CaParv,'k')        #plot CaParv vs time as a continuous black curve
251  plt.plot(time,MgParv,'k--')      #plot MgParv vs time as a dotted black curve
252  plt.plot(base_x,base_y,':k')
253  Ymax=400                         #set the scale for the y-axis
254  plt.ylim(-Ymax, Ymax)            #set the y-axis limits
255  plt.xlabel('time (ms)')
256  plt.ylabel('changes on Parv (\u03BCM)')
257  plt.text(100,-300,'\u0394[MgParv]')
258  plt.text(100,+300,'\u0394[CaParv]')
259  plt.savefig("Ca_Dynamics_3",dpi=200)
260
261  #plot the changes on the Pump in a 2-panel figure and label accordingly
262  plt.figure()
263  plt.subplot(2,1,1)               #plotting traces of Ca bound to the pump
264  plt.plot(time,CaPump,'k--')      #plot CaPump vs time as a dotted black curve
265  plt.plot(time,2*Ca2Pump,'k')     #plot 2xCa2Pump vs time as a continuous black curve
266  plt.plot(base_x,base_y,':k')
267  Ymax=60                          #set the scale for the y-axis
268  plt.ylim(-0.1*Ymax, Ymax)        #set the y-axis limits
269  plt.ylabel('\u0394[Ca] bound to Pump (\u03BCM)')
270  plt.text(75,5,'\u0394[CaPump]')
271  plt.text(135,46,'2x\u0394[Ca2Pump]')
272  plt.title('\u0394[CaPump], 2x\u0394[Ca2Pump], \u0394[CaPumped]  (One AP)')
273  plt.subplot(2,1,2)               #plotting trace of concentration of Ca pumped
274  plt.plot(time,CaPumped,'k')
275  plt.plot(base_x,base_y,':k')
276  Pmax=40                          #set the scale for the y-axis
277  plt.ylim(-0.1*Pmax,Pmax)
278  plt.xlabel('time (ms)')
```

```
279  plt.ylabel('\u0394[CaPumped] (\u03BCM)')
280  plt.savefig("Ca_Dynamics_4",dpi=200)
281
282  #plot the total amount of SR Ca release and the rate of release in a 2-panel figure
283  plt.figure()
284  plt.subplot(2,1,1)
285  plt.plot(time,CaTotal,'k')
286  plt.plot(base_x,base_y,':k')
287  Ymax=500                    #set the scale for the y-axis
288  plt.ylim(-0.1*Ymax,Ymax)
289  plt.ylabel('\u0394[CaTotal] (\u03BCM)')
290  #calculate the rate of SR Ca release
291  CaRelease=1.*CaTotal     #'1.*' makes sure space is allocated for a new array
292  CaRelease[0]=0
293  for i in range(1,CaTotal.size):
294      dt=time[i]-time[i-1]
295      CaRelease[i]=(CaTotal[i]-CaTotal[i-1])/dt
296  plt.title('\u0394[CaTotal] and (d/dt)\u0394[CaTotal]  (One AP)')
297  plt.subplot(2,1,2)
298  plt.plot(time,CaRelease,'k')
299  plt.plot(base_x,base_y,':k')
300  plt.xlabel('time (ms)')
301  Rmax=200                    #set the scale for the y-axis
302  plt.ylim(-0.1*Rmax,Rmax)
303  plt.ylabel('(d/dt)\u0394[CaTotal] (\u03BCM/ms)')
304  plt.savefig("Ca_Dynamics_5",dpi=200)
305  print("\nlast value of CaATP = {:.5f}".format(CaATP[-1]))
306  print("last value of CaTrop = {:.5f}".format(CaTrop[-1]))
307  print("last value of Ca2Trop = {:.5f}".format(Ca2Trop[-1]))
308  print("last value of CaParv = {:.5f}".format(CaParv[-1]))
309  print("last value of MgParv = {:.5f}".format(MgParv[-1]))
310  print("last value of CaPump = {:.5f}".format(CaPump[-1]))
311  print("last value of Ca2Pump = {:.5f}".format(Ca2Pump[-1]))
312  print("last value of CaDye = {:.5f}".format(CaDye[-1]))
313  print("last value of CaPumped = {:.5f}".format(CaPumped[-1]))
```

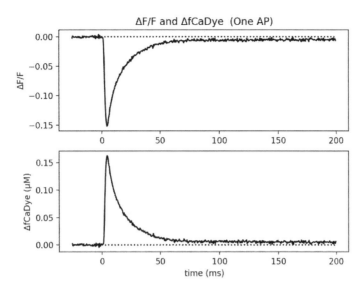

Figure 13.2 Upper: experimental measurement of the furaptra ΔF/F signal during a twitch of a frog fiber at 16 °C (averaged record from 5 experiments). Lower: Δf_{CaDye}, the fraction of furaptra in the Ca^{2+}-bound form during activity, calculated from the ΔF/F signal with Eqn. 13.2. The peak value of Δf_{CaDye} (0.16) corresponds to a peak concentration of Ca^{2+} bound by the dye of ~12 μM.

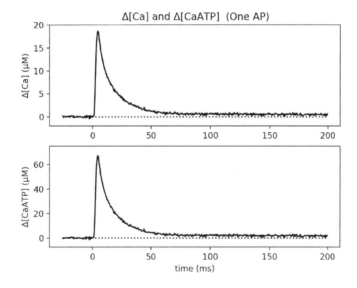

Figure 13.3 Upper: experimental estimate of $\Delta[Ca^{2+}]$ during a twitch of a frog fiber at 16 °C, calculated from the furaptra Δf_{CaDye} signal in Fig. 13.2 with Eqn. 13.3. Lower: estimate of Δ[CaATP] during a twitch, as calculated in Ca_dynamics.py. The Δ[CaATP] waveform has the same shape as $\Delta[Ca^{2+}]$ but is 3.60 times larger.

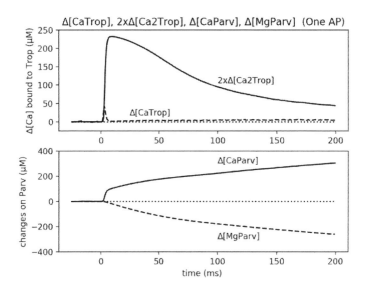

Figure 13.4 Upper: model estimates of Δ[CaTrop] and 2×Δ[Ca$_2$Trop] during a twitch of a frog fiber at 16 °C, as calculated in Ca_dynamics.py. Lower: estimates of Δ[CaParv] and Δ[MgParv], as calculated in Ca_dynamics.py.

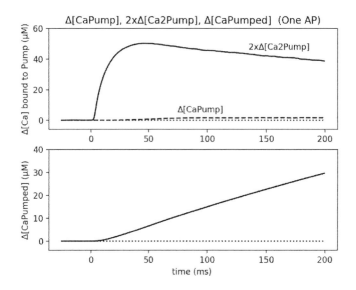

Figure 13.5 Upper: model estimates of Δ[CaPump] and 2×Δ[Ca$_2$Pump] during a twitch of a frog fiber at 16 °C, as calculated in Ca_dynamics.py. Lower: model estimate of Δ[CaPumped] (the cumulative amount of Ca^{2+} pumped by the SR Ca^{2+} Pump), as calculated in Ca_dynamics.py.

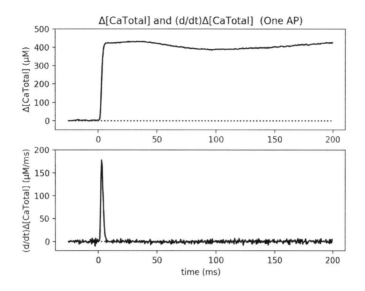

Figure 13.6 Estimates of Δ[CaTotal] (upper) and (d/dt)Δ[CaTotal] (lower) during a twitch of a frog fiber at 16 °C, as calculated in Ca_dynamics.py.

fE = 0.00826
f_E_and_H(CaR) = 0.74441
fCaPump0 = 0.00566
fCa2Pump0 = 0.00404
fMgPump0 = 0.12294
fMg2Pump0 = 0.12294
sum of pump states = 1.00000

fCaATP0 = 0.00002
fCaTrop0 = 0.00569
fCa2Trop0 = 0.00147
fCaParv0 = 0.25771
fMgParv0 = 0.68043

last value of CaATP = 2.12960
last value of CaTrop = 4.49386
last value of Ca2Trop = 21.95192
last value of CaParv = 305.05938
last value of MgParv = -260.38752

last value of CaPump = 1.66307
last value of Ca2Pump = 19.37624
last value of CaDye = 0.47158
last value of CaPumped = 29.61188

Program Notes

The program divides into 5 main sections, which are demarcated by the commented dashed lines in program lines 71, 156, 168, and 200.

- The first section of the program contains the user-defined functions. The first function is Ca(t), which is used by four of the remaining functions: F_ATP(y,t), F_Trop(y,t), F_Parv(y,t), and F_Pump(y,t). The latter 4 functions (i) are called by odeint (the ordinary-differential-equation solver imported from the 'scipy.integrate' module) and (ii) require the value of free [Ca^{2+}] as a function of time in order to calculate the time-dependent changes in the concentration of Ca^{2+} bound to the various myoplasmic Ca^{2+} buffers (ATP, troponin, parvalbumin, and the Ca^{2+} pump) -- and, in the case of parvalbumin, the change in concentration of Mg^{2+} bound to parvalbumin. The np array dCa (which is set in line 165) holds values of $\Delta[Ca^{2+}]$ only at the time points of the measurement of $\Delta F/F$, whereas odeint requires values of [Ca^{2+}] at time points other than just the measured ones. To satisfy the requirements of odeint, Ca(t) uses the function 'np.interp' to obtain interpolated estimates of [Ca^{2+}] at all required time points. This function takes values at a discrete set of data points (i.e., dCa, which is known at the values in the array 'time') and uses these to estimate the values required at the other time points.

- The user-defined functions in the first program section include three other functions: Factor_CaE, f_E, and f_E_and_H. These functions, which were explained in Section 9.8 of Chapter 9, are used to calculate the various states of the Ca^{2+} pump under resting conditions based on Scheme 9.5 of Chapter 9 and the reaction rate constants in Table 13.2.

- The second section of the program contains the statements that (i) set the total concentrations of the various constituents and (ii) calculate the resting fractions of the constituents in their various states from the values of resting [Ca^{2+}] (0.05 µM), resting [Mg^{2+}] (1000 µM), and resting [H^+] (0.1 µM) (lines 73-76). Calculations for (ii) are based on the reactions given in Table 13.2 and equilibrium relations of the type discussed in

Chapter 9. This section of the program ends by printing to the console information about the resting state(s) of the various constituents.

- The third section of the program is very short. It reads from disk the measurement of the furaptra $\Delta F/F$ signal in frog fibers activated by an action potential at 16 °C. This trace, which was previously stored on disk as a two-column numpy array in file 'frog_dff.npy', was averaged from 5 experiments, which gave very similar $\Delta F/F$ signals. The first column of the array contains the time points of the measurements, the values of which are relative to the time of the external shock that initiated the fiber action potential (which is time point 0.0 in the data file). The second column of the array contains the measured values of $\Delta F/F$ at the corresponding time points. The $\Delta F/F$ measurement, in combination with Eqns. 13.2 and 13.3, is used to obtain the Δf_{CaDye} trace (line 162) and the $\Delta[Ca^{2+}]$ trace (line 166). For the $\Delta[Ca^{2+}]$ trace, the value of FDHM (full-duration at half maximum, i.e., the time between the half-rise and half-decay of the trace) is 9.6 ms (=12.2 - 2.6 ms). The Δf_{CaDye} trace is multiplied by the indicator concentration in line 165 to obtain the $\Delta[CaDye]$ trace, which is the change in the concentration of Ca^{2+} bound to the indicator; at line 198, the $\Delta[CaDye]$ trace is one of the summands in $\Delta[CaTotal]$. $\Delta[CaTotal]$ contains the sum of the changes in all of the myoplasmic Ca^{2+} concentrations as well as the concentration of Ca^{2+} that is removed from the myoplasm by the SR Ca^{2+} pump.

- The fourth section of the program uses the information in the second section of the program to set the initial conditions for the four function calls to odeint. As noted above, the calls to odeint use the information in the $\Delta[Ca^{2+}]$ trace (i.e., the array dCa in the program) in combination with the value of resting $[Ca^{2+}]$ (denoted 'Ca0') to calculate the time-dependent changes in the amount of Ca^{2+} bound to ATP, troponin, parvalbumin, and the Ca^{2+} pump. These amounts, which are referred to one molecule of each type, are then multiplied by the concentration of each type to yield the relevant changes in concentration units. In the case of parvalbumin, the function F_Parv(y,t) also calculates the change in the amount of Mg^{2+} bound to parvalbumin. In the case of the pump, the calculation of the amount of Ca^{2+} pumped by the SR Ca^{2+} pump is carried out in function def F_Pump(y,t) by integration of the rate of SR Ca^{2+} pumping minus that in effect at the resting level (line 47) and then multiplication of the last array returned by F_Pump(y,t) by the pump concentration (line 194), thereby referring the result to concentration units. This amount is then included in the calculation of the $\Delta[CaTotal]$ array (line 198).

- The fifth section of the program generates the plotted output. The statements used for these plots and their labels are of types that have been explained previously.

Model Accuracy. The accuracy of the model calculations obviously depends on (i) the accuracy of the values listed in Tables 13.1 and 13.2, and (ii) the assumption that troponin, parvalbumin, ATP, and the SR Ca^{2+} pump suffice as the major intrinsic Ca^{2+}-binding molecules of myoplasm to be considered. The information in these tables draws upon a wealth of information from the muscle literature and is thought to be reasonably accurate and complete (see, e.g., references in Robertson et al., 1981; Cannell and Allen, 1984; Baylor et al., 1983; Hollingworth et al., 2006).

The accuracy of the calculations also depends heavily on the accuracy of the experimental measurement of $\Delta[Ca^{2+}]$. As described elsewhere (Baylor and Hollingworth, 2011), furaptra is one of a small number of Ca^{2+} indicators that are thought to be capable of reporting an accurate measurement of the large and rapid $\Delta[Ca^{2+}]$ that occurs in skeletal muscle fibers in response to an action potential.

The relevance of the model calculations to the normal physiology of muscle cells also depends on the experimental condition of the fibers. For the furaptra experiments in frog fibers, the indicator was introduced by micro-injection into the middle of a normally-functioning fiber, the health of which was always checked after injection. Action potentials were elicited by direct stimulation of the fiber with a pair of external electrodes located near the injection site (cf. Fig. 12.11 in Chapter 12). To minimize the influence of fiber movement on the $\Delta[Ca^{2+}]$ measurements, the fibers were stretched to a long sarcomere length (3.5-4 µm). The fibers in the experiments typically gave reproducible Ca^{2+} signals for several hours following the injection of indicator. Thus, the physiological state of the fibers used for the measurements of $\Delta[Ca^{2+}]$ is thought to have been essentially normal.

Physiological Interpretation

According to the calculated results in Fig. 13.6: (i) $\Delta[CaTotal]$, the total concentration of Ca^{2+} released from the SR in response to a single action potential in a frog twitch fiber, is ~425 µM (where concentration units have been referred to the myoplasmic water volume), (ii) the peak of $(d/dt)\Delta[CaTotal]$, i.e., the peak rate of SR Ca^{2+} release, is ~175 µM/ms, and (iii) the FDHM of the Ca^{2+} release waveform is ~2.2 ms (= 4.4 - 2.2 ms). If there were no errors or omissions in the model, the $\Delta[CaTotal]$ trace in Fig. 13.6 should rise to a peak value and remain constant thereafter. The fact that the $\Delta[CaTotal]$ trace does not stay constant, but oscillates slightly after reaching an early peak, indicates that the model calculations have some error.

Possible sources of this error include: (i) the fact that the model is a spatially-averaged one rather than a spatially-resolved one, (ii) the possibility that $\Delta[Ca^{2+}]$ estimated from furaptra has some error (for example, a slight movement artifact might contribute to the $\Delta F/F$ measurement during its falling phase, when significant tension is developed by the myofilaments), (iii) the possibility of an error in one or more buffer concentrations, reaction schemes, or reaction rate constants in the model (Tables 13.1 and 13.2), and (iv) the possibility that a myoplasmic Ca^{2+} buffer of some significance has been omitted from the model. Overall, however, the conclusion that, under physiological conditions at 16 °C, an action potential causes the SR Ca^{2+}-release channels to open for 2 to 3 ms while releasing 400 to 425 µM total $[Ca^{2+}]$ into the myoplasm appears to be reasonable.

Interestingly, the 2.2 ms value noted above for the FDHM of the $(d/dt)\Delta[CaTotal]$ waveform is about half that of the rise time of an average Ca^{2+} spark recorded from the same preparation at a slightly warmer temperature (4.6 ms at 18 °C; see Chapter 12). Since the latter value is thought to reflect the average open time of the SR Ca^{2+} release channels under the conditions of a Ca^{2+} spark, it follows that the SR Ca^{2+} release channels, when activated by an action potential, open for a substantially briefer time than during a Ca^{2+} spark. As noted in Chapter 12, this difference is likely due to a difference in the effectiveness of the process of Ca^{2+} inactivation of Ca^{2+} release. With an action potential stimulus, the increase in myoplasmic free $[Ca^{2+}]$ that occurs near the triadic junctions is rapid and reaches higher, longer-lasting values than occurs during a Ca^{2+} spark. This large, rapid rise in $[Ca^{2+}]$ is likely to be more effective in inactivating the SR release channels than the rise in $[Ca^{2+}]$ during a spark; thus, it is expected that the open time of the release channels during an action potential will be briefer than during a spark.

Because of this negative feedback mechanism, the amount of Ca^{2+} released by an action potential can be limited to that which gives nearly full occupancy of the troponin Ca^{2+} regulatory sites and thereby a nearly full activation of the myofilaments. According to the Ca^{2+}-troponin occupancy traces in Fig. 13.3 (traces labeled '$\Delta[Ca2Trop]$' and '2x $\Delta[Ca2Trop]$'), ~230 µM Ca^{2+} is bound to the troponin Ca^{2+}-regulatory sites at 9 ms, the time of the peak occupancy of troponin by Ca^{2+}. Since less than 1% of the regulatory sites are occupied with Ca^{2+} in the resting state (see printed output above from Ca_dynamics.py), the model estimate of the peak occupancy of the Ca^{2+}-regulatory sites in response to one action potential is ~97%, almost all of which involves troponin molecules that have both of their Ca^{2+}-regulatory sites occupied.

In Fig. 13.3, the time of peak of the $\Delta[Ca^{2+}]$ trace is 4.5 ms whereas that of the $2\times\Delta[Ca_2Trop]$ trace is 9 ms. Although the $\Delta[CaTrop]$ trace decreases during the time period 4.5 to 9 ms, the $2\times\Delta[Ca_2Trop]$ trace increases much more than $\Delta[CaTrop]$ decreases. Thus, the binding of Ca^{2+} to troponin contributes substantially to the decline in $\Delta[Ca^{2+}]$ during this time. Also, substantial amounts of Ca^{2+} bind to parvalbumin and to the SR Ca^{2+} pump at times after 4.5 ms (Figs. 13.3 and 13.4). Therefore, Ca^{2+}-binding to parvalbumin and the Ca^{2+} pump also contributes significantly to the decline of $\Delta[Ca^{2+}]$. Less than 1 µM Ca^{2+} is pumped by the Ca^{2+} pump during the first 9 ms after the action potential and less than 7 µM Ca^{2+} is pumped during the first 50 ms. It follows that most of the falling phase of $\Delta[Ca^{2+}]$ is due primarily to a redistribution of released Ca^{2+} among the various myoplasmic Ca^{2+} binding sites, not to the removal of myoplasmic Ca^{2+} by Ca^{2+} pumping.

As noted in Chapter 9, Ca^{2+}-binding to parvalbumin in response to a sudden rise in $[Ca^{2+}]$ proceeds in two phases: a fast phase, during which Ca^{2+} binds to the parvalbumin molecules that are free of Ca^{2+} and Mg^{2+}, and a slow phase, during which Ca^{2+} binds to parvalbumin molecules that become divalent-ion free when Mg^{2+} dissociates from parvalbumin in response to the perturbation of the resting-state by the rise in $[Ca^{2+}]$. The distinction between these two phases of Ca^{2+} binding by parvalbumin is clear in Fig. 13.4.

Also of note is that the peak of $\Delta[Ca^{2+}]$, ~18.5 µM, is small compared with the peak of $\Delta[CaTotal]$, ~425 µM. Thus, most of the Ca^{2+} that is released into the myoplasm is bound by Ca^{2+}-binding sites in the myoplasm, with only a small fraction of the released Ca^{2+} remaining free. Stated qualitatively, $\Delta[Ca^{2+}]$ is only the 'tip of the 'iceberg'. Similarly, the peak value of $\Delta[CaDye]$, ~12 µM (= 0.16 x 75 µM), is small with respect to the total amount of SR Ca^{2+} release. Thus, the presence of the furaptra in myoplasm at a concentration of 75 µM produces only a minor perturbation of the normal Ca^{2+}-buffering properties of myoplasm and is not expected to modify substantially the overall Ca^{2+} dynamics that would occur in the absence of the indicator.

Line 47 of Ca_dynamics.py calculates, for one unit of the Ca^{2+} pump, the rate of Ca^{2+} pumping during activity relative to the resting rate of Ca^{2+} pumping. Note that this is the only line in the program where the rate of Ca^{2+} pumping in the resting state is referenced. The program assumes implicitly that, in the resting state, the small rate of Ca^{2+} pumping is balanced by a small leakage of SR Ca^{2+} through the release channels, thereby resulting in a stable level of resting $[Ca^{2+}]$. This leakage could arise, for example, from a small frequency of spontaneous Ca^{2+} sparks (e.g., Hollingworth et al., 2001).

The Return to the Resting Condition. At 200 ms after onset of the action potential, i.e., at the end of the traces in Figs. 13.2-13.6, $\Delta[Ca^{2+}]$ is estimated to be ~0.4 µM above baseline and declining very slowly. The actual elevation of $[Ca^{2+}]$ above the resting level at 200 ms may, in fact, be slightly smaller than 0.4 µM. The reason is that furaptra has a slight sensitivity to Mg^{2+}, and $[Mg^{2+}]$ is expected to rise slightly during activity due to the exchange of Ca^{2+} for Mg^{2+} on parvalbumin (i.e., the time of the slow phases of the $\Delta[CaParv]$ and $\Delta[MgParv]$ traces in Fig. 13.4). Thus, a small rise in $[Mg^{2+}]$ likely makes a small contribution to the maintained furaptra $\Delta F/F$ signal at 200 ms in Fig. 13.2. The final return to baseline of the $\Delta[Ca^{2+}]$ trace and of the other traces in Figs. 13.2-13.6 involving Ca^{2+} binding is not well-resolved with furaptra and undoubtedly takes tens of seconds (not shown). This time course can be resolved satisfactorily with a high-affinity fluorescence Ca^{2+} indicator such as fluo-4 (cf. Nelson et al., 2014). The slow return of the traces to baseline is explained by the slow rate of turnover of the SR Ca^{2+} pump when $[Ca^{2+}]$ is elevated only slightly above the resting level (see Fig. 9.9 of Chapter 9). Exercise 13.4 encourages the reader to explore these issues in his/her own *Python* program that incorporates many of the elements of Ca_Dynamics.py.

13.3 MODEL ESTIMATES IN RESPONSE TO A TRAIN OF ACTION POTENTIALS

As noted above, the process of Ca^{2+} inactivation of Ca^{2+} release appears to have a strong and rapid action to inhibit SR Ca^{2+} release in response to the rise in $[Ca^{2+}]$ elicited by one action potential. One would expect, therefore, that the amount of Ca^{2+} release elicited by a second action potential initiated shortly after a first action potential would be substantially reduced. In fact, this is the case (not shown; see, e.g., Hollingworth and Baylor, 2013). For example, if a second action potential is initiated within 10 ms of a first action potential, the amount of Ca^{2+} released by the second action potential is estimated to be less than 20% of that released by the first. Ca^{2+} releases in response to subsequent action potentials elicited at a frequency of 100 Hz are even smaller. These reductions take place even though the SR still contains large amounts of releasable Ca^{2+}. This strong effect of Ca^{2+} inactivation of Ca^{2+} release has been observed in all skeletal muscle fiber types examined (slow-twitch, fast-twitch and superfast-twitch) and all species examined (frog, fish, and mouse).

As mentioned in Chapter 12, the Ca^{2+}-inactivation process serves a major physiological function. The object of the EC coupling mechanism is to raise myoplasmic $[Ca^{2+}]$ to a level that permits nearly full activation of the myofilaments. Allowing $[Ca^{2+}]$ to rise to substantially higher levels has no advantage. Doing so would be energetically wasteful and risk the toxic effects of sustained high $[Ca^{2+}]$ levels, e.g., such as that which impairs mitochondrial function when $[Ca^{2+}]$ is high.

13.4 EXERCISES

Exercise 13.1 The text states that the peak rate at which Ca^{2+} is released from the SR (i.e., the peak value of the $(d/dt)\Delta[CaTotal]$ in Fig. 13.6) is ~175 μM/ms. Estimate the peak rate at which Ca^{2+} is returned to the SR by the SR Ca^{2+} pump by either (1) estimating the maximum slope of the $\Delta[CaPumped]$ trace in the lower panel of Fig. 13.5, or (2) estimating the peak of the $\Delta[Ca2Pump]$ trace in the upper panel of Fig. 13.5 and multiplying that number by the appropriate constants.

a) What is the ratio of the peak rate of release to the peak rate of pumping?

b) Qualitatively, why do you think the first number is so much larger than the second?

Exercise 13.2 From anatomical counts of the number of foot proteins in frog twitch fibers (Franzini-Armstrong, 1975, 1980), the estimated concentration of SR Ca^{2+} release channels, if referred to the myoplasmic water volume, is ~0.3 μM. If the Ca^{2+} sites responsible for Ca^{2+} inactivation of Ca^{2+} release are located on the SR Ca^{2+} release channels and if there as many as four such sites per release channel, would you expect that inclusion of these sites as another Ca^{2+} buffer in the Ca^{2+}-dynamics model described in the text would significantly affect the modeling results shown in Figs. 13.3-13.6?

Exercise 13.3 (a) From the concentration of RyRs given in Exercise 13.2, calculate the peak rate of SR Ca^{2+} release per RyR in response to an action potential. (b) How does this rate compare with the single-channel Ca^{2+} flux through an open RyR as measured in bilayer experiments under ionic conditions that are approximately physiological, namely, 0.5-1 pA. (c) From your answers to (a) and (b), estimate the fraction of the RyRs that open in response to an action potential.

Exercise 13.4 As discussed in the text, the program in Section 13.2 illustrates use of the information in Tables 13.1 and 13.2 in conjunction with a measurement of $\Delta[Ca^{2+}]$ made with an appropriately-chosen Ca^{2+} indicator to model the Ca^{2+} dynamics in skeletal muscle during EC coupling. The approach uses $\Delta[Ca^{2+}]$ to estimate Ca^{2+}-binding to the myoplasmic Ca^{2+} buffers, the rate and amount of Ca^{2+}-pumping by the SR Ca^{2+} pump, and the amount and rate of SR Ca^{2+} release. The logic of the analysis can be used in reverse. Suppose that a waveform for the rate of SR Ca^{2+} release is given, which, by integration with respect to time, also gives a waveform for the amount of SR Ca^{2+} release. From the rate of Ca^{2+} release and the information in Tables 13.1 and 13.2, one should then be able to calculate Δ[Ca^{2+}] and Ca^{2+}-binding to the myoplasmic Ca^{2+} buffers (ATP, troponin, parvalbumin, the SR Ca^{2+} pump, and, if desired, a Ca^{2+} indicator) and to calculate Ca^{2+}-pumping by the SR Ca^{2+} pump, including rate and amount.

Using the program in Section 13.2 as an aid, implement a *Python* program of the type suggested in the previous paragraph, including making plots of the various time-dependent waveforms. Assume that the rate of SR Ca^{2+} release (Rel_Rate) satisfies the following function for t > t0:

$$\text{Rel\_Rate}(t) = R \times \left(1 - e^{-(t - t0)/t1}\right)^{P1} \times \left(e^{-(t - t0)/t2}\right)^{P2},$$

where t0 = 1.15 ms, R = 11,900 μM/ms, t1 = 1.5 ms, t2 = 0.75 ms, P1 = 5, and P2 = 1. Note: t0 is a 'time-offset' parameter; a value of t0 = 1.15 ms matches the time delay of Rel_Rate to the time delay of the SR Ca^{2+}-release waveform calculated in Ca-dynamics.py, i.e., the time between the initiation of the action potential by the external stimulus and the onset of Ca^{2+} release. The selection of the other parameters is explained in the next paragraph.

Suggestions
1) Start by making a plot of the Rel_Rate(t) function after setting the parameter values to those given in the preceding paragraph; then integrate Rel_Rate(t), e.g., with a call to odeint. This part of your program should reveal that the Rel_Rate(t) waveform has a peak value of ~180 μM/ms, a FDHM of ~2.2 ms, and an integrated amount of release of ~425 μM, i.e., that this function gives good agreement with the amount and rate of SR Ca^{2+} release estimated with Ca_Dynamics.py in Section 13.2. It is then expected that the remaining Ca^{2+}-dynamics waveforms calculated in your program (i.e., the calculations of Δ[Ca^{2+}], Ca^{2+}-binding to ATP, troponin, parvalbumin, the SR Ca^{2+} pump, and the Ca^{2+} indicator, as well as the rate and amount of Ca^{2+}-pumping by the SR Ca^{2+} pump) will be in good agreement with the corresponding waveforms calculated in Ca_Dynamics.py.

2) Build up your program 'brick by brick', i.e., add one small logical step at a time and confirm that this step does what you think it does before adding the next step.

3) Pay attention to how Ca^{2+} binding to the various Ca^{2+} buffers in the resting state is

handled and also to how Ca^{2+} pumping by the SR Ca^{2+} pump is handled. Use Ca_dynamics.py as a template for how to proceed.

4) For convenience, model Ca^{2+} binding to the indicator with a one-step reaction scheme similar to that for ATP but with the following rate constants: k_forward = 10^8 M^{-1} s^{-1} and k_reverse = 9600 s^{-1} (hence, Kd = 96 µM, the same as for furaptra in Ca_Dynamics.py). Doing so allows the logic of Ca^{2+} binding by the indicator to be treated in your model like that of Ca^{2+} binding to the other Ca^{2+} buffers rather than needing it to be treated as a separate special case.

5) Use odeint to solve the required system of differential equations. Note, however, that, in Ca_Dynamics.py, $\Delta[Ca^{2+}]$ is known; hence the call to odeint to solve the rate of Ca^{2+} binding to ATP is independent of the call to odeint to solve the rate of Ca^{2+} binding to troponin, which is independent of the call to odeint to solve the rate of Ca^{2+} binding to parvalbumin, etc. Thus, a series of independent calls to odeint are made in Ca_Dynamics.py. In contrast, for the program in this exercise, $\Delta[Ca^{2+}]$ needs to be solved in the call to odeint at the same time that the changes in all the other variables (which depend on $\Delta[Ca^{2+}]$) are being solved. This situation arises because the amount of SR Ca^{2+} release is what is known and a change in the binding of, say, Ca^{2+} to ATP affects the calculation of $\Delta[Ca^{2+}]$ and hence the calculation of the binding of Ca^{2+} to troponin, etc. This means that you will need one call to odeint to solve the whole system of equations at once. The text below gives a suggested version of the function to be called by odeint to solve for all of the variables of interest at once.

```
#F_Ca has the formula for all changes during activity (called by odeint)
def F_Ca(y,t):
    dy=[0]        #dy[0] will hold (d/dt)dCa after the other changes are accounted for
    dy.append(0) #dy[1] will hold (d/dt)ATP
    dy.append(0) #dy[2] will hold (d/dt)CaTrop
    dy.append(0) #dy[3] will hold (d/dt)Ca2Trop
    dy.append(0) #dy[4] will hold (d/dt)CaParv
    dy.append(0) #dy[5] will hold (d/dt)MgParv
    dy.append(0) #dy[6] will hold (d/dt)CaPump
    dy.append(0) #dy[7] will hold (d/dt)Ca2Pump
    dy.append(0) #dy[8] will hold (d/dt)MgPump
```

```
dy.append(0)  #dy[9] will hold (d/dt)Mg2Pump
dy.append(0)  #dy[10] will hold (d/dt)CaDye
dy[1]= kCaf_ATP*(Ca0+y[0])*(ATP-y[1])-kCar_ATP*y[1]
dy[2]= kCaf1_Trop*(Ca0+y[0])*(Trop-y[2]-y[3])-kCar1_Trop*y[2]\
    +kCar2_Trop*y[3]-kCaf2_Trop*(Ca0+y[0])*y[2]
dy[3]= kCaf2_Trop*(Ca0+y[0])*y[2]-kCar2_Trop*y[3]
dy[4]= kCaf_Parv*(Ca0+y[0])*(Parv-y[4]-y[5])-kCar_Parv*y[4]
dy[5]= kMgf_Parv*Mg0*(Parv-y[4]-y[5])-kMgr_Parv*y[5]
dy[6]= kp1*(Ca0+y[0])*(Pump-y[6]-y[7]-y[8]-y[9])+km2*y[7]-(km1+kp2*(Ca0+y[0]))*y[6]
dy[7]= kp2*(Ca0+y[0])*y[6]-(km2+kp9)*y[7]
dy[8]= kp3*Mg0*(Pump-y[6]-y[7]-y[8]-y[9])+km4*y[9]-(km3+kp4*Mg0)*y[8]
dy[9]= kp4*Mg0*y[8]-km4*y[9]
dy[10]= kf_Dye*(Ca0+y[0])*(Dye-y[10])-kr_Dye*y[10]
temp= CaRel(t)-2*kp9*(y[7]-Pump*fCa2Pump0)   #net rate of Ca entry into myoplasm
dy[0]= temp-dy[1]-dy[2]-2*dy[3]-dy[4]-dy[6]-2*dy[7]-dy[10] #entry rate minus binding rate
return dy
```

Note that, in function F_Ca, the equation for dy[0] (the rate of change of free [Ca^{2+}]) is left until last. Why?

6) Confirm that calculations with your program out to 200 ms after SR Ca^{2+} release yields waveforms that are in reasonable agreement with those in Figs. 13.2-13.6.

7) Now extend the calculation time of your program out to a number of seconds (e.g., to 10 s after SR Ca^{2+} release). Are free [Ca^{2+}] and the other variables back to baseline? If not, how long does it take for the activity of the Ca^{2+} pump to restore free [Ca^{2+}] and the other variables essentially to the baseline levels?

A Next Step. Suppose one wanted to implement the program approach suggested for Exercise 13.4, which applies to a spatially-averaged model, to a spatially-resolved model. To do so, one would need a model that divided the half-sarcomere into a number of small compartments. This would permit setting the values of variables in the model that are not distributed homogenously throughout the half-sarcomere to different values in different compartments (i.e., to values appropriate to specific regions within the half-sarcomere). For example, the sites of SR Ca^{2+} release would logically go in some compartments but not others, and similarly for the sites of SR Ca^{2+} pumping and the location of the troponin molecules (whose location coincides with that of the thin filaments).

For such a model, one would also have to take into account the diffusion of the various diffusible constituents (free Ca^{2+}, ATP, parvalbumin, and the Ca^{2+} indicator), which are found in all compartments. Whenever the concentrations of the latter variables differed in adjacent compartments, net diffusive movements between compartments would take place. For example, [Ca^{2+}] would rise first and highest in the compartments that contained the release sites, and then [Ca^{2+}] would rise in the other compartments due to diffusion -- and similarly for the concentrations of the other diffusible constituents. A model of this type is called a 'reaction-diffusion' model and requires specification of the diffusion coefficients of the relevant constituents as well as a means of solving a large number of first-order differential equations simultaneously. If, for example, a model along the lines of Exercise 13.4 were expanded to have, say, 20-30 compartments, the use of odeint would require that several hundred initial conditions be specified and that a function be called that specified the rates of change of the same number of variables. Examples of spatially-resolved models of this type for Ca^{2+} dynamics during EC Coupling are given in the reports by Cannell and Allen (1984) and Baylor and Hollingworth (1998). These models were implemented in languages other than *Python*, but implementation in *Python* along the lines suggested should also be possible.

Exercise 13.5 To investigate how the Ca^{2+} dynamics in muscle cells differs in slow-twitch, fast-twitch, and superfast-twitch fiber types, the reader is encouraged to download the interactive self-study teaching program called 'CalDyx', which is available from the journal *Science Signaling* (8(362):tr1; Feb 3, 2015).

CHAPTER 14

THE MUSCLE REFLEX ARC: A PEAK INTO THE NERVOUS SYSTEM

Chapter 1 introduced the subject of cell physiology from a broad vantage point. Subsequent chapters have focused on much narrower topics, usually events and mechanisms involving single cells, portions of single cells, and, often, single molecules. Here, we return to a broader view. The examples concern several types of excitable cells that work together to carry out a specific function. Our primary example is the muscle stretch reflex, which involves signal processing in the nervous system, sensory reception, propagation of electrical signals along axons, cell-cell communication at synapses, and activation of motor units.

14.1 A QUICK TOUR OF THE MUSCLE REFLEX ARC

The stretch reflex might be considered the first line of defense in maintaining posture. We begin with a brief tour of its elements, using the stretch reflex at the patellar tendon of the human knee as an example.

Anatomy. We will initially be concerned with 3 types of nerve cells: an alpha motorneuron (α-motorneuron), a gamma motorneuron (γ-motorneuron), and a IA sensory cell (pronounced "one a"; also written 'Ia'). The cell bodies of these neurons lie in or near the spinal cord. We will also consider 2 types of muscle cells: a spindle muscle fiber and an ordinary muscle fiber. The spindle fiber is so named because of its shape: bulgy toward the middle, tapered at its ends. The spindle fiber is also called an 'intrafusal' muscle fiber (i.e., a fiber within the spindle), whereas the ordinary muscle fiber is sometimes called an 'extrafusal' muscle fiber (i.e., a fiber outside the spindle). The anatomical arrangement of these cells is diagrammed in Fig. 14.1.

The muscle cells in Fig. 14.1 reside within the *rectus femoris* division of the quadriceps muscle. This muscle stretches from an origin on the pelvis to an insertion on the tibia via the knee cap and the patellar tendon. The muscle fibers in the quadriceps are innervated by a branch of the femoral nerve that originates from roots in the lumbar region of the spinal cord.

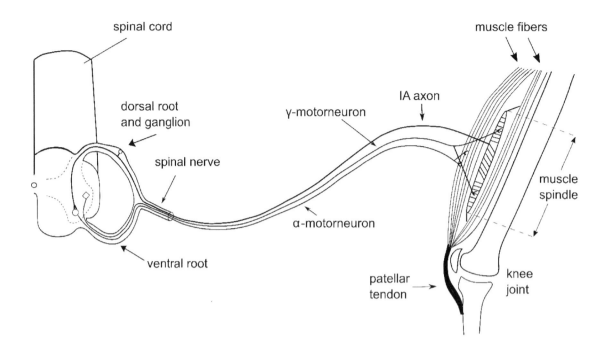

Figure 14.1 Cells participating in a stretch reflex. The axons of the 3 types of nerve cells run in the same nerve trunk. The cell body of the γ-motorneuron, located in the ventral horn, is diagrammed as a diamond shape. The spindle muscle fiber is shown disproportionately enlarged in the diagram; it has a bulgy central portion and tapered ends (hence, the name 'spindle'), with tiny tendons that insert onto the regular muscle fibers. There are many spindles within the muscle.

The Reflex. The knee-jerk reflex can be elicited by a tap on the patellar tendon just below the knee cap. The tap causes a small, rapid increase in the length of the quadriceps muscle. This stretch of the muscle is detected by small sensory structures, the spindles, which are embedded in the muscle. A spindle, as described below, is composed of small muscle fibers (the spindle fibers) and the nerve endings of the motor and sensory nerves that are attached to them. Stretched spindles generate electrical signals, called 'generator potentials', in the sensory nerve endings within the spindle.

The function of the generator potential is to trigger an action potential in the axon that extends from the sensory nerve ending in the spindle. These are the IA axons. The Roman numeral I implies a large (10-20 μm diameter) fast-conducting axon; A means it is connected to the spindle. Once initiated, this action potential propagates quickly along the IA axon to the spinal cord. In the spinal cord, it has, among other connections, synaptic endings on α-motorneurons. The synapse there is between a IA fiber pre-synaptically and an α-motorneuron post-synaptically. This is an excitatory synapse mediated by the transmitter glutamate, which is released from the IA ending upon arrival of the action potential. The glutamate diffuses to and binds to receptors on the α-motorneuron. These receptors are chemically-gated ion channels that elicit a depolarization. This synaptic depolarization is an excitatory post-synaptic potential ('epsp', pronounced "e - p - s - p"). If enough IA fibers and their synapses are active, the combined synaptic potential is large enough to generate an action potential in the cell body of the α-motorneuron and its axon.

The action potential in the axon of the α-motorneuron travels peripherally, again through the femoral nerve, to the neuromuscular junctions (nmjs) on muscle fibers in the quadriceps. A motor axon is indistinguishable functionally from a sensory axon in the sense that both axons can carry action potentials in either direction. Under normal circumstances, action potentials in the IA fibers are generated in the spindles and travel to the spinal cord, while those in the motorneurons are generated in the spinal cord and travel peripherally. Each α-motorneuron makes one nmj on each of, typically, many tens to hundreds of muscle fibers in its motor unit. Thus, this α-motorneuron and its innervated muscle fibers constitute a *large* motor unit.

As discussed in Chapter 11: (i) the nerve ending of the α-motorneuron is the presynaptic element of the nmj and the muscle fiber is the postsynaptic element; (ii) activity in the nmj causes a local depolarization of the muscle fiber, the endplate potential (epp), at the muscle membrane located opposite the nerve ending; and (iii) the epp triggers an action potential in the muscle fiber, just as did the generator potential in the IA axon and the epsp in the α-motorneuron. Because the safety factor for generation of the muscle action potential is large, an action potential in the α-motorneuron will, under normal circumstances, reliably initiate an action potential in all of the muscle fibers in its motor unit.

As described in Chapter 12, the action potential in each muscle cell of the active motor unit propagates from the muscle endplate to both ends of the fiber; simultaneously, it invades the transverse tubules and initiates Ca^{2+} release from the sarcoplasmic reticulum throughout the fiber volume. The released Ca^{2+} activates the contractile apparatus, causing the fibers to generate force and to shorten. Shortening of the muscle fibers cancels out the stretch that initiated the reflex a few milliseconds before. Thus, this reflex functions as a rapid *negative feedback* control loop. The purpose of the reflex is to maintain posture: if the knee starts to buckle, the quadriceps is stretched, and a reflex contraction ensues that serves to re-extend the knee. All skeletal muscles, as well as eye muscles, have very similar stretch reflexes, which are essential for accurate control of posture and movement.

14.2 DETAILS OF THE STRETCH REFLEX

Spindles. The spindles relay information to the spinal cord about muscle length and how fast muscle length is changing. Each spindle, of which there are many in the quadriceps, contains several small spindle muscle fibers (i.e., intrafusal fibers), roughly a centimeter long. Each spindle fiber functions as a component of an adjustable sensory organ. In essence, it serves as an adjustable elastic scaffold around which the spiral ending of the sensory nerve fiber is wrapped (Fig. 14.2).

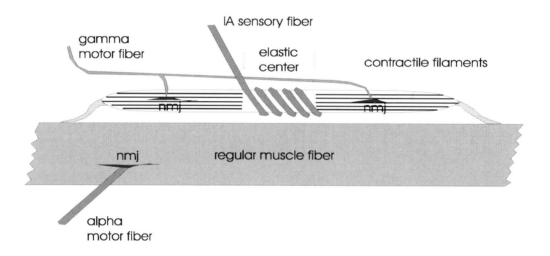

Figure 14.2 Diagram of a spindle muscle fiber in relation to a regular muscle fiber. The spindle fiber is innervated by both a sensory neuron and a motorneuron. (Note: a nerve axon is also called a nerve 'fiber'.)

The adjustability is provided by the fiber's contractile filaments, which are located mainly away from the center of the spindle fiber, toward its tapered ends. The tiny tendons at the ends of each spindle fiber insert onto the connective tissue surrounding the regular muscle fibers (i.e., the extrafusal fibers). The regular fibers are much stronger than the spindle fibers and much longer, extending from tendon to tendon. Because of the attachments of the spindle fiber to the connective tissue of the regular muscle fibers, the length of the spindle fiber is determined by the length of the much stronger regular fibers. Since the regular fiber is uniform, the part to which the spindle fiber is attached is representative of the whole regular fiber, and, should the regular fiber shorten or lengthen, the spindle fiber will also shorten or lengthen. Mechanically speaking, the spindle fiber is organized in parallel with the regular muscle fiber.

The spindle fiber's contractile filaments are made up of actin and myosin. As mentioned, the center of the spindle fiber has few filaments; rather, it is elastic. Spiraling around the elastic center is the ending of a sensory nerve fiber. Some spindle fibers have class IA sensory axons attached to their endings, and others have class II axons (which are smaller than class I). Class II endings are usually to the side of the elastic center and do not have a spiral ending. We focus here on the class I fibers. When the muscle lengthens, the spindle fiber is stretched with it. The stretch is concentrated on the elastic center and hence the IA ending, because the contractile ends of the spindle fiber resist stretch. The stretch of the spiral ending of the nerve cell causes it to depolarize (see below); as noted above, this depolarization is called a generator potential. The generator potential is localized to the vicinity of the nerve ending and spreads only a mm or two along the nerve cell away from the ending. If the depolarization is large enough, however, it will drive to threshold the membrane potential of the nearby region of cell membrane that contains a high concentration of voltage-dependent sodium channels, thus setting off an action potential. This region is the location of the 'node of Ranvier' that is nearest to the spiral ending.

The nodes of Ranvier are short regions of axon that lack the myelin that covers the bulk of the IA axon (see below); they are found approximately every 1-2 mm along the length of the axon. At each node, the myelin disappears and a short region of axon membrane, which contains a high concentration of voltage-dependent sodium channels, is uncovered and exposed to the ECF. The action potential generated at the first node of Ranvier moves electrotonically (i.e., passively, according to cable theory) along the myelinated portion of the axon to the next node, where the amplitude of the action potential is reinforced by inward sodium current, which reinforces the further spread of the action potential, and so forth at successive nodes along the way. This method of propagation is called 'saltatory conduction' ('saltatory' means 'jumping') and contrasts with the type of uniform propagation that occurs in unmyelinated axons such as the squid giant axon and the smallest-diameter axons found in vertebrate animals. This action potential propagates rapidly along the myelinated axon to the spinal cord, and the information carried by the action potential is that "a stretch has occurred" in the IA cell.

Adjustability. As mentioned, the sensitivity of the spindle is adjustable. With contractile filaments present, the mechanism is simple. Suppose the two ends of a spindle fiber are held in a fixed position by their attachments to the regular muscle fiber, which is a very strong cell and resists a change in its length. If the membrane of the spindle fiber is depolarized, there will be a rise in myoplasmic $[Ca^{2+}]$ and shortening of the sarcomeres on the myofilaments, which are found mainly towards the ends of the spindle fiber. This shortening stretches out the central elastic portion where the IA ending is located, thus heightening its sensitivity to any additional stretch.

Depolarization of the spindle fiber is brought about by activity in the small γ-motorneuron ('γ' in this context means 'small', with an axon diameter of 4-8 μm), which synapses on the two ends of the spindle fiber. γ-motorneurons are completely different in function and connections from the α-motorneurons. Like α-motorneurons, the cell bodies of γ-motorneurons are located in the ventral horn of the spinal cord (Fig. 14.1). Unlike α-motorneurons, γ-motorneurons innervate only the contractile ends of the spindle fibers and have no connection to the regular muscle fibers. Further, the γ-motorneurons are activated by a completely different pathway; for example, they do not receive synaptic input from the IA sensory fibers. Instead, their primary input is from the higher centers in the brain -- the motor cortex and cerebellum -- that plan and control voluntary movement.

Importance of Adjustability. Consider what would happen if there were no adjustability in the spindle. Suppose that the brain commanded a movement that required a substantial shortening of the quadriceps by means of activation of its α-motorneurons. As shortening proceeded, the spindle fibers would shorten proportionally, taking tension off the spiral ending in the center and decreasing its sensitivity to stretch. Eventually the point would be reached at which the sensory ending would be slack. At this point there would be no feedback from the muscle about further changes in length, and movement would be in danger of becoming clumsy. To prevent this, the γ-motorneurons are commanded to fire by the higher brain centers that plan the voluntary movement -- so-called 'α - γ linkage' -- and the firing of action potentials by the γ-motorneuron causes the contractile ends of the spindle fibers to shorten, taking up the slack. Then, even though the overall length of the spindle fiber decreases as the regular muscle fibers shorten, the center of the spindle fiber remains tense, maintaining the sensitivity of the IA ending. Thus, the input from the γ-motorneuron makes it possible for the spindle to send information to the spinal cord about the muscle position and length over a wide range of motion.

Notice that, in principle, there are two ways that the brain could command the regular muscle fibers to shorten: by directly activating the α-motorneurons or, indirectly, by activating the γ-motorneurons. The latter path would cause a contraction of the ends of the spindle fibers, activation of the IA ending, and hence a reflex contraction of the regular muscle fibers. In fact, this seems not to happen. Rather, the brain directly activates the α-motorneurons to cause muscle shortening, and at the same time activates the γ-motorneurons so the spindle fibers can maintain their intended function.

The IA Sensory Ending in the Spindle. This ending, which spirals around the elastic center of the spindle fiber, contains mechanically-sensitive ion channels that open in response to stretch. These channels are non-selective cation channels, with a P_{Na}/P_K ratio of approximately 1. As for the channels at the nmj, when they open, the flow of cation current will depolarize the nerve ending because entry of Na^+ will exceed efflux of K^+, thereby producing the generator potential.

The Axon and Cell Body of the IA Sensory Nerve. The cell body ('soma') attached to this axon is located outside the spinal cord, in a nearby ganglion, the dorsal root ganglion (DRG). From the soma, a single axon extends for a short distance and then branches (Fig. 14.3). One branch goes into the spinal cord (a short distance away), the other out to the spindle (a long distance away).

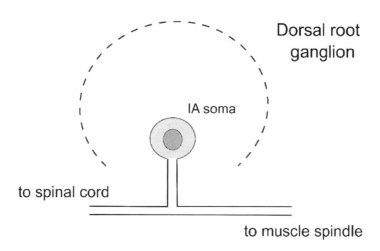

Figure 14.3 Schematic showing the location of the cell body of a IA sensory nerve in a dorsal root ganglion (DRG), which is located outside the spinal cord.

An action potential initiated by the spiral ending in a spindle travels straight to the spinal cord; it also happens to invade the soma, but this has no function for the reflex. The soma has no synapses; its functions include metabolic support, including synthesis of proteins. The ending of the IA axon in the ventral horn is, like all chemical synapses, a tiny voltage-controlled secretory organ. The purpose here is to release glutamate, which is packaged in vesicles. Once released, the glutamate diffuses a short distance across the synaptic cleft and acts on receptor molecules located in the membrane of the α-motorneuron. Again, these receptors molecules are chemically-sensitive cation channels that open in response to the binding of transmitter, causing an epsp in the α-motorneuron.

Information Carried by the Sensory Axons. As noted, an action potential in the IA fiber signals that the muscle has lengthened. But what kind of length change is signaled: small or large, slowly or quickly developing? The answer is that the pattern of action-potential firing conveys information not only about the size of the length change but also about the rate of change of length ('velocity').

This information is diagrammed schematically in Fig. 14.4. It is supposed that the muscle is stretched at uniform speed for a brief time, after which the muscle length is maintained constant (trace labeled 'Length').

In Fig. 14.4A, the frequency of firing in the IA axon (upper traces) has, for didactic purposes, been decomposed into its length (i.e., position) component and its dynamic (i.e., velocity) component. The length component depends only on the total stretch. The velocity component is small for a slow stretch, large for a fast one. True velocity is only approximated by the velocity component of firing.

The actual firing frequency, which is approximated by the upper trace in Fig. 14.4B, is the sum of these two components. The frequency is low at rest, rises to a peak during lengthening, and, once the length change is complete, settles out to a lower steady value that is proportional to the length change.

[Note: some spindle fibers are innervated by smaller axons (type II axons) that convey only a length signal. These spindle fibers are histologically distinct, but we will ignore the details.]

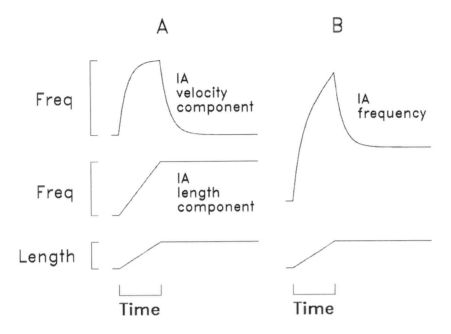

Figure 14.4 Schematic of the time-dependence of action potential firing by IA sensory axons in response to a sudden increase in the length of the muscle (lowest traces). A. The frequency of firing (upper two traces, left) includes components proportional to the length change and, with some adaptation, to the rate of change of length (velocity component). B. The overall IA firing frequency (upper trace, right) is the sum of the length component and the velocity component.

The α-motorneuron and its Synaptic Inputs. Fig. 14.5 shows a drawing of an α-motorneuron. It has five general regions:

- The <u>dendrites</u> extend from the soma or cell body to receive synaptic input from the various sources that influence generation of action potentials by the α-motorneuron.
- The <u>soma</u> itself also receives synaptic input, and provides general metabolic support to the remainder of the cell.
- The unmyelinated <u>initial segment</u> of axon, which emerges from the axon hillock (a slight bulge between the soma and the initial segment), has a high concentration of Na$^+$ channels and is thought to be the site where action potentials are initiated. The initial segment also receives many 'inhibitory' synapses. As the name implies, inhibitory synapses function to inhibit action-potential generation.
- The <u>axon</u> is the output pathway of the α-motorneuron and can extend for as much as a meter to reach the cells in its motor unit; it is myelinated for most of this distance.

- The axon terminal is the unmyelinated branching termination of the α-motorneuron, which synapses onto the various muscle cells in the motor unit.

As noted, the main function of the nerve terminals is the secretion of neurotransmitter, in this case, acetylcholine.

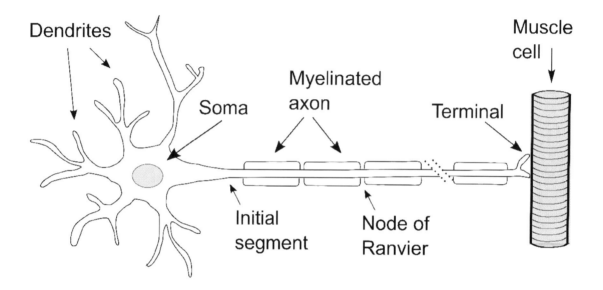

Figure 14.5 Schematic of an α-motorneuron, with anatomical regions labeled; termination is at a synapse on a skeletal muscle cell (only one fiber in the multi-cell motor unit is diagrammed). The pair of diagonal dotted lines denotes a break in the depiction of the long myelinated axon.

A major task carried out in the soma is the bio-synthesis of the ion channels that underlie the signaling capabilities of the cell. These proteins are inserted directly into the membrane of the endoplasmic reticulum (ER) as they are synthesized. Vesicles carrying the membrane proteins bud off from the ER and travel to the Golgi apparatus for further processing, e.g., glycosylation. The finished proteins are carried in vesicles that bud off from the Golgi and are transported to specific destinations in dendrite, soma, or axon.

There is a continuous traffic of vesicles being inserted into the surface membrane by exocytosis, and of material being taken back from the membrane in endocytotic vesicles. The latter may contain not only membrane proteins but also useful substances such as signaling molecules absorbed from the extracellular fluid. Membrane proteins destined for the axons and nerve terminal are carried by specific transport systems to locations as much as a meter away. There is also a retrograde system for carrying the absorbed substances and proteins destined for recycling from the nerve terminal or dendrites back to the soma. The plasmalemma of the large axon is wrapped with myelin (see next section). As noted in Chapter 5, myelin functions as an electrical insulator to lower membrane capacitance and thus improve the electrical signal-carrying abilities of the axon as well as improve its metabolic efficiency.

The Nmj and the Regular Muscle Fibers. The function of these elements should be clear from previous discussions, including Chapters 11 and 12.

Overall, the Stretch Reflex Provides Negative Feedback on Length and Velocity. Because the reflex has a sensor for both muscle length and velocity, when length and/or velocity of lengthening increases, the reflex causes a control action of opposite sign: the muscle contracts, or contracts more strongly, to counteract the change. Conversely, if the muscle should shorten on its own, for example, in response to a sudden lightening of the load, action potentials in the reflex arc will decrease, thus promoting lengthening by exerting a relaxing effect on muscle tone due to a reduction in firing in the sensory axons and hence in the α-motorneurons.

It should be noted that a strong stretch reflex will occur if there are many good reasons for the γ-motorneurons to fire (i.e., lots of excitatory input from the spindle afferents) and no reason not to fire. On the other hand, even if the excitatory input from the spindle afferents is strong, input from inhibitory interneurons might override the excitatory input. For example, if one were to step on a hot coal at the same time that the knee was buckling, the buckling might continue due to inhibition of the stretch reflex through signals from pain receptors on the bottom of the foot.

14.3 MORE ABOUT MYELINATION

Myelination of nerve axons is one of the great evolutionary discoveries of vertebrates; a few members of invertebrate phyla also discovered myelination. In an unmyelinated axon, such as the squid giant axon, the action potential propagates in a spatially continuous (smooth) fashion along the axon, as discussed in Chapter 8. An important limitation that applies to this mechanism is that, to achieve a fast speed of propagation, the unmyelinated axon needs to be of large diameter. In the case of the squid giant axon, the fast propagation velocity of 25-50 meters/sec is achieved because of the large diameter of the axon, 0.5 to 1 mm. While achievement of a fast propagation velocity by means of a large axon is an acceptable solution for the squid, which requires only a small number of high-speed axons, it represents an unacceptable volume requirement for a vertebrate animal, which requires large numbers of high-speed axons to control the many different motor units within its many different skeletal muscles. Myelination is the solution found by evolution to meet the simultaneous requirements of a small diameter axon and a fast propagation speed.

As mentioned, regions of active membrane with voltage-dependent sodium channels are located primarily at the nodes of Ranvier rather than extending uniformly along the axon's length, as occurs in an unmyelinated axon. The regions between the nodes of Ranvier ('internodal regions') have been wrapped many times during development by Schwann cells, which are neuronal support cells, with the result that the internodal regions have many layers of insulating membrane between the intracellular and extracellular solutions. Myelin is the final result of this insulation process (Fig. 14.6). Chemically, myelin is about 40% water; the non-water components are ~75% lipid and ~25% protein.

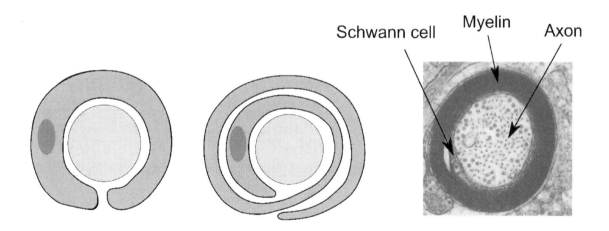

Figure 14.6 Developmental changes in the internodal regions of a myelinated axon (transverse view). Left: myelination begins with a support cell known as a Schwann cell (darker gray, with nucleus shown) wrapping around a nerve axon (lighter gray). Middle: during development, the Schwann cell wraps around the axon many times. Right: the final result is that the internodal region contains many layers of Schwann-cell membrane that separate the ICF from the ECF. [Credit: Raine (1984); magnification, 32,000.]

Since the pathway to ground for current flow across the internodal region must cross many lipid bilayers rather than just one, electrically the internodal region has (i) a greatly increased effective resistance, since resistances encountered in series are additive, and (ii) a greatly reduced effective capacitance, since capacitance is inversely proportional to the distance between the conducting regions, i.e., between the solutions on the inside and outside of the cell, which, because of the myelination, are far apart. The reduction in membrane capacitance of the internode is the more important of the two effects. The lowered capacitance means that less ionic current is required to charge and discharge the membrane capacitance as the action currents spread along the interior and exterior of the axon during propagation. The increased membrane resistance of the intermodal region implies that the space constant λ ($= \sqrt{r_m/(r_i+r_o)}$; see Chapter 7) for spread of an electrical signal is larger than would otherwise apply, since it is more difficult for current to leak out of the cell interior across r_m. The combined effect is to greatly improve the speed of propagation of the action potential.

At each node, the opening of the Na^+ channels generates inward current to drive continued spread of the action potential along the axon. At comparable temperatures, a propagation speed of 25 m/sec can be attained by a 16 μm diameter myelinated axon compared with a 500 μm diameter unmyelinated axon, which represents approximately a 1000-fold smaller volume requirement. Conversely, for an identical axon diameter of 16 μm, a myelinated axon conducts its action potential 5-10 times faster than an unmyelinated axon.

For axon diameters below about 1 μm, the unmyelinated axon usually conducts its action potential faster than a myelinated axon; thus, below this diameter, axons are usually unmyelinated.

Besides the increase in speed of propagation of the action potential, a major advantage of myelination over non-myelination is less energy consumption per action potential. Since the average membrane capacitance per unit length is many times smaller in a myelinated axon than an unmyelinated axon, the net entry of Na^+ ions per unit length of axon to produce a 100 mV depolarization is also many times smaller in the myelinated axon. Thus, much less ATP consumption is required by the Na^+/K^+ pumps on the surface membrane to re-establish the Na^+ and K^+ concentration gradients that power the action potential, which are dissipated slightly during each impulse.

14.4 RECIPROCAL INNERVATION

Most joints have one set of muscles to extend the joint, and another set of muscles -- an opposing or 'antagonistic' set -- to flex it. Extending a joint, then, involves not only exciting the extensors but inhibiting (turning off) the flexors. The nerves for this control rely on an anatomical arrangement called 'reciprocal innervation' (Fig. 14.7).

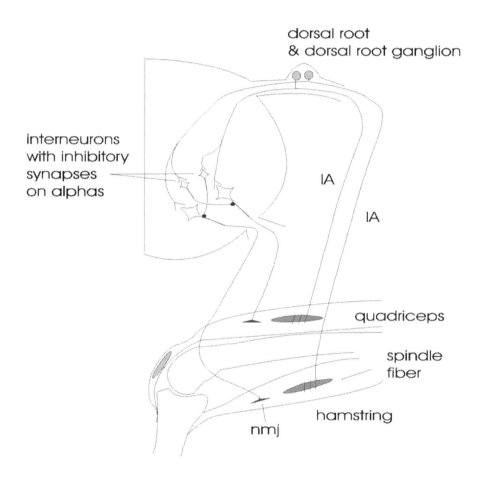

Figure 14.7 Anatomical arrangement for reciprocal innervation of muscles about the knee joint.

The inhibition makes use of interneurons in the spinal cord that, when excited, release the inhibitory neurotransmitter glycine onto α-motorneurons, in this case, to the flexors. The glycine released by the inhibitory interneuron generates an inhibitory postsynaptic potential ('ipsp') that slows the firing of the α-motorneuron, thus tending to relax the flexors. The ipsp is caused by the opening of chloride channels, which pass chloride current to keep V_m below threshold for the action potential. In the case of the antagonistic pair of muscles found at the knee joint, a tap to the patellar tendon will increase firing in the α-motorneurons going to the quadriceps and decrease firing in the α-motorneurons going to the hamstrings, thus allowing the antagonistic muscles to work in a coordinated fashion. The complementary activation and inhibition pattern occurs when the flexors are called to action.

14.5 THE GOLGI TENDON ORGAN

The Golgi tendon organ is another type of mechanically-sensitive sensory organ found in skeletal muscles. It is interposed between the regular muscle fibers and the tendon (Fig. 14.8) and serves as a force sensor. The nerve endings of the organ are buried within the tendon, and there are many of them in most muscles.

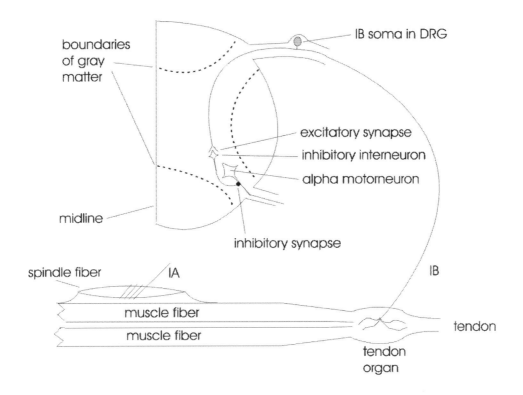

Figure 14.8 Anatomical arrangement that mediates inhibitory effects by the Golgi tendon organ and the IB sensory cell.

Conceptually, the tendon organ is simply an elastic element that is stretched when the fibers within the muscle produce force -- similar to the central part of a spindle fiber minus the contractile ends. Mechanically, however, the tendon organ is in series with the muscle fibers and the tendon. Its purpose is to keep track of the force produced by the muscle fibers -- obviously a quite different function from the spindle, which reports length and velocity of lengthening. The tendon organ is innervated by a large and therefore fast-conducting sensory nerve fiber called 'IB' (pronounced "one b"; also written 'Ib'); I because it's large (12-20 µm diameter), and B because its sensory ending is in the tendon organ. There is no motor innervation to the organ.

Contraction of the muscle causes stretch of the sensory ending, which causes a generator potential that, if sufficiently large, generates action potentials in the IB fiber -- very similar to the events in the spindle. The larger the force, the larger the generator potential and thus the more frequent the generated action potentials. These action potentials travel back through the IB axon to the spinal cord, passing by the dorsal root ganglion where the cell body of the IB axon is located, and carry the message that "the force on the tendon is rising in the muscle". In the cord, the IB sends branches to higher brain centers and, most importantly for the discussion here, a branch that synapses on an inhibitory interneuron in the ventral horn. At the synaptic ending on this interneuron, an excitatory transmitter, probably glutamate, is released. This causes an epsp in the dendrites of the interneuron, leading to an action potential in the interneuron axon. This action potential travels a short distance to reach a synapse on an α-motorneuron going back to the same muscle. This second synapse is inhibitory; the likely inhibitory transmitter, again, is glycine.

Overall, the Golgi tendon organ and its connections provide *negative feedback* on force. Thus, an increase in muscle force leads by this pathway to a relaxation of the muscle. The most dramatic use is to prevent the muscle from tearing its tendon from bone, but it is also essential for control of forces employed in delicate motions.

14.6 PATHOLOGY AFFECTING THE MUSCLE REFLEX ARC

If injury, e.g., due to a stroke, compromises certain motor centers in the brain, spasticity and/or rigidity can result because of altered function of the muscle spindle. Both symptoms can be explained by excessive firing of γ-motorneurons. Spasticity occurs as a result of exaggerated tendon reflexes, which causes jerky motion of the limbs. This 'hyperreflexia' results from an excessive firing rate in the γ-motorneurons that innervate the spindle fibers that support IA endings. The excessive γ-firing leads to hypersensitivity of the IA endings, which then give abnormally large signals in response to quick changes of muscle length. Rigidity, in contrast, is the result of excess firing in the γ-motorneurons innervating spindle fibers that support class II sensory endings, which respond only to length, not the rate of change of length. As a result, the type II sensory fibers fire rapidly and steadily, which causes a steady excessive drive to the α-motorneurons. This produces a 'tonic' (i.e., steady) contraction of the normal muscle fibers -- hence rigidity.

14.7 EXERCISES

Exercise 14.1 The text states that the initial segment of an α-motorneuron is a site where this neuron receives substantial inhibitory inputs. Why would this be a particularly effective location for the placement of inhibitory synapses -- e.g., compared with locations somewhere on the dendritic tree of the α-motorneuron?

Exercise 14.2 Figs. 14.7 and 14.8 show that the effect of an inhibitory interneuron to suppress firing of the α-motorneuron is by means of an inhibitory action on the membrane of the initial segment of the α-motorneuron. If the inhibitory neuron were to make contact on the terminal ending of the IA sensory axon that drives this α-motorneuron and reduce the peak of the action potential in that nerve terminal, would this action also be expected to reduce the ability of the α-motorneuron to generate an action potential?

Exercise 14.3 Suppose that an action potential at room temperature propagates along a myelinated nerve at 25 m/s and that the time between the half-rise and half-decay of the AP is 0.4 ms. Recall that a temporal waveform propagating in space has the same shape in the space domain as in the time domain after an appropriate scaling factor is applied to relate the two domains. If the spacing between the nodes of Ranvier along the axon is 1.5 mm, how many nodes are included between the half-rise and half-decay of the spatial waveform of the AP? Would it make sense physiologically that the propagation of the AP along the myelinated axon would depend on the inward current generated at more than one node?

APPENDIX A

INSTALLATION OF PYTHON 3

Python exists in two main versions, Python 2 and Python 3. They have some incompatibilities and the use of Python 3 in combination with a package called 'Anaconda3' is recommended. For a free download, go to either www.python.org or www.anaconda.com. Instructions are given there for an open-source distribution of Python 3 and Anaconda3 for Windows, Mac, and Linux platforms. The distribution from either site is similar, as is the installation process for the different platforms. A summary of the installation process for a Windows platform is given below in two parts; similar processes should apply to the other platforms. Part A is for machines running Windows 7 or Windows 10 and part B is for machines running Windows XP. **Note, however, that the details of the installation procedure will undoubtedly vary over time.**

For installation information on other platforms (and for more installation information on a Windows platform), the website: https://fangohr.github.io/blog/ is recommended At this site, click the 'Python' tab, then the link opposite the section '2016, September 14' entitled 'Installation of Spyder, Numpy, Sympy, Scipy, Pytest, Matplotlib via Anaconda (2016)'. The reader may wish to read this installation information in conjunction with the information in parts A or B below before proceeding with an actual installation.

A. Installation of Python 3 on a Machine Running Windows 7 or Windows 10. At the time of this writing (2019), the latest version of *Python* available for these platforms is Python 3.7.2. Use of the Integrated Development Environment (IDE) called *Spyder* that is part of the Anaconda3 package and comes with the download is highly recommended.

- At www.python.org, under Downloads, choose Windows, and click the option to download. This selects a version of *Python* that is packaged with Anaconda3. The file that is downloaded for a Windows 64-bit machine is named 'Anaconda3-2018.12-Windows-x86-64.exe', whereas that for a Windows 32-bit machine is named 'Anaconda3-2018.12-Windows-x86.exe'. (The names may differ in years later than 2019.)

- Go to the download directory on your machine and double-click on the appropriate download file; say 'yes' to the question about proceeding with the installation.

- Wait some minutes as the installation and setup process is carried out. It ends with a message that the setup was successfully completed. (Feel free to skip the installation of code for MS Visual Studio if you are asked and do not plan to use this).

- Find the program 'Anaconda Navigator' on your machine (it may be in the sub-directory 'c:\Users\ ...\Appdata\local\continuum\Anaconda3') and run it. On the home tab in the App pane on the right, scroll to the *Spyder* title and click the 'install' button. At the time of writing (2019), this installs *Spyder* 3.3.2.

- Within Anaconda Navigator, click on the Launch Tile for *Spyder*, which brings up the *Spyder* IDE. This will be your working environment for writing and running *Python* programs. The Editor is shown on the left-hand side. On the upper right-hand side is a pane with tabs for Variable Explorer, File Explorer, and Help. On the lower right-hand side is a pane with the IPython Console. Note that the top line of the IPython Console gives the version of *Python* that is running. With this console, you are now in contact with the *Python* Interpreter and you can start typing in commands to *Python*. For example, on the Console line that says 'In[1]', try typing '2+3' followed by the 'enter' key and see if the Console responds '5'. If so, you are off and running.

- You may want to pin Anaconda Navigator to your task bar to allow for quick launchings of *Spyder* by means of Anaconda Navigator.

Several More Things
With the *Spyder* IDE running, go to the menu bar at the top and click on Tools and then Preferences. On the left-hand side of the new window, click on 'Current working directory'. This will open a new pane on the right-hand side to allow you to set the current working directory. Below the heading 'Console directory', under "The working directory for new consoles is:", select the button that says 'the following directory' and, in the option box, enter the name of the directory where you would like to load and save your *Python* programs. This will now be your default directory when you work with *Python*. You can still access and run *Python* programs from any other directory on your computer.

While still in the Preferences window (or go back to it if you have closed it), on the left-hand side, click on 'IPython Console'. In the new pane on the right-hand side, select the 'Graphics' tab. Under the panel 'Graphics backend', change the 'Backend' option from 'Inline' to 'Automatic'. This will allow graphics plots to appear in their own window rather than be plotted 'inline', i.e., as output to the Console. When in their own window, plots have available extra tools that are not available inline, including zooming in on, moving, and rotating figures. A very useful feature is that, by positioning the cursor on a plotted curve, you can also see a readout of x-y data values on curves.

While still in the Preferences window, on the left-hand side, click on 'Editor' and, on the right-hand side, select the 'Advanced settings' tab and click on 'Edit template for new modules'. This will bring up in the Editor a file called 'template.py'. It contains several suggested "good-practice" comment lines with which to start all of your *Python* programs. (That they are comment lines is indicated by their enclosure within three double quotes. Such program files are also called "script files".) The suggested lines include one for automatic date creation (because of the presence of the characters "%(date)s") and another for automatic author identification (because of the presence of the characters "%(username)s"). You can now close the Preferences window.

Next click on the Editor panel -- or you can do this at a later time -- and add any other initial lines to 'template.py' that you would like to appear at the start of your programs. These can be additional comment lines or actual coding lines. Then save 'template.py' in the usual way. [Note: 'template.py' is saved in a directory different from your working directory. However, when you are in the Editor at normal times and open a new program file (e.g. by hitting 'Ctrl' + 'n'), the contents of 'template.py' will be brought up under a name such as 'untitled0.py', and the "%(date)s" and "%(username)s" fields will be filled in automatically with values of the date and user name. You can then save this file in your working directory under the name of your choice and begin entering your new script.]

To make active these three changes to 'Preferences', close *Spyder* and relaunch it. You are now ready to starting writing and running your own script *Python* programs. For more information about proceeding, see Chapters 3 and 4. Also recommended is the book by Kinder and Nelson (*A Student's Guide to Python for Physical Modeling*). Among other things, the appendices in that book include information about error messages and recovering from errors and how *Python* handles variables and objects internally, implements functions, and keeps track of the scope of variables.

B. Installation of Python 3 on a Machine Running Windows XP. At the time of this writing (2019), the version of *Python* that is available for this platform is Python 3.4

- Go to 'https://repo.continuum.io/archive/' and download 'Anaconda3-2.3.0-Windows-x86.exe'.
- Find 'Anaconda3-2.3.0-Windows-x86.exe' in your download directory and run it; select the option "install for me". The installation will go to a new directory, 'C:\Anaconda3'.

- Within a command-prompt window, go to 'C:\Anaconda3' and type 'conda update conda'. This will provide any necessary updates to your installation.

- Set up a shortcut to 'C:\Anaconda3\Scripts\spyder.exe' and then run it. This will launch your working environment for writing and running *Python* programs. On first launch, it may take several minutes to bring up the *Spyder* IDE. You will now see 3 main panes in the IDE. The Editor is shown on the left-hand side. On the upper right-hand side is a pane with tabs for Object Inspector, Variable Explorer, and File Explorer. On the lower right-hand side is a pane with the IPython Console. The top line of the IPython Console gives the version of *Python* that is running, e.g., Python 3.4.3. With this console, you are now in contact with the *Python* Interpreter and you can start typing in commands to *Python*. For example, on the Console line that says 'In[1]', try typing in '2+3' followed by the 'enter' key and see if the Console responds '5'. If so, you are off and running. **Note**: the initial output lines to the Console give some tips for getting information about available features in *Python* and *Spyder,* including a quick reference guide, a help guide, and a brief reference about the graphical user interface.

Several More Things
Go to the menu bar at the top of the *Spyder* IDE and click on Tools and then Preferences. On the left-hand side of the new window, click on 'Global working directory'. This will open a new pane on the right-hand side. Under the panel 'Startup', select 'the following directory' and enter the name of the directory where you would like to load and save your *Python* programs. This will now be your default directory for working with *Python*. (You can still access and run *Python* programs from any other directory on your computer.)

While still in the Preferences window (or go back to it if you have closed it), on the left-hand side of the new window, click on 'IPython Console'. In the new pane on the right-hand side, select the 'Graphics' tab. Under the panel 'Graphics backend', change the 'Backend' option from 'Inline' to 'Automatic' and click 'ok'. This will allow graphics plots to appear in their own window rather than 'inline', i.e., as output to the Console. When in their own window, plots have available extra tools that are not available inline, including zooming, moving, and rotating figures; by positioning the cursor on a plotted curve, you can also see a readout of x-y data values on curves.

While still in the Preferences window, on the left-hand side, click on 'Editor' and, on the right-hand side, select the 'Advanced settings' tab and click on 'Edit template for new modules' and click 'ok'. This will bring up a file called 'template.py' in the Editor. It has several suggested "good-practice" comment lines to start all of your *Python* programs. (That they are comment lines is indicated by their enclosure within three double quotes. Such program files are also called "script files".) The suggested lines include one for automatic date creation (because of the presence of the characters "%(date)s") and another for automatic author identification (because of the presence of the characters "%(username)s"). You can now close the Preferences window.

Next click on the Editor panel -- or you can do this at a later time--and add any other initial lines that you would like to appear at the start of your programs. These can be additional comment lines or actual coding lines. Then save 'template.py' in the usual way. [Note: 'template.py' is saved in a directory different from your working directory. However, when you are in the Editor at normal times and open a new program file (e.g. by hitting 'Ctrl' + 'n'), the contents of 'template.py' will be brought up under a name such as 'untitled0.py', and the "%(date)s" and "%(username)s" fields will be filled in automatically with current values of the date and user name. You can then save this file in your working directory under the name of your choice and begin entering your new script.]

To make active these changes to 'Preferences', close *Spyder* and relaunch it. You are now ready to starting writing and running your own script *Python* programs. For more information about proceeding, see Chapters 3 and 4. Also recommended is the book by Kinder and Nelson (*A Student's Guide to Python for Physical Modeling*). Among other things, the appendices in that book include information about error messages and recovering from errors and how *Python* handles variables and objects internally, implements functions, and keeps track of the scope of variables.

APPENDIX B

DERIVATION OF FICK'S FIRST AND SECOND LAWS OF DIFFUSION

Fick's First Law

Consider an imaginary rectangular boundary of area A located at x0 along an axis, x, within a medium, e.g., water, that contains molecules of a specific type (Fig. B.1). Let $N(x0 - \Delta x/2)$ denote the number of molecules at a distance $\Delta x/2$ in the –x direction from the boundary and $N(x0 + \Delta x/2)$ denote the number of molecules at distance $\Delta x/2$ in the +x direction from the boundary.

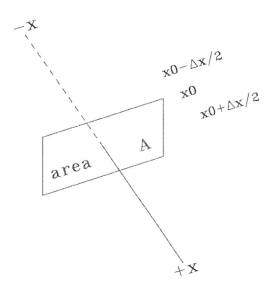

Figure B.1 Diffusion in one-dimension across a boundary of area A that is perpendicular to x.

Suppose that, due to thermal motion, in each small time interval Δt, each molecule moves randomly a distance Δx in either the -x or +x direction (i.e., along the direction perpendicular to the boundary) from its initial position. (We ignore movements in the y and z dimensions.) Then, during Δt, half the molecules at $x0 - \Delta x/2$ move a distance Δx in the -x direction (and therefore none of these cross the boundary A) and half the molecules move a distance Δx in the +x direction (and therefore all of these cross the boundary A); and, similarly, for the molecules at $x0 + \Delta x/2$. The net number of molecules that cross the boundary in the +x direction in Δt is then $(N(x0-\Delta x/2) - N(x0+\Delta x))/2$. Thus, the estimated flux J across the boundary in the +x direction during the interval Δt is:

$$J = - \frac{N\left(x_o + \frac{\Delta x}{2}\right) - N\left(x - \frac{\Delta x}{2}\right)}{2 A \Delta t} . \quad (B.1)$$

Let $C(x0-\Delta x/2)$ and $C(x0+\Delta x/2)$ denote the concentration of the molecules at $x0-\Delta x/2$ and $x0+\Delta x/2$, respectively. Then, $C(x0-\Delta x/2) = N(x0-\Delta x/2)/(A \cdot \Delta x)$ and $C(x0+\Delta x/2) = N(x0+\Delta x/2)/(A \cdot \Delta x)$. Rewriting Eqn. B.1 in concentration units, we have:

$$J = - \frac{\Delta x \left(C\left(x0 + \frac{\Delta x}{2}\right) - C\left(x0 - \frac{\Delta x}{2}\right)\right)}{2 \Delta t} = - \frac{\Delta x \, \Delta x \left(C\left(x0 + \frac{\Delta x}{2}\right) - C\left(x0 - \frac{\Delta x}{2}\right)\right)}{2 \Delta t \, \Delta x} . \quad (B.2)$$

Defining D (the diffusion coefficient) as $\Delta x^2/(2 \Delta t)$ and taking the limit as Δx and Δt approach zero, one obtains Fick's first law (Eqn. 2.2 in Chapter 2):

$$J = - D \frac{dC}{dx} , \quad (B.3)$$

where D has units of (distance)^2/time (e.g., cm^2/s).

It is not obvious that $\Delta x^2/(2 \Delta t)$ should converge to a defined number as Δx and Δt approach zero. However, Δx^2 and Δt are linearly related. Specifically, the average distance the molecules will move from their original location by random movements is related to the square root of the time allowed for the movement. For example, as shown in the program Example4_1.py at the end of Chapter 4, the average distance a molecule moves from its original position by random steps of a given size is proportional to the square root of the number of steps (the latter being a proxy for the time of the movement). Equivalently, time is proportional to the square of the displacement. Thus, it is reasonable to conclude that $\Delta x^2/(2 \Delta t)$ is constant as Δx and Δt approach zero, and therefore that D is a well-defined constant.

Fick's Second Law

Fick's second law follows from the first law and the assumption that the number of molecules is conserved. Consider the flux into and out of a box of volume $A \cdot \Delta x$ located at x0 (Fig. B.2).

DERIVATION OF FICK'S FIRST AND SECOND LAWS OF DIFFUSION

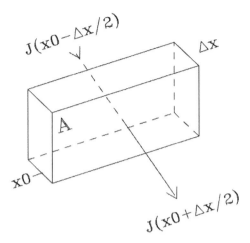

Figure B.2 Flux along the x dimension into and out of a box of volume $A \cdot \Delta x$.

Let $J(x0 - \Delta x/2)$ denote the flux that enters the box on the -x side during a time interval Δt, and let $J(x0 + \Delta x/2)$ denote the flux that exits the box on the +x side during Δt. Because (i) $C(x0) = N(x0)/(A \cdot \Delta x)$ and (ii) the number of molecules is conserved, we have, at x0, that:

$$\frac{C(t + \Delta t) - C(t)}{\Delta t} = \frac{(J(x0 - \Delta x/2) - J(x0 + \Delta x/2)) A \, \Delta t}{\Delta t \, A \, \Delta x}. \tag{B.4}$$

Thus:

$$\frac{C(t + \Delta t) - C(t)}{\Delta t} = - \frac{(J(x0 - \Delta x/2) - J(x0 + \Delta x/2))}{\Delta x}. \tag{B.5}$$

Taking the limits as Δx and Δt approach zero yields:

$$\left(\frac{\partial C}{\partial t}\right) = -\left(\frac{\partial J}{\partial x}\right). \tag{B.6}$$

Substituting from Eqn. B.3 gives:

$$\left(\frac{\partial C}{\partial t}\right) = D \left(\frac{\partial^2 C}{\partial x^2}\right), \tag{B.7}$$

which is Fick's second law for one dimensional diffusion (Eqn. 2.3 in Chapter 2).

APPENDIX C

DERIVATION OF THE NERNST EQUATION

This derivation follows that given by Bernard Katz in the book "Nerve, Muscle and Synapse". (For an alternative derivation, see Note 2 of Exercise 8.14.)

The Nernst equation applies to a particular ion species (e.g., Na^+, K^+, Cl^-, Ca^{2+}, etc.). It calculates the ion's equilibrium potential (E_{ion}) from the ion's concentrations on the two sides of the membrane, i.e., given that ion's concentrations, it calculates the value of membrane potential (V_m) at which that ion species would be at electrochemical equilibrium.

As noted in Chapter 1, according to the modern convention, V_m is defined as the electrical potential inside the cell with respect to that outside the cell. The general form of the Nernst equation (Eqn. 5.2, Chapter 5) is then usually written:

$$E_{ion} = \frac{RT}{zF} \ln\left(\frac{[ion]_o}{[ion]_i}\right). \tag{C.1}$$

E_{ion} is the equilibrium potential, R is the universal gas constant (8.3145 Joules K^{-1} $mole^{-1}$), T is temperature in degrees Kelvin (K), F is Faraday's constant (96,485 coulombs per mole), z is the charge on the ion species (+1 for K^+, -1 for Cl^-, +2 for Ca^{2+}, etc.), and $[ion]_o$ and $[ion]_i$ are the ion concentrations on the outside and inside of the membrane, respectively. In principle, ion activities rather than ion concentrations should be used in Eqn. C.1; however, the activity coefficient (which is used to scale concentration units to activity units) is approximately the same for ions on the two sides of the membrane and therefore cancels out in the equation.

The derivation relies on equating (i) the electrical work needed to move a specific quantity of ions across the membrane with (ii) the chemical work needed to move the same quantity of ions in the opposite direction. This equation is then solved for E_{ion}. To simplify, we deal with one mole of ions of valence z.

(i) The electrical work needed to move a mole of ions from inside to outside the cell at V_m is $-z \cdot F \cdot V_m$. At $E_{ion} = V_m$, the work is $-z \cdot F \cdot E_{ion}$. (Note: in terms of electrical work, a negative value of V_m means that energy must be supplied to move positively-charged ions from inside to outside; conversely, the movement of negatively-charged ions from inside to outside is a source of energy. And vice-versa for a positive value of V_m.)

(ii) The chemical work (equivalently, the osmotic work) to move a mole of ions from outside to inside the cell can be calculated from a consideration of an analogous case -- that of reversibly compressing a mole of an ideal gas. Suppose that a mole of gas is contained in a cylinder with a moveable piston of area A at one end. If Δx denotes a small displacement of the piston in the direction to concentrate the gas in the cylinder, an input of a small amount of mechanical work (Δw) is required. Because work is force times distance and because the force against which work is done during the displacement is pressure (P) times area, $\Delta w = P \cdot A \cdot \Delta x$. Equivalently, $\Delta w = - P \cdot \Delta V$, where ΔV denotes the change in the volume of the gas (a negative value in this case). We suppose that the gas is compressed slowly and reversibly (i.e., without heating) so that all of the work is directed to change the volume of the gas. Then, the total work W done in compressing the gas from an initial volume V0 to a final volume V1 is given by:

$$W = - \int_{V0}^{V1} P \, dV . \qquad (C.2)$$

From the gas law applied to one mole of gas, $PV = RT$. Hence $P = RT/V$ and:

$$W = - R T \int_{V0}^{V1} \frac{dV}{V} = R T \ln \left(\frac{V0}{V1}\right) . \qquad (C.3)$$

Because volume is inversely proportional to concentration:

$$W = R T \ln \left(\frac{C1}{C0}\right) , \qquad (C.4)$$

where C0 and C1 are the initial and final concentrations of the gas, respectively.

An analogous argument applies to the calculation of the chemical work to concentrate solute molecules in water. For example, we could imagine that the piston is a rigid membrane that is permeable only to water and separates two solutions whose solute concentrations are identical in the initial condition. Pressure is then applied slowly to one side of the piston to concentrate the solute on the other side by allowing the water to escape back to the side to which pressure is applied. Eqn. C.4 then gives the osmotic work to concentrate the solute.

Equating the electrical work with the chemical work gives $-z \cdot F \cdot E_{ion} = RT \ln (C1/C0)$. Substitution of $[ion]_i/[ion]_o$ for $C1/C0$ and rearrangement gives Eqn. C.1.

APPENDIX D

FITTING OF MODEL PARAMETERS IN PYTHON

As mentioned at the end of Chapter 3, when the parameters of a quantitative model are to be adjusted to fit a data set, it is common to use a least-squares fitting of the model to the data to obtain "best" estimates of the model's parameter values. In *Python,* the function 'curve_fit' from the 'scipy' module is available to do a least-squares fitting of this type.

The *Python* program below illustrates use of the function curve_fit. The example is based on the model and data set discussed in Sections 3.4 and 3.5 of Chapter 3. The model, which is defined by Eqn. 3.1, calculates a one-dimensional diffusion profile for the initial condition of a bolus of substance introduced into the middle of a long structure of small cross section -- in this example, for phenol red introduced into the middle of a frog skeletal muscle fiber. The data set, which is given in lines 8-9 of the program Example3_5.py, consists of the 7 ordered pairs of numbers specified by the np.arrays x1 and y1. The x values are the distances (in cm) from the site of injection of phenol red, and the y values are the concentrations (in mM) of phenol red at the corresponding locations. All measurements in this experiment were made at 100 min (= 6000 s) after the injection.

The program is listed next, followed by its graphical output, its printed output, and the Program Notes. The line numbers are not part of the program itself.

```
1  # -*- coding: utf-8 -*-
2  """
3  Python 3.7
4  Curvefit_dapp.py
5  Description: use scipy.optimize to fit Gaussian curve to phenol-red diffusion data
6  """
7
8  import numpy as np
9  import matplotlib.pyplot as plt
10 from scipy.optimize import curve_fit
11
12 #define the function for calculation of a Gaussian curve
13 def my_1D_gaussian(x,D,M):
```

```python
14  return M*np.exp(-x**2/(4*D*T))/(np.sqrt(4*np.pi*D*T))
15
16  #specify the data set for the phenol-red concentrations along the muscle fiber
17  x1=np.array([-0.090,-0.039,0,0.036,0.092,0.136,0.183])        #distance (cm)
18  y1=np.array([0.2810,0.5965,0.7184,0.6138,0.2939,0.0778,0.0259]) #conc. (mM)
19  T=6000    #time (s) after injection of phenol red into the muscle fiber
20
21  #plot the data set and print a header label for the inset
22  plt.plot(x1,y1,'ok')     #'o' for circle; 'k' for black
23  plt.plot([], [], ' ', label="value:    D       M")
24  #set the x and y limits of the plot; label the axes and give a title
25  plt.xlim(-.2,.2)         #set xlimits for the plot
26  plt.ylim(0.,1. )         #set ylimits for the plot
27  plt.xlabel('distance from injection site (cm)')
28  plt.ylabel('phenol red concentration (mM)')
29  plt.title('Curve-Fit Example: 1D-diffusion profile at {:d} seconds'.format(T))
30
31  D=5.e-7    #initial guess for diffusion coefficient D (units of cm^2/s)
32  M=0.1      #initial guess for total amount of phenol red (units of mmoles/cm^2)
33
34  X=np.linspace(-0.2,0.2,500)    #define a dense x-axis for the model calculation
35  Y=my_1D_gaussian(X,D,M)        #calculate the gaussian profile on X
36  #plot Y vs. X as a black dashed line
37  #also print the initial guesses of D and M in the the inset
38  plt.plot(X,Y,'k--',label='initial:   {:.3e}  {:.4f}'.format(D,M))
39
40  #Now fit and print the parameters D and M in the function my_1D_gaussian,
41  #constraining the fit to the region of 1e-8 <= D <= 1e-6 and 0 <= M <= 5
42  popt,pcov=curve_fit(my_1D_gaussian, x1, y1,bounds=\
43    ([1e-8,0.],[1e-6,5.]))
44  #popt contains the least-squares fitted values of D, M
45  D,M=popt[0],popt[1]
46  print("fitted values: D = {:.4e}; M = {:.4f}".format(D,M) )
47  p_sigma=np.sqrt(np.diag(pcov)) #gives approximate SD errors of the fitted paramters
48  print("std dev/error: D,  {:.4e}; M,  {:.4f}".format(p_sigma[0],p_sigma[1]) )
49
```

```
50  #calculate and plot the gaussian profile based on the fitted values;
51  #also print the final (=fitted) values of D and M in the header
52  Y=my_1D_gaussian(X,D,M)
53  plt.plot(X,Y,'k',label='fitted:   {:.3e}  {:.4f}'.format(D,M))
54  plt.legend()  #show the requested information in the legend
55  #plt.show()
56  plt.savefig("curvefit_dapp.png",dpi=200)
```

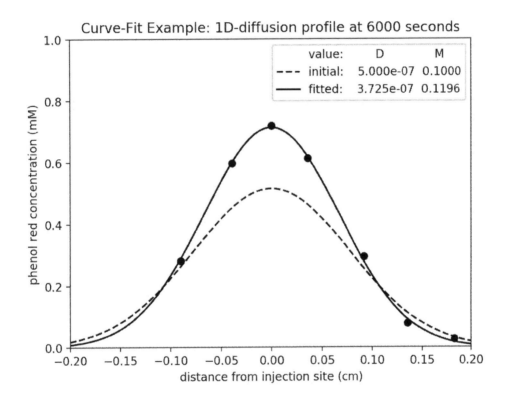

Figure D.1 Experimental measurements of a phenol-red diffusion profile (circles) and two Gaussian curves: an initial estimate (dashed) and the least-squares fitted one (continuous).

fitted values: D = 3.7251e-07; M = 0.1196
std dev/error: D, 1.1770e-08; M, 0.0016

Program Notes

The principal feature in this program is the use of the function curve_fit, which is imported from scipy.optimize and called in line 42. Line 42 also assigns the values returned by curve_fit to the variables popt (short for parameters to be optimized) and pcov (short for parameter covariance matrix). Prior to the call to curve_fit, initial values are assigned to the parameters to be optimized, D and M, which is done in lines 31-32.

Use of the curve_fit function starts with the assumption that it will be passed 3 principal arguments: the name of the function involved in the optimization, the data that correspond to the independent variable of the function, and the data that correspond to the dependent variable of the function (i.e., to the return value of the function). In this example, the three arguments in the call to curve_fit are: my_1D_gaussian, the x1 array, and the y1 array. Since my_1D_gaussian is a function of 3 independent variables (x, D, and M), the latter 2 variables, i.e., D and M, must be the parameters to be optimized for the data x1 and y1.

Keyword arguments are also allowed in the function call. In this case the keyword argument 'bounds' is used. The values for bounds given in line 43 limit the search of the variables to be optimized to specific ranges. The ranges are given as a tuple of two lists (a list of two lists is also allowed); the first list holds the lower bounds of the variables in the search (the first for D, the second for M) and the second list holds the upper bounds.

Line 45 unpacks the fitted values of D and M from the array returned to popt by curve_fit. Line 47 makes use of the other return value of curve_fit, namely, the covariance matrix for the fitted variables. In this case, since the values of 2 variables were adjusted, the covariance matrix is a 2x2 matrix (i.e., a 2x2 numpy array). The diagonal values of this square matrix give uncertainty estimates -- roughly, variance estimates -- for the fitted parameters. The square roots of the diagonal values thus estimate the standard deviations of the fitted parameters. For this fit, the standard deviation of D is about 3% of D and that of M is about 1% of M.

Curvefit_dapp.py can be modified in straightforward ways to address other approaches in the fitting. Suppose, for this data set, that the exact location of the injection site has some uncertainty relative to the location of the x measurements. If so, it is easy to include a distance offset (call it 'x0') as an additional parameter to be optimized. In this case, the function my_1D_gaussian would be defined as a function of 4 variables (x, D, M, and x0), and 'x' in line 10 of the function definition would be replaced by 'x-x0'. An initial guess would then also be assigned to x0 (e.g. x0=0.). Lower and upper search limits for x0 would then also be appended to the values included in line 43 (e.g., -0.2 in the first list and 0.2 in the second). If these modifications are made, Curvefit_dapp.py returns a best-fitted value of 0.0010 for x0, with a standard deviation of 0.0010 for x0. The fitted values of D and M, and their standard deviations, differ only slightly from the values obtained without inclusion of x0 as an adjustable parameter.

As another example of the flexibility of curve_fit, suppose that time T in this experiment is not a fixed number (e.g., 6000) but varies in a known way at each measurement location. As above, my_1D_gaussian would be set up to calculate concentration given values of x, T, M and D. In this case, however, rather than the definition specified in lines 9-10, my_1D_gaussian would be defined with the expectation that the "second" variable passed to curve_fit (i.e., the independent data variable) is actually a tuple of two independent variables:

```
def my_1D_gaussian(Z,D,M):
    x,T=Z
    return M*np.exp(-x**2/(4*D*T))/(np.sqrt(4*np.pi*D*T))
```

If the distance, time, and concentration data happened to be the following:

```
x1=np.array([-0.090,-0.039,0,0.036,0.092,0.136,0.183])      #distance (cm)
t1=np.array([5850.,5900.,5950.,6000.,6050.,6100.,6150.])    #time (s)
y1=np.array([0.2810,0.5965,0.7184,0.6138,0.2939,0.0778,0.0259]) #conc. (mM)
```

then line 42 of the above program would be replaced by:

```
popt,pcov=curve_fit(my_1D_gaussian, (x1,t1), y1, bounds=\
```

Again, the fitted values of D amd M (and their standard deviations) obtained in this version of the program differ only slightly from the first fitted values.

The fitting of models to data is obviously a broad and important subject. The reader may be interested in investigating a commercial package called 'MLAB' (short for Modeling Laboratory, available from Civilized Software Inc., Silver Spring, MD). The curve fitting features in this software are powerful and include, for example, the ability to provide least-squares estimates for parameters of models that are defined by differential equations.

Exercise D.1 Based on the least-squares-fitted parameter values obtained in Curve_fit.py, add statements to the program to calculate and print the sum-of-squares deviation between the model predictions and the data.

APPENDIX E

KINETIC RESPONSE OF V_M IN A ONE-DIMENSIONAL LINEAR CABLE

Section 7.8 of Chapter 7 introduced one-dimensional cable theory for the analysis of the electrical properties of a long cylindrically-shaped cell or cell process with constant values of c_m, r_m, r_i and r_o (cf. Fig. 7.6). Fig. 7.7 shows how V_m, the normalized steady-state change in membrane potential, is expected to vary with distance in response to a maintained step of current injected into the middle of the cell/cell process. This appendix extends the results in Fig. 7.7 by considering the time-dependence of V_m during its build-up to steady state. As before, λ and τ denote the time constant and space constant of the cable, respectively, and V_m is calculated in normalized distance units X ($= x/\lambda$) and normalized time units T ($= t/\tau$). (See Exercise 7.9 for an example of how to convert V_m from normalized units to unnormalized units.)

To calculate the time-dependence of V_m in response to a current step, we use Eqns. E.1 and E.2 below, which are derived by Hodgkin and Rushton (1946) (see also Rall, 1969, and Jack et al., 1975). As with Eqn. 7.12, with $X = 0$ defined as the location of the current-injection site, the form of the solution differs according to the sign of X:

If $-\infty < X < 0$:
$$V_m(X,T) = e^X [1 + \text{erf}(X/(2\sqrt{T}) + \sqrt{T})]/2 - e^{-X} [1 + \text{erf}(X/(2\sqrt{T}) - \sqrt{T})]/2, \quad (\text{E.1})$$

and if $0 < X < \infty$:
$$V_m(X,T) = e^{-X} [1 - \text{erf}(X/(2\sqrt{T}) - \sqrt{T})]/2 - e^X [1 - \text{erf}(X/(2\sqrt{T}) + \sqrt{T})]/2. \quad (\text{E.2})$$

Here, $V_m(X,T)$ is the change in V_m at distance X and time T normalized by the steady-state change in V_m at $X=0$. The function $\text{erf}(x)$ -- also called the 'error function' -- is defined as:

$$\text{erf}(x) = \left(\frac{2}{\sqrt{\pi}}\right) \int_0^x e^{-y^2} dy. \quad (\text{E.3})$$

As pointed out by Hodgkin and Rushton (1946), Eqns. E.1 and E.2 (i) are symmetrical pairs that differ only in the sign of X and (ii) satisfy the one-dimensional cable equation (Eqn. 7.9) and the relevant boundary and continuity conditions.

432 APPENDIX E

For the case of a step of current applied for a long time and then suddenly broken (i.e., returned to zero), the time-dependence of V_m beginning at the break of the current can be obtained by superposition (e.g., Hodgkin and Rushton, 1946) and is given by:

If $-\infty < X < 0$:
$$V_m(X,T) = e^X [1 - \text{erf}(X/(2\sqrt{T}) + \sqrt{T})]/2 + e^{-X}[1 + \text{erf}(X/(2\sqrt{T}) - \sqrt{T})]/2, \quad (E.4)$$

and if $0 < X < \infty$:
$$V_m(X,T) = e^{-X}[1 + \text{erf}(X/(2\sqrt{T}) - \sqrt{T})]/2 + e^X[1 - \text{erf}(X/(2\sqrt{T}) + \sqrt{T})]/2. \quad (E.5)$$

The next *Python* program calculates a number of $V_m(X,T)$ waveforms with these equations; the line numbers are not part of the program itself. Figs. E.1 to E.4 show the program output. For the 'make' of a current step, Fig. E.1 shows V_m as a function of distance X for several times T, and Fig. E.2 shows V_m as a function of time T for several distances X. Figs. E.3 and E.4 show analogous results for the 'break' of a current step. Calculations with these equations are in excellent agreement with experimental measurements confined to the linear range of the cellular response (e.g., Hodgkin and Rushton, 1946).

```
1  # -*- coding: utf-8 -*-
2  # cable_kinetics.py: calculations and plot of Vm(X,T) for Appendix E
3
4  import numpy as np
5  import matplotlib.pyplot as plt
6  from scipy.special import erf  #this works with vectorization, so use this
7
8  def V_minus_on(X,T):  #cable solution for normalized Vm if X<0; current make
9      return 0.5*np.exp(X)*(1+erf(X/(2*np.sqrt(T))+np.sqrt(T)))\
10         -0.5*np.exp(-X)*(1+erf(X/(2*np.sqrt(T))-np.sqrt(T)))
11
12 def V_plus_on(X,T):  #cable solution for normalized Vm if X>0; current make
13     return 0.5*np.exp(-X)*(1-erf(X/(2*np.sqrt(T))-np.sqrt(T)))\
14         -0.5*np.exp(X)*(1-erf(X/(2*np.sqrt(T))+np.sqrt(T)))
15
16 def V_minus_off(X,T): #cable solution for normalized Vm if X<0; current break
17     return 0.5*np.exp(X)*(1-erf(X/(2*np.sqrt(T))+np.sqrt(T)))\
18         +0.5*np.exp(-X)*(1+erf(X/(2*np.sqrt(T))-np.sqrt(T)))
```

```python
19
20  def V_plus_off(X,T):  #cable solution for normalized Vm if X>0; current break
21      return 0.5*np.exp(-X)*(1+erf(X/(2*np.sqrt(T))-np.sqrt(T)))\
22          +0.5*np.exp(X)*(1-erf(X/(2*np.sqrt(T))+np.sqrt(T)))
23
24  N_steps=int(1e3)+1              #density of steps for the calculation
25  xmax=4.0; dx=(xmax)/N_steps     #distance range for the calculation
26  xm=np.linspace(-xmax,-dx,N_steps) #x distances < 0
27  xp=np.linspace(dx,xmax,N_steps)   #x distances > 0
28  tmax=3;dt=tmax/N_steps          #time range for the calculation
29  tp=np.linspace(dt,tmax,N_steps) #t values
30
31  #calculate and plot Vm(X) at different times T; make of current step
32  x_loc=0.84*xmax                 #x-location on plot for labels
33  Tx=[0.02,0.1,0.3,1.0,10.]       #T values for calculation
34  Ty=[0.138,0.325,0.540,0.822,0.98] #vertical locations of labels
35  plt.figure()
36  plt.xlim(-xmax,xmax)
37  plt.ylim(0,1.1)
38  plt.xlabel("distance (X)")
39  plt.ylabel("Normalized Vm")
40  plt.title("Vm Spatial Response: Make of Current Step")
41  plt.text(x_loc,1.05," T", fontsize=12)
42  for i in range(0,5):            #calculate and plot the curves for 5 selected X values
43      T=Tx[i]
44      plt.plot(xm,V_minus_on(xm,T),'k')
45      plt.plot(xp,V_plus_on(xp,T),'k')
46      plt.text(x_loc,Ty[i],"{:.3}".format(T), fontsize=12)
47  plt.savefig("Cable_x_on.png", dpi=200)
48
49  #calculate and plot Vm(T) at different distances X: make of current step
50  x_loc=0.90*tmax                 #x-location on plot for labels
51  Xx=[0.001,0.1,0.3,1.0,3.]       #X values for calculation
52  Xy=[0.99,0.835,0.67,0.295,0.055] #vertical locations of labels
53  plt.figure()
54  plt.xlim(0,tmax)
```

```
55  plt.ylim(0,1.1)
56  plt.xlabel("time (T)")
57  plt.ylabel("Normalized Vm")
58  plt.title("Vm Temporal Response: Make of Current Step")
59  plt.text(x_loc,1.05,"   X", fontsize=12)
60  for i in range(0,5):            #calculate and plot the curves for 5 selected T values
61      X=Xx[i]
62      plt.plot(tp,V_plus_on(X,tp),'k')
63      plt.text(x_loc,Xy[i],"{:.3}".format(X), fontsize=12)
64  plt.savefig("Cable_t_on.png", dpi=200)
65
66  #calculate and plot Vm(X) at different times T; break of current step
67  x_loc=0.81*xmax                 #x-location on plot for labels
68  Tx=[0.001,0.1,0.36,1.0,2.]      #T values for calculation
69  Ty=[0.96,0.63,0.38,0.14,0.05]   #vertical locations of labels
70  plt.figure()
71  plt.xlim(-xmax,xmax)
72  plt.ylim(0,1.1)
73  plt.xlabel("distance (X)")
74  plt.ylabel("Normalized Vm")
75  plt.title("Vm Spatial Response: Break of Current Step")
76  plt.text(x_loc,1.02,"   T", fontsize=12)
77  for i in range(0,5):            #calculate and plot the curves for 5 selected X values
78      T=Tx[i]
79      plt.plot(xm,V_minus_off(xm,T),'k')
80      plt.plot(xp,V_plus_off(xp,T),'k')
81      plt.text(x_loc,Ty[i],"{:.3}".format(T), fontsize=12)
82  plt.savefig("Cable_x_off.png", dpi=200)
83
84  #calculate and plot Vm(T) at different distances X: break of current step
85  x_loc=0.90*tmax                 #x-location on plot for labels
86  Xx=[0.001,0.5,1.0,2.0,3.]       #X values for calculation
87  Xy=[0.92,0.59,0.35,0.12,0.035]  #vertical locations of labels
88  plt.figure()
89  plt.xlim(0,tmax)
90  plt.ylim(0,1.1)
```

```
91  plt.xlabel("time (T)")
92  plt.ylabel("Normalized Vm")
93  plt.title("Vm Temporal Response: Break of Current Step")
94  plt.text(x_loc,1.01,"  X", fontsize=12)
95  for i in range(0,5):           #calculate and plot the curves for 5 selected T values
96      X=Xx[i]
97      plt.plot(tp,V_plus_off(X,tp),'k')
98      plt.text(x_loc,Xy[i],"{:.3}".format(X), fontsize=12)
99  plt.savefig("Cable_t_off.png", dpi=200)
```

Program Notes. Lines 24-29 set up the space and time domains for the calculations. The main work of the program is done in lines 45, 62, 80, and 97, where the four user-defined functions (Vm_minus_on, Vm_plus_on, Vm_minus_off, and Vm_plus_off) are invoked in vectorization calls. As noted in line 6, the erf function from the module 'scipy.special' can be used with vectorization calls. The other program statements (e.g., that generate and save the plots) are similar to those explained in other programs discussed in the main text.

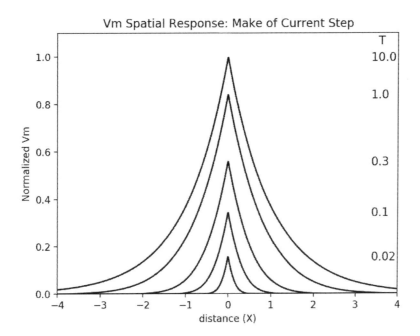

Figure E.1 Theoretical calculations of V_m, the normalized membrane potential response of a cellular process that satisfies the assumptions of one-dimensional cable theory. The curves show the spatial distribution of V_m at the indicated (normalized) times T for the 'make' of a current step.

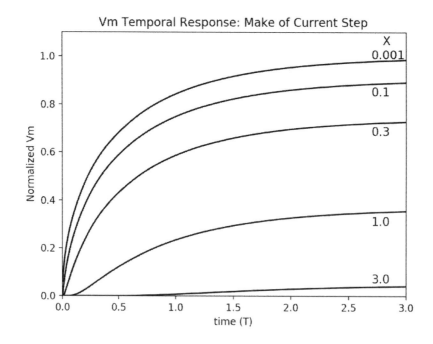

Figure E.2 As in Fig. E.1, except that the curves show the time course of V_m at the indicated values of (normalized) distance X for the 'make' of a current step.

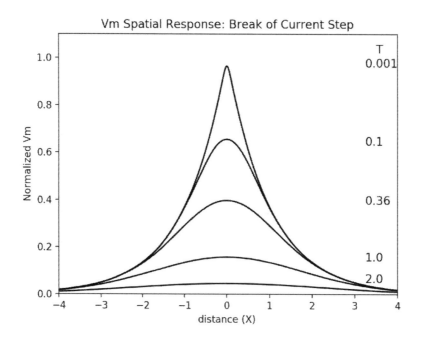

Figure E.3 As for Fig. E.1 except the calculations are for the 'break' of a current step.

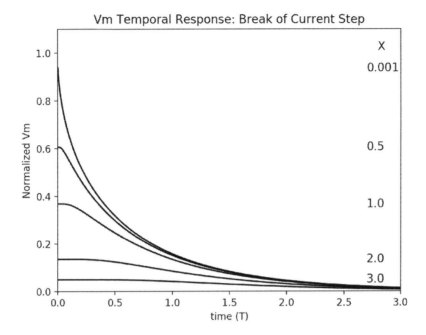

Figure E.4 As for Fig. E.2 except the calculations are for the 'break' of a current step.

Exercise E.1. Use Eqn. E.2 to determine the limiting value of normalized Vm(X,T) for the make of a current step when T = 1 and X approaches zero from the plus side. Compare this value with that when t = τ for the case of a single-exponential function f(t) that starts from zero and rises to one, i.e., f(t) = 1 – exp(-t/τ). Use Eqn. E.4 to do the analogous calculation for Vm(X,T) during the break of a current step and compare this with the value of the function f(t) = exp(-t/τ) when t = τ.

Exercise E.2. Show that Figs. E.3 and E.4 can be calculated with appropriate use of the functions V_minus_on and V_plus_on (which are based on Eqns. E.1 and E.2) without the need for the functions V_minus_off and V_plus_off (which are based on Eqns. E.4 and E.5). Hint: because the cable is a linear electrical element, a negative current step will produce a V_m that is minus that of a positive current step. Hence, for example, V_minus_on(X,10)-V_minus_on(X,T) should equal V_minus_off(X,T) since 10·τ corresponds to essentially infinite time, i.e., steady-state. Thus, V_minus_on(X,10)-V_minus_on(X,T) should be equivalent to the function for a current 'break'.

Exercise E.3. This exercise investigates what might be considered an unexpected property of Eqns. E.1 - E.2. Suppose that these equations apply to a cell or cell process that is stimulated by a step of current initiated at X = 0 and T = 0. Write a *Python* program that determines for a number of values of normalized distance X (e.g., 5 or more) the normalized time T that is required for V_m to reach half of its steady-state value at X (the function V_plus_on(X,T) in the program above may help in this effort). Next make a plot of these half-rise times vs. X. Notice that the relation is almost linear, with a slope, which has units of a propagation velocity, of ~1/2. Thus, knowledge of this slope in combination with (unnormalized) time course measurements of V_m at several (unnormalized) values of x provides a method for relating λ and τ. For example, if λ were known by some other means, the collective V_m time-course measurements would provide a method for estimating τ -- and, conversely, if τ were known by some other means, a method for estimating λ.

Exercise E.4. Use the curve_fit function described in Appendix D to fit a straight line to the values you obtained in Exercise E.3, thereby obtaining a least-squares estimate of the slope and intercept of a line fitted to your values. Is the fitted slope ≈ 0.5?

Exercise E.5. The 'erfc' function, also known as the 'complementary error function', is defined as 1 – erf (cf. Eqn. E.3; also notice that the term under the integral sign specifies a Gaussian curve). Make a plot of erf(x) and erfc(x) for values of x between, say, -3 and 3.

Notice the similarity in shapes between these functions and the curve defined by the data points in Fig. 4.1 (ignoring the noise in the data points in Fig. 4.1). Can you think of a reason why the latter curve might be related to the integral of a Gaussian function? (Hint: the starting curve in Fig. 4.1, i.e., the gray right-angle waveform, can be approximated as an appropriately-scaled sum of a large number of identical, very narrow Gaussian curves positioned uniformly between x = 0 and x = 350. These curves, if interpreted as diffusible profiles, will spread out with time according to the laws of diffusion, e.g., their spatial extent will increase with the square root of time.)

APPENDIX F

CALCULATION OF A PROPAGATED AP WITH THE HH MODEL

A membrane action potential (AP) occurs simultaneously and uniformly over a long length of axon. Chapter 8 calculated and discussed two membrane action potentials for a squid axon based on the Hodgkin-Huxley model (HH model) of membrane excitability. This appendix extends these calculations to a propagated AP in a squid axon, the type that occurs under physiological conditions.

The theoretical basis for the calculation of a propagated AP combines the HH model for a patch of axon membrane with the equations of one dimensional cable theory (Section 7.8 of Chapter 7). The *Python* program below calculates a propagated AP using the procedures of Hodgkin and Huxley (1952d), with the exception that their time-saving method to calculate the falling phase of the AP and its return to baseline (see below) has been ignored.

During a membrane AP, no current flows along the core of the axon or along the extracellular solution because, at all times, the membrane potential (V_m) is the same along the length of the axon. The situation is more complicated with a propagated AP because, in this case, V_m varies with both location (x) and time (t). The spatial variations drive local-circuit currents (sometimes called 'electrotonic currents'; Chapter 7) along the axon core and, equally and oppositely, along the extracellular solution. These local currents serve to successively raise V_m to threshold in adjacent regions of the axon as the AP moves along the membrane with a constant propagation velocity. This velocity, denoted 'θ' (Greek 'theta'), has units of m/s (or, in the program below, cm/ms).

For a membrane AP, once the stimulating current ceases, the membrane current (I_m), which is the sum of the ionic current (I_{ionic}) and the capacitive current (I_c), is zero, i.e.:

$$I_m = I_{ionic} + I_c = 0. \qquad (F.1)$$

Stated qualitatively, if the net ionic current is inward, the loop of current is completed as an outward capacitive current (which moves V_m in the positive direction); conversely, if the net ionic current is outward, the loop of current is completed as an inward capacitive current (which moves V_m in the negative direction).

In contrast, during a propagated action potential, I_m is usually different from zero because of the local-circuit currents. By cable theory, I_m satisfies:

$$I_m = I_{ionic} + I_c = (a/(2\,R_i))\,(\partial^2/\partial x^2)V_m. \quad (F.2)$$

Here, a is the axon radius and R_i is the specific resistance of axoplasm (the resistance of the extracellular solution has been ignored). If these constants are expressed per unit length of axon, Eqn. F.2 becomes equivalent to Eqn. 7.5.

In general, $I_c = C_m\,(d/dt)V_m$, and, in the HH model (see Chapter 8):

$$I_{ionic} = n^4\,\overline{G}_K\,(V_m - E_K) + m^3 h\,\overline{G}_{Na}\,(V_m - E_{Na}) + G_{leak}\,(V_m - E_{leak}). \quad (F.3)$$

The latter two equations can be combined with Eqn. F.2 to yield:

$$(a/(2\,R_i))\,(\partial^2/\partial x^2)V_m =$$
$$n^4\,\overline{G}_K\,(V_m - E_K) + m^3 h\,\overline{G}_{Na}\,(V_m - E_{Na}) + G_{leak}\,(V_m - E_{leak}) + C_m\,(\partial/\partial t)V_m. \quad (F.4)$$

Eqn. F.4, with two independent variables (x and t), is a partial differential equation that has no ready solution. However, for an AP propagating with a constant velocity θ, the waveforms of V_m in space and time are scaled versions of each other. For propagation in the +x direction, $V_m(x,t) = V_m(x - \theta t)$, and for propagation in the -x direction, $V_m(x,t) = V_m(x + \theta t)$. In either case, $V_m(x,t)$ satisfies:

$$(\partial^2/\partial x^2)V_m = (1/\theta^2)\,(\partial^2/\partial t^2)V_m. \quad (F.5)$$

Hence, $(a/(\theta^2\,2\,R_i))\,(d^2/dt^2)V_m =$
$$n^4\,\overline{G}_K\,(V_m - E_K) + m^3 h\,\overline{G}_{Na}\,(V_m - E_{Na}) + G_{leak}\,(V_m - E_{leak}) + C_m\,(d/dt)V_m. \quad (F.6)$$

Eqn. F.6, with one independent variable (t), is an ordinary differential equation and can, in principle, be solved by numerical integration. Several complexities arise in doing so, however. First, as pointed out by Hodgkin and Huxley (1952d), θ is not known prior to the start of the calculation. It is therefore necessary to guess an initial value of θ before starting the integration. If the selected value of θ is too small, the developing solution may initially be approximately correct, but soon V_m goes to -∞ (an obvious error); conversely, if θ is too large, V_m goes to +∞. Thus, the calculation must be repeated as θ is successively refined until a satisfactory value is found -- ideally one that brings V_m at the end of the calculation back to the starting potential.

A second complication with the numerical integration concerns the calculation of the initial rise of the propagating AP waveform, i.e., the 'foot' of the AP. Hodgkin and Huxley note that it is reasonable to assume that, at the foot of the AP: (i) V_m can be approximated as a rising exponential that starts from a small voltage offset V_0 above the resting potential V_r, i.e., starts from $V_m = V_0 + V_r$, where V_0 is, say, 0.1 mV; and (ii) any effect that V_0 has on the resting values of n, m, and h at the start of the AP are small enough to be ignored.

[Note: with these assumptions, the exact value assumed for V_0 has little effect on the final value chosen for θ. For example, as determined in the *Python* program below, if V_0 is 0.001 mV rather than 0.1 mV, the final value selected for θ is different by <0.03%.]

The program below incorporates the assumption of Hodgkin and Huxley (1952d) that V_m rises exponentially from a small offset V_0. If G_0 denotes the resting conductance of the membrane, then, neglecting any small changes in the gating variables n, m, and h during the start of the calculation (i.e., assumption (ii) above), Eqn. F.6 can be rewritten as:

$$(d^2/dt^2)V = K \{ (G_0/C_m) V + (d/dt)V \}, \qquad (F.7)$$

where V denotes the change in membrane potential relative to the resting potential and the constant $K (= 2R_i\theta^2 C_m/a)$ has units of s^{-1} (or, in the program below, ms^{-1}). [Note: in contrast to the program below, all AP simulations by Hodgkin and Huxley (1952d) were carried out as V_m relative to V_r.]

The solution to Eqn. F.7 is given by Hodgkin and Huxley (1952d):

$$V = V_0 \exp(\mu t), \qquad (F.8)$$

where μ is the positive solution to Eqn. F.9 (which is a quadratic equation) and has units of s^{-1} (or ms^{-1}):

$$\mu^2 - K\mu - K G_0/C_m = 0. \qquad (F.9)$$

[Note: given a reasonable choice for the value of θ and hence K, the other solution for μ in Eqn. F.9 has a negative value and can be ignored.]

The *Python* program HHAP_prop.py implements these numerical procedures to calculate a propagated AP for a squid axon. As in Chapter 8, the resting potential is assumed to be -65 mV, and this value is included explicitly in the formulas and procedures of the calculations. The temperature of the calculation, 18.5 °C, was selected to match that of the propagated action potential calculated by Hodgkin and Huxley (1952d). The values of the constants a, R_i, and C_m (0.0238 cm, 35.4 ohm cm, and 1 µF cm^{-2}, respectively) were also chosen to match those used by Hodgkin and Huxley. Their propagated AP calculation is shown in Figs. 15A and 15B of Hodgkin and Huxley (1952d) and is also reproduced as Figs. 8.2A and 8.2B in Chapter 8. The reported value of θ for their calculation, rounded to 3 significant figures, is 18.8 m/s, and the reported value of K is 10.47 ms^{-1}.

The program listing for HHAP_prop.py is given next, followed by the figure produced by the program and the Program Notes. The first 57 lines of the listing are the same as those in HHAP.py (Section 8.6 of Chapter 8), so are omitted here. The program lines after the call to odeint (line 122) are also omitted; these statements simply plot and save the figure and are similar to those in other programs explained in the main text. As before, the line numbers are not part of the program itself.

```
58  #set up the initial conditions for Vm, n, m, and h as a function of temperature
59  def Set_conditions(Temp):
60      Vm_init=Vr
61      n_init=n_infinity(Vm_init)
62      m_init=m_infinity(Vm_init)
63      h_init=h_infinity(Vm_init)
64      Wm_init=Wr
65      return [Vm_init,n_init,m_init,h_init,Wm_init]
66
67  #F contains (d/dt) formulas for Vm, n, m, h and (d/dt)Vm in the call by odeint
68  def F(y,t): #where y is a 5-member list with the initial conditions in its call
69      dy=[0,0,0,0,0]   #create a 5-member list of the derivatives to be returned
70      dy[0]=y[4]                                    #dVm/dt (mV/ms)
71      dy[1]=alpha_n(y[0])*(1-y[1])-beta_n(y[0])*y[1]   #(d/dt)n (per ms)
72      dy[2]=alpha_m(y[0])*(1-y[2])-beta_m(y[0])*y[2]   #(d/dt)m (per ms)
73      dy[3]=alpha_h(y[0])*(1-y[3])-beta_h(y[0])*y[3]   #(d/dt)h (per ms)
74      dy[4]=K*(dy[0]+I_ionic(y[0],y[1],y[2],y[3])/Cm)  #(d/dt)(d/dt)Vm (mV/ms^2)
75      return dy  #this returns d/dt of Vm, n, m, h, and dVm/dt
```

```
 76
 77  #specify the basic constants to use in the calculation
 78  Vr=-65.              #resting membrane potential is -65 mV
 79  ENa=Vr+115.          #ENa is 115 mV above resting Vm (mV)
 80  EK=Vr-12.            #EK is 12 mV below resting Vm (mV)
 81  Eleak=Vr+10.613      #Eleak is 10.613 mV above resting Vm (mV)
 82  GK_max=36.           #maximum K conductance (msiemens cm^-2)
 83  GNa_max=120.         #maximum Na conductance (msiemens cm^-2)
 84  Gleak=0.3            #leak conductance (msiemens cm^-2)
 85  Q10=3.0              #Q10 value to adjust rates of alphas and betas
 86  Cm=1.0               #membrane capacitance (microfarads cm^-2)
 87
 88  Wr=0.                #set Wr = resting (d/dt)Vm to 0 for now; below set to >0
 89  a=0.0238             #radius of axon in cm (as for Fig. 15 of HH, 1952d)
 90  R2=35.4              #specific resistance of axoplasm, in ohm cm (ditto)
 91  #theta=1.88          #propagation velocity stated by HH, in cm/ms (ditto)
 92
 93  theta=1.87346468027364666    #refined value of theta for this calculation (cm/ms)
 94  K=(1e-3)*2*R2*theta**2*Cm/a  # constant to simplify the calculation (per ms)
 95  #Hodgkin and Huxley's stated value of K is 10.47 (per ms)
 96  #which would correspond to theta = 1.876 (cm/ms); see rounded value in line 91
 97
 98  #parameters for setting up time grid for the solution (ms)
 99  t_start=0; t_end=3.0; N_steps=int(1e4)    #start and end times; N_steps
100  dt=(t_end-t_start)/float(N_steps)         #time increment per step
101  t=np.linspace(t_start,t_end,N_steps+1)    #time grid for solution
102
103  #set temperature and initial conditions for calculating the resting conductance
104  Temp=18.5                     #temperature for calculation in degrees C
105  R_factor=rate_factor(Temp)    #adjust all rates according to R_factor
106  y_init=Set_conditions(Temp)   #set initial conditions based on Temp
107
108  g0=Gleak+GK_max*y_init[1]**4+GNa_max*y_init[2]**3*y_init[3]
109  g0_overCm=g0/Cm               #constant used by HH (1952d)
110  #use the quadratic formula to get the relevant root of u in Eqn. F.9 (=Eqn. 32 of HH (1952d))
111  u=(K+np.sqrt(K*K+4*K*g0_overCm))/2
```

```
112
113  #adjust the values of V and r for the start of the calculation
114  dV=0.1              #offset V by 0.1 mV to start the calculation
115  def f(t):           #function for mimicking HH's start of V
116      return dV*np.exp(t*u)
117  Wr=(f(dt)-f(0))/dt   #offset in W for starting the calculation
118
119  #solve the deq's with adjusted initial conditions (new values of Vr and Wr)
120  y_init[0]=Vr+dV
121  y_init[4]=Wr
122  y=odeint(F,y_init,t,hmax=1e-5)  #the slice y[0,:] will contain the solution for Vm
```

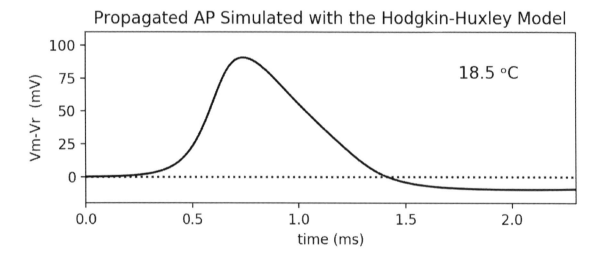

Figure F.1 A propagated action potential at 18.5 °C simulated with the Hodgkin-Huxley model. The calculation is based on Eqn. F.6 in the text and is generated by the program HHAP_prop.py. The value of θ (line 93 of the program), if rounded to 3 figures, is 18.7 m/s, which is close to the value reported by Hodgkin and Huxley (1952d), 18.8 m/s. The corresponding value of K in HHAP_prop.py is calculated in line 94 and, if unrounded, is 10.44112560936491 ms^{-1}. The value of K reported by Hodgkin and Huxley is 10.47 ms^{-1}.

Program Notes

As in HHAP.py, the function odeint from the scipy.integrate module is used to perform the integration, and the first column in the array y returned by the call to odeint contains the solution for V_m, which is plotted in Fig. F.1 relative to the resting potential. Use of odeint requires that initial conditions be specified for the system of simultaneous first-order equations to be integrated. In HHAP.py, this is done by the user-defined function Set_conditions, which specifies the initial values of V_m, n, m, and h. In HHAP_prop.py, an additional condition is required because of the use of the extra variable W_m, which is defined as $(d/dt)V_m$. This variable is needed because, as pointed out in Section 6.2 of Chapter 6, if odeint is used to solve any differential equations of order 2 or higher, the latter must be recast as one or more first-order equations. In this case, with $W_m = (d/dt)V_m$, the term $(d^2/dt^2)V_m$ in Eqn. F.6 can be replaced with $(d/dt)W_m$. The function Set_conditions (line 59) therefore sets 5 initial conditions rather than 4 (the 5th being that for W_m). Correspondingly, the function F(y,t), which is the function called by odeint in line 122, contains formulas for calculating the rates of change of 5 variables (V_m, n, m, h, and W_m) rather than just the 4 in HHAP.py (V_m, n, m, and h).

As defined above, $K = 2R_i\theta^2 C_m/a$ and $W_m = (d/dt)V_m$; thus Eqn. F.6 can be rearranged as:

$$(d/dt)W_m = K [(d/dt)V_m + I_{ionic} / C_m]. \qquad (F.10)$$

Eqn. F.10 gives the formula used to calculate $(d/dt)W_m$ in function F(y,t) in HHAP_prop.py (see line 74).

Because numerical integration of Eqn. F.6 is very sensitive to any small errors in the calculation (e.g., as noted, a small error in θ sends V_m in the calculation toward either -∞ or +∞), the call to odeint (line 122 of HHAP_prop.py) includes the optional keyword argument 'hmax'. This argument, which was discussed in Sections 6.2 and 6.3 of Chapter 6, is set to a small value, 1e-5, thereby changing the step size in the integration routine from the default value to a much smaller value. The accuracy of the integration is thus increased at the cost of increased time to complete the integration.

Comparison with the Results of Hodgkin and Huxley
As indicated by the values in the table below, the propagated AP shown in Fig. F.1 is in good agreement with that in Fig. 15A of Hodgkin and Huxley (1952d). The first 6 values listed under the column "HH (1952d)" were estimated by this author from ruler measurements of the AP tracing in Fig. 15A of Hodgkin and Huxley (1952d) and the associated calibration bars in Fig. 15A. The full-duration at half-maximum is calculated as the time of half-decay from peak minus the time of half-rise to peak.

Action Potential Properties (18.5 °C)	Fig. F.1	HH (1952d)
peak amplitude, positive phase (mV)	90.6	91.0
time of peak amplitude (ms)	0.74	0.73
time of half-rise to peak (ms)	0.57	0.55
time of half-decay from peak (ms)	1.06	1.05
full-duration at half maximum (ms)	0.49	0.49
peak amplitude, negative phase (mV)	-9.7	-9.6
conduction velocity θ (m/s)	18.7346…	18.8
constant $K = 2R_i\theta^2C_m/a$ (ms^{-1})	10.4411…	10.47

The Falling Phase of the Propagated AP

Because the AP calculations of Hodgkin and Huxley (1952d) were made many decades ago, only relatively-primitive calculation devices were available to assist in the calculations; thus, the numerical integration of even one such AP was a very time-consuming and tedious undertaking. For this reason, once a propagated AP had been calculated through its time of peak by standard integration procedures, Hodgkin and Huxley chose to adopt a less tedious strategy for the calculation of the later phases of the propagated AP. (Hodgkin and Huxley note that this shortcut strategy was not applicable to the rising phase of the propagated AP.) This alternate method used the falling phase of a membrane AP as a template, with the values of $(d^2/dt^2)V$ calculated at each step of the integration from the time differences in $(d/dt)V$. The estimates of $(d^2/dt^2)V$ for the propagated AP were then refined by means of a secondary procedure, which is described in the last paragraph on p. 524 of Hodgkin and Huxley (1952d). The final result for the later phases of the propagated AP was similar to that calculated for a membrane action potential and agreed satisfactorily with experimental measurements of propagated APs.

Difficulties with HHAP_prop.py in the Calculation of the Later Phases of the AP

Hodgkin and Huxley's time-saving method for calculating the later phases of a propagated AP (previous paragraph) appears to have worked well (Fig. 15B of Hodgkin and Huxley, 1952d, and Fig. 8.2B in Chapter 8). In HHAP_prop.py, the standard integration procedure available in odeint was used throughout and a difficulty with the integration emerges if the calculation time is extended much beyond that shown in Fig. F.1. At such later times, $(d/dt)V_m$, $(d^2/dt^2)V_m$, and the rates of change of n, m, and h are generally small; in consequence, the stability of the integration becomes very sensitive to small errors in the calculation (e.g., truncation errors). In HHAP_prop.py, the errors are such that it was not possible, with *Python*'s 64-bit floating-point precision, to find a value of θ for which V_m at time points significantly later than those shown in Fig. F.1 did not move to either +∞ or -∞. An attempt to remedy this deficiency in HHAP_prop.py was to use a 10-fold smaller value for hmax in the call to odeint; this did not, however, extend the time of a valid integration significantly beyond that shown in Fig. F.1.

[Note: *Python* has an alternative differential-equation solver, namely, the function 'solve_ivp' from the scipy.integrate module, which has greater flexibility than odeint, including a number of integration algorithms from which to choose, such as high-order Runge-Kutta methods and an Adams/BDF method with automatic stiffness detection and switching. Use of solve_ivp with these various methods did not yield a simulation that was valid at times substantially greater than achieved with odeint. These results, as well as those of Hodgkin and Huxley, are consistent with there being an inherent difficulty in achieving a full numerical solution to Eqn. F.6 if standard integration procedures are used with floating-point numbers whose precision is no greater than 64 bits.]

Comparison with the Results of FitzHugh and Antosiewicz

FitzHugh and Antosiewicz (1959) also simulated propagated action potentials in a squid axon with the HH model. Their calculated AP waveform at 18.5 °C (lower panel of their Fig. 5; time scale, 0 to 2.5 ms) is very similar to that in Fig. F.1 (time scale, 0 to 2.3 ms). The values they report for θ and K, 18.74 m/s and 10.437847 ms^{-1}, respectively, are also close to the values 18.73 m/s and 10.441126 ms^{-1} determined in HHAP_prop.py if the latter values are rounded to the same number of significant figures reported by FitzHugh and Antosiewicz (see program line 93 and legend of Fig. F.1).

As found by Hodgkin and Huxley, FitzHugh and Antosiewicz encountered difficulties in the use of a standard numerical integration procedure at times after the peak of the calculated AP. These difficulties were presumably due to limitations in the accuracy of the calculations, which, in the case of FitzHugh and Antosiewicz, were carried out with an IBM 704 computer with 36-bit floating-point precision. To continue the simulation of the later phases of the AP, FitzHugh and Antosiewicz replaced their standard integration procedure with a numerical interpolation procedure (as did Hodgkin and Huxley). An apparent advantage of the calculations with the *Python* program of this Appendix is that, with 64-bit resolution for the floating-point calculations, the simulation can be continued with standard integration procedures until about the time of the nadir of the undershoot of the AP.

Overall Conclusions

On the time scale shown, the simulated AP in Fig. F.1, which was calculated with standard methods for numerical integration, is in good agreement with the simulated AP in Fig. 15A of Hodgkin and Huxley (1952d) and that in the lower panel of Fig. 5 of FitzHugh and Antosiewicz (1959). On longer time scales, numerical integration of the highly non-linear equations of Hodgkin and Huxley with standard techniques and no more than 64-bit resolution becomes problematic if the complete return of the AP waveform to baseline is the desired endpoint of the calculation. Nevertheless, these various simulations confirm that the mechanism of propagation of the AP, including the AP's approximate time course and propagation velocity, is well explained by the experimentally-measured membrane conductances and passive electrical properties of the axon. The design of the axon appears well-suited for its function of transmitting a large physiological signal over distance at high speed.

Exercise F.1 At what times, if any, during a propagated AP is the total membrane current zero? How does your answer compare with that for the case of a membrane AP?

Exercise F.2 In Fig. F.1, the peak of the propagated AP is 90.6 mV above the resting potential whereas the corresponding peak of the simulated membrane AP in Chapter 8 is 96.9 mV above the resting potential. Why should the former peak be smaller than the latter? (Hint: recall Exercise 7.8 in Chapter 7.) Based on your reasoning, how would you expect the amplitude of the undershoot to differ in a membrane vs. propagating AP?

Exercise F.3 If the resistivity of axoplasm were somewhat larger than the value used in HHAP_prop.py, would you expected this to affect the value of θ that provides a solution to Eqn. F.6 and, if so, how?

Exercise F.4 Repeat the simulation in HHAP_prop.py by starting the foot of the AP with a 0.001 mV offset above the resting potential rather than a 0.1 mV offset. How is the estimate of θ affected by this change? Discontinue your calculations after you have refined your estimate of θ to a reasonable number of digits.

Exercise F.5 Repeat the simulation in HHAP_prop.py at 6.3 °C (the reference temperature for the kinetics of n, m, and h in the HH model) and see if the calculation is reliable for a larger fraction of the AP time course. Although the specific resistivity of axoplasm is expected to be temperature-sensitive, keep the value of R_i (= R2 in HHAP_prop.py) at 35.4 ohm·cm in your investigation. You may wish to compare the results of your simulation with that of FitzHugh and Antosiewicz (1959) (see the upper panel of their Fig. 5 and the values at 6.3 °C in their Table 3).

Exercise F.6 Amend the plot in HHAP_prop.py to show the waveforms for I_{Na} and I_K during a propagated AP. How do these waveforms compare in amplitude and time course with those during a membrane AP at the same temperature if the latter AP is elicited by a brief stimulus that is moderately above threshold?

Exercise F.7 This exercise expands on Exercise F.1. Amend the plot in HHAP_prop.py to show a waveform that is proportional to the total membrane current during a propagated AP. (Hint: you will need to calculate and plot the first difference of trace y[:,4].) Determine when this waveform is positive and when it is negative, and state what is the physiological significance of the periods of positivity and negativity.

Exercise F.8 Let f(t) denote the waveform of the propagating AP in time, e.g., as calculated in Fig. F.1. Assume that θ for this AP is 18.7436 m/s, as found in HHAP_prop.py at 18.5 °C, and that the AP is propagating in the +x direction. Let g(x) denote the waveform of this propagating AP in space and make the assumption that the peak of the AP occurs at x=0 at a particular moment in time. Make a plot of g(x), including a distance calibration on the x-axis.

Exercise F.9 Use HHAP_prop.py to investigate how θ for a propagated AP is expected to depend on the radius of the axon. Determine your values of θ to an appropriate number of significant figures to answer the question without needlessly refining the estimates of θ.

APPENDIX G

PHYSICAL CONSTANTS AND COMMON UNITS

A. Physical Constants

Constant	Abbreviation	Value
Gas constant	R	8.3145 joule/(mole · K)
Elementary charge	e	$1.6022 \cdot 10^{-19}$ coulomb
Avogadro's number	N	$6.0221 \cdot 10^{23}$ (particles)/mole
Faraday's constant	F	$9.6485 \cdot 10^{4}$ coulomb/mole
Boltzmann constant	k	$1.3806 \cdot 10^{-23}$ joule/K

B. Quantities and Common Units

Quantity	Units	Abbreviation	Equivalent Units
Distance	meter	m	-
Time	second	s	-
Temperature	kelvin	K	-
Charge	coulomb	Q	$6.2415 \cdot 10^{18}$ e
Energy	joule	J	volt · coulomb
Voltage	volt	V	joule/coulomb
Current	ampere	A	coulomb/second
Resistance	ohm	Ω	volt/ampere
Conductance	siemens	S	ampere/volt
Capacitance	farad	C (or F)	coulomb/volt

C. Other

Quantity	Abbreviation	Usual Units
Diffusion coefficient	D	m^2/s (or cm^2/s)
Membrane permeability	P	cm/s
Flux	J	moles / ($cm^2 \cdot s$)
Time constant	τ	s (or ms)
Space constant	λ	m (or mm)

REFERENCES

Adams, B. A., Tanabe, T., Mikami, A., Numa, S. and Beam, K. G. (1990). Intramembrane charge movement restored in dysgenic skeletal muscle by injection of dihydropyridine receptor cDNAs. Nature 346(6284):569-572.

Aggarwal, S. K. and MacKinnon, R. (1996). Contribution of the S4 segment to gating charge in the Shaker K+ channel. Neuron 16:1169-1177.

Alberts, B., Bray, D., Lewis, J., Raff, M., Roberts, K. and Watson, J.D. (1994). Molecular Biology of the Cell (3rd Edition, Garland Publishing; New York and London).

Albillos, A., Dernick, G., Horstmann, H., Almers, W., Alvarez de Toledo, G. and Lindau, M. (1997). The exocytotic event in chromaffin cells revealed by patch amperometry. Nature 389:509-512.

Anderson, C. R. and Stevens, C. F. (1973). Voltage clamp analysis of acetylcholine produced endplate current fluctuations at frog neuromuscular junction. J. Physiol. 235:655-691.

Armstrong, C. M., Bezanilla, F. M. and Horowicz, P. (1972). Twitches in the presence of ethylene glycol bis (β-aminoethyl ether)-N,N'-tetraacetic acid. Biochim. Biophys. Acta 267:605-608.

Armstrong, C. M. and Bezanilla, F. (1973). Currents related to movement of the gating particles of the sodium channels. Nature 242:459-461.

Armstrong, C. M. and Bezanilla, F. (1977). Inactivation of the sodium channel. II. Gating current experiments. J. Gen. Physiol. 70:567-590.

Armstrong, C. M. and Hollingworth, S. (2017). A perspective on Na and K channel inactivation. J. Gen. Physiol. 150(1): 7-18.

Barrett, K. E., Barman, S. M., Boitano, S. and Brooks, H. L. (2004). *Ganong's Review of Medical Physiology* (23rd Edition, McGraw-Hill; New York).

Baylor, D. A. and Fettiplace, R. (1979). Synaptic drive and impulse generation in ganglion cells of turtle retina. J, Physiol. 288:107-127.

Baylor, S. M. (2015). CalDyx: an interactive self-study teaching program on calcium dynamics during excitation-contraction coupling in skeletal muscle cells. Sci. Signal. 8(362):tr1.

Baylor, S. M., Chandler, W. K. and Marshall, M. W. (1979). Arsenazo III signals in singly dissected frog twitch fibres. J. Physiol. 287:23-24P.

Baylor, S. M., Chandler, W. K. and Marshall, M. W. (1983). Sarcoplasmic reticulum calcium release in frog skeletal muscle fibres estimated from Arsenazo III calcium transients. J. Physiol. 344:625-666.

Baylor, S. M. and Hollingworth, S. (1998). Model of sarcomeric Ca^{2+} movements, including ATP Ca^{2+} binding and diffusion, during activation of frog skeletal muscle. J. Gen. Physiol. 112:297-316.

Baylor, S. M. and Hollingworth, S. (2003). Sarcoplasmic reticulum calcium release compared in slow-twitch and fast-twitch fibres of mouse muscle. J. Physiol. 551:125-138.

Baylor, S. M. and Hollingworth, S. (2011). Calcium indicators and calcium signalling in skeletal muscle fibres during excitation-contraction coupling. Prog. Biophys. and Molec. Biol., 105:162-179.

Baylor, S. M., Hollingworth, S. and Chandler, W. K. (2002). Comparison of simulated and measured calcium sparks in intact skeletal muscle fibers of the frog. J. Gen. Physiol. 120(3):349-368.

Berg, J. M., Tomockzyo, J. L. and Stryer, L. (2002). *Biochemistry* (5th Edition, Freeman and Co.; New York).

Bezanilla, F. (2018). Gating currents. J. Gen. Physiol. 150:911-931.

Bittner, M. A. and Holz, R. W. (1992). Kinetic analysis of secretion from permeabilized adrenal chromaffin cells reveals distinct components. J. Biol. Chem. 267:16219-16225.

Block, B. A., Imagawa, T., Leung, A., Campbell, K. P. and Franzini-Armstrong, C. (1988). Structural evidence for direct interaction between the molecular components of the transverse tubule/sarcoplasmic reticulum junction in skeletal muscle. J. Cell. Biol. 107: 2587-2600.

Boron, W. F. and Boulpaep, E. L. (2009). *Medical Physiology, A Cellular and Molecular Approach* (2nd Edition, Saunders; Philadelphia, PA).

Boyd, I. A. and Martin, A. R. (1956a). Spontaneous sub-threshold activity at mammalian neuromuscular junctions. J. Physiol. 132:61-73.

Boyd, I. A. and Martin, A. R. (1956b). The end-plate potential in mammalian muscle. J. Physiol. 132:74-91.

Burdyga, T. V. and Kosterin, S. A. (1991). Kinetic analysis of smoothmuscle relaxation. Gen. Physiol. Biophys. 10(6): 589-598.

Cannell, M. B. and Allen, D. G. (1984). Model of calcium movements during activation in the sarcomere of frog skeletal muscle. Biophys. J. 45:913-925.

Chandler, W. K., Rakowski, R. and Schneider, M.F. (1976). Effect of glycerol treatment and maintained depolarization on charge movement in skeletal muscle. J. Physiol. 254:285-316.

Cheng, H., Lederer, W. J. and Cannell, M. B. (1993). Calcium sparks: elementary events underlying excitation-contraction coupling in heart muscle. Science 262:740-745.

Cochet-Bisseul M., Lory, P. and Monteil, A. (2014). The sodium leak channel, NALCN, in health and disease. Front. Cell. Neurosci. 8:132.

Collander, R. (1954). The permeability of Nitella cells to non-electrolytes. Physiol. Plant. 7(3):420-445.

Colquhoun, D., Dionne, V. E., Steinbach, J. H. and Stevens, C. F. (1975). Conductance of channels opened by acetylcholine-like drugs in muscle end-plate. Nature 253(5488):204-206.

Davis, J. P., Tikunova, S. B., Swartz, D. R. and Rall, J. A. (2004). Measurement of Ca^{2+} dissociation rates from troponin C (TnC) in skeletal myofibrils. Biophys. J. 86:218a.

del Castillo, J. and Katz, B. (1954). Changes in end-plate activity produced by pre-synaptic polarization. J. Physiol. 125:586-604.

DiFrancesco, D., Ferroni, A., Mazzanti, M. and Tromba, C. (1986). Properties of the hyperpolarizing-activated current (i_f) in cells isolated from the rabbit sino-atrial node. J. Physiol. 377:61-68.

Dittman, J. S. and Regehr, W. G. (1998). Calcium dependence and recovery kinetics of presynaptic depression at the climbing fiber to Purkinje cell synapse. J. Neurosci. 18:6147-6162.

Dodge, F. A., Jr., and Rahamimoff, R. (1967). Co-operative action of calcium ions in transmitter release at the neuromuscular junction. J. Physiol. 193 (2):419-432.

Douglas, W. W. and Rubin, R. P. (1963). The mechanism of catecholamine release from the adrenal medulla and the role of calcium in stimulus-secretion coupling. J. Physiol. 167(2):288-310.

Douglas, W. W. (1968). Stimulus-secretion coupling: the concept and clues from chromaffin and other cells. Br. J. Pharmacol. 34:451-474.

Doyle, D. A., Cabral, J. M., Pfuetzner, R. A., Kuo, A., Gulbis, J. M., Cohen, S. L., Chait, B. T. and MacKinnon, R. (1998). The structure of the potassium channel: molecular basis of K^+ conduction and selectivity. Science 280(5360):69-77.

Eisenberg, B. R. and Peachey, L. D. (1978). Helicoids in the T system and striations of frog skeletal muscle fibers seen by high voltage electron microscopy. Biophys. J. 22:145-154.

Ellis-Davies, G. C. (2003). Development and application of caged calcium. Methods Enzymol. 360:226–238.

Fatt, P. and Katz, B. (1950). Some observations on biological noise. Nature 166:597-598.

Fatt, P. and Katz, B. (1951). An analysis of the end-plate potential recorded with an intracellular electrode. J. Physiol. 115(3): 320–370.

Felder, E. and Franzini-Armstrong, C. (2002). Type 3 ryanodine receptors of skeletal muscle are segregated in a parajunctional position. Proc. Natl. Acad. Sci. 99:1695-1700.

Fernandez, J. M., Neher, E. and Gomperts, B. D. (1984). Capacitance measurements reveal stepwise fusion events in degranulating mast cells. Nature 312(5993):453-455.

FitzHugh, R. and Antosiewicz, H. A. (1959). Automatic computation of nerve excitation – detailed corrections and additions. J. of the Society of Industrial and Applied Mathematics 7(4): 447-458.

Franzini-Armstrong, C. (1975). Membrane particles and transmission at the triad. Fedn. Proc. 34: 1382-1389.

Franzini-Armstrong, C. (1980). Structure of the sarcoplasmic reticulum. Fedn. Proc. 39:2403-2409.

Franzini-Armstrong, C. (2018). The relationship between form and function throughout the history of excitation-contraction coupling. J. Gen. Physiol. 150:189-210.

Furshpan, E. J. and Potter, D. D. (1959). Transmission at the giant synapses of the crayfish. J. Physiol. 145:289-325.

Gage, P. W. and Quastel, D. M. J. (1966). Competition between sodium and calcium ions in transmitter release at mammalian neuromuscular junctions. J. Physiol. 185:95-123.

Geroski, D. H. and Edelhauser, H. F. (1984). Quantitation of Na/K ATPase pump sites in the rabbit corneal endothelium. Invest. Ophthalmol. Vis. Sci. 25(9):1056-60.

Giannini, G., Conti, A., Mammarella, S., Scrobogna, M. and Sorrentino, V. (1995). The ryanodine receptor/calcium channel genes are widely and differentially expressed in murine brain and peripheral tissues. J. Cell. Biol. 128: 893–904.

Gifford, J. L., Walsh, M. P. and Vogel, H. J. (2007). Structures and metal-ion-binding properties of the Ca^{2+}-binding helix-loop-helix EF-hand motifs. Biochem. J. 405(2):199-221.

Grabner, M., Dirksen, R. T., Suda, N. and Beam, K. G. (1999). The II-III loop of the skeletal muscle dihydropyridine receptor is responsible for the bi-directional coupling with the ryanodine receptor. J. Biol. Chem. 274, 21913–21919.

Gutierrez, G. J. and Marder, E. (2013). Rectifying electrical synapses can affect the influence of synaptic modulation on output pattern robustness. J. Neurosci. 33:13238-13248.

Hagiwara, S. and Byerly, L. (1981). Calcium channel. Annu. Rev. Neurosci. 4:69-125.

Hamill, O. P., Marty, A., Neher, E., Sakmann, B. and Sigworth, F. J. (1981). Improved patch-clamp techniques for high-resolution current recording from cells and cell-free membrane patches. Pflugers Arch. 391(2):85-100.

Hall, J. L. and Baker, D.A. (1977). *Cell Membranes and Ion Transport* (Longman Group; New York and London).

Hanke, W. and Miller, C. (1983). Single chloride channels from Torpedo electroplax. J. Gen. Physiol. 82:25-45.

Hille, B. (2001). *Ion Channels of Excitable Membranes* (3rd Edition, Sinauer Associates; Sunderland, MA).

Hille, B. and Campbell, D. (1776). An improved Vaseline gap voltage clamp for skeletal muscle fibers. J. Gen. Physiol. 67:265-293.

Hirschberg, B., Rovner, A., Lieberman, M. and Patlak, J. (1995). Transfer of twelve charges is needed to open skeletal muscle Na^+ channels. J. Gen. Physiol. 106:1053–1068.

Hladky, S. B. and Haydon, D. A. (1970). Discreteness of conductance change in bimolecular lipid membranes in the presence of certain antibiotics. Nature 225: 451-453.

Hodgkin, A. L. and Horowicz, P. (1959). The influence of potassium and chloride ions on the membrane potential of single muscle fibres. J. Physiol. 148(1):127-160.

Hodgkin, A. L. and Huxley, A. F. (1952a). Currents carried by sodium and potassium ions through the membrane of the giant axon of Loligo. J. Physiol. 116:449-472.

Hodgkin, A. L. and Huxley, A. F. (1952b). The components of membrane conductance in the giant axon of Loligo. J. Physiol. 116:473-496.

Hodgkin, A. L. and Huxley, A. F. (1952c). The dual effect of membrane potential on sodium conductance in the giant axon of Loligo. J. Physiol. 116:497-506.

Hodgkin, A. L. and Huxley, A. F. (1952d). A quantitative description of membrane current and its application to conduction and excitation in nerve. J. Physiol. 117:500-544.

Hodgkin, A. L. and Katz, B. (1949). The effect of sodium ions on the electrical activity of the giant axon of the squid. J. Physiol. 108:37-77.

Hodgkin, A. L. and Rushton, W. A. H. (1946). The electrical constants of a crustacean nerve fibre. Proc. Roy. Soc. Lond. B 133:444-471.

Hoffmann, E. K., Lambert, I. H. and Pedersen, S. F. (2009). Physiology of cell volume regulation in vertebrates. Physiol. Rev. 89, 193–277.

Hollingworth, S., Baylor, S. M. and Marshall, M. W. (1993). Voltage dependence of calcium transients measured in mouse fast-twitch muscle fibres. J. Physiol. 259:232P.

Hollingworth, S., Peet, J., Chandler, W. K. and Baylor, S. M. (2001. Calcium sparks in intact skeletal muscle fibers of the frog. J. Gen. Physiol. 118:653-678.

Hollingworth, S., Chandler, W. K. and Baylor, S. M. (2006). Effects of tetracaine on calcium sparks in frog intact skeletal muscle fibers. J. Gen. Physiol. 127:291-307.

Hollingworth, S. and Baylor, S. M. (2013). Comparison of the myoplasmic calcium movements during excitation-contraction coupling in frog twitch and mouse fast-twitch fibers. J. Gen. Physiol. 141:567-583.

Hoshi, T. and Aldrich, R. W. (1988). Voltage-dependent K^+ currents and underlying single K^+ channels in pheochromocytoma cells. J. Gen. Physiol. 91:73-106.

Imagawa, T., Smith, J. S., Coronado, R. and Campbell, K. P. (1987). Purified ryanodine receptor from skeletal muscle sarcoplasmic reticulum is the Ca^{2+}-permeable pore of the calcium release channel. J. Biol. Chem. 262:16636–16643.

Inue, M., Saito, A. and Fleischer, S. (1987). Purification of the ryanodine receptor and identity with feet structures of junctional terminal cisternae of sarcoplasmic reticulum from fast skeletal muscle. J. Biol. Chem. 262:1740–1747.

Ishida, I. G., Rangel-Yescas, G., Carrasco-Zanini, J. and Islas, L (2015). Voltage-dependent gating and gating charge measurements in the Kv1.2 potassium channel. J. Gen. Physiol. 145:345-358.

Islas, L.D. and Sigworth, F. J. (2001). Electrostatics and the gating pore of Shaker potassium channels. J. Gen. Physiol. 117:69–89.

Jack, J. J. B., Noble, D. and Tsien, R. W. (1975). *Electric Current Flow in Excitable Cells* (Oxford University Press: London).

Jentsch, T. J., Stein, V., Weinreich, F. and Zdebk, A. A. (2002). Molecular structure and physiological function of chloride channels. Physiol. Rev. 82(2):503-568.

Katz, B (1966). *Nerve, Muscle and Synapse* (McGraw-Hill; New York).

Katz, B. (1970). On the quantal mechanism of neural transmitter release. Nobel Lecture, December 12, 1970.

Kettlun, C., Gonzalez, A., Ríos, E. and Fill, M. (2003). Unitary Ca^{2+} current through mammalian cardiac and amphibian skeletal muscle ryanodine receptor channels under near-physiological ionic conditions. J. Gen. Physiol. 122:407-417.

Kinder, J. M. and Nelson, P. (2015). *A Student's Guide to Python for Physical Modeling* (Princeton University Press; Princeton, NJ).

Klein, M. G., Cheng, H., Santana, L. F., Jiang, Y.-H., Lederer, W. J. and Schneider, M. F. (1996). Two mechanisms of quantized calcium release in skeletal muscle. Nature 379:455-458.

Konishi, M., Hollingworth, S., Harkins, A. B. and Baylor, S. M. (1991). Myoplasmic calcium transients in intact frog skeletal muscle fibers monitored with the fluorescent indicator furaptra. J. Gen. Physiol. 97:271-301.

Konishi, M., Suda, N. and Kurihara, S. (1993). Fluorescence signals from the Mg^{2+}/Ca^{2+} indicator furaptra in frog skeletal muscle fibers. Biophys. J. 64:223-239.

Kozono, D., Yasui, M., King, L. S. and Agre, P. (2002). Aquaporin water channels: atomic structure molecular dynamics meet clinical medicine. J. Clin. Invest. 109:1395-1399.

Kretsinger, R. H. and Nockolds, C. E. (1973). Carp muscle calcium-binding protein. II. Structure determination and general description. J. Biol. Chem. 248: 3313-3326.

Kuffler, S. W. and Yoshikami, D. (1975). The number of transmitter molecules in a quantum: an estimate from iontophoretic application of acetylcholine at the neuromuscular synapse. J. Physiol. 251(2): 465–482.

Kugler, G., Weiss, R. G., Flucher, B. E. and Grabner, M. (2004). Structural requirements of the dihydropyridine receptor alpha1S II-III loop for skeletal-type excitation-contraction coupling. J. Biol. Chem. 279(6):4721-4728.

Kuo, A., Gulbis, J. M., Antcliff, J. F., Rahman, T., Lowe, E. D., Zimmer, J., Cuthbertson, J., Ashcroft, F. M., Ezaki, T. and Doyle, D. A. (2003). Crystal structure of the potassium channel KirBac1.1 in the closed state. Science 300:1922-1926.

Kuschmerick, M. J. and Podolsky, R. J. (1969). Ionic mobility in muscle cells. Science 166:1297-1298.

Labarca, P., Coronado, R. and Miller, C. (1980). Thermodynamic and kinetic studies of the gating behavior of a K^+-selective channel from the sarcoplasmic reticulum membrane. J. Gen. Physiol. 76(4):397-424.

Lai, F. A., Erickson, H. P., Rousseau, E., Liu, Q. Y. and Meissner, G. (1988). Purification and reconstitution of the calcium release channel from skeletal muscle. Nature 331:315–319.

Lansman, J. B., Hess, P. and Tsien, R. W. (1986). Blockade of current through single calcium channels by Cd^{2+}, Mg^{2+}, and Ca^{2+}. Voltage and concentration dependence of calcium entry into the pore. J. Gen. Physiol. 88(3):321-47.

Lewis, C. A. (1979). Ion-concentration dependence of the reversal potential and the single channel conductance of ion channels at the frog neuromuscular junction. J. Physiol. 286:417-45.

Liley, A. W. (1956). The effects of presynaptic polarization on the spontaneous activity of the mammalian neuromuscular junction. J. Physiol. 134:427-443.

Lollike. K., Borregaard, N. and Lindau, M. (1995). The exocytotic fusion pore of small granules has a conductance similar to an ion channel. J. Cell Biol. 129(1):99-104.

Luo, F., Dittrich, M., Stiles, J. R. and Meriney, S. D. (2011). Single-pixel optical fluctuation analysis of calcium channel function in active zones of motor nerve terminals. J. Neurosci. 31(31):11268-1128.

Marx, S. O., Ondrias, K. and Marks, A. R. (1998). Coupled gating between individual skeletal muscle Ca^{2+} release channels (ryanodine receptors). Science 281(5378):818-821.

Millar, A. G., Zucker, R. S., Ellis-Davies, G. C., Charlton, M. P. and Atwood, H. L. (2005). Calcium sensitivity of neurotransmitter release differs at phasic and tonic synapses. J. Neurosci. 25(12):3113-3125.

Miller, C. (1983). Integral membrane channels: studies in model membranes. Physiol. Rev. 63(4): 1209-1242.

Miller, C., Bell, J. E. and Garcia, A. M. (1984). The potassium channel of sarcoplasmic reticulum. In *Ion Channels: Molecular and Physiological Aspects*, W. D. Stein, Ed. (Academic Press; Orlando, FL), pp. 99-132.

Montal, M. and Mueller, P. (1972). Formation of bimolecular membranes from lipid monolayers and a study of their electrical properties. Proc. Natl. Acad. Sci. 69:3561-3566.

Naitoh, Y. and Eckert, R. (1969). Ion mechanisms controlling behavioral responses of paramecium to mechanical stimuli. Science 164(3882):963-965.

Nakai, J., Dirksen, R. T., Nguyen, H. T., Pessah, I. N., Beam, K. G. and Allen, P. D. (1996). Enhanced dihydropyridine receptor channel activity in the presence of ryanodine receptor. Nature 380, 72–75.

Nakao, M. and Gadsby, D. C. (1989). [Na] and [K] dependence of the Na/K pump current-voltage relationship in guinea pig ventricular myocytes. J. Gen. Physiol. 94(3):539-65.

Neher, E. and Marty, A. (1972). Discrete changes of cell membrane capacitance observed under conditions of enhanced secretion in bovine adrenal chromaffin cells. Proc. Natl. Acad. Sci. 79(21):6712–6716.

Neher, E. and Sakmann, B. (1976). Single-channel currents recorded from membrane of denervated frog muscle fibres. Nature 260:799-802.

Neher, E., Sakmann, B. and Steinbach, J. H. (1978). The extracellular patch clamp: a method for resolving currents through individual open channels in biological membranes. Pflugers Arch. 375(2):219-228.

Nelson, F. E., Hollingworth, S., Rome, L. C. and Baylor, S. M. (2014). Intracellular calcium movements during relaxation and recovery of superfast muscle fibers of the toadfish swimbladder. J. Gen. Physiol. 143:605-620.

Nelson, B. R., Wu, F., Liu, Y., Anderson, D. M., McAnally, J., Lin, W., Cannon, S. C., Bassel-Duby, R. and Olson, E. N. (2013). Skeletal muscle-specific T-tubule protein STAC3 mediates voltage-induced Ca^{2+} release and contractility. Proc. Natl. Acad. Sci. 110 (29):11881-11886.

Newman, M. (2012). *Computational Physics*. CreateSpace Independent Publishing.

Noceti, F., Baldelli, P., Wei, X., Qin, N., Toro, L., Birnbaumer, L. and Stefani, E. (1996). Effective gating charges per channel in voltage dependent K1 and Ca21 channels. J. Gen. Physiol. 108:143–155.

Pape, P. C., Jong, D. S. and Chandler, W. K. (1995). Calcium release and its voltage dependence in frog cut muscle fibers equilibrated with 20 mM EGTA. J. Gen. Physiol. 106(2):259-336.

Patlak, J. B. and Horn, R. (1982). Effect of N-bromoacetamide on single sodium channel currents in excised membrane patches. J. Gen. Physiol. 79: 333–351.

Peachey, L. D. (1965). The sarcoplasmic reticulum and transverse tubules of the frog's sartorius. J. Cell. Biol. 25 (3, part2):209-231.

Penner, R. and Neher, E. (1988). The role of calcium in stimulus-secretion coupling in excitable and non-excitable cells. J. Exp. Biol. 139:329-345.

Peinelt, C. and Apell, H.-J. (2002). Kinetics of the Ca^{2+}, H^+, and Mg^{2+} interaction with the ion-binding sites of the SR Ca-ATPase. Biophys. J. 82:170-181.

Perni, S., Marsden, K. C., Escobar, M., Hollingworth, S., Baylor, S. M. and Franzini-Armstrong, C. (2015). Structural and functional properties of ryanodine receptor type 3 in zebrafish tail muscle. J. Gen. Physiol. 145(3):173-184.

Proenza, C., O'Brien, J. J., Nakai, J., Mukherjee, S., Allen, P. D. and Beam, K. G. (2002). Identification of a region of RyR1 that participates in allosteric coupling with the 1S (Cav1.1) II-III loop. J. Biol. Chem. 277, 6530–6535.

Protasi, F., Paolini, C., Nakai, J., Beam, K. G., Franzini-Armstrong, C. and Allen, P. D. (2002). Multiple regions of RyR1 mediate functional and structural interactions with 1S-dihydropyridine receptors in skeletal muscle. Biophys. J. 83:3230–3244.

Raju, B., Murphy, E., Levy, L. A., Hall, R. D. and London, R. E. (1989). A fluorescent indicator for measuring cytosolic free magnesium. Am. J. Physiol. 256:C540-C548.

Raine, C. S. (1984). Morphology of myelin and myelination. In *Myelin*, P. Morell, Ed. (Plenum Press, New York), pp. 1-50.

Rall, J. A. (2020). A perfect confluence of physiology and morphology: discovery of the transverse tubular system and inward spread of activation in skeletal muscle. Adv. Physiol. Educ. 44:402-413, 2020.

Rall, W. (1969). Time constants and electrotonic length of membrane cylinders and neurons. Biophys. J. 9:1483-1508.

Ríos, E. and Brum, G. (1987). Involvement of dihydropyridine receptors in excitation-contraction coupling in skeletal muscle. Nature 325:717-720.

Robertson, S. P., Johnson, J. D. and Potter, J. D. (1981). The time-course of Ca^{2+} exchange with calmodulin, troponin, parvalbumin, and myosin in response to transient increase in Ca^{2+}. Biophys. J. 34:559-569.

Rolfe, D. F. and Brown, G. C. (1997). Cellular energy utilization and molecular origin of standard metabolic rate in mammals. Physiol. Rev. 77(3):731-758.

Sakmann, B. and Neher, E. (2009). *Single Channel Recording* (2nd edition, Springer; Boston, MA).

Sakmann, B., Patlak, J. and Neher, E. (1980). Single acetylcholine-activated channels show burst-kinetics in presence of desensitizing concentrations of agonist. Nature 286:71-73.

Schneider, M. F. and Chandler, W. K. (1973). Voltage dependent charge movement in skeletal muscle: a possible step in excitation–contraction coupling. Nature 242:244–246.

Schoppa, N. E., McCormack, K., Tanouye, M. A. and Sigworth, F. J. (1992). The size of gating charge in wild-type and mutant Shaker potassium channels. Science 255:1712–1715.

Schredelseker, J., Di Biase, V., Obermair, G. J., Felder, E. T., Flucher, B. E., Franzini-Armstrong, C. and Grabner, M. (2005). The β1a subunit is essential for the assembly of dihydropyridine-receptor arrays in skeletal muscle. Proc. Natl. Acad. Sci. 102(47):17219-17224.

Schredelseker, J., Dayal, A., Schwerte, T., Franzini-Armstrong, C. and Grabner, M. (2009). Proper restoration of excitation-contraction coupling in the dihydropyridine receptor beta1-null in zebrafish relaxed is an exclusive function of the beta1a subunit. J. Biol. Chem. 284(2):1242-1251.

Shirokova, N., Garcia, J. and Ríos, E. (1998). Local calcium release in mammalian skeletal muscle. J. Physiol. 512:377-384.

Shtifman, A., Ward, C. W., Yamamoto, T., Wang, J., Olbinski, B., Valdivia, H. H., Ikemoto, N. and Schneider, M. F. (2002). Interdomain interactions within ryanodine receptors regulate Ca^{2+} spark frequency in skeletal muscle. J. Gen. Physiol. 116:15-31.

Simon, S. M. and Llinas, R. R. (1985). Compartmentalization of the submembrane calcium activity during calcium influx and its significance in transmitter release. Biophys. J. 48(3):485-498.

Singer, S. J. and Nicolson, G. L. (1972). The fluid mosaic model of the structure of cell membranes. Science 175(4023):720-731.

Stevens, C. F. and Wesseling, J. F. (1998). Activity-dependent modulation of the rate at which synaptic vesicles become available to undergo exocytosis. Neuron 21:415–424.

Stuart, G. J., Dodt, H.-U. and Sakmann, B. (1993). Patch-clamp recordings from the soma and dendrites of neurons in brain slices using infrared video microscopy. Pflugers Arch. 423:511-518.

Sudhof, T. C. and Rothman, J. E. (2009). Membrane fusion: grappling with SNARE and SM proteins. Science 323:474-477.

Takekura, H., Bennett, L., Tanabe, T., Beam, K. G. and Franzini-Armstrong, C. (1994). Restoration of junctional tetrads in dysgenic myotubes by dihydropyridine receptor cDNA. Biophys. J. 67, 793–803.

Takekura, H., Paolini, C., Franzini-Armstrong, C., Kugler, G., Grabner, M. and Flucher, B. E. (2004). Differential contribution of skeletal and cardiac II-III loop sequences to the assembly of dihydropyridine-receptor arrays in skeletal muscle. Mol. Biol. Cell. 15(12):5408-5419.

Takeuchi, A. and Takeuchi, N. (1960). Further analysis of relationship between endplate potential and endplate current. J. Neurophysiol. 23: 397:402.

Tanabe, T., Beam, K. G., Powell, J. A. and Numa, S. (1988). Restoration of excitation-contraction coupling and slow calcium current in dysgenic muscle by dihydropyridine receptor complementary DNA. Nature 336(6195):134-9.

Tanabe, T., Beam, K. G., Adams, B. A., Niidome, T. and Numa, S. (1990). Regions of the skeletal muscle dihydropyridine receptor critical for excitation-contraction coupling. Nature 346:567–569.

Tanabe, T., Takeshima, H., Mikami, A., Flockerzi, V., Takahashi, H., Kangawa, K., Kojima, M., Matsuo, H., Hirose, T. and Numa, S. (1987). Primary structure of the receptor for calcium channel blockers from skeletal muscle. Nature 328:313–318.

Tsugorka, A., Ríos, E. and Blatter, L. A. (1995). Imaging elementary events of calcium release in skeletal muscle cells. Science 269:1723-1726.

Turner, T. J., Adams, M. E. and Dunlap, K. (1992). Calcium channels coupled to glutamate release identified by ω-Aga-IVA. Science 258:310-313.

von Ruden, L. and Neher, E. (1993). A Ca-dependent early step in the release of catecholamines from adrenal chromaffin cells. Science 262:1061-1065.

Wang, L. Y. and Kaczmarek, L. K. (1998). High-frequency firing helps replenish the readily releasable pool of synaptic vesicles. Nature 394:384-386.

Widdicombe, J. H., Basbaum, C. B. and Highland, E. (1985). Sodium-pump density of cells from dog tracheal mucosa. Am. J. Physiol. 248(5 Pt 1):C389-398.

Zhang, M., Liu, J. and Tseng, G-N. (2004). Gating charges in the activation and inactivation processes of the hERG channel. J. Gen. Physiol. 124:703-718.

INDEX

A

acetylcholine receptor (ACHR), 115, 253, 275, 302
   single-channel recording, 265, 274–77
acetylcholinesterase
   defined, 296
   muscle, 295–96
action potential
   all-or-nothing property, 184
   brief survey, 177
   function, 177
   mechanism, 197
   membrane, 183–84
   motorneuron, 291
   need for, 172
   paramecium, 16
   propagating, 179, Appendix F
   simulations, 190–95, Appendix F
   skeletal muscle, 301, 325–27, 334–35
   speed of propagation, 15
   squid giant axon, 179, Appendix F
   threshold, 184, 294
active zones, 292, 309
anticholinesterase inhibitors, 300
aquaporins, 31–33
Azo1, 65

B

baroreceptor, 6
basal lamina, 295
basement membrane, 295–96
bicarbonate (HCO_3^-), 2
   extracellular concentration, 4
   intracellular concentration, 4
blood capillaries, 42
blood pressure, 5–7, 37, 42
Brownian motion, 14

C

Ca^{2+} channel. *See* calcium channel
cable theory, 167–72, Appendix E
caged calcium, 310
calcium (Ca^{2+}), 2
   extracellular concentration, 13
   intracellular concentration, 13
calcium binding sites, 223, 243
   calcium pump, 237, 338
   EF hand, 243–46
   parvalbumin, 223, 229, 244, 345
   phosphorylase kinase, 217, 233
   recoverin, 217, 244
   troponin, 216, 233, 244, 364–65, 383
calcium channel, 252, 257, 260, 292, 304, 309, 336, 339
   CaV_1, 260, 336
   CaV_2, 260, 292, 304, 309
   L-type, 260
   N-type, 260
   P-/Q-type, 260
   R-type, 260
calcium dynamics, muscle
   defined, 361
   model, 361–66
   simulation of, 367–80
calcium inactivation of calcium release, 345, 352, 354, 385

calcium pump, SERCA
   definition, 235
   kinetic model #1, 235–37
   kinetic model #2, 249–50
   location, 338
calcium pump, surface membrane, 139, 358
calcium signaling, 15, 17, 328, 344, 362
calcium sparks
   defined, 350
   differences in different fiber types, 354
   relation to muscle twitch, 354
calmodulin, 217, 243
capacitance, 105
capacitive current, 105
capacitor, 105
cardiac muscle, 177, 23
carotid body, 7
carotid sinus, 6–7
carrier protein, 33–35, 295
cell membrane, 2, 12
   damage, 16–18
   fluid-mosaic model, 10
   structure, 8–11
charge, 102–3
charge immobilization, 207
chemical synapse
   calcium dependence of transmitter release, 307–10
   compared with electrical synapse, 310–12
   defined, 291
   structure, 292–94
chloride (Cl^-)
   extracellular concentration, 4
   intracellular concentration, 4
choline transporter, 295
circuit diagrams
   HH model, 181–82
   introduction, 145–48
   passive membrane, 163–65
competitive binding
   definition, 223
   kinetics, 228–30
   steady-state, 223–26
conductance, 109–10
confocal imaging, 350–54
cooperative binding, 231
   Hill equation, 232
   kinetic model, 233–35
curare, 298, 300
current, 102–3

D

differential equations
   solving in *Python*, 122–26
   systems of, 120–21, Appendix F
diffusion, 14, 35, 43, 51, 58, 60
   derivation of Fick's laws, 417
   diffusion-limited, 222
   facilitated. *See* facilitated diffusion
   simple, 21–26
   simulated, 87–92
diffusion coefficient
   "electrical", 172
   defined, 21, 418
   experimental estimation, 60–62
diffusion potential, 13, 101
dihydropyridine receptor (DHPR), 260, 327
dorsal root ganglion
   action potential, 178
   structure, 399, 408
driving force, 112, 114, 145, 165, 333

statement, 110–11

d-tubocurarine. *See* curare

E

ECF. *See* extracellular fluid
ECF and ICF, 3–5
EF hand, 243–46
electrical synapse
    compared with chemical synapse, 310–12
    defined, 291
    structure, 291
electrocardiogram (EKG), 100
electroencephalogram (EEG), 100
electromyogram (EMG), 100
electrophysiology
    basic introduction, 99–114
    skeletal muscle, 332–35
electrotonic coupling, 175, 178, 296, 335, 397
endocytosis, 291–94, 313
endplate, 263, 296, 298, 395
endplate potential, 298–300
equivalent circuit. *See* circuit models
erf function, Appendix E
excitation-contraction coupling
    amphibians vs. mammals, 339
    calcium sparks, 350
    defined, 325
    Luigi Galvani, 325
    mechanism, 337, 339
    summary of steps, 327–28
    timing sequence, 344
    voltage sensors, 335
    voltage-clamp studies, 346–49
exocytosis, 312–15
extracellular fluid, 3, 100, 337

extracellular voltage, 100, 169

F

facilitated diffusion, 33–35
feedback
    electronic, 180
    negative, 5
    positive, 181
Fick's laws of diffusion
    derivation, 417
    first law, 21–23
    second law, 24–26
first-order differential equations, 121–23
fitting of model parameters. *See* least-squares fitting
fluo-3, 350–52
fluo-4, 385
flux, 21, 28
free $[Ca^{2+}]$. *See* free calcium concentration
free calcium concentration, 13, 219, 305, 340, 343
furaptra, 341, 342, 362, 366, 382

G

Galvani, Luigi, 325
gating currents
    K^+ channel, 208
    Na^+ channel, 206–7, 208
Gaussian curve, 24, 45, 51, 58, 171, 267, 305, 427
glutamate receptor, 254, 284
glycine receptor, 253, 254
glycosylation, 260
Goldman-Hodgkin-Katz equations

flux equations, 133–34
voltage equation, 138–39
Golgi tendon organ, 407–8
G-protein-coupled receptor, 10, 253
gramicidin, 261

H

half time, 112–14
Hill equation, 231–32
Hodgkin-Huxley model, 184–89
    action potential simulation, 190–95
    voltage-clamp simulation, 198–201
homeostasis, 5–8
hypertonic, 39
hypotonic, 39

I

ICF. *See* intracellular fluid
inactivation, 197, 202, 207, 284
indicator dye
    calcium, 65, 341, 362, 363
    pH, 61
interstitial fluid, 4
intracellular fluid, 3
ion channels
    conductance, 109–11
    defined, 105
    families, 251–56
    functions of, 251
    gating, 252
    gating charge, 213
    gating currents, 206–7
    gating models, 274–77
    methods of classification, 252–56

    structural motifs, 256–60
    structure, 104, 257, 258
isopotential, 181
isotonic, 39

K

K^+ channel. *See* potassium channel
kainate receptor, 254
keyword argument, 49
Kirchhoff's laws, 148

L

law of electroneutrality, 119
least-squares fitting, 64, Appendix D
limiting steepness
    release of neurotransmitter, 309
    sodium and potassium conductance, 205–6
    SR calcium release, 348
lipid solubility, 29
lymph, 37

M

magnesium (Mg^{2+}), 2
    extracellular concentration, 226
    intracellular concentration, 226
mass action
    example with calcium, 217–19
    law of, 216–17
mast cells, 313–15
membrane capacitance
    capacitor charging, 111–14
    statement, 105–8
membrane conductance

definition, 109–10
  equivalent circuit, active, 182
  equivalent circuit, passive, 164
membrane current
  definition and discussion, 102–8
membrane permeability, 26–29
  lipid solubility, 29–31
membrane potential
  definition, 12
  origin and discussion, 99–102
membrane resistance
  cable theory, 167
  statement, 110–11
membrane voltage. *See* membrane potential
Michaelis-Menten equation, 35
miniature endplate potential, 300–302
motorneuron, 291, 393–94
  alpha motorneuron, 324, 399, 401
  gamma motorneuron, 393, 398
muscle charge movement, 346–48
muscle reflex, 394–96
  anatomy, 393–94
  IA axon, 399–401
  muscle spindle, 396–97
  pathology, 408–9
  spindle muscle fiber, 393, 396, 398, 400
  α-motorneuron, 401–3
  γ-motorneuron, 393
muscle structure
  light microscope, 329
  mechanical coupling, 339
  triadic junction, 336, 338
  T-system, 331
  ultrastructure, 330
myelin, 107, 113
myelination, 403–5

myotonia congenita, 360

N

Na/K pump'. *See* sodium-potassium ATPase
Na^+ channel. *See* sodium channel
negative feedback. *See* feedback
negative-feedback system, 5–7
Nernst equation
  proof, Appendix C, 421–23
  proof, Boltzmann approach, 213
  statement, 108–9
neuromuscular junction (nmj)
  anatomy, 294–97
  endplate potentials (epps), 298–300
  miniature endplate potentials (mepps), 300–302
  statistics of epps and mepps, 307
NMDA receptor, 254
node of Ranvier, 397, 404

O

oncotic pressure, 42
ordinary differential equation. *See* differential equations
osmosis, 35–38
osmotic balance, 117–20
osmotic pressure, 35–40
  osmotic pressure equaton, 37

P

paramecium, 15
partition coefficient, 26–31
parvalbumin, 223, 229, 244, 345

pCa
  definition, 219–20
permeability, 12–13
  permeability vs. conductance, 165–66
phenol red, 61, 63, 348
phospholipids, 8
phosphorylase kinase, 217, 233
physical constants, Appendix G
physiology
  cell, 1–3
  defined, 1
  molecular, 2
  organellar, 2
plasma membrane. See cell membrane
plasmalemma. See cell membrane
Poisson probability. See probability distribution
Poisson process
  definition, 272–74
  examples, 273, 274, 303
potassium (K^+)
  extracellular concentration, 4
  intracellular concentration, 4
potassium channel, 104, 109, 110, 198, 206, 254, 257, 258, 278, 282
  inactivation, 284
probability distribution
  binomial, 278, 287
  negative exponential, 273, 289
  Poisson, 266–68
  standard normal, 271, 321
propagated action potential, Appendix F
pump-leak model, 137
Python. See also topics in Table of Contents
  introduction to *Python*, 43–64
  odeint function, 124
  Python elements, 67–87
  setup for solving deqs, 120–26
Python programs
  one-dimensional cable kinetics, Appendix E
  calcium dynamics in skeletal muscle, 367–80
  calculation of diffusion profile, 60
  diffusion profile vs. data set, 62
  Hodgkin-Huxley membrane AP, 190–94
  Hodgkin-Huxley propagated AP, Appendix F
  Hodgkin-Huxley voltage clamp, 198–201
  least-squares fitting, Appendix D
  input/output of text and numbers, 56
  one-dimensional diffusion, 43–49
  osmotic balance in cells, 126–30
  passive response to current step, 152–55
  passive response to voltage step, 158–61
  Poisson probability distribution, 266–68
  propagating action potential, Appendix F
  simulated one-dimensional diffusion, 87–91
  SR calcium pumping, 237–41
  two-dimensional diffusion, 51–53

Q

Q_{10}, 189
quantal content, 297
quantum, 297

R

random number generator, 92, 288
reciprocal innervation, 406–7
recoverin, 217, 243
resistance, 110
reversal potential, 115
ryanodine receptor (RyR), 255, 327, 337–39

S

Schwann cell, 297, 404
serotonin receptor, 253
signaling mechanisms, 15
single channels
    conductance, 110
    currents (ACHRs), 263–66
    simulation (ACHRs), 271–72
single-channel recording
    artificial bilayers, 261–63
    chloride channel, 280–81
    glutamate receptor, 285
    patch clamp, 263–66
    SR potassium channel, 278–80
    voltage-dependent potassium channel, 284
    voltage-dependent sodium channel, 281–82
skeletal muscle
    calcium dynamics, 361–63
    calcium transient ($\Delta[Ca^{2+}]$), 328
    cross-bridges, 328
    dihydropyridine receptor (DHPR), 327, 336, 337, 338, 339
    EC coupling, 328
    excitation-contraction coupling, 328
    fiber types, 323
    Galvani, Luigi, 325
    introduction, 325–27
    motor unit, 325
    myosin, 328
    ryanodine receptor (RyR), 327, 337–39, 351–54
    structure, 328–31
    terminal cisternae, 330, 337, 338
    thick filaments, 328
    thin filaments, 328
    triads, 327, 336
    tropomyosin, 328
    troponin, 243, 328, 345, 362-65, 383-84
smooth muscle, 323
SNARE proteins, 292–94
sodium (Na^+)
    extracellular concentration, 4
    intracellular concentration, 4
sodium channel, 112, 198, 206, 255, 257, 260, 281, 295, 296, 397
    activation, 133, 197, 206
    deactivation, 206
    inactivation, 197, 202, 207
sodium pump. *See* sodium-potassium ATPase
sodium-calcium exchange, 139
sodium-potassium ATPase, 11
    cell volume, 136–40
    effects of block, 140–41
    function, 11–12
    ribbon structure, 11
space constant, 169, 170, 172, 300, 405
spindle muscle fiber. *See* muscle reflex
squid giant axon
    action potential, membrane, 183–84
    action potential, propagated, 179, Appendix F
    simulations. *See also* Hodgkin-Huxley model
    voltage clamp technique, 180–82
Starling forces, 42
stopped-flow experiment, 249
stretch reflex. *See* muscle reflex
striated muscle, 323
synaptic vesicles
    docked vesicles, 292
    recycling, 294
    reserve vesicles, 292
    structure, 296

synaptobrevin, 294
synaptophysin, 294
synaptotagmin, 217, 293

T

techniques
    artificial lipid bilayer, 261
    caged calcium, 309
    calcium indicator dye, 342–43
    confocal imaging, 350
    glass microelectrode, 150
    patch clamp, 150–51, 313
    voltage-clamp, general, 156–58
    voltage-clamp, squid giant axon, 180–81
tetraethylammonium (TEA), 255
tetrodotoxin (TTX), 255
Thomsen's disease. *See* myotonia congenita
time constant, 114, 155, 166, 169, 186, 222, 275, 300
transcellular fluid, 4
transporter protein. *See* carrier protein
tropomyosin, 217
troponin, 217, 243, 355, 362-65, 383–84

U

ultrafiltration, 36

V

VAMP family, 294, 307
van't Hoff equation. *See* osmotic pressure equation
vascular pores, 42
vectorization, 48, 54, 195, 270
voltage, 99
voltage clamp. *See also* single-channel recording
    skeletal muscle, 349
    squid axon, 180–81, 198–206
    theoretical, 156–63
voltage dependence
    neurotransmitter release, 309
    sodium and potassium conductance, 205–6
    SR calcium release, 348–49
voltage signaling, 15
voltage steepness
    neurotransmitter release, 309
    skeletal muscle calcium release, 348–49
    sodium and potassium conductance, 206

W

water
    body water, 3
    equilibrium, 35
    osmosis, 35–38
    permeability, 3

Made in the USA
Columbia, SC
03 December 2020